A Life in Movies

MICHAEL POWELL

A Life in Movies

AN AUTOBIOGRAPHY

ALFRED A. KNOPF *New York* 1987

THIS IS A BORZOI BOOK
PUBLISHED BY ALFRED A. KNOPF, INC.

Library of Congress Cataloging-in-Publication Data

Powell, Michael.   A life in movies.

1. Powell, Michael. 2. Moving-picture producers and directors—Great
Britain—Biography.
I. Title.
PN1998.A3P648   1987   791.43'0233'0924   [B]   86-46015
ISBN 0-394-55935-5

Manufactured in the United States of America

FIRST AMERICAN EDITION

Movies are the folklore of the twentieth century.
— Hein Heckroth

CONTENTS

BOOK ONE

Silent

All my life I have loved running water. One of my passions is to follow a river downstream through pools and rapids, lakes, twists and turnings, until it reaches the sea. Today that sea lies before me, in plain view, and it is time to make a start on the story of my life, to remount it to its source, before I swim out, leaving behind the land I love so much, into the grey, limitless ocean.

Yet, although I love grass and trees, woods and forests, hills and rivers, with the passionate love of an Englishman for his island, I shall not be afraid to swim out over those awesome depths. I have lived a long time. I have seen men and women, far better and cleverer than I, crippled by illness, killed by chance, and I have been allowed to achieve the summit for which I aimed and the rewards that come with success in a profession that never existed until we invented it.

I have had perfect health. I have had friends without whom I would have achieved nothing, for I have no personal ambition and I am too proud to beg or to intrigue. I have loved and been loved. "From too much love of living" . . . how does it go? I know so much verse by heart that I am bound to misquote:

> From too much love of living,
> From hope and fear set free,
> We thank with brief thanksgiving
> Whatever gods may be,
> That no life lives forever,
> That dead men rise up never,
> That even the weariest river
> Winds somewhere safe to sea.

I remember André Maurois quoting those lines in the first French novel that I ever read, bought off a bookstall in 1929 in Chamonix, where I was working on location for a film with a background of winter sports. Maurois's lovely heroine, Odile, with whom I fell in love, spoke the phrase in English "the weariest river", then repeated in French "*la rivière la plus lasse*", and I shivered with pleasure at the writer's skill in finding in another language the exact words from Swinburne's dying fall.

Today, the day that I start to write my story, is January 1, 1980. I was born in September 1905, on the day after the Feast of St Michael, after whom I am named. My mother intended me to be born on the saint's day, but I fooled her. It was not to be the last time that she planned with loving care for her younger son and that he let her down.

I am seventy-four years and thirteen weeks old. At my age each week is important. Seventy-four is not a great age, but it is a respectable age, the sort of age when you realise that there are certain things that you have always intended to do – read the whole of the Comédie Humaine, *climb Kilimanjaro, follow the Douro from the Gredos to the Atlantic – most of them unlikely to be accomplished. I am not in my workroom in the cottage in Gloucestershire, the cluttered little room on the first floor which looks out on the walnut tree by the garden path; I am in the ground floor flat provided for the Artist in Residence at Dartmouth College, Hanover, New Hampshire, by the Hopkins Center for the Arts – Heavens! – yet another capital letter – whose tall windows look out on East Wheelock Street. The house of which this flat is a part is built on a brick foundation and is painted white with green shutters. Most of the other houses on this side of the street, leading up the hill to the campus, are the same. Pine trees push close to the houses like patient dogs, waiting for a chance to get in. As for Isaac Wheelock, he was a local worthy. I came across his name on a bronze plaque where his virtues were extolled, while I was wandering about the deserted campus yesterday.*

I have always sworn I would never spell "art" with a big A, and here I am doing it before I have written a thousand words. Art with a big A makes professionals uneasy. All art is one, and there is no difference in the mystery of the craft, only in the hand and eye of the craftsman. I have listened to many passionate debates about my own profession by those who are in it and those who were trying to get into it. Is film-making art? Well, if telling a story is not art I don't know what is. There are always people who confuse the binding with the content of a book. Perhaps, if I tell my story truly, this life in art that has extended over sixty years, I shall find out whether I have misspent my life or not; for make no mistake, on this January morning in New England, I feel that I have nothing to apologise for! By the time that I finish the job, I may sing a different tune. An autobiography may be a revelation to the reader, it is certainly a rediscovery for the writer.

Today came the first snow of winter. It is a very light fall – students returning early with hopes of a skiing weekend are disappointed. Still it is only Thursday. Normally, I am told, at this time of the year there would be two or three feet of snow in the town of Hanover. The ski slopes are up in the White Mountains, thirty miles away, and a thousand feet higher. Not that it concerns me, although it may concern my son Columba, when he joins me later on from England. I am not a sportsman. I walk, climb mountains, shoot and fish, because that takes me into wild and lonely places to meet cunning and hard-headed individuals. But the indisputable fact that I am here in New England by invitation, at the end of my life, is part of my story which started on September 29, 1905 with the struggle to be born.

My British passport, gold lettered and stiff with the royal coat of arms on its cover, announces that I was born at Canterbury, Kent, and this legend has accompanied me throughout my life. It has been useful. It has an uncompromisingly British Anglican ring. Everyone has heard of Canterbury if only because they murder archbishops there. In point of fact I was born five miles from the cathedral city in a red-brick farmhouse, Howlett's Farm, which faced the dusty white road that ran from Bekesbourne to Littlebourne accompanied by a coy little brook, which appeared and disappeared according to the flow of water, which was affected by dry summers and winters. It was a tributary of the River Stour, a weedy stream which wanders through lush country, passes through Canterbury and reaches the sea at Pegwell Bay, near Sandwich, on the east coast. Our eccentric little stream was called the Nailbourne. It ran, when it could, through land on the far side of the tennis court which my father had laid out in the meadow opposite the farm. Two great cedars of Lebanon stretched protective arms over my perambulator where I lay, swathed in shawls, listening to the thud of tennis balls, cries of "Love all!" and "Sorry, partner!" and shouts from my father of "Out of the way. Let me take it!" answered by protesting cries from my mother, on the wrong side of the court as usual. Within a few yards the Nailbourne vanished into dense beds of nettles surrounding a ruined cottage, whose broken flintstone walls inspired my mother to call it Nettle Abbey, so that the humble building acquired a dignity on its deathbed that it never had in life. A picnic at Nettle Abbey was one of my mother's favourite excursions, to escape from duties which bored her, to play with two sons who adored her.

My father and mother were Worcestershire-born. They had married there and their first home was a snug little farm on the River Teme in the village of Leigh called Bank Farm. There my elder brother, John Miles, was born, and there my mother learnt to be a farmer's wife, to manage the dairy, to churn butter, and to make round cheeses for the market, which she christened Leigh Lumps and which became, on moving to East Kent, Bekesbourne Bumps. My father moved to Kent because he was a hop farmer, and Kent and Worcestershire are great hop-growing counties. He left Leigh because it was too close to his father, who had been a severe parent and was proving a critical neighbour. In Kent he would be far enough away from his father to go his own way. The other reason he decided to move was a scandal in my mother's family.

My mother was born Mabel Corbett. My maternal grandfather was Frederick Corbett, a prominent solicitor of Worcester and from 1882–3 its mayor. He and his brothers were of yeoman stock, that had farmed and practised country professions in and around the village of Chaddesley Corbett since the Normans came. Our particular ancestor had as his crest a raven proper. This raven, in its French form, "*le corbeau*", begat the long line of Corbetts, which continues to this day: in my case by the lineaments of my Corbett ancestors, for I take after my mother and can see traces of other resemblances in the photographs of my grandfather and of my Danish great-grandfather whose name was Horne and of whom I know nothing, to my shame. Frederick Corbett was a vigorous man, ambitious for his large family, five girls and four boys. He shone like a comet above his native city and his fall, when it came, was all the more shocking. In 1902, a man in his sixties, he was charged with embezzling his clients' money, arrested, convicted, and sent to prison. It was the sort of incident that shakes a provincial city like Worcester to its Roman foundations.

All this happened some years before I was born. When I became conscious of my surroundings I was a Man of Kent. I knew that and was proud of the fact that I had been born east of the River Medway. I was sorry for those Kentish Men who lived out their miserable lives on the left bank in places like Sevenoaks, Tonbridge and Bromley, which latter borough was reported to be not much more than a suburb of London. We Men of Kent, I knew, had always been in the centre of everything with Dover and the Cinque Ports to our south and the North Foreland and the great wide mouth of the River Thames swallowing and spewing out shipping to our north. Our Kentish coast was the haunt of smugglers and excisemen. It was full of caves in the white chalk, and Dover Castle was the strongest and most important castle in the world. My brother, on the other hand, although my elder by two and a half years and an object of veneration, had been mysteriously born in Worcestershire: a county with a cathedral, true, though not to be compared with ours at Canterbury; an inland county and city that was a good 150 miles away and which could only be reached by going up to London. (London was always "up".) You then crossed London to Paddington Station and went down to Worcestershire. (Worcestershire was always "down".) My curiosity was further provoked by my parents' frequent references to Worcester and their respective families. My father usually spoke in tones of recrimination and talked about "old Corbett and his precious bunch of blue stockings" (my mother's sisters, who had received a superior education paid for by "old Corbett's clients", no doubt, and who since their father's disgrace were now cast to the four winds or to the London County Council, which was much the same thing, to earn a crust), while my mother, who had been the prettiest of the five sisters and her father's favourite, was more prone to reminisce about the social life of Worcester, of the myriad friends whom she had left behind there, of the Three Choirs Festival, when the cathedrals of Worcester, Hereford and Gloucester pooled their resources, of Edward Elgar, great composer and family friend, and of her adored brothers, with special emphasis upon Geoffrey, who was doing so well in the Indian Civil Service, and Alan, who had volunteered for service in the Boer War and had now married and settled down in South Africa and was doing so well too.

That was all very well, but I was more intrigued by my Uncle Edward, a solicitor like his father, but quite obviously the only artist in the family. In person he always reminded me of a shaggy dog. When other men were bent over their desks, his door, decorated with the legend "back in an hour", was almost permanently closed. He had the wanderlust. He was to be seen frequently at Shrub Hill railway station, which was on the main line to London, watching the trains go by. The climax to these dreams quite swept me off my feet, when I was told how one day he sprang impulsively upon the London express and spent the day in London wandering around the docks among alleys with names like Wapping and Old Stairs, ending by signing on as supercargo in a clipper bound for Australia. The legend "back in an hour" on his door remained there for two years.

These scraps of information were constant in memories of my childhood, that is to say from the time when I started to make sense of my elders' nonsensical conversations, say at the age of three, until the 1914–18 World War, which separated my parents and finished our farmhouse life for ever. My parents and relatives – I saw much more of my Corbett uncles and aunts than I did of my Powell connections – never chose to rattle this skeleton in the Corbett closet and nobody that I can remember ever sat me down for a serious talk. It was probably thirty years before anybody enlightened me and the pieces of the puzzle came together, probably when I took a house for my mother in the Berkshire pinewoods at a safe distance from the London blitz in 1939 to make a home for my beloved grandfather in the 98th year of his life. He first appeared in the lives of my brother and me when he came from London to stay for a week or two, a bent figure in black, with balding white hair and a bristly white beard and moustache which caused me distaste when I kissed him. He wore a black or dark grey city suit, probably a thick Cheviot, and a billycock hat. We were in our beds (or more probably out of them) in the little rooms with a communicating door which looked out on the apple plantation on the other side of the road. He gave us two identical books, a copy for each of us of *Coral Island* by R. M. Ballantyne, and always every year that he came he would repeat the ritual. *The Gorilla Hunters* was certainly one title, and probably 20,000 *Leagues under the Sea* was another, with coloured illustrations. He bought the books, he told us, in his light-toned airy voice, with a hint of amusement in it, in Paternoster Row; and Paternoster Row, which is hard by St Paul's Cathedral and Ludgate Hill is where book publishers have had their stalls since Shakespeare's day (although the publishers were moving westward) and was still the very best place in the world to browse over books and pick up bargains: a Corbett custom.

Whether my grandfather was ever a tall man I have no means of knowing, for when I knew him he was already bent and marked by hard prison life. What is certain is that Frederick Corbett was a very strong man and that one of his sons, my uncle Alan, the South African one, was still kicking at the age of 102. My mother reached the respectable age of ninety-seven, and all her sisters lived as long as they felt inclined. They were strong stock. In his photograph in the oak frame he sits very erect in a chair at a table with his eyes looking calmly over the head of the photographer. He looks as if he can see the Malvern Hills through the windows of his office; and when I look at the long line of the Malverns, which I often do when I drive along the Cotswold escarpment where it looks across the Severn Valley to Wales, I remember how he used to look out of the window of his office in Worcester and see it was a bright, windy day, a day for the hills, and he would order his dogcart to be brought round and he and his groom would drive at a spanking pace to Malvern where he would hand the reins to the man, jump down and walk along the five tops from end to end until he came to where the dogcart was waiting for him and so back to the city and his desk smothered in papers. Now! who told me that, I wonder? I think it may have been himself.

He was a keen mountain climber, at a time when Englishmen were only just taking up the sport. He had climbed with Edward Whymper and it was from him that I heard the story of the first ascent of the Matterhorn, and the tragedy which spoilt the triumph of that memorable day. Every summer he took some of his own children with him and with Fanny, his wife, to Zermatt or Chamonix, and my mother was thrilled to be allowed to accompany him up Monte Rosa. He was one of the early members of the Alpine Club and his son Geoffrey was an active member after him. I remember how my uncle, on long leave every four years from India, with his wife and son, used to spend a month in Switzerland before arriving in England, with exotic presents for his nephews and nieces. Geoffrey went on to found the Himalayan Club and to organize the 1933 attempt on Everest. At that time, he was in the running for the Governorship of the Central Provinces.

My grandfather insisted upon higher education for his girls as well as for his boys, and it was largely owing to his active support that Miss Alice Ottley was able to start her famous Worcester school for girls. Her first pupils were Corbetts, Webbs and Beales who were all close neighbours or cousins and were to form distracting pieces of the jigsaw puzzle of my Worcester connections for the rest of our mutual lives. By the time I knew them they were mostly married and their newly acquired surnames added to my confusion and does still. Casual explanations by my mother that Blanche Beale and Jenny Huxham were sisters did nothing to clear the fog. Once when on a visit to Worcester, while my Great-Uncle Albert Webb was alive, I accompanied my mother down to the shops at the bottom of St Katherine's Hill, ignorant of the hundreds of memories that must have been passing through my pretty mother's mind as she trod the familiar pavement. At the shoemaker's shop she gave instructions for the mended shoes to be sent to her at Mr Albert Webb's "for Mrs T. W. Powell". The old craftsman looked up at her with affection and sympathy and murmured, "Miss Corbett, as was?" It was as delicate a reminder that she and her father and her once illustrious family were not forgotten and were still regretted, as if he had swept off a plumed hat and bowed to the ground. I was about eight at the time.

My Corbett aunts were people. They had and have the greatest influence on me, second only to my mother. My uncles were scattered about all over our casual Empire. Geoffrey in India, Roger in New Zealand, Alan in South Africa, Edward, who at that time was happily travelling for Lee & Perrins and had succeeded in selling Worcestershire Sauce to the Chinese, there, here and everywhere. But my aunts, when the crash came, took up teaching and never married. Annie, the eldest, was a geologist. Ethel took Middle English and the Icelandic Sagas and studied Russian. Muriel, the youngest, known as Noo-noo to her sisters, went straight from school to teaching. Grace, my godmother, went into business managing a big laundry belonging to Herbert Tomlins, who had married her cousin Ursula, known to me as "Ula", and was possessed, I gathered, of unbounded wealth in her own right. Her four sons were the cousins I came to know best and still do.

I was rich in aunts. Corbett aunts. My Powell aunts and uncles, though goodlooking and charming, were two-dimensional. Only my Uncle Clarence took an interest in us, and it was more in my brother than in me. Clarence Powell was one of the early pioneers of aviation, and when I was about fifteen he was working for the Sopwith Company. He had a small yacht on the upper Thames and one summer took me and my cousin Dick for a week's cruise. Shortly after that he went to America, to Canada, I believe, and never returned. Like all the Powell men, my father included, he had weak eyesight, and my chief memory of him is of his piercing eyes, behind steel-rimmed glasses. Of the two remaining brothers, one was a pilot on the Irrawaddy River, in Burma, a member of that close and skilled fraternity that kept the traffic moving up and down the great river, with its eternally shifting channels, which, before the railroad, had always been the main highway of Burma, from Rangoon to Bhamo. The remaining eldest brother farmed Lower Wick near Worcester, a rich farm on the River Teme. I knew him as Uncle Bertie.

My Corbett aunts, by the time I was born, were entrenched all over the Home Counties. Annie at Clapham, with a weekend cottage at Farleigh on the Surrey Downs; Ethel with her mother, in Forest Hill, a suburb of South-East London adjacent to the Crystal Palace, not far from Dulwich; Grace at her laundry in Kilburn, North London, just off the High Road near the underground station; Muriel, who worked at Reading High School, sharing a house in the village of Mortimer, Berkshire, with a fellow teacher. Owing to the long school holidays they were able to pay frequent visits, and were especially welcome at the time of the hop-picking, which like the *vendange* in the wine countries depends greatly on casual labour. My father grumbled at the visits of his sisters-in-law but, as he was seldom at home except in the hunting season and at harvest time, he could hardly complain, and he liked Annie ("ought to have been a man"), Grace ("a good sort"), and Muriel ("pretty as paint") – but not Ethel, whose massive intelligence and formidable opinions could always make him run for cover to the billiard room.

The farm where I was born was the home farm of Howlett's estate, which is now a safari park. The big white house in the park meant little to me, but I have a vivid memory of a large mound by the road, obviously man-made, with a mysterious door that was always shut and barred. I was told it was the ice house, where blocks of ice from the lake were stored in winter, deep in the earth, and where it was dangerous for little boys to go. I believed them. But I went and peered down into the pit all the same, when I found the door ajar one day.

I imagine that when my father escaped to Kent he rented Howlett's Farm on a short lease while looking around for something more suitable, for within a few years we were to move to the much larger Hoath Farm. Howlett's is now two cottages and may well have been then. I visited it with my two sons about twenty years ago. It is now part of the Woolton estate and is well looked after. I found it sympathetic, but I could see how it must have seemed cramped and cottagey to an ambitious man like my father. I had told my sons about the deep well in the yard and how my brother and I used to lean perilously over the rim and peer down the brick-lined sides to where far, far below – it was said to be ninety-eight feet to the water – two small heads could be seen reflected in the mirror of the water; and how bricks, dropped down, if the bailiff was nowhere around, would hit first one side then the other and so on – boom . . . boom . . . ba-boom! until with a hollow-plunge into the water, the mirror broke. But when we ventured into the yard there was no longer a well house with a bucket and chain. It was cemented over and I could not be sure even where it had been.

Howlett's was all bottom-land and was not a large farm for that part of the world. Our neighbours at Woolton were Percy Mount and his gay, bustling wife, and on the other side the large family of Maxteds.

There were about thirty acres of hops which involved the most work and were the most risky investment. I have said that my father was an ambitious man, but he was also a gambler. He gambled with cards, at games of skill, on horses, at roulette, or on anything else. The ordinary life of a young gentleman farmer didn't interest him. Not for him the local point-to-point steeplechase, or the Hunt Ball. He dreamt of the Derby, the Grand National, and the Trocadero and the Criterion (referred to, of course, as "the Troc" and "the Cri") of London and of Monte Carlo; and he knew that in a good year at the right price he could, with a bit of luck, clear a couple of thousand pounds on his hops and nip off to Monte Carlo to double it, or halve it, or lose it.

No other crop could do this for him. No wonder he and the men were always at work in the hop gardens during the early part of the year. Joe Wood, the bailiff, had come with my father from Worcestershire, as also had Coleman the head waggoner, who looked after the dozen or so workhorses. The rest were Men of Kent. I always think of Joe Wood as a strong man, in corduroys tied below the knee with a string, a corduroy waistcoat, and a round tweed hat jammed over his eyes. The rest of his face was covered with a heavy beard. He looked old to me and was I suppose about thirty, the same age as my father. He had two daughters, Annie and Lizzie, who used to play with us and kept guinea-pigs. Lizzie had red hair.

Hop-growing is a big capital investment in time and in material. Every five years or so all the tall posts have to be renewed: the old posts are grubbed out and stacked for firewood or fencing, and the new posts, as big as telegraph poles, have to be sunk in rows in the ground, their butts soaked in creosote to protect them from borers. Two stout strands of wire, at shoulder height and at the top, connect the poles. These wires are to be the main support of the heavy vines. Every year, after the poles and wires have been inspected and, where necessary renewed, the hop garden has to be restrung with the thick white hemp string that came in huge balls which we loved to finger. The string was threaded in criss-cross patterns between the parallel wires. Joe Wood, a corduroyed giant on stilts of his own manufacture, would check the upper wire, striding along between the rows, a ten-foot-high colossus. When the vines flowered and when the dusty bunches of hops were forming heavy on the bine, there was constant spraying by a lumbering Behemoth of a machine, with sprouting candelabra of acorn-shaped nozzles, which burst into life when the patient horse started his walk down the rows. It seems to me that the disinfectant was mostly soft soap and harmless, for many a time we have been drenched by not jumping free in time, but came to no harm beyond smarting eyes.

When nine months' work and care and a little bit of luck had led to September and the annual hop-picking, we all knew our duties. My brother and I, when old enough, were tally-men both at Howlett's and later at Hoath Farm. Visiting aunts, cousins, friends and my mother were press-ganged as pickers. Down from the East End of London came the families who looked on the hop-picking as their only paid holiday of the year and who took over the long sheds which were cleaned out and whitewashed for them every year. Special trains to Kent were laid on, and the hop-pickers brought all their own gear – kettles, enamel cups, plates, tin knives, forks and bedding. It seems to me they were supplied with blankets and many of them filled sacks with hops to sleep on and enjoyed a scented, dreamless sleep. Children and babies abounded – also cats, which are transportable, even if the cat doesn't think so! In a few hours this flood of Cockneys had subsided to a normal level, a seasonal price had been agreed with the group of leaders (which always included a couple of gipsies), and the picking started.

Each family, or group of friends, took over a row and worked their way along it, pulling down the loaded vines with a crash and a twang of wires, often leaving the crown of the vine bobbing on the topmost wire well out of reach. The vines would be thrown across the picker's knees and the hops picked off into boxes, baskets, often umbrellas stuck in the earth by their ferrules, hats, newspapers – anything that could hold a hop. At intervals these were emptied into bushel baskets supplied by the management. When brimming full the boys would trudge to the end of the row and empty their baskets very gently and carefully into the big five-bushel baskets that were standing there. The reason for the delicate care was not consideration for the hops but to prevent them sinking down in the big basket by their own weight, and thus taking more baskets to fill it. Two overseers with curved knives mounted on long poles patrolled up and down to be appealed to when a new vine was being pulled down. With a twist of their knives they could cut the string and it was they who brought down the crowns left hanging in the air. All the families worked well, for they were paid for piece work, but the speed of the Cockney women was lightning, like their wit. I can hear now the shouts of repartee mixed with the crashing fall of the vines, the muttered jokes about the family in the next row, accompanied by cries of "Tally! Tally!" as the baskets filled, the shrieks of laughter and the furious quarrels, shouted through the curtains of vines. Our job as tally-men was to accompany the open waggons drawn by four horses down the lanes at the end of the rows to inspect the picked hops and complain if there were too many leaves and vines among the hops, to give the big baskets which had been so carefully filled a vigorous shake so that the general level was a true one, to supervise the five bushel baskets of hops as they were emptied into the big sulphur-coloured sacks destined for the oast house, and finally to mark and initial the bright yellow tally card belonging to each family and stamp on the cover the name of the estate.

It can be imagined what disputes flared up, what insults were volleyed and returned over the marking of the cards. I am talking about the Cockneys from the East End, with whom everything ended with a laugh. With the gipsy families it was a different story. They cheated brazenly and outrageously, they stole anything left about and the children never stopped begging. Nobody minded, nobody ever expected them to be different: they were the gipsies; that was how they were: Ishmaels, with their own secret language that nobody understood. Until one day my Uncle Edward, back from selling Worcestershire Sauce to the Patagonians, started talking Romany to two of the men, for when he was a student he had gone off into the Welsh mountains once or twice with a band of gipsy tinkers and at another time, inspired by George Borrow, he had spent six months with the gipsies of Spain. Then what a change we saw in the handsome, silent men, who had always scowled, watched their women work and their children beg and said never a word. Suddenly they were talking with animation and listening to our uncle with attention until he strolled off with them to brew tea and talk of mutual acquaintances in Spain and Central Europe, and on Epsom Downs.

When the great waggons were loaded high with the bulging sacks of hops (and it was an art to pile them so that their own weight kept them from toppling off), they were secured with ropes fore and aft and we were allowed – or rather I was allowed, because my brother at twelve was getting a bit old for joy rides – I was allowed, then, to ride on the very top all the way to the oast house, on the corner of the road to Fordwich, the village which I later used for some of the scenes in my film *A Canterbury Tale*. There were two kilns for drying the hops and ample space on all three floors for handling, drying and pocketing the whole of Mr Thomas William Powell's crop. The distance from the hop garden (they call them hop fields in Shropshire, the ignorant furriners) was about a mile: up the hill from the brook, along the high wall of the polo grounds (rented by the Army: Canterbury is a garrison town of repute), past the Pudding Gates, where each brick gatepost was crowned with an enormous cement pudding, and so down the slope, with the brake shoe creaking and groaning to stop with a lot of whoaing and jingling fairly under the open door on the top floor where the hoist swung ready for the sacks. My brother has got there first on his bicycle and has got permission to work the hoist to my speechless envy. Down comes the hook on the end of its chain, several rope-slings looped over it. Already the waggoners are seizing the full sacks and roping together three or four at once. On a signal the hoist tightens and the sacks rise to the height of the third floor. Now comes the tricky bit. The sacks have to be raised until the men in the oast house can grab them, when the trick is to lower away at just the right moment so that willing hands can swing the heavy sacks in and on to the third-storey floor. My brother is equal to the challenge. Machinery always works for him. He's not a Corbett. He's a Powell. He could never sell Worcestershire Sauce to a Chinese. He already wears glasses. Like Father.

The oasts were ready and waiting. Most people are familiar with the exterior of an oast house, with its tall conical towers, surmounted by white-painted cowls, weather vanes which turn in the wind, typical of the landscape of Kent and Worcestershire. I suppose not many have been inside. The drying chamber under the cowl was slatted and floored with sacking to allow the fumes of the sulphur to mount up, penetrate, and dry the hops. You had to be careful to walk on the beams when turning the hops over or dragging them in. The sacks from the hoist were hustled across the oast house floor, untied and emptied into the kiln where men with wide wooden shovels distributed the flood of hops evenly to a depth of about three feet. As each kiln was filled to the satisfaction of the foreman the wooden entrance doors were banged shut and latched. Now came the time I loved when, in the late afternoon, we would help the old watchman, Beech, to break up the black sticks of charcoal and set them under the wide iron pans on top of the brick ovens. Then it was the turn of the thick, bright yellow sticks of sulphur to be broken and set in the red-hot pans to burn with a bluish flame, sometimes visible, sometimes not. The weird smell of the burning sulphur, the glow of the red-hot charcoal under the pans, the fumes mountaining up into the darkness overhead, were all wonderfully medieval and evocative, and the final touch of romance was provided by old Beech, producing from a sack carefully selected potatoes, which he set to roast in the charcoal with fingers as impervious to fire as a salamander's. We ate them with salt which he had in a screwed-up paper and you can imagine my joy when, in reading *Puck of Pook's Hill*, I came upon exactly the same scene as I have just described – potatoes, salt, hops, children, and all in Kipling's story "Dymchurch Flit".

My brother rode us both home, I standing on the step of his bicycle with one leg, kneeling with the other on the carrier, my hands on his shoulders. "Just put them lightly on my shoulders," he grumbled. "Don't hang on as if you are drowning. You'll have us both in the ditch."

We shot down the hill and round the corner into our lane, skirting the rushy pond which was supposed to be "awfully deep" and the dingle which I have always associated with "Mumper's Dingle", where George Borrow and Isopel Berners lived in *Lavengro* and *The Romany Rye*. The lane ran straight after the wood, with the meadows of Little Barton on our right and our own farmland, strawberry fields and hop gardens on our left. They had planted poplar trees as windbreaks for the hops. As we neared home I could see the tall beech tree with the seat at the top which was my favourite place for reading. Then the long scummy pond was sliding by, with the ducks single-filing off to bed, led by Francis Drake. White railings appeared and there was my mother, as usual working in her garden until the last glimmer of light. We were home.

Hoath Farm was and is a square of comfortable house, standing back twenty feet from the road, with gardens on one side and a group of farm buildings – barns, sheds, dairy, coach-house and stables – on the other. Parts of the house are three or four hundred years old. The farm had been modernized just before 1910. There was an engine in a shed with a tall chimney to turn machines and a complicated series of wheels, axles and leather belts to harness the power to cake-cutters, revolving drums for cleaning mangold-wurzels, and to the itinerant, lumbering machine that threshed the corn.

My father farmed about four hundred acres, mostly arable, with large orchards and about forty acres of hops. There was a dairy herd and their pastures were within easy reach of home. The new house pleased my father. There was room for a billiard room, there was a fair-sized hall and dining room, with plenty of room for a big mahogany table from his father's home. Across the hall was a large stone-paved kitchen and, leading off it, a scullery with slate-shelved larders and a big copper in one corner for boiling clothes. My mother was allowed her drawing room on the first floor – with windows overlooking the farmyard, it was true, but with room for her Worcester china, for miniatures in little silver frames, for porcelain figures and for watercolours of faltering execution, but cherished because of the executioners. The windows were protected from winter weather by folding white shutters which, after the long summers, unfolded to reveal nests of earwigs and moribund flies. There was only one bathroom, at the top of the first flight of stairs, and only one water-closet at the farthest end of the long corridor which held the house together. Hip baths were still in use, as were chamber pots. The tin hip-bath, in front of a coal fire in a cast-iron grate, with a towel-horse draped with warm towels behind it, is still my idea of heaven. The cans of hot and cold water, the security from draughts, the warmth of the fire, the thought that with a bit of luck you might get into your mother's brass bedstead, with the detachable balls on the ends of the bars which rolled all over the floor to be retrieved with a great deal of laughter and scrambling under the bed, formed part of a ritual which represented comfort, security, friendship, and dependent independence, for none of the servants thought of themselves as servants – not Norah, the great red-faced cook, nor Emily, the house-parlourmaid, nor Miss Eagles, my governess, nor Joan, the scullery maid. They were part of the house and shared in its triumphs and its changes.

Howlett's Farm had been a cramped dwelling place in comparison with my father's ambitions. Hoath Farm had a spacious medieval feel about it, *la vie du château*, after the small rooms and cottage passages of Howlett's. I was about four when we moved and I remember sitting – or being seated – on top of a pile of carpets and furniture.

My most vivid memories of the smaller house where I was born are all connected with fire: the day we burnt the rick down, the day I fell into the fire, and the blacksmith's forge, which seems to have vanished, for I find no trace of it today. Perhaps he was an itinerant blacksmith, but it seems to me that he was a permanent fixture, along the road in the direction of the railway viaduct of the London and South Eastern Railway, where we tried to time our walks to see the splendid boat-train – chocolate and cream – dashing towards Folkestone and Dover, and on one occasion the Royal Train, and our Bekesbourne stationmaster in a top hat borrowed for the occasion from my father, which got blown out of his hand by the wind of King Edward's impatience to get to Carlsbad and Lily Langtry.

My father was fond of sports, because he was good at them and was socially inclined. We saw little of him, so that threat "Your father will hear of this" was a very real one. We addressed him when he crossed our paths as "Father". "Dad", "Daddy" or "Pa" would have been unthinkable, in the Powell tradition. (We were taught to address my mother's father as Grandpa, and he was "Pa" to all his Corbett sons and daughters.) My dear mother had many names, culled from our mutual readings: "Mummy Mouse" (Beatrix Potter), "Best Beloved" (Kipling), "Dearest" (*Little Lord Fauntleroy*), "Marmie" (*Little Women*) and best of all the two syllables which are the first word that every child in the world utters and that every woman loves to hear.

My father was sociable and attractive, masculine, popular with both men and women. He was what the French call *très sportif* – he got a great deal of pleasure out of playing and winning, and showed it. He was about six feet tall and heavy-set; he had been in the rugby football team at Bromsgrove and can be seen with arms crossed staring narrowly at the photographer, but almost unrecognisable to us without his glasses. He looked keen and observant with his rimless pince-nez spectacles, but when he took them off to polish them with a silk handkerchief, or to rub his eyes with his knuckles, the difference was striking; that he was romantic I knew from the books he read; but without his glasses he looked defenceless. His world never saw him like that. As for my mother, I have the impression that she never knew him at all – from which her sons profited, for she played with her little boys and let other women tramp around the golf course in oversize tam o'shanters, or swoon admiringly at my father's cannonball tennis service. She was, however, a fearless horsewoman, and I have a vivid mental picture of her, a diminutive figure in her dark riding habit, veil, and hard hat, perched on top of The Terror, or The Giantess, immense sixteen or seventeen-hand horses loaned to us by the Army in return for their keep. East Kent hunting mostly consisted of ups and downs: up the slippery chalk hills in the misty North Sea rain, to slither down the other side, sitting well back on your horse's buttocks. Either that or splashing along the rides cut through the chestnut saplings, which were a feature of our part of the world. Arthur Marchant, a jolly man who owned a brewery and looked as if he did, whom we liked, swore that he would follow my mother anywhere. "She'll ride at anything and put that monster of a horse at it, and if it's too high for him he'll just smash his way through, and your mother on him, and me right behind them both."

The day we burned the rick down I was in the pinafore stage. My most treasured possession was a little four-wheeled waggon, painted in gay colours, with a swingletree for my patient brother John to pull it by, while I rode in it entranced. We decided to have an unofficial picnic in the rickyard at Howlett's. It was at our back door and it must have been in September when the corn was in and the yard was full of ricks, built on stone pillars clear of the ground and the stacks of corn waiting to be threshed. In a fatal moment John suggested that we build a fire and roast potatoes as we had learned to do at the oast house. It must be borne in mind that I was three and my brother two and a half years older. He built a fireplace of bricks and kindled a fire with straw and laid on some bits of tarred wood, while I watched in admiration. The fire caught the tar and roared up, the flames ran along the ground scattered with ankle-deep straw and caught the nearest stack. While my brother was trying to stamp out the train he had lit I can recollect myself running roaring into the kitchen and the cook's apron. By now the alarm bell on the stables was being rung by Joe Wood and men were running. "Let the stack go!" John, white-faced but brave (he didn't try to hide) helped drag the garden hose and get the water going. The corn stack was completely destroyed, the other ricks scorched but saved. My little waggon stood where I had abandoned it, a charred skeleton which collapsed on being moved.

It was the most awful event of my young life. I was too small to be blamed (although I am sure I had been an enthusiastic accomplice) and my brother was locked in our bedroom "until your father comes back from Canterbury". He let down a string from the window to which I attached a basket – I may have had the help of Ernest, son of the waggoner – with a very red apple in it; or it may have been a tomato. When my father returned John got a good thrashing and there was talk of boarding school. My part in the arson was ignored. It was all very terrible. We were devoted brothers. When I was first taken out in my pram, John introduced me to mutual friends: "This is Icky-Micky." Now, most unfairly, he was treated as a corrupter of innocence, when it was much more likely that I had corrupted him. He was a serious responsible boy. A Powell.

The day that I fell in the fire was not so serious for me as it was for my little sister. Breakfast at Howlett's was a crowded meal. First of all my father was there, and he filled the room. There were always one or two farm pupils; there might be a guest, there was my brother and me and all the dogs, of course, who would crowd in and get stepped on. The dining room was small and the mahogany table, as I have said, was large, and in winter there was a huge fire of logs burning in the open chimney. Mahogany chairs, with horsehair upholstery, surrounded the table with armchairs at each end for my father and mother. At her end was a tall brass coffee-urn with a glass dome that misted over when the coffee percolated. But recently my mother, who was pregnant, took her breakfast in bed. My father was reading the racing news, the pupils were munching and John was dispensing coffee into willow pattern breakfast cups. I was without supervision.

It was my favourite game to be a locomotive on the South Eastern and Chatham Railway with sound effects, also doubling the porter on arrival at the stations – "Sandling Junction! Change here for Hythe, Sandgate, and Romney Marsh", etc. – and since there was nowhere else to get up steam, I was running round and round the table. One of the men put his arm out playfully like a signal to slow me down. I cannoned off it and fell face down onto the blazing logs. One of the pupils, a Mr Stacpole (a relative of de Vere Stacpole, author of *The Blue Lagoon*, we had been told), was seated opposite, and quick to see the mishap and facing the right way, he jumped the table and snatched me out of the fire before I collapsed. I had instinctively put out my hands to save my face. They were badly burnt.

I had a good pair of lungs and I would seldom have a better occasion for airing them. My mother, struggling out from under a breakfast tray, insisted on my being brought to her, while someone put the horse in the trap and went to fetch Dr Morris from Littlebourne. When he came, he wrapped my hands in lint and boracic powder and my chief recollection of the episode is the pink and blue lint and how important the bandages made me feel. By that time I had quite got over my fright. My mother suffered a delayed shock and had a miscarriage. She had no more children. We boys badly needed a sister and a daughter would have made my mother's life happier.

I had better explain the phrase "horse and trap", for there can't be many people left alive who are familiar with it. A trap, besides being many other things, is a light, two-wheeled carriage as opposed to a four-wheeled dogcart with which everyone is familiar as the main means of locomotion in any authentic Sherlock Holmes story. A trap was a very smart vehicle indeed. It was sprung for comfort and built for speed, with two large wheels covered with solid rubber tyres. It was primarily intended for two, but the seat was adjustable, so that two small boys could sit back to back with the driver and his companion and watch the road streaming away behind them. Our trap was painted in a scheme of yellow and black, with black stripes on our yellow wheels like a tiger. Our horse was a Welsh cob, a smart, sturdy animal, a real cob, with hogged mane and tail. His name was Umslopagaas: known as Sloppy.

In those days before the 1914 war and before the automobile, it was important to know how to drive. Management of the horse, or horses, came first. If you couldn't back a horse into the shafts and harness it up you had no business driving it. If you didn't know what to do when a young horse got its leg over the traces, or when a riding horse clamped its teeth shut to stop you putting a bit between them, then you had no business being in the saddle. If you couldn't turn into a driveway without taking the gatepost with you, you were unpopular, unless you were young, female and pretty. The next important thing was consideration for other people, in particular pedestrians and cyclists. We were taught to slow up, stop, or signal our intentions and pass the time of day. Not in modern English lanes. It is no longer a privilege to drive an automobile there. It's a dog fight. But what I miss most is the courtesy which was part of every driver's training.

With us there was no question of anybody but my father (and Woodcock, the groom) driving the trap. It was the equivalent of a sports car later on. But the automobile was already knocking at the stable door. By 1912 my father possessed a tourer, a French Darracq, a formidable piece of machinery with huge brass carriage lamps and a *tonneau* cover which buttoned up around the driver and his passenger delightfully like an aeroplane of that vintage. With my vivid imagination we flew all over East Kent, my brother at the steering wheel. It was fifty years later that I really did fly in an Army helicopter at no more than an owl's height over the fields and woods, the villages and streams I knew so well. We took off from

Thanet, headed for Romney Marsh and flew down the whole length of the Marsh to Camber Castle, which looks across to Rye on its hill. I had never realized before how big the Marsh is. I knew how beautiful it was, with its great skies, its small perfect churches that John Piper has immortalized and its wall against the sea, for the Marsh is many feet below sea level. I knew its miles of golden sands at Dymchurch, and weary pebbles at Dungeness, the little railway and the Martello towers; but we seemed, as the sun set and the Marsh fell under shadow, to be droning like a great bee over a continent. No wonder the Marshmen say that the world consists of Europe, Asia, Africa, America and Romney Marsh. At last we turned and headed straight back over the countryside that I knew from the back of a pony. We passed over Barham Downs, where the water tower crowns the height, over the Nailbourne, over Howlett's and Woolton and Hoath Farm. I was seeing them all again: those familiar and beloved fields and woods and farms streamed by below me "following darkness like a dream". We were hedge-hopping like a witch in *The Ingoldsby Legends*. But because I knew every squashy yard of the bank by the brook, because I knew the fields which were good or heavy going for my pony, because I had had my face stung so often by the hazel rods whipping back in the woods, it all seemed closer and more familiar. There is no land like the land of your childhood. I once asked John Masefield what countryside he had in his head when he wrote *The Midnight Folk*, a film I always wanted to make, and he answered: "Ledbury. Where I was born and where I was a boy."

"Then Wicket Hill is one of the Malverns?"

"Either the Beacon or Clee Hill."

Greatly daring I asked, "If I make the film would you mind if I make it in East Kent, in the country I knew as a boy?"

"Not a bit. If that's where you were a boy I quite understand you would want to make it there."

He was that boy until he died. Like me.

Although the headwaters of our little river often failed, so that Patrixbourne and Bekesbourne Brook ran dry under their many bridges, I was informed by the gardener that the river was still there. "See, Master Mick, 'ow green the grass is in the bed o' th' brook. That's because the stream's there. 'E's sunk into the ground, but 'e's runnin' down there in the chalk." This fascinated my imagination, already stimulated by the terrifying underground river in *Allan Quatermain* and by rivers like the Mole, whose burrowing proclivities turned sedate Surrey in my mind into that garden bright with sinuous rills, "where Alph the sacred river ran through caverns measureless to man". I can sit for hours looking into the Fontaine de Vaucluse, where the river springs full grown from those mysterious limestone caverns. The strength and power of that column of water is like some great artery pulsating and, whereas rivers are friendly to man, so that he can forgive them their periodic and destructive outbursts, I have the feeling that if the Vaucluse dried up, or were tampered with, some great catastrophe would follow. I was shocked when Cousteau's skin-divers profaned the sacred fountain to which the Romans had built an altar, as they did to the Mistral, that bright, cold, impersonal wind and ruthless god, who rides remorselessly down the Rhône hurrying to the Camargue and Les Saintes-Maries-de-la-Mer flattening the Mediterranean with the weight of his breath, buffeting Cap Corse and, repulsed by those splendid cliffs, pouncing upon Genoa. I waited in suspense to hear that the intrepid frogmen had vanished, devoured by fabulous monsters who would vomit out pieces of their indigestible rubber suits. But no! They returned to the herb-scented air of Provence, complaining of the cold and saying that "there was nothing there". Nothing there! How the ghosts of Julius Caesar's Legions must have pitied them . . .

Below Howlett's, and in particular at Nettle Abbey, there were strong springs, and by the time my painted waggon (perhaps it was even early enough for my perambulator) had trundled the mile to Littlebourne, there was always water under the brick bridge which carried the road to Wingham Well, where our Auntie Chrissie and our Uncle Will farmed from a long, black-and-white timber and plaster house. Chrissie was my father's sister. A Powell.

On great and memorable days we pushed on through Littlebourne following the little river to Wickham and Ickham, both of which villages had a tall mill, many storeys high, built of weatherboarding and painted white. I loved everything about those flour mills: the deep, calm millpond where the weeds waved and the coarse fish rose to the flies; the iron grating to catch weeds and tree branches that might damage the millwheel, placed where the still water of the pond got sucked down into the chute; the great undershot wheel itself, dripping and turning the heavy iron machinery of the mill; the millrace between narrow slippery stone walls down into the pool below the mill . . . these all come back to me at any mention of a water mill and my first baby words were about "the rushing water" of Ickham and Wickham. Thirty-six years later in the middle of the second great European war, I dragged my film unit down to the Nailbourne Valley, or the valley of the Little Stour, as it is called by foreigners like the Ordnance Survey, to get shots of my nursery memories. One of the great wooden mills was gone – burnt down, I fancy – but the other was still there, as fine a piece of timber building as ever and it is in the film *A Canterbury Tale* as long as it lasts – the film I mean.

The racket in the flour mill was immense when the wheel was turning and the corn was being ground. The whole structure shook with delight, like a horse on a frosty morning. The air was dusty with flour. The wooden chutes and trap doors, down which the corn and the flour slid, banged and rattled like trap doors in a pantomime chase. The leather belts, which connected wheel to flying wheel, slapped and whirred. I would toil up to the topmost floor by the shaky ladders to see the sacks of grain emptied into the hopper to be sucked out through the funnel at the bottom when a gate was opened, to drop down a chute onto the roaring millstones – for they did roar, like the raging lions in *The Rose and the Ring*, when my mother read it to us. The miller would open wonderful little doors for me to see the grain, or the flour, falling to its destiny. The upper and the nether stone, in their square timber box with the grain-chute in the centre above the hole in the upper stone, were sacred objects, the inner sanctum of the mill. There were always two or three spare stones around, some used, some old, and the miller would expound on the different texture of the stones and how they reacted on each other, and how the nether stone was the hardest.

Bread is a sacred thing and a mill is a temple where the grain we have sown is ground to flour. I used to finger the fine and the coarse flour with respect, as I do today in the health shops. To think that we should have to be reduced, poor, pinched creatures of the supermarket that we are, to deciding between bread that gives us life and bread that turns sour and mouldy in twenty-four hours. Only a very short while ago, every stream had its series of water mills; wheels were turning wheat into flour long after the sails of the windmills had stopped turning. I can understand the passing of the windmills: those huge sweeps of louvred oak, descending like a titan's flail, mounting into the sky like a gesture of his hand and arm; the wooden tower on its brick or stone foundation that shook and trembled in the wind that came racing at forty or fifty miles an hour over the Downs; the smock-mills that could be turned by handling a heavy sweep into the wind – and most of all their stance high on the ridges like a fleet of galleons, glorious, but doomed. But that the local folk, who owe their life and existence to the river, who have strolled and loved and fished and flirted in its meadows, who have gathered bunches of watercress from its chalky beds, who have spent hours lying on a narrow wooden footbridge with a hand trailing in the cool water – that they can bear to see their water mills go, is hard for me to understand.

Towards the end of Hitler's war I was in the Western Isles of Scotland making a film from a story of Emeric Pressburger's for which my Irish wife supplied the title, *I Know Where I'm Going*:

> I know where I'm going
> And I know who goes with me,
> I know whom I love
> But the dear knows whom I'll marry.

I was astonished to see that one of the principal cargoes of MacBrayne's steamers to the Isles during the War was bread from Glasgow. It was strange enough to import factory loaves of bread in peacetime, but it was incredible in time of war. When we came to Colonsay, a thickly populated island, with a Big House, modern cottages, a shop and an inn, one of the first things I saw was a water mill in ruins. It had been allowed to collapse; Lord Strathcona was a good landlord, and so long as the steamer called every three weeks or so with its Glasgow goodies, there was no urgent need for a miller and a baker when a dentist came twice a year from the mainland:

> See you the little mill that clacks
> All busy by the brook?
> It has ground its corn and paid its tax
> Ever since Domesday Book.

That was in 1908 in Burwash in Sussex, England.

Lower down, our little Stour left the villages and millponds behind and wandered through water meadows, thick with buttercups and cowslips, to join the big Stour, where there was an island, with four poplars, placed so soberly, that it was at once dubbed Bedpost Island by my mother. Here we came one summer for a camping holiday and here it was that I first felt the urge to write. I was seven and three-quarter years of age according to the note scribbled on the back of a photograph of the diarist by my mother; so it was the summer before the 1914 war, the summer before everything changed. She had evidently been impressed by my wanting to keep a diary and by my application to the job, for to paraphrase Dr Johnson, it is bad enough to have to start to write, it is even worse to have to get on with it. She made an enlargement of the photograph and I found it among her treasures together with the original diary in pencil in an exercise book.

Agust the 8. 19.13 Camping Out.

We came here at one a-clock on Fridy and had dinner and then waited fo the dray which was bring our things but as it didunt come mummy went off on her bicle as she came down the hill into wingham she looked back up the other hill which led to ashe and saw the dray just deserpearing over the hill so she went after it and broght it back, it had got to the hill and couldn't get up and so had to go back fora norther horse and then went up the rong hill, we have got 5 tents and a canoe or boat and a wash-tub to bathe in. There are five of us and Bit and Pupsey seven. The first of the tents in the kithichen, the 2 Aunty-noos and Dapney's, the 3 Johns and mine, the 4 the Glory-Hole, the 5 mummy's.

The "glory-hole" was the contemporary term for a place to store objects that might come in handy. I had forgotten that there were five bell tents. It must have been quite an impressive camp in those lush water meadows of the Stour. At the back of the exercise book is a list of the stores we had brought with us. It is entitled: "Cook-house". I quote from it because it shows at an early age my passion for detail, which has driven many a prop man mad, and my relish for lists and expeditions. It must be remembered that the date is the summer of 1913.

Cook - house .

Cooking Stove ,
Coffee pot ,
Kettles ,
Picnic Boiler .
Billy can .
Soft Soap .
Silver sand .
Tool bag .
Saucepans .
Cups & saucers .
Iron .
Cauldron .
Mustard .
Sugar .
Jam .
Matches .
Cakes .
Plates .
Mallets .
Basins .
Dish cloths .
Hammock Chairs .
Marmalade ,
Chutney .
Tomatos .
Butter

Tea .
Cocoa
Birds Custard Powder
Milk Can
Knives and Forks .
Spoons .
Jugs ,
Bowls .
Bowl of string .
Bread .
Pepper Pot .
Biscuit tins
Dog Biscuit
Drinks
Soap
Salad Dressing
Milk Pan
Flower .
Bovril .
Condensed Milk .
Pineapples .
Teapot .
Vinegar .
Funnel .
Bread Board .
Lemons .

The tents were Army pattern in white canvas with a central pole, and were loaded, along with boxes and baskets of crockery and bedding and provisions, on one of the farm drays drawn by two horses.

I believe the land was farmed by my Uncle Will Maxted, so Chrissie, my father's sister, would have been there. It was a gathering of the clan: Chrissie's children were there, and Edith Powell, my Uncle Jack Powell's wife, with her children, including my cousin Daphne (who was a beauty), plus other cousins, aunts and John and myself. My Uncle Jack was never visible. He was "on the Stock Exchange", spent most of his time in London, and was the envy of my father until he went broke, when he became overnight "that fool Jack".

My father was always outspoken about his relatives, either direct or by marriage, and his fury when his favourite sister, Chrissie, came to stay at Howlett's and married "that fool Will Maxted" continued well into the twenties. We boys liked Will very much. He had a red Indian motorbike and sidecar which was more than enough to make him attractive; and he was kind and good-humoured and tolerant, which our father was not, unless he happened to remember that he ought to be, usually after winning at auction bridge. Chrissie was considered pretty but I never thought so; she was all curls and teeth and ear-rings and she had the Powell nose and an affected way of speaking, which was compared silently with our mother's tender voice whose tones were as warm as sunlight. Of course my father proved to be right, as he usually was about men and women, and when the slump came after the war was over, Will went to the wall and the large family of girls had to leave their black-and-white farmhouse and scatter over the land to earn their living. But by that time, I was in films and in France and I only learnt of it from my father's brief remarks and from meeting my cousins on my return to England.

It is time for me to attempt a portrait of my father and mother as they appeared to an observant little boy in those days before the Great War of 1914, when families were large and prosperous and the British Empire encircled the earth. Lots of my friends and relatives still think it does.

Ladies first: a principle my father subscribed to, like Mudie's Lending Library, but didn't believe in. He had a way of ushering in – or ushering out – a lady which flattered her without committing him.

I look like my mother: but I only know it after seeing our faces merge and meld as we grew old together. It's natural that children resent being told how like they are to people. I remember thinking "How can I be like my mother when she is she and I am me?" A boy called Brockwell who was in my House at the King's School, Canterbury, an elegant and superior boy, whom I admired, said to me after a Founder's Day, or some other visitation of parents, "Powell! Why are you so absurdly like your mother?" I answered hotly that she was much taller than me; but what my mother's height (she was five feet four inches) had to do with her shaming likeness to myself is a mystery to me until this day.

My mother was small, slender and fair, with little swift feet and bright eyes: hence Mummy Mouse. She had been her father's darling and I suspect she might never have married Tommy Powell if it hadn't been for the crash. She was one year older than my father. They were born on December 18 and 19, so on one day in the year they drew level for twenty-four hours and my mother made great play of it. John always knew our mother's birthday. I could never remember which of them came first. And I can't now.

To her sisters she was May and I loved to hear them call her May. It suited her so well. She had the Corbett sense of the ridiculousness of life which helped them to take things, welcome or unwelcome, in their stride. She hated to be indoors. Although her drawing room was full of cabinets of Worcester china, whole sets of tea and dinner plates, dishes, cups and saucers, even soup tureens, figurines of hunters and shepherdesses, cake-plates with scalloped edges, candle sticks like mushrooms, she would find any excuse to picnic in the barn, or in the garden, or even up a tree, with her two boys.

She was a good photographer: first with a square box Brownie, and then later on with a postcard size folding Kodak. (I would love to have got those cameras into the Black Museum of *Peeping Tom*, but I did at any rate include my first film camera, a 35mm Eyemo, hand-operated, made by Bell & Howell, who gave it to me for posing with it on skis and photographing my own feet. I also put my original 16mm Kodak camera into my son's hands in the film.) When I was a boy I never had the slightest interest in cameras myself, and I don't think I ever had one in my hands until the film business got me, fifteen years later. My father certainly had little mechanical flair and had once cut the top joint of his third finger off in a chaff-cutter; we used to ask him, when he was in a good mood, to show us the stump. My brother could take a camera to pieces or anything else to pieces (he should have gone to Canada with his Uncle Clarence) but Mother was the only one with an eye. We had the usual studio photos of us done by Fiske Moore, the photographer of Canterbury, and indeed he did a very lovely one of my mother looking like a Canterbury Belle, but the ones I love are her own work. In the War she had no time, and film was expensive, or rationed – everything was rationed in the First World War, from the beginning. But a dear old man, an itinerant photographer, who made a living travelling around the army camps and was universally known as "Snap 'Em", was able to get a quota of negative filled in, and it is thanks to him that my memory of these years is so detailed.

Ours was a house full of dogs and cats, canaries and goldfish, rabbits and white mice, all possessed of aggressive personalities, and insisting on regular meals and lots of attention. Sometimes they got too much of it. Once I was discovered in the white rabbit's hutch bawling because I had eaten "dear Bun's currants" and didn't like the taste of them. The goldfish got overfed with ants' eggs and the white mice were exiled after raising a family in my father's collar-box. The canaries lived in the kitchen window and sang to the cats purring in the steel fender and there was usually an orphan lamb or two in the boiler cupboard next to the kitchen range, whom we were allowed to feed on the bottle and who butted with their woolly heads on the cupboard door when they felt hungry, which was about every half-hour.

Like all children brought up on a farm in those days, I don't think we really loved animals. I mean that it wasn't an all-embracing love like our mother's. There were animals that were useful, animals that were harmful, animals that were pets, and animals you ate. We loved our ponies, Mister Bun and Fubsy, but then we had to look after them, groom them and muck them out, and it is natural to love whom you serve, without thinking very much about it. We used to tease the dogs until they were frantic. Pupsy, the long-haired English collie, was highly strung, and when her soprano bark was heard outside the door, asking to come in, we delighted to call out, "Wipe your feet, Pupsy! You can't come in till you wipe your feet!" which made her leap up and down with impatience and scream hysterically, "Nobody loves me – loves me – loves me! Everyone hates me – hates me – hates me!" until my brother got up, a piece of Meccano in his hand and let her in, when she would rush to my mother and pant all over her: "Sorry! Offly, offly sorry!"

Bit, the little terrier, half Aberdeen, half brindled ratcatcher, was full of fight like most terriers, and a terror in the rickyard. Our favourite game was to lure him into the big scullery and tease him with long hazel sticks from the vantage point of the top of the copper, until he would yell with rage. If he managed to grab the end of the stick with his teeth a tug of war would ensue which he would often win, for, like the Lobster in *The Water Babies*, Bit would never let go. The advantage of the scullery was that you could leap from copper to big well-scrubbed white wood table, from table to stone sink, and back again, with the raving sweating imp of a dog always close below you, telling you what he would to to you if he caught you. Norah the cook said it was bad for his temper but I think he enjoyed it as much as we did. And what terrier worth his salt ever had a good temper? James Cagney, for instance?

But my mother really loved animals and they loved her. That's the difference. She loved flowers. She loved birds. She gave them personality. Or rather, she made them a gift of her own. Some of it has rubbed off on me, but it is only now, after a long and selfish life, that I realize how much I owe her and how little I have given her the credit for it. She is in every foot of film I ever shot. She is in everything I ever wrote. She is the author of this book.

She was a great garden-maker. She would make or remake a garden and then move on. If she had been able to have a settled life and home, with enough money to plan and look ahead, I fancy she could have become as famous as other women who have fostered rare and slow-growing plants, like Gertrude Jekyll (or Gertrude Stein). But as she was always on the move, from 1919 to 1968, when she died, she left behind her a continuing legacy of beauty and creation. She planted fruit trees and flowering shrubs, she created vegetable gardens and fish ponds, she lugged great barrowloads of stones to make rockeries on which she could grow the Alpine plants her father had dug with her in the Alps. She waged war on moles, slugs, snails, blight and all the pests that beset good English gardeners; and after a few years she would move on and it was all to be done again, in new soil, with new problems, but perhaps this time in a garden with a south-facing wall, on which she could train espaliers of fruit and coax old-fashioned wallflowers to grow in the crannies between the bricks.

Her first garden was a patch at little Bank Farm in the village of Leigh, where the tempestuous River Teme rolls waggon-loads of silt down from the Welsh Hills. It was far from the Worcester she knew and loved, but still within sight of the lofty tower of the Cathedral. She won second prize for a rose that year – I think it was "Beauty of Bath".

Worcestershire is typical of the Shires, heavy clay and rounded hills. Kent is chalk, where chestnuts and hazels flourish. The shallow streams are green with watercress. At the farm where I was born, there was only a vegetable garden with sunflowers lining the fence. It was when we moved to Hoath Farm that she came into her kingdom. It had a rose garden, and a tennis lawn, and a kitchen garden surrounded by a crumbling red-brick wall, with a huge mulberry tree, split apart and riveted by an iron bar, dropping its luscious purple fruit to stain the gravel paths. We stayed there the whole of World War I, and she shocked her sons by gardening in her absent husband's breeches.

For a season after the war was over, she took a house at Hythe, a tall, narrow house on the seafront, which had no garden but the sea, which when she lay in bed seemed to roll right up to her windows, giving her great satisfaction, particularly in a sou'westerly gale, which filled the garden with shells and pebbles, the same gales that roared through the 500-year old oaks of the New Forest, where she next went to live. The Red Cottage was near Ringwood, a little market town on the River Avon, where I was eating my heart out as a bank clerk. The forest soil was sandy, and the New Forest ponies came in the winter to ask for bread.

There was a brief sharing of a house on the edge of Ringwood, too near to shops and conveniences to please my mother, but there was a flower garden bordered with eschscholtzias and marigolds. When I was moved to the Bournemouth bank, it was to a mean little house on the outskirts of the town. It had a small lawn which my mother at once dug up.

Moving westward, and now into Thomas Hardy country, she found Turling Farm at the head of Poole Harbour in Dorset, but after a few years doubled back eastward to be near her son once more, and found Redleaf Cottage, Chalfont St Peter, Buckinghamshire, a cottage tucked away in a fold of the ridge that runs along the Colne River valley, where Denham's great film studios rose among the water meadows, buried in beech woods, on a narrow lane, no near neighbours, my dear mother's ideal of a cottage. Until she found Orchard Cottage, Bramley, Surrey, on a wooded ridge where the narrow lane runs from Hascombe to Bramley and where Miss Gertrude Jekyll cultivated her famous garden, and English chestnuts shed their prickly husks.

Still in the Home Counties, she moved to Berkshire with its gravel pits, casual gorse and scattered pines, where my grandfather, Frederick Corbett, in 1939 spent his last year of life doing *The Times* crossword every morning. Then north to Scotland, to a shepherd's cottage – The Linn, Tynron, Dumfriesshire, where my mother went to look after Land Girls for the duration of World War II. A linn is a waterfall, and the cottage was poised above, the deep glen below. There was no garden.

The Scots have a way of winning your heart, and after the war was over I bought Milnton for my mother, the home of her dreams. The land was bordered by the Tynron Burn. There was a walled garden, a squat comfortable house and two cottages. Two glorious copper beeches, always my favourite tree, stood between the house and the burn. The pasture was all bottom land and flat, a rarity in those hills, and was about seven acres. For a few years my mother was happy, but my father died and I inherited his hotels, and we went less to Scotland and she found it lonely and after an illness moved south to a small house in Hove, next door to Brighton, and only a few hundred yards from the English Channel. Her sister Ethel had retired there from school teaching and they shared the house with its owner, and my mother grew roses, until Ethel died. Her final move was to Weybridge in Surrey, where she was near her sister Grace and the Tomlins family, whose roots reached back to the Worcester of her girlhood. She took over the garden, and was gardening when she died.

With the upheavals caused by two great wars and the virtual liquidation of the middle classes, I suppose that my volatile mother's frequent moves were common to many other families; but what I remember is the energy and the cheerfulness that she showed for every new move, the pleasures and the adventures, the new friends and the new things, that she created out of adversity, out of changes of plan, and above all of the unpredictable changes of fortune of her selfish will-o'-the-wisp of a son, who had fallen in love with the movie business and was finding it hard to reconcile his ideals with the realities of his celluloid mistress.

My mother was a great reader. You couldn't be a daughter of Frederick Corbett and not be a lover of books. Her sisters were scholars. My mother loved poetry and romance, novels and essays. She could never stray far from human contacts. She couldn't afford to buy expensive editions and I would hate to part with the pocket libraries that crowded her shelves. I have them still: the Canterbury Poets, Everyman's, little red Nelsons, the World's Classics, the *Rubáiyát*, George Borrow and Maurice Hewletts that slipped into your pocket. Their familiar faces (for a book's back is its face) smile up at me from every secondhand book box that I turn over, like lost dogs in Battersea Dogs Home. Must I add to their number? Not I. My sons can dump them in the Village Hall and help to buy an outing for the Women's Institute after I am gone. I have twice sold all my books and pictures. I have never sold hers.

One of the great influences of my life, and on the lives of my Corbett aunts and uncles, was Louisa May Alcott. *Little Women, Good Wives, Little Men* and *Jo's Boys* came to Victorian children like a sudden wind that leaped across the Atlantic and blew delightfully fresh and lively air into the stuffy nurseries of the Old Country. There were other New England writers that became our nursery classics. My Uncle Geoffrey's first demand, when he returned from a spell of pro-consulship in India, was always for a copy of *What Katy Did* by Susan Coolidge to take to bed. We all knew the *Katy* books by heart: *What Katy Did, What Katy Did at School*, and, *What Katy Did Next*. I think that my love for America, for the real America that surrounds me now as I sit writing in New England, was born and fostered by these revelations of kindness and frankness, of respect between girls and boys, of love for your neighbours and patience with old and sometimes difficult people. I glimpsed a country like ours, talking the same language, but peppering and salting it with unusual, sometimes old-fashioned words and phrases; breeding youngsters that were not afraid of responsibility and could control their emotions, while behind their brightly coloured faces and figures I sensed a vast country of rivers and plains and forests full of promise, even after a devastating civil war when brother had fought brother over the greatest unresolved issue in the history of man.

This is what *Little Women* meant to us in England and the Katy books were as much beloved. However, I should state that the Elsie Dinsmore books stuck in our craws. We never liked them.

My father was not a reader – or not, at any rate, at this time of his life. He was an active man, a doer. He played a part all his life and got away with it, triumphantly. He was romantic. He was shrewd about his own doings and simple about other people's. He had a great admiration for talent: he didn't understand it, but could enjoy it in others. He was a biggish man, assertive, unexpectedly tender on occasion, attractive to women because he was so uncomplicated. To a child he was a noise: a big noise. To me he always seemed to be banging doors, slapping down cards, and calling out strange phrases like "Where do we go for bees and honey?" or "Come on, partner! If you don't know which are trumps, play the card next to your thumb!"; or to my mother, "What are you doing messing? You trumped my king!" to which she would reply, with spirit, "It's your own fault for shouting at me."

I first got on to him, I think, by studying the old photographs in heavy albums and silver frames which littered the house. This was after we moved to Hoath Farm: even I don't claim to have started being a Peeping Tom before the age of ten, although I do know that it was on the stairs in the hall, stairs painted white, with Kidderminster carpet and brass stair rods, with a white-painted panelled wall on one side, thickly hung with coloured, framed, sporting prints from the *Bystander* Christmas numbers, that I suddenly realized that sex ruled the world: that all the extraordinary behaviour that I had witnessed in grown-ups for the past ten years was caused by the physical attraction of male for female, which I knew all about from the farmyard, but had not associated with sporting prints and Kidderminster carpets. (My Great Uncle Webb was, it seems to me, "in carpets" and may well have been the donor of the thick, flowered stair carpet to the upper regions.) What had caused this experience I can't remember, nor imagine, which is disappointing, and I have once or twice thought, when passing the Hoath, of stopping, knocking at the door, and asking if I might look around, in the hope of some revelation when I stood once more upon the stairs – for that there was a sexual revelation and that it was revealed to me there, I have no doubt. But the particular door that opened in my mind is now shut.

The photograph of my father that gives him away is a framed portrait of an alert, nervy young man, clean-shaven (as he and his brothers were all their lives), in a tweed knickerbocker suit, with stockings, gaiters and boots, a flat tweed cap, and a horn-handled riding crop, the kind that is useful for opening gates. He has taken off his glasses, and his unprotected short-sighted eyes stare at the camera. He looks like the younger son of a farming family trying to be a man-about-his-country-town, and that is what he was, whether the town was Worcester, Canterbury, or Monte Carlo.

His father, old John Powell, was supposed to have brought up his sons with severity and was rated a hard man. My only memory of him was when I went to stay at Upper Wick, together with my mother, to be a page at my aunt's wedding. My cousin Pat was a bridesmaid and we had a splendid time exploring the farm buildings at high speed. My grandfather looked like Allan Quatermain (but all Victorian grandfathers, except Frederick Corbett, looked like heroes in a Rider Haggard novel) and he hardly spoke to us. Later on when he was dead, and his wife was living at Malvern, she seemed gentle and charming, so perhaps there was some truth in the stories of his grimness. She was a dab hand at making cakes and was delighted with greedy little boys.

My Uncle Bertie farmed Lower Wick, and it may have been there that we slept, at my Aunt Stella's. She was a large, friendly woman, had the Catholic religion in a big way, and let Bertie run the house to suit himself. There was a huge stone-flagged kitchen with a scrubbed table and racks of bacon and dozens of hams hanging from the oak beams. Chickens and kittens, dogs and guinea fowl, wandered in and out – nobody ever shut a door. It was just the same thirty-eight years later when I brought my film unit to Shropshire to make Mary Webb's Gone to Earth. We all came over one evening to visit my Aunt Stella and she proceeded to cook bacon and eggs for the lot of us. It is the only time I have ever seen forty eggs sizzling in a pan, while my cameramen reached up to the sides of bacon above and cut off succulent slices as directed. Cameramen are always hungry.

My uncle Bertie was a quiet man, as befitted the eldest of the five Powell brothers. I am sure he hardly ever left Lower Wick and was quite happy about Stella's activities so long as she didn't try to convert him to the Roman Catholic faith. Of course she tried. All the Powell wives tried, in one way or another, for one purpose or another, to alter their husband's character and way of life. But the Powells are Marchers: descendants of Welsh borderers and cattle thieves: close-mouthed raiders and throat-slitters; folk that tell their wives and families nothing and spend the winter in front of a blazing fire, beasts in the barn, doors bolted and barred, waiting for the spring in the fat valleys of the Welsh Marches.

It must have been with some despair that my mother took a look at her first-born, John, and realized she had produced another Powell. There was no mistaking the narrow Celtic head, the weak eyes, and as he grew, the light slender body. She need not have worried. My brother had a sweet disposition and a passion for mechanics and invention which kept him busy and happy all his short life. He was as patient and generous an elder brother, as I was a maddening, moody younger one. Our relationship, loving but erratic, was to be a pattern for the partnerships and collaborations that later on shaped my life and work.

I have already hazarded a guess that my father's reason for moving to Kent was to get away from his father. He was a great get-awayer. He spent the next few years getting away from his wife: the 1914 War was a golden opportunity to get away from wife and family. His first job in the War, training remounts for the cavalry, took him to Folkestone, and from Folkestone it was only a step across the Channel to where the action was.

Service abroad, in his beloved France, took him ever further away from his prewar destiny, and when a brother officer persuaded him to come in with him as co-owner of a hotel, he "got away" for ever and proceeded to act his new role with gusto and considerable success for the rest of his life.

My father was a selfish man. He rode rough-shod over everyone and it was astounding that he made so few enemies. The fact that he kept all his women friends as long as they lived is a clue. There was no malice in him. He was close, but not secretive. He was tight-fisted, but not mean. He was sociable, but not effusive. He had no depths, but no shallowness either. He was attractive in his person, light on his feet, a good ballroom dancer, a considerate host, an appreciative guest, a good partner at contract bridge, a bold gambler. He liked to win, but was a good loser. A woman might do worse.

Except one woman – my mother. On the credit side she had her two sons, but not for long. She had a comfortable home, but not for long. She had a husband who no longer loved her, perhaps had never loved her, as my mother understood love, and who had all the attractions that a man needs to make otherwise sensible women fall in love with him. She had clothes, possessions, position, for all of which she cared nothing. She had friends and these she did care about: she made new and faithful friends throughout her long life. On the debit side were the wounds inflicted upon her warm generous heart and no man to help or heal it; her quick brain with no man to sharpen her wits on; her fearless spirit and fierce determination to reach a goal with no man to applaud it. Ferocious feminists in America – you can start a crusade at the drop of a girdle in this country – will reply, "What did she need a man for?" – and the answer is always the same as in Jacques Feyder's film of *La Kermesse Héroïque*, when Françoise Rosay snorts that very question and the young wife answers, "*Vous savez bien.*" My mother didn't need a man like my father: but she was stuck with him, and with her two boys; and the War made their separation a duty, and the loss of the farm a necessary sacrifice.

I loved my mother, but I have never put myself in her place until now, in 1980, twelve years after she died. The decisions, the uprootings, the pilgrimages, the discussions, the temporary refuges, the changes of plans, the hopes, the despairs, the embarrassments of a homeless family in snug and settled England, meant nothing to a schoolboy but novelty. It was all very exciting for me and humiliating for my mother. John was more responsible. He could be consulted. I could only be cuddled.

One last image of me and my mother and then I must return to Hoath Farm. It was on Salisbury Plain. A cold sou'westerly wind is blowing showers of rain across those eternal ups and down. There is no shelter of any kind. Ahead (to a total optimist) lies Stonehenge. My mother is determined to get there. She has never seen Stonehenge, because she married the wrong man, and she is hell-bent on getting there now. She leads the way on her bike, with its loaded basket and Thermos flasks and its three speeds. The wind is rising to gale force. She has to stand on the pedals of her bike to keep forging ahead. She peers through the grey squalls. It can't be far. And then she looks over her shoulder. She falters. What she sees is me, the future film director of heroic adventures, of dogged endeavours, of superhuman sacrifices in the name of art, the director whose name is a by-word as "the man who kills actors", the man who dragged film units up to Baffin Land and down to Montevideo – to get unique scenes, it's true, but mainly for the fun of going there. She sees a twelve-year-old-boy in her wake on his battered bike, trying to keep up with his leader's furious pedalling, the tears streaming down his face, his hands blue on the handles, his bare knees raw in the wind, his . . .

She stopped. She dried my tears. We drank some hot tea. She gave up her struggle when the goal was almost in sight. She gave it up for me. We went back to Salisbury. She didn't get to Stonehenge until seven years later. But when she did, she took a sleeping bag and slept there.

I must have been about four or five years old when we moved from Howlett's where I was born, to Hoath Farm. I remember sitting on top of a pile of rugs and carpets on an open dray. They were familiar by their colourings, their bare patches recalling the rooms they had covered. Here is the Turkey carpet from the dining room, and my mother's Axminster from her withdrawing room. Here are the green nursery rugs; and the antelope skins sent by my Uncle Alan, known to his family as Bulbo (does any child still read *The Rose and the Ring*?). Here is a great roll of stairway carpet, for there are two staircases in the farmhouse. And there cracking and uncoiling, like Kaa the Python in *The Jungle Book*, is the roll of linoleum off the kitchen floor.

Coleman, the head waggoner, cracked his whip and the ponderous dray started to roll as the harness tightened and Ginger and Pickles and Jemima strained at their collars. The iron tyres of the gaily painted wheels gritted on the dusty road. I think it was the March Quarter Day. I sat on my carpet throne and watched my baby days go by. I had been haunting the smithy, watching the blacksmith check the shoes on the horses. Coleman brought them down, two at a time, with his son Ernest, who was about my age, both riding side-saddle on their broad glossy backs. I think that those huge, warm, docile bodies, with the massive ridge of backbone, and the long mane of hair to clutch hold of, were the earliest memories of most country children in those days. At the forge the men examined the feet of the horses, looking for loose or worn shoes, hooking the farmyard litter out of their feet, checking for any signs of thrust in the "frog" of those great hooves, as big as dinner plates. I watched the work as the smith shaped the red-hot shoe and plunged it again and again into a tin of cold water, making clouds of steam. *Bang! Bang! Bang!* with the hammer, then the shoe, seized by pinchers, was applied to the horny sole of the horse's foot, giving off evil smelling smoke as the hot iron seared it. The smith seized his knife and pared away some of the horn, then reheated the shoe and, while he held it rigid on the anvil, his boy punched holes for the nails. One last fitting, the shoe was nailed home, and the projecting ends of the nails twisted off and filed down.

"Doesn't it hurt Smiler?" I asked each time I witnessed a shoeing and always got the answer:

"Not a bit, Master Mick. It don't hurt 'im no more'n you having your nails cut."

"But I hate having my nails cut."

Our new home had its own oast-house on the Sandwich Road, and John and I haunted it during the hop harvest, especially during the pocketing. It was the nightwatchman's job to turn the hops over several times during the night, wielding his wide wooden shovel until they were dry, but not too dry, brown but not too brown. They smell intoxicating and they are ready to be "pocketed". This is a responsible job and is usually supervised by Joe Wood, the bailiff: a hop-pocket burst by careless handling is a disaster. These are huge cylindrical sacks about ten feet long and two and a half feet across, made of stout burlap and closed at one end. The other is tucked over and around an iron ring which sets into the floor and holds the mouth of the pocket open for the press. The press is a round cast-iron ram which fits the pocket exactly. Both ends of the pocket are tested with great care by the bailiff before he gives his nod. The cooked hops have been shovelled out of the kilns and gathered into great drifts kept in place by boards. At the bailiff's nod the men start shovelling into the pocket until it is full and the guides of the press are buried in surplus hops. A shout from the bailiff, the men stop, the ratchet is let go and the heavy press plunges down into the pocket. He lets it go until it stops itself. Two men take the wheels and start turning. Down and down goes the press, the burlap groaning, the hops becoming a solid mass at the bottom of the pocket until the men can turn no more. "Her'll do!" from Joe Wood.

The press is wound up to the top again and the action is repeated. At last the pocket is crammed full and the open end has to be sewn up. One of the older men has been waiting to do this. He has the big needle, the string and his knife all ready. Now comes a tricky moment. The heavy and swollen pocket has to be lifted up a few inches so that the surplus burlap can be freed from the iron ring and the mouth sewn securely up. Last of all the ends of the burlap are gathered into "ears" for handling. The bailiff shouts, "Look out below!" the pocket is freed and falls with a thump to the storey below, which is just the right height for loading a waggon. By the end of the morning the dray has been loaded with what looks like a dozen huge sausages and is on its way to Canterbury. At some time during the pocketing a sample of the packed hops has been collected by Joe in a small wooden box. One sniff of the contents and a fingering of the dried hops by an expert will settle the price of the load and decide whether Monte Carlo will see my father, or Margate.

It must have been March 1910 when we moved, because I know I learnt to read between the age of five and six and we were already established at the Hoath and at a more convenient distance from Canterbury. Bekesbourne, except for its railway station, was remote, but now we were only two and a half miles from the town and my mother arranged for me to go to Fröbelheim, a kindergarten in St George's Place, conducted by two ladies who guaranteed that by the Fröbelheim Method any child could be taught in one year to read and write. They were as good as their word. My brother, being two and half years my senior, went to the Misses Sankey, spinsters who kept a dame-school in the street opposite Court's Stores; he rode in on Mister Bun, a sturdy blue roan pony, which he stabled with Mr Crowhurst, the vet, as I was to do so later on Fubsy. I was a bit young to ride my first pony, Old Barney, to school, so for the whole scholastic year my mother popped me on the carrier of her bicycle and rode furiously to Canterbury, down our lane to the main road, passing by Chartham Asylum, down vertiginous St Martin's Hill, past St Martin's Church which was, we were told, the oldest church in Christian England (which didn't stop me always wanting to go out during the sermon to pee in the graveyard), past Simon Langton's School, an uproar of rough boys and even rougher girls, to Fröbelheim. How she managed to get us both back again and what she did all the morning while I was at school, I don't remember and probably never knew. I think it was only mornings that I attended.

As soon as I could read, I was bought a new pony, an Exmoor mare, who must have arrived in winter when her coat was shaggy, to have been named Fubsy, after Kipling's *Law of the Jungle*:

> Oppress not the cubs of the stranger,
> But treat them as sister and brother,
> For though they are little and fubsy,
> Maybe the Bear is their mother.

Mr Finn's brother, who lived at Faversham, on the north coast of Kent, bought her for me. George Finn was a Canterbury estate agent, as well as a farmer on his own land, and he became my father's friend and benefactor, when the war burst upon us. He was a tall, fine-looking man, slow and stately, competent and kind, and we were to meet again during the Second World War, when I was directing *A Canterbury Tale*. His son Hugh, who farms intensively and with genius 650 acres of land at Nackington just outside Canterbury, came with his family to see the film again the other day. But Nackington farmhouse itself, with its 400-year-old ships' timbers, its tiled roof, and its lovely gardens, is no more: the new by-pass road has obliterated it and cut the farm in two.

I had learnt to ride as soon as I could sit a pony. Woodcock, our groom, took me on a leading rein first, along the cart-track of our farm, then along the dusty white lanes, full of chances for a pony to start cutting up, which Old Barney ignored. He'd seen it all. It was a different matter with Fubsy. She was a high-spirited, mischievous pony with an observant eye and a mouth of brass, once she got the bit between her teeth. She would shy at anything. She was a devil to round up, and when you groomed her you took her into the yard or a loose-box, for in her stall she stood on your feet; and when you got unwarily between her and the wooden partition wall she would lean heavily against it and crush you in between. I loved her. *Il y a toujours un qui baise et un qui tend la joue.* Fubsy loved nothing but her stable and a handful of oats.

I was always falling off in those days. I was a dreamy boy and given to long reveries during which I saw and heard nothing. It annoyed my brother and it annoys people still. Fubsy would feel the grip of my knees weaken, the reins slacken, would choose her excuse – a blown leaf, an abandoned agricultural implement, a gate swinging in the wind – give a stiff-legged jump of exaggerated surprise and off I would go onto the road or into the ditch, and off she would go at a brisk trot homewards, her reins swinging, me running after her yelling, frantic that she would catch her legs in the reins and bring herself down on the road and break her knees. With luck we would meet one of our men who would bar the way with outstretched arms, and after a bit of dodging bring her to a halt, when she would at once start to eat great mouthfuls of cow parsley, which she was forbidden to do with a recently cleaned bit in her mouth.

One morning she had a once-in-a-lifetime opportunity when we met a marching company of Territorials complete with bugles and drums that burst into sound as we came around the corner of the lane. That time she really bolted and I came off and was dragged by one stirrup for a hundred yards or so before the safety catch released. But I wasn't hurt except for a bang on the knee which made me an interesting cripple for half the summer holiday, hobbling about on crutches (two croquet mallets). Water on the knee, they called it.

I have led an active life and, in my eighties with all my wits and teeth about me, you could call it a charmed one. A film director has not time for fear. The perfect set-up, the perfect shot, that is all he has time for. I have had some near shaves along with my camera-crews. I can't say that any of us were impressed by them. Very occasionally one of us runs it a bit too fine, as happened to my old and dear friend Skeets Kelly, on The Blue Max, *when his chopper sliced into another over the Irish Sea. We can imagine it. We salute him. But it doesn't make us any less determined to take just that extra bit of risk to get just that extra bit of perfection in the shot. Our sense of curiosity is greater than our sense of caution. Every cameraman and every director has his memory stuffed with images: images that have been created or attained by fellow artists. His life is a constant search to improve those images, to invent new ones, to add to the common stock of story telling. In the course of doing this he takes unjustifiable risks, but he doesn't see it that way. The great innovators have always been fearless. You may call them, if you wish, foolhardy.*

I have had all my life a priceless gift of detachment. I have fallen off haystacks, out of trees, over cliffs. I have been nearly drowned, shot and hanged. I have been in countless car crashes without getting a scratch. I have been alone in an office with Louis B. Mayer. I always weighed 150 lb and now weigh 160. But I still take the same size in shirt collars. And I still take a calculated risk.

When we were making The Edge of the World *on the remote island of Foula, one of the Shetland Isles, it was before the Second World War and we were young. Most of us were studio-bound craftsmen. The actors were from the theatre. I had knocked about the world a bit, but only two of us could be said to have the pioneer spirit: one was an Irishman, Niall MacGinnis; the other a Scot, Finlay Currie – "Mac" and "Finn", after the first week in camp. Finlay was an old trouper who had already had several careers in the legitimate theatre, had toured the world with famous actor-managers, was a favourite actor of Edgar Wallace's and was launched by me into the big time of films, to be later starred by David Lean as the convict Magwitch in* Great Expectations, *after which he became first choice for all American directors who were casting apostles or saints for Biblical spectacles. On the island we thought he was very old indeed (he was rumoured to be over sixty), and since he was big and heavy, moved with deliberation, and was blind in one eye, we feared he might die on us before we finished the film. We need not have worried. He was as strong as an ox and had thirty more years of work in him. We met briefly in this later apostle period, in the gentlemen's toilet at Claridges after the first night of* Ben Hur.

"How are you, chief?" he asked, shaking his mane of hair. He had played Peter (or St Paul) in the film and was already cast in the next epic as Paul (or St Peter). "Meet Chuck Heston. He's a great admirer of yours."

We nodded: we couldn't shake hands, being otherwise engaged.

Niall MacGinnis died some years ago, of cancer, and I still can't accept it. When I first knew him he was a powerfully built young man, tall and graceful, dark as nightfall, with one of the most musical voices I ever heard in a man. He was a natural actor; it was impossible for him to make a false move, or mistime a line. He had a Dublin intonation, and to hear him sing, "Alive! Alive-o-o! Alive! Alive-o-o-o! Cockles and mussels – alive! alive-o!" the vowels echoing in your brain, was an enchantment. In the camp that we built on Foula, Niall and I were in the same hut. We became friends, and I learnt that his other vocation was to be a doctor; and a doctor he eventually became and a doctor he died, although he continued to act. When I led a film unit to Canada to make 49th Parallel, *there were four of my Foula brothers with me and Niall was one of them. He played one of the German seamen, Vögel the baker, and was a tower of strength in other capacities. He couldn't hold his drink, though. When the other men got happy or pissed, Niall went berserk. I remember on the trawler off the north coast of Labrador the engines broke down when we were surrounded by icebergs. The boys had a party and Niall cut his forehead open on the capstan. It was a deep gash which just missed the eye, and following his instructions I cleaned it out with a toothbrush dipped in permanganate and put a clip on it. We were both proud that there was no scar.*

The last time I saw Niall was at his farm in the Wicklow Hills, near Dublin, when I was planning Return to the Edge of the World. *John Laurie, who had played the leading part in the film, agreed to go back to Shetland with me, and I wanted Niall to be the narrator and appear with John and me and my wife in the new film. The scheme was to bind the old classic black and white film between coloured covers, adding a prologue and an epilogue. My wife Frankie was on the original expedition and came with me from Dublin to find Niall and make sure he would join us in search of our youth. It was a dark and damp winter evening; we had to ask our way and got contradictory answers several times before we parked the car in a steep and stony farmyard and groped our way towards a house with a dim light in the window. It reminded me so much of other nights on Foula that I couldn't resist peering through the panes and, sure enough, there was Mac sitting reading and someone else moving in the shadows cast by the oil lamp. It could have been the Haa (Scots for "the Hall", the Laird's house) on Foula, forty years before.*

We knocked and were welcomed. We drank tea and ate cake and stated our mission and Mac agreed to go with us, provided he got enough notice to find someone to look after his practice for a couple of weeks. We talked of old deeds and planned new ones and then suddenly Mac was dead and I had to return to Foula without him. John Laurie, who as a young man had played an old man, was now an old man playing a young one. We tramped the hills together and talked of Belle Chrystall, who had refused to join us, preferring to leave her 1936 image the way it was, and of Eric Berry, who had become very plump and was touring America playing the Chinese Emperor in some musical show. And now John is dead, too. I am glad he came with us. A good companion, quoting Carlyle to the last.

In 1936 when we made the film, Eric Berry had spent the whole four months on Foula in a battered armchair in the Haa reading, except for the rare occasions when he was on call. "Robbie", the part he played, gets killed in the third reel of the film, so after a couple of months there was little but the cliff-climbing shots to do. When summoned by a breathless messenger Eric would mark his place in the current book, amble out to the location, listen to my enthusiastic description of the spectacular nature of the shot, scramble through it and go back to his book again. He was short-sighted and could do nothing without his glasses. He was only conscious of a void full of noises, wheeling seabirds and the thunder of Atlantic rollers on the rocks 600 feet below him. It was just as well. We all took chances. There is no earthly reason why an actor who, like most of our English film actors, is an actor in the theatre, should do his own stunts in films. There is no reason why he should be asked to behave as if he were an acrobat, but being an actor and a show-off, he likes to have a go. Still, when I had Eric sprawled on the tip of a waterfall where Hoevidi Burn plunges over the ledges to drop into the sea, where boats looked small as toys far below, it occurred to me that I might be taking advantage of his amiable nature, and I sent Hamish and Syd Streeter down with ropes onto the ledge below to catch him when he fell. The sequence finished, Eric changed his wet clothes, asked for his glasses and trudged back to base to resume his reading.

The only excuse for my behaviour, which became a legend, is that I never asked anybody to take a chance that I wouldn't take myself. Generations of cameramen and actors will bear me out. As for my mother, in my boyhood days she was forever bandaging and binding my cuts and sprains, rubbing dock leaves on my nettle stings, and drying my tears. I became stoical, resigned to my clumsiness, and you couldn't get a tear out of me after I was six. To this day when I hit my bald head on a stone lintel, or cut my thumb off my hand with a saw or bury an axe in my boot, it is a point of honour with me to say nothing. Behind the mask, I curse my ineptness. When my mother read us stories, my brother liked G. A. Henty. I was reported to have said, "I befer Greek Smiffs". The Greek myths appealed because of their outright paganism, the superhuman tasks accomplished by their heroes, and their stoicism. My particular hero was Theseus, whose father's sword was hidden beneath a giant rock until the boy should be strong enough to lift it. My mother said she saw me struggling to lift something far beyond my strength and, approaching unobserved, she heard me say between my teeth in Theseus' words, "If my heart comes out of my body it shall come up!" I seem to recognize the man in the boy.

The four years at the Hoath, up to August 4, 1914, were formative ones. The farm was manageable and it prospered from the combination of my father's drive and ambition and Joe Wood's care and admiration. The family prospered also, although there were no additions to it. My brother was already showing his bent for mechanics and was Meccano-mad, which involved vast expenditure on miniature girders, nuts and bolts, gears and motors. This was the heyday of Basset-Lowke, a firm which made and marketed scale models of every type of steam engine, each part constructed on a special jig which produced pistons, wheels and undercarriages correct to a thousandth of an inch. The founder of the firm lived and died in London, in Melbury Road, Kensington, in the tall red-brick house opposite the one we later lived in and which serves, in my film *Peeping Tom*, as the home of the fiendish Professor Lewis, who used to drop lizards on his son's bed to study his reflexes. I only found this out when I was making the film in 1958. The occupants of the basement flat asked me in and showed me the hatchway in the wall, opening into the garden, which had been constructed by the equally obsessed Basset-Lowke for his private model railway engines to steam around the rockeries, flowerbeds and fishponds, returning, unless signals were set against them, to the basement room, which was one vast, busy terminus like Paddington Station. My brother's similar expanding interests over the floor of the hall and the billiard room were too much for my father, who decided we were to have a playroom to get us out from underfoot. He must have had a good harvest that year for a playroom we got, a sectional hut about ten feet by twenty erected in the paddock outside the back door which was one of our favourite play places, because superannuated hop poles were stored there like Indian wigwams and it was possible, by carefully adjusting the poles one at a time, to make an opening to the interior large enough to wriggle inside. When the playroom arrived my brother at once constructed a wide shelf running around it with a drawbridge across the door, to carry his four railroad tracks, and I was continually being pressed into service to alter points and work signals.

Some spectacular railroad smashes resulted from such an optimistic appointment. My idea of playing was to be up a tree, preferably a beech tree, with my head in a book. So when coaxed or bribed to come down and be a signalman the book came too. "Fuzzy! Will you put that book down and attend to the job?" I had a huge mop of golden curls of which my mother was proud, and was called Fuzzy by my straight-haired, bespectacled brother whose hair was rich mouse.

The garden at Hoath was divided like Caesar's Gaul into three parts: the flower garden (which included a lawn tennis court), the kitchen garden, surrounded on four sides by a high red-brick wall, on the top of which it was my delight to play follow-my-leader (so long as it was I who led) and the Wilderness, a grove of trees and bushes beside the duck pond, where there was a swing and a stile into the hop garden. This was my special domain. I had a seat at the top of a beech tree, suitably stocked with oranges and apples, according to the season, which gave me a view across the hop vines to the white towers of the oast house. I would stay up there until called in to meals, or summoned by John to admire his latest steam engine that could be connected to a minute circular saw to cut up logs as thick as pencils!

I was now riding to school every morning on Fubsy, John riding Mister Bun. We groomed and saddled up our ponies ourselves, and I usually had time to gallop around the orchard and the lower meadow to check my mole traps. A glance would tell me that a trap was sprung and I would jump off, throwing the reins over Fubsy's head to trail on the ground, having been assured by Wild West tales that cowboys trained their ponies to stand so. Whether they did or not, I had trained Fubsy to do it. Pulling on gloves, to disguise the smell of human sweat, I pulled the trap out of the ground and five to one there was a dead "velvet-coated gentleman" in it, to be dropped into my satchel. I reset the trap, replacing the turf and sprinkling loose earth over it so that no chink of daylight should penetrate into the mole's dark tunnel. Then off to the next one, often with only one foot in the stirrup, Fubsy was so fresh and eager to go. When I rode back to the stableyard I would find my brother looking at his new wristwatch. If there was time I handed over my catch to Old Beech to be skinned, pegged out on a board, and dried. It was typical of me that I was good at catching moles and bored at having to skin them. When there were a hundred skins I would check the market for moleskin waistcoats, which varied like any other market, but I seem to remember that the going price before the 1914 War was lowest at fourpence a skin, highest at ninepence. Anyway it was mine, and as my pocket money was fourpence a week it was big money. But I don't remember that I gave kind, patient Old Beech (who was probably about forty years old) any of it.

Off we would go, Mother waving (all the Corbetts were great wavers), at a brisk trot along the lane by the duckpond, where Francis and his snow-white wives were gabbling and dabbling in the rich black mud and green scum. In a minute or two we had reached the field gate into Little Barton. My brother opened it, using the horn handle of his riding crop to unlatch the gate and then hold it open. Fubsy, impatient and cocksure as usual, would crowd up, pushing her unmannerly way through to a snort of contempt from Bun and a whisk of his hogged black tail which didn't impress Fubsy at all. She had a long tail down to her fetlocks and what a job it was to comb the dirt out of it, too! We cantered along the farm road to clatter through the cobbled yard of the farmhouse, and out into the carriage road, which led under an enormous oak, downhill to St Martin's. There we had two choices. We could turn left, join the Dover road, and follow it to Canterbury, or we could turn right and come out at the foot of St Martin's Hill on the Sandwich road, which was shorter but which meant we would run the gauntlet of the rude boys and girls of the Simon Langton School who considered little toffs on ponies ideal targets for orange skins, apple cores and, occasionally, stones. My brother's reply was to turn his pony, which was a big one, and ride straight through the enemy to scatter them, while Fubsy flashed by, her little hooves striking sparks out of the flints, her tail and mane tossing, to wheel into Upper Chantry Lane, where the Crowhursts lived in their tall Victorian house, "The Paddock". The stableyard gates were always welcomingly open, and I clattered in, unable to stop Fubsy going straight into her loose-box, so that I had to duck and lie along her neck to avoid knocking my head off on the lintel. John and Mister Bun would follow. We were usually late, so there was no time even to off-saddle; we slipped the bits out of the ponies' mouths, the Crowhurst groom would do the rest. We hurried through the narrow streets to the cattle market under the city walls, passed through the Dane John Gate, down Burgate and around the corner to the little school kept by the Misses Sankey: Miss Helen and Miss Mary.

Why do I see Miss Helen in mauve ruches and Miss Mary in striped shirts? Miss Helen was slim and eager. She was artistic and drew rather well. She had a lined face full of laughter, and dark hair gathered on top of her head. Her eyes were bright and observant and saw a long way. She held herself well – I can never see her slouching – and I suppose she was about forty. Miss Mary, short and square, was more formidable. She was shrewd and capable. Did she have glasses? If she did they were steel-rimmed. She reminded me of a badger. She was always smiling but it was only an expression. It meant nothing. They were good teachers.

My brother had been their pupil for two years when I started going to the Sankeys' School. He was soon to go to the King's School (Junior) but he remained a day boy. We still rode together to Canterbury, although we no longer shared our midday meal at the Crowhursts', as arranged by my mother. The family consisted first of Mr Crowhurst, the vet, a figure straight from Trollope. Vigorous, deliberate and rotund, with a fuzz of reddish hair and beard, red-rimmed eyes, gold-rimmed spectacles on a chain. No small talk. We never knew whether he knew we were there or not, although he carved the meat at the table: it was often bullock's heart, stuffed and braised. (I almost wrote *always* bullock's heart because I have such a vivid memory of it, but perhaps that was because I detested bullock's heart; I was a finicky boy and had an annoying gift of sicking up at once anything I was forced to eat, like fat or gristle.) Then there was Mrs Crowhurst, who had the most vivid, twinkling eyes, set in a weather-beaten face. She was slim and active and I seem to remember that she could handle a dogcart better than a man. Her daughters, Nancy and Marjorie – Marjorie was the elder but it was always Nancy and Marjorie – were our first girlfriends, outside of cousins. They were not pretty, but they had charm and were kind, and Nancy was a friend in a thousand, first to John who was about her age, and then to me, as she still is. They were always inventing private jokes which they shared with us and when I was in the Cathedral choir, in an Eton collar and a white pleated surplice, they sat opposite in the public seats and did their best to make me laugh. As we had no sisters, their companionship and high spirits were what we needed.

Besides being dreamy I was shy and reticent, and it was an agony for me to ask a favour, to assert myself, or to ask to go to the toilet. I would avoid it as long as possible and once, on the long run from the stables to the school, nature caught up with me and I shitted myself. I still remember the miserable dilemma I was in and how I tried to clean myself up in the public lavatory which I had just failed to reach. I arrived at the Sankeys' smelling like – well, not like violets – crept into my seat (we all had desks with flip-up seats) and hoped nobody would come near me. Miss Mary was the first to sniff and finally homed in on me. "Michael! Have you stepped in something horrid?" Sniff! I stammered something about smelling of the stableyard. By this time it was impossible for me to do the obvious thing and appeal for help and a bath. So I sat there the whole morning with everyone giving me a wide berth. When I got to the Crowhursts' at lunchtime I saddled my pony and rode uncomfortable home, without lunch, and not returning for afternoon school. The stupidity of my reflexes made a great impression on me: proved by my remembering it so vividly after all these years. It was as formative as My Egg.

My Egg was a boiled egg – four minutes. My father made many new friends in the 1914 war and among them were the Johnstons of Billericay in Essex. Daphne Johnston was as beautiful as she was kind and when I was a boarder at Dulwich College in 1921, she invited me to spend the weekend. I had never been a country house guest on my own and my chief worry was how or what to tip the butler. I needn't have worried. He pocketed my half crown without hesitation or thanks. It was arranged that I should return to school on Sunday evening and that I should have an egg for my tea as I was a travelling schoolboy who would report back too late for tea. The ladies were out and I was alone in the library when Keith, Daphne's brother, came in from exercising the horses. Tea was served. "Ha! Boiled eggs," he said. "Good," he said, and ate my egg. I munched bread and butter, scones, cake, but the egg rankled. It rankles now. It is the same as when I hit my bald head on concrete. I say nothing. I can say nothing. I can't even groan. Why couldn't I say to Keith, "Steady on! That's my egg. Your butler will get you a dozen boiled eggs, but that four-minute egg is mine"? I couldn't then; I couldn't now. A friend to whom this story was told was always afterwards quick to spot the expression on my face over some frustration. "It's your Egg!" she would cry pointing a finger, "It's your Egg!"

Years later, in a production of Jean Anouilh's *The Lark* at the Lyric Theatre, Hammersmith, a young actor walked onto the stage and with superb insolence captivated the audience as the Earl of Warwick. Richard Johnston was the son of Keith, the eater of my egg. When we became friends I told him the story. He didn't find it amusing nor even interesting. He was no analyst. He was an extrovert, a lordly handsome extrovert, like his father, whom I knew, but whom, of course, he never knew as I knew him. He had no Egg. Neither of them had an Egg. They just ate other folks' eggs.

Although born, brought up and partially educated in a famous cathedral town, it was some years before I realized that I had an eye. Canterbury is full of famous churches and fascinating ecclesiastical architecture, but is otherwise not noticeably devoted to the visual arts. It is above all a place of pilgrimage, and for us farming families a market town, baaing and mooing twice a week with sheep and cattle in their pens under the Roman walls of blue-grey flintstone. One took for granted the High Street and the narrow, medieval lanes – Butchery Lane, Mercery Lane (always confused in my infant mind with Nursery Lane), that pushed their way between the overhanging black-and-white houses. You can see them in my film when the marching soldiers turn left to their route to the Cathedral. My temple was the public library – the Beaney Institute – just as Goulden's Lending Library was my mother's. I would often swap books two or three times a day. My first act was to check down the Jules Vernes on the Indicators – red was Out, blue was In – to see if I had at last hunted down *Michael Strogoff* or Part Two of *The Mysterious Island*. These were all profusely illustrated with vivid engravings, at least fifty to a volume, and they led me to the bound volumes of *Punch* and of the *Strand Magazine* which lined our bookcases. This was when it dawned upon me that I had an eye – and that not everybody has one or takes pleasure in using it. I found I could identify any artist or illustrator by his line without looking at his

signature. For instance H. R. Millar (the E. Nesbit stories) and Sidney Paget
(*The Adventures of Sherlock Holmes*) took precedence for me over the
writers! (I can see Emeric Pressburger's grim smile as he reads this. *He* is the
writer half of our collaboration.) Those days before the movies were the
heyday of the illustrator. Weeklies like *Sketches by Boz* and *Punch* had
always been as much visual as literary, but it was the publication by George
Newnes in 1891 of the monthly *Strand Magazine* that was the watershed.
The *Strand* jogged along for a few months, neither making nor losing
money, then in July appeared the first instalment of *The Adventures of
Sherlock Holmes* by Arthur Conan Doyle, with vivid illustrations by
Sidney Paget, and the magazine took off. Both my grandfather and my
uncles told me that on the City platform at Forest Hill Station, crowded as
usual with businessmen, with umbrellas, gloves and top hats, waiting for
the 9.15 to London Bridge, they had seen every man of them, on the day of
publication with his head in the *Strand Magazine* devouring the latest
Adventure. In the crowded carriages six a side, every man was either
reading Sherlock Holmes or discussing him. Just as with Jules Verne the
pictures, as much as the text, created the immortal folk figure. The lean
face, the deerstalker, the Inverness cape, captivated the world. Here in
Dartmouth College ninety years later students glance at me, amused but
respectful, as I stride by in my Inverness cape and deerstalker hat. In
Munich, as I trudged across the icebound city with my valise, looking for a
hotel, a band of students seized my cases with a chorus of "*Guten Abend,
Herr Sherlock Holmes*" and escorted me right up to the reception desk
of the Vier Jahreszeiten Hotel. I am convinced that Holmes and Watson
would never have become household heroes without pictures. For the first
time, and all over the world, a storyteller's images, as well as his words,
were known and recognized. Sidney Paget and Arthur Conan Doyle were
the parents of the silent film, the sound film, the colour film, TV, video tape,
of all the audio-visual storytelling inventions of the next ninety years.

We paid our tribute to them, Emeric and I, in 1942 in our film *The Life
and Death of Colonel Blimp*. In the course of our researches into the Boer
War period we discovered (probably from the bound copies of the *Strand*
which I still possess and which ornament the top shelves of my workroom)
that *The Hound of the Baskervilles* was coming out in monthly instalments
at the exact time of our hero's return to England with the Victoria Cross he
had earned in some South African skirmish. The German newspapers at
that time were publishing anti-British propaganda stories, refuted by
Conan Doyle, who had been in South Africa as a war correspondent. We
sent our young officer, charmingly played by Roger Livesey, first to see
Conan Doyle, then to the War Office, where he found that his superior,
Colonel Betteridge, was only interested to know what happened in the next
episode of *The Hound of the Baskervilles*.

"Did this Conan Doyle fellow tell you what's going to happen, eh?"

"Yes, sir. There's another murder."

"Not the Baronet!?"

"No sir. The Baronet is safe."

"Good, good. I'm glad." Then as an afterthought, "Now, look here young fellow! Forget these ideas of yours! Don't get mixed up with newspapers. It isn't done. You got a damn good VC. Lie low for a bit!"

The *Strand Magazine* had many imitators, sponsored by other publishers: *Pearson's Mag* with its yellow cover, and *The Adventures of Captain Kettle*. Cutcliffe Hyne's hero, the aggressive little red-bearded master mariner, was a genuine creation. Then there was Guy Boothby with his Doctor Nikola, who dabbled in Asiatic magic and theosophy. There was the *Windsor Mag*, styled for the would-be sophisticates in county families, with pictures of smoothly smug, beautiful people, which reached its zenith after the 1914 war, with the class-conscious novels of Dornford Yates. And there was always, when all else failed, a new variation on the theme of the private investigator. When Conan Doyle, bored by the insistent demand for more Holmes stories, abruptly killed off his hero in *The Final Problem*, even the *Strand* did not disdain to commission "Martin Hewitt, Investigator" from Arthur Morrison, a writer who knew the East End of London as a social investigator. Conan Doyle soon had to bring Holmes back to life (and Baker Street) in a new series, *The Return of Sherlock Holmes*.

The mushrooming movie business kept pace with the illustrated mags. Their answer to the monthly instalment was the Serial. In the movies' twice-weekly change of programme there were usually a Western, a Comedy, the News, and an episode of a Serial ("Episode 6: The Deadly Spiders"). Oh! those Serials! *The Exploits of Elaine*, *The Perils of Pauline*, *The Crimson Stain*, and oh! those Westerns! Bronco Billy, Tom Mix, William S. Hart . . . Well? Aren't they still with us on the TV screens? They *were* the movies for most of us. When my friend William K. Everson published his book *American Silent Film*, under the imprint of the Oxford University Press, I sat up all night reading it, and yet as the hours sped by a vague unease possessed me: Griffith, Chaplin, Fairbanks, yes! Cecil B. DeMille and Erich von Stroheim, quite so! But where, oh, where, were the Serials? Where were Houdini, Antonio Moreno, and Eddie Polo. Ha! A bright thought! He's left them for the final chapter: he's giving Serials, deservedly, a chapter to themselves: a chapter stuffed with suspense; a chapter terminating with: "CAN SHE ESCAPE FROM CERTAIN DEATH ON THE FACE OF THE LOG-JAM? COME AND SEE THE NEXT EPISODE AT THIS THEATRE NEXT WEEK!" Reassured, I read on. Chapter 19, "Transition to sound", was gobbled in a few minutes. It was an apology, more or less, for a distressing but inevitable development of a thing that was perfect

already. But there were only a few pages left! How can Bill deal with
Serials, with *my* Serials, in a page or two? I turned the page: Appendix!
Chronology! Index! By all the Famous Players and Lasky himself there is
no chapter on the Serials, neither at the end nor at the beginning! I can't
believe it! Bill Everson, the most dedicated film historian alive, has written
off the Serials! I telephoned him. I wrote to him. I pinned him down, in
sorrow as well as anger. I pointed out what he had done to Ruth Roland,
Pearl White, George B. Seitz and a score of others of my friends. He
admitted it. And what was his explanation? The Oxford University Press
had thought the book too long and something had to go. Had to go? Go?!
The Serials, the joy of my youth, had to go? Because Queen Victoria's reign
was intolerably long would Geoffrey Cumberlege be in favour of dropping
Palmerston from the chronicles of her reign? Faugh! Pooh! Stuff! It would
need the pen of Thackeray to invent enough ejaculations and snorts to deal
with this decision, forced upon my friend by the mandarins of Oxford, so I
will quote David Everett (1770–1813):

> Large streams from little fountains flow,
> Tall oaks from little acorns grow.

and leave it to the conscience of the Oxford University Press to put it right
in the next edition. I shall nag the Oxford pundits until they do.

I am a craftsman, and a craftsman I shall remain until I die. I know only
one craft, the craft of making films. The art of telling a story to the largest
audience that ever said, "Tell me a story!" The work of art that we call a
feature film, a major motion picture (was there ever a minor motion
picture?), gives employment to many craftsmen, perhaps two hundred
clever men and women who are intimately involved in the texture of each
film. Each is an expert in his field, and most of them, while giving of their
best, are convinced that they could direct the film better than the director. I
used to think so myself. A director has only a superficial skill in the various
departments which serve the film, a smattering of the vocabularies; he is a
jack of all trades, a man for all seasons. Usually he is an expert in one
department: he may have been a journalist like Alexander Korda, a sketch
artist like Hitchcock, an actor like Laurence Olivier, a film editor like
David Lean, a genius like Charlie Chaplin, and he or she (we don't have
enough women directors) will lean heavily at first upon this slender prop of
specialized knowledge in the arguments with his fellow craftsmen; but a
director very soon learns that his function is to get the essence of all these
clevernesses up there on the screen, and if he can't do that, then all the rest
of his abilities aren't worth a damn and he is letting down his fellow
craftsmen.

And how does the film director do this? With a heart of steel, the patience of Job, the cunning of the fox, the energy and agility of a cat, the loneliness of the long distance runner; with love, compassion and imagination, with detachment.

In the early days of film-making in Hollywood, directors sprang up from nowhere: they took control in the way a born soldier takes over from a professional in an emergency. Perhaps they were not conscious of what they were doing; they certainly had little idea that they were artists. I am not writing about directors from the theatre like D. W. Griffith, or from the Cockney music hall like Chaplin, but of men from nowhere, who took control with complete assurance of this new form of storytelling and who, within a year or two, were commanding and deploying vast resources of men and money with the confidence of a General George Marshall or a Winston Churchill.

When movies started to talk these men took it in their stride. It was a new weapon for their armoury, that was all. These old-timers had a breath-taking self-confidence. And horse-sense. A director like Woody Van Dyke could go from *Tarzan of the Apes* to *Marie Antoinette*, from *White Shadows on the South Seas* to *The Thin Man*. He was told by the studio heads of MGM to direct some retakes of a Greta Garbo film. At the time she was the company's biggest star. She came on the set. It was a staircase. She was punctual. Garbo was always punctual. Van Dyke was seated in his chair looking at the script of the film. She said, "Good morning." He said, "Mornin', honey," without looking up. "The script says you come through that door" – he pointed to the top of the stairs – "and you go out of that door" – pointing to the door across the splendid baroque hall at the bottom of the staircase. Garbo was used to working with Clarence Brown, a first-rate director and diplomat who handled her with kid gloves: "Miss Garbo, this," "Madame Garbo, that," but she said "Shall we try it?" Van Dyke said, "Sure!" She went up the stairs and went through the action: "How was that?" "Swell. Now the script says you have a change of costume and you come in that door and go out the other." She was puzzled. "Aren't you going to shoot the other section first?" "Oh, we got it." A pause. Garbo looked at him. "Mister Van Dyke, don't you ever rehearse?" He was already back in the script and answered without raising his eyes; "Listen, honey, how many ways are there of coming down a staircase?"

Another formidable professional was Jack Conway. Was it by luck or judgment that Metro-Goldwyn-Mayer in its great days had Victor Fleming (*Gone With the Wind, For Whom the Bell Tolls, The Wizard of Oz*), Van Dyke and Conway all under contract at the same time? Perhaps only supremely confident and quite fearless men could take Louis B. Mayer at their own valuation, not his. When Jack Conway was directing *A Yank at Oxford* in England at Denham Studios he was working with a cast of distinguished British actors, most of them from the theatre, who were inclined to be a bit snobbish about the American approach. One of them was a fine old actor called Edward Rigby who would later play the Wheelright in *A Canterbury Tale* – extraordinary how this picture keeps on cropping up! – and one day, waiting for the sun, he said to me, "Do you happen to know Mr Jack Conway, Michael?" I said no, but knew who he was, of course. "What about him?" Rigby started to chuckle: "He really taught me a lesson. I was playing Robert Taylor's 'Scout' in *A Yank at Oxford* [Oxford "Scout" – a term for servant, valet, guide, philosopher and friend to undergraduates in College rooms]. As soon as I got the script I leafed through it and could see it was just feed." (Edward Rigby was a beautiful actor with a distinguished record. He had created the old skipper in *Anna Christie* in London: "that old debbil sea".) "But," he went on, "there was one scene which had a little more juice in it for me and I thought, 'I'll show them!' When it came to that scene I gave it all I'd got and when the director said, 'Cut,' I just stole a glance at him out of the corner of my eye and he was looking at me, sitting in his director's chair, and he beckoned to me and said, 'Come here, Pop.' So I went and stood in front of him, thinking maybe he wanted to say a word or two of appreciation, and it wouldn't hurt if Mr Robert Taylor should hear it. But he beckoned again and I had to come close and lean down to him before he whispered to me, 'Pop! That was *so* good, I want just a quarter of it.'"

Here the old actor started to chuckle until he had a fit of coughing, amongst which I could still distinguish the words "just a quarter of it". Meanwhile I meditated on the tact and sympathy which had enabled a rough, tough leader of men like Jack Conway to appreciate the motive behind the old actor's flamboyance. He knew how to share it with him and get just as much as he could from him without exposing him to ridicule.

Now I have a confession to make. I have been cheating. It is January 1, 1981 and I am writing these lines in Hollywood, California. It is exactly one year since I sat down to write my autobiography in No. 36, East Wheelock Street, Dartmouth College, New England, scribbling a thousand words a day before putting on my heavy boots to slip and slide up the hill to the Department of Film Studies to hold a class or analyse a film. For a month this was the pattern of my life. Then my son Columba arrived from England. He is a painter and a poet and there is no room in one apartment for an autobiographer, a painter and a poet. I became cook-housekeeper. My student class were starting to make their project film: a condensed dramatization of Ursula K. Le Guin's The Tombs of Atuan. We prepared it like a professional film with the key technical jobs assigned to, or claimed by students. They insisted that I direct it. We used the stage of a big theatre at the Hopkins Center. It took about seven days. The sets and costumes, props, were all made by the students, helped by Berni Vyzga, the theatre's art director. The only outsider to be co-opted into the production was a young dancer from a local ballet school, who played the Priestess.

Suddenly term was over and Tom Luddy had invited me to California. I flew with Columba to Los Angeles where we were met by a limousine so black and big that Columba giggled: "You could roller skate in it." Francis Ford Coppola had just taken over a famous old independent studio lot on Santa Monica Boulevard in Hollywood, rechristened Zoetrope Studios. Only Francis and Dean Tavoularis knew what a zoetrope is or was (Dean is a Greek as well as Francis's chief designer). We stayed at the house Dean had rented on Highland Boulevard. (They none of them had a home in Los Angeles, they all came from San Francisco, four hundred miles northward.) For a week I shared with Francis the pangs of running a new studio. Then I flew north to lecture to the Pacific Film Archive, part of my programme. At George Lucas's invitation we crossed the Bay to see what he called "my facility", a special effects department planned with impressive thoroughness, financed by the success of Star Wars and just completing the effects for the sequel, The Empire Strikes Back. And this was only the start of George's success: he was already being sued by his agent, the Hollywood equivalent of winning the Nobel Prize.

Invitations poured in: to the Santa Fe Film Festival to present The Edge of the World, to Denver (another film festival) to show A Matter of Life and Death, to New York to discuss a Broadway musical to be based on The Red Shoes and before I left for London, a definite invitation from Francis to join him in the fall as Senior Director in Residence at Zoetrope Studios. Who could resist? Suddenly, I was home, in Gloucestershire, at my square pedestal table with the flaps, behind my French chestnut bureau, stuffed with papers and photographs, around me shelves from floor to ceiling, full of books, notebooks, typescripts, diaries and cardboard boxes. It was high summer out of the window, a gentle rain was falling after a long dry spring, the walnut tree had moved in very close and I could not see the village, only green, green foliage. The giant horse chestnut trees at the back of the cottage rose up like cliffs, the slope of the land so steep that I got the impression I was looking up at a green sea cliff with the creamy white blossoms looking like sea-birds nesting in the crannies.

Of all the memoirs I have read, I love best Châteaubriand's Mémoires d'Outre-Tombe. His life was a series of hair-raising successes and exhilarating failures. He had no sooner become rich and powerful than he was friendless and out of a job. He had no sooner discovered that he was one of the freshest, most influential, and most charming writers alive, when *he had to sell his books and pictures and beat a retreat from La Vallée-aux-Loups. Best of all he made the discovery that his life was all of a piece – it took place in space not in time: he dates a section of his memoirs as 1842, the year it is being written, and settles down to share with you the smallest details of his disgrace by Napoleon in 1810, stepping lightly and masterfully to and fro across the intervening years. And yet he never loses control either of his personality or of his many friendships. His manners are perfect. His loyalties are constant. His prejudices are peculiar to himself. His books and poems are unread: his autobiography is immortal.*

This scavenger whom you glimpse following in his footsteps, this cleaner-upper, impaling odd bits of film on the end of his pen, is me. The only thing Châteaubriand and I have in common is a contempt for conventional chronology and complete recall of things that interest us. "Time? What is time?" asks the Heavenly Messenger in A Matter of Life and Death, *"a mere tyranny!" He was a Frenchman like Châteaubriand (who was a Breton, come to think of it).*

I left myself a few pages back biting my pen and staring out of the window at the walnut tree, and the story of my life in movies is still waiting to be told.

I hope I can do it. I must do it. Because there is nobody else who can. I am the cinema. I fell in love in 1921 when my celluloid mistress was the most beautiful, fascinating, irresistible object in the world. She was universally beloved. No barrier of language existed for her. She crossed all frontiers. The Soviet revolutionaries entrusted her with their ideals to scatter around the world. The great Max Reinhardt and his disciples seized hold of her with enthusiasm to bring us his myths and fairy tales. The Italians stunned us with extravagant spectacle; the French dazzled us with wit and realism; the Swedes brought us their introvert tales glittering with icicles; and the Americans bought up all the films and their makers and set them to work making bigger and better movies, distributing them, exhibiting them, selling them, creating the greatest storytelling market in the world, creating the film industry 1921–81. That was where I came in, this is where I am now. I'm still in. They can't get rid of me. There must be a purpose. It must be that I am to tell the story of the movies before I – fade out.

So, on January 1, 1981 I take up my pen again. It is August 4, 1914, the start of the First World War, as the newspapers are quick to tell us. I am eight years and ten months old.

It had been a long, hot summer. The hops were two weeks ahead and the spraying of the vines against insects and disease was continuous. It looked like being a record harvest. Our few acres of strawberries blushed with berries, and we grew tired of helping with the picking, even though we got paid for it. I don't remember any talk of war or any special movements of troops except the usual summer manoeuvres by the volunteer regiments – the Yeomanry – amateur soldiers with their own organization and headquarters, about whom the usual jokes were made that they met to drink beer together for fifty weeks of the year, so that they could sweat it off in two weeks of summer manoeuvres. But that was peacetime talk. This volunteer army was our only reserve in wartime. The tiny regular army, the "contemptible little army" so disparaged by the German Emperor, Kaiser Wilhelm II, was already being rushed across the Channel to the aid of the French. The Yeomanry regiments, most of them cavalry with their horse-drawn transport, were moving up in support to train, to outfit, and to defend the coast.

The white cliffs of Dover were only ten miles away from our farm gates. On the morning after war was declared in a solemn proclamation by King George V, when my father was absent in Canterbury at the Corn Exchange, a commandeered Daimler automobile, an open tourer, with a khaki-clad driver and a corporal sitting beside him, drew up in the dusty road outside Hoath Farm. On their shoulders we boys read in brass letters "1st Sussex". On the back seat was a long, lean, elegant Anglo-Irishman, studying a map of East Kent, who introduced himself to my flustered mother – she was jam-making – as Captain the Honourable Blakiston-Houston, Billeting Officer of the 1st Sussex Yeomanry, and could he please inspect the premises, as the field opposite – he pointed to the Collard's meadow on the other side of the road, that sloped down to the apple orchard – had been assigned to the Regiment as a camping ground and Hoath was an obvious choice for HQ. While my brother chatted to the driver, who soon had the bonnet open and discovered that John knew far more than he did about German carburettors, I followed the tall figure of the Adjutant – he was six foot three – and his Corporal, who noted down on a pad the observations thrown out by his superior officer. Captain Blakiston-Houston had a pleasant drawling voice and loads of charm, which was not without effect upon my mother. He requisitioned our playroom on sight as an ideal Orderly Room – "You have the telephone, Mrs Powell? Good? I'll have an extension put in tomorrow." I rushed to tell my brother that we had lost our playroom! Or more accurately his playroom, for it was entirely taken up by his model railways. He took it calmly. He was already putting childish things away. He was a Powell.

I returned to the house just in time to see my mother and the elegant officer coming down the stairs.

"Well now, Mrs Powell, our Colonel, the Earl of March, will have the room by the bathroom that looks on the farmyard." (My mother's drawing room!) "How many more of our officers would you be willing to take?"

My mother hesitated, half-excited, half-appalled, at the speed at which things were happening, then hazarded:

"Well, I think we could squeeze in two more."

"Oh, Mrs Powell, I'm sure you can do better than that. Shall we say six?"

The next day the Advance Guard arrived in the persons of Lieutenant Bloxham, the Quartermaster, a big man with a big moustache, the Veterinary Officer, a small man, Irish, with blue eyes in a wizened face and the bow legs of a horseman, and their crew. In no time they had Collard's meadow marked out with posts and flags: here the rows of tents for the men: here the mess tents, the cookhouse, the latrines, the horse-lines – have I said that the 1st Sussex Yeomanry was a mounted regiment? – here the Officers' Mess and the Sergeants' Mess and the Chaplain's and the Doctor's tent; and already the military waggons were rumbling up the road and turning into the meadow through a gap ruthlessly hacked out of the hedge, iron-shod wheels rumbling on the wooden bridge hastily constructed by the sappers over the ditch. I was everywhere at once, getting in everybody's way, escaping injury by a miracle, asking questions, running errands, giving information and getting it. My brother was philosophically packing up and moving his models and his railways out of the Orderly Room, where the Regimental Sergeant Major (RSM), a personage of enormous authority and presence, was already installed at a trestle table loaded with files. The Regiment had arrived with their horses and transport at Canterbury Barracks and were to march in tomorrow.

After breakfast next morning I scurried across the putting green, up the path through my mother's rosebeds and by the white painted pigeon-house – we kept white fantails – into the Wilderness and up my favourite beech tree (there is nothing like a clean, smooth beech tree for climbing) to the top where I had constructed a seat and a cupboard out of the remains of a farm cart and small cider barrel. Taking a pear from my store I settled myself comfortably. From this height I could see over the trees and bushes that rimmed the duck-pond to the meadow. The Commissariat had arrived, and the cooks already had their big boilers and cookers set up in the open air and were embarked on that never-ending job of Army life, peeling potatoes. The white canvas bell tents, eight men to a tent, similar to the three tents we had borrowed for the Wingham Camp at Bedpost Island the year before, had been set up in two long lines, and shirt-sleeved men were struggling with big mess tents under the eye of the RSM stalking up and down, cane with a polished nob under his arm. Other men were digging trenches for drains and for the water pipes which were being connected up to our farm supply for watering the horses and supplying the cookhouse and the canteen. A dray from the brewers stacked high with barrels of beer was being unloaded with a great deal of cheerful shouting, an Italian ice-cream salesman with his cart gaily painted in Neapolitan colours and drawn by a donkey was already doing a brisk trade, with ice cream wafers, and our Canterbury photographer, Old Snap 'Em, who usually turned out only during the hop picking, having smelt business from afar, arrived on his bike and side-car and was already taking down names and addresses of his new customers, only to be summarily ordered off the meadow by the RSM, who thundered that it was now a Military Camp and that, by rights, he should confiscate Old Snap 'Em's equipment, as giving "hinformation to the Henemy"!

At this point, having eaten three pears and been joined by my brother, I glanced up the road towards the oast house and nearly fell out of the tree. A cloud of white dust was moving towards us, together with the ring of bridles, the squeak of harness, the grinding of the iron tyres of gun-limbers on the road and the wonderful sound of three hundred horses' hooves moving together at a smart trot: the Regiment was coming!

I went down the beech tree as if it were a staircase. Seven seconds was the established record from perch to beech-mast, timed by my brother with the stopwatch he had received for his tenth birthday. I shot through the gap in the fence separating the Wilderness from the hop garden. It was made of split chestnut withies, wired together into rolls like carpet, which were then unrolled, set upright and supported at regular intervals by stout stakes. They were good enough to keep out animals; they couldn't keep in boys. I ran along the edge of the pond, which petered out into a dry dingle, littered with holed kettles, tins, rusty coils of wire, and a bathtub. By the time I got to the five-barred gate leading to the road, the leading files were halted and the mounted officers were holding a conference.

The Regiment had marched up from Canterbury Barracks and were dusty and sweaty. They looked pretty splendid to me. Even John was impressed. Colonel the Earl of March, son of the seventh Duke of Richmond and Gordon, was a black-browed, black-moustached terrier of a man. He rode at the head of his regiment, many of whom were tenants and servants from his Goodwood estate in West Sussex. Captain the Honourable Blakiston-Houston, his Adjutant and personal friend, rode half a length behind the CO's staff, and messengers were at their horses' heels. Then there was a gap followed by the First Company Commander at the head of his men. The long column of men and horses, with the gun-limbers bringing up the rear, two soldiers seated on their boxes arms folded, stretched for five hundred yards down the road. The horses tossed their heads impatiently and changed feet. Some impatient animal would take advantage of the slackened rein and surge forward, cannoning into the file ahead, earning a reprimand from his Sergeant – "Keep your distance, Stillingbourne!" – and a frown from his Company Commander. By now, some of the officers whom we already knew surrounded the Colonel, who was visibly irritated. With a brusque "Lead the way then!" he turned his mare – she was a beauty and about fifteen hands at the shoulder, her muscles moving under silky black skin – and crossed the wooden bridge into the camp site, the mare dancing at the sound of her dainty hooves drumming on the boards. Commands rang out all down the line – "Number One Company! Forward at a walk! Walk! . . . Number Two Company! . . ." and so on. We hung on the gate until the Rear Guard had passed and turned like the rest into the meadow, then we rushed back to the house to tell the excited female staff that the Regiment had arrived: ". . . and there are hundreds of men and hundreds of horses . . . and they have about fifty remount horses as well as baggage animals . . . they have mules . . . and they have a blacksmith of their own . . ."

"That's the Farrier-Sergeant," said John knowledgeably. "Of course they have to have their own smith. You could hear the loose shoes clicking all down the line. I counted seven!" Have I said he was a Powell? Practical.

Soon the farmhouse was echoing with men's voices as the officers were shown their bedrooms, and their servants invaded the big kitchen with bags and boxes of rations for Norah to make use of. The billiard room was to be the Officers' Mess. My mother and Emily hurried to and fro with a preoccupied air, while shouts of laughter and maidenly giggles coming through the swing door to the scullery and larder made it evident that whatever the mistress might think, this invasion of bronzed men, with their soft Sussex accents, was welcome in the kitchen.

The fine weather continued. Within a week the Camp in the meadow was as orderly as a busy village where everything is regulated by the bugle calls. We boys soon knew most of the Regiment by sight and rode our ponies over to the horse-lines as if we had been used all our lives to be part of an active professional community. A big Union Jack hung from a staff on the wall of Hoath Farm, and an armed sentry marched up and down challenging intruders with "Who goes there?" Norah's canary was singing *fortissimo*. We were at war.

I was soldier mad. If the 1st Sussex had been an infantry regiment, I probably wouldn't have been so crazy, but you can imagine what a regiment of cavalry meant to a boy who had been brought up on a farm where horses were as much a part of the daily round as his own family. Coleman, the head waggoner, and his teams were the most important workers on the farm. Besides, I was a mounted man myself! A small boy could never have kept up with infantry on their exercises, or on a route march, but astride my pony, Fubsy, it was more a question of the cavalry keeping up with me! There was no chance of keeping either of us out of the

Camp. From the beginning Fubsy and I were part of the scene. "The one and only Micky," murmured Captain the Honourable Blakiston-Houston, chewing on his pipe, while he looked me up and down after some outrageous piece of cheek, such as complaining that my name was missing from the list of the Sergeant's Mess. (This was after my mother had procured khaki cloth, shoulder plates, and a set of brass buttons and made me a uniform to which the Quartermaster-Sergeant added Sergeant's stripes.) A snapshot of me at this time, taken by my mother, shows me in khaki shirt, corduroy breeches, leather gaiters, boots, curls under the brim of a Scout hat tipped rakishly backwards, riding crop swinging negligently from my hand, a cool grin on my infant face, a sarcastic retort trembling on my tender lips. Fubsy was just such another. She had a high spirit, a flowing mane and tail, and thought a great deal of herself. I was proud of her appearance and kept her well groomed in summer. Exmoor ponies are tough and full of guile and quick on their feet. Some of the soldiers asked if they could ride her bareback for a lark. She had them all off and the one who managed to stick on, she ran away with to her stable and scraped him off her back as she bolted under the stable door.

When the Regiment first arrived nobody knew how long they would be encamped. The 1914 war started like the 1939 war, with the battering-ram of an armoured German invasion force. The neutrality of Belgium was violated and the Germans were only stopped on the Marne by the famous Paris taxicabs bringing up the reserves and the arrival of England's "contemptible little army". Except for the Boer War and various skirmishes in different parts of a negligently acquired Empire, the British had not been involved in a major war for a hundred years. They couldn't even hate the Kaiser. After all, he was Queen Victoria's grandson and had been a figure of fun for the press for ten years, with his telegrams and his posturings and his uniforms. A few men like Haldane, Fisher and Erskine Childers took him seriously and preached the gospel of a strong Navy to keep the Kaiser's fleet bottled up in the Kiel Canal. But thoughts of a long war of attrition and exhaustion, of England brought to her knees by U-boat warfare and the ruthless sinking of neutral ships, were shared by very few men; and when H. G. Wells and Bernard Shaw denounced the War and pleaded for peace at any price for Europe's sake, they were denounced as traitors and given white feathers.

If anyone thinks that a nine-year-old boy couldn't have known all this and had no vivid picture in his mind of what was going on in those days before radio and television, he only had to look at the stout, green-bound volumes of the *Bystander* 1914–18 which are on my shelves today. There in photographs, articles, reports and cartoons – especially cartoons – today's reader can follow week by week, year by year, England's surprise turning to horror, horror to contempt, contempt to fear, fear to hatred,

hatred to intolerance, intolerance to cruelty and revenge. We children never looked at the daily newspapers, but we read the *Bystander* and *Punch*, with the full-page cartoons by Bernard Partridge superbly drawn, ineptly subtitled, e.g.:

> Kaiser: (To the King of the Belgians) So you see! You've lost everything!
> Albert: Not my soul!

And we read the *War Illustrated* in fortnightly parts, and other periodicals. We knew what was going on: but it seems to me that it was the naiveté of glossy mags like the *Bystander*, with their photographs and chit-chat and desperate attempts to keep peacetime pleasure alive, that was most informing to an observant little boy.

These feelings were intensified over the next eighteen months when my father took me with him once or twice to stay for a weekend with the Gilardis, who ran the Grand Hotel at Folkestone, a huge ornamental luxury hotel standing on top of windy cliffs beside its sister caravanserai, the Metropole. Mr and Mrs Gilardi were cultivated people, members of the powerful international Society of Hoteliers and Restaurateurs who were on familiar terms with European royalty, aristocracy and their Jewish bankers, and who wielded more influence and real power in many capital cities than the court chamberlains. Before the war the Grand had been my father's escape valve when a bad year of hops made "Monte" out of the question. I had been a guest at their daughter Lola's sixteenth birthday party and mightily impressed by her gift to me of an articulated wooden snake, painted green and black with a forked tongue flickering in its jaws. There was a tinted photograph of Lola on the cabinet in the drawing room: a thin, intense girl with big eyes. I was not prepared for the tall, creamy young woman, full of energy and laughter, wearing dead white make-up and a silver frock that left nothing to the imagination, who took me by the hand, gave me bound volumes of *Punch* to read, and showed me a bed made up behind a screen in the Gilardis' own suite, apologizing at the same time that there was nowhere else to sleep, the hotel was so full. And full it was with gay girls and "temporary gentlemen" (as the young enlisted Second Lieutenants were called), full of officers going over to France at – hush! hush! – midnight; full of champagne parties in the restaurants and in the rooms that linked breakfast to breakfast; full of hollow-eyed men, returning from Mons or Arras, who went to sleep in the lobbies; full of celebrations and weeping, of laughter and anger, the noise of breaking glasses, the orchestra playing "Hitchy Koo! Hitchy Koo! Hitchy Koo!" in the ballroom, and dozens of gramophones in the rooms playing "There's a Long, Long Trail a-Winding" and "Keep the Home Fires Burning", full of the idiocy and despair, the selfishness and generosity, of human beings caught in the whirlpool of war.

In 1944, during another world war, I was on the island of Mull in the Hebrides, shooting scenes at Loch Buihe Castle for *I Know Where I'm Going*. The day had dawned fine and without wind, and I had proposed that we sail in Ian Mackenzie's huge open motor-boat from Carsaig up the coast. Any of the unit who wanted to could come, I said, and most of them did. That south coast of Mull is a fine sight from the sea: granite cliffs rising and falling but never less than 500 feet high; not a house, nor harbour, all the way to the Sound of Lochbuie. The brief winter sunshine shone all day and by the time we finished all the scenes we had to do the wind had got up and Ian was looking at the sky and at his watch. A message came down to me from the Castle: "Did I remember Lola Gilardi?" She and some friends were dining there that night, and if I couldn't stay for dinner would I have a drink, said the Laird, and tell them "about the filming". I sigh today when I think of my refusal. Lola Gilardi! Of course I remembered her! I had not seen her since that weekend thirty years before, but the fragrance of the beautiful, kind young woman, her sense of fun and her vitality, remained with me all my life. I had heard of her through stray remarks of my father's. She had not had a happy life. And now here she was in the Western Isles asking if I remembered her. She was one of my most cherished memories, and was I now to see her, thirty years older? Good heavens! She must be fifty! Were we to stand and look at one another over a glass of whisky, while I asked questions about the haunting and romantic story that I and two beautiful women were conjuring up out of the sea and mountains of Mull? The sun was near the horizon, the wind was blowing against the tide, the boat was overloaded; I sent apologies and we shoved off, while the rest of the unit went by bus. It was a dangerous sail, and standing with Pamela Brown by the mast, I looked at Ian's watchful face as he spied the waves and kept as close to the rocks as he could. It was dark when we turned in under the jetty at Carsaig. They were waiting for us with lanterns, and all the way images had been forming and changing in my mind, like the patterns in a kaleidoscope; and I reflected how we survive, not in our consciousness, but in other people's. Still, I was glad I had escaped, and now, thirty-six years later, I am sorry.

I think what caused my confusion was that Lola and all the times she existed for had become part of a pattern in my life of shadows. Lola, the warm, breathing human Lola, was ragtime and the 1914–18 war. When I saw the film *The Dark Angel*, which had a sequence of two lovers parting at wartime Dover, the severe nine-year-old critic within me said: "It wasn't at all like that. They haven't got the atmosphere at all. No, not at all." Lola existed for me, but I had no idea that I existed for Lola, and this was probably the part of the experience that most confused me. The sudden revelation that somebody else knows something about you that you thought was only known to yourself is a shock.

Today a letter was sent on to me (here in Hollywood) from a lady who lives in Folkestone, Kent, England. Here it is:

> Dear Michael Powell,
> Do you recall on the Polo Ground at Canterbury, when you were a very small boy, your pony bolted when you were riding with your mother and brother? You were thrown and your foot was caught in the stirrup and your pony continued to gallop with your head down and your flaxen curly head bumping on the ground?! My governess and I watched it all in horror lest your head should be kicked as well as thumped! Obviously it all did you no harm?

The lady, "Yours very sincerely – Mary Skinner", had seen my 1944 film *A Canterbury Tale* on BBC 2 and felt emboldened to share with me at last her memory of this incident. Her account of it was exact and I hasten to absolve Fubsy from any participation in it. I was trying out Mister Bun, my brother's big blue roan pony, who was inclined to fits and starts when he was fresh and the weather cold. There had been heavy rain, and the tunnels that crossed the field where the drains lay were full of water. I was a bit doubtful about handling Bun, for I had never ridden him before. When I shook the reins he bounded forward from a standing start and off I went. The stirrup leathers caught on the usual safety catch (which I have never yet known to work), and I was dragged yelling through the pools and puddles of water on the field, with Bun's iron-shod hooves flashing around me. The more I yelled and bumped the faster Bun went, until the safety catch at last worked and left us both free. Bun stopped and began to eat grass. My brother and mother came to sweep up the remains. I lay where I had fallen, soaked through, furious. My brother pulled me up and examined my head. "No damage," he reported to my frantic mother, then to me: "You had better stick to Fubsy." Spoken like a Powell.

It remained one of the memorable incidents of my boyhood – one of the narrow escapes that colour a lifetime. The polo ground was on the road to Littlebourne and Wingham. I never passed without remembering my lucky escape, even years later when we were making the film. It was something unique, something that nobody knew but I, and here was a dear lady, who had carried the memory of it for more than sixty years and thought of me still as a little boy with golden curls, just as I remember the dark eyes and creamy skin of Lola Gilardi; and then they talk of the time passing! It is we who pass. Time remains.

When the "Old Contemptibles" (as the regular soldiers were later known) went overseas, the Yeomanry were left to guard England, especially the Eastern Approaches. Our 1st Sussex was only one of a hundred camps, from the Wash to Portland Bill. None of them knew what they might be called upon to do. For the present the Germans were held in the First Battle of Mons; a line was beginning to form through Arras and Beauvais to the North Sea. Thanks to Admiral Jackie Fisher we had a strong Navy; but the prospect of invasion was very real that autumn, particularly in East Kent. The sea at Sandwich was only eight miles away from the Hoath. "The Terriers" camped in our meadow and were short of every kind of equipment, including firearms and ammunition, so they concentrated on bayonet practice, taking turns at the rifle-range, on keeping fit and exercising their horses, in all of which my brother and I took part. By the time the autumn rains came, all England knew we were in for a long war. The Collard's meadow turned into a sea of mud, on which duck boards dismally floated, and Army contractors arrived to build a permanent camp of huts that would weather the winter of 1914–15.

One of the commands which I loved and understood was "Make much of your horses!" You don't think there was such a command in the cavalry of World War I? Well, there was. After a long exercise we would return to Camp. We would form up. "Company, dismount!" "Company, 'shun!" "At ease!" "Make much of your horses!" And the boys – for they were most of them Sussex boys – would run their hands over sweating necks, loosen throat lashes, slip the bridle out of soft mouths, rub their faces along velvet noses and, if nobody was looking, swap a kiss or two. Even Fubsy was partial to a kiss, if nobody was looking.

It was not to be expected that my father, with his passion for being "in the swim", would keep out of uniform. As a farmer he was exempt from call-up, and his age, in those Georgian days, made active service out of the question, but men had to be trained, there were still cavalry regiments, horses were still "bringing up the guns". He was an expert horseman, and after discussion with Blakiston-Houston, he joined the Buffs, a famous Kent regiment, took the King's Commission, and was posted as Second Lieutenant in charge of remounts to the camp at Shorncliffe on the white cliffs of Dover, almost, as he pointed out to my mother, in the front line; almost, as she pointed out, in the Gilardis' suite in the Grand at Folkestone, three miles away. Anyway, he was in uniform, with a polished leather Sam Browne belt and smart leather gaiters that the old groom, who had taken over from Woodcock, had to learn to bring to a high stage of lustre; and he was in a famous regiment, not Yeomanry, and no longer had to feel inferior in his own house to the Sussex invaders. My mother at once discovered a booklet on the Buffs and gave one to each of us boys. I have mine yet. It is bound in brown paper and has illustrations, one of which is of an ancestor of mine, Lieutenant Latham, defending the Colours at Albuera, in the

Peninsular War. According to the text, after a sabre duel with a French dragoon, in which he had one arm severed, he snatched up the flag and parried further attacks with the staff. My middle name is Latham so I took a personal interest in the gallant Lieutenant (for he survived his wounds and lived to a ripe age), more than did John, whose middle name was Miles, after an ancestor whose name appears as one of the signatories in the warrant for King Charles I's execution. I discovered about this time that my uncle, Geoffrey L. Corbett, of the Indian Civil Service, also had Latham as his middle name, although to this day I don't know anything about the Latham connection in our family. It was enough for me that I was a Royalist and a Corbett. John was a regicide and a Powell.

By 1915 I had a uniform tailored by my amazing mother – as I have already noted. I had learnt to wind puttees so that they didn't unwind on a long route march (puttees are easier to wind if you are infantry because you start at the boot and wind upwards, fastening the tape below the knee, whereas horsemen, who grip the saddle with their knees, reverse the technique, finishing with the tape around the ankle). I also had a pair of bright spurs, the rowels of which had been filed down at the suggestion of the Farrier Sergeant, who had seen Fubsy express her views on the subject by standing on her head as soon as she felt the spur. As soon as I got back from school I would fling off my "civvy-suit", hop into my uniform, report to the Orderly Room, then nip over to the Sergeants' Mess which, by now, was a big comfortable hut, full of my most intimate friends, one of whom would be sure to stand me a fizzy lemonade in a bottle with a glass marble as the stopper. There I would read Company Orders, listen to professional chat and hear the latest rumours. The rain drummed on the roof, the iron stoves at each end of the hut glowed red-hot, while I listened to letters from brothers or fathers with their mostly humorous descriptions of trench warfare and their incredible stories of the Christmas Truce when both sides ceased firing and English and Germans met and fraternized in No Man's Land, then went back next day to killing each other.

The 1st Sussex stayed with us nearly two years. At first they expected to go overseas. They lived from month to month. I heard that the Colonel, Lord March, was pulling all sorts of strings at the War Office. But cavalry regiments had been proved to be no earthly use in Flanders, where the first and last cavalry charge had already taken place. Transport was a different matter. Horses and their postilion-mounted men were doing invaluable work, bringing up the ammo, bringing up the field-guns, under fire. The automobile was fast becoming the vehicle of the "gilded staff" but the regular officer still rode, if he could find a mount, and transport and farmwork behind the lines was horse-drawn. The war was expanding overseas. The Middle East was, as ever, the cockpit. The epic of Gallipoli and the disaster of Churchill's gamble in the Dardanelles was only just being digested; it looked more and more to those in the know as if the regiment was destined for the Mediterranean area.

On one never-to-be-forgotten day on summer manoeuvres (it must have been in September 1915, for the harvest was in and the stubble fields not yet ploughed), I and my pony charged with the Regiment. Horses and men were in a high state of fitness; we had ridden across Thanet for about six miles and had arrived in open country. The summer had been dry, and the soil was hard and firm, ideal for the cavalry manoeuvres. I didn't realize what was going on until one of the sergeants told me. The officers had been summoned to a conference and a ring of mounted men surrounded the Colonel. I cantered my pony over and was just in time to put in a plea for me and Fubsy. It was dismissed. "Too dangerous!" was the verdict. That settled it. I shut my mouth and rode away to take up a position on the right wing where the Colonel couldn't see me. The horses were getting excited. They knew what was coming. The long line stretched right across the field, with the company commanders three lengths ahead of the troopers, their horses wheeling and dancing like swifts on a summer evening. A distant voice drawled: "First Sussex! Prepare to charge!" My heart beat fast and Fubsy snorted as the company commanders ordered: "Number One Company, at a walk – forward!" "Number Two Company . . ." and so on. The whole line was in motion, our eyes on the distant line of dummies, our ears straining for the next order. The horses were hard to hold. They tossed their heads, their bits jingling, the leather squeaking, flecks of foam flying from their mouths. "Number One Company! Trot!" We were off, followed by the other two companies, Fubsy's toes twinkling, her head high, her heels clicking, the dust rising in clouds behind us. The distant voice of the Colonel drawled "First Sussex, Charge!" The company commanders flung over their shoulders "Out swords!" The long straight swords rasped out of the sheaths and flashed in the sun. "Number One Company, Number Two Company, Number Three Company – CHARGE!" We were off! The horses bounded forward screaming with excitement, their riders trying to keep control to ride stirrup-to-stirrup as the line wavered and bellied. The sound of the drumming of those hundreds of pairs of hooves on the parched land is with me still. One of the young company commanders stood up in his stirrups, waved his sword and screeched: "View halloo!" as if he had sighted a fox. A roar came from the men behind him, a roar of excitement mixed with swear words and even more atavistic sounds as they bore down on the enemy, slashing and thrusting at the row of poor dummies, checking and wheeling their foaming horses and cannoning into their friends. Fubsy and I had kept up with Number One Company throughout, although my sword was only an ashstick with a hand-guard on it, one of a pair my brother and I used to fence with. Ashstick, or no, I did fearful execution with it and was nonchalantly wiping off the blood and guts of Lieutenant Latham when Captain Blakiston-Houston cantered up and said in passing "Well ridden, Micky! You had better keep out of the Colonel's way. He's cross with you." I nodded and slipped Fubsy a lump of sugar out of my pocket.

I claim to be the only director alive who has ridden in a cavalry charge, and I have always held a grudge against Tony Richardson, a man of the theatre, not a man of films, for directing *The Charge of the Light Brigade* instead of me.

Looking back on those martial years I wonder that my character was not more influenced by the experience of living in a world of men. When I was not in camp, among my fellow horsemen, I was in the house, surrounded by officers and their batmen. I heard of intrigues and love affairs. Occasionally of tragedies. Even the Colonel was said to be greatly taken with the charms of my prettiest cousin, Daphne. She was a Powell. And if the Colonel, who was the son of a duke and aged about a hundred, could fall in love, then any mating was possible. Our officers, being Territorials (Reservists), were mostly mature men, some of them married, which made complications even more on the cards. There was one suicide over money – a young, handsome officer whom we all liked. In the hutments, of course, I heard all kinds of dramas discussed freely, but I knew them already from Kipling's *Soldiers Three*. I seem to have been quite untouched by it all. This was partly due to the love and care of my mother; partly to the simple kindness of these men who were most of them friends and neighbours and who still thought of the War, if they thought of it all, as a crusade to be won, after which they could "make much of their horses".

And then one day in 1916 they were gone: gone overseas, somewhere in the Middle East. I seem to have heard that the first thing that happened to them was that they were parted from their horses. After all the training, the grooming, the tedious journey out in the troop transport, the ship rolling in the Bay of Biscay, the horse-lines in her bowels, stifling as the convoy crept along the coast of Africa – after all that, to arrive at Alex and to be told to hand over their mounts to an impersonal remount officer and to re-embark as foot-soldiers for an unknown destination – what a tragedy! A small one in those years of tragedy, but because I was so close to it, because I had seen love and trust between men and animals, it has haunted me all my life. They trust us and we let them down.

Who is it who tells that story of the veteran horses of the Peninsular War? After long service with the Dragoons, when peace came they were shipped home and turned out to grass, honourable pensioners for the rest of their lives. I think it was in Yorkshire. Anyway it was big rolling cavalry country, the sweet, short turf covering, like a carpet, beds of ironstone.

One day there was a tremendous thunderstorm preceded by sheet lightning that lit up the landscape with flashes of heavy artillery. The old warhorses ceased to graze and raised up their heads. The thunder rattled in the distance, then driving the storm clouds before it roared and rolled. Lightning zigzagged across the sky and, attracted by the ironstone, several bolts tore into the ground, exploding like cannon shell and starting fires. What did the old cavalry horses who had seen and survived Albuera, Torres Vedras and Waterloo do? They formed up in a line, wheeling and stamping and taking up their positions, as if ghostly riders had gauntletted hands on their reins, and there they stood facing the enemy, until the storm was over and they could turn to grazing again.

When the 1st Sussex went overseas the 2nd Sussex Regiment took their place, but it was not the same. By now nobody had any ideals or illusions left, except the politicians. Nobody expected any more that the war would be over by Christmas. After that first spontaneous gesture of man to man there were no more Christmas truces. 1916 was a black year. The U-boat campaign was a German success; food rationing, fat rationing, and every other kind of rationing was in full force. Even on the farm we felt the pinch but not, of course, as they did in the towns and cities. At sea, the Battle of Jutland had been fought and was neither a defeat nor a victory. Being islanders we had a reluctant admiration for the German Navy. Curiously enough the first film I made with Emeric Pressburger, in 1938, a month or two after Munich, had Conrad Veidt as a U-boat commander hero in the First World War; and the first sequence of the film showed him returning to Kiel, the German base, after a successful trip sinking merchant ships, "paving the bed of the sea with the finest food the world produced"; to be told by a *maître d'hôtel* that he could have boiled carrots for supper since it was a meatless day. The film, which opened the week that the 1939 war was declared, was a huge success. It is only now as I write that I realize that my other hero figure, the purest and most fanatical in all my gallery of fighting men, is Captain Langsdorff, of the German pocket battleship *Graf Spee*, played by Peter Finch. Peter confessed to me that of the parts he had played, this was one of the most hypnotic. Every now and then, he said, there is a part which, more than another, acts you, rather than you acting it. A demon takes over. The doomed man becomes a tragic figure and the actor grows in stature. And then, my mind and my pen wandering further back, I realize that the very first film I ever worked on was *Mare Nostrum*, and that the hero was a merchant ship's captain, who fell for the charms of a Mata Hari, she to die before a French firing squad, he at sea. And then I start musing how salt water ennobles the passions of the men who fight on its surface. Our earth, torn and blood-soaked, does not do that. Perhaps it is because our sea is the mother of us all.

My father went overseas. He had found his war work, transferring from the Buffs, and a chair-polishing job, to the RASC (Royal Army Service Corps), growing food for the army. They made him a captain and *"le Capitaine Povvell"* was soon a name of power in Normandy and Brittany. It was exactly the right job for him: energetic, ruthless, tireless, talking franglais, an astonishing mixture of French and English. With complete assurance he travelled everywhere, ordered and commandeered, bred beef cattle and pigs, raised poultry and organized collective farms over a huge area. He was sociable and unscrupulous which endeared him to the old Norman peasants. He finished the war a Chevalier du Mérite Agricole for services to French agriculture.

My brother was now at Dulwich College, a school in the south-eastern suburbs of London. I viewed this step with suspicion. The only good thing I knew was that the school was founded by an actor, Edward Alleyn, a contemporary of Shakespeare's. It stood in Alleyn's unchanged meadow-lands and woods on the slopes of Sydenham Hill, which was crowned with Joseph Paxton's Crystal Palace, created for the Great Exhibition and transported there from Hyde Park. A school that was dominated by a crystal palace, I felt, couldn't be all that bad. But the main reason for my brother's transfer was the fact that my maternal grandmother, Fanny Corbett, now a dumpy old lady in black shawls, rustling petticoats and lace caps, had come to live at 241 Devonshire Road, Forest Hill, a small house in a long ribbon of speculative housing on the side of the hill: the sort of house, with basement kitchen, front and back garden, front door ornamented with coloured glass and brass knockers, that changed hands for about £250 sterling in those days. Here she made a home for her schoolteacher daughter Ethel, only ten minutes' walk from the High School; here came my grandfather on Sunday from the office room that he rented in No. 1 Wardrobe Court, where he eked out a slender living from journalism; here descended my uncles on their infrequent visits to England from all over the Empire; and here my brother John was to live and go to Dulwich College, over the hill, as a day-boy for the duration of the war. I rather fancy that my Uncle Geoffrey, who was becoming a great man in the Indian Civil Service, paid the school fees, but I am not sure. I know that he came to the rescue of mine, later on. My father was a great quoter of adages, and "Out of sight, out of mind" was one of them. Such men flourish in wartime, leaving their families to shift for themselves.

I myself was now a Scholar at the King's School, Canterbury, founded when St Augustine's church was a wooden building. It stands in the cathedral precincts, and the vast shadow of Bell Harry Tower falls across the quadrangle as the sun sinks. The buildings of the school are half-monastic and half-modern. There is an arched entrance from the busy street and another entrance for pedestrians around the transept of the cathedral. It is part of the old cloisters of the monastery and at night you passed through a long vaulted tunnel, lit by flickering gas jets, where the sound of your footsteps followed you. It was haunted. It was called the Dark Entry.

You came out, usually at a panic-stricken run, into the peaceful Green Court, where masters of the School and dignitaries of the Cathedral Church – canons, major and minor, deans, precentors, prophets, priests and deacons – lived, if not in harmony, in charming houses around two sides of the wide green lawn. The school was not so much planned as piled up around a gravel courtyard, the Quad, and was half red brick and half Kentish flint. The Assembly Hall was built magnificently over the archways between Green Court and Quad, and with three hundred other boys you pushed and panted up the wide stone medieval staircase that gave access to it. The cathedral was, of course, our chapel.

The school uniform was striped trousers, black coat and waistcoat, starched Eton collar, black tie (until you got your colours) and a straw hat, stiff, hard, with a wide brim and a broad ribbon, blue and white striped, around the crown, which was the principal reason for my son Columba refusing to attend his father's old school forty-five years on.

Scholars – King's Scholars, to give us our correct appellation – wore over all a short black gown with no sleeves and pleated at the back, medieval in pattern and not inelegant. I rather enjoyed swishing about in it, and far from giving me any feeling of inferiority – for the award of a scholarship was essential for my mother to pay the fees – the reverse was the case. I had passed the examination with ease and felt I was paying my way.

The Junior School was separated from King's by a high iron fence lined with elms. There was a gate through which masters passed to and fro, and occasionally scared rabbits of boys carrying messages through hostile country; or perhaps a lordly prefect from the Senior School, with down on his lip and his hands in his pockets, a gesture totally taboo in Junior circles. The Seniors were objects of interest to us Juniors when we were outdoors playing; to them we did not exist, particularly if you, a Senior, were unfortunate enough to have a younger brother, a Junior, who could at any moment ruin your social standing by calling you by your Christian name, or worse still by the name you answered to in the bosom of your family. We Juniors had a separate entry through a high wall into the cathedral cloisters, wide enough for the choristers, of whom I was one, to parade two by two in our starched white surplices on Sundays. We pattered down the cloisters, turned right to enter the cathedral and scuffled into our stalls in the chancel, under the eye of the Verger, who preceded with his cross-crowned staff. Above us and behind us were the oak choir-stalls, where the violet cassocks of the boys of the Choir School appeared and disappeared as they joked and ducked behind the high pews. The stalls for the Dean and Precentor and other important prebendaries were in the screen which separated the vast 200 foot nave from the chancel. They provided the main objects of entertainment for us. We knew all their mannerisms by heart. We would place bets on who would doze off first during the sermon.

The Headmaster of the Junior School was the Reverend H. V. Tower, MA, and I owe him and his wife a great deal. He was quick, sturdy, clean-shaven and "mod", where the Headmaster of the Senior School, Algernon Latter, was tall, dark, ferociously moustached and "trad". Tower was a classical scholar and had a pretty wife. I can't remember whether Latter had a mate but if he did she must have been a lioness. Mrs Tower had auburn curls and invited selected small boys to tea with French conversation – which started me off well in French. Even at that early age I was socially and sexually inclined. I appreciated Mrs Tower's efforts to raise the tone of the Junior School. In my opinion it needed it.

I was a cultivated small boy. Thanks to my mother and her sisters I had read and had read to me, poetry and legend, biography and fiction. During my early years Arthur Mee's *Children's Encyclopaedia* was being published in fortnightly parts, and we owned the run of the numbers in red bound volumes. Lavishly illustrated and brilliantly presented to its child readers, there had never been anything like it as an educator. I have already mentioned, I think, the bound volumes of the *Strand Magazine*, of the *Cornhill*, and *Temple Bar* which crowded my grandmother's shelves from floor to ceiling, and the weekly numbers of *Punch* and the *Bystander* which dabbled in politics and hints from the fashionable world; not to mention my father's fascination with the life of "Town" and "Monte", the glimpses of that world that I had been given at the Grand at Folkestone, and the talk I had overheard during the last two years of war, and preparation for war, by the "temporary gentlemen". I read and I listened and I remembered what I read and heard. The experience of farm life, of books, and of the life of the camp and barracks combined to make me a disconcerting little boy in conversation.

It was about the middle of the war, 1916, that I became a boarder at the Junior King's School at Canterbury. It is now – and was at the time my son Columba was considering its possibilities – outside Canterbury, two or three miles downstream of the River Stour, in the village of Sturry; but at the time I am writing about, it was in the centre of the town and, so far as I was concerned, ideally situated, not more than four hundred yards from the two libraries that I patronized: the already mentioned Beaney Institute, a public library, and Goulden's, a stationery shop with a lending library of modern novels, where my mother had a ticket which allowed me to take out two books at a time. Frequently on half-holidays I would take out two novels, say by Edgar Jepson or E. F. Benson, devour them standing at the counter or walking about the town, return and change them for two more and so on through the afternoon until I had read eight novels with two extra for reading after prep that same evening. It was just as well that I ate novels, because in this period of the War and at boarding school there was precious little else to eat: no butter, only "bread and scrape" (thin slices of grey bread with margarine); two meatless days a week and usually, when there was meat, boiled mutton; steamed pudding without jam or treacle; tea without sugar and with condensed milk. Ugh! Of course we each had tuck boxes (chests of wood with your name stencilled on it and very necessarily padlocked), which my mother filled on my return to school with home-made jams and cakes and preserves, made with sugar and flour from the Army canteen, so that for a week or two I was host to town boys. But it was no magic box – the bottom was soon reached, and after that goodies had to be smuggled in, as Mr Tower believed in "share and share alike" in the interests of *esprit de corps*.

He taught us Latin and he made it a living language. It lives with me still. He made us hear and see the bustle of the Roman marketplace. He introduced us to Roman slang and proverbs and supplied us with racy equivalents in English (*Carpe diem* – "make hay while the sun shines"). He taught us to know the date by calculating it from AUC (*ab urbe condita*), the date of the founding of the city – the Roman way as opposed to the Christian. He made us write down pages of everyday words and phrases before he would take us with Julius Caesar through the Gallic Wars and he would talk for hours about the Roman invasion of Britain (55 BC – an easy date to remember) and about the Roman walls of Canterbury and the forts at Richborough and Pevensey.

It was exactly the kind of teaching that appealed to me, and I learnt more of value from the Reverend H. V. Tower than from any subsequent teacher. It seemed to me that he could have been a great headmaster but I gather he opted for the Church or, at any rate, for Church politics. He was Secretary to the Bishop of London at Lambeth Palace shortly before he died.

Very little remains in my memory of the other masters except for Godfrey the music master, a character as eccentric as any of the characters that appear and disappear in my films. He was either Scottish or Northern Irish, and larger than life. I can see his great, ill-shaven face, red and weather-beaten, with craggy eyebrows over blazing blue eyes. His hair was pepper-and-salt and cropped short. It seems to me that he always wore the same suit of clothes: a brown tweed knickerbocker suit, the jacket in the Norfolk style with a belt of the same material, the breeks buckled below the knee. He loved to teach us to bawl out traditional songs like "Aken Drum":

And he rode upon a ladle
A ladle! A ladle!
He rode upon a ladle
And his name was Aken Drum.

This quaintly named hero also "ate up all the bawbie baps"; although it wasn't until I was in Scotland, in Sanquar, on my search for an island for *The Edge of the World*, that I found out that a "bawbie" was a threepenny bit and a "bap" was a sourdough bun.

Godfrey loved ballads and would chant "Phadraig Crohoor" and "Cockles and Mussels" with a passion that transformed him:

O Phadraig Crohoor was a broth of a boy
And he stood six foot eight
His arm was as round as another man's thigh
'Twas Phadraig was great.

And I can still hear his musical, whisky-harsh baritone half-crooning, half-whispering:

For the green grass is growing
O'er Phadraig Crohho-oo-oor!

He was a figure of fun to most of the boys, and we were inclined to bait him, rather as one baits a bull, half-fearfully, because he would not hesitate to throw his song book at the head of an unruly or unmusical pupil. Also he was armed with his conductor's baton and would certainly use it to keep order. He never wore a mortar-board and gown like the other masters, so seemed to be closer to us: a big truculent bear of an old boy. It was my first experience of an artist; except for my Uncle Edward, of course, who was selling Worcestershire Sauce to the South Sea Islanders in order to learn Polynesian.

In the Junior School we wore caps with blue stripes and a red badge; in the Senior we wore the big, strong, straw hats that I have already mentioned, that revolted my son. If he had seen how far and how high you could throw them from the steps of the School Library on a windy day, he might have become reconciled: when the broad brim caught the wind it could glide a hundred yards. I made my mark that Easter term, as a storyteller. I can't remember how it started, but it was discovered that I had a huge repertoire of stories by heart, mostly by Edgar Wallace, Rudyard Kipling, Rider Haggard and other prolific writers of romance and adventure. The "Sanders of the River" stories were almost inexhaustible and very popular: they were coming out in the *Windsor Magazine* with fine black and white illustrations by Maurice Greiffenhagen. I was in a large dormitory, divided up into individual cubicles of pitch-pine – one bed, chest of drawers, hooks, tuck box to each cubicle, a green baize curtain to draw across the entrance, a red blanket on the bed. A prefect slept in the cubicle nearest the dormitory door to keep order. To save energy, lights were put out early, when nobody felt sleepy, and the boy next to me would call out: "Powell will tell a story." Other voices would take it up: "Story! Story!" and in the pause during which I remained modestly silent the prefect's voice would be heard magisterially, "All right, Powell! Let's have it!" and I would lie back on my bed, my hands behind my head, and in a clear voice like my mother's I would tell another man's story in my own way.

It is interesting to me now to realize that I was even then an interpreter rather than an originator. I was a good narrator. My mother's readings aloud had taught me the value of pauses, of change of voice, of change in speed. I was never one of the school that holds a book should be read like a book, without emotion, without participation. I had a photographic memory and knew a lot of poetry by heart. Sometimes I would refuse to tell a story and would announce, amid groans of horror, that I proposed to recite "The Rime of the Ancient Mariner" or the *Rubáiyát*. But when I persisted, the magic rhyme soon quieted them. "The Ballad of East and West" became a favourite performance, with Henry Newbolt's "Drake's Drum" and "He Fell Among Thieves" and Alfred Noyes's "The Highwayman" runners up. I would drum on the wooden partition of the cubicle – Rub-a-dub-dub! Rub-a-dub-dub! – before the lines

> He'll drum them up the Channel
> As he did so long ago!

And the boys – remembering the war, which was by no means over, and the part that the Navy had played in the U-boat campaign, which would have starved us out if the Americans hadn't come to save us, and thinking no doubt of the fathers, brothers and uncles who had disappeared in Flanders mud, and the sisters and mothers who were away from home in the hospitals and first-aid stations – would take up the drumming on their partitions, "Rub-rub-a-dub! Rub-rub-a-dub!" and shout in the dimness of the night lights: "He'll drum them up the Channel – Rub-a-dub-dub! Rub-a-dub-dub! As he did so long ago!" and shout out: "Recite it again Powell! Say it again!" and the noise would die down and I would clear my throat and in a hushed voice start:

> Drake he's in his hammock and a thousand miles away.
> (Capten, art tha sleepin' there below?)
> Slung atween the round shot in Nombre Dios Bay,
> An' dreamin' arl the time o' Plymouth Hoe.

And then the door would open and the housemaster would put his head in and say: "What's going on here? I could hear you in the Common Room. What's going on, Tyrwhitt-Drake?"

And the prefect, who had been drumming Rub-a-dub-dub with the rest of us would answer: "Nothing, sir. It's only Powell has been doing a bit of reciting."

To which: "Oh! You seem to have dramatic talent, Powell."

"No, sir."

"I hope you are not going to display it in my English class?"

"No, sir."

"What was the subject of your performance?"

"'Drake's Drum', sir!"

A silence. Then: "Hmm! 'Drake's Drum' . . . He'll drum them up the Channel, eh?"

"Yes, sir."

Footsteps back to the door. "No more drumming! D'you hear Tyrwhitt-Drake? Goodnight all."

A chorus of "Goodnights" and I would lie there staring up into the darkness getting drunk on rhymes, while the dormitory slept.

It was the year 1918, and of our summer holiday at Canford Cliffs. England was exhausted by the war. The Allied armies were still reeling from the nearly successful German breakthrough. Nobody was to know that the end was so close. My brother John, fifteen and a half and a keen member of his school's Officers' Training Corps, was already looking forward to army camp and to being called up in a year's time. The nation was fed-up with mismanagement. The average expectation of life of a "Tommy" on the Western Front was three weeks; for an officer, ten days. The only hope was the Americans who were arriving in force "Over there".

My mother, seeing her world crumble about her, was determined to have one last holiday with her sons. When John came home from his military training on Salisbury Plain she had it planned. There was hardly any transport for civilians, and what there was couldn't be counted on. We were to bicycle, all three of us, all the way from Kent to Dorset, carrying everything with us, to spend the whole of August in a wooden chalet by the sea. What a cavalry commander she would have made!

It had all been arranged with Jenny Huxham, Jenny Beale as was, my mother's schoolfellow in Worcester and her oldest friend. Jenny had married Edward Huxham, who was in the National Provincial Bank and was now Manager of the Bournemouth branch, a position of some importance. At that time Bournemouth was in Hampshire, not in Dorset as now, when the county boundaries have been adjusted. (There were, no doubt, good reasons for this, but for me, Bournemouth will always be Bournemouth (Hants) and Dorset will always start at Sandbanks. I am sure that Shakespeare, seeing what has happened by re-drawing the maps of Warwickshire, Gloucestershire, Oxfordshire and the Cotswolds, would be of my opinion.)

Sandbanks is a spit of sand about a mile in length, upon which the winter storms of that tricky piece of salt water known as the Solent had piled up pebbles until it bade fair to close the mouth of great Poole Harbour, the finest natural harbour for small ships between the mouth of the Hamble and Torbay. It is supposed to be ninety-eight miles around if you include its various creeks, and it is fed by two rivers, Thomas Hardy's Piddle and the Frome at Wareham. The area was to play a significant part in my life. To the north the shore was low and green; to the west the open moorland mounted to Egdon Heath; to the south was the long rampart of the Isle of Purbeck, which wasn't an island but had all the character of one; to the east the long line of the sandstone cliffs of Bournemouth, cut with numerous deep and lush ravines, called locally "chines", crumbling away into golden sands and into Sandbanks itself, upon which, in the course of time, bathing huts, then beach huts, then bungalows, then houses, had been built with one central road for traffic giving access to the Point, where the tides ripped through at eight to ten knots twice every twenty-four hours and where a ferry was established that could take foot passengers over to Studland on the opposite bank where they were faced with a three-mile trudge along Shell Beach before reaching Studland village. At the landward end of this spit of sand become a town, were a few pine trees, a lot of sand and several modest wooden chalets facing the sea. One of them called "The Look Out" was booked for us by Jenny Huxham for the whole of August, after which time John was to join a study group organized by his Dulwich form master, "Spud" Dalton, somewhere in the Home Counties.

To dream, for my mother, was to plan: to plan was to act. John had scarcely twenty-four hours at home before we were off on our loaded bikes, wobbling badly until we had become accustomed to the weight. We were to stay at pubs on the way but we carried all our food for the journey, my mother's leather-covered Thermos flask, her folding Kodak camera, and all the necessary apparatus for brewing frequent cups of tea. Both my mother and John had three-speed gears; my bike was an ordinary model, so that I complained bitterly on hills. Our route was the Pilgrims' Way.

So early one morning, on a warm August day, accompanied by a great deal of hand-waving from Emily, the only survivor of our staff, we took the familiar road to Canterbury, John in the lead, my mother next and myself toiling in the rear. When the bikes were loaded, there had been a readjustment of tyre pressures under the mildly despotic eye of my brother. After a mile or two, we got used to the balance and John actually rode his top-heavy machine down St Martin's Hill. Have I told you about the time that old Barney bolted with the pony-cart down St Martin's Hill? No? Well, perhaps it's better left to the imagination. (St Martin's is steep, and had a gradient of one in five.) After last-minute purchases in the town, which included a bicycle pump and a puncture repairing outfit insisted upon by John, and spurred on by the jeering remarks of the Kelsey boys, who opined that our mother might get to Bournemouth but that *we* would "conk out" in ten miles, we left Canterbury by the West Gate and made for Harbledown (Chaucer's Bob-Up-and-Down).

It is fifty-six miles from Canterbury to Southwark, where the Canterbury Pilgrims assembled in Chaucer's day. It is my recollection that the courtly and witty poet was not presented to us as such by our English masters: rather he was forced into our consciousness in a bowdlerized and anglicized version which we automatically resisted. But my mother had read us most of the *Tales* and Arthur Mee had presented them to us in prose, so we agreed readily enough with my romantic parent when she insisted on us riding the Pilgrims' Way until it got too close to London, when we headed south-west for Guildford, keeping our height along the steep slopes of the North Downs. We stopped that night at Ightam Mote, a famous black-and-white sixteenth-century manor house still in Kent, but on the borders of Surrey. It had become an hotel. It was surrounded by a wide moat full of water-lilies. It must be off the main road, for although I have been close by a hundred times, I have never been there again.

The next day we came to Guildford and the winding River Wey passing by Merrow Down. We made a detour to see St Martha's Chapel on the hill. Anyone who travelled with my mother had to be prepared for numerous detours made for their literary or historical associations. To this particular one we owe the opening shots of my film *A Canterbury Tale*. As we flew down the hill into Guildford we were chanting:

> There runs a road by Merrow Down,
> A busy road today it is:
> An hour out of Guildford Town
> Beside the River Wey it is.

And as we posed for photographs on the high, bustling ridge of the Hog's Back, we looked down on the extravagant loops of the river which had inspired the letter "S" in "How the Alphabet was Made", and we quoted:

> The Wey that Taffy called Wagai
> Was almost ten times bigger then,
> And all the Tribe of Tegumai
> They cut a noble figure then.

My mother and I loved Kipling for *The Jungle Book* and the *Just So Stories*; my brother for *The Day's Work*, for *.007*, for *Steam Tactics* and for

Farewell Romance!
While all unseen
Romance brought up the 9.15.

Machinery, engineering, construction – all the arts and crafts of the new century developed rapidly by the war – were his field. I admired him deeply for his patience, for his thoroughness, and for his invention. I felt certain that he would join my Uncle Clarence in the budding aircraft industry. I was a dreamer. He was the dreamer whose dreams came true. It was the loftiness of his vision and his dedication to the future, while we looked back on the past, that made my mother so happy that her plan had worked. For four weeks the family would be together again. After that, who knew? Except that the world we knew would never be the same again.

I believe that my mother knew instinctively that she had lost my father, that he would never return to Hoath Farm and to his prewar life. His brief letters – "Passed by Censor" – how could the Censor read, I wondered, his dashing impatient handwriting, sprawling about twenty words to a page, when it sometimes took his whole family a morning to decipher them? – were enigmatic about the future. He was grateful to George Finn for running the farm during the war years, and I daresay, knowing George Finn and his son Hugh, who is one of the most successful intensive farmers of this century, that he had reason to be thankful. But he was already talking of the plans of a brother officer to buy a hotel in France when the war was over and "he might go in with him", without actually specifying how he would or could combine the two careers of hotelier in France and hop farmer in East Kent. The French were "top-hole". Their cheeses, their wines, their women, were marvellous. "Any other nation would have been crushed by the war. Not the French." If a smart man kept his eyes open after the war was over, there would be pickings. His job took him about all over Northern France and he could see the way the wind was blowing. My mother read the letters and her heart sank. This was not the life for a daughter of Frederick Corbett. But she put a brave face on it as she always had to and as she always did.

We stopped another night in Hampshire, in the New Forest at the Inn of the Trusty Servant – the Minstead Arms – little knowing that we would soon, my mother and I, live only a few miles away on the Ringwood side of the Forest. None of us had been there before. John's camp on the edge of Salisbury Plain was our nearest point of contact. We were not disappointed. The New Forest was wonderful: the great oaks, the deer, the wild ponies, the miles of unfenced grassy glades and seas of green bracken, already yellowing; the sheer size of it all, the varieties of butterflies dancing in the sunshine, the sensation of being in a part of old England that had not changed or felt the plough since *Domesday Book* was compiled, the Forest where Red William died of an arrow, shot by an unknown hand, where outlaws could hide and be undetected, where children – for like all good families we had read *The Children of the New Forest* – could have incredible adventures among Roundheads and Cavaliers and emerge unscathed. It was beyond our dreams. "Pure Maurice Hewlett," my mother was heard to say. "I knew I ought to find room in my bag for *Forest Lovers*."

My mother was going through a sentimental attachment at the time for a tall, gentle poetic officer in command of a searchlight battery on the top of Tyler Hill, overlooking Canterbury from the north. My godfather lived there, a very gay sportsman whose influence over my father had always been deplored by my mother in the years before the war. As he always came up with magnificent Christmas and birthday presents for us boys, we could not understand our mother's exasperation when my father would abruptly announce that he was "going up to Town" or "down to Monte" with Whitey. Anyway it was at the house of this gay deceiver, this Mephisto, now a bit faded after a misspent life, that my mother met the man she should have married.

Maurice Hewlett's novel *Open Country* was a combination of modern free love with medieval trimmings like a tapestry woven at Kelmscott in the studios of William Morris. Hewlett was widely read for his romances of the age of chivalry: *Richard Yea-and-Nay, The Forest Lovers* and *The Queen's Quair*. They were dangerous books for my lonely, deserted mother to read. The hero and heroine were pure, rather like figures in a tapestry: diluted George Borrow, Isopel Berners, sketched in watercolour.

My mother and "G.W.T.P." read and wrote verses together, strolled in the woods hand in hand, wrote each other long literary letters – did all the proper things that lonely middle-aged lovers brought together by war should do. I remember him as a moustached and unmilitary-looking officer with a walking stick; and after the war as a clean-shaven, delicate-looking country gentleman who could have been a parson. There are faded snapshots and faded letters. He was married, of course.

There is no doubt that my mother loved him; but whether he loved her I have no means of telling. They were about the same age and she survived him by twenty years. They wrote to each other until he died in the Lake District, where he had his home.

The next day we had only a twenty-mile ride to Bournemouth from "The Sign of the Trusty Servant". He's a bit rare now but the sign is still there. He has deer's feet to run fast with messages, and a pig's head, because a pig will eat anything, and a padlock on his snout, because he can keep his mouth shut; and – I don't remember the rest but take a day off! Go and see for yourselves. Go to Minstead and wander through the Forest on a summer's day: you won't be disappointed, even if you never look at the sign or think that a good servant is a survival of an exploded feudal system.

By noon, we were being greeted with shrieks by Jenny and her daughter Peggy who was a honey and about my age. Philip was at school and Edward Huxham was (in a hushed voice) "at the bank". After lunch we all cycled down to Sandbanks, about four miles, and were introduced to the hut we were to occupy: "The Look Out".

The wooden cottage straddled a low cliff. Surprisingly you climbed up a short ladder to enter it from the pine wood and you climbed down a long ladder to the beach on the far side. It faced the sea; the spring tides reached to the foot of the steps. It was all pure sand. Far away to the south-east was a white line that Peggy said was "The Needles" on the Isle of Wight opposite us, and quite near was Studland Point with two pillars of chalk, "Old Harry" and his "Wife" walking into the Solent together. It was the cabin of one's dreams. Even John was rushing about, opening doors, asking questions, climbing down with me to the beach, while the women were unpacking, lighting the Valor Perfection oil-burning stove, testing the water supply and inspecting the neighbours. There were a few other cabins scattered about among the pine trees, in no sort of order, refreshing to eyes that had been regimented. The road from Parkstone to Poole, which forked to Sandbanks a few yards back, ran down to our door, then petered out into the sand and seaweed, razor fish, dried sea skates and cockleshells. And that was all. It was a heavenly place.

The five weeks that we were to spend there seemed to stretch on for ever. John and I had lost touch with one another at a vital time when he was at Dulwich College. Before that we had never been separated. I was passionately loyal to King's School, where the boarders were the élite and the dayboys dismissed as dayboys. At Dulwich, I suspected, the reverse was the case. How could it be otherwise when surrounded by suburbs like Tulse Hill, Herne Hill, Forest Hill, Denmark Hill – and, most importantly, Sydenham Hill from whose heights on a clear day you could see the North Downs lying like a great wave about to break over the Weald of Kent? John was Modern. I was obstinately Classical; and the Classics were part of my loyalty to King's. I hated all games except Rugby Football; I enjoyed jogging back covered in mud from the playing fields out of town to the hot showers in the monastic changing rooms of the school. In rugger, your position on the field is a rough guide to your character. From the first try-outs I was either full-back or wing three-quarter: a loner. So it wasn't really loyalty to "the old school" that I felt. It was loyalty to place: to the narrow streets of Canterbury, to the High Street and cattle markets that are no more, to the Christchurch Gate opposite Kit Marlowe's statue in the Butter Market, to Cave's café, to the Cathedral standing amid the hushed green lawns of the precincts, to the vast silence of the nave, where a chair dragged across the echoing flagstones made one think of Becket's body dragged by armoured men, pierced and slashed with swords, to die before the altar in the side chapel. All this I have tried to get into the last twenty-five minutes of *A Canterbury Tale*, guided by Emeric's noble dramatic instinct, inspired to dozens of small touches, glimpses of textures, effects of sunlight and shadow, and above all by love and grateful memory for having been born a Man of Kent.

If a boy of thirteen can feel this in his bones, how much more can a boy of fifteen and a half. But John had no special feeling, so far as I can tell, for Canterbury. He was delightfully different from me. He was a Powell. And perhaps, besides kinship in blood, there is a kinship of place, and he might have come back after many years abroad to look for a home within sight and sound of Worcester Cathedral's bells instead of Canterbury's. Here, at Sandbanks, he was freed of his engineering projects, of his scale models and his blueprints and his textbooks, and discarding his spectacles, became once more my hero and my teacher. For I am selfish and impulsive; he was considerate and careful. If a thing doesn't come easily to me I have no use for it; he would never use a tool or toy until he had taken it to pieces to see how it worked and put it back together again. Above all, in his tenderness to my mother and his sense of responsibility for his family, he was a man already.

It had been arranged that at the end of the Sandbanks holiday we should all three go up to London, by train this time, the "Bournemouth Belle", with our bikes in the guard's van, my mother and I to stay until term time with my grandmother and my Aunt Ethel at Forest Hill, John going on to Ashingdon to join his study group. I was fond of my grandmother, held Ethel in awe, and admired the tiger's skin whose head with fierce glass eyes and yawning jaws (one of the teeth was loose) hung on the wall in the narrow entrance hall. At once I dived into the bound volumes of the *Strand*, always my first act at Devonshire Road. I was only heard of at mealtimes.

Suddenly our little world was thrown into confusion. John was ill. That didn't seem to be anything to fuss about. He was a bit delicate. He was subject to colds. But after all that sea-bathing and sunshine of "The Lookout" he would soon shake that off. I went on reading *The Adventure of the Blue Carbuncle*. Then my mother disappeared with Ethel up to town and I was left with my grandmother. I learnt that John had appendicitis. His housemaster had been late in diagnosing it. There had been a panic. He had been rushed to Guy's Hospital; he was there now, my mother and Aunt

Ethel were with him. That's all right, I thought, if mother was there John would be all right. At teatime we heard Ethel's key fumbling in the lock of the front door. I jumped to open it. She brushed by me, ran to her mother, and fell into her arms, crying with all the violence of pent-up feeling: "Our little Johnnie's gone!"

The appendix had burst, peritonitis had set in, everything had been done too late, my brother was dead. My grandmother comforted Ethel, cried with her, clasped me to her, got up with dignity, went upstairs to change her white lace shawl for a black one, locked herself in the bathroom, had a delayed heart attack brought on by the shock of Ethel's sudden entrance, and died. We had to get a man to break the door down.

I am not a great man. I am not a clever man. I am not a man at all, but a truculent and dreamy small boy who is determined to impose his view of the world upon any audience he can get. To do this I use anything and anybody, and there is no doubt that I would have used my brother's cleverness if he had lived. I fancy that his career would have been in aeronautics with his Uncle Clarence, and that by the time I was thirty and made my first important film (*The Edge of the World*) he would have been a great man in Canada or America.

As I am writing this it is snowing outside and snowing in my heart when I think of John. He was buried by my mother's wish in the churchyard at Ashingdon, a country churchyard, the kind that she loved. I think she must have already given up Canterbury in her heart and saw ahead of her constant attempts to make a home, constantly thwarted by the gipsy-like existence of an independent film-maker. I seem to remember that she visited John's grave from time to time, but never with me.

A death in the family, particularly of a fellow adolescent who has no power of decision or influence on one's own destiny, has an effect on a child quite unlike that on an adult. When I was born, John was there. He was part of the scene. We grew up together. Our age and our tastes separated us. We liked one another, teased one another, shared family jokes – then suddenly he was gone. I had not lost a brother, an elder brother, I had lost a piece of myself. I didn't know what to do or how to express my sympathy for my mother. Should I be weeping for brother and grandmother as my mother and aunt were weeping? I didn't feel like weeping. There was just a gap and a sense of bewilderment. I searched around and found a book of poetry with some translations from Schiller. I pondered over a lament by some maiden pacing a stormy shore and brought the words of the final stanza to my mother, hoping they would do what I had no words to do:

For the sweetest balm for the broken hearted
In their dreary waste of years
When the soft delights of love are parted
Is love's lament and tears.

What earthly use this was to my poor mother I don't know.

Of more practical use to my mother was the fact that I learnt to cook. After the funeral her strong spirit broke. My Aunt Ethel had to return to her duties at the High School, and I was left to look after my mother until she was well enough to travel to Canterbury. My *plat du jour* was usually Welsh rarebit, washed down with pots of strong tea. My mother survived the diet and I acquired a lasting interest in cookery.

I don't remember that my father came over for the funeral. I don't think he did. He was proud of John, of his brains, of the fact that his brother Clarence thought a lot of John and planned to get him into Sopwith's; and that he looked like a Powell. But his practical attitude to life, the fact that the war was nearly over, that he had already decided on a new career in his early forties must have weighed against a decision to cross the Channel. I doubt if it would have occurred to him that my mother needed him. I'll give him the benefit of it, though.

My grandfather, Frederick Corbett, continued to come on Sundays to play his games of patience, using two full packs. I think the variety was called Miss Milligan. It took the whole surface of the dining table and the eight columns very rarely came out. He never said a word to either of us about John, which was strangely comforting. But his light-toned voice when he left to go back to his truckle bed in the City, turning at the glass-fronted door, under the flickering gas-jet, to say "Good night, May," said everything.

It was customary in those days for boys to wear a broad band of black stuff on their arm out of respect for a death in the family. When I returned to school a week late, I am afraid it gave me importance in my own eyes. Human beings are like that. I was soon to be deflated, however. Unknown to me, discussions had been going on among the Corbetts about my future and the future of 241 Devonshire Road. The little house was to be sold. Ethel would find a flat for herself and for my grandfather on Sundays. And I was to be taken away from King's and sent to Dulwich as a boarder at the Blew House, "Spud" Doulton's House.

There were various reasons for this from the planners' point of view and I gathered them one by one with a dawning sense of outrage that I was not being consulted – I, a member of His Majesty's Forces! – and the deeply felt knowledge that I wouldn't be listened to if I were. "Tommy" (my father) was not coming back from France when the war was over. (The signing of the Armistice was only six weeks away and all that folk could think of was peace.) Hoath Farm was to be sold. My mother would either join my father, or find somewhere for the present in England to make a home for me. Meanwhile money was short. My Uncle Geoffrey offered to pay my school fees if I took John's place at Dulwich College and in Ethel's home at weekends.

Now that I examine for the first time the motives of all concerned, I pin them on Ethel. Beneath her stern, intellectual personality of a scholar and disciplinarian, was an emotional, passionate, frustrated woman. Her dramatic entrance with the news of my brother's death had been a revelation to me. It had killed her mother. Her brothers and sisters decided that the only way to settle Ethel as the new family centre in London was to give her – me! She had been passionately fond of John. *Ergo*! She was to be passionately fond of me. A John Miles Powell Prize was to be founded at Dulwich to be competed for by members of the Upper Fifth, and was, of course, won by me in due course.

When these decisions were imparted to me by my mother, with an effort to make them palatable, I don't think that I protested or argued, but deep down, in my inmost being, I was shocked and despairing. I still feel it now that I am old. I had always had a deep sense of place; if anything has so far come out of these pages it is the feeling that I was part of a known world. It has kept me in this country, where I was born and brought up, long after it had been made clear to me that my devotion was not reciprocated. I love England. I have mirrored England to the English in my films. They have not understood the image in the mirror. I am writing these lines in a foreign country (only, to paraphrase a line from *Colonel Blimp*, it isn't a foreign country, it's Hollywood) because for the last ten years I have been made to feel an outcast by my own people. I was "too big a risk". I was "too independent". I wanted my own way. I was all the things that have made my films different from my contemporaries' films. I have grown up. Audiences have grown up. Films have stayed in the nursery.

There was nothing to be done. All the moves were planned. I decided that I wouldn't be a chessman. I had always felt more Corbett than Powell and now suddenly the Corbetts were deciding my life. They were responsible for my leaving the farm, for my pony being sold, for my leaving Canterbury and the grey, monastic King's School for the piles of red brick, ornamented with finials, cloisters and a clocktower, called Dulwich College, London SE23. Greek was optional on the Classical side at King's. I had only taken Latin. At Dulwich I would have to learn Greek, which meant going back to the lowest form in the senior school and working my way up again from the first declension. Only a Latin snob like myself can appreciate my disgust.

The Armistice was signed on November 11, 1918, in a railway carriage at Compiègne, we were told; and at last the guns were silent. When the wind was in the south-east we had heard them muttering, when the Germans were stopped on the Somme; and again only a few months ago when they broke through to Arras. But now they were silent, and "demobbed" was a new word in the language. My father had bought a half-share in a hotel in Chantilly: the Manor House. His partner was a colonel and his wife, "a jolly good sort". My mother and I were to come out at Easter next year to see for ourselves. Chantilly had a racecourse, training stables and a famous château. I perked up and decided that the Powells had a future superior to the Corbetts, with their humdrum curriculum and London suburban trees that looked all right until you climbed them and found yourself covered in soot.

My mother decided that, like Mr Asquith, she would wait and see. Meanwhile she studied French and forced me to make French conversation. We had all picked up some French in the war, Entente Cordiale and all that: and I had a phrase book, *French, Troops, for the Use Of*, which was handy if you were driving a horse-drawn limber, or were wounded in hospital, or just lost in a blasted landscape like General Clive Candy and his driver Murdoch on that November morning when the guns ceased firing in *Colonel Blimp*. By the middle of December my indomitable mother had packed and stored our furniture, handed over the Hoath to the new tenants, and was waiting to take me to spend Christmas with Aunt Ethel in Forest Hill, where she had taken a flat in a tall, brick-built Victorian house in the London Road, only a few doors from the Horniman Museum, where I spent most of my time. I remember nothing about our journey except that we brought our black and white long-haired cat, Booey Angel, in a basket: he made a mess in the kitchen and was assured by everyone ever so many times that it was not his fault. After five hours in a basket, who wouldn't?

Forest Hill is a shoulder of Sydenham Hill, which in those days was crowned by the Crystal Palace. It is both steep and high. Carriage roads lined with villas that boasted coachhouses and large gardens full of laurels, zigzagged up its flanks. From the top there was an inspiring view of the Surrey hills to the south; while to the north, on the other side of the River Thames, were the hazy heights of Hampstead, Highgate and the long, even rampart of the Stanmore escarpment, where Fighter Command was later to be established to guard London in the next World War. The side of the hill facing north, from Forest Hill to the Brighton railroad, a distance of about two miles, was green farmland and included a golf course. There were no farms, as I remember, but trees and hedges, pastures and meadows, until the slope of the hill became too steep for husbandry and the woods began. All this was College property, bequeathed by the famous Edward Alleyn, who collected oil-paintings as well as press cuttings. He was a contemporary of Shakespeare's and his big successes included

Malvolio and Richard III. The Dulwich Portrait Gallery, though small, is choice and lies in the village. It gave a good excuse for strolling that way, then suddenly whipping around the corner, out of sight and out of bounds, to the second-hand bookshops of Herne Hill. A carriage road crossed the farmland and climbed up the Sydenham Hill. There was a toll-gate with a little octagonal toll-house opposite the College. There was a lane up to the golf club, which was only a shack. There were the usual paths. The road that ran to join the London Road, where the tall trams ground groaning up Forest Hill, was called Dulwich Common and, on the other side of the road, was Dulwich Park, famous for its rhododendrons and its swans; one of the loveliest little parks in London. Queen Mary used to have the greys harnessed to drive around the park in blossom-time. I can see her now, her back straight as a poker, her toque firmly nailed to her head with formidable hatpins, her face covered by a veil with such large violet spots that she looked as if she might be contagious, bowing graciously to the occasional curtsey and the frequently doffed hats.

This then was to be my new kingdom, and all that Christmas I explored it. In the course of a polite visit to my temporary housemaster, who had a tall house on Dulwich Common (there was no room in the Blew House until the next winter term), I had learnt that College boarders were not allowed to wander over the estate, so it was up to me to get to know all the paths and hiding places intimately before donning the College cap which was dark blue with pale blue stripes on it and a crest in front. At least it was better than the King's straw hat which was to become a stumbling block to Columba's academic career. I soon found that one of the big elm trees that lined the lane to the golf club was hollow and that there was an entrance for boys about fifteen feet up. Owls were using it and it was full of débris and knot-holes which could be enlarged into spy-holes with a pocket-knife. I took possession of this watch-tower, expelled the owls by stretching wire netting over the entrances and slanted the spy-holes so that I could see up and down the lane, for masters who played golf used to cycle along it without ever raising their eyes above their handlebars. This outpost once established, I had a retreat from the busy haunts of men. As for the rest of the estate, it was only a matter of keeping close along the hedges to avoid observation, or along the edge of the dark woods, into which one could melt when hailed by some busybody.

Auth Ethel, being a scholar, a sentimentalist and a bookworm, had kept all the books from Devonshire Road. My mother was a great addict of circulating libraries (as I think they were called in those days) when Mudie's was still at the corner where New Oxford Street meets Shaftesbury Avenue, and the Times Book Club was still in Wigmore Street. But my aunt bought most of the novels she read. They were of the Maurice Baring, William de Morgan (*Alice for Short*) type of story – long, discursive, good-mannered and, I suspected, superficial. But she also had Chekov and Turgenev and all the new poets, and to the year of her death, many, many years later, I knew that I would receive on my birthday from Aunt Ethel, a little book of verse or essays, or a short novel that I had never heard of and which I should have been sorry to have missed (Frank Kendon's *The Cherry Minder*, Osbert Sitwell's *A Place of One's Own*, Eliot's lectures, or a deliciously insulting pamphlet by Ezra Pound). Then there were the Early English, Scandinavian and Russian textbooks which I pored over, and big books of the Sagas like *Burnt Njal* and William Morris's *The Earthly Paradise* and all the classics, mostly in the Everyman editions, with copious notes. I decided that I had enough reserves to keep the enemy at bay for the present and started Easter term at my new school with the comfortable knowledge that my father wanted my mother and me to join him at Chantilly for the Easter holidays. The coast of France at Cap Gris Nez had been a familiar sight all my short life. It would appear and disappear like an Impressionist painting as I sat playing with the pebbles on Dungeness. Sometimes the haze cleared and the coastline moved nearer and we knew this as a sign of rain. France and Flanders had been in our minds and on our lips for more than four years. Now we were going there. Perhaps to live there.

The boat-train ran non-stop from Calais to Paris in two and a half hours. My father was to meet us at the Gare du Nord. I was standing in the corridor watching the stations flash by and trying to catch a glimpse of the countryside when we burst out of the woods and crossed a narrow valley by a high viaduct. I had time to see that there was a stream and that the slopes on each bank were thick with market gardens. In the distance there was an ornamental lake. Then we were thundering through a station and I snatched CHANTILLY from the signboards!

"Mummy! Mummy! It's Chantilly! We're passing through it."

My mother joined me with one finger keeping her place in her book. But the little town had already disappeared and the forest, green and orderly and French, not in the least like our dear shaggy New Forest, had taken over. My mother was going back to her seat when I exclaimed, and she turned in time to see the forest fall away into a deep valley, filled with another lake, and a single white château, which seemed to float on its surface like a solitary swan.

"The Château de la Reine Blanche," announced my mother, thumbing her Baedeker. "It's only a mile or two from the town. It will make a nice walk through the forest." My mother always had to have an objective for her walks. I said nothing. But I had found my Guermantes and had fallen under the spell of France.

In forty minutes we were being greeted boisterously by my father, no longer in uniform. Being listed as a farmer he had got demobbed early, but he would have wangled it anyway. He wore a *béret basque* with a metal crest of The Buffs pinned on it, a blazer with the crest of Bromsgrove School on the breast pocket, tweed plus-fours, a canary-coloured cardigan, brown brogues, thick wool stockings and carried a thick stick. He had scrounged a pair of horn-rimmed glasses from the Yanks and given up his pince nez. The new glasses made him look a bit owlish for my taste, but younger. We were to board a local train for Chantilly almost immediately. I had just time to sample the delights of a French station buffet before we were hustled on board. The heavy luggage and packing cases were coming by *la grande vitesse*, they were consigned direct to Chantilly as instructed, and to our surprise turned up three days later. We had all we needed with us.

My first impression of Chantilly was the sound of iron-bound wheels and iron-shod horses's hooves over the *pavé* in the main streets of the town. The side streets were simply untarred roads with stone gutters under the trees lining the street, but the main streets were paved with blocks of stone about eight inches square and weighing two kilos which had seen service all through the war; and, indeed, the town and the country around were still on a war footing. Compiègne, where the Armistice had been signed in the famous railway carriage (resurrected later by Hitler), was only a few miles away and was our municipal town. Army vehicles, horse-drawn and motor-driven, passed through the streets all day. The men were starting to come back but most of them were still in uniform or in parts of uniforms. I wandered about, gaping at everything, very struck by the immense number of mules – animals of which I had little experience. Everyone was very cordial. I suppose an English schoolboy to them was as rare a sight as a mule to me. The proprietor of the café on the corner stood me a *sirop*. A woman in the pâtisserie bought me a packet of very hard, small candies. I learnt to say "Bo'jou" and to touch hands on every occasion.

The Bar Le Manoir was on the High Street and was one of the oldest houses in the town. Half-timbered and lattice-windowed, it was small and panelled with dark wood. There were two bar-rooms. Behind the little house was a stone-paved courtyard which had been a stableyard. An outside stone stairway led up to a bedroom which was my father's. A narrow and steep inside staircase led to two rooms and a bath over the bar. An iron door led through the kitchen and scullery into yet another courtyard, beyond which was a tall, three-storeyed, very French house with high shuttered windows, a large dining room and a salon with creaking parquet floors. It looked south into a walled garden with white railings, through which the beautiful Chantilly racecourse could be seen. In fact there were two houses back to back and connected by passages: the old Norman bar on the street, and the elegant mansion on the *pelouse*, as we learnt to call the racecourse. The Manor House Bar (English was more chic, said my father, and more suitable when more than half the big trainers were English, as were most of their stableboys) had been bought freehold, while the French house was on a lease. I knew nothing about father's partnership with the Colonel and whether there was a company jointly owned, or what, but I am sure that my father had the best of it. He wasn't a Welsh Marcher for nothing. I have a clear memory of Colonel – let's call him Drake. He didn't look like a colonel; he looked like a nervous businessman. He had a lined, brown face with black hair smoothed down with pomade, and the eyebrows of a comedian. He was slight, of average height and usually wore a well-cut suit and well-shined shoes in contrast to my father's *sportif* outfit. Mrs Drake was large and beautiful, creamy and pregnant, gay and popular. As far as I remember, racing had started again, and Easter was one of the big meetings at Chantilly, when the French Derby was run and the Prix de Diane. The Manor House seemed to be well known, and all the other hotels, cafés and bars were jumping on race days.

The racecourse of Chantilly has one of the most beautiful settings in the world. It is surrounded by forest. Broad rides for horsemen radiate to the east and south, stretching for miles, meeting and crossing other avenues, starting new cross roads, new radiations. The forest seems immense. It is beautifully kept. Early in the morning the training stables empty out their long string of horses, mounted by lads. They cross the town and enter the forest. At first I used to lie in bed in the early morning and hear the ring of their hooves on the *pavé* as they followed each other in single file. It seemed interminable. Later on, when I knew a few people and made friends with the Carter boys, I joined them and passed, like them, through the grandiose arch at the end of our street, which is all that is left of the royal stables of the Grand Condé, Duc d'Aumale, Prince of France. The road leads down, then up again, bordered by green turf and, quite suddenly, the Château appears, floating on its ornamental lake, close at hand, the fat carp swarming under the white stone bridge that crosses the moat, the walls and towers, the blue-tiled roofs, the pinnacles and the rows of windows reflected in the glassy water. It is one of the most harmonious landscapes I know, and coming early in my experience as it did, I often get an urge to see it again – to ride my horse down the street, imagining I am one of three hundred horses and horsemen, all expectant, all young, all gone to the knacker's yard, where I shall one day dreamily follow.

Diana, whose Prize is one of the great sporting trophies of France, stands on her pedestal at the crossroads in the forest named after her, Le Carrefour de Diane. The forest is a hunting preserve. On *journées de chasse* the use of the forest is restricted and all the formal etiquette of stag-hunting is deployed, exactly as depicted in the huge tapestries in the château. The huntsman uses an enormous horn to marshal his forces. An English huntsman would smile grimly when he saw this massive, great circular affair of shining brass which finally emits a very unstirring TOOT! But there is nothing antiquated about the hounds, the stag and the riders as they gallop up and down the allées, shouting to one another, while clouds of fine dust rise behind them veiling the low sun. It is a breathtaking sight to see the stag, as I have more than once, burst from the undergrowth into one of the broad rides, pause and listen, then trot calmly down it, pause again, then melt into the trees. The hounds seem larger than our Exmoor hounds which are the only staghounds that I know.

From my very first day it was made clear to us that no slackers would be tolerated around the hotel. We all had to pitch in. Outside the bar door, in the courtyard, my father showed my mother and me a low door with a curved top to fit the archway over stone steps leading down to the cellar.

"This is going to be your job, Mick. You're the cellarer and you keep the key on you. If you go out leave the key with me or with the barman. You're responsible, mind! It's your job to check the stock after every weekend and order up replacements. Newman (the barman) will tell you about the bar and the *maître d'hôtel* will tell you what's wanted in the *salle à manger*."

By now we were down in the vaulted cellar, which must have been several hundred years old. An attempt had been made to make shelves out of cases and there were already medieval niches in the walls, but cases of wine and loose bottles of cider and beer were all over the place. I felt my mother's disapproval, but my tidy soul rejoiced at the idea of bringing order into the cellar and handling bottles labelled with famous names which I had already savoured in books.

"Keep the red and white wine on opposite sides so that you can go straight to them. The champagne and the *vins mousseux* in a place by themselves. They're mostly for *jours de fête* and marriages. The cider's popular – good Norman stuff; I get it from a farm I know and bottle it. It sells at a franc a bottle. The beer's poor stuff. The French can't brew beer. Not enough hops in it. Liqueurs and all that hair-oil muck we keep in the bar and a few bottles down here. So get busy, you young monkey, and get some order into the place. And don't leave the key in the lock."

Of course I did. Often. I still do. I open or shut a door and think perhaps of Yeats's lines: "Old woman, old woman he never shuts a door, but one opens", and start dreaming and walk away, leaving the key in the lock. It used to drive my son Kevin mad. It drives urban Americans mad. They are great lockers of everything.

So this is why I know about wine. At fourteen and a half I was the *sommelier* of the Manor House at Chantilly, and later on at la Voile D'Or at Cap Ferrat. I loved my cellar. I cleaned it out and whitewashed it and spent most of my holiday down there. It was dry and cool. I improved the lighting with the help of the *plongeur*, a greasy boy of about my own age who did all the washing-up of plates and vessels. (He had an immense stone bath for the job, and his first task in the morning was to skim all the grease off it and top up the filthy residue with hot water.) I made an inventory and I cut labels out of cardboard to go over the bins and racks. We didn't have much vintage stuff, the Burgundies and Bordeaux that the fathers of French families like to make such a fuss about on festive occasions in a good *moyen* restaurant, but we had a lot of excellent Loire wines – Vouvray and Pouilly, and that clean, cheap, stony wine from the north bank that goes so well with shellfish. Our champagne stocks were good and came from Epernay, which I have always preferred, and, in particular, from Ay, a favourite of my father's, a small vineyard (*Homm of Ay*) but so much the more personal in its loving handling of their champagnising (what an odd word, but it's the correct one in English). My father loved the rich wines at the heart of Burgundy – Beaune and Pommard – and already at that time he had started a relationship with Bouchard Aîné et Fils at the Hospice de Beaune. Unlike most English wine-drinkers, with their traditions of claret and port, my father was luke-warm about the great Bordeaux, although he knew his way around the châteaux and admired simple wines with a firm personality like Saint-Estephe or a hearty masculine wine like Château Margaux; but what he loved for a special treat were the great yellow wines of Bordeaux, Château d'Yquem and Barsac, sweet as Tokay, elegant as Chateaubriand (the author, not the steak), with their peculiar combination of heavy perfume and lightness on the tongue. I admit its quality, although I don't much care for Yquem with food; it is better drunk in fine crystal in the sunshine, when the heat of the day and the sun itself is declining. Then, as you raise your glass against a background of rolling vineyards and appreciate the sun's warmth striking against the tall, cold glass and the dragon yellow heaviness of the wine – ah! then – you are bound to agree with my father that there is something special about Château d'Yquem.

I imagine him looking over my shoulder and nodding approval of the sentiments, even if he thinks I am being a bit long-winded. "What you doin' messin'? Cut the cackle and get to the 'orses!"

Muscadet! That was the northern Loire wine that I was trying to think of, much better known now than it was then, perhaps because even the wines of Tours, which have to be drunk quickly – and which *are* drunk quickly by the locals – are no longer as cheap as they are good.

Immersed as I was in the day-to-day running of the hotel and bar, I hardly paid attention to my parents' relationship. Boys are not usually made that way. The war had separated them like so many other people, and now the Armistice – for the Peace of Versailles which was to bring about the next World War was not signed yet – had brought us together again. Without John, I think that I sensed rather than knew, that their marriage was moving towards a crisis and had been for a long while. After a valiant effort to be a farmer's wife, my mother had seen my father slip more and more under "Whitey's" influence. He spent more and more of his time at Folkestone and in London. The war had been an escape for him, not a hindrance. A whole new world had opened up for him and, when Colonel Drake invited him to come on in, he hadn't hesitated, and if he thought of my mother at all, it was "She's got Mick. He'll be at school for a few years yet. If she doesn't want to pitch in here with us, she'll have to stay in England and make a home for Mick."

About this time I became conscious of two small people who were like characters out of a novel. They were there and they were not there, although I am sure that my mother had pinpointed their presence early on. They were a mother and daughter and lived in two rooms over the bar. Madame was in black, with an apron, and always mending or hemming something. Mademoiselle resembled a parrot as to her profile, which she was proud of, because she was Norman. She liked to use a particle before her name, when she thought it was safe to; and she always used it on the flyleaf of her books. She was sensitive and intelligent; she was also patient and sly. No doubt she had been my father's mistress, but she was after bigger game than that. For the present she was cordial, as her position was equivocal: neither she nor her mother had official status in the hotel: the Drakes didn't like them, but the old girl was useful and they tolerated them, only complaining about the valuable space they occupied at weekends.

A small tragedy helped the Norman invaders considerably. Mrs Drake was a vivid personality, was popular, and loved parties. There was dancing in the salon to the gramophone every night, and to a small orchestra at weekends and on *jours de fête*. Money was still plentiful, everybody gambled on horses, there were big wins and big parties and all that goes with parties, whether the time is 1919 A.D. or B.C. Not surprisingly, Colonel Drake was jealous of his lovely wife and worried because she was carrying his child. Even I could see trouble coming, as I had been witness to a slanging match or two and, with my Army experience behind me, I was no stranger to intrigue. One night there was a big scene: banging on doors, feet on stairs, broken glass, drunken shouts, fisticuffs – the lot. Mrs Drake had a miscarriage and lost her child.

It shows my innocence that, when everyone was sleeping it off next morning and the doctor had left, leaving a nurse behind him, I came up from my cellar carrying some cider and asked my mother, as she passed by: "How is the little stranger?" It stopped her in her tracks. She said "Darling – of course you didn't know. Mrs Drake's baby is dead. It was born dead." She touched my cheek and I felt a fool.

The Normans saw their chance and moved into the breach, Mademoiselle taking over the running of the French House, her mother appropriating the keys of the *lingerie*, which meant that every piece of linen used in the house was dispensed by her. They were not the sort, once established, to retreat. It was an invasion, not yet a conquest.

There was a cinema at Chantilly. There were local cinemas everywhere in those days. Chantilly was not a large town, but I think it had two. The one near us was down a side street and advertised that it was open for business by an electric buzzer which rang until the show started. I can hear that remorseless bell shattering the calm under the plane trees whenever I think of Chantilly. It is curious how the French, most sensitive of nations, are insensitive to noise, particularly if it is a new and splendid noise that stands for Progress.

The films were mostly serials, like the French films I had seen at the Palais de Luxe in Canterbury. One of my earliest movie images is of Fantomas, the Master Crook of Paris. When he wasn't wearing white tie and tails, a cane, a top hat, and an opera cloak, he was in black tights with a black mask, performing incredible feats of hide-and-seek with the police. The image that stays with me is of an open cistern of water in the attic of some house. The police dash in, in pursuit of Fantomas, and find nobody. Baffled, they withdraw, but the Chief takes one last look at the cistern, sees a straw floating on the surface of the water, gives it an idle flush. Aha! we all think. And sure enough! As the last policeman goes, the water stirs and bubbles and the black form of Fantomas appears from the depths, between his lips the straw through which he has been breathing! I can see now his black figure, glistening like a seal's, smiling triumphantly at the camera. For, in silent films, one learnt to "register" to the camera.

Candy and the movies have always gone together, and in the intervals at Chantilly girls moved up and down the aisle chanting *"pochettes surprises! . . . esquimaubriques!"* There were frequent intervals. In 1919 most films were short comedies. In addition they were playing an interminable serial in fifteen episodes of *The Three Musketeers*, and there was another serial starring the famous French boxer Georges Carpentier. I believe that d'Artagnan was Aimé Simon-Girard, and as a movie historian I ought to check it with the dates, but I really don't think it matters. Aimé Simon-Girard was in practically every romantic French costume film of that decade and the Musketeers serial may have been a year later. The Carpentier film I remember well. He was not an actor of any kind, but he was charming, and his flattened nose on his pretty face gave him a different look. The film was full of stunts, of course. All serials had to be full of stunts: jumping on and off moving trains, onto moving automobiles, fights on the edge of high buildings, all the tricks of the trade, from Georges Méliès to Superman. Carpentier moved obligingly (he had a pleasant smile) through the scenes, and we all thought he was splendid. Films were tinted then: the predominant colour of the Carpentier serial seemed to be green.

The Musketeers did their stuff in a sort of Old Master yellowish-brown, suitable for cloak and rapier adventures. Night scenes, of course, were blue.

When I went back to school my mother went with me. No crucial decision had been taken and, as far as I know, there had been no showdown about the Normans. It didn't look as if the Drake-Powell partnership would last, and, since my mother had all the Hoath furniture and other belongings in store, and I had at least another two years in school, it seemed sensible to find a house in East Kent for the present. My father naturally suggested rakish and modern Folkestone. My mother settled for Hythe.

Not only Hythe but her feet in the sea. There used to be a row of tall grey houses, five storeys high and one room wide, facing the English Channel, with only the narrow beach road between the windows and the pebble beach, which shelved rapidly, so that the waves in winter, striking the slope of shifting pebbles, hurled cartloads of them onto the road and sometimes through our windows. Little did my mother care. She always said that she never knew what luxury was until she lay in bed, on the third floor of the gaunt grey house, propped up with pillows and looking straight out over the waves rolling in. We had the end house in the row. The price was about £400. They were probably the silliest houses ever designed for silly people. We loved ours. Not many years ago I went looking for those houses on the seafront, but they had gone. I believe they had all fallen into the sea.

Hythe is one of the Cinque Ports which are, as everyone knows, Romney, Hastings, Hythe, Sandwich and . . . and, Good heavens! I have forgotten the fifth port. Here in Hollywood, where I am writing these words, who can help me? Is it Deal? Is it Dover? Is it Ramsgate? The official residence of the Warden is Walmer Castle but Walmer is not a port. Their harbours are mostly dried up, the sea has retreated as at Rye. Hythe is no longer a port; it has its harbour at Sandgate, which, in winter, is bombarded by the sea. In my day there were horse-drawn trams that bumped along enchantingly by the sea, the tram-lines full of pebbles; they finished, as far as I remember, at Sandgate, where the coast suddenly mounted into a cliff at Folkestone. At Sandgate the tides swept in with tragic force; there was something about the shelf of the coast. Time and again the sea-wall at Sandgate was pounded to rubble and the sea-front road closed. Out at Dungeness, the pebbles come together for many miles. At the point where the lighthouse was and the radar station is, the pebbles go off sheer like a cliff into the sea. Big ships can come in close to this pebble cliff which falls sheer into tides of fantastic power and speed, where the depth at a distance of a hundred feet from the shore can float big ships. It's an eerie place. The whole force of the Channel tide hits it. You're miles from anywhere. It is the physical strength of the tide, the rolling stones, the urgency of Dungeness, which is impressive; the feeling that the restless tide is part of England.

In January 1921 something happened to me. I had been at Dulwich College in the Blew House for two years. I had started in the lowest form (no Greek!), but since I was already a bit of a Latin scholar and could learn anything by heart (including algebra) I shot up the school and won the John Miles Powell Prize as planned. My time at Dulwich was not creative; it was practical. There were two French masters who were, I think, from Alsace-Lorraine. They had a German accent to their French. They were passionately French and they were passionately good. My French was conversational and I had started to read newspapers in the holidays. They taught me grammar. They were wonderful teachers. They made me love French prose. I don't remember that they taught me much poetry. Perhaps they shared the opinion of André Gide, who, when asked to name the greatest of French poets, replied "Victor Hugo, hélas!" But I owe to these two brothers the magical gift of Proust and Michelet, Molière and Marivaux, Raymond Queneau, Marcel Aymé, Marcel Pagnol, Stendhal and Mérimée in the original, because they taught me to think in French. I salute them here and now.

For the Christmas holidays of 1920–21 I had invited a boy called Richardson to stay with us. I can't remember why. I was not particularly fond of him and as far as I know I never saw him again after leaving school. Perhaps my mother suggested that I invite someone to keep me company and I picked out Richardson. He was tall, quiet, good-looking and a success with my mother. Unknown to him he was a chosen instrument.

His parents must have been well off. He had money to spend, which was certainly not the case with us. I was already an avid second-hand book buyer and every penny went on little editions of G. K. Chesterton, Hilaire Belloc and H. G. Wells who, excitingly, was a fellow inhabitant of Hythe and could be seen cycling through the lanes of Romney Marsh, perhaps to call on Henry James at Rye, or on Joseph Conrad in his farmhouse. Richardson, the plutocrat, had wasted several shillings on magazines and left them lying about: one of them was called the *Picturegoer* and had a photograph of a girl called Ivy Close sitting on a luge in the snow. She was starring (it said) in Abel Gance's film *La Roue*, one of the first great railway films. It was Volume 1, Number 1, of a new one-shilling monthly devoted to the art of the movies. I opened it at an article entitled "Chasing the Sun with Bryant Washburn". I read.

I read how the author of the article had met by appointment at a London hotel the company that was making the film and its star. He was a well-known American light comedian and had appeared in a series of comedies with Laura La Plante (a splendid showbiz name!). He was lively and tended towards the kind of plumpness that goes with curly hair and a straw hat: what was to be, soon, the P. G. Wodehouse leading-man type. Having enacted innumerable complications in Saratoga Springs and other resorts of the Four Hundred, he had now come to London to rehash the same scripts over here in "olde Englande". That was where the title of the article came in. The company had reckoned without the weather, the fabled British weather. They set up in Park Lane. The sun went in. They packed everything into cars and vans – cameras, reflectors, costumes, actors – and moved to Windsor. It rained. They returned to London and scaled the heights of Hampstead Heath where Pearly Kings and Queens had been waiting all day. They ran into a thunderstorm. They returned to Hyde Park. The weather had been perfect all day but now the sun had sunk behind the trees. Cheerfully, they announced the time of the call next morning and adjourned to the bar. The author of the article was a W. A. Williamson.

I was fascinated. Somehow the journalist had succeeded in conveying the camaraderie of a film company, the complete absence of class or wealth distinction, the combined enthusiasm towards a common end. And the end was art; the end was to tell a story; the end was to go out into the real world and turn it into a romantic fantasy world where anything could happen. That was what G. K. C. did with his books and his short stories of Father Brown; these people were doing it with their cameras and their lighting. It was obvious to me that, as Americans, they were baffled by the British weather. They were used to a summer in which the sun shone all day. They didn't know, as I knew, that there was no secret to learn about shooting exteriors in England. You just go out and set up and whatever the weather you stay put. One of us will tire first and it won't be me. I got a fabulous reputation later for my luck with weather. The luck consisted in this. Being there.

There were other articles in that *Picturegoer* about making films, including one about, I think, the Stoll Studios at Cricklewood, which were big in their day and where I believe some ambitious war films had been made and famous battles refought. The British tended towards a documentary approach even then. I returned to the article about chasing the sun. I could have shown them! But, again, what fascinated me was the attitude: the planned yet flexible operation, led by the director, to seize the moment, to take advantage of something pictorial or surprising, to snatch your scene out of the streets, to turn the light of common day into something beautiful and entertaining. This was for me! I never had the slightest doubt that I was meant to direct films from that day to this. Ten years later I made my first film.

I started collecting data.

I became (what wasn't yet called) a film-buff. I woke up to the fact that the mild rural English film dramas of H. M. Hepworth – films like *The*

Forest on the Hill (by Eden Philpotts), starring Gerald Ames, James Carew and Chrissie White – had been discussed and (perhaps) even planned; that racing films from Broadwest, starring Stewart Rome and Violet Hopson, which were almost a carbon copy of each other, had actually been produced and directed. They had been "shot" somewhere. Somewhere, a director had been fired because he had "lost the sun". I no longer guessed about these things. I knew. D. W. Griffith's *Intolerance* was playing on the pier at Folkestone. I went to see it. It was the greatest experience I had had. There has never been a film director like Griffith. The screen title – "Out of the Cradle, endlessly rocking" endlessly repeated – I knew it was Walt Whitman without Griffith telling me. I saw the film again that week and began to understand the use of narrative titles in silent films: "Brown Eyes, ah me! ah me!" . . . the massacre of St Bartholomew . . . the walls of Babylon . . . Elmo Lincoln, the Mighty, the king's two-sword man, cutting off a head with one sweep of his blade . . . Constance Talmadge as the Mountain Girl . . . Mae Marsh as the twentieth-century persecuted heroine . . . and, with all this spectacle and glamour, the feeling that a strong hand held the reins, that the shrewd, calm eyes of the director had scrutinized every detail, giving the actors the opportunity of rising to heights they had never scaled before.

"Out of the Cradle, endlessly rocking" – Lillian Gish, who had starred in Griffith's 1914 production of *The Birth of a Nation* had nothing to do in *Intolerance* but rock the cradle and how beautifully she did it! Every line of her body contributed to the tenderness of the scene. I saw her the other day, March 31, 1981, on the stage at the Oscar Awards ceremony, in a huge theatre in Westwood. She filled it. She stood straight and made the others look like pygmies.

It didn't take me long to arrive at my conception of a director's job. An ordinary member of the movie-struck public identifies first with the actors and actresses. I went through the usual phase of filling notebooks with the names, ages and sexes of a lot of hard-working and, until now, totally obscure members of the legitimate and variety theatrical profession. I wish I had those exercise books, with the gilt crest of Dulwich College on the cover, neatly filled with names like Bessie Barriscale, Earle Williams, William Farnum and Nita Naldi, accompanied by long lists of every film in which they had appeared.

It was David Wark Griffith who made up my mind for me that I was going to be a movie director and would settle for nothing else. When I met Lillian Gish at Dartmouth College in New Hampshire, where I was teaching in the winter term of 1979–80, I pulled out my card case and showed her a United States ten-cent stamp that I always carried in it. On it was the portrait of a man in a broad-brimmed hat, the face of a man who would go anywhere and be afraid of nothing. Beyond him loomed a movie camera. The stamp was superscribed: "D. W. Griffith Moviemaker". She said: "I lobbied for years to get that stamp issued. I guess I wrote and saw more than two hundred congressmen, senators, newspaper men. I had some of the stamps made up in a plastic medallion for key rings. I still have a few. I'll send you one." It is on my key ring now, bless her.

D. W. Griffith Moviemaker. It's enough.

I told nobody of my intention to be a movie director. It was a far cry from Hythe to Hollywood. It would seem that there could be no possible link between a dreamy English schoolboy and this new and mighty entertainment business that was comprised in the one word HOLLYWOOD. But the link was there, it was predestined, and three events forged it.

My father bought the lease of an hotel in the South of France . . .

My mother gave way to his persuasions and prepared to sell the house at Hythe and join him at Cap Ferrat . . .

I was told I must leave school and find a job.

At Chantilly the Drake–Powell partnership had broken up and the Normans reigned supreme. The season started at Easter with the first race meetings and continued throughout the summer. Besides the races there was a beautiful golf course and the château was a must for tourists and still is. But when the schools went back, the good season was over, the hotels shut down everything but the bars, and the rain and winds of autumn stripped the forest of leaves. The only busy life left was in the training stables; and in the bars of an evening.

One winter like this was enough for my father. He had a little car, a Bignon Sport. He had his gratuity from the Army and he had done well at the races. He threw a mistress into the car, stuffed his money in his pocket and drove down to the Riviera, to his beloved Monte Carlo. They put up at the Eden Hotel at Cap d'Ail and went to Monaco to play the tables at the Casino. My father's game was baccarat but that night he played roulette. His girlfriend brought him luck. He won. He won a lot. The next morning they went out to celebrate. They drove along the lower coast road – La Petite Corniche – which winds hysterically along the huge cliffs of the Alpes Maritimes, in constant competition with the railroad and the trams which ground their way from Nice to Ventimiglia in those days. The other coast road – La Grande Corniche – climbed up from Nice by zigzags to about 4000 feet, marched along the tops, with splendid views over the back country of Savoy and a glimpse, if you were lucky and an early riser, of the cliffs of Corsica sixty miles away across a sea as blue as indigo. It was the Route Napoléon: it had also been the route of Julius Caesar and of Frederick Barbarossa. When the Bignon got to Beaulieu-sur-Mer, a tidy little town much loved by the English, my father's eye was caught by the sight of the fishing port of St Jean Cap Ferrat about a mile away, where the peninsula juts out into the sea. He followed the coast to the Hotel Bristol, crossed the railway line of the PLM by the iron bridge and mounted the rocky road of the Cap. After a couple of false turns he came down the hill onto the Port where the restaurant Caramello stood on the *place*. It was famous for bouillabaisse. But my father didn't fancy saffron, garlic, pistou and bony rascasse for a celebration. On the other side of the Port there was a terrace, palm trees and a long white hotel with green shutters and a sign reading "Hotel du Parc". They went there.

They drove up onto the terrace where a few people were lunching, ordered a bottle of champagne and were welcomed as *confrères* by the proprietor, who was his own *maître d'hôtel*. He was Italian and he couldn't wait to get back to Bordighera, which he could see forty kilometres along the coast if only Cap Martin didn't stick its neck out so far. They lunched. The terrace with its palms and olive trees and its view back towards Beaulieu was superb. The lunch was not. The proprietor took a *digestif* with them and continued to complain. He had the finest terrace with the finest view on the Côte d'Azur and yet people driving out here to lunch preferred to cram into that rusty old glass box of Caramello where it was well-known that rats regularly fell off the wall into the bouillabaisse – *"Tiens!"* Did we know the latest Caramello story? A cockroach had fallen into the bouillabaisse! "What's this, Caramello?" cries a patron. Caramello picks it out with his dirty finger and thumb. "Speciality of the house!" he says, pops it into his mouth and crunches it up with every appearance of satisfaction! How can you compete with a fellow like that?

My father and his girlfriend walked down to the end of the terrace, which was partly protected from the Mistral by glass. They looked out over the sea, nursed to the calmness of a lake by the long breakwater of the Cap. Below them the little port was crowded with gaily painted, long, heavy fishing boats, full of gear, ready for the night's fishing. There were a few small yachts; the harbour was too small and too shallow to accommodate the big ones that anchored in Villefranche harbour on the west side of the Cap. Opposite them the great mass of Cap Roux separated Beaulieu from Eze-sur-Mer. The mountain village of Eze, on its lonely fortified hill (the Moyenne Corniche road was not yet engineered because of the war, but a start had been made on the great viaduct which spans the gorge of Eze, and the unfinished pillars could clearly be seen), then the Tête du Chien, the dog's head which dominates the whole of that magnificent coast, then Cap d'Ail, Garlic Cape, then the Rock of Monaco, Cap Martin, Roquebrune and the blue hazy heights of the Italian Riviera beyond. My father looked at the violet light which bathed Cap Roux, as the sinking sun projected long shadows across the cliffs. The proprietor shrugged his shoulders. "It's a superb view. Superb. But you can't eat it. I would sell out tomorrow if I could. My brother-in-law wants me to join him but I haven't the capital."

My father fingered the thick wad of notes in his wallet. "How much capital would you need?" he asked.

Well, he got the lease, and with it thirty years of sunshine. He never would tell anyone how much cash he put down, but what chance had a Piedmontese *restaurateur* against a Welsh cattle-thief? He was to take over at the end of the Season and he needed help. In those days the Riviera was the haunt of the rich and famous and the Season was a winter season. Nobody who was anybody would have been seen dead there in the summer months. It was too hot. All the grand villas, all the terraces and colonnades, all the fountains and ornamental pools, all the gardens full of oranges and lemons, loquats and figs, bougainvilleas and geraniums, were silent and deserted. The idea of lying in the sun to make your body as much like an African native as possible would have been greeted with shrieks of horror. There were no swimming pools and no holidays with pay. This was the preserve of the rich and they meant to keep it that way.

In August these charming people were in Scotland or in Yorkshire or in Austria, shooting things. Others were curing themselves from the effects of overeating at Vichy, Karlsbad and Bad Ischl. In September the potential cannon-fodder for the next World War returned to the sado-masochistic monasteries known to the British as public schools (whereas nothing could be more private) and the new Season got under way with a series of Coming Out balls for their sisters.

On the Riviera, things were stirring. There were usually one or two severe thunderstorms in November, and after that cooler weather the days were short, the tiled rooms were chilly, but the sun shone. The first Riviera cuckoo was Serge Diaghilev, returning in December from his annual world tour to take up the winter quarters for himself and for his Ballets Russes, so hospitably provided by the Société des Bains de Mer et de Monte Carlo that runs the Opera House, a little jewel of a theatre in the same building as the gambling rooms and built by the same architect who built and decorated the Paris Opera. Those who have been exposed to the film *The Red Shoes* will recognize similarities with the Ballets Lermontov. In the twenties the surviving Russian Grand Dukes still had plenty of money. In the winter they returned to their Riviera homes accompanied by their mistresses – soon, now that they were freed from the Tsar's control, to be their Grand Duchesses. Matilda Kchessinskaya, the former *prima ballerina assoluta* of the Imperial Ballet, was the most popular, as she was certainly the most outspoken and extravagant. Her palace in Leningrad had been big enough to accommodate the Revolutionary Committee when they took control of the city. The Grand Dukes had always loved the Riviera. The Russian Quarter in Nice was extensive, with its fine Orthodox church on the hill to the east of the Boulevard Victor Hugo, where thousands of dependants of their Russian masters could worship. Those who got out, or who were already out of Russia when the Revolution took power, had vast resources in France in the shape of funds, properties, works of art, and jewellery. They also had hundreds of dependants and were accustomed to service which was little better than slavery. I remember a very proper and respectable housekeeper who said to me: "Prince . . . ? An animal. He shits in his chamber-pot and leaves it under the bed." These "animals" were also extremely friendly with their servants and looked after them as long as they had a gold watch to sell. In Nice these Russian men and women, many of whom were Ukrainians or Cossacks, opened restaurants and cabarets. The less fortunate became film extras (for the Victorine Studios in Nice were already turning out films), others found their way to Paris and became taxi drivers. Kchessinskaya herself married Grand Duke André and lived very happily with him at Cannes until he died. I remember her mobile face and tremendous laugh and her audible criticisms of the new crop of ballerinas – Nikitina, Nemchinova *et al.* – from her place in the centre of the stalls. She went back to teaching ballet in her last years in Paris. Margot Fonteyn told me she travelled to Paris around 1935 to take some lessons from the ballerina who had been Petipa's favourite dancer and had seen the young Pavlova create *La Mort du Cygne*.

In the last week before Christmas, the foreign servants arrived ahead of their masters and mistresses and there was a great hanging of drapes and banging open of green-painted shutters and a bustle in the huge kitchens which had been dark and cold for so long. Housekeepers were seen at the Galeries Lafayette with lists in their hands! The cooks (who all got commissions on the meat and fish and vegetables they bought) were busy in the old market of Nice, meeting old friends, making new ones, and hearing all the gossip. The Opera of Nice was hopefully presenting its repertoire. The casinos were trying to appear busy while waiting for the big gamblers.

Suddenly about December 23 everyone was there! The Train Bleu, the luxury sleeping-car express which left Paris Gare de Lyon in the evening and found itself running alongside a sparkling blue sea washing over red rocks in the morning – I write sleeping cars, but there was precious little sleeping in the cars in my day – was twice its usual length in order to handle all the fashionable people coming for the Winter Season on the Côte d'Azur. By Christmas Eve there wasn't room to be had between Menton and Cannes and everyone (who was anyone) was in Monte Carlo to attend the first big party of the Saison d'Hiver, Le Réveillon de Noël. From then on it was one party after another; and gambling; and getting engaged, and getting disengaged every night. The lovely early spring of the Alpes Maritimes filled the valleys up in the mountains with fruit-blossoms. The days got warmer. The flowers got cheaper. Lent was upon us. The London season was at its height. Day by day one missed familiar faces. Easter was around the corner. It was time to go north before your complexion was ruined. Dust-sheets were drawn over the lavish furniture. Shutters were closed on the empty rooms. The gardens bloomed in their full glory with nobody to congratulate the gardeners. By Good Friday everybody who was anybody had gone north, only to meet again at Ascot, Longchamps and Chantilly. My father had gone north, too, to open the Manor House.

Now that he had two bases, one in the North and the other in the South of France, he could cut his losses. As soon as the number of guests at St Jean Cap Ferrat dropped below a certain profitable level, he closed the hotel, deaf to the protests of the few clients left, and headed north. He usually drove, and took several days about it, figuring that two hundred kilometres a day in an open sports car was about a good average, and usually taking a new route depending on whether Easter came early or late that year, for the roads through the mountains of Savoy and the Dauphiné were not all open by the middle of April. He was never a gourmet (unlike Emeric, my future partner, who will drive two hundred miles in the morning to lunch at a certain three-star restaurant and another two hundred miles in the afternoon to dine at another), but he liked to eat the local specialities – crayfish in the mountains, truffles in omelettes in Périgord, sausages in Dijon, pocketing the menus to compare what the other fellow was giving for the price – and above all to drink the local wine and taste the local cheese. I have already quoted his dictum on the wines, cheeses, and women of France which invariably produced a scream of protest from his female auditors: "*Après tout! Vous pouvez bien nous citer les premières!*" He loved to pull up at some little bistro in the middle of the morning and order a bottle of the local wine and some of the local cheese, if it were in the mountains, and savour their distinctive flavours while sitting in the harmless sunshine of spring on those rickety chairs which the French seem to have a monopoly of. (Who was it who said that everything in France looks twice as bad as it is, and everything in Germany looks twice as good as it is?) But whatever his route (and I accompanied him many times), whether by the mountains, by the Rhône Valley, or by the Auvergne (the bleu d'Auvergne is the king of cheeses), he always arrived at Beaune, stayed the night at the Hospice de Beaune, made a stately call upon M. Bouchard to taste new and old vintages and order Burgundy for the cellars of the Manor, some cases of which we would pack into the back of the car, before proceeding to Epernay to order our champagne.

So now my father – "*le Capitaine Powell*", for you can be sure that my father hung on to his Army rank, as a limpet to a rock, just as he took care to sport always in the buttonhole of his tweed Norfolk jacket the rosette of a Chevalier du Mérite Agricole – needed my mother and needed her furniture. Whether he needed the furniture more than my mother is a moot point. She decided to take a chance on that, sold the house at Hythe, shipped the furniture to Marseilles, made arrangements for me to travel to

Beaulieu when the Easter holidays started, and took a second class ticket herself. Being my mother, she couldn't pass through Paris, which she had only seen once when travelling with my grandfather to Zermatt, without breaking the journey to see Notre Dame. As a consequence she missed the train and there was nobody to meet her when she arrived at the station after the sixteen-hour journey Paris – Lyon – Méditerranée. It was dark, but she got a horse-drawn fiacre to drive her to St Jean, where the hotel was dark and still. The bell didn't work but banging on the door awoke my father, who opened it dressed in a Chinese robe (as she wrote to me subsequently) "like Chu Chin Chow." It soon became abundantly clear that he had been in bed with the Norman, whose presence so far south of her territory had not been advertised.

My mother was a woman of spirit and announced in the morning her immediate departure and plans for divorce. He persuaded her to postpone them. The Norman took off for Chantilly, where the bar and the little old house ticked over all winter to get the big house ready for Easter. The furniture arrived. I arrived.

I had a couchette coming south: that is to say I was in an ordinary, comfortable second-class compartment which was made up, by the attendant, into two bunks or four according to the seats reserved. I shared my compartment with a Frenchwoman and was in an agony of embarrassment. She ignored my embarrassment, shared my sandwiches, shared a half-bottle of PLM wine of unbelievable nastiness, and later shared my bed. I decided that things were looking up. "They order these things better in France." She got off at St Raphael.

Unlike my poor mother I was met. By her. Over a huge water-ice at the *pâtisserie* opposite Beaulieu railroad station she brought me up to date. She had already written off the furniture with my father. She would help to get the new hotel in order and then return to England. She would not go anywhere near Chantilly. She had already written to her oldest and most faithful friend, Jennie Beale, to warn her husband, Edward Huxham, that she would be asking him to use his influence to get me into the National Provincial Bank in the autumn. We had been pushed around long enough. We were going to stand on our own two feet. In addition, she was going to divorce my father.

I went over to the Corbetts. I loved this indomitable small person. She had been the pet of her father, the successful lawyer, the mayor of Worcester. She had been the wife of a successful hop-farmer and had been somebody in the county. She had borne her husband two sons and brought them up. She had survived the war and all its upheavals. She had loyally supported him in this new career, which was not her kind of life at all and which was not at all the kind of life she would have chosen for me. But enough was enough. We were going to hang on to each other and live in

England until I was old enough to make up my own mind. (It was already made up, but she brushed that impossible dream aside.) We had no money except what was left from the sale of the house. It would carry us through to the autumn. After that we should have to live on what I could earn. We soon found out what that was. Twelve pounds a month.

I couldn't believe it. Twelve pounds a month! I had never earned anything in my life, and nobody knew better than I how unfitted I was for the life of a bank clerk. When Emeric wrote that joke, in our film *A Matter of Life and Death*, about millions of people on earth thinking it heaven to be a clerk, I had grave doubts about it, even when the enchantingly grave Kathleen Byron, as the Angel, spoke the line. A boy who aims to emulate D. W. Griffith has not got the qualities that make a good clerk. Still – twelve pounds a month! And two can live cheaper than one. When I was a very little boy, my mother told me, I took her arm in a burst of affection and quoted the words of a popular song:

> You and I together, love
> Never mind the weather, love.

It seemed that the moment had come to repeat these sentiments.

Meanwhile there were *les cafards*.

Le cafard is what the Foreign Legionnaires used to get when the delights of Bou-Saada started to pall and there was nothing to do except shoot your toe off, or wait for next payday: it means the miseries, the blues, the hump; it also means a cockroach. When the leaseholder of the Hôtel du Parc moved out he left the basic bedroom furniture at a valuation, but he also left *les cafards* – about thirty thousand of them, who had grown fat and shiny on the scraps of food scattered by careless scullions. They feared the light, but rejoiced in the dark. There was a trapdoor in the big stone-floored kitchen which was their hide-out. Here they watched and waited and planned their dreadful sallies. When we became aware of this hidden army in our midst we resorted to direct action, hand-to-hand combat. Armed with those long bushy brooms made of esparto grass, or something similar, which the French household used to possess and which are useless as brooms, but excellent as an object of offence and defence, we would turn out all the kitchen lights and hide in the long passage that ran the length of the hotel. Soon a whispering noise was heard:

> But e'er three shrill notes the pipe uttered
> You heard as if an army muttered.

The army was on the move! We waited a minute or two more. "Lights!" yelled my father. "Yoicks! Tally-ho! Go for 'em!" For the naked bulbs revealed a fearful sight: a moving sea of black forms scuttling all over the kitchen, and panic-stricken by the light, scuttling back the way they came to meet new waves of infantry coming over the top. I have never seen so much vermin in my life except once, by moonlight, in Albania. Our brooms were excellent weapons of offence, but inadequate for such a plague of Egypt. Stamping and whacking we cut them off from their bases and killed hundreds, but there were thousands more. My father had underestimated the amount of dirt an unsupervised Italian kitchen staff can get into every cranny of an old-fashioned kitchen. We had to get an expert in. He came from Nice, from the Old Town, no stranger to *les cafards*. We thought he would take weeks. Within forty-eight hours there was not a *cafard* in the place. Whatever spell he used it was powerful and effective. Or perhaps he got Caramello to eat them?

The original Hôtel du Parc was a square building three storeys tall, standing on the low cliff which is not more than thirty feet high to the south of the port. It faced, therefore, backwards to the coast and did not get the sun in winter until it was high. In summer this was a blessing, because the tall rooms with their tiled floors and Italian decorations painted on the plaster walls remained cool. In 1921, as I have explained, there was no advantage in this, so the white house dreamed away the summer months with shutters closed and entrance gate shut with a board stating "*Fermé*" attached to it by a piece of wire. After a few years someone had extended the entrance terrace over the rocks to the sea and constructed a few apartments and sheds under it for the use of the fishermen. They had run out of money before finishing it; there was no restaurant, but kitchen and *salle à manger* were all added on with a design about as aesthetic as a mobile home. The terrace was not glassed-in like Caramello's, and the whole shape of the property had an engagingly haphazard and unfinished look about it. There were no steps down to the sea but I early on discovered that by slipping over the low wall you landed on a ledge about a foot wide which led to an iron-barred gate belonging to the villa next door (later on owned by the son of Henri Matisse). It was easy to drop from the barred gate and land on the rocks beside the fishermen's shit-house.

So far as I know I was the only one to use this simple stairway and I continued to use it for the next fifty years. During those Easter holidays of 1921 I explored the Cap and the Pointe St Hospice. If you will imagine a spread hand placed upon the Mediterranean close to Beaulieu, the curving thumb is the Pointe St Hospice and the larger, higher part, made by the four fingers, is Cap Ferrat. The Port St Jean is where the thumb joins the rest of the hand. If you will come with me up onto the Moyenne Corniche (which is now the most popular and beautiful of all the coast roads) you will see Cap Ferrat below you, exactly like that, with the deep and beautiful bay of Villefranche to the east, with probably a big ship or two and certainly a big yacht at anchor. Or better still and with less effort you can see Moira Shearer in *The Red Shoes* climbing up towards stardom with that fabulous seascape below her. My mother and I discovered a large empty reservoir on the top of the Cap with a great crack in the concrete. It was supposed to be an emergency water-supply, but since those days we get our water from the mountains. Most of the villas were shuttered so we could explore the wonderful gardens. We made one friend and two acquaintances.

The friend was Bussell, the head gardener and agent at Maryland, a villa which stood high among olives and cypresses, on the hill opposite the hotel. It was a Florentine-style house, with an entrance patio of rose-red Carrara marble also seen in *The Red Shoes*. It is my dedication to Bussell's memory. He was a landscape gardener of genius and a kind and faithful friend. The Germans murdered him in the Second World War.

The first acquaintance was a bulky figure in a linen jacket and a Panama hat who used to set up his easel and little campstool every day at about eleven o'clock, when the sunlight fell upon the rosy walls of a fisherman's hut standing above a stone ramp leading down to the harbour, with the port and the church in the background. He wasn't a particularly good painter but was better than the average amateur, and he must have been somebody for he was staying as a guest at one of the great villas and he was a friend of Beau Warwick's and Somerset Maugham's.

The second acquaintance was a big American whom I met when exploring what I thought was the ruin of a palace just behind the hotel, with its own private harbour. The entrance gate, an archway built of Cyclopean masonry, was unfinished, and there were high fences alongside the gardens bordering the narrow road which wound up to Cap St Hospice and the cemetery. But the rocks on the seafront were no obstacle for me. There was a tower of the same white-and-rose-coloured Cyclopean blocks about a hundred feet high, with a huge arched doorway at the base, as big as a cathedral doorway, opening onto a stone platform as big as a theatre stage and washed by the sea. A woman was dancing on it, in bare feet and a gauzy sort of dress. She wasn't dancing to music, she made her own. A very large man was climbing about over the piles of marble and granite and pieces of worked stone which had evidently come in by the sea gate, like me. I said, "Hello!" He said "Hello!" He was Paris Singer and this was Isadora Duncan. He guessed I was the son of the British captain that had bought the hotel. I admitted it. I asked him if he was rebuilding the villa, whether he was going to live there. He corrected me, amiably. They were living there. That is to say this was one of the places they lived in. That was their flat at the top of the tower, there! With the big stone balcony! I said there must be quite a view from there and he said there was an elevator. It must have been the only elevator in Cap Ferrat. As for the rest of the villa it was never going to be finished. It wasn't a ruin: it had been planned like

that. The idea was to be suspended in a modern luxury flat high above a
ruined palace with its feet in the sea. The marble colonnades would end
nowhere. The Sienese frescoes would moulder away. The Spanish grilles
would rust. The Andalusian tiles would remain in their opened crates. And
when the big storms of winter came, or when the Mistral whipped up the
waves of the Mediterranean, they would wash over the stone platform
where Isadora was dancing and into the great hall at the foot of the tower
which had been designed to looked like *une cathédrale engloutie* and he
would light hundreds of candles and sit there drinking, while Isadora
danced naked for him with the breaking waves as a backdrop and the foam
swirling around her ankles. What did I think of that? I said it sounded
swell. I went up with them from the drowned cathedral – I am not sure
whether there was an organ installed there or whether he only planned to
have an organ, or whether he intended a pianola with those charming rolls
of paper perforated with dots and dashes that simulated performance at a
piano, or an organ. ("I was seated one day at the organ." Does any line of
prose or verse so perfectly hit off the period as "The Lost Chord"?) And as
soon as we got into the elevator the wind howled and wailed like one of Mr
Lefanu's Irish banshees. Some freak of planning willed that the elevator
shaft of Paris Singer's superb tower became a cave of winds. He never
seemed to mind, and Isadora was so used to being a part of the natural
phenomena that she would have noticed nothing (she was a very good sort
and full of lice); but Singer's daughter, Winaretta, who lived in another of
his palaces (a spirited imitation of the Palace of Versailles at Torbay in
Devon, where her husband was Commodore of the Yacht Club), hated the
place, although she loved the Paris Palace at 2 Place des Vosges, and was
glad to see the great tower pulled down. For it was pulled down, after the
war, that great tower that was built to stand for a thousand years, with its
red-tiled roof, hand-made tiles weighing ten kilos apiece . . . Gone, all gone!
The high stone balcony to which a Renaissance prince would have been the
only possible improvement (and after all Singer was one), the great echoing
cathedral crypt with its high Norman arches, the great oak doors swinging
and banging as the icy Mistral stormed down the Rhône Valley and out to
sea . . . gone, all gone.

Singer had another of his palaces in London, just off Sloane Street, or in
Cadogan Gardens, or in both Sloane Street and Cadogan Gardens, for it
was two houses turned into one, with a front entrance on the street and a
back entrance which was more discreet. I had occasion to visit it during the
Second World War. Nobody was living there; I was given the keys and
went alone. There was not even a caretaker, I suppose because of the Blitz.
The palace was the usual Singer jumble of good and bad, good furniture
and bad pictures, but the most striking and characteristic work of art was
the elaborate swimming pool on the ground floor decorated in the Moorish

style with marvellous mosaics, gauzed drapes and a raised platform near the pool for the dancers. There had been no attempt to tidy up, or drain the pool, everything had been left as it was for years: a torn curtain sagged across the marble floor and the surface of the pool was covered in scum. I envisaged a glassy-eyed Pasha, reclining on the cobwebbed cushions, staring at the forms of undulating skeletons performing at the edge of the pool, reflected dimly in the scummy water. Pure Bosch!

That was in 1941 and I had met him, surrounded by masons, carvers, and fresco painters, twenty years before. Most of his workmen at Cap Ferrat came from Italy, from Siena and Pisa, where all these crafts went back hundreds of years, but there were a lot of local craftsmen, too, and some of them I was to meet and work with later on. Nice became part of France as late as 1850, and the frontier between France and Italy has altered three times in the last hundred years. When Italy came belatedly into the war on the side of Hitler, local Italian troops, stationed ready at the frontier, marched in. They met with a poor reception from their cousins, sisters-in-law and grandmothers, who leant out of their windows emptying chamber-pots onto the heads of their marching relatives, screaming "Nino! Go home, Beppo! For shame, Luigi! Aren't you ashamed to break your old grandmother's heart?"– accompanied by many suggestions of an acrobatic nature, which sound all right in Italian, but are not reproduce-able in English, or even in American, Italian being the expressive and imaginative language that it is. Mussolini, in particular, was invited to do a number of things, which even a trained contortionist would have found difficult to accomplish.

Singer was not a sociable man, but he was, perhaps, a lonely one, and he got into the habit of dropping in at the hotel. We were not open that season, but the bar was open and I had painted "Nunc Bibendum" over the french window, which was the entrance from the terrace. As Bibendum is the name of the little figure made up of pneumatic tyres in the Michelin guides my father tolerated this bit of classicism, but our discussions over the aperitifs were mostly to find a new name for the hotel. The Hôtel du Parc was ridiculous. We wanted a name which should be romantic and should suggest the harbour and the sea. An unofficial committee consisting of our family, Singer, the barman, and the solitary painter, who turned out to be the Right Honourable Winston Churchill, met daily to discuss this important problem, but I don't remember which of us hit on *La Voile d'Or*. I thought I did. We decided finally, in order to avoid coming to blows, that it was a collaboration.

La Voile d'Or it was! And *La Voile d'Or* it still is.

Now that my parents had definitely come to a parting of the ways, they were remarkably friendly. When I look back on the twenty years they had been married, there doesn't seem to have been any time for friendship. It had all been stress and strain, incompatibility, constant moves, raising a family, and ending up with the war and one ewe-lamb. My mother wanted a divorce because she had hopes of marrying again and providing me with a more suitable father – as if suitability were any way to choose a father! My father didn't want a divorce, because he would have to pay for it; and because he would then be open to attack on his tender flank, if he had one. But my mother was determined, and when she was determined she was a Corbett. He agreed to a divorce.

My future was discussed but I was not a party to the discussions. Edward Huxham had got me accepted by the National Provincial Bank and I was posted to Ringwood, a little market town on the River Avon in Hampshire, on the edge of the New Forest. I was to report in October 1921 after the school summer holidays were over. I was sorry about leaving school because I was good at it. My two hours' prep every evening usually took me twenty minutes and I spent the rest of the time reading history. I had already decided to try for a university scholarship and to specialize in history, seeing nothing incongruous in my two ambitions. However, that hope was knocked on the head. I was to be a bread-winner.

It was agreed that I should spend holidays with my father, whenever possible. The bank allowed two weeks to juniors, unpaid. It was a bit of a change from the fourteen weeks of school holidays. But it was the common lot. And it didn't sound as if Ringwood was overloaded with work. Perhaps I could keep a pony?

The end of the holidays came. We left my father whitewashing the kitchen and travelled back to London together. No doubt there were soon Normans instead of cockroaches. It should be obvious to anybody who has read so far how very unwise it is to assume that teenage boys are unobservant. In my day we were seen but not heard; and we saw a lot.

I went back to Dulwich for my last term and won the Powell Memorial Prize (a Greek testament), as I have already mentioned. I spent most of my time, when not in class, up a tree reading a book. I had realized that if I got my house football colours the prefects could not make me play games, or watch other people play games. I was a fast wing three-quarter at rugby football, won my colours after a few games and, after that, only turned out when shamed into it. As for cricket, in spite of P. G. Wodehouse's school stories, I despised it, as I despised all compulsory games. As for watching other people play games (the great British exercise) when you could be ferreting through some second-hand bookshop, or sneaking into a movie at Brixton, it was not my scene.

My Aunt Ula and my Aunt Grace lived and worked on the other side of London in Kilburn and, I think, Brondesbury. At any rate Ula's house was a big, detached villa with a garden and carriage-house in Willesden Lane.

They were wonderfully kind to me during my years in London. I was leading a rather isolated life for a boy, and a house full of male cousins was just what I needed. At one of the constant parties I was given a book by Ula, *The Blazed Trail* by Stewart Edward White, which opened up a new world for me and which had a direct connection through me with other people's lives. It was a novel about land-looking and logging in the Upper Michigan Peninsula, and the author was obviously a man of wide experience and varied interests. Up until now I had read very little fiction except Kipling. The American output was poor compared with Europe. I had read Frank Norris and Jack London. The Paris-germinated explosion was around the corner, but I couldn't know that. Stewart Edward White only wrote about what he knew, like the other Americans I had read, but he had no message, nor sermon to preach, unless it was the Kipling theme of the importance of the day's work and of the rules of the game. I searched out other books by him and discovered that he had written, besides novels, a series of semi-autobiographical books about travel in the northern woods, in the California Sierras and in East Africa, where he had gone to hunt big game. (I would hazard a guess that his books influenced the young Hemingway, although his *Up in Michigan* and White's Michigan are a World War apart.) This mixture of photographic realism and strenuous adventure was very much to my taste, as many rueful actors, both dead and alive, could testify. I owe its development in me to Aunt Ula and S. E. White, in that order.

Herbert Tomlins, my Aunt Ula's husband, always busy and always harassed, looked to me like an artist, a poet or writer, and perhaps he was, but fate had decreed that he should own and be owned by a large laundry. His eldest son, Bernard, my cousin, was a graphic artist and suffered from poor health. I liked him. He had remarkably observant and malicious eyes. Martin left home early for the Merchant Navy. Leonard was a lazy feline dilettante: we exchanged books and literary criticism. David was a saint. He became a British general practitioner, which in the Thirties was practically the same thing. He only retired in the 1970s, and he deserves – both he and his wife, Pamela, deserve – to live for ever.

Aunt Grace managed the laundry and was always full of delightful stories. On one occasion, a doll was found in a hamper of bed linen. She was undressed, her clothes and underclothes were washed (they needed it), ironed and mended, and she was returned with a note describing her experiences. Another time a cat and her newborn kittens added a bit of variety to the daily check-in. Grace was a tall, powerful woman – a friend to me all my life – who lived to be nearly a hundred, helping my cousin David and his wife to keep the kind of open house which Ula had kept before them. Heaven knows how many lives and souls these two families saved in their long, generous existence.

After leaving the field to the Normans, my mother had reopened communications with the tall, gentle, moustached Searchlight Officer who must, I think, have been the true love of her life, although she never confided so to me. He was now back in civilian life, minus his military moustache, and living near Bassenthwaite in the Lake District. He was married, and I can't imagine what was in the mind of the two lovers when it was arranged that my mother and I should pay them a visit in the long summer holidays before I started work. I can see that I was a necessary piece of camouflage (a term which the war had popularized) if we were all going to be under the same roof, but it was such a transparent stratagem (to everybody but the two lovers, even to me) that it must have been the only way they could meet. His wife (who had hypertrophic eyes) was the kind of wife who automatically starts packing for two when her husband announces that he has business in town, or in Paris, particularly in Paris. She was certainly not a woman to have any illusions. I think she was contemptuous of the sentimental attachment and of this way of handling it, and she may even have seen some humour in it. She was an intelligent woman, and I enjoyed my conversations with her.

As an instance of how reckless the lovers were in their happiness at being together, one day as I came downstairs I saw them reflected in a mirror over the mantelpiece, kissing each other good morning behind the screen which stood at the entrance to the dining room. (I wonder how many film directors and cameramen have thought themselves clever to have worked out that particular shot? At least a thousand.) I went straight on in, and, as they sprang apart, kissed my mother myself. I was a sophisticated little boy, in some ways.

The only local people who came to the house during the weeks we were there were rock-climbers. Perhaps they were asked for my sake. Anyway, it interested me. I was contemptuous of games, but this passion for scrambling up rock faces was something I could understand. I had my grandfather and my Uncle Geoffrey as examples and I had a good head for heights. As I listened to the talk of these enthusiasts and looked at the photos by the Abraham brothers, I began to wonder whether this might not be a way of escaping from the life of a bank clerk. There was a keen little man called Wilson, a terrier in glasses, who lent me climbing books and took me out to scramble up boulders. I can hear, now, his cheery "Hullo, Michael! How be?" He was killed climbing alone a few years later. Then there was Thompson, a big, heavy man with one paralysed hand and arm, who insisted on going everywhere that any sound man could go. And there was Miss Ward, a long, thin woman in corduroy knickerbockers and woollen stockings, who climbed like a cat. The great day came when we all walked to Wastwater, to the inn, where the walls of the bar room were scratched with the nailed boots of climbers using the picture rail to do a hand-traverse around the room. After breakfast, we climbed the slabs on Great Gable, and I remember the exhilaration of seeing the sullen lake a thousand feet below our boots.

I am approaching what I always think of as the Dornford Yates period, as one might say of a geological formation: "Ah, yes. Jurassic." Or: "Hum! Pleistocene." Recognisable, but obscure, to any but the expert.

Dornford Yates was a very dangerous writer; he was a snob and a humourist. I never met him except in his books. He started out, like Michael Arlen, but without Arlen's irony, by writing lightly and amusingly about charming people. His short stories about a social group, the Pleydells and the Mansels, were published in the *Windsor Magazine* and effectively illustrated by Norah Schlegel – tanned Englishmen, fair ladies, dressed by Reville. They had all been in the War, officer class of course, and they were rich, they were idle, they were very good company. One of them – Adele – was an American, so that Sargent could paint her. The tales were of brief encounters, or of experiences shared abroad, while touring the Continent in expensive automobiles. They scored a bullseye, not so much with the class they depicted, as with the honest, hard-working, middle class, whose only chance of spending a winter abroad at Biarritz, with all the trimmings was a hundred thousand to one. The stories were stylishly written, but the insidious thing about them was their humour. Dornford Yates's chief clown was an ex-war hero called Berry. Berry Pleydell – a bit too good to be true, especially as a landed gent and magistrate. At judicious intervals, his author would create a set-piece for him, usually involving his long-suffering wife, Daphne, in physical disasters, or else providing him with a hilarious monologue about his experiences. Berry and Co. became best-sellers. Gradually Dornford Yates shifted his ground: more sentimentality, less humour. The most colourless member of the group was built up into a Shining Knight, capable of anything, afraid of nothing, but a bit of a witch-hunter. It was interesting, in that mournful decade of the 1930s, to compare the transformation that came over those two doughty champions of the upper-middle class, Buchan's Richard Hannay and Yates's Jonathan Mansel. They became bores. Dare I say, Blimps?

In 1921 they were young – well, not yet middle-aged – in habits, or in spread. They had put the War behind them forever, as we all wished to do; they were full of high spirits and they felt – and we agreed – that they had earned their right to a little idleness. But these were the people who broke the General Strike in 1926; and whose children would fight in Spain in 1937 and win the war against Hitler with American and Russian help.

I think I am trying to say that the middle-class self-styled educated Englishman is frivolous and a snob. I am one of them. We are so anxious not to wear our heart on our sleeve that we sometimes have no heart at all. We are so anxious to believe that all is right with the world that we have ceased to be one of its leaders. Everyone recognizes our good intentions and despises us for thinking that good intentions are enough. The Americans look on England as a museum. No, not a museum: a junk shop. In the years between the Wars, Thomas Mann wrote for Germany, Proust and Gide for France, Hemingway for America . . . and P. G. Wodehouse for England.

I never knew how my mother's gentle romance ended. His wife had a sardonic eye, and she knew her husband well enough to know that he would settle for marriage and a deck-chair in the end. That is how I remember him: sitting smiling in a deck-chair, his long legs crossed, a Panama hat on his head, a cup of tea in his hand and an embarrassed smile on his clean-shaven lips. My poor mother! An adventurer for a husband, a sheep for a lover, and a son mad about the movies. But nothing got her down. She was fifty that year and her life was just beginning.

She had found, and rented for a year, a furnished cottage on the edge of the New Forest, up the hill towards Picket Post, near Ringwood. It may well have been on forest land, which would have given us something under manorial rights, such as a villein's right to run his pigs, or to cut bracken, or graze ponies, for they run wild in the Forest. It was called the Red Cottage, a long shack at the end of a lane and I couldn't find a trace of it when I went back with Frankie, nearly sixty years later. There are a lot of big, bourgeois houses around there among the laurels and rhododendrons, and the Red Cottage may have been the gardener's cottage of one of them. It was long, two-storeyed, one room wide, and the trees came up to the doors and windows. So did the ponies, asking for apples. You came in by a wicket gate and O. Henry, our tabby kitten (Booey Angel was no more!), used to wait for me to arrive, lying along a branch of the wisteria tree that hung across the gate. He would catch my cap in his claws if he could. We had a Belgian hare as well – a terrific personality as Dutch and Belgians are, who loved to play with the cat but would stand no nonsense. They would be lying in front of the fire, blazing with pine cones, then suddenly Benjy would be off to the foot of the ladder-like stairs and pause for a catch-me-if-you-can look at Henry. Henry would roll over, uninterested. Then suddenly he would launch a furious attack on Benjy, who would nip upstairs. We would hear them scampering along the corridor, all the mats and carpets flying, then a rabbit cataract down the stairs and a rush up to the fire where they would fling themselves down, panting, paws extended. When Benjy was hungry, he would go into the scullery beyond the stone-flagged kitchen, where empty saucers, or perhaps sardine tins, would be waiting replenishment. He would take the saucer in his teeth and bang it on the stones to tell us that he wanted a little service. And he got it!

We stayed a few days with Jennie and Edward Huxham before digging in at Ringwood.

The great day came when we moved into the Red Cottage and I presented myself at the bank. As a set-up it was almost too good to be true. The manager was an alcoholic and hardly ever seen; the accountant, Mr Jones, had bushy eyebrows and moustache and looked at me over his glasses. There was a junior clerk who looked like a caricature of all junior clerks from the time of Chaucer onward. And there were two female clerks. They had taken over during the last years of the war and were scheduled to be demobbed sooner or later, as the men came back. Meanwhile they really ran the branch. Their names, I learnt, were the Misses Calcott: Connie and Mear.

Meanwhile I had been examined from behind the battery of calf-bound ledgers. What Connie and Mear saw was a slim, grave youth, with piercing blue eyes, a high intellectual forehead, and a firm mouth like his mother's (of course they couldn't know that yet, as I had vetoed any suggestion that she should accompany me on this first day). The important thing to find out was whether I played tennis. I was put to work copying letters and presently a dazzlingly pretty girl came in. She was a slim, blue-eyed blonde with naturally curly hair, and with a firm bony handshake, an athlete's hand. She was introduced by her aunts: "This is Inkie." I at once joined the queue, which I soon found out stretched all around the block. I and my mother were asked to tea that afternoon – "We're usually home by half past four, unless there's something wrong with the balance" – and I learnt that Inkie's mother was called Mrs Ingledew, and the house – "It's the big, brick house on the corner – you pass it when you cycle down from the cottage" – was called Kooringa and was open house to the neighbourhood.

For the next two years I was always in love – that wondering, idealistic, adolescent love that radiates throughout your entire being. I never dreamed of physical consummation. I went to sea only to be sick. I played tennis – I who despised games – and hockey (a savage pastime) and croquet (even worse). I went to dances, I who was born with two left feet and no sense of rhythm. I went to Grand Costume Balls as Douglas Fairbanks in *The Mark of Zorro*. I went on picnics to Mudeford, where the Avon pours into the Solent under the long line of Hengistbury Head. I went to our local cinema every day the programme changed, and I cycled to Bournemouth and Boscombe to see films like Fritz Lang's *Die Nibelungen*, which would never by any stretch of the imagination play the Town Hall at Ringwood. What did I see there? Well, they mostly seemed to be British films, so perhaps we were part of somebody's empire – someone like Sir Oswald Stoll, or Walturdaw. I remember being impressed by a Herbert Wilcox production, *Flames of Passion*, starring Mae Marsh (specially imported from the USA) with Herbert Langley and directed by Graham Cutts. Langley was an opera singer and had appeared in *The Bohemian Girl*, a comic opera by Balfe from the same stable; so perhaps he was working off his contract. He was stagey. C. Aubrey Smith was also in *The Bohemian Girl* as a gypsy. He looked like a guards officer in unconvincing disguise on a special mission. I was already thinking like a director. I remember a splendid serial, starring and directed by George B. Seitz, something like *Skyriders*, with lots of production and a stunt a minute. Grant Whytock mentioned him the other day, when we were walking around Hollywood:

"Nice fellow," Grant said. "Never any trouble and popular with everybody."

I had last seen him diving from a burning house with the heroine in his teeth, fifty years before. And they say the cinema is one of the ephemeral arts!

All this little society was governed by the conventions and traditions of Dornford Yates, whose popular books poured from the presses of Ward Lock: men were kind, chivalrous and gallant; women were elegant and brave; meals were always on time; one liked landscape and architecture, but one never talked about art: one talked about money, money, money; it was a very small world. Like ours. Except that none of us had any money. Nor expected to. Whom was I in love with? Inkie, of course. I am still in love with Inkie (she sent me a card for her eightieth birthday and I reciprocated), and with Fluffy, with Esther, with my cousin Peggy, with Eileen, with any female amiable enough to encourage me, or rather, not to discourage me. I had no image of myself as a lover. I was just in love with love.

Fortunately for my education, I travelled down to Beaulieu-sur-Mer every Easter (never ceasing to wonder at living so near to Beaulieu in the New Forest, pronounced Bewley, especially annoying to Americans) to help my father shut up the Voile d'Or and motor up France with him to Chantilly. The Winter Season was still the big thing on the Riviera. There was a racecourse at Nice, beside the River Var, where the airport is now; and there was another at Cannes. My father took me with him to the newly opened Sporting Club de Monte Carlo, and we played baccarat until three in the morning, I drawing the cards from the shoe, my father directing. It is always considered luckier to have somebody else draw the cards. The rich Greeks used to come down with their mistresses, and I have seen an impassive Greek millionaire sit at the table between two beautiful women, each one with jewelled bracelets up to their elbows, each one drawing as and when he indicated. He would lose 5 million francs and win them back again without any sign of emotion, and occasionally he would pass big banknotes to the croupier, who would nod his thanks, or to one of the women, who would stuff the notes into her handbag. We won that night, my father and I, five or six hundred pounds sterling. As we drove back to Cap Ferrat, muffled up in the open car, he roared: "You brought me luck, Mick. But don't go gambling on your own. You haven't the talent for it." He was quite right, and I have never had any inclination to gamble, but I thought it was rather bad taste to say so, with his wallet bulging with the money I had won for him.

My father was very much in demand on the coast as a bridge player and dance partner, even though he so obviously played to win. ("Must play another rubber. I haven't won my dinner yet.") Occasionally, I used to accompany him to one of the villas, where I was made welcome for his sake and shown the library or the terraces and left to amuse myself. There were all sorts of famous people on the coast in the Season. It was entertaining to realize that this rather comic Lady de Bathe, wife of the amiable Suggie de Bathe, was the celebrated Lillie Langtry, who had once acted for the silverminers in Virginia City.

My friend Bussell – we all called him Boss – took me on far more interesting visits to villas near Grasse, where he had built the terraces and landscaped the gardens, and sometimes we would take a load of orange trees for planting, or a truck full of huge stone olive-oil jars, bought for a song, to be filled with earth for growing bougainvilleas and geraniums. Once he proudly showed me the staircase of tall cypresses at Maryland and said: "I planted those, Mick, carrying them up the steps, two at a time, one in each hand." There was no water at Maryland, or at least not enough to make a cascade, so he had created a glen, with a steep fall, and slabs of rock and channels just like the bed of a stream, and had sown forget-me-nots to make a waterfall of blue flowers at just the right time of the year.

I often saw Serge Diaghilev at the Casino of Monte Carlo, although I don't believe that I ever saw him gamble. The theatre at Monte Carlo is part of the Casino complex, and it was the custom to stroll into the Rooms during the lengthy intervals between the ballets, to see and be seen, and to win or lose a few thousand at the tables. Diaghilev knew everybody and was always on the lookout for backers. What I remember about him were his exquisite manners. He was always in control of himself, always the most important person in the room. Alexander Korda had the same gift of effortlessly and charmingly taking the centre of the stage.

In a few days, the Season ended and my father and I would start off north. If Easter came late one year and the high passes were free from snow, we would tackle the Route Napoléon over the mountains, and come down to the valley of the Rhône by Grenoble. I much preferred this to the coast road by Avignon, stopping usually at Aix-en-Provence. In the mountains, my father would make fascinating detours to show me the Gorge de Verdon, or the thrilling landscape of the Dauphiné; and we would stop at unpretentious inns. The Paris main road meant stopping in some town like Chalon-sur-Saône, and watching my father play belote with the locals in the café bar which would be attached to the Grand Hotel. Once, however, he surprised me by making a detour through the Auvergne and showing me the Gorge du Tarn, a wild and wonderful river, full of whirlpools which he swore we would one day explore by canoe (he was a keen canoer). But we never did – any more than we descended the Dordogne, which is now, I suppose, a classic French canoe river, but was then relatively unknown and unexplored.

"It beats the Wye to a frazzle!" my father would exclaim. "There's only one really tricky lot of rapids on the Wye at Symond's Yat, but the Dordogne's" (with ghoulish relish) "got twenty kilometres of 'em!"

When he was a young farmer in Worcestershire, he and his school friend Quarrell used to send their white painted canoe, which they had built themselves out of orange boxes, to a point above the white water, using a dray pulled by two farm horses. It took the horses all day. Then they would get the canoe into the water and come down to Chepstow in twenty minutes.

When he was sixty-five, he volunteered to show some sceptics at the Voile d'Or that he knew something about canoeing. The River Var was in spate after storms in the hills. He took them all twenty kilometres up the river to where it came out of the mountains to race down its wide, stony channels to the sea. He put the canoe into the rushing water, leapt in and shot out into the current. They all rushed back to their cars and raced down the main road, trying to keep him in sight. He had got a big start on them, and they kept on sighting him and losing him, screaming like maniacs. He got to the sea before they did. Right side up. The drinks were on them that night.

The Norman had gone ahead of us to prepare Chantilly and was there when we arrived. I had a few days to inspect my cellar and then I returned to Ringwood and my love affairs.

My mother had kept in touch with her sisters and their friends, and it was rare, during the school holidays, not to have one or more of them to stay with us. It was good for me to have this constant contact with the family background, although it was an exclusively feminine one. My Uncle Geoffrey's son, Richard, was still with his parents in India (we had a photo of him with his Sikh servant); my Uncle Alan's son, Michael MacGregor, was newborn and living in Pretoria. Geoffrey and Alan had met for the first time in years at the Commonwealth Conference in Canada after the War, which forged the Commonwealth out of the British Empire. It was like a story by Kipling.

We saw little of our Powell connections. They were out of our orbit, and it wasn't so easy for them to get away as it was for my schoolmistress aunts.

However, the wind was changing. I must have been the most unpromising bank clerk in the world, although I struggled through my work conscientiously, but even I could feel that something would have to be done about the Ringwood branch. The visit of a bank inspector blew the gaff. The Manager was retired on pension. Mr Jones was made a deputy and in due course a sleek, efficient individual, with "new broom" written all over him, took charge. We were no longer certain of being at Kooringa at half past four for tennis.

On top of that I was moved to Bournemouth to be under the eye of Edward Huxham. I had been in the bank three years, and Foreign Exchange and Banking Law were still a mystery to me. They still are, although I know a little bit more about overdrafts. Nobody could blame me for learning nothing at Ringwood, my (honorary) Uncle Edward announced, but if I was to make banking my life's work I must PASS EXAMS! This pronouncement and the move to a big town got my adrenalin working. I was caught for life if I didn't act, and act swiftly.

On my next visit to Chantilly, I broached the subject to my father. I had never made any secret of my strange love for the cinema. He didn't understand it, but he was sympathetic. As for my feelings about being a banker, he was in complete accord: "Last job in the world for you," he declared. "I'll tell you what. I met Leonce Perret, the film chap, and his girlfriend Huguette Duflos. I'll ask him to give you a screen test! How will that do?"

With a sinking heart I agreed. How could I explain that I felt my métier was to be behind the camera (like Perret), not in front of it (like the voluptuous Duflos)?

The amiable Perret agreed, and on the day, we went to the film studios at Joinville. At that period, cinematographers were changing over from filtered sunlight to artificial lights, and the studios were made of glass like a huge greenhouse, with blinds to control the glare, like one they used to have in a photographer's portrait studio (I have photographed whole films like that too). I felt at once the strange fascination of a film studio: the mixture of art and artifice, of technique and temperament, of a dream factory. I felt at home.

The test was a farce. I don't know whether there was any film in the camera. Anyway, I was too busy looking around me to be able to collect myself and improvise something. Perret, a kind, portly individual with a good eye for spectacle (he had recently had a big success with a spectacular production of *Koenigsmark*) suggested that my father come on with me. With alacrity my father leapt in front of the camera, shook hands with me, whirled me round and walked me up to the camera with his arm around my shoulders, to the applause of Perret and his cameraman. I didn't get the contract, but I made a friend. I reminded Perret of the incident two years later when I was shooting the stills on his production of *Morgane la Sirène*, still with Duflos, who was still wrapped in furs, feathers and sequins.

Many people have wondered why I don't make tests and why, when I am forced to do so, I am so considerate to the unfortunate shrinking actors whose career may depend upon the audition. This is why.

Anyway, that test got me the entrée into Paris film studios and I was able to get glimpses of film units at work. It was enough. I knew I could handle this. I no longer went to the movies for entertainment. I went to criticise and to learn.

In Ringwood I had been in a backwater and happy to be so. In Bournemouth, I was surrounded by good libraries and by bookstalls which sold the *Saturday Evening Post, Photoplay,* and *The Stage.* I became America-mad, like most of my contemporaries in Europe and Soviet Russia. I rediscovered my old friend Stewart Edward White in the *Post* and made new ones like James Warner Bellah and Mary Roberts Rinehart. It was evidently the thing to have three names.

American films had made great strides in the years I had been an aficionado. Serials and two reelers had turned to features. Great directors had arisen, rivalling the German, Swedish, French and Italian filmmakers. Young Rex Ingram had fired the world with Valentino in *The Four Horsemen of the Apocalypse* and Ramon Novarro in *Scaramouche.* Henry King, who was to lead his craft with fifty years of superb storytelling, had made *Tol'able David* and *Romola,* starring Lillian and Dorothy Gish, and young William Powell, from the stage, as Tito. The great companies in New York and Hollywood – Paramount, Famous Players, Metro-Goldwyn-Mayer, United Artists – were forming and snatching each other's stars and directors. I followed all this and treated it as deadly serious and professional, while my elders mocked. I wrote to my father that I had seen a film called *Enemies of Women,* from a book by Blasco-Ibáñez, starring Lionel Barrymore as the sort of Russian prince I had sat next to at the Sporting Club. The exteriors had been shot at La Vigie, the strange circular villa that crowned the hill at Cap Ferrat, opposite us at the Voile d'Or. Somehow this was the spur. Americans (it was Alan Crosland) were shooting great romantic films in my backyard. I had just gotta get into the film business!

Meanwhile, my valiant mother, acquiescing to Edward Huxham's plans, had taken half a house in a new and ugly road of new and ugly houses on the outskirts of Bournemouth. The address, which was Ulverston, Chigwell Road, was as ugly as the house. We furnished it on the "never-never" from the Times Furnishing Company. I still have some of the pieces, and they are as solid as ever.

Before leaving Ringwood, we had moved down from the Red Cottage to a house in the valley which we shared with a couple called Tidy: Waldo and Elfrida. They had a daughter, Waleen. They had been our nearest neighbours at the White Cottage, in the same lane. Waldo was ex-Navy and a sick man. Elf was pretty and bustling and efficient. I met her again, in

WRNS officer's uniform in the next war, looking even prettier and even more efficient, with Waleen in tow, now nineteen. We gave Waleen a part in *Colonel Blimp* as Miss Hunter's sister, whom Blimp takes to the theatre. She was right for the part, but her pretty mother, twenty years earlier, with her delightful common sense, would have been even righter.

How my mother managed to run the house and give me money for magazines and cinemas and a few – very few – gramophone records, I have no idea. I think she had one or two small legacies about that time, and I know she had one later on, which helped her to buy Turling Farm. There were so many films that I HAD to see. One of them was *Woman to Woman*, one of the first international British successes. It was a drama starring Clive Brook and Betty Compson. The producer was Michael Balcon, the co-producer Victor Saville, the director Graham Cutts, and the art director, a new name on the credits, Alfred Hitchcock. I filed these names away, knowing that I was going to see a lot of them – and they of me.

My taste was improving, not so much in the visual arts as in literature. Aunt Ethel had got me used to *The Times Literary Supplement* every weekend, and she continued to send her copy on to me so long as I was in the bank. It had become a necessary part of my life, and with my retentive memory it gave me wide terms of reference that led me on to collateral reading. I gobbled up Shaw and Lawrence, discovered Richard Aldington, Aldous Huxley and Compton Mackenzie. I had begun to appreciate publishers. Up till now I had only cared that their books stay in one piece. Mills & Boon were a case in point: they didn't. Now I wanted to know who Martin Secker was. And what a private press was.

But all that quiet literary stuff was to go by the board when I met my father again at the railway station in Beaulieu. He was as excited as I was.

"You've got your chance, Mick. It's an American company making a big film here in Nice. They were filming all day yesterday in Villefranche, using a French submarine from Toulon. Some of them came over to St. Jean to look around. They came onto the terrace, and I asked a few of them to dinner at Maxim's, nine o'clock sharp. I told them you knew all about films, and they laughed. They seem a friendly lot."

I couldn't take it all in. "An American company? What American company?"

"Metro, I think they called it."

"Metro," I gasped.

"They've been filming all round the Méditerranée for the past few months – Naples, Pompeii, Barcelona, Marseilles, and now they're here to finish the film at the Victorine Studios in Nice."

"The Victorine?"

"It's in the Californie. On the hill, above the *chemin de fer*. You've never been there."

"What's the film?"

"*Mare Nostrum.*"

My throat went dry.

"It's Rex Ingram," I whispered.

"Who?"

"He made *The Four Horsemen of the Apocalypse*. He made *The Prisoner of Zenda*. He made *Scaramouche*."

"Did he, by Jove!"

"Is he coming tonight?"

"No idea. I asked them all. No good doing anything by halves. We'll go into Nice this evening, you and me, and hang around the Ruhl Bar. They're staying at the Ruhl, so there are always some of them in the bar. We'll play it from there."

The little car shot through Le Port like a bullet, roared up the stony road and swung into the entrance of the hotel, sending the gravel flying. My father always made a big thing of his arrival on the terrace.

"*Le Capitaine Powell est arrivé! Avec son fils.*"

I was a questionmark in the Port. Was I going to be the heir-apparent of the hotel, or was I not?

André Caramello, son of the hero of the "*Mange-Cafard*" episode, was a friend of mine. We were – are, I hope – the same age. We were both enthusiastic fencers – with foils – *le fleuret*. We used to fight Musketeer fights on the Port. He was always trying to find out my intentions. The Voile d'Or was a prize. Twenty-four rooms! *Bien!* But it was the huge terrace they all had their eyes on. With parking! And parking was beginning to be the start and finish of a hotel's success or failure.

At the Ruhl Bar, my father was greeted by the barman as an old friend. Henri knew everybody's secrets and was banker and father confessor to all the bums, pimps and whores on the coast. Visiting celebrities stayed at either the Negresco or the Ruhl. If they were Russian, or new to the Coast, at the showy Negresco, an ice pudding of an hotel on the Promenade des Anglais. If they had been in Nice before, they stayed at the Ruhl, which was opposite the Jetée Casino, a stroll to the Casino Municipal, and thirty seconds to Madame Regina's well-kept establishment in the Rue de France. My father ordered a Manhattan for himself, and a gin fizz for me. "And go easy on the gin, Henri, *c'est mon fils, vous savez.*"

Meanwhile I looked around.

A big, heavily built man, swarthy and dressed like a sailor, was standing at the bar, talking quietly to a thin, sardonic-looking man with a beaky nose, remarkable eyes and the hairy hands of a craftsman. As I watched, he nodded agreement to the big man, put his hand in his Norfolk jacket pocket, pulled out a handful of small cards, and made a note. As the big man looked around the bar I recognized him. It was Antonio Moreno, one of the Latin Lovers then so popular, but whom I knew better as the daring hero of countless serials, in particular *The Iron Test*. He was a good actor and an attractive man, but not in the same glamour school as Valentino or Novarro. I knew that Moreno was co-starring opposite the divinely blond Alice Terry in *Mare Nostrum*, which I hadn't read, but knew to be by Blasco-Ibáñez, the author of *The Four Horsemen, Enemies of Women*, and *Blood and Sand*, and who was certainly the most successful author of the decade. He was a Socialist, or even better (since he was Catalan), an anarchist. He lived in exile on the Riviera like most politically minded Catalans of that or any period.

At that moment, two men whom my father knew came in: one was a typical Syrian businessman, with a close-clipped moustache and an equally close-clipped smile. The other was tall, slender and spoke with an American accent although he was French. My father introduced them as Fred Bacos and John Daumery. They were, to my chagrin, not artists or technicians but business managers and organizers. However, they introduced us to the other two and we were soon in a group of movie people.

I have a bad habit (and a rude one) of never hearing the name of a stranger when I am introduced, and being too shy to have it repeated. I have always admired Americans who, confronted, as they are every day, with the most surprising polyglot surnames, can seize someone's hand and say firmly: "I didn't quite catch the name," and what's more, nail it down. In this case, I didn't need to ask Tony Moreno's name, but his companion's name escaped me. I caught him once or twice looking at me disconcertingly, with a quizzical expression, when my father claimed that I knew everything there was to know about films.

We arrived eventually at Maxim's with a mixed bag of moviemakers, who were not interested in my father's diplomacy on my behalf, but were not averse to a free meal at one of the best night club restaurants on the coast. The band was good, there were hostesses, and my father, who loved parties, whatever the excuse, danced every dance with a beatific smile on his lips, his eyes half-closed behind his horn-rimmed spectacles. The slim, sardonic companion of Moreno had not accompanied us, but he turned up later in the evening with a ravishingly pretty girl and sat watching us, while she danced with everyone else. Apparently he didn't dance. Once or twice I caught the same ironic look in his eyes as he watched our progress. Finally, he said to me: "So you want to be in the picture business?"

I muttered something.

He said: "This little party's going to set your father back a few francs."

I agreed.

"Just exactly," went on this Satanic character, "what do you want to do in movies? And what sort of help do you and your father expect to get from Fred Bacos and John Daumery?"

I stared dumbly.

"Here's my card," he said. "Come early in the morning to 155 Promenade des Anglais. Ask for me."

A few minutes later he left. I sneaked a look at the card. It read "*Harry Lachman*", and in small print "Chevalier de la Légion d'Honneur", and a Paris address.

The address on the Promenade des Anglais was that of the office of the American Express, which was as legendary in Europe as the *Saturday Evening Post*. I didn't sleep. I caught the early tram from St Jean and was in Nice by 8:30. The film company had temporary space at 155. You must picture tall, rattling french windows overlooking the Promenade, and a room full of sunlight. The parquet floors of the apartment squeaked everytime anyone walked over it. The door had a buzzer on it. There were several French girls working and typing. I sat and waited.

A tall, lean, black-haired young man in a tweed suit came in. He couldn't have been anything but American. He said to the nearest girl, who happened to be pretty as well as young: "And how are you this morning?" He sounded as if he cared.

She answered, typing rapidly, "Very well, thank you."

He said, as if it were the answer he had been hoping for all night: "I am glad to hear you are feeling so well." Then, turning to me, he said: "Hello."

I said I was waiting for Mr Lachman.

"You a friend of Harry's?"

I explained.

"Sure he's got the Legion of Honour. He's a great painter. He's got three of his pictures in the Luxembourg. He was all through the war in Paris. He's a great photographer, too. He's shooting our stills on the film. You a photographer?"

I explained that I wasn't much of anything. Yet. But I hoped to be.

He looked at me with the kindest, shrewdest eyes I had ever seen on a man and said: "Sure you will. Just stick around."

The door crashed open and Harry Lachman put his head in. "Powell!" he said.

I jumped up and tripped over a loose bit of parquet. The young man caught and steadied me. "This your new assistant, Harry?" he asked.

Harry snapped: "What do I want with an assistant?" Then to me, fiercely: "We can't afford to pay you anything, you know!"

I didn't know what to say. I only knew that I stood on the threshold of a new and wonderful life, half in and half out, and that I must, I *must*, cross that threshold.

"Can you speak French, Powell?"

I said I spoke French; and a little, a very little, American.

"What do you think, Howard? He speaks American."

"Might come in useful. Never know. He could help out in the publicity department."

"OK, Powell. You can stick around. We'll pay you a hundred francs a week. OK?"

It was about five dollars in 1925. I was already being asked to make sacrifices for my art. The bank was paying me about five times as much.

"When do I start, Mr Lachman?"

"Now! You call me Harry, I call you Powell." To Howard: "I'm going to the Victorine." To me: "Come on."

His car was parked outside. It was a red Fiat. We got in and drove like hell along the Promenade.

"What are we working on?" I asked professionally.

Harry gave me one of his black grins. "We are working on about four things at once, owing to a lack of ordinary foresight and elementary organization in the company."

We turned up a stony road lined with villas built on spec by a hopeful local builder. Harry took a left at the end on two wheels, just scraping by a big truck coming down the centre of the lane. We were running along beside the main railroad track, the lane rising to a stone bridge over the tracks. A fierce right wrenched us onto the bridge, a ferocious left wrenched us off it. An iron gate appeared in the wall. It was closed and Harry sounded his horn. The guardian ran out, the gate groaned open, Harry shouted: "*Merci*, Angelo!" we drove up a road full of potholes and stopped in front of a white villa, French style, with a curving double stairway leading up to a terrace. Harry vanished inside and I looked about me.

The Victorine had obviously been a rich man's villa. The grounds were about ten acres in extent. Most of it had run wild, but the kitchen garden was still there. There were olive trees and loquats, and yucca and agave, and one very tall and slender palm tree in the centre of the plot. In fact, it was exactly like a back lot in Hollywood, and it is only now, looking back after all these years, that I realize how much at home the homeless Hollywoodian gipsies must have felt: for they didn't belong in Hollywood, they hadn't been born there; they had migrated there from New York or Chicago, beckoned by the giant forms of Griffith, Mack Sennett, Thomas H. Ince and Charles Chaplin. It had been a new Gold Rush, with fortunes being picked up among the orange groves of Hollywood and Vine. To those who had followed Rex Ingram to the Mediterranean to make *Mare Nostrum*, Nice was not all that different.

In 1925, the Victorine had been a film studio for some years and for the same reason that D. W. Griffith and the others went westward: for the sunshine. There were three small glass studios about sixteen by twelve metres. There was one large studio, about twice as big, of which the glass panel had been blacked out so that artificial light could be used inside. All the studios had big rolling doors for servicing, and blinds for controlling the density of light from outside. There were rows of cabin-like dressing rooms attached to the studios. There was a second villa, once a factor's or gardener's villa, now the production offices of the company, for I saw people going in and out and heard the sound of typewriters and telephones ringing. At the top of the gentle slope, behind the white villa, there was a long barn-like building which stretched a good sixty metres and evidently housed the carpenters' and plasterers' shops. Most of the activity seemed to be centred around there. I could see lights and generators through the open doors and a shifting crowd of people, and I could hear American voices.

Harry reappeared just as a procession of women entered the villa carrying costumes, props, make-up, blond wigs, and all that goes into making a film star. Evidently Alice Terry was working today. My heart beat faster, for where she was, her director husband could not be far away. Harry was making one of his notes. "Come on, Powell!" He led the way up the stony road to where the crew was working.

Half of the carpenters' shop had been taken over and converted into a film set. The floor of polished parquet was protected by dust-cloths. It was evidently a sort of palace. A pretentious chandelier hung in the middle of the set, although I could see no ceiling. Arc lights were fizzing and blazing and, in order to get the set clear, people were jammed all around the walls. There was some question of the adjustment of the chandelier, which was on a pulley, and there was a lot of shouting.

At the far end of the set were my heroes, the camera crew. A glance told me they were using a Bell & Howell camera mounted on a tripod. Around the camera were a chunky chief electrician chewing gum, a pair of pliers in his belt, gloves on his hands; a calm, bespectacled prop-man, with a belt containing every conceivable gadget, from a sheath-knife to a whisk-broom; an Irish-looking assistant director, who was doubled up over some joke he had told the assistant cameraman, a tall, bony, blond young man, whom I took to at once; while, through the camera, a thin, worried-looking man, in a hat and suit, in contrast to the other men's rough clothes, was squinting, as he tried to align the chandelier, in the centre of the set, with an object suspended over the camera. Behind him, a calm dark man, with the face of a priest, was standing in his shirtsleeves, waiting his turn to look through the camera. I crept around behind them and discovered that the object over the camera was a miniature ceiling, built in false perspective to fit over the top of the camera, and by careful adjustment make the set appear like a ceilinged room. I was to do a lot of this foreground miniature work later on, on *The Thief of Bagdad*, for Korda, and the amusing link to me, as I look back to that first day, is that the priest-like miniature-maker,

Walter Pahlman, had done the miniature work on Douglas Fairbank's *Thief of Bagdad* two years before. So my first day in movies was centred on a trick shot as, I have no doubt, my last will be.

Harry Lachman appeared at my elbow and addressed the worried cameraman as Johnny. I realized that this was John F. Seitz, who had photographed *The Four Horsemen, Scaramouche,* and all Rex Ingram's great movies. I had never even held a Kodak in my hands at that time, but I already knew most of the big names and felt the difference between Billy Bitzer's harsh realism and Johnny Seitz's impressionism, which was to reach its fullest expression in Billy Wilder's *Double Indemnity* thirty years later. I have always been amazed at the apparent sophistication of these early cameramen, but it must be remembered that they worked with sunlight before sun-arcs, used huge sheets of gauze to filter the light, and, through half-closed eyes, were already studying the problems of telling a story with actors in a natural setting. Those pioneers of motion picture storytelling – and you must remember, that at the time I crept on a film set, the art was only ten years old – were also pioneers of surrealism, for every film is surrealistic to a certain degree. What could be more pleasing to Artaud, or Apollinaire, than the scene in Charlie's *The Pilgrim,* where he converts his brother Syd's bowler hat into an ice pudding? As for Luis Buñuel, my master, the only film-maker I would defer to, from *Un Chien Andalou* to *The Discreet Charm of the Bourgeoisie,* he has known from the beginning what most of us have only learnt in brief moments of vision and clarity.

A foreground miniature ceiling is the most tricky of all objects to line up. It must be at a calculated distance from the camera. The focus between it and the set has to be split, and each adjustment of this focus necessarily upsets the delicate marriage of set and ceiling. Johnny muttered savagely to himself (he was the gentlest and kindest of men), and threw his soft hat on the floor. I picked it up.

"This is Powell," announced Harry. "His father owns a hotel at Cap Ferrat, and he's a film fan. Rex says he can stick around. Give him something to do."

They looked at me. The tall assistant cameraman grinned and asked: "What's your name?"

"Michael."

"You English, Mike?"

"Yes."

"Well, I'm Gordon Avil, and this" (the Irish assistant director) "is Joe Boyle, and this" (the tough electrician) "is Chris Bergsvik, and this" (the bespectacled prop-man) "is Ray Moyer."

"How do you do?" I said.

I handed Johnny his hat and he gave me a sweet smile, without actually seeing me.

"Guess you'd better be a grip today," announced Ray Moyer, handing me a mop.

"OK," I said.

"Do you know what a grip is, Mike?" asked Gordon, who seemed to have appointed himself my guardian. I shook my head.

"It means you're one of the camera department. It's a very responsible job. And if anyone tries to put anything over on you, you come to me or to Mr Seitz here."

Johnny muttered despondently, something about being ready, while Walter Pahlman looked through the lens.

"See that floor?" said Ray to me. "Every time they come in that door, they track dirt in and leave footprints across the floor. Make it your job to clean 'em up."

There was a stir outside. Rex Ingram and Alice Terry entered the set.

Rex was about twenty-nine and was one of the best-looking men I had ever seen. He had straight black hair and eyebrows, a perfect profile, and was about medium height. His eyes were remarkable, a dreamer's eyes. He wore a gold bracelet on his left wrist. He was dressed in khaki, long pants and a bush shirt with short sleeves. Bare brown feet in sandals. Long slender fingers and toes.

Alice wore a dress of the period of the Great War, about 1916. I think it was grey silk with a lot of fussy accessories. The hat, which had a wide brim, didn't suit her and she knew it. She sat down and, while her dresser held a mirror, worked on it. She was only a few yards away. You can bet I used my eyes. She was more beautiful than I had expected, because of the charm of her natural expression, which was full of fun. She had blue eyes. Her parts in her husband's films hardly allowed much gaiety: the Princess Flavia; the heroine of *The Four Horsemen*; the persecuted Countess in Sabatini's story; the missionary's daughter in *Where the Pavement Ends*; and now the doomed Mata Hari-like character, a siren and a spy, she was playing in *Mare Nostrum*, had not prepared me for this natural, gay young woman whose voice had a lilt in it. I stared and stared, until she suddenly caught my eye, and seeing a new face, gave a look of inquiry. I became very busy.

Rex was talking to a mountainous Frenchwoman, a cruel caricature of a German secret agent, wearing a kimono over a dress of mannish tweed. I heard him call her Madame Paquerette. She only spoke French. (In the days of silent films, actors played in their own language, whatever the nationality of the character he or she was supposed to be portraying.) Harry was beside him. It was clear to me, even then, that Harry was cultivating Rex. He was not afraid of him, as most of his unit were, and he was a personality and an artist in his own right. They walked over and Rex sat down in his canvas chair next to Alice. I mopped up their footsteps.

"This is Powell, Rex," said Harry, with a leer. "He's college trained, and he's British and he knows every picture you ever made, and some you didn't. Say how-d'you-do, Powell."

I couldn't speak. Alice looked up from her mirror. Rex took me in at a glance. "Do you live on the Coast, Michael?"

I said that my father had a hotel.

"The Voile d'Or," said Harry. "You remember, Rex. You went over there when you were shooting the submarine at Villefranche."

Joe Boyle said: "We're ready, Rex."

Alice got up and went across to Johnny to say good morning. I heard her laugh and saw him give a reluctant smile. They were very fond of one another, and understood each other perfectly. I myself came to know Alice well. Without great technique, with very little training, and with nothing but her wit, charm and intelligence to guide her, she had arrived, as Rex Ingram's wife and leading lady, at the summit of this new profession of screen star. She was the image of the unattainable, "*la princesse lointaine*". On the screen, her head held high, higher than head had ever been held, she lost lover after lover magnificently. We admired this superb creature and longed to comfort her, while knowing she was out of our reach.

There have been proud blonde ladies before and since, but Alice was in a class by herself. She was human, and her public sensed it. God knows, she was allotted part after part that, in other hands, on other figures, would have been just walking clothes-horses. Alice's humour always came through. Rex didn't help her: he never gave her little, tender, useless things to do. But even in the most ornamental and useless part, we could feel Alice's warm heart beating: without great projection she shared with us her emotion; and she never made a false move. I have only worked with one other woman who had this gift of imaginative sympathy to the same degree as Alice. If she is reading these words, she will recognize herself.

The sequence on which we were working was the one in which Alice, as the blonde siren working for the Germans, is briefed by the head of the local espionage bureau in Naples. On that first day, I saw some of the typical Ingram trademarks. Every one of the faces in the sequence, even the passer-by in the corridor, had been hand-picked. They registered with the clarity of individuals in a crowd etched by Goya or Daumier. I soon learnt that this was a passion of Rex's. It is one of the reasons why I do my own casting to this day. Not that I haven't worked with casting departments – but departments are impressed by credits, experience and by actors who are "hot". We movie directors are looking for faces. Even voices take second place to faces.

The next thing that impressed me was Rex's patience. He knew what he wanted from each shot, he was working with professionals who each knew what he wanted, and he was prepared to wait until he got it. He sat in his chair and people came to him, chatted, asked questions, and went away. Howard Strickling, my friend from the publicity department, appeared with a youngish, donnish-looking man who was carrying a few sheets of typescript for Rex to read. I heard him called Willis. I had already sneaked a copy of the script from Gordon Avil, and I knew that Willis Goldbeck had written it. He had been at Yale with Rex. Howard saw me wielding my mop and called out: "Hi there, Mike." I mopped away. I was an accepted member of the film company – of the great, world-famous film company of Metro-Goldwyn-Mayer!

Or of Metro-Goldwyn at any rate. The distinction was impressed upon me later – fifty-six years later – by Grant Whytock, editor of all Rex's great films.

"That was the old Metro lot," he said the other day, pointing to a huge carpark between Cole and Cahuenga Boulevard, right opposite the splendid Art Deco building of Technicolor in East Hollywood. "*The Four Horsemen* was shot there."

"And *The Conquering Power* and *Black Orchids*?" I asked, confidently. But I had "struck out".

"It was the remake of *Black Orchids* that was made there – *Trifling Women. Black Orchids* was made first by Rex at Universal. It got murdered by the front office for being too erotic. So Rex remade it when he joined Metro and made it twice as erotic. That Barbara La Marr," he added with relish, "was quite a gal! But I was telling you about Louis B. Mayer. He and Rex never did get on, and when the merger happened, and Goldwyn stormed out to build his own studios, that left Mayer on top of the heap. But Rex was their money director, and after Louis B. wouldn't let him direct *Ben-Hur* and gave it to Niblo, Rex refused to have Mayer's name on his pictures. You'll see if you look at them. It's Metro-Goldwyn presents, but no Mayer."

What a business, I thought. Goldwyn joins Mayer, leaves his name on the company, and never makes a picture for them; and his name isn't even Goldwyn, it's Sam Goldfish. So Rex, loyal to the old Metro company, lets Goldwyn's name ride, but picks a quarrel with Mayer. But who had the last word? Mayer.

I fancy that Harry Lachman had from the first intended me to be his assistant. He had no authority to hire or fire: that belonged to John Daumery, the production manager, or to George Noffka, who was Metro's representative on the spot. But once I was on the lot and doing a job, in those easy-going days – not that I notice much difference in the situation today, film-makers are a lot of gipsies by nature – he thought he could annex me to the department of which he was already head in his mind. His actual position with the company was stills photographer, which included portraits, for he had a European reputation – Havrah of Paris – as a portrait photographer; but his aim was to direct, and he was prepared to step upon anybody's neck to achieve that end. Rex was all-powerful and acknowledged no master, and he was Rex's friend. An assistant who spoke English and French and who was amiably willing to work for nothing, could only add to Harry's prestige at present. He would look after my expenses; and later he would get me on the payroll.

At lunchtime everybody – Italian craftsmen, Niçois extras, wardrobe and hairdressers, actors and American film unit – all ate at long wooden tables under roofs of palm leaves. The company paid. We were considered to be on location.

"This is one of the things we've got to get right," announced Harry, slipping in on the bench beside me, with a plate containing *salade de tomates aux anchois*. He never ate much. I was up to the elbows in pasta: they do ravioli pretty well in Nice.

"What's wrong with it?" I asked.

I gradually learnt that the film unit, after shooting all round the Mediterranean, notably at Naples and Barcelona, had fixed on Nice for some studio interiors. In those days, on the right bank of the River Var, which empties into the sea by the airport today, there was a small glass film studio at St Laurent du Var, and there they had built the interiors of the Barcelona house, a stone-flagged living room and a kitchen hung with bunches of herbs, strings of onions and garlic. A Spanish character actor, Uni Apollon, played the usual Blasco-Ibáñez patriarch in these scenes, and as he was old and heavy it had been decided to complete his part in Europe. The rest of the interiors would be shot at Metro in Hollywood. But meanwhile Harry and a local lawyer, a young sporting type named Corniglion-Molinier, had conceived the idea of renting the much bigger Victorine Studios nearer Nice, on the near side of the River Var, and completing the whole film in Europe. This had been the original intention of MGM when they started to film *Ben-Hur* in Rome in 1924, with Charles Brabin directing. But the unit was soon recalled by Louis B. Mayer, who replaced the director and made the film at the new studios in Culver City. A lot of the Rome equipment, notably generators and lights, had been taken over by the *Mare Nostrum* unit. No doubt, Mayer would have recalled Rex to Hollywood too, but Rex was a law unto himself.

All this I gradually learnt during the next few days, and some of it I have worked out now, many years later. The unit were only just getting used to the idea that, instead of hightailing it back to Hollywood to complete the picture, we were going to complete it in Nice at the Victorine. The plan included a modern laboratory, a cutting room, and a projection theatre; and an enormous tank, about thirty metres square, for the shipwreck scenes and the mythological scenes.

Before I go any further, I had better give you a synopsis of the story. *Mare Nostrum* was an anti-war film. Seven years after the First World War ended, Europe's writers and thinkers were still reeling from the shock. Some, like Thomas Mann, were beginning to publish. Wasserman had written *The World's Illusion* and Oswald Spengler had declared *The Decline of the West*. Erich Maria Remarque's book, *All Quiet on the Western Front* had become a best-seller, but first of them all was the old Catalan anarchist with his *Four Horsemen*, which Rex, and June Mathis, his mentor and screenwriter at Metro, had turned into a box-office hit. Vicente Blasco-Ibáñez became a big name and when Metro bought *Mare Nostrum* it was naturally to Rex that they turned to make it, and it was equally natural that he should accept the task without going too deeply into the difficulties and dangers of another war film.

The story is a tragedy. Captain Ulysses Ferragut is a Spanish merchant trader who commands and owns his ship. He is married, with a twelve-year-old son, when the War comes and the price of freights soar and it looks as if he will make a fortune. He is constantly at sea, and sees little of his family. He meets in Naples a fascinating woman Freya, who becomes his mistress. She is a German agent whose job it is to persuade him to take fuel oil to a secret rendezvous with a U-boat. He does so and his son, who comes to look for him, is killed when the same U-boat torpedoes the passenger steamer on which he is a passenger. Ferragut seeks revenge. His blonde mistress is denounced by her own people and shot before a French firing squad. Ferragut succeeds in encountering the U-boat and sinks it, but loses his ship and his own life in the action. A fine and sombre tale, but dangerously late in joining the queues of other war stories.

Films were a new thing, but they were already showing a perilous tendency to exhaust their potential audience. It was probably with this thought in mind that Rex and Willis Goldbeck had adopted from the book a mystical introduction, told by his old grandfather to Ulysses Ferragut as a boy, of the sea goddess Amphitrite, whom the old man claims to have seen one night driving her white horses over the foam, standing in a sea chariot formed by one gigantic shell. This figure of Amphitrite becomes an obsession with the young man, and he seems to see her likeness in the face of the woman who betrays him. In a final apotheosis the drowning man sinks to the bottom of the sea and his mistress Amphitrite rises to meet him and take him in her arms.

This was pretty heady stuff for a first picture, and looking back I am not surprised that I never had much of a taste for kitchen-sink drama.

Harry had finished his lunch and was scribbling one of his eternal notes on his pack of blue cards. When the note had been followed up, he tore the card in two and threw it away. He told me to copy him, but he soon gave that up. I lost the pencil, lost the cards, or lost my head.

"Come on, Powell," he said.

We went to a laboratory building, a square brick building among the olive trees. It was being gutted.

"We're putting in new tanks," Harry explained. "The old ones are slate and are full of sludge. The dailies have to go to Paris to be developed and printed."

We ran up some outside stairs.

"This is the stills department."

He entered his domain and I started a friendship that lasted until death.

"This is Tomatis."

A thin, solemn-looking young man was peeling glossy eight-by-ten prints off a vulcanite plate. He had an incredibly lined face for so young a man – he was about thirty – and a quizzical manner which masked a keen sense of the ridiculousness of all authority. He had big, brown, observant eyes. He was Niçois and spoke the patois with all his friends, who were more Italian than French. When he spoke French, as he did in answering Lachman, he spoke it correctly. He also spoke with precision and authority about his métier. He was a craftsman. Harry was giving some instructions about the development of some glass negatives he had exposed in Barcelona. Tomatis listened. If he agreed, he said "*C'est bien*" in a deep, hoarse voice. If he did not agree he gave his reasons.

Harry jerked his thumb in my direction. "*Il va vous aider.*"

Tomatis looked benevolently at this fair, solemn English boy, who looked as if he had just come out of the egg. "*C'est bien, M. Lachman.*"

He held out his long, thin fingers and we shook hands. For the next three years, this office and this darkroom were to be my refuge.

"Come on, Powell."

The cutting room – cutters were cutters, then, not editors – was on the second floor of the laboratory building, like our stills department; it was large, light, airy, clean and well equipped with spools, winders, film cans, film joiners and all the toys which are now in common use in every home, but which then were the tools of a new and mysterious craft. Grant and Leota Whytock were both at work. I had noticed Grant during the morning when he looked in to ask Rex a question. He was a firm-looking man, about thirty, with a bristly moustache and a vigorous crest of black hair. He wore a brown knickerbocker tweed suit and looked like a character out of a Booth Tarkington novel. He was kind and quick to smile, and very sure of himself.

Leota, his wife, was fat and full of fun. He called her Ota and so did all of us kids around the lab. She wore huge glasses with thick lenses and was always ready to help us and join in our games. She and Grant were a great team. They had worked on all of Rex's films since the Universal days – the days of the young director's *Crimson Skies* and *Black Orchids*, so offensive to the bosses of Universal because they were directed with sophistication and taste by a visual artist.

"Tell me, Grant," I said to him the other day. "Have the big studios always had the personality that they seem to have now?"

"What do you mean?"

"Well, MGM was Rolls-Royces, and Warners was Ford sedans, and Paramount was mobile homes; but Universal seems to me to have always been Universal, where they make films to make money and for no other reason."

A slow smile from Grant. "You might say they have always been like that. Yes. Rex would have agreed with you. Not that his films didn't make money. He could have written his own ticket with Marcus Loew and Nick Schenck. Louis B. was told to give him everything he wanted after *Scaramouche*. When he said he was going to finish *Mare Nostrum* in Europe, they just pulled out the chequebook and said, how much?"

I was taught to handle film by Grant and Ota. I was taught order and method and accuracy: I, the despair of the National Provincial Bank! They were kind and patient. Above all, they taught me to look at film and to love it – to love and to know every image on the couple of hundred thousand images that create the atmosphere and tell the story of a feature film. They cut by hand and eye, very rarely by measurement, except when a fade out or a lap dissolve had to be specified in the final cut. Most dissolves and fade outs in the early days were planned and made in the camera, and it was quite common for me to be sorting out – in company with Gordon Avil, in his camera room where he kept his precious equipment, and sometimes slept when we were working late – a dozen or so loaded magazines on which were written in wax pencil instructions like "Alice dissolve to Amphitrite. Scene 65. Dissolve starts at 275 feet on Counter, ends at 283 feet 8 frames"; and we would prepare for the filming next day of the other half of a scene shot in Pompeii two months before and held in the camera.

I was always running sequences from the film under the indulgent eyes of Grant and Ota. I learnt to turn the film on the spools slower or faster over the light table, and could soon spot the change of density, or of colour. (We had tinted films in those days, and Rex, being a painter, was always experimenting with tints. He never made a film in colour, more's the pity.) In a short time I knew the film almost as well as they did. The Pompeii sequence had amused me. There is a room in the dead city, a brothel or a private bath, that is full of pornographic images. The guides make a great fuss about ladies not being admitted, in order to get a handsome tip. Tony Moreno, as Ferragut, falls for this ploy and meets two ladies coming out of the forbidden room: Alice, of course, as the seductive Freya, and Madame Paquerette as the mountainous head of the German bureau, complete with tweed suit, Bavarian hat, and shooting stick. It is the sort of joke that Rex liked to make to give the American bourgeoisie a bit of titillation.

"Mr Ingram," I addressed him respectfully, a film later, during the shooting of *The Magician*, "is female companionship essential for an artist?"

Harry snorted. Alice, who was not working that day and was running her hands through her lovely chestnut hair, rolled over on the grass and laughed at me. Rex smiled and said: "Powell, you will not get far in life without tail."

He translated for the benefit of Dardé, the peasant sculptor, a huge man invariably clad in a workman's smock and beret. He was modelling in clay a huge statue of a faun. He nodded, and getting up, crossed over and handed me the drawings on which he had been working while we talked. They were all erotic, highly-charged and explicit sketches of men and women making love in various positions, and they were observed with tenderness and in great detail. He dealt them out to me one by one like a pack of cards, and Alice looked over my shoulder. Here a magnificent woman lay and smiled up at the naked man who had his hand between her legs. There a girl sat astride a youth who had his face buried in her thighs, flinging her hands with ecstasy into the air. There a couple embraced each other with their tongues and were so locked together that it was impossible to tell whether they were male or female. There were a dozen others. All were spontaneous, earthy, passionate, innocent. I sat with my face scarlet, trying to appreciate the drawings as drawings, an obvious virgin. Alice took pity on me.

"You're not to make fun of Powell," she announced, "just because he doesn't jump on every girl he sees. He's been brought up to respect women, and quite right too! Get me a glass of soda-pop, Micky."

I made my escape.

That was a year later. I must go back to my first week at the Victorine. For three days I was walking on clouds.

On Thursday I got fired.

It was those bloody glass negatives of Barcelona.

We – the still department – were short of offices. The production office and the MGM office took up all the space in the gardener's cottage. Grant had knocked three other offices into one to make a projection room with a thirty-foot throw. Harry took over a couple of dressing rooms in a row, attached to one of the large studios. The usual long stone corridor serviced the rooms. It had an entrance from the lot, and there was a tricky little step. Carrying the glass plates, I tripped over it and dropped the lot. The smash was terrific, out of all proportion to the size of the plates. Out of thirty or forty stills of Tony Moreno looking around Barcelona – the Port, the Cathedral, the Gaudí church – only two were intact. Harry turned on me like a demon. His rages were rare, but volcanic when they erupted.

"Get off the lot! Go home! Get out of my sight! No! Don't try to pick 'em up! Get out! Get going! Don't ever come back!"

I slunk away, more miserable than I had ever been in my life. My things were still in the still department. I told Tomatis what had happened. He clicked his tongue in sympathy. "*Disparaissez!*" Keep out of sight! Good advice, but how? Where? If I went off the lot, out the gate, I might never be allowed back. My name would be listed as a pariah, a glass-smasher.

Lachman's voice was heard outside calling for Tomatis. "*Tomatis! Viens! J'ai besoin de toi!*" Tommy jerked his head and I took refuge in the darkroom. Harry came into the other room and I heard myself described as a clumsy camel. "*Ce salaud de Powell. Le chameau à cinq pattes!*"

Tomatis answered briefly, and they went away to pick up the pieces and see what could be salvaged. I was determined not to leave the lot. It seemed a very long day. Gordon came down to unload his magazines and I sneaked over and told him what had happened. He knew it already. Harry had told everybody.

"He'll get over it," said Gordon. "Just stick around. He'll forget about it. Do you want a lift to Nice with the truck?"

"I'm not going to leave the lot," I said. "They might give orders to Auguste at the gate. I might never get back in again."

"Have you got any food? Where are you going to sleep?"

"In one of the dressing rooms."

"Here's some chocolate. I'll bring some chow in the morning. Keep your pecker up."

Gordon's matter-of-fact acceptance of my predicament, and his evident belief that I only had to "stick around" (that immortal phrase which has started so many cinematic careers) to be accepted back into the fold, cheered me up a little. As soon as the lot started to clear, I sneaked a telephone call to St Jean, and said we would be working all night.

When my father had succeeded in getting me taken on by the movie company, he considered his duty done and closed the hotel, in spite of the protests of the few remaining guests, and took off for Chantilly with a mistress summoned peremptorily from his pool of temps. I was to stay with the Bussell family at Maryland. The big house was shuttered and dust-sheeted for the summer. The family – Boss, his wife, Violet (Viso), Lily and Nero the dog – were in the gardener's cottage. Both the girls worked. Tonia, the Italian girl from Florence, a handsome brunette with a sweet disposition, slept in one of the back bedrooms of the big house and I slept next to her. We used to shout to one another, but there was no romance. Tonia was affianced to a house painter.

I ate with the Bussells, so my hundred francs was partly spent on the little yellow trams that groaned their way along the winding, narrow coast road from St Jean to the Place Masséna in Nice. There another tram, perilously overloaded, with people hanging on to each available projection, banged and swayed its way to the Californie. The bus run by MGM to get people to the studio was mostly for office staff, who kept office hours.

I had put off writing to my mother until the weekend (my father had already sent her a brief note). I had already overstayed my leave at the bank. Those doors were now closed to me. And now how was I to tell her of the inglorious end to my motion picture career? And what was I to do, marooned on the Côte d'Azur out of season? Look for a job? Join my father at Chantilly, at the Manor House run by the Normans? But I didn't really consider these ghastly alternatives. There was only one profession for me in the world.

The night passed slowly. At first the dressing rooms were stuffy. Then they were cold. I couldn't switch on the light. It would have alerted the nightwatchman. The labs were locked at night.

At last I heard the workmen arriving, shouting to each other in Niçois. The machine shops started up. I crept out feeling and looking scruffy, and ran down to the lab. Tomatis had brought me a *pan bagnat*, a crusty Niçois sandwich of half a yard of French bread soaked with olive oil and garlic, and loaded with tomatoes and slices of raw vegetables. I ate it down to the last ring of onion. Gordon arrived with croissants and brioches from his hotel and a Thermos of hot coffee. A council of war followed. It was agreed by both of them that I couldn't go on hiding on the lot. I was bound to be spotted, sooner or later, and then they would have a real reason for firing me. But I had only been fired from the stills department by Harry. I could still come back to the camera department and be a grip.

"I'll teach you how to load," said Gordon optimistically. "We could do with another assistant, now we're in the studio."

Encouraged by a full stomach, I put a brave face on it and helped push the camera gear up the hill to the set.

Johnny Seitz had to be told, of course. He nodded absently and gave me a sweet smile. I was a very industrious grip. They even let me track the camera, set up on a platform built over an automobile chassis with pneumatic tyres. By the time Harry looked in on the set, everyone knew the situation except Rex, who was deep in script revisions with Willis Goldbeck. Harry gave me one of his sidelong black looks, and I shook in my sandals. He slouched over to the camera crew.

"You seem to have made some friends, Powell," he growled, and that was all. If not forgiven, I was at least excused.

Do you wonder that I have a special feeling about Americans? But how near the hotel business was to gaining another Escoffier!

Three golden years rolled by.

No young man starting to work in his chosen profession could have been luckier than I was. It goes without saying that every artist in Europe was interested in movies and that the Americans, with their enthusiasm, their money, and their *savoir faire*, were looked upon as the natural leaders in this new art form. Rex, with his own studios, directing and producing a great story, with all the modern gadgets available from America, was in the position of an independent prince. The Victorine Studios became a Mecca for writers, actors, artists of all kinds. I made stills of them all.

Harry and Tomatis had soon taught me enough of the art of squeezing a bulb to make me official stills photographer for Howard Strickling's publicity department. Harry had originally taken on this chore for Rex along with many others, but in his march towards the general manager's job he intended to be in the publicity groups of the famous, alongside Rex and Alice, instead of setting up the camera. Tomatis, of course, was really the cameraman, he was a professional, and anyway, he had to develop the eight-by-ten negatives and rush prints of them to show to the famous visitors. He took good care that I exposed in the middle of the scale and let me do the social stuff of getting a group together. In no time I was an old hand; and when Gordon gave me a heavy old black four-by-five Graflex camera that belonged to the camera department – they used it to record make-ups and costumes for the script-girl – I really felt that I was somebody. Everybody likes to be photographed. The photographer has power over people. We are feared as much as we are loved. I learnt this lesson.

Taking stills brought me into remote contact with Rex. He was bored by famous people, but justly vain about his good looks, so it was fairly easy to get him to pose. He knew vaguely who I was, and since I had been to Dulwich College he assumed I was literate. I never disillusioned him about Dulwich College. I was literate because I was a Corbett, that's all. Later on when I was entrusted with production stills, which sparked off the slightly exotic thrill of focusing Alice's beautiful figure upside down in the ground glass, he saw me reading the script.

"Well, Powell, what do you make of it?"

I said it was a very good adaptation of the novel.

"Oh! You read the novel?"

"Yes, Mr Ingram."

We had finished the sequences with the secret agents and moved down to the big studio. The scene was Alice's apartment, where she keeps her sailor lover enthralled while the days pass and his ship's officers wonder what has become of him. This was the sort of scene where music was a help, and a three-piece orchestra stood by to give a rendering of the "Serenata Toselli" while Tony Moreno wallowed like a stranded whale in Alice's arms. The scene was very mild, really. Alice didn't share Barbara La Marr's enthusiasm for rolling about on perfumed divans, and Rex had been warned by the front office not to go too far with the torrid love scenes in the book. Not that Rex would have listened to their warning if Valentino, or even Novarro, had been playing opposite Alice. And anyway, Hollywood had been taught a new and sophisticated attitude to sexual relations by, of all people, Charles Chaplin in *A Woman of Paris*. It was just that not a spark of sexual fire passed between honest Tony and statuesque Alice. They were "just good friends". By now I was used to the conventions of silent films, in which the actors improvised their dialogue. Tony was not good at this.

In desperation, Rex invented a bit of business with an atomiser. As the lovers lay on the couch together – in those days only Erich von Stroheim succeeded in bringing the bedroom into his pictures, and even he couldn't get away with a scene *in bed* – Alice languidly sprayed her mouth with perfume and then turned the spray on Moreno's manly lips. She got away with it. That lovely woman had such humour that she could get away with anything.

"Powell!" said Rex one day as I passed him on the lot, my camera on its tripod balanced on my shoulder, my camera case with the big slides and the accessories in my other hand. "Grant Whytock wants some help with the titles now that Willis has gone back. Give him a hand, will you?"

A silent film – at any rate most American silent films – had lots of titles. It's an easy way to tell, or to comment on, a plot, and American movie distributors were in a hurry to cash in at the box office. They underestimated their audience and insisted on spelling out the plot. The great German director F. W. Murnau, one of the greatest of all film directors, had succeeded in making a film with Emil Jannings, most famous of German actors, without a single title; and Lupu Pick had filmed an adaptation of Ibsen's *The Wild Duck*, a very talky play on the stage, with the minimum number of titles because he had been content to show what the actors thought and felt. *Mare Nostrum* seemed to have about 150 titles, and now that the film was coming together, Grant felt that a lot of them were unnecessary. I agreed with him, and was not backwards in expressing my opinion, now that Willis was safely back in New York.

So now I had a foot in two departments, and the right of entry to Gordon's camera room. I was consolidating my position. As Harry's assistant, it was one of my jobs to order from Paris boxes of expensive printing paper in large formats. Harry knew the old dictum: big picture, big artist. After a portrait session with Alice (who hated them, but once coaxed into one would change hats and costumes all day) Harry would blow up the most striking ones on soft, creamy paper and show them to Alice and Rex when they were surrounded by a crowd. Harry had no intention of hiding his light under a bushel. I used to walk up to the production office to order the art paper, dictating my order to the prettiest of the young secretaries, the one whom Howard Strickling had picked out at 155 on my first day. She was a dear little girl, intelligent and modest, with burning eyes in a pale triangular face. Her name was Netty d'Abbadie.

I dictated: "Schmitz Kodak Paris, 17 Rue François Premier, Envoyez deux boîtes Kodura crème, deux boîtes Kodura blanc, 30 à 40," and thought that the destiny of the stills department was in my hands. It all added to Harry's prestige, even though George Noffka had to countersign the order on an MGM invoice. They all knew that Harry had Rex's ear, but they didn't know quite how to deal with this painter from Chicago, who looked and talked like a blue-chinned Mephisto, wore the prestigious ribbon of the Légion d'Honneur in his buttonhole, and was known to be a famous artist, even though nobody ever saw him with a canvas and a box of colours.

The broad lines of Harry's strategy, mapped out with Eddie Corniglion-Molinier (whom readers of Michael Korda's *Charmed Lives* will recognize when he pops up at Antibes, twenty-five years later), was to persuade Rex to stay in Europe to make his films, to buy the Victorine Studios, and make Nice a centre that would rival Hollywood and incidentally make their fortunes. But whereas Harry only wanted to direct and make the sort of films that appealed to his sensual and imaginative talent, Eddie was interested in money. Their two ambitions contributed in the course of time to Rex's downfall, although the idea was bankable enough and initially prospered. But their scheme depended on the benevolence of Louis B. Mayer, and Louis B. was not the man to forgive or forget an insult. Rex was king at the box-office, but a king who had fought for his crown and who thrived on opposition. He was an artist, a humanist, a man of many interests, with a lovely wife who adored him. Take away the opposition and he was bound to make mistakes. He had not got the temperament of an emperor. He liked to make decisions but shirked the responsibility of weighing them first. More Julian than Hadrian.

Henri Menessier was art director on *Mare Nostrum*. He was a plump, dapper man with pince-nez spectacles, full lips and warm, observant eyes. He was already an old-timer in the business. He was a Frenchman and may have done the sets of Rex's *The Conquering Power*, which was the film title of Balzac's *Eugénie Grandet*. (Here is a homeless thesis, waiting for some keen student to adopt.) The only time I ever met somebody who knew him was at the Telluride Film Festival at the ghost town in the Colorado mountains, when Ben Carré was the guest of honour and showed us *The Blue Bird*, which he had art directed for Maurice Tourneur around 1918. It was a fantastic production, but unfortunately Maeterlinck sends me to sleep. Ben was about ninety-something, so we talked about Percy Day, the great matte painter and film illusionist, whom he knew, and then I asked him if he had known Menessier. He was an old man and the fuse was slow burning, but suddenly he went off like a bomb with "Menessier! Menessier! Henri Menessier! Of course I know him! We came to America together! Henri Menessier!"

I tried to learn more, but that was all I could get out of him then. And now Ben is dead.

Menessier was a meticulous art director, not an inspired one: more theatrical than cinematic. Naturalism was the obvious solution for early film directors ("A tree is a tree! Shoot it in Griffith's Park!") except in Germany, where the mighty shadow of Max Reinhardt lay across the theatres and film studios; and to a lesser extent, because the northern light and the northern setting were dramatic in themselves, in Scandinavia. Nobody who ever saw Mauritz Stiller's *Sir Arne's Treasure*, or Victor Sjöstrom's *The Secret of the Monastery*, will ever forget their composition. But in France the French landscape and the French face seemed inexhaustible: no need for surrealism until Cavalcanti and Renoir came along, and not having enough money to finish their films made *La P'tite Lili*.

Rex Ingram was no innovator: his sets were massive, accurate and full of detail. According to Grant Whytock: "Sometimes Rex would decide that detail was what he wanted, and then he'd have Ray Moyer running around and there'd be shots of watches and snuff-boxes and spinets, like in that sequence with Lew Stone in the château in *Scaramouche*. But mostly he'd leave it to Johnny Seitz to get the set across. Rex was interested more in people."

My two instructors in the art department were John Birkel, the chief of construction, and Walter Pahlman, head of the trick and model department. Both of them were typical wood and metal craftsmen – spare, powerful, considering men not given to small talk, with deep-set eyes, and a skin with that curious sheen that betrays the metalworker. Of all film technicians, I admire the chief of construction most of all. I have schemed and intrigued to get the best of them on my films with a mixture of perfidy and cunning that other producers lavish on their leading ladies. These craftsmen, these engineers, these leaders of men, have to solve problems that introduce entirely new theories of dynamics into the handling of masses of steel and water and wood; and this has to be achieved in a controllable way for the safety of the actors and so that the scene can be repeated as often as necessary. A chief of construction thinks nothing of building out a camera platform over Victoria Falls, or of constructing a revolving steel-framed moving stairway to carry twenty people and the camera crew from heaven to earth. We trust our lives to him, and he never lets us down.

John Birkel was very insistent that he was a Luxemburger. Perhaps he always worked with Menessier. I never knew. He wore a hard-crowned straw hat with a ribbon at all times. He went swimming in it. He went to bed in it – or he looked as if he did.

Walter Pahlman was a much more devious man. He had a considerable sense of humour. I seem to remember he was quite an engineer. A slide rule seems to be his magic wand in my memory. I have said that he was an experienced trick-man, but I have the impression that he needed a cameraman more interested in optics than John Seitz. Johnny was a painter in light, in the tradition of drawings and gouaches by the masters. There were scenes in *Scaramouche* worthy of Watteau, in *Mare Nostrum* of Monet. The mythological scenes needed a much harsher treatment. They were planned and executed as classical; they should have been done by de Chirico. There should have been a direct relation between the fabulous Amphitrite legend and the brutal fate of Ferragut. Rex was soaked in art and the theatre, but he didn't have the sense to employ top talent at the time when he was at the top.

So Walter Pahlman to me was a technician, not an artist; he needed a good artist to lead him on to solve his problems. Even Harry couldn't do that. And Harry felt instinctively that this department of production was one where he could make his influence felt. But he was too much of a painter, too much of an impressionist. Douglas Fairbanks had been on the right track when he called in Joseph Urban for the sets of *Robin Hood*, and William Cameron Menzies for the silver silhouettes in *The Thief of Bagdad*. In *Mare Rostrum* Rex sensed what he wanted, but he didn't ransack Europe for the craftsman who would execute it for him. I learnt a lesson from that.

I write at such length and with such affection about the men and women I worked with at the Victorine, because I am telling you at the same time about the craftsmen I worked with when I was in a position to choose my own path and give them the opportunities they had been trained for, that they had been waiting for. I can never get over my luck in starting with a great man like Ingram and his Hollywood band. The target I aimed at made me a pain in the neck to a lot of people, but led a lot of actors, actresses, designers, composers and cameramen to heights of achievement that they wouldn't have otherwise attempted. I had worked as an apprentice with the best in Europe and America, but still I wanted more. When my chance came, I aimed high. We didn't always hit the Gold. But we were always on target.

A slim, serious young man with thinning blond hair, the beginnings of a moustache, and fierce blue eyes seems to be emerging from the 1920s. He stands about dreaming, as likely as not, but he can be extremely active when called upon. Occasionally people, even his friends, are fooled into thinking he is practical, but they soon find out their mistake. He takes the long view. He sees what is going on but makes no attempt to change things. He is widely read and has the sarcastic wit of a bookish young man. Sex has not troubled or enriched his life.

I learnt the language of my chosen profession (or did it choose me?) with incredible speed. In three months I knew the tricks of the trade of half a dozen departments. I was shooting and developing stills (under the eye of Tomatis), making enlargements, splicing film for Grant Whytock (checked by Ota), loading film for Gordon Avil, interpreting for Johnny Seitz, who as premier lighting cameraman of America was much sought after by Messieurs Debrie and Eclair to try out their movie cameras, and by Claude Rignon, inventor of the 3-D camera (the first of many), who wanted to shoot alongside our Bell & Howell and show us the difference. There wasn't any. I pored over blueprints, scale models and perspective drawings in the art department; I spent hot nights watching the walls of the water tank rising, and at the same time, in the trick workshop, the creation out of rubber and bath sponges and plaster of Paris, of the goddess Amphitrite and her cockleshell chariot with its four white horses, and in the carpenters' shops the building of the wooden wave-making machines which would line the big tank when it was finished and would be backed up by aeroplane propellors to blow the top off the waves. I ran errands in three languages and started sleeping in dressing rooms (legitimately this time) in order not to miss anything. Nobody bothered, so long as I was Harry's problem child. But when time-cards were introduced and a time-keeper's office installed and run by the accountant Langenfeldt (father of the famous cameraman), my salary suddenly shot up from a hundred frances a week to six times as much, and I was told that if I wanted to stop over nights I had to clock out first. It made no difference. The studio and the production was mine: my life, my work, my future, my love, my mistress. There was no room in my heart and head for anyone but my mother. To her I used to pour out the thoughts of this silent young man and the observations of his baby blue eyes.

Harry Lachman had campaigned successfully up to this point. He was general manager designate of the Victorine Studios, which were at present on lease to MGM for *Mare Nostrum*, and he had little doubt that he and Eddie Corniglion-Molinier would persuade Rex to make it his permanent base. He still had his apartment in Paris; he went up there from time to time to renew his contacts, and was on excellent terms with Laudy Laurence, the extrovert head of MGM in Paris. Some of the most talented members of Rex's class at Yale were with MGM.

I gradually became aware of a group of talented Americans in Paris. Howard Dietz was head of publicity and exploitation in New York and spent his spare time – and a good deal of the company's – writing the books and lyrics for musical comedies with Arthur Schwartz. I had met him with the Murphys at Antibes where they kept open house. Howard Strickling was part of this network; he was attached to Rex from Paris, and was to go back to Hollywood later on to be personal press representative of Louis B. Mayer. With Howard Dietz in New York were a bunch of brilliant and witty journalists, writers, and new publishers like Simon and Schuster. I knew many of them from the pages of *Variety*, the show-biz newspaper, and one day Howard introduced me to Frank Scully, a genuine *Variety* mugg, who thought as he wrote and wrote as he thought: a big, tall, handsome Irishman, with a massive face, like a Roman emperor. He talked in a continuous slow stream of words, made up of jokes, puns, remarks about politics and people, news items, while unexpected similes and new-minted metaphors crackled and exploded into the listener's ears. I can well believe the story about Frank, when he went to London at the height of the talkie boom, being entertained to lunch by Walter C. Mycroft, head of the scenario department at BIP, who said, over cigars: "Well now, Mr Scully, could we see some of your dialogue?"

To which Frank said:

"You've been listening to it for two hours. I'll bill you."

He was talking the first time that I met him at the Victorine, as someone might talk of discovering El Dorado, of a new novel by an American writer living in Paris, *The Sun Also Rises*. As I listened to him tell how, at last, America had produced a novelist who was not only the equal of the best, but who epitomized so accurately the new American that was emerging after the War, with such an ear for speech, with such a sensuous feeling for place, that he was going to create a whole new generation of Americans in his image, I became as excited as if I too were an American. He promised to lend it me. Howard was reading it now.

"What does the title mean?" I asked.

"I guess it's about a man," he said in his gentle drawl, "who gets his balls shot off in the war and by the end of the book finds that life is still worth living."

No English novelist that I knew, except Richard Aldington, would tackle a theme like that. I wished more than ever that I was American. They seemed to be going places. With balls.

I owe Frank many things. He made me a faithful reader of *Variety*, by which I mean the Chatter, the news items and the by-lines with an occasional item signed by Sime Silverman, the editor, himself. I learnt this new language.

I also read *The Times Literary Supplement* as a corrective and out of devotion to Aunt Ethel. Frank, in spite of his splendid appearance, was a martyr all his life to a bone disease that necessitated amputating first one leg, then the other. He never lost his spirit. He never stopped talking and writing. It's typical of him that after his first amputation he persuaded

Simon and Schuster (old school friends from Bryant High School in New York City) to issue the first books of crosswords ever published, and dreamed up the title *Fun in Bed* for a later collation.

He had come to the Riviera for his health, to interview Isadora Duncan, and to ghost a life of Bernard Shaw by Frank Harris. He stayed to write some of our best publicity stories and to feature me in one of them for the Associated Press as "College Trained Mop-Boy Joins Rex Ingram."

Like many autocrats, Rex surrounded himself with a court of oddballs, among them dwarfs, hunchbacks, apes and clowns.

The other day (in 1981, fifty-six years later) I had a date with Tom Luddy at a New York hotel in the East Fifties to meet Kenneth Anger, the genius who made *Scorpio Rising* and whose New York flat is a shrine to Valentino. Kenneth was very high at the prospect of weekending with Tennessee Williams in the Deep South. The décor of the hotel was early De Mille, somewhere about the period of *Male and Female*. I was just leaving (Tom was on the telephone of course), when Kenneth exploded across the lobby. "Have you read the new book about Rex Ingram? Thank *God* for it anyway! It's incredible that one of the *greatest* of film directors has been *ignored* and *forgotten*! But this *book*" – (I don't write like this ordinarily, Kenneth talks like this) "it's only a sort of *record*, for God's sake! Nothing about the dwarfs and hunchbacks!", he cried. Whereupon he vanished to catch his jet and left me meditating on his words.

Yes, I thought, there is certainly very little in Liam O'Leary's devoted and painstaking book that touches on the bizarre taste for deformity that was shared by my late master, Rex Ingram, with the court of the Infanta Margareta Teresa of Spain.

In one of the early scenes of *Mare Nostrum*, Captain Ferragut returns from a voyage to his home in Barcelona. When the fiacre draws up at the big stone house two dwarfs, who are sitting on a bench outside, see him and rush to greet him with the same affection as was shown to the other Ulysses by his hound Argos. They shoulder his baggage and march with it into the house – and out of the film. They are never seen again. This is their sole appearance after Grant Whytock had finished editing the film.

The hunchback dwarf, John George, had been a permanent member of Rex's troupe for some years. He was a well-known Hollywood character and a good actor. He had been in circus films and mystery films. I remember him in a wonderful Lon Chaney film, where the star played an armless knife-thrower. His target was Joan Crawford. She was about sixteen. John George, who was probably Mexican-Spanish or even Greek, had a beautiful face with fine eyes. He had been one of the strolling players in *Scaramouche*. Rex had dragged him, rather disastrously, into *The Prisoner of Zenda*, and had cast him, more successfully, in a sinister part in *Trifling Women*. I particularly remember his tall Parsee-like hat.

Shorty, as the second of the two dwarfs came to be called, because his name was Abu Ben Harish, was different. He was not an artist or a gipsy, but an Arab buffoon. He had been one of the court jesters of the Bey of Tunis, who had given him to Rex while he was filming exteriors for *The Arab*, Edgar Selwyn's play, which sparked off Rex's obsession with Arabs and Islam. Shorty was a misshapen dwarf, pretty strong, with a barrel-like body on short legs. His expression was mobile and he was shrewd. He was to be Rex's court jester for all the years I was with him.

It is hard to believe that Rex brought John George 8,000 miles for one scene in the film, but that was how it worked out. All his other scenes, mostly unscripted, ended up on the cutting room floor. Grant was a martinet when it came to the story.

"We never used to allow the director in the cutting room," he said firmly to me the other day. If Rex liked to have freaks around that was his business. He was the director. It was his picture. Grant was the editor. Snip! Snip! Face on the cutting-room floor.

Both Rex and his friend and fellow director Erich von Stroheim shared a taste for the bizarre and the erotic, the morbid and the perverse. What artist doesn't? Hans Andersen, for instance. Rex always asserted, keeping an eye out for Alice, that his favourite film was *Trifling Women*. A richly mounted Grand Guignol exhibiting the luscious charms of Barbara La Marr, it was all moonlight on tiger skins and blood dripping onto white faces, while sinister apes, poison, and lust kept the plot rolling. There was a famous Hollywood ape actor called Joe Martin.

"That Joe Martin!" says Grant. "He always had his hand up the girl's skirts, if you didn't watch him, and he was just crazy about Barbara. He bit Eddie Connelly in the arm and it took three of us twisting his balls to make him let go. Eddie wouldn't work with Joe after that and I don't blame him. We had to do the last scene with a split screen."

He refers to the final scene of the film when the old Baron, played by Edward Connelly, lies stiff and dead in his chair, before a table piled high with grapes, caviar and champagne, while Joe Martin climbs into the opposite chair and toasts the glassy-eyed corpse with a glass of wine.

Did I hear someone murmur something about the orgy in *Tales of Hoffmann*?

John George went back to Hollywood to a distinguished career in movies, but Shorty stayed on to be teased and provoked and kicked around like a football. He knew his place and invited the treatment. He was made of rubber. He had a huge head and torso, no legs to speak of and was smart. He wore Arab dress. If Rex wanted a butt for a joke, or just a punching ball, Shorty was always on hand. He made actors uneasy. Naturally, I have heard even Alice speak sharply about "Rex's damn dwarfs" getting more attention than the job in hand. Usually, however, she accepted them as one of Rex's aberrations and pretended they weren't there.

All this was everyday stuff to Kenneth Anger, whose mother had been wardrobe mistress on the Metro lot at the time when Valentino and Rex Ingram were the two rising stars on the Hollywood scene. For me it was the stuff of legend. It still astonishes me that men and women have lived their lives, been born and died, in the lifetime of the cinema. It is as if children suddenly discovered that their nursery walls contained the world. One day soon those innocent days when the American film-makers trekked across the country to Hollywood will be as difficult to imagine as the world of Molière and his theatre is to a drama student. But there are still men who remember when Westerns were being made by rugged pioneers like Thomas H. Ince, directed by young John Ford and his friends, a guard sitting by a cave in the Malibu Cliffs, which was the negative vault, with a shotgun to deal with hijackers. A few hours of California sunshine was long enough to complete a Western and a stream of negatives flowed east to the nickelodeons.

"And Hollywood, those days," says Grant Whytock, "wasn't even called Hollywood. That was a big orange farm belonging to some Easterner. She called it Hollywood after her Eastern property. But the township was first called Colegrove."

"Is that where Cole Avenue gets its name?" I ask, thinking how I cross it twice every day in my walk from my apartment on Waring Avenue to the Zoetrope Studios on North Las Palmas.

Walter Strohm backs up Grant. "Sure there used to be an orange grove there," he observes as we leave the San Diego Freeway and slide down the steep pitch to Hollywood and Vine. "I used to walk to Hollywood High through the orchards."

Walter Strohm is one of my oldest friends in movies, and he's a walking encyclopaedia on Hollywood, Pasadena and Los Angeles history. As for his knowledge and experience of Europe, Asia and Africa, in the service of MGM, it is extensive and peculiar. He appeared one day in 1925 at the Victorine Studios in vacation time, as if he had just strolled in from America – which he had. He was a year younger than me but he was already old in the business, and we took to one another. I have a still of Walter leaning against the old olive tree near the Lab. He wears an open-necked white shirt, knickerbockers belted at the knee, like Grant's – it must have been the fashion that year – and a completely natural, charming grin as he faces the camera. His family had been Los Angelenos for a couple of generations. His grandfather had been Fire Chief, and when Metro started to grow, his father became their location manager, for it wasn't easy in those early days to get permission to shoot scenes for films. The élite of Los Angeles and, above all, Pasadena, which was millionaire pasture (and where the fashionable racetrack was), looked down on film people as a lot of circus roustabouts, which of course is what we are, essentially. So Walter had grown up on the old Metro lot, running around and showing visitors the sights for which they tipped him five dollars, as I did. Now the new MGM had moved out of Hollywood to Culver City and I wanted to hear all about it. It was the first time someone my own age had swapped film gossip with me, and once again I noticed the frankness and generosity of Americans: they were incapable of meanness or shyness, they didn't care who you were, they only cared what you were and they expected the same from you. I compared them silently with my kind but class-conscious countrymen, with their oblique and tongue-tied approach to conversation, and decided there was no room for introverts in my profession. I would change all that. And so I did – for a time.

I was learning fast, thanks to the patience and kindness of my teachers. Even Harry, apparently the most impatient of men, was communicative to me about art. He took me with him when he went to call on Matisse in his flat on the Promenade, just where the road curves around the Citadel of Nice, the Point Rauba Capeu in Niçois ("Point Snatch Your Hat"). I had met quite a few painters on the coast, especially Bonnard, who was gentle and tongue-tied. He said to us: "A house painter said to me the other day, M. Bonnard, you're a painter. The first coat of paint, that goes on by itself, eh? But what about the second?"

Matisse was something new. He looked and talked like a professor and was methodical. He had card indexes for all his paintings, and we were engaged in photographing all the canvases he could round up, in Nice or in Paris, and reducing the stills to a size no bigger than postage stamps to stick on the cards. He appeared as a serious, bearded man with glasses, very methodical in his hours of work, which he had to be because he had no studio. He painted in the apartment and by noon the sun had come around the cliff and was shining through the windows. I remember his quiet voice whenever I see one of that series of paintings, the tall french windows opening onto the Promenade, and the models, like big cats, that he liked to paint over and over in different colour combinations. (Has there ever in the history of art been such a revelation of form and colour as the Matisse retrospective at the Grand Palais in Paris in the 1970s?) When it came to the great paintings and then the great collages, when the old wizard could no longer paint, it was like Beethoven bursting into colour with his Sixth and Ninth Symphonies.

I went to see Matisse not long before his death, in his big, airy flat in the Palais de Cimiez, above and beyond Nice. It was an old family hotel turned into apartments. He was sitting up in bed, in a clean white nightgown, cutting out these marvellous shapes in coloured paper and directing a troop of girls, students or friends, where to place them on the composition on the wall. Sometimes they had to climb a ladder to pin them where he indicated, and then he would look with pleasure at their legs. I had come to ask if he was interested in doing a new décor for the ballet *Schéhérazade*, with music by Rimsky-Korsakov, for a group of art films that I was planning. He was enthusiastic. "*Nous allons essayer cela! Nous allons faire un coup.*" But those films were never made.

All that summer of 1925, we were preparing for the trick shots and for the sea scenes of *Mare Nostrum*. I think all the dramatic and intimate scenes of the story had been shot before the summer solstice. I had not expected the high dry temperature of Nice in the summer. In those days we didn't go chasing the sun with consequent damage to our epidermis. The heat come on us gradually. But when it came it was oppressive. Metal became too hot to touch. We had to surround the camera with ice to keep the film emulsion from melting. The lunch hour was extended to two and three hours so that everyone could sleep or go swimming. I could no longer sleep in a dressing room. They were like ovens; there was no air-conditioning. It was accepted in the villas, if not in Nice, that in winter the marble floors were cold, in the summer the rooms were too hot. I was by now clocking-in like other workmen at the studio. Greatly daring, I took a bedroom in Nice, in a rather dubious house in the Rue du Paradis, central but cheap.

I knew few people, and those I did know had taken to the mountains. I had a few acquaintances on the beach. The English colony frequented the Plage Negresco and I had met George Busby and his wife, Alma. George was a champion high-diver, a fine swimmer and very social. He was an accountant at Barclays Bank. He had ambitions to be with Rex but feared to take the plunge; he looked before he leapt, as I was to find out later when we worked together. Alma was a beautiful woman, like a glorious basket of hot-house fruit. I eyed her and timidly envied George.

There were other friends. One afternoon as I was mooning up and down the Rue du Paradis, a huge yellow French open sports car, built on the same opulent lines as Mrs Busby, drew alongside me. It was not a Hispano-Suiza, but something like it. I know this will drive the automobile fans mad, and if there is a second edition of this book I will try to find the answer to this particular quiz, but it was a very superior model, with a great deal of wasted space, with an exhaust that went vroom-vroom like in a *Saturday Evening Post* story, but with a French accent. What *was* the name of the maker? Oh! well, no matter.

It was the Fieldings. I had vaguely seen them around on the lot as friends of Rex's. There were two boys and a girl. They were dressed carelessly, carefully, like English undergraduates of the period, when the tone was set by the Prince of Wales: light-hearted, sportive, long coloured woollen scarves and Fair Isle knitted sweaters. The sister was rather striking, with an oval face framed with dark curly hair and an angelic forehead. There was something exotic about them in spite of their Englishness and their Catholicism, for the boys had all been to one of the great English Catholic schools, Stoneyhurst or Ampleforth, that we used to play at rugger and who nearly always murdered us (no doubt remembering the Battle of the Boyne). When I met their mother I realized what the quality was. She was beautiful and imperious, Circassian perhaps, or Parsee, a widow and a great personality. They lived in a large villa above the railway line, on the way to California. It was called Château Fielding.

In the yellow bombshell (unfortunately anonymous) was a large man I hadn't seen before, who was older and tougher than any Fielding I knew, but obviously a Fielding. This was Mike, who lived in America and had been a crime reporter, it was said. Beside him sat his sister, Aline, giving me a dazzling smile. In the back seat was another girl, American, Eulalie (yes, girls really were christened Eulalie before the First World War), wedged between Claude and Gerald Fielding.

"We're going on a navel picking party," said Claude. "Want to come along?"

I was a shy young man and made even more so by my life as a devotee-recluse, so I made some excuse and didn't go along with these dazzling young people. But Aline saw through me, of course, and was determined to befriend me, and the boys were crazy about Rex and about films and I was a bit of a mystery, and obviously on the inside, so the next time they came to the studio they sought me out and carried me off to Château Fielding, which turned out to be a huge French villa, richly and heavily furnished, with a staff of servants and a glorious garden terraced out of the red rock of the hillside. It was on this occasion that I met Mrs Fielding.

They transformed my life. No young man ever had such thoughtful and generous friends. In fact, they treated me as one of the family and I spent more time there than at Cap Ferrat. The war scattered us, as it did everyone, and brought terror and disaster to some of us, but the Fieldings and especially Aline (or Arleen as she called herself when she changed her name on some craze for numerology) and Claude (who changed his name to Paul), will never be forgotten by me for their charm, their gaiety and their kindness at a time when I needed friends.

And then there came the great friend. His name was Leonti Planskoy and he had a League of Nations passport. Lee Planskoy when he talked of his year at the Massachusetts Institute of Technology, when he spoke of White Russia, and the escape of his family through Harbin; Leonti when he appeared operating an arc-light for Chris Bergsvik during the month's night shooting on the tank, where we filmed the sea scenes.

We had built towers around the tank for the arc-lights, but we were short of operators; not many French or Italians knew how to keep the flame of a burning arc constant (it's a question of adjustment of the distance between the glowing tips of the carbons), and Planskoy, who had been working on the first trials of panchromatic film in France, was welcomed by Johnny and Chris. He was on the top of a high wooden tower, and I saw one of the girl extras climb the ladder to join him. After a while the light spluttered and went out.

"What's up, Lee?" hailed Chris.

"Changing carbons," shouted Lee and soon I saw the girl retreat down the ladder.

"Was that Poupette who climbed your tower?" I asked Lee later.

"Yes."

"What did she want?" I asked somewhat foolishly.

"Well, what do you think? I kept the arcs steady as long as I could, but she was too good for me."

For the next ten years Lee was closely concerned with my – can't call it a career, unless you mean the careering from side to side of a runaway automobile with a somnambulist at the wheel. Lee was cynical, he was an idealist, he was a sensualist, he was Russian. He was sceptical, he was analytical, he was well read, he was a technician. Having been hauled out of Russia at the Revolution by his family, he was naturally sympathetic to Lenin and Communism. He was always quoting Lenin's dictum: "Communism is Socialism plus Electricity", and he watched the progress of the great hydro-electric scheme at Dnieperstroi with personal concern. With him I went to all the great Soviet silent films, admiring their vigorous images, dynamic cutting and forthright acting, more than their political preaching. We talked of these films – such as Pudovkin's *Mother*, and Turin's *Turksib* – as art and discussed their dynamics from an intellectual point of view, not realizing that the films were intended for a population largely illiterate and susceptible only to a bombardment of images. What humanity there is in *The General Line*, what humour in *Bed and Sofa*, what lyricism in *Earth*! To see them now is to realize the idealism and hopes of the Revolution. See them, and weep with Pasternak and Mandelstam for what could have been – for what was, for a time.

Dear Lee! I can see him now, seated at one of the little rickety tables of the café on the corner of the Boulevard Victor Hugo and the Rue de France. He is talking, and the constant cigarette in his long, nervous fingers stained with chemicals and nicotine scatters ash over his suit, which he brushes off from time to time. He has a pale, mobile face, large and oval, with a long, inquisitive nose and eyes that are usually narrowed to Oriental slits, though whether this is due to a trick of heredity or the smoke of his eternal cigarettes, I can't be sure. He speaks several languages fluently and reads all the foreign newspapers, so he is remarkably well misinformed. His English has no trace of an American accent, although he learnt it in Boston. He flattens his vowels in an amusing way, and for years I longed to come across a brand of vodka he spoke about, which was steeped with red paper in a bottle until it became the colour of the paper. It was only the other day that I concluded that Lee was talking about red peppers, not paper.

I met Lee at a fortunate time for me. Rex's world was a separate little world that revolved around him. It was a selfish world, if you like. Rex was an artist, but an amateur artist, a show-off; a bit of an actor, because of his good looks, but not a good actor; a showman, certainly, with a sure instinct for and appreciation of the theatrical. He was loyal to his likes and dislikes, and his friends were loyal to him. This fascinating new art, this Eldorado for showmen, this Gospel according to Mack Sennett, had attracted to the Pacific coast a mixed crowd of people of all ages and experience, but there were very few Rex Ingrams among them (Alan Crosland perhaps, or Mitchell Leisen). This formidable young man – he made his first film, and wrote the scenario too, in 1916, when he was nineteen – had inspired admiration among his fellow technicians and alarm among the executives of Universal by his sophistication, his classical contempt for bourgeois points of view, his outspoken anti-Semitism, and his indulgence in frankly erotic and perverse sequences which dared the censors to intervene. Of course the censors did intervene, the Studio censors, and many were the clashes between Rex and the heads of Universal before they parted company. Rex made Metro's first big success, *Shore Acres*, and had already been promised *The Four Horsemen of the Apocalypse* by June Mathis, the Irishwoman who was artistic head of the new company; but he still had to deliver one more quickie feature (they were five-reelers) to Universal, and according to Grant Whytock, "he sure left them a few problems if they wanted to put the picture out." I asked Walter Strohm what he thought about Rex. "Oh, he was like a god to us, Micky. Me and Bob Carlisle – he was Grant's brother-in-law – were always around the studio lots from the time we were kids. My father worked for Laemmle at Universal, when Irving Thalberg was a secretary there. Later on, he moved over to Metro: Universal was the first of the great, big busy assembly-line studios, producing and renting. They shipped out East more than fifty reels of finished film a week. It was a factory. The old Metro was a little company. They never had a film in the big time, playing first run on Broadway, until Rex made *Shore Acres*. It had been a Broadway hit and Rex made it a good picture. Then when he made *The Four Horsemen*, using fourteen cameras on the war scenes and shooting a million feet of film, he could have anything he wanted. He didn't change. He went on in his old way, with his old friends, with Grant and Ota cutting his pictures, doubling as assistant and script-girl when occasion arose. He used to have a house on Sunset Boulevard, next door to the Catholic church, and I'd see him under the pepper trees smoking his pipe, strolling down to the Metro lot on Cahuenga Boulevard. When I came to Europe and joined you all on *Mare Nostrum,* he was just the same. He sent messages to my father and gave me good advice about going to UCLA and working part-time at MGM to keep in touch. Which I did."

"In the old days did Metro have the Lion as their trademark?"

I was thinking of the MGM notepaper I knew so well, with Leo the Lion framed in the motto *"Ars Gratia Artis"*, as he is on the screen.

"No. They had a parrot."

"A parrot!" I squawked.

"It was animated and it threw up the letters M-E-T-R-O one by one."

I digested this pearl in silence. A parrot!

"Do you remember Harry Lachman's parrots?" I asked out of the blue.

"Of course I do. He had two big coloured ones, all red and blue."

"Those were macaws."

"And a little white one who used to raise his crest when he was excited."

"The sulphur-crested white cockatoo."

Harry had stands for them with drinking and eating cups, and they used to scream under the olive trees until the typists complained. He was devoted to them and they to him, and when he was talking to the big coloured macaws he looked remarkably like one, with his beaky nose and sidelong glance. He knew it and it amused him. Harry was a generous warm-hearted man and he hadn't an atom of vanity about him. He ignored what he had achieved and was determined to become a film director. But he never let Rex know. Not then.

Lee Planskoy was my antidote to the politics of this little kingdom, just as later on Hein Heckroth was my contact with European art, when England, my England, threatened to smother me, or starve me out. Lee felt with me that all the arts were part of this new art of the cinema and it was our job to know what was going on and bring nothing but the best to our storytelling. We knew that Rex was undecided what film to make next. We had spent weeks shooting the ship scenes and the submarine scenes and the ship models and finally the beautiful allegorical scenes (in the big studio) when Captain Ulysses Ferragut sinks down through the weeds and drowned ships into the arms of the goddess Amphitrite. It necessitated wires and harnesses and flying tackle and all sorts of properties, as well as a big tank of water, double-sided with glass, for the camera to shoot through. Grant was getting fretful. "If Rex doesn't get what he wants soon, we'll run out of film. We're shooting nine to one for these slow-motion effects. We'll never be able to match the negative! We'll end up with 150,000 feet of film just for this one sequence." And we did.

Meanwhile I was writing the final titles. Someone had to do it. Grant and Ota were up to their eyes in film, Rex was lazy, Willis was in New York working on the script of Rex's next picture, *The World's Illusion*; so the chore fell to me. Can a duck swim? Grant had recently invented the direct cut for reaction. It was the custom in silent films to show the actor talking for a few frames, then insert a title so that his words could be read, then cut back to the same actor as he finished speaking. Grant found that it was more direct and often worked better to cut to the other person in the scene, or to a general reaction, from the title itself. He had often done this in *Scaramouche*. But of course this put a whole new emphasis on the words, and the titles had to be rewritten. So here was I, after six months in the business, writing and rewriting the story of a major film. Did I doubt my capacity? Not for a moment! I would trudge up to the villa with my pages of titles and demand Rex's approval or advice. We shared a taste for the mystical, macabre works of Arthur Machen, of which I had already discovered a complete set in Rex's library, so there was a bond between us; and although he had no time to write the titles himself, he was always ready to spend time with me (except one day when I stumbled upon him with his arms full of Alice).

Besides spoken titles and editorial titles (like "Later that evening . . ."), we had an unusual number of narrative titles on *Mare Nostrum*, and Rex was prepared to spend hours over the right word, or the rhythm of a sentence. The other day, Walter and I (he was driving me from Hollywood for a weekend at Yosemite) chanted together: "Between Europe and Africa, stretching from Asia to the Atlantic Ocean lies the Mediterranean, land-locked and tideless, known to the ancients as Mare Nostrum – OUR SEA."

When Louis B. Mayer saw the completed film, he cabled Rex: "It's a travelogue, take out a thousand feet and you have a swell picture." It was like a cold douche for the lotus-eaters, but Mayer was right. Grant made the cuts by telegraph, using the negative key-numbers as references for the negative cutters in New York and the picture opened on schedule. It got good reviews, but was not a big success with the public. The timing of the story was unhappy. The American public were sick of tragedy about War, they wanted a new approach and got it with King Vidor's *The Big Parade*. It was probably the reception given to *Mare Nostrum* that turned Rex away from another war film and drove him at short notice into making *The Magician* by W. Somerset Maugham, for I can't think of any other reason, except that it was a sort of horror film, a macabre plot of the kind the Germans did so well, with a chief character based upon Aleister Crowley. I know that Rex really wanted to make another Somerset Maugham story, *The Moon and Sixpence*, also owned by MGM, and much later it was made into a talkie by Al Lewin, starring George Sanders as Gauguin. I only wish he had. He had the combination of talents and also the sheer bloody-mindedness to put such a rich character on the screen. Whom did he think of to play Gauguin, I wonder? There was no language barrier in those silent days. he had the pick of Europe to choose from . . . Conrad Veidt?

But to make that story into a film would have meant a truce with Mayer. MGM had been advised by June Mathis to buy the book, and she was no longer a supporter of Rex's. She would have no part in his personal feud with Mayer. And *Ben-Hur*, starring Ramon Novarro, Rex's discovery, was going to be a huge success. June Mathis went over to the big battalions.

Walter Strohm tells me she spent a lot of time on the Culver City lot when he went back to Hollywood, after spending the summer with us in 1925. Production was at its peak; there hadn't been anything like the chariot race for spectacle since the huge Italian epic films, when Enrico Guazzoni staged *Messalina* and Pastrone made *Cabiria* – which was, I suppose, the reason why MGM first decided to make *Ben-Hur* in Rome and then changed their minds. Walter's father was scouring California for Roman locations, and Walter's own triumph was the discovery of a location for the Appian Way – near San Diego.

Walter went on to follow Rex's advice about going to college and getting his degree, while keeping in touch with the film business. As a matter of fact he never lost touch – how could any boy in California in the twenties? – and I would hear his name from time to time over the next fifteen years as he marched steadily up the production stairway of MGM and became chief of the whole production office in the great days when MGM was releasing a new picture every week of the year, with MORE STARS THAN THERE ARE IN HEAVEN! As my own name became better known, I would hear of Walter and get messages and tales about him, for he was in the middle of every crisis that rocked MGM from *Trader Horn* to *Mogambo*, from *Quo Vadis?* to the second *Ben-Hur*. But it is only now in 1981, at his house looking down on Laguna beach, that we are able to swap yarns, and say, "Do you remember?", and ask Grant Whytock and Howard Strickling over the telephone to corroborate some episode.

Walter's family have been Los Angeles residents for five generations, counting all the grandchildren. His grandfather, Tom Strohm, married in December 1876 and was Fire Chief of the beautiful little city of L.A. His son, Walter's father, joined Laemmle at Universal in 1919, as I have mentioned, when young Irving Thalberg was planning to marry into Metro. Not many people knew their way around California in those days; in the film business they were mostly incomers from the East; so Strohm just naturally became location manager. And Walter just naturally followed his dad, when he moved over first to the Metro lot, then to Culver City. He admits to me that he appeared at the Victorine that summer just like a little dog following his master. Just like me. Rex was the greatest that he knew, and he wasn't going to lose touch with him while he was in Europe. He came to stick around and sit at Rex's feet. Just like me. We have both done a lot of silly things in our lives, but we both agree that was the most sensible thing we ever did. A man needs a master to look up to, to set standards of achievement in his profession. Rex was our master.

Mare Nostrum had been a costly film, mainly because of the time it took to shoot. Usually Rex worked quickly on locations, scattered from Valencia to Naples; the delays while we were refitting the studios and the lab, the establishment of our own trick department, and all the night exteriors had taken us over budget. We had been nine months on the film. The final cost, I seem to remember from a conversation in the office, was $650,000, a huge sum. *Scaramouche* cost less that half that. This was probably another reason why Rex got quickly on with another film. He was being pressed to buy the Studio (I am not sure whether MGM bought it for Rex, or whether his advisers formed a company to buy it, which is more likely), and obviously as the owner of the studio, he was in a strongly independent position.

I knew nothing of all this at the time, though I overheard a lot. I am piecing it together now, in the light of all the other gallant attempts at independence that I have shared in: Michael Balcon's 1930's season with Gaumont-British at Shepherd's Bush, Korda's spectacular invasion of England and the building of Denham Studios, Arthur Rank's bid for world empire during the war; the founding by Powell and Pressburger of Independent Producers, the return of Korda after the war, the decline and fall of Rank in the fifties, and now in the eighties the domination by the far-sighted, cool-headed George Lucas with *Star Wars* and his block-busting partnership with Steven Spielberg, which owes so much to Walt Disney; and finally, the daring risks run by Francis Ford (*Apocalypse*) Coppola in the cause of independence, with his fiercely personal studios in Hollywood, where I am writing this book. I walk to work each morning from my apartment near the Paramount Studios passing the old Metro lot on the way, identifying with those giants whom I knew fifty years ago.

I remember *The Magician* because it was the first film on which I worked from start to finish. I think that Rex wrote the script of the film, but I can't be sure. I may have had a hand in it myself. The decision to make it was certainly taken before my father opened the hotel for Christmas 1925. It was the first Christmas I had ever spent away from my mother.

Grant stayed on with Ota to edit the film: he remembers that they were packed and ready to go home when Rex asked them to stay. Others had gone back to Hollywood already: Chris, the electrical gaffer, Ray Moyer (who later got an Academy Award for his set dressing), Walter Pahlman. My bosom friend Walter Strohm had gone in November, back to UCLA and MGM. But I had seen, once and for all, what it meant to be making a feature film with a group of expert craftsmen, led by a director who knew what he wanted, and nothing else could satisfy me until I achieved that aim myself.

I have seen Rex Ingram's *The Magician* recently, in the private projection theatre of a Hollywood collector. It was a good print and I was surprised at how little I was surprised. It was a horror film made at a time when very few were made in America. I suppose Tod Browning, with *The Unholy Three*, and, later, *Freaks* (1932), and Rex's own *Trifling Women*, were the only outstanding achievements in that genre. Germany led the field with Murnau's *Nosferatu*, Paul Wegener's *The Golem*, and Robert Wiene's *The Cabinet of Dr Caligari*. Of course, Rex had seen these and many others, and he yearned to emulate them. But Maugham's story defeated him; and his own good taste.

Here it is.

Metro-Goldwyn (without the Mayer) presents Rex Ingram's production of *The Magician*, directed by Rex Ingram. The usual cast and credits before the film. Opening title: "Paris". Fade in a shot of the Place de la Concorde, which both Grant and Harry Lachman claim to have shot. There had been an argument between Harry and Johnny Seitz about whether the obelisk in the shot should be framed on the left of the picture or dead centre. The centre party won. *Fade out.* We are in a large studio on the Left bank, a sculptor's studio. Alice is working on a gigantic clay image of a smiling faun, about four metres high and weighing half a ton. Rex had commissioned it from Dardé, whose powerful forms impressed the art world. Harry found him for the film.

With Alice in the studio is her girlfriend (played by Gladys Hamer, an English actress), who is supposed to supply comic relief. She doesn't have much opportunity. Almost immediately the armature supporting the great shaggy head of the faun breaks. The clay cracks (suspense shot of the break in the clay widening, about to fall). It falls, half-burying Alice and injuring her back. She is paralysed. A doctor, a friend of the family, a thankless part played by Firmin Gémier, the director of the Odéon Theatre (another of Harry's friends), calls in a young surgeon (played by Ivan Petrovic) who, in a brilliantly done operation sequence, relieves the pressure on the spine. He falls in love with Alice's lively spine, and in two dissolves and a fade they are courting in the Jardins du Luxembourg.

Short pause to introduce Ivan Petrovic.

I never knew whether the charming and polished Ivan was Yugoslav, Polish, or Ukrainian, and it doesn't really matter, except to the encyclopaedists. He was a dull actor, handsome, good-mannered, anxious to please, whose clothes never seemed to fit him. Alice rather fancied him, and he must have been a relief after the spoilt child Novarro and the heavy

Latin *maître d'hôtel* Valentino. Not that Alice couldn't take them all in her stride if she'd cared to. But she didn't care, although she enjoyed playing them off against Rex's bits of nonsense. She was a one-man woman. Anyway, Petrovic was cast as the brilliant young surgeon-lover and wandered through the subsequent scenes in the manner of an innocent bystander caught up in an insurrection.

New readers start here.

At Belfort, in the Vosges, stands a famous statue of a lion and there is a replica of him at one of the gates of Paris. A fair is held there every year, and the square is filled with tourists and Parisians. Rex, like most film directors, adored fairs, carnivals, circuses and carousels. I would like to state here and now, that the sight of any young director's carousel shots, except those in Hitchcock's *Strangers on a Train*, makes me want to throw up. It's too much like taking candy from a baby. So, prefaced by the inevitable montage sequence from Grant Whytock, our party meets Oliver Haddow, a sinister figure in regulation costume for wizards: black slouch hat, black cloak, ebony cane and very hypnotic eyes – Paul Wegener, the German actor who had recently played and directed *The Golem*, an ancient Jewish legend, and made a huge success of both chores. His formidable physique had been the basis of the Golem's shape, like a child's grotesque toy, hacked out of wood with a pocket-knife, crowned with a square mop of hair that fell to his shoulders. I feel sure that Rex would have played Conrad Veidt in the part, if he had not recently seen *The Golem*, and then I should have met Connie at the time when he was reputed to be the most brilliant actor and most interesting heterosexual in the German theatre. But Wegener was chosen, and so we were saddled with a pompous German whose one idea was to pose like a statue and whose one expression to indicate magical powers was to open his huge eyes even wider, until he looked about as frightening as a bullfrog.

The figure of Haddow, in Maugham's book, was supposed to be based on Aleister Crowley, who had quite a vogue among impressionable undergraduates: he dabbled in sorcery and claimed to have celebrated the Black Mass with conspicuous success, several well-authenticated demons being known by his disciples to be his familiars. If Crowley himself had played the part it might have been more entertaining. The sheer eccentricity of the man would have carried him through, as it did Captain Knight in *I Know Where I'm Going*. Crowley, besides being monstrous and outrageous, was also witty and charming, with a capacity for drinking other hard drinkers under the table with mixtures such as absinthe spiked with calvados. But Wegener, alas, contributed nothing to his part but a theatrical presence, a formal European politeness and clouds of smoke from cigars which would never have passed the local pollution test. He rarely spoke on the set, but every so often his "*Ali, meine Zigarren!*" would send his Turkish manservant scurrying to bring a new stogie which he would light with anxious care, while Wegener puffed, his eyes closed to Oriental slits.

The sequence at the fair marks my debut as one of Rex's clowns. My angelic seriousness must have amused him, for he suddenly announced on the night of the shooting that I was to be included as comedy relief, Gladys Hamer presumably having been found wanting. I was clapped into a make-up chair, covered in Leichner make-up, had my head shaved, was allotted a battered suit of clothes, a pair of glassless spectacles, a toy balloon, and a bag of bananas – I have said that Rex's comic sense was rudimentary – and was told to be funny. I tried. There is a still of the cast of *The Magician* all lined up like a lot of dummies before one of the fairground booths. Wegener is posing for his portrait by a silhouette artist. Opposite him Alice, in mink and toque, is staring, already half under his influence. Petrovic, next to her, glares protectively in a grey Homburg. Gémier does his best to look casual: he is used to being the centre of any group. Gladys is pulling a funny face. Last, and most certainly least, is Mike Powell, the college-trained mop-boy turned actor, the man who made it to in front of the camera from behind it:

"Go get 'em, Micky!" breathes Gordon Avil as he runs a tape out to my ear, "go act 'em off the screen!"

I stand there in my morning coat and baggy trousers, my mouth open (I was a sufferer from adenoids in my early years), staring through those false spectacles at the silhouette artist. What is passing through my mind at this incredible moment in my career? Nothing. But at least I know where the camera is. The Magician steps forward and presents Alice with his silhouette image: "With my compliments." She reacts to his hypnotic eyes. The scene changes to a snake charmer's tent, where the Magician again demonstrates his power. A pretty Arab girl (one of Rex's entourage and actually a Cuban, Rosita Ramirez) is bitten by a deadly viper.

"How on earth did you get Rosita to react so well?" I asked Grant, who directed the necessary close-up.

"Stuck a pin in her ass," he said with modest pride.

"Did you often direct pick-up shots for Rex?" I asked.

"All the time. When Rex was really interested there was nobody like him, but he got bored easy. Take *Where the Pavement Ends*. It . . ."

"Was that shot in Tahiti?" I asked.

"Florida. Florida and Cuba, and we only went to Cuba because of the waterfalls. That's what I wanted to tell you about. There isn't a flatter state in the USA than Florida, and here was this waterfall sequence where Novarro chucks himself over, so we went to Cuba. Right behind the hotel where we were staying there were some low falls, great for close-ups. So Rex shot Alice and Ramon and said to me and Johnny, 'You fellows go find a high waterfall,' and went back to bed. So we took a car as far as we could go and then the locals took us as far as they could and then we went on as far as we could, but we couldn't find those falls. So we started back home – and suddenly, bingo! There are the tallest falls you've ever seen and there's only an hour of sunshine left. So we doubled Alice and Ramon – Hell! it was only long shots! And we came back to the hotel around midnight, dead beat, and Rex was playing billiards with some local political guy and he says: 'Did you find the waterfall?' and we say, 'Yes,' and that's the famous death falls sequence of *Where the Pavement Ends*."

My methods are different: the difference between the artist and the craftsman. Rex couldn't shoot anything that didn't interest him. I am interested in everything. In Rex's place, I would have vanished with a local guide into the Cuban jungles until I found the waterfall, come back and dragged my reluctant company of actors and technicians to the scene. Heroic stuff, but the end product is the same by both methods. I had seen the film and been moved by the passionate ending. It justified the means.

To return to *The Magician*.

The Magician pursues Alice and forces his attentions on her. Using the faun's head, which lies broken in a corner of his studio, as an image of lust and power, he conjures up a sort of witches' sabbath, staged by Stowitts, the American dancer. He also danced the faun. Stowitts had been Pavlova's partner for several Latin-American seasons, and had an amazing body and an imagination of the very first order. We built a huge set of rocks and trees on the studio lot and shot nights for nearly a month, using twenty boys and twenty girls, naked except for a few gauzy rosebuds. It was a memorable session. Most of the girls came from a summer school up at St Paul, run by and for pupils of Miss Margaret Morris. They found the experience of a pagan film set highly enjoyable after the classical restraint of Miss Morris's studio on Primrose Hill. One of the young male dancers, James, has remained a friend all my life.

Rex became bored with the Faun Dance after a few conversations with Stowitts, and Harry Lachman directed the rest of the sequence. It was his debut as a creative director. His talent for pictorial images had a cutting edge to it: some of his images were memorable, and he persuaded John Seitz to go further in lighting effects than anything that great lighting cameraman had done since *The Four Horsemen*. When I was in Niagara not long ago, I was introduced to a collector who possessed a print of the Inferno sequence of *Dante's Inferno*, which Harry directed for Fox in 1935. It starred Spencer Tracy. The influence of our Faun Dance sequence was very striking. Shot for shot, images and style were the same. The cameraman was Harry's Hungarian-born cameraman from Paris, Rudolf Maté, who had shot *La Belle Marinière* with Jean Gabin. But the lighting was Harry's, as I could testify. If he had stayed in Europe, Harry would have become one of the Masters. His individuality was stamped on every composition in his films. He followed no one. He blazed his own trail. But in the talkie Thirties, when Hollywood had monopolized the new medium, and prizes of all kinds were glittering on the trees, America was the goal for talented Europeans; and although Harry was born a Chicago Jew, he was one of the most European of artists – far too European to survive an encounter with a vulgar and brutal genius like Darryl F. Zanuck.

Alice and Haddow, of course, appeared in the Faun Dance as virginal victim and satanic sorcerer. Rex always liked to scandalize the front office with a touch of eroticism, or a pinch of anti-Semitism, and with Stowitts giving an excuse – "He's a great classical dancer" – Rex and Harry went as near to raping Alice as that stately lady ever got on the screen. Alice enjoyed it thoroughly and looked about sixteen in floating white chiffon. In fact, we all enjoyed ourselves hugely; and the Fielding brothers, as fauns, had fewer inhibitions than anybody and were greatly in demand. It was the start of Gerald's career. There's nothing like a bit of rape and nudity to get the adrenalin flowing.

Back to the tale. Alice is about to be married to the young Doctor, when she disappears, hypnotically summoned by the Magician. A telegram arrives. She has married him!

Title: Monte Carlo.

An unknown gambler is winning at all the tables, his companion a beautiful blonde who plays his stakes for him. Guess who! They are recognized by the faithful Petrovic, and his even more faithful friend Firmin Gémier, who have been turning Europe upside down looking for Alice, when any scenario writer could have told them Monte Carlo was the place to look, besides being within sight of Somerset Maugham's villa at Cap Ferrat. (My father used to play billiards with Willy, but after complaining that not one of the Villa Mauresque's billiard cues was straight and bringing his own cue, he was never asked again.) The dogged duo track the Magician and his hypnotized victim to his lair, a lonely tower in the mountains, where the caretaker is – guess what? – a dwarf, a hunchbacked dwarf called Henry Wilson, especially imported from England to be the subject of Rex Ingram's sport. Like all dwarfs he was always anxious to prove that he was as good as, and better than a sound, ordinary man. In the course of the climax to the film he was soaked to the skin, rolled in mud and water, hurled off rocks, hung in chains and was finally blown up in the explosion that demolished the castle – all to his great satisfaction and Rex's sadistic amusement. (Claude Fielding found the English dwarf infinitely entertaining and would lead him on to extol his prowess in words which he would then repeat for us verbatim: "Didja see us last night, Mr Fielding? Oh! we didn't 'alf 'ave a time of it. I 'ad the clothes all ripped off me and they 'ung me up in a tree and 'ad ravens croaking at me, very weird like, and there was me swinging in the air more than 'alf a hower while they got the wind machines and the hoses on me. Fell off twice. See that scar? I got that in the fight when they put me in the cupboard. I'm all covered in scabs. Real beauties. Got a cracker on my back. Want to see it?"

It is hardly necessary to state that our hero arrives at the tower in the nick of time, just as Alice, a virgin bride, natch, is about to give her blood as one of the conventional but necessary ingredients of the Elixir of Life. In a murderous struggle between the rivals, the Magician falls into his own furnace and is carbonized. The tower burns, and blows up as the lovers escape through the village below. As the Magician dies his power over Alice does too. She recognizes and remembers her faithful lover and true husband.

We all had a swell time making *The Magician*, but looking back it was a mistake for Rex to write his own adaptation of the book. Words are concrete things. Craftsmen tend to take them literally: that is why I and my fellow craftsmen hold frequent discussions over the script during pre-production, all heads of departments present, so that they can ask questions of the director, so that he can explain what he has or has not got in mind, how he proposes to interpret the words on the paper, with their assistance. *The Magician* was a naturalistic production. They took a tall tale and made it taller by telling it in real exteriors and natural settings. I am pretty sure that Rex originally dreamed of something on the lines of Murnau's *Faust* or *Nosferatu*. In that case the décor should have been imaginatively unreal from the opening shot. John Seitz's elegant and beautiful lighting, based upon close study of the Old Masters, was wrong for a piece of Gothic horror like *The Magician*, which called for the German Karl Freund's, or Hoffman's use of light and shadow. At the time I was too young and inexperienced to formulate these ideas, but I felt them and I had the German film-makers to guide me and reassure me and lead me finally to *The Red Shoes* and *The Small Back Room* and *The Tales of Hoffmann*.

Grant Whytock kindly allowed my performance as an actor to remain in the final cut, but my hair has never recovered from the shaving. I have been bald every since and so have suffered none of the pangs of other men as their barber looks more and more contemptuous of their thinning locks. As Frank Scully wrote in his book in 1955: "Among us lotus eaters of the Côte d'Azur was one Micky Powell, who looks much the same now as he did then, thirty years ago", and he printed a photograph to prove it. Now another twenty-five years have passed and – like Colonel Blimp – I still haven't changed. But I'll print no photograph.

Another lesson I absorbed, rather than learned, from *The Magician*, was to distrust, in films of imaginative power, a mixture of studio settings and location shooting. The strange little hill towns in the back country of Nice – Peille, Tourette, Sospel – half Italian, half Moorish, and totally Mediterranean – would seem ideal settings for a fantasy, but the village street finally constructed for the film, dominated by the lonely Magician's tower, was far more successful than all the romantic jumble of the Alpes Maritimes. Much later, when I came to the Côte d'Azur after the war to shoot exteriors for *The Red Shoes*, I showed how to use a fairytale landscape in a fairytale way; but when I made *Black Narcissus*, I had made the decision to make it a studio production in order to create and control the atmosphere from start to finish. No matching of studio sets with real exteriors shot in Nepal! And yet, when it was done, it was so convincing that people who knew the Himalayas have told me where the picture was shot. "We recognized the Palace and the costumes of the people." I happen to know that Rex loved that film, for he told me so, when I saw him for the last time.

About this time, Easter 1926, I saw my first British film unit in action, and I was proud of them. The film was *Roses of Picardy*, a story of World War I, and it was directed by Maurice Elvey, England's top director, who had made many films in the South of France. His yearly scheme, a sound one, was to come down to the coast with his unit in the winter, and shoot the exteriors for three or four films in the blessed Riviera sunshine, usually thrillers by writers like A. E. W. Mason or E. Phillips Oppenheim. This took about six weeks, after which he returned to England and shot the interiors of the films at Cricklewood Studios in London, home of Sir Oswald Stoll's film company, frequently using the same cast, or alternating the villain's part for the hero's with actors like Warwick Ward or Gerald Ames. But what had Picardy to do with the South of France? Simple. We had built a picturesque village street for *The Magician* and left it standing as a permanent set on the studio lot, in the Hollywood manner. An efficient and well-informed production manager like Victor Saville soon heard of this and leased the setting and its facilities for a month.

An art director appeared – probably one of the Arnold brothers – and the village was tranformed into a black-and-white Normandy job. In three weeks' time everything – costumes, props, and drilled soldier extras – was ready. Elvey arrived with every shot worked out. Saville supplied all and more than the script demanded. Shells burst, buildings collapsed, a 1917 bi-plane swooped down along the street, the pilot's gunner firing his machine guns over the panic-stricken peasants; in four days they had wrapped the whole job up and gone back to England. I was thrilled and impressed. Elvey's dynamic presence had shown me another side of film direction: no remote controller, he was in the thick of it, imposing the tempo on the action, getting what he wanted the first time, working to a plan and a slender budget. Saville's tall figure, in lounge suit and an English felt hat, was impressive in a different way. He was the planner, the chief of staff, whose job was to provide the director with everything he would need before he asked for it. He never hurried, he was supremely confident, he was everywhere at once, and it was obvious that he looked upon the correct direction of the men and the things as just part of an efficient operation, properly conducted, to show a profit as soon as the negative was delivered to the distributors. I was watching the development of a brilliant producer and director, cool-headed, detached, kind and thoughtful, meticulous and far-seeing, who would never make an unsuccessful film, nor direct a good one.

Louis B. Mayer is said to have liked *The Magician* when he screened it, but it was not a success. I suppose it was almost the first of those mysterious hybrids, an American film made in Europe with a script which satisfied neither public. Curious that Rex, who was so sure of himself in Hollywood, where he was a young giant, should lose his touch in Europe, where his reputation as a film-maker was immense. All the cleverest artists in Europe longed to be asked to write, or design, or direct films, and they came in pilgrimage to Nice to talk to the Master. Perhaps this made him humble and unable to resolve his own problems.

For this was to be a fateful year for Rex. It was in the interests of a great many people that he should stay in Europe and make the Victorine a Mecca for film-makers. He was surrounded by people who were bound to agree with him, and Rex had always thrived on opposition. He had been in Europe long enough to be uncertain of his aims. In Hollywood there was no uncertainty. You did it for the money. Even Marcus Loew, the almost legendary tycoon at the head of MGM, couldn't save Rex if he had three failures in a row. Rex went back to the USA to confer with him and his associates in New York.

The first intimation that I had about their decision came from Harry.

"Powell! I've got a job for you. Do you know what a Trappist monk is?"

"They take a vow of poverty and silence, I think."

"Right! You're going to be one for a bit. Here's your train ticket to Montélimar. Here's the address of the monastery. They are bound by their rules to receive you for three days. Learn what you can and try to take some stills. It may get you kicked out. Photographers are forbidden, but you'll have to risk that. You look such a fool that you'll probably get away with it."

I looked cautiously at the ticket. It was for the round trip, so I wasn't being taken for a ride. My spirits rose. My mother had written to me suggesting that we meet in Paris to save money. She had a lot to tell me about the farm she had found for sale at the top end of Poole Harbour. Perhaps I could combine the two trips and MGM would pay. I confided in

Harry. He agreed. He probably paid the difference out of his own pocket. Being Harry, his bark was worse than his bite. He was always doing kindnesses for people who made ambition their excuse for climbing on his shoulders.

"Harry! Why does Rex want the dope about an obscure order of monks? Is it for a film?" I asked.

"*The Garden of Allah*."

"D'you mean the novel by Robert Hichens?"

"That's it. Don't you approve?"

"It's tripe and it's been done before."

"And it'll be done again. MGM owns it."

"Do you mean to say that Rex and Metro have agreed that as his next picture?"

"Yes. Now bugger off and catch the train."

Robert Hichens was a best-selling novelist once. It is hard to believe it now. He specialized in second-rate plots of *femmes fatales* acting like crazy in bogus settings in the Levant. *Bella Donna* was also one of his, filmed with the impressive Pola Negri writhing all over a houseboat on the Nile, before she finally got her come-uppance. In the library of the vast, dustcover-shrouded villa where I had stayed my first summer at the Studio, I had leafed through Hichens' *The Garden of Allah* among all the other trash that crowded the shelves, accumulated for guests who "wanted something to take to bed". However, it was true. Rex had agreed to film this pre-1914 piece of pulp; this in 1926 with every writer in Europe wishing to be filmed. Well, we should just have to get on with it.

"Will we go to North Africa, do you think?"

"*We* will go. But I doubt whether Louis B. Mayer will insist on your going."

Harry was quite properly damping me down. But he was really as excited as I was. Rex making another big film meant more power and money for his own ambitions. For Frank Scully and he were already making plans for a film, or a series of films, together.

Harry was right about another thing, too. United Artists did remake *The Garden of Allah* as a talkie with an up-and-coming young producer in charge, the son-in-law of Louis B. Mayer, David O. Selznick. The French have a charming word for a pretentious piece of shit, a flop, a turkey: they call it a *navet* (a turnip), and when it is embarrassingly awful it becomes a *super navet*. D. O. Selznick's production with Marlene Dietrich and Charles Boyer was a *super-super-super navet*.

I was now clear what my mission to Montélimar was all about. The hero of *The Garden of Allah* is a Trappist monk, who has broken his vows and left the monastery. The action of the piece takes place in Algeria, in the monastery of Staoueli, near Algiers, and in a small town on the edge of the great Libyan desert, Bou-Saada. The runaway monk meets a beautiful woman who loves him in return, knowing nothing about him. She becomes his mistress. They are befriended by a sheikh, a man of power and authority who also loves this woman. One can see what the heads of Metro saw in it. But for a man who wanted to make *The World's Illusion* and *The Moon and Sixpence*, it was just a bunch of bananas.

Unfortunately Rex loved North Africa and was becoming fascinated by Mohammedanism. He compared religions and was modelling in clay a pietà of Christ held in the arms of the Buddha. At the same time he was playing practical jokes on Shorty and was not above acting Sultan to the Niçoise bathing girls at *La Grande Plage Bleue*. I watched him, fascinated by the opposing elements in his character. He had the most marvellous eyes, pensive and far-seeing, even when he was laughing and joking in the middle of a crowd of people. There was always a remote air about him, except when he was on the set, directing. Then he looked happy and young. Off the set, the lines between his eyes would return. He wore a gold bracelet on his wrist and a thin gold chain on his ankle.

All this I meditated on as the train rumbled across Provence. A boy in his twenties is not usually intent on the actions of his elders, nor on the reasons for their actions, particularly when every day brings something new, but I was already beginning to understand the immense power and wealth wielded by the handful of men who controlled this new medium, mushrooming in a few years from the nickelodeon to the supercinema, and who owned the studios, the films, the distribution companies and the theatres.

Every artist has to be alone with his art, but Rex Ingram was like some lonely swimmer landing upon a steep, shelving beach, feeling each receding wave tug at his weary feet as he struggles to get above the tide-mark, knowing that one big wave will roll him over and drag him, scrabbling on the rolling pebbles with his bleeding fingernails, back into the ocean, to swim a little longer before he disappears. I vowed then and many times since that I would manage to keep my independence and make the films I wanted to make without incurring the additional burden of a war with my financiers that I could never win. We shall see whether I kept that vow or not.

I was kindly received by the monks at La Trappe in the hills near Montélimar. The guest brother, or almoner, is allowed to speak out of necessity, and this one was quite a chatterbox. He showed me my cell and then took me on a tour of the monastery. It was simple and small, more like a working farm than a religious retreat. There were about thirty monks. Their day started at 4:00 a.m., and finished at 8:00 p.m. I managed to get a few stills with my small camera, but they weren't much good. The place was too small and humble for a Robert Hichens novel. Pity we didn't take the hint.

I sent my roll of film to be developed by Tomatis and took the train for Paris. My mother was waiting for me at the little hotel she had found. It was a great reunion. I showed off all my new knowledge. We took one another's picture – I had brought my studio portrait camera for the purpose. We went to the Théâtre du Vieux Colombier to see Ivan Mosjoukine in *Kean*. We went up the Eiffel Tower. We walked miles and she told me her plans.

One of the great-uncles had died and left legacies to all of Frederick Corbett's scattered and hard-working daughters. My mother's share was £625. One of her exploits when freed from me had been a tour of southern England on her bicycle. She carried a hammock and slung it between trees in the New Forest and elsewhere with a mackintosh to pull over her when it rained. What a mother for a man! When exploring the Hamworthy Moor, which lies at the western end of Poole Harbour, she discovered a farm, a smallholding, just where the train from Poole crosses a neck of the great harbour on its way to Dorchester and Weymouth. It was in Mother's favourite country, the Thomas Hardy country, and the moors were an outlying piece of Egdon Heath. You could look across to the Isle of Purbeck, but best of all from my mother's peculiar point of view was the fact that you had to open two locked gates and cross the railway line by an unmarked crossing to get there. Four hundred pounds would buy Turling Farm. Should she buy it?

"Buy it," I said, little knowing what the future held for this magnificent youth who talked familiarly about Rex and Harry and MGM, saying: "Oh, here's a picture of the new Swedish actress that we have signed up. Her name is Greta Garbo. She's Mauritz Stiller's girlfriend."

Mother and I had four days together. The photograph she took of me was in profile. I am wearing a cloth cap and a blue raincoat and I think I'm terrific. Then we went our separate ways, my mother to Southampton, where she had left her bicycle, myself to the Victorine. I don't think she ever spoke of my father. John's death had wiped him out, and she concentrated all her love on me. She had asked me if there was any special girl, and I had dismissed the question as absurd: girls were a dime a dozen around a film studio.

"Yes, darling, but somebody special . . . you will write to me if there is, won't you?"

I returned to find a bustle of activity. The script had arrived (by Willis Goldbeck again), and was being analysed. Alice and Petrovic were already approved for the main parts, and a handsome French actor with a commanding presence, Marcel Vibert, was playing their Mohammedan saviour. (I forgot to explain that the big scene of the film is a sandstorm in which the lovers nearly lose their lives, but instead find their souls, thanks to the sanctuary provided by the Sheikh.) Rex was already holding casting sessions for faces. This was one of his great strengths, and his films were famous for their stunning close-ups of human types. Few of them were regular actors: he would bring them in off the street, from bars, from fairgrounds, from the mountains. He would coach them and costume them and insist that the cameraman light them for the effect he wanted. These flashes of human faces that belonged to people who had suffered and laboured and been through disappointment and degradation, were fascinating to this young Irish-American, with regular features and handsome as a god.

It had already been decided that there would be a reconnaissance trip to Algeria: to Algiers, on the outskirts of which was the monastery of Staoueli, also to Biskra and the desert town of Bou-Saada, which was one of the outposts of the French Foreign Legion. The trip was mainly for the Art Department and for Rex and Willis to pick locations and explore the haunts of the Bedouin. The hot weather time was approaching with temperatures of 120 degrees in the desert: the studio scenes would be shot first between September and Christmas. In January, the African weather would be cool and clear for the exterior scenes with the actors.

This was a big project and Rex took it seriously. It was the sort of simple tale that he liked, and it gave him scope for big, sweeping sequences. Grant and Ota, alas, had by this time gone home for good. Another American editor, Arthur Ellis, who had the round, clean-shaven face of a comedian, arrived to take over the cutting room. Harry was in supreme charge of everything by now and he had Rex's ear. There was no doubt that things were much better organized. I think our budget was about half a million dollars.

Everyone was swept up in the preparations. The two Fielding brothers, Claude and Gerald, both had parts as Arabs, and Claude at least had a fine scene as a jealous lover. I was cast in my old part as an innocent tourist. I was told to work it up myself, and was given a tropical outfit complete with solar topee and a butterfly net. I went through the script and wrote myself into several sequences, including a scene with Alice in a crowded railway coach. My new pages passed through the production office without comment and became part of the schedule. But my attempts to write myself into the exteriors were spotted by Harry.

Unknown to me, and because of the scenes in *The Magician*, Frank Scully had already proposed to Harry a series of two-reel comedies to be called *Travelaughs*. The scheme was to fill a coach with a bunch of funny-looking tourists, most of them borrowed or stolen from Rex's current productions, and run them around the Riviera (which was always good for quaint hilltowns, the Monte Carlo Casino and bathing girls) and involve them in adventures and escapades. Now that I was to follow up *The Magician* fiasco with a part in a much bigger production, my prestige got a boost; and since I had no objection to breaking my neck, it was decided that I should do all my own stunts, from a parachute drop to jumping from a moving automobile onto a railroad train. But I anticipate.

We had a new lighting cameraman on *The Garden of Allah*, Lee Garmes, an exciting talent, one of the new type of cameramen who no longer thought in terms of painterly and theatrical compositions and lighting but of the style of the film as a whole, moving in on the departments of design and direction, making sure that their voices would be heard in any major decision. Later, in 1933, he would become famous with one film, *Zoo in Budapest*, a simple story about a boy and a girl (played by Loretta Young) on the run, which gave him the chance he needed. I remember the luminous quality of the images and the image of the fugitives intercut with slender-legged white cranes standing in the water. I know that Rex and Harry were unfairly disappointed with Johnny Seitz's work on *The Magician*, and wanted to work with one of the new men and yet—and yet—when I saw *Double Indemnity* thirty years later, one of the most brilliant and sophisticated films that even Billy Wilder ever made, John F. Seitz was the lighting cameraman.

Lee Garmes arrived. We were all curious to see him for great things were expected of his collaboration with Rex. Lee was young, round-faced, cheerful, and looked more like a politician than a lighting genius. But he was a lighting genius, particularly in the sympathetic lighting of his close-ups. Alice never looked lovelier. And he was fast and sure of himself. He and Harry got on together. That year the firm of Bell & Howell, whose movie cameras were unmatched for steadiness and service, brought the Eyemo hand camera into production. On the Continent, hand cameras had been in use for some time, and Lee Planskoy, with other students from the Sorbonne, had used them for Abel Gance in the big scenes of *Napoléon*. Lee tells me that they used SEPT cameras, containing only seven metres of film. You wound them up like a toy, and you could start them going and jump on a horse, or throw them from the battlements for others to catch, and although most of the resultant cuts were short, there were some marvellous glimpses of the fighting and confusion.

The Eyemo was a beautiful camera taking a hundred feet of film, solidly made, easy to handle. The first models only had one 35mm lens, but they soon produced a turret fixture with three lenses of different focal lengths. This was necessary if we hand-cameramen were to shoot alongside the main camera-crew. Lee was open-minded and as interested as Harry in finding new angles, or in picking up details that might interest the director. I soon learnt how to handle the Eyemo and with Tomatis as my teacher, I managed to sneak some good shots into the dailies. From that moment, when I had seen my own shots on the screen and watched Arthur Ellis cut a few feet of my shot into the film, I was lost to all other worlds. I was a movie brat, for ever.

The production was a handsome one and went smoothly, even in the sandstorm sequences. Sawdust was used instead of sand and even camels jibbed at that. We were back with the rows of aeroplane propellors again, filling the air with sawdust, choking and blinding the actors. Shorty, of course, was having a fine time. He was in the film playing the fool in front of the camera for a change. His huge head and squat body were effective in the scene in the tomb, where the lovers shelter from the sandstorm.

Alice was as good as ever, although the part was not a patch on Freya in *Mare Nostrum*. Petrovic never got near his part. He had little imagination, and I imagine was too overawed by the set-up to bring something original to his work. I told him once he had only two expressions: with his mouth open, and with his mouth shut. He agreed. He was an amiable man.

Our largest and most interesting set was a café in the Souk of Algiers. Our Arab extras in the scene were authentic and were controlled and interpreted for by a uniformed figure complete with tall turban, riding boots and a whip. He had an intelligent face with large features and huge, sad eyes. I forget his name, but I remember him vividly.

There were other unforgettable faces in the crowded scenes, all hand-picked by Rex. There were dancing girls, Ouled-Naïls, some authentic, some not. There was a beautiful creature called Ayesha. There was a tall, monkey-faced woman who danced with a bottle on her head. And there was me.

Yes. There he sat: the Eternal Tourist. A figure out of a comic strip. Taking it all in. Reacting. I could never understand why Rex thought I was funny. I guess I was just the stock figure of the eccentric Englishman that American (and maybe Irish) audiences like to believe exists. Jules Verne has him too. In any case, my scenes were left in by Arthur Ellis, including the sequence I had inserted when I come through the window of the railway train. What's more, I achieved my first screen credit at the bottom of the cast list: "A Tourist: Michael Powell."

The scene in the moving train taught me something: instead of the train rolling into the station, it is just as effective to have the station rolling towards the train. This is a stage trick, just as effective in a film studio. Until back projection and front projection of naturalistic scenes was perfected, it was the standard way and, at a pinch, I used the same trick in *49th Parallel*, when I had to shoot the Raymond Massey baggage car sequence in Montreal in a studio about as big as a hen-coop. We travellers sit in the stationary railway compartment while the scenery flew by. Out of the corner of my eye I can see grips by the dozen running, bent over so as not to be seen, offering up telephone posts, palm trees, camels' humps, what have you, until at a carefully orchestrated signal they begin to slow up and the team of grips (which probably included Harry Lachman and half the front office) who are pushing the railway station get under way. It runs on rails. Puffing and sweating they roll it along to meet the train. It is crowded with extras, desperately trying to keep their balance and look nonchalant, and failing to do either. They look as frightened and unsteady as a bunch of tourists in the Haunted Castle at Disneyland, when the planks begin to shuffle back and forth under their feet. Except for Alice. Nothing can shake that queenly poise. Like a statue she stands as her chariot comes to a halt opposite us. We in the carriage all simulate a slight jerk as if it were the train that stopped, not the station. Several of the extras outside stagger, but not Alice. She opens the carriage door, steps in and sits down opposite Petrovic, who is doing his best to look like an unfrocked Trappist monk in a well-cut lounge suit. A butterfly passes the window and dances in the sunshine (prop-man with fly on fishing rod). I sight it and plunge out in pursuit. Need I say that I miss the train, pursue it and make a jack-in-the-box entrance through the window? I have hinted that Rex's gags were rudimentary.

Harry proved to be a false prophet. When we came to the exteriors, I was the only member of the cast to get to the Sahara. Louis B. Mayer evidently did not blacklist me. Or maybe it was the fact that I was Harry's assistant, also the stills cameraman, also the focus puller for the camera unit, also the representative on location of the cutting room, all for 650 francs a week. (How much was that in 1927? Maybe thirty dollars.) I was also playing my part. Harry had something to do with it, I am sure. He was already planning his *Travelaughs*: desert shots from the film could be put in. Marcel Lucien had gone ahead of us, deep into the desert, to get his shots of mounted Bedouin, hundreds of them, crossing the sandy mountains. Burel, Abel Gance's cameraman, would have joined us but was still working on *Napoléon*. Lee Planskoy was working as an extra in the Siege of Toulon sequence. Burel was to shoot Rex's next film, *The Three Passions*. Rex was slowly becoming Europeanized under the guidance of Harry. Anyway, when the ship sailed to Algiers in January 1927, I was on it.

The monastery of Staoueli proved to be partly a commercial affair, where the liqueur for which it was famous was bottled and sealed and which was a sort of tourist attraction. The monks had handsome, clean – too clean – grey robes with black hoods. Petrovic looked well in them. (Perhaps he should have been a monk, not an actor.) Algiers I loved. It was French and yet not-French, beautiful, intriguing, French, clean, dirty and French. I was not to see it again until we entered it, with General Darlan, in 1942, during the Allied landings in North Africa.

Many films have been made in the Casbah, but nobody has used it more effectively than Julien Duvivier in *Pépé le Moko*, with Jean Gabin.

Duvivier was a great director. He loved and understood people and he had a talent for putting them into a landscape without losing their importance as human beings. Scale is everything in making a film. Lose the sense of scale and you lose your audience. His two versions of *Poil de Carotte*, both silent and sound, were perfect in this respect. His *Carnet de Bal* was the finest of all the anthology films (in which a group of people, brought together by a device, reveal their lives and characters). He never tried to be original: he just was. He was the supreme professional and sensualist, like Bonnard starting fresh every morning to draw for the thousandth time the body of his beloved, always the same, always different.

Rex's Casbah was partly the real thing, partly a studio setting, the usual mixture in those days, when naturalism was confused with realism. The struggle was still being fought between theatre and film, between – if you care to adopt the conceit – the actors and the dreamers, between technique and the technicians, between words and images. Silent films flowered in a decade of astonishing and unforgettable achievement, then withered at the trumpet of sound. Jolson spoke, and silent films, the most perfect form of communication ever invented and perfected by man, were dead. But not and never to those of us who worked on them. Let my works bear witness for me.

In my films, images are everything; words are used like music to distil emotion. The ballet sequence in *The Red Shoes*, the whole of *The Tales of Hoffman*, the defusing of the bomb in *The Small Back Room*, the movement of ships at sea in the *Graf Spee* film, the whole of *The Edge of the World*, more than half of *Black Narcissus*, the trial in Heaven in *A Matter of Life and Death*, are essentially silent films. Did I write that silent films are dead? When Abel Gance's *Napoléon* (made in 1927) and revived by Kevin Brownlow, is sold out for every performance in the largest hall in Los Angeles in 1981? When I see and hear people who have come to smile and wonder at the technical trick of a screen triptych, of one giant screen expanding into three, and then find instead that they are totally gripped by the art of the Master, who shows us everything – emotion, action, men, women – in stunning images, and finally burst into spontaneous applause when the screen enlarges for the battle scene? They come out of the Hollywood Shrine, now, today, fifty-four years after Abel Gance hurled these images onto the screen, together with his own personal view, they stream out, these 1981 audiences, talking not about a technical innovation, but about a man and a film. There's hope for all of us, then. Silent films are dead but they won't lie down. Have we neglected a Sleeping Beauty for half a century? Are we at last giving ourselves time to think?

The actors (I don't include myself among them) returned to Nice. Alice to New York with her sister Edna, the unit (I include myself) went by bus to Bou-Saada. It was my first important location trip.

Our opening shot, on which I had to pull focus, started with a pair of Arab tribesmen prostrating themselves as the muezzin summons them to prayer, then pulled back and up to show hundreds of others, all facing towards Mecca, each kneeling on a little square of carpet in the prescribed manner. For this shot we had built an elevator in sections in the studio which we assembled in Bou-Saada, in an open space just outside the little town. In the book the town was Biskra, but it had become a tourist trap and lost its simple charm. Bou-Saada was an outpost town on the edge of the desert, and looked it. The tower which contained our elevator was mounted on wheels with pneumatic tyres, which was a mistake to begin with. They should have been solid rubber. One of the tyres blew and the tower swayed worse than Pisa. This wasted some days. The wheels ran on planks so that as the camera rose in the air to a height of about twenty metres, the tower would be rolled back manually to compensate for the steepness of the angle. Anything more hair-raising for a complete neophyte couldn't have been invented. But I thought of my mentor, Gordon Avil, the kindest, most thorough master that a young technician could ever have, to whom it never occurred that anybody would find difficulty in doing anything – and I pulled focus as if my life depended on it. It probably did.

The tricky moment on a shot like this is the start, when every foot that is travelled by the camera makes quite a big adjustment to the focus necessary. Marcel Lucien was second unit cameraman, but Monroe Bennett was operating and his patience was inexhaustible as we chalked up vital statistics on the planks and on the cross-pieces of the elevator tower. After days of sweat and preparation The Day was suddenly there and we were shooting before I had time to be scared. I shall remember the faces of the two leading Arabs to my dying day, kneeling there in the sand, hour after hour, while we lined up the shot. It was on the second take that the tyre blew out. We were forty feet up at the time. We laughed. Oh! youth! youth!

I never saw a final cut on *The Garden of Allah*, until I saw the completed film early in 1928 at the Tivoli Cinema in the Strand in London. I believe it opened that super-cinema. (Exhibitor veterans, correct me if I'm wrong!) I went to see if I were still in the picture, whether my name was still on the credits. I was. It was. Rex bore me no grudge for leaving him to go with Harry. But Harry himself, on whom he leaned, and Corniglion-Molinier, that smart and charming lawyer – he didn't forgive them so easily.

Perhaps only Tai Lachman knows the inside story of those stormy pioneer months in 1927, and she won't tell or be quoted. It was Matisse who introduced the beautiful Chinese opera singer to Harry in his Paris studio. Harry, with his passion for the rare and exotic, fell in love immediately. We boys were jealous. We looked to Harry for our future, and here was Harry, the black, cynical seducer, the witty Casanova, raving about a Chinese girl as if he were a student. We listened with scepticism, Matisse or no Matisse. Then she came to Nice and we all rolled over with our paws in the air. She was everything that Lachman and Matisse had said and more.

She has forbidden me to write about her. "Write about Harry, but not about me," she says. She lives on a fabulous corner site in Beverly Hills. Harry bought it when he came to Hollywood in the years before the war, when his European films had unrolled a carpet for him to the studios of Hollywood. Tai has the most sensual of voices. Her voice alone used to drive Harry into raves, until we roared with ribald laughter. She was a contralto, and was studying with Barthelemy. She had power and imagination. She was a good artist. Is there greater praise? But like us she was swept off her course by that demon Lachman. Does she regret it? Do I? Not me! It is wonderful to be trusted, even more wonderful to be led. I have worked for and with many men and women, but never with a bad artist, never with a bad leader, from Rex Ingram to Francis Coppola. Luck? No. Only the best will do for me.

The location trip to Bou-Saada completed the work on the film and we returned to the Victorine, but not before Harry had shot enough film on me to complete a *Travelaugh* in North Africa. He only had to separate me from the other tourists in some vaguely North African location (there are plenty on the Côte d'Azur and even more in that strange territory of the Camargue) and *bingo*! I was off on a chase across the Sahara to the Congo! This two-reeler was called *Camels to Cannibals* (I smell Frank Scully there!) and the Congo scenes were shot with the blackest of Senegalese soldiers from the barracks near St Raphael, and I now remember that I ended up blacked all over, dressed in a grass skirt, a solar topee and an Eton collar, assisted by Shorty, Rex's jester, as an amiable baby gorilla.

For the first part of the chase across the Sahara sand-mountains I was on skis, which I borrowed from a Tyrolean tourist who happened to be passing through. I only remember it because I shot my own feet sliding over the sand-dunes on skis, using the Eyemo hand camera and the Bell & Howell Company used a cut-out of me in my tourist outfit operating the Eyemo in a full-page ad in the *American Cinematographer* for July 1927. There weren't many American cinematographers at the time who photo-graphed their own feet and lived to talk about it, and when it becomes generally known I expect to be elected an Honorary Member of the ASC.

While we were in North Africa, Lee Planskoy was in Northern France working with Abel Gance and Marcel l'Herbier. Together with René Clair, these directors represented a formidable talent, and in a few years they made France the leader of the avant-garde cinema. I shall never forget being bowled over by the wit and invention of René Clair's *Paris Qui Dort*.

From his first short film in 1923, this civilized and enchanting man created his own cinema world and never betrayed it, to the end of a long career and a long life. (He died in 1981, and I sang his praises to Francis Coppola, who knew his films from the archives, but had never, like me, gasped as a cold douche of wit and wisdom took my breath away in a film like *Le Chapeau de Paille d'Italie*, or *Les Grandes Manoeuvres*.) Of Abel Gance I have already written: he was to other directors what Richard Wagner is to other composers. You can't argue with a thunderstorm. But Marcel l'Herbier, the third member of my French triptych, was, in some ways, the most interesting of all. He was a true avant-garde man, bringing theatre, painting and literature, as well as the latest and trendiest of movements, to his films. He was also a student of technique, and in *Le Diable au Coeur*, which he was shooting in Brittany, on location, with the English actress Betty Balfour, he was using Panchromatic film for the first time in Europe. Lee, who knew the curve of an emulsion when he saw one, was his technical adviser, and full of this new quality in photography he came back to join Harry and put his experiences into practice.

The Garden of Allah cutting copy was only waiting for our location scenes in order to be completed and shipped off to New York, where the negative would be cut. This time, Rex went with his film to show it personally to Marcus Loew and Nick Schenck. I never heard what happened after that. MGM treated the film as an important one, but it was a disappointment to Rex Ingram fans: beautiful to look at, but the story creaked; marvellous atmosphere, but little action: Alice as beautiful and moving as ever (and her silk caftan started a new fashion), but Petrovic was as responsive to her love as a plate of Jello. The Metro bosses liked and admired Rex. He had given them some of their biggest hits, and they must have pleaded with him to give up his European petty kingdom and come back to Hollywood, which was already being rocked with rumours as formidable as an undersea earthquake, about the coming of sound.

But returning to Hollywood meant returning to the new studio at Culver City where Louis B. Mayer and his strong-arm boys had already seized supreme power. Returning to Hollywood meant manoeuvring for authority with Irving Thalberg, whom he had ignored at Universal and who was now the production whiz-kid at MGM and married to Norma Shearer, their Number One star. Returning to Hollywood meant confrontation for subjects, for stars and starlets, with up-and-coming producers as ruthless and as crude as any petty conqueror that ever burst out of Asia dragging kings and concubines at his chariot wheels. Returning to Hollywood meant returning with Alice to a dream-factory where the wheels were turning relentlessly, ever faster and faster, and where even to stand still you had to run until your lungs were bursting, where formidable figures with strange names were building a vast industry, where orange groves and avenues of pepper trees were being bulldozed to make way for Hollywood and Vine and the Brown Derby.

Is it any wonder if Rex, in this changed world, looked longingly back to Nice and the Victorine, so like his early years in Hollywood? In Nice, his white villa stood in the middle of his own studio, surrounded by olive trees hundreds of years old, where his half-finished clay pietà awaited him in the shuttered studio, shrouded in damp cloths, faithfully renewed every morning and evening by Thibault, his seaman janitor? It was a fateful moment. In a few months, Warner Brothers and Vitaphone would be household words and the world of European art, theatre, and cinema would be shaken to its foundations. Berlin, Paris, Moscow, London, Rome would cease overnight to have any international significance as centres for film-making. It would be Hollywood or bust! Rex chose and was bust.

He may have made overtures to United Artists when he was in Hollywood. I am only guessing, but they would seem to have been natural partners for such an individualist. But Doug and Mary were mature sweethearts now, thinking twice before they risked a picture; Chaplin was Chaplin and would always be Chaplin; and the great D. W. was suffering the fate of all masters: pupils had learnt their craft from him and had gone on to eclipse him. Rex returned to New York for one more interview with Marcus Loew. He still hoped to get a one-picture contract out of Metro and make *The World's Illusion* in Europe. He was unsuccessful. MGM were no longer interested in the subject. They were looking for subjects for Greta Garbo. If Rex was to find a backer for a European film starring his wife, it would have to be in London. He probably tried to buy *The World's Illusion* from Marcus Loew, but MGM weren't selling.

The big studios, what are now called conglomerates, as if they were some kind of geological phenomenon (which they resemble in their intensity and ugliness), very seldom appreciate the treasures that they own. They mark them down instead. In the J. Arthur Rank Organisation, only some literary-minded accountant, if there can be such a thing, knows what wonderful films are lying, stifled, moribund in the files marked "Project Purchased". Ditto and even worse for Korda and London Films. So just imagine what potential entertainments are accumulating dust at MGM. I remember being told by a friend who represented an American major (as they are humorously called) in London, that he had received a cable: "BUY FOR SINNERS ONLY". He made inquiries, obtained the book, started to read it, then cabled his principal: "Do you realize this is a book about the Oxford Movement?" (It was a sociological study of a religious movement.) A few days passed. Then he got a cable: "BUY IT ANYWAY."

In Nice, Harry and Frank Scully were now running in top gear. Harry had got a distribution contract from Ideal Films in London for his two-reelers, and although I am sure he was using his own money for production, he had the assurance of collecting an advance on delivery. He hadn't changed his simple life-style and MGM had taken care of his expenses, so he had saved all his salary, which as chief executive, was considerable, and he spent it all on learning to direct.

"People always had an idea that Harry was a financial wizard, because he drove such a tough bargain for Rex with all the people who worked for him" (Tai says). "But Harry knew nothing about making money for himself, and when he had it he spent it like a drunken sailor. He had no call to bail you boys out, you and Lee Planskoy, and take you to London with him. He just did. He felt responsible for you and he took you with him."

To complete his *Travelaugh* team, Harry had snapped up all the freaks and lovelies and starlets that hung around Rex's court. Gerald Fielding supplied romance. Marianne and Poupette, sex (the latter had worn a strategic rosebud in the Faun Dance). Basil Hambro, villainy. Madame Paquerette, grotesquerie. Shorty and a number of other freaks did their stuff. And we made up the scenario as we went along. I did all the stunts. I got lost, climbed palm trees, parachuted with an umbrella off cliffs, fell off a ship into the sea, leapt from camels to canoes, from automobiles to railroad cars, and ended up on a flowery float as the King of the Carnival of Nice.

I also got my first assignment as a director. There was a little town called Carros on a hill on the west bank of the Var, once the frontier between France and the kingdom of Savoy. It is a steep hill and the town crowns it, its walls looking sullenly across to the terraces and villas of the hills behind Nice, the *arrière-pays* beloved of the Niçois, where there are thousands of little valleys and paths, and dozens of secret stills where the local *marc* is brewed from the stones and skins and residue of the grapes – all quite illegal and tasting all the better for it. How many times have I driven my old Harley-Davidson World War I motorbike, usually with Tomatis in the battered sidecar, up rough roads to the shack where some old school friend of his was presiding over the big, copper alembics, heated by fire and cooled by running water, so that the warmish flat-tasting grappa, distilled, in great drops, into the waiting funnel. Then there would be a tasting with judicious nods, and wine would be opened, and Tomatis would mix his own brand of *pastis*, pure poison, cloudy and brown in a glass of water, and we would eat raw vegetables and anchovies and garlic.

Harry had sent me out with Marcel Lucien, his cameraman on one memorable day, to "get some shots of hill-towns – and don't waste any film". I didn't. I took one of our tourists with us and worked out, with

Marcel, a series of dissolves in the camera, which gave an impression of Carros in about twenty seconds. Harry was astonished. He looked at me with new respect.

"Powell! That wasn't bad," he said.

I also got married.

Her name was – but what does it matter what her name was? It lasted three weeks. She was beautiful, young, strong, healthy, American – and just about the last person to be made happy by me, and vice versa.

In 1927 I was slim, arrogant, intelligent, foolish, shy, cocksure, dreamy and irritating to any sensible woman who had her fortune to make and a family to plan.

Today I am no longer slim.

We got married one lunch hour at the Anglican church in the Boulevard Victor Hugo. I had to escape from the studio at St André de Nice, travel by tram to the Place Masséna, run to the church (about half a mile), run back again, wait for a tram, and get bawled out by Harry for leaving my cutting-room (Lee Planskoy and I were cutting the circus film that Harry was directing). I told Lee. He was horrified.

"Where are you going to live?" he asked.

"I suppose Avenue des Orangers" (where I had a room).

"But what are you going to live on?"

I hadn't thought of that either.

For Harry had broken with Rex. Had refused to give up his own dreams of direction in order to run the Victorine for Rex while Rex was making *The Three Passions* with Alice Terry for Gaumont. Neither man was wise. Rex lost a valuable friend and executive who was afraid of nothing and nobody and always spoke the truth. Harry lost a friend and the use of a big studio with all its invaluable assets, tangible and intangible, to help him make his experimental little films for almost nothing. He had fallen in love with an act by a clown, a wire-walking act that he had seen in a circus. (Harry, like Rex, was crazy about circuses. They send me to sleep. Except for E. A. Dupont's *Variétés*, I have never seen a circus film which didn't start me yawning from the first reel.) Harry had got all he could out of *Travelaughs*, which were being finally edited in London. (My last big scene before I gave up film-acting was a solo faun dance which I dreamt up and performed with my girlfriends from Margaret Morris, in the olive grove that used to exist beside the path on Cap Ferrat that follows the coast.)

Harry had to find a studio, or some place he could use as a studio, and half an hour out of Nice, up a little stream which is a tributary of the Paillon, he found a small, empty factory, built for a local entrepreneur who had changed his mind, and which was high enough and long enough to film the circus scenes in. He rented it and we moved in. The owner was the proprietor of the Café and his family name was Musso, a typical Niçois name. I remember when I came into their little café for the first time we all liked each other at first sight. "*Il est sympathique*" was Madame Musso's opinion. She should have told my wife. Not that it would have saved the marriage.

My parents reacted differently. My father put a notice in the local paper to the effect that he would not be responsible for my debts. That was the Welsh side of him. My mother, for whom it was certainly a shock and a disappointment, packed up my books and small belongings that she had kept for me through all her wanderings and came with them to Nice, on the assumption that I would be setting up house there. She knew nothing of Rex's altered status, nor of Harry's burning his (and our) boats, so far as the Victorine was concerned. I had written regularly and enthusiastically about our progress and my prospects, and she must have thought that I had my father and job in the hotel to fall back on. Even my mother, who knew me better than anyone, would not have imagined that, at the riskiest time of my fortunes, I would up and get married to an American girl with a widowed mother if I didn't want to or have to. For the amazing thing is that I didn't want to. Or have to. Perhaps I was in love with the mother. She was a very nice woman. She came from Puerto Rico.

My wife and I lived together for three weeks – by which I mean that I sometimes saw her at night, but more often not – then a flat became vacant and she moved into it, announcing that for the present she had no desire for me to follow her. This was a relief, as Harry was shooting hundreds of feet of film of the high-wire act, and Lee and I were working night and day to keep ahead of him. We had committed ourselves, Lee especially, influenced by his experience with Abel Gance, to what I call cannonball cutting. It was all very impressive and impressionistic, but a little difficult to follow. Winter was upon us. Christmas was not far away and it looked unlikely to be a merry one. Help came from England, of all places. British International Pictures had taken over the Elstree Studios in Hertfordshire, about twelve miles outside London. There was a village called Borehamwood. There was a shortage of directors, of technicians, of stories, of scripts, above all of experienced directors. Harry's production values (supplied at MGM's expense) on his two-reel comedies, had impressed Wardour Street. He was offered a contract by BIP. He took it. He took us with him. Without a thought for my wife, parents, flat, personal belongings, notes, scripts, stills and clips of movie film, I stumbled onto the train for London, which was like a foreign city to me. We arrived in the first week of January 1928 and set about looking for lodgings. Harry and Lee accompanied me. Whenever a nice-looking girl answered the door Harry, who as a young painter had starved in London as well as in Paris, would whisper: "She'll do. Ask her to sleep with you. All the English girls have to sleep with you, their houses are so cold."

We eventually settled for a grim room in Sussex Gardens near Paddington Station. The next day we went by Underground to a sooty, brick, Gothic Revival cathedral called St Pancras Station, and took a battered suburban train to Borehamwood, an ugly village in the ugliest part of Hertfordshire. There was wet snow on the ground. The only shoes I had were sandals. The only name I knew was Alfred Hitchcock.

BOOK TWO

Sound

At the time that we arrived at Elstree the silent film was at its zenith. In the glorious period between 1912 and 1928, the new medium threw up fantastic showmen who projected exciting new images onto the silent screen:

D. W. Griffith and Abel Gance
Rex Ingram and René Clair
Erich von Stroheim and Josef von Sternberg
Fritz Lang and Victor Sjöstrom
Carl Dreyer and Jean Renoir
Alfred Hitchcock and Anthony Asquith
Ernst Lubitsch and Charlie Chaplin
Douglas Fairbanks and Mary Pickford
Walt Disney and Mickey Mouse
Buster Keaton and Max Linder
Laurel and Hardy
Eisenstein and Pudovkin
John Ford and Fred Niblo
Allan Dwan and William Wellman
Cecil B. DeMille

. . . to pick a handful of memorable names out of hundreds that are forgotten.

What a blazing glory of talent and impudence! These men created the motion picture, the silent motion picture, long before a black-face comedian started to cry for his "Mammy". These pioneer directors came from everywhere and nowhere. From Vaudeville, from the circus, from the gutter. They took silent movies for their own. The sky was the limit. When I was sixteen these men were gods to me.

I am writing this sixty-five years later and the names come up as fresh and green and inspiring as ever. I need no reference books. They are the creators and designers of my medium, they are my Leonardo, my Chardin, my Daumier. They saw instinctively the limitations and advantages of a two-dimensional picture. Where there is no depth movement must be lateral, particularly in comedy. The pioneers soon discovered that the camera can photograph thought as well as action. They discovered the power of mime. They discovered that in this wonderful medium, emotion could be shared between the actor and actress, the director and the audience. The comedians discovered that there was a different speed of the camera for every piece of business. This was a new way of mocking the human condition and audiences roared for more. Silent film comedy became the most sophisticated theatrical art since the commedia dell'arte.

D. W. Griffith and Abel Gance grabbed spectacle and melodrama from the theatre to make the super film: *The Birth of a Nation, Intolerance, La Roue, Broken Blossoms, Way Down East, Napoleon, Orphans of the Storm*. Their films came thick and fast – spectacular, dramatic and enormously successful. But the genius of the silent cinema was Charlie Chaplin. Almost single-handed he created the silent cinema. Laughing and crying, the whole world took him in its arms and Charlie, the little Cockney clown, understood the importance of the medium, and knew that he had a mission. He was not just the master of his medium, he was its servant. As soon as he could he built his own studio and became his own boss. He moved from shorts to features. His rivals predicted disaster – he triumphed. Like the Pied Piper he led the way and others followed. They danced from one-reelers to two-reelers and from two-reelers to six-reelers. Great clowns like Buster Keaton emerged, full of invention and incredibly ambitious. Laurel and Hardy and their directors raised knockabout and slapstick to the level of high art. With these two great clowns, the movies probed to the roots of laughter. Now – remember that these were all silent films, with the minimum number of sub-titles for the information of the audience.

But why do I call them silent films? Our films were never silent. From the earliest days of the nickelodeon, a tinkling piano behind a dusty palm tree had accompanied the action on the screen. The movies and music went hand in hand from the beginning. If you have never seen James Cruze's *The Covered Wagon* lurch and strain and fight its way across the prairie on the screen, to the accompaniment of a banjo strumming in the orchestra pit:

> Oh, Susannah! Oh don't you cry for me,
> For I'm bound for Californiay
> With my banjo on my knee

played on the screen by a freckle-faced boy, you will never be able to capture the experience. Much was left to the imagination in the early films, but the music never! Sheet music accompanied the distribution of the big films. For the big love stories like *Bella Donna,* or *The Prisoner of Zenda,* the manager of a motion picture palace was expected by the distributor to hire a violinist for the scenes of passion or renunciation, and a drummer with all the usual percussive effects, for the battle or chase scenes, in addition to the indefatigable pianist. These inventive musicians performed miracles of synchronization with the action on the screen, providing added entertainment for those of us in the audience who were betting they would never make it. But they always did, coming in with a final bang of the drum and the cymbals.

All this is forgotten today, even by students of the silent film. I went to a showing of an important silent film the other day, of which I had very tender memories, and to my horror it was shown just like that – silent. My host said:

"Well, what do you think of it? Doesn't it stand up well?" I said, "How can it! You didn't even have a piano! The last time that I saw it, sixty-one years ago, it was with full orchestra! I remember the musical themes!"

He was dashed. He said. "Of course, I've seen Kevin Brownlow's reconstruction of *Napoleon* with full orchestra, but I thought . . ."

I quelled him with a look. "When I saw Herbert Brenon's film starring Pola Negri as *The Spanish Dancer,* it was in a flea-pit in Nice in 1926 with a six-piece orchestra, and that wasn't even a first run! And when Doug Fairbanks presented *The Three Musketeers* in London, it was at the Drury Lane Theatre, with a twenty-piece orchestra! And an elaborately cued effects track with whip cracks, and galloping hooves, all in sync. There was wonderful chase music. And you think silent films were silent! The only thing silent about them were the actors. It was paradise!"

That was the silent film, that was! The greatest medium of communication, the greatest storytelling medium that has even been invented. No language barrier – dialogue, descriptions, information, quotations, were all conveyed by the means of sub-titles inserted in the film. Each nation had a free hand over the titles, according to the quickness of their audience. Some used more titles, and some less. A list of the titles accompanied the film cans to every country of the world. In a few hours they were translated into Chinese, Czech, Castillian Spanish or Double Dutch, and cut into the film. As if by the wave of a magician's wand, the new audiences could experience the film as if it were made in their own language. It never occurred to them that it wasn't. The first film directors used a lot of sub-titles, because a lot of the first films were from classic novels or from history. But distributors and exhibitors kept abreast of public taste and very soon told the directors that enough was enough. And then as directors learnt their craft they began to resent the custom of inserting narrative titles into action sequences and they began to exploit new conventions and found ways of telling the story without the use of titles.

Then came the Russians and the Bolshevik Revolution, with the necessity to instruct and entertain at one and the same time a shrewd but illiterate population. They did this either by rhythm or through constant, unwearying repetition, or by the use of vast spectacles to impress, inform and stimulate their audiences. Then there were the propaganda films like *The Battleship Potemkin* and *Mother*, whose directors had learnt a great deal from the study of D. W. Griffith, using montage of images and a direct appeal to the emotions. All of us in Europe went mad about the Russian Revolutionary films and our editing was changed forever and for good. All at once, as if Europe were still in the nineteenth century, the power of the film as propaganda and as entertainment was realised by politicians as well as by artists, and Europe thrilled as if it were a new Reformation. And then, when nation was talking to nation in the most direct and simple way, the blow fell. Synchronised speech had arrived. Movies had become talkies.

Alfred Hitchcock already had a European reputation in 1928. He was the only British director who had. He was seven years my senior, crowding thirty; like me, he had got his first chance to direct abroad, in his case in Germany. After his precocious début as art director on *Woman to Woman*, when he used storyboard technique – action sketches rather than conventional designs, for he had no formal architectural draftsman's training – he had worked in Berlin and been offered the chance to direct *The Pleasure Garden*. Back in England he turned his German experience to good account with *The Lodger*, an atmospheric thriller about a mysterious young man who could conceivably be, in his spare time, Jack the Ripper or Mack the Knife, or any of the murderous sex maniacs so dear to the home-loving Germans. Hitch had already started on his mission to scarify the bourgeoisie, and had cast England's favourite matinée idol, Ivor Novello, as the Lodger. All the British mothers doted on Ivor Novello. He was as beautiful as a god and so well-mannered! They were appalled at Hitch's casting, but secretly delighted. They went to see the film in droves. Hitch, as usual, had it both ways.

But he had not yet recognised his own genius. He was an artist who could do one thing supremely well. He thought he could do everything. It took him some years to learn from his mistakes. But in the making of them, and in the years that followed, he was the most inventive, mischievous, inspiring hobgoblin in movies, and movies were all the better for him. The film industry (as it is rightly called) wouldn't have been the same without him. He was the great debunker. Three great artists have saved the film business from going completely off the rails in my time, three great humanists as well as great craftsmen: Charlie Chaplin, Walt Disney and Alfred Hitchcock. Hitch's greatest strength was that he never proclaimed himself as a teacher. On the contrary. He was the eternal Cockney barrowboy who knows it all, watching with a sardonic eye the world passing by, addressing his customers as "Guv'nor", in a tone which combined a declaration of independence with subtle insult. That was Hitch.

When the *Travelaugh* team came to Elstree, it was January 1928. Al Jolson had spoken on the screen three months before, and "You ain't heard nothing yet!" had entered the language. After three years in the South of France working for MGM, then striking out for ourselves as independents, we had accumulated a couple of hand cameras, a couple of stills cameras, a dozen negatives of two-reel comedies (they were already dated because of American sound-shorts), and the clothes we stood up in. We soon found that sandals and linen trousers were unsuitable for the bleak fields and muddy lanes of Hertfordshire. Unlike most British studios, before and since, the British International Pictures Studio had not sprung up around the nucleus of a country house with gardens, landscaping, and other amenities. Elstree was a charming little village with one main street and was gradually being destroyed by the traffic passing through to the North. The railway station was a mile away to the east and a few industries had established themselves there, with two or three avenues of houses for the workers, a pub or two and the film studios, which stood on the main road in a wind-swept field with all the discreet charm of a jam factory. If you ask me why the Borehamwood film studios (which were to include, later on, the Whitehall Studios and the British and Dominion Studios, and the MGM British Studios, making about twenty stages in all) should be called Elstree Studios, I can only tell you that you are now in England, where custom takes precedence over common sense, and the reason lies buried in the mists of time.

Harry Lachman, our leader, and Frank Scully, our roving *Variety* reporter, were solvent. Harry had a contract as director with BIP. Frank had titles to write for Ideal Films, who were distributing our two-reel comedies. Lee Planskoy and I were broke, but since we had never been anything else that didn't worry us particularly. Harry told Simon Rowson of Ideal Films that he had to find me a job. Simon looked sadly at me.

"Ten pounds a week," suggested Harry.

"Five," said Simon, automatically, and five it was: about twenty dollars. I was back where I had started.

My job was to be a reader in the story department of BIP at Elstree Studios, which meant going there by steam-train every day. I forget whether they paid our fares. I doubt it. I had nothing but contempt for all story departments, and I knew from my MGM experiences that no director worth his salt ever asked a story department to find him a story, or read their reports and synopses when they did. But that didn't matter. I was in. And once inside the studios I would soon find my niche. I already considered myself a director – more than Harry, who was a painter after all. I just knew I was a director, and couldn't understand why people didn't stand in line to offer me a film. I was twenty-three. Time was marching on.

Harry took Lee Planskoy with him as his personal technician. He knew that Lee's knowledge of optics was something that he, with all his showmanship, could never achieve. Lee was born with a slide-rule in his mouth; he received all the American scientific magazines, and could talk on equal terms with Ernest Schufftan, Werner Brandes, Karl Freund and other great German cameramen. Harry needed this, and he needed us both in the studios with him. He was used to us, in spite of our criticisms of his technical mistakes. These were frequently caustic. He knew that he was an elderly amateur and we were movie brats.

The story department of BIP fulfilled my worst fears. It was a Sargasso Sea of hopeful scriptwriters, an Isle of Lost Scripts. Its boss was a woman, Mrs Boyd. She was cheerful and hopeful and orderly. I looked at her with disgust, poor woman. She was doing a good job, which made it worse. What did she know of stars on the screen and in your eyes? Had she ever thrilled to the word "Action!" or staggered back into the world of reality on the magician's word "Cut!" How could a film studio, with its vast, shadowy spaces and its pools of light, the echoing voice of the assistant director calling "Quiet!" – how could it mean to her what it meant to me? It was my life, my home. I looked at my fellow readers. I can only remember Sydney Gilliat and Roger Burford. I gathered that Sydney had a powerful father in Fleet Street. That accounted for him. He was a dour, silent, chunky young man, with very observant eyes that gave nothing away. Roger was tall and thin and bespectacled, and it was whispered that he was married to a novelist! The rest are shadows to me.

I was frequently absent without leave from Mrs Boyd's department and got warned several times before I found my chance. By that time, I had got to know my way around the various stages. The escape of

German liberals from the Nazis had already begun. The great German director E. A. Dupont had a contract with BIP and was directing *Moulin Rouge*. Alfred Junge was one of his art directors. Arthur Robison, whom I revered for his experimental film *Warning Shadows*, was directing in the studio the first version of Liam O'Flaherty's *The Informer*, with Lars Hanson. The setting of tall, narrow tenement streets and tiny rooms was interesting and quite unlike anything I had seen before. Anthony Asquith, the son of the British Prime Minister, had completed *Shooting Stars* with Brian Aherne and was directing the same actor in *Underground*. Lee and I decided that he and his unit were the most professional on the lot. Norman Walker had just finished an ambitious war drama called *Tommy Atkins*. Thomas Bentley was doing one of the Dickens novels. Two efficient Americans were working at Elstree: Denison Clift and Tim Whelan. And then there was Alfred Hitchcock.

Hitch had recently finished a film based on an Eden Philpotts play, *The Farmer's Wife*, and was now directing Betty Balfour, England's ersatz Mary Pickford, in a comedy called *Champagne*. Rumour said that he was far from happy. He had signed a longterm contract with BIP after the success of *The Lodger* and *The Ring*, and was getting a big salary for the first time in his life. But he had no control or choice of subject: he had to make what the studio assigned him. He hated the frothy story *Champagne*, he hated Betty Balfour as a "piece of suburban obscenity", and he was expressing his irritation by refusing to let any stills cameraman come onto his set and take photographs for the publicity department. When a stills man arrived and asked to be allowed to make a still, Jack Cox, the cameraman, would yell: "Throw the breakers!", the lights would dim out and Hitch, getting ponderously up from his chair (he was an immensely fat young man, not tall, but weighing over two hundred pounds) would stumble and kick over the tripod of the clumsy eight-by-ten stills camera, which went down with a crash. This had been going on for a month. Nobody knew what to do about it. Not Joe Grossman, the studio manager with a permanent twitch of head and shoulder. Not John Court Appleby Thorpe, the general manager of BIP. Not John Maxwell, the Glasgow-born chairman of the company, a Scottish lawyer, forgotten now, but one of the pioneers of the British cinema. They all said that somebody should do something about Hitch and stayed well away from the *Champagne* stage and its *enfant terrible*.

When I heard this, I knew it was my chance. By this time, I had realised that there were only freelance photographers working at Elstree, and the best of them, Fred Daniels, a photographer and publicist, was working exclusively for E. A. Dupont. I went to the chief accountant's office. He was a good man named Nicholson. He knew who I was, of course.

I said: "I'm your new head of the stills department. I have my own cameras and I'm going to fix up a studio for portraits in that open loft in the roof of Stage One. I want a chit from you to show Drapes and the stills lab."

He said, rather amused: "What makes you think we need a permanent stills photographer?"

I said: "Ask your publicity department. Ask Harry Lachman – he handled all Rex Ingram's publicity. And I'll get you stills from Alfred Hitchcock's picture."

He said: "If you can do that, you've got the job."

"How much do you pay?"

He hesitated. "Twenty pounds a week. *No* overtime."

"Done."

I had my Akeley tripod with the hand grips and the special head. It was a fine piece of craftsmanship, and I knew that the whole camera unit would know what it was and covet it. The big camera with the Bausch & Lomb lens was in the case with the loaded slides and the usual gadgets. I hefted the tripod on my shoulder, picked up the case and made rather a noisy entrance onto the *Champagne* set. It was a scene in a manager's office. Betty Balfour was applying for a job. Everyone looked at me, including Hitch, who was sitting in his director's chair twiddling his thumbs. He really was the fattest young man I had ever seen. He had a fresh, rosy complexion, his dark hair was sleeked back, and he was correctly dressed in a suit with a watch-chain across the waistcoat. He wore a soft hat. He observed me out of the corner of his piggy eyes sunk in fat cheeks. There was not much that Hitch missed with those piggy eyes.

Hitch had got a loyal and tight little unit together (the first rule of self-preservation for a director) and they took their cue from Hitch, and dead-panned me.

Hitch had met Harry Lachman and probably knew or guessed who I was. Anybody who had worked with one of the great American firms was of interest at Elstree. When the scene was over he said: "Stillsman!"

"Yes, Mr. Hitchcock."

"Do you want a still?" It was a static scene. I shook my head. The afternoon wore on. Twice, Hitch looked at his new stillsman invitingly, and twice, I sadly shook my head. Jack Cox, the lighting cameraman, was a quick worker. He was a big, cheerful man, in a business suit like Hitch's and with an aggressive crest of dark hair. He opened his eyes very wide, which gave him a surprised expression. He was kind and genial. About teatime, some interesting action occurred, and I said: "I'd like a still, please."

Jack looked at Hitch, who nodded. I set up my camera on the bored actors and addressed Hitch, who had never moved from his chair, where he sat Buddha-like.

"Mr Hitchcock, do you mind if I kill some of the lights?" I asked.

Jack stared. Everyone stared. The gaffer looked at Jack. Jack looked at Hitch.

Hitch said: "Mr Cox, do you mind if the stillsman kills some of your lights?"

I said: "It's OK for the movie, but a still doesn't need all that light. Kill Number 18, Number 22, Number 29, and both the sun-arcs."

Hitch twiddled his thumbs. The order was obeyed. The gaffer was a young man, good-looking, eager. Why does his face suddenly leap up before my eyes?

I said: "Mr Cox, would you give me some back light from the near rail?"

Jack said: "16. On Miss Balfour. Spread it."

I said: "And a softer filter for Miss Balfour." Betty looked grateful.

Jack switched on an arc-light and the gaffer put a silk on it.

I said to the actors: "Action, please!" They looked blank. I said: "Go through the action, and when I say 'Hold it!' hold it! Action!" They went through it.

"Hold it!" I took a still. "Could I have another, Mr Hitchcock?"

"Very well, Mr Powell." He had known who I was all along. I had underestimated him.

I explained to the actors: "The stills are to sell the story outside the cinema. You need to overact in a still. Action!" They got the idea and this time I was happy.

"Thank you, Mr Hitchcock."

"Thank *you*, Mr Powell."

They started rehearsing. I went off to see Nicholson.

"I got the still," I told him.

"You did? What did Hitch say? Did you have any trouble?"

"No trouble. Have I got the job?"

"I suppose so." I went off to the story department. Mrs Boyd was out of the room. I started to pack up my papers. Sydney grunted: "Leaving us?"

"Yes. I've got a job on the floor."

"Good for you!"

I went back to the set. They were just about to wrap up. I followed suit.

Hitchcock heaved himself out of the chair. "Would you care to join

Mr Cox and myself in a beer, Mr Powell? This is Mr Eliot Stannard, the author of this dreadful film." Stannard was a dark, wildly handsome, untidy man, with "Fleet Street genius" written all over him. He could talk like an angel and forever. I shook hands all round. We went and had a beer at the big pub by the railway station. I had never tasted English beer before. I had never been in a pub. I had made a friend.

After a few weeks of travelling between Elstree and London in grimy suburban railway carriages, with a long walk in the rain, snow and shit at the end, Lee Planskoy and I decided to live near the studio, at any rate until Spring. Now that I had a living wage, we looked around and found a bungalow in White House Avenue, a dead-end lane which backed onto the studio lot. It had the double advantage that we could fall out of bed into work, and the low fence which separated our garden from the studio was no obstacle to the steady stream of extra girls that Lee was always leading up the garden path.

Lee's technique was a mixture of science and sadism. When he hunted a woman, his concentration was something to marvel at. He would take her hand, kiss it formally, hold onto it, examine it, exclaim at the beauty of the fingers, the colour of the nails, the slender wrist, the ... he could keep this up as long as the object of his sensual approach enjoyed the game. If she withdrew her hand somewhat smartly (as sometimes happened, even to Lee), then he would redouble his formality, stand very tall (he was tall), bow from the waist, rush to open doors and move chairs, light cigarettes and inhale the lady's perfume as a connoisseur of perfumes ...

"Guerlain? No! No! Chanel Cinq? Or Six? Perfect for you. Not every woman can wear such a heavy perfume. But you can! Don't you think that ... but no! It's cheeky of me!" Of course, she would fall for this.

"Your lipstick. You have such a beautiful mouth. It could stand a brighter red than Number 12. Let me try it on you!" (He had lipsticks lying about everywhere.) "Here's a tissue. Wipe that off. Now! Let me show you. That lovely upper lip needs to be fuller. See? Look in the mirror!" And so on, through a complete seduction scene ("I have just the right colour of nail varnish in my room") – to the lock of his bedroom door snapping shut, followed by the most astounding "View halloos" mixed with the bounding of mattresses, chairs, or even tables, offstage.

He had endless ploys in the game of love. He would ignite desire between some cold maiden's legs, by pretending profound disillusionment, quoting Baudelaire: "Toujours le même mouvement ridicule!" Or he would stoke the fires under some willing victim by giving his imitation of a French freight train getting under way, spoken in female undertones that indicated most clearly that whoever got the most pleasure out of sexual intercourse, it was not the male participant:

(Sleepily): *"Fais pas ça . . . fais pas ça . . . fais pas ça!"*

(Half awake): *"Pas si vite . . . e! Pas si vite . . . e! Pas si vite . . . e!"*

(With enthusiasm): *"O! Que c'est bon! O! Que c'est bon! O! Que c'est bon!"*

(Screaming): *"Yoo-oo-oo-ooh!"*

Never, of course, taking his slanting Slav-eyes away from his victim's, nor ceasing to slide an exploring hand up her leg.

My friendship with Hitchcock developed. I met Alma, his wife, a tiny blonde girl, who wrote his scripts under her professional name of Alma Reville. They invited me to their country cottage for the weekend. Shamley Green is a hamlet in the tidy woods and narrow lanes of Surrey, near the village of Bramley, famous for its apples. Ten years later my mother took a cottage there, because it was near the River Wey and the Hog's Back, along which the Pilgrims' Way runs to Farnham and Winchester. (My mother should have written a literary guide to English highways and byways.)

Hitch and Alma's cottage was picturesque, half-timbered, and they were proud of it. They were kind to me, asking me down frequently. I never could understand what they saw in that moody, silent boy. I think that it was my association with great men and great films. Something had brushed off. Like me, Hitch adored films and had great ambitions. Like me, he was impatient with the men who financed the struggling British film industry, looking inward instead of outward. For Hitch as for me, the whole world was our audience, or we failed.

His next film was to be *The Manxman*, adapted by Stannard from a wordy novel by Hall Caine, a Manx writer. It contained strong scenes and the unusual atmosphere of the Isle of Man and its Old Norse customs. The young fisherman-hero was a good part for Carl Brisson, whom Hitch had made a star in *The Ring* and the girl was to be the enchanting Anny Ondra, a Czech actress and cabaret star who had made a name for herself in Berlin. She was the tall, blonde, lovely girl with a sense of humour who is the heroine of most of Hitch's films: Ingrid, Grace, Tippi – and I expect that Hitch wanted to play her in *Champagne* until the British distributors insisted on Betty Balfour. Anny's real name, by the way, was Anny Ondrakova. She was a neat chick.

As I had appointed myself head of the stills department it was my job to arrange portrait sessions, and this introduced me to all the contract stars of British International Pictures. They were not a very exciting lot. There were several films shooting on the floor of the studio, and Lee and I made the tour of them together. I would grab the director and introduce myself and then bring up Lee, introducing him, according to the fantasy of the moment as "Dr Planskoy, who is preparing his version of *The Brothers Karamazov* with puppets", or "Lee Planskoy, an assistant of René Clair's". The prop-man would be ordered to bring chairs and we would sink into them, whispering in French, and would stay just long enough to get the actors, director and cameramen into a state of nerves.

There was one interesting portrait session I remember, arranged by a German cameraman called Werner Brandes. His star must have been playing a ballerina, because she was in a *Swan Lake* costume with feathers. I was pleased with the portraits, for she knew how to pose. She was married to Alex Korda, at that time a little-known Hungarian director, and she emphasized the difference in their importance by spelling her name with a "C" – Corda.

There was one other experience in my days as a stills photographer at Elstree that I would have been sorry to have missed. I had succeeded in getting a stills studio rigged up, and one morning I was doing a photo session of some dumb blonde. In an attempt to make her interesting, I had torn the clothes off her and covered her with balloons. But she had no sense of humour and I was getting nowhere. I became aware that I was being watched by a dapper, light-boned, self-assured young man, very neatly dressed, with a carefully trimmed, small moustache. He introduced himself as Christopher Mann and said he was an agent. One of his clients, a young actress called Madeleine Carroll, was to play the leading part in a film to be made at Elstree. It was called *The Firstborn*. He wanted to bring Miss Carroll to my notice: he thought she had a great future. He mentioned with modest pride that she had proved herself as an actress at the famous Manchester Repertory Theatre. He was from Manchester himself. He needed portraits of her for publicity.

There was something about his brisk matter-of-factness that I liked. I said I would look out for her.

In due time, this budding star arrived at Elstree for photographic tests, and I was on hand with my camera. So was Christopher Mann, but he kept out of the director's eyeline. The director's name was Miles Mander. He was the author, scriptwriter and director of the picture. He was also the leading actor. He and Madeleine were to play husband and wife. The other characters were mere silhouettes. I shot my stills. She was provincial, beautiful and inexperienced. I decided that this was a *ménage à trois* that might be worth watching. But I was already sorry for Christopher Mann.

Mander was a sadist. Of course, most men are sadists, give or take a little, and women subscribe to it, but most men have some sense of shame. Miles Mander had none. (No more than old Renoir, the painter and father of Jean Renoir the film director, who said in an interview: "I paint with my prick.") A film director, of course, has unique possibilities for sadistic pleasures. But as writer, director, actor, Mander had it three ways. It was easy for him to humiliate Madeleine in public and take advantage of her innocence in a bathroom sequence, which exposed her to a gaping crew and delighted the dark recesses of his libido. He knew he could have her whenever he wanted, so he spent the whole time during the making of the film in exposing and humiliating her in explicit bedroom scenes, where he dragged her about and did everything short of laying her in front of the camera. He was his own leading man, remember. It was interesting to watch.

Miles Mander was a clever, ingenious man who, coming from nowhere in particular, had written and starred in his own play in the West End and made a personal success. Straight actors looked at him a bit askance. He made *The Firstborn* from his own play, and he soon went to Hollywood, which was where he belonged. The last time I saw him at the Berkeley Grill, he was lunching with Merle Oberon, who had been discovered by Alex Korda just then, when she was an unknown Anglo-Indian girl with the kind of Eurasian beauty that one sees in dreams. Intimates of Mander told me that he carried his public sadism home with him and would never lay a girl if he couldn't first strap her to the bed and beat her till she howled for mercy. It's possible. But he must have been very good in bed to make up for the beatings. He was a thin, elegant man with the eyes of a ferret, a curly moustache, and a mannered way of speaking that suggested a cavalry colonel. Altogether an unforgettable character, particularly to the ladies.

Although Madeleine was a bit confused by her association with Mander, Chris remained her manager and she soon became the brightest and most popular star in England, pure and ladylike, a schoolboy's dream, until she met Alfred Hitchcock and Robert Donat on *The Thirty-Nine Steps* in 1935. They soon knocked the stuffing out of her demure, lifeless, saintlike image, and she revealed that she had a sense of humour. Miles Mander had given her sex appeal. She became a world star and deserved it. She had staying power – she was from Birmingham.

Although I was titular head of the stills department, it was agreed by Hitch and me that I should personally shoot all stills on his pictures, and go along with him on location hunts. We were already exchanging ideas for future pictures. When it came to shooting *The Manxman*, only two scenes were shot on the Isle of Man. Hitch was not enthralled by local colour, except in city streets. Mostly, we shot around Minehead in Somerset, and in North Cornwall. The truth is Hitch was bored. One day he threw a playscript at me to read.

"What is it, Hitch?"

"It's a play by Charles Bennett." he said. "Very good, but his Act III is rotten. Charles never could write an Act III. See what you think of it. We might work on a script of it together."

I looked at the title: *Blackmail*. I read it and came back to Hitch with enthusiasm. "It will make a swell movie."

"What about the third act?"

"To hell with the third act. We'll make it a chase. Films don't need a third act."

It was about a beautiful, innocent blonde – I was already in love with Anny Ondra, so that part was easy – who is taken by a charming painter to his studio and invited to strip off. When he tries to rape her, she stabs him with a pair of scissors and by bad luck kills him. She escapes unseen, as she thinks. Her fiancé is the detective who is put on the case. A blackmailer appears who has seen her enter and leave the flat. The girl has nobody to help her and becomes desperate. Her fiancé discovers that she is being blackmailed and begins to suspect the truth, but, when he corners the blackmailer, the man panics, runs into the traffic and is killed. The play finishes on a question-mark. Will he denounce his girl, who has killed in self-defence, or not? Probably not. But in that case, he will have to resign from the police. Good stuff. But Act III *was* weak.

The invitation from Hitch, whose acute sense of cinema I admired, was the best thing that had happened to me in England. I started to make notes right away and discussed the part with Anny Ondra, while taking romantic still photographs of her charming face and body in the woods of Somerset. Hitch occasionally came with us and looked moodily on.

"You don't want to take all those solos of Anny," he said. "You want to get a boy with her in the hay and she's pressing up against him to feel his cock against her leg." He loved to talk bawdy: it made up for his gross, clumsy body. I am sure he wanted Anny as much as I did. But she, alas, was in love with someone else. Once, when we were talking together, she took my head and looked into my eyes and said: "Powell! Why are you not older? You could direct me." I was tongue-tied. Dear Anny! She married Max Schmeling, the boxer. I hope she had a happy life.

As soon as we got back from exteriors to the studio scenes of *The Manxman*, Hitch and I started writing the script of *Blackmail*. He and Alma had a London apartment in a tall, sooty brick house, one of a continuous line of houses in the Cromwell Road – I think Number 155 – that back onto the underground railway, like a cliff. Theirs was the top flat, so that the thunder of the passing trains was distant, like the waves on the pebbles of Sandgate beach. I always imagined it was here that the body was deposited on top of the train from the open window in one of my favourite detective stories, for the trains would frequently stop there at a red light, and I would check how easy it would be to push the body out. Fifteen seconds, I reckoned.

Since *Blackmail* was a London story, our collaboration was perfect. Quite apart from being a Cockney from the East End of London, Hitch's knowledge of London was peculiar and delightful, east of Temple Bar. Towards the West End he had in his films a more conventional approach because, to him, it only meant eating well in expensive restaurants, or going to the theatre to see some actor or actress who had made a hit. But with the lower-middle-class Londoners of our film, shopkeepers, barrow-boys, hawkers, match-girls, hangers-on at the tails of the garment business, policemen, detectives, reporters, copper's narks, thieves and pickpockets, he continually delighted me with the extent of his knowledge and the sharpness of his observation. He had already decided that Donald Calthrop, a complex and brilliant actor, would play the blackmailer. Calthrop came of a famous and gifted theatrical family: he despised films, but liked the money, two opinions that have often combined in a superb piece of screen acting.

When we came to the chase through the streets, I broached an idea that I had been maturing for a while.

"Hitch! Don't let's do an ordinary chase through the streets like you did in *The Lodger*. Let's take it into some bizarre location that is entertaining in itself."

"What do you mean? What do you think Michael means, Alma?" Alma looked encouragingly at me.

I had been thinking of my visits to the British Museum Reading Room to see my grandfather, and the impression that had been made upon me by his bent figure, at his desk, dwarfed by the height of the shelves and topped by the glass dome over the whole vast room, and I went on: "Let's have him slip into the British Museum at night and get chased through rooms full of Egyptian mummies and Elgin Marbles, and climb higher to escape, and be cornered and then fall through the glass dome of the Reading Room and break his neck."

Hitch, being a Londoner, had never been near the British Museum Reading Room, but he saw the possibilities of the idea, and so I think I can make a modest claim to being the inventor of the Hitchcock Climax, unveiled to the world through the chase in *Blackmail*, and which led us all on many a delightful dance from Tower Bridge to Mount Rushmore, from the Statue of Liberty to you name it.

Meanwhile, Lee and I had separated, although neither of us lost touch with Harry Lachman, who had struck up a friendship with Monty Banks, an Italian-American comedian (Montebianco) who had made a name for himself in Hollywood with two-reelers full of pratfalls and stunts. He was now in England and Harry was soon to direct a picture for him.

Lee had become enthusiastic about film trick-work. Till now there had been no great hurry about developing trick processes for general use in storytelling, but with the coming of synchronised sound, when sound effects and dialogue became the masters for a dozen years, and action became more and more confined to the studio, trick-work became important. The aim was to convince the audience that a film had been made in real locations, when it was actually a combination of actors in the studio being superimposed upon real backgrounds by various means such as back projection, front projection and what we called "matte painting".

Lee had found a sponsor for his trick-work experiments in Jerry Jackson. Jerry was a young New York lawyer, Jerome Jacob Jackson, destined to join his father's law firm and marry a nice Jewish girl, already picked out by his mama. He escaped. Nathan Burkan sent him over to London on a special mission as the representative of Nick Schenck, the president of United Artists, and one look at London in 1928 was enough to infect Jerry with Anglomania. Jerry was good-looking, thirty, quick-witted, kind, generous, and as forthright about sex relations as any lady could wish. It was like taking an Irish-bred stallion from the banks of the Boyne and turning him out on Kentucky blue grass.

The London office of United Artists, presided over by Murray Silverstone, gentle, hard-working and cosy, was an indulgent guardian. Jerry looked around. Being fresh from New York he knew all about the coming tidal wave of Sound which was going to turn the poverty-stricken, out-of-date British film industry upside down in the next eighteen months. Jerry decided to be a film-maker. In London.

Lee took me to meet the man who was to be my partner for the next seven years and my best friend for ten years. Jerry's headquarters was a poky office over a shop in Gerrard Street, Soho. There was a street market outside. Inside were a secretary, Jerry, and a projectionist with a film threaded up.

"He wants you to look at it," explained Lee, picking strands of tobacco off his long, thin lips (he had recently taken to rolling his own). "It's German, it's silent and nobody wants it." (How often must a similar short, damning phrase have been spoken in New York when they later screened our films I *Know Where I'm Going* or *Colonel Blimp* and looked at each other in dismay, before the inevitable remark: "This will take some selling.")

We went in, shook hands, and Jerry looked a bit startled at the youth of his new editor. The film was screened. It starred Lilian Harvey and Robin Irvine and was directed by Lupu Pick. It was a comedy, a thin one, even its title, *A Knight in London* seemed to apologise for it. I could almost hear the pun being explained to its German producers: "Knight – keine Nacht ist, aber *A Night in London* ist nicht gut. Mit 'k' ist besser für England." Then, desperately: "It's a joke!" The polite blank faces nod hopefully. It is an English joke.

I knew Lupu Pick as a fine director in Germany. He looked like a Chinaman. His film was beautiful to look at because it had Lilian Harvey, and the photography was up to UFA's best standard. (UFA was the principal producer and distributor in Germany with studios at Neubabels-burg, whose boss was Erich Pommer.) Harvey had a neat little body and elfin eyes and there was a pretty scene where she took a shower. Robin Irvine was a polished young comedian with a style of his own (he died prematurely, or he would have certainly gone to Hollywood); but tasteful nudity only seemed to make the film more respectable (Lupu Pick had excellent taste), and respectability without titillation has seldom been box-office. The film needed Ernst Lubitsch's enchanting vulgarity. I cut it from eight reels to five, collected fifty pounds in the hand (an enormous fee for me) and notified Nicholson at the studio that I was visiting my father in the South of France for Christmas.

"I can't promise to hold your job open for you," he said, no doubt thinking of the way Hitch had adopted me into his unit.

"Oh, that's all right," I said loftily, never dreaming he might mean it.

The reason I was returning to France was not to see my wife, who was now with her mother in Georgia, USA, dancing on tables and cutting up generally – she was reportedly known as Gay Powell – but to see Peggy.

Peggy was twenty and I was twenty-three, and there had never been a union like ours since the completion of the Union Pacific Railway. She was American and a darling. She had a helmet of golden hair cut in a bob, traces of puppy fat, and was working her way around Europe in the splendid way that American girls were doing after the First World War had redressed the balance of the Old World. Curiosity had brought Peggy to Elstree as an extra, and as I was romantic about American girls it was love at first sight. She had a job looking after a child which was taking her to Nice, to Cimiez, the health resort on the hill behind the city. I followed her.

My father was cautiously glad to see me. He abandoned caution when he learnt that I had a round-trip ticket.

I never went near the Victorine. When I look back now, it is hard to say why I neglected the master and the studio that I loved. I think that I felt I had betrayed them by choosing to follow Harry's star. Instead, I saw a lot of Tomatis, who had opened a little photo-shop at the Pont Magnan, not far from his flat on the Avenue de la Californie where he lived with his wife and two sons. He kept me posted with all the latest action and deluged me with questions about the English scene. He was one of several men I was to meet in my profession whom I have loved and admired for their love of their job and their fellow men.

Rex had completed *The Three Passions*, based on a novel by Cosmo Hamilton, and it was not, apparently, a box-office hit. I never saw it. He was now deep in preparation and research for an all-Arab film about tribal war in the Atlas Mountains, called *Baroud*. Andrews Engelmann, the monocled U-boat captain of *Mare Nostrum*, was to give a superb performance in it as a Riff warrior. Rex was faced with a tough budget, and was no longer backed by MGM. He had heard from Grant Whytock, who was acting supervisor on *White Shadows on the South Seas*, that music and effects would have to be added to his films, and some key scenes reshot with synchronised dialogue, if the film were to be acceptable in the USA. He decided to play the leading male role, a French officer, himself, trusting to his profile to carry him through the love-scenes with Rosita Ramirez. Unfortunately, Grant wasn't there, pin in hand, to stimulate them both. Alice had gone home to see to their property and check on the chaotic scene in Hollywood. She reported suicides and ruin stalking through the colony, as contract after contract was torn up, or forcibly settled. Broadway actors and actresses from the legitimate theatre were in demand. Suddenly, it was no longer *faces*, it was *voices*. Directors of imagination and flair were pushed aside by an influx of dialogue directors. Stars of vaudeville and burlesque were smartening up routines which had served them well for many a year, to sell this new talking-picture market for astronomical fees. Money talked.

Most of this I learnt from Gerald Fielding, who had decided on an acting career after his success in *The Garden of Allah*. He had thrown in his lot with Rex. A few years earlier his romantic good looks, guided by Rex, would have made him a star. He had poise and temperament. But he was an image, like Valentino, not an actor, like Ramon Novarro: and the days of images were numbered. Our wonderful silent world, shining and as iridescent and insubstantial as a soap bubble, was exploding and vanishing before the heat of the microphone. Overnight, the magic shadow show had faded and the realities of the American voice had taken its place. Charlie Chaplin had already announced that he would never speak in a film. What? Never! Well . . . hardly ever. Others, with vast investment in the movie business, announced that they trusted to the loyalty of their public. They were disillusioned.

When I returned to England, I found that the realities of the sound revolution had reached Elstree and was rocking it like Hollywood. Hitch was in production with *Blackmail* and told me that he was already insisting that British International Pictures find the money to add sound-effects and some dialogue scenes to it. In the end, he shot the picture retaining all the intimacy and imagery of a silent film, in which the director always had the camera in the right place. Then he reworked it as a sound film, a style which was to stay with both him and me for the rest of our working lives. For us, a movie would always be a piece of visual entertainment with sound and dialogue heightening it.

It is almost impossible for one of the Old Silent Brigade like myself to explain to you postwar generations, stunned by radio, sugared by television, with an occasional movie on the side, what the coming of sound meant to a maker of silent film. But I will try. Perhaps I should start by telling you that most of the leaders in the industry thought that films with synchronised sound were just a flash in the pan. (Some flash! Some pan!) They pointed to the huge grosses that silent films had been piling up that year, and said there was no reason to think that the public wanted talkies. They soon changed their tune and joined the mad scramble to get in sync. America led the world, as usual. If a rich and successful entertainment industry like the motion picture business had to be redesigned and recapitalised, the Americans had the guts and the money to do it. Studios had to be redesigned and sound-proofed. Theatres had to be equipped with sound projection. It entailed the investment not of a few millions, but of hundreds of millions. The new technicians moved in. There was panic among the stars. Sound was king. Money talked.

British inertia had a field-day. The leaders of the industry were watching which way the American cat would jump. "Nasty talkies! Go away, nasty talkies!" – but the nasty talkies wouldn't go away. Suddenly, giants with weird names like Western Electric and RCA were saying "Fee, Fi, Fo, Fum, I smell the blood of an Englishman!" and bleeding them white with royalties. "Sound-proof and equip your studio, sir? Certainly, sir! Sign on the dotted line, sir. Take your place in the line, sir. Yes, that long line, sir. When do we deliver, sir? In about a year, chum, if you're lucky."

All over Europe, sound-synchronised films were sweeping the board. They didn't have to be talkies. Some of them were semi-talkies, some of them had only one scene that was a talkie, others had synchronised sound-effects and music. But the old silent film, the glorious old silent film, was dead. Studios were going dark all over Europe. Technicians were out of work. Overnight, the American market had vanished. All over the world, people were demanding talkies in their own language. An art that spoke a universal language had ceased to exist. Money talked.

Hitch was always ahead of the game. Somehow, he had got hold of some German equipment and was shooting synchronised sound scenes to be included in the final version of *Blackmail*. It was to be billed and sold as Britain's first talkie. What a showman he was! I went down to Elstree to see him. He was shooting extra sound scenes between Anny Ondra and Cyril Ritchard, her seducer in the film. Anny had a Czech accent you could cut with a knife, so Hitch had hired a bright young actress, Joan Barry, to speak Anny's Cockney lines off-camera, while Anny mouthed them in front of the camera. It was a mad idea, but it worked. Hitch was listening to the scene on a dud set of earphones, judging by his expression. He waved to me and I waved back, then I looked around. Where was Jack Cox? Where was the sound-proofed camera? I edged carefully around the set to where the camera was presumably hidden, and found it in a sort of sweat-box which contained the camera and the whole camera crew. In front was a thick glass panel through which they were shooting, which could hardly have improved the quality of the black and white film, however much they cleaned it with alcohol. At the rear was a trap-door through which they crawled. As I arrived there, it opened and I saw Jack Cox's rear end coming out of it. He was always a very natty dresser, even on the set, but he had discarded coat and tie and waistcoat and was pouring with sweat. No wonder: there were three of them inside this sound-proof box. He saw me and groaned.

"Look what they've done to us, Micky! We're shooting through glass, ordinary plate glass an eighth of an inch thick, with my beautiful Cook lenses! I've lost ten pounds in the last three days. Look at this bloody box!" He gave it a kick. "And Hitch is asking for a mobile camera. Mobile, I ask you!" He gave the offending box two more kicks.

I had lunch with Hitch in his office.

"Silent films are a dead duck, Micky," he said. "Nobody wants 'em. The big American companies are cutting their losses on the films already made or planned. Sound is the only thing making money. I had my head in the sand like everybody else. Ostriches. That's what we were, you and I. Ostriches."

"It was great while it lasted, Hitch. We got the camera moving, we had it running, we had it flying. Once the camera learnt to move, to pan, we could do anything, couldn't we?"

He nodded. "We'll get the camera moving again."

"Amen," I said.

I soon found that I was out of work as well. Even my cherished but ponderous eight-by-ten stills camera was out of date. My job had been taken over by Fred Daniels, an action photograher, a stills pioneer, who despised posed stills. I got a call from Harry Lachman. The film he was directing for Monty Banks was one of the last silent film comedies to be made, *The Compulsory Husband*. They were about to leave for Chamonix in the French Alps, where the exterior sequences would be made. I joined Harry in my usual capacity as stills photographer, location editor, interpreter, assistant director and stuntman. Those were innocent days.

A sequence where Monty Banks gets on skis which run away with him, kept me busy doubling the star. My resources were limited, even by *Travelaugh* standards. I remember there was one sequence where Monty finds himself heading straight for a peasant's house surrounded by a fence. A boy with a luge opens a gate in the fence just in time for Monty to shoot through. A girl opens the front door of the house and he continues on in. Inside the house is an old lady cooking. He upsets her. A man opens the outer door in time for him to shoot out into the yard. An old man with a beard has just finished mending the garden gate. Monty gets straight through it, smashing the gate to smithereens and sending the old man into a snowdrift. I was the boy with the luge, the girl at the door, the mother cooking, the peasant entering, and the furious old man in the snowdrift as well.

I had read little French during the year I had been in England. I had hardly read *at all*. At Chamonix I bought a copy of *Climats* by André Maurois, and it started me reading again. All my old passion for books returned, and I started a plan of reading in both languages which still continues. It has been one of the great joys of my life. It has kept me humble. I have only to see that faithful, tattered French paperback, published by Grasset, among the shelves of French books in my cottage, to remember Chamonix and Maurois with gratitude. He wrote well, and he wrote simply, but his phrases were often memorable and his two love stories are completely believable. Very few people, since Benjamin Constant, have written better.

While we were in Chamonix shooting slapstick, Lee, back in London, had struck up a friendship with the great German cameraman Karl Freund, the only man in international cinema who was fatter than Alfred Hitchcock. He had invented a sort of tricycle to carry the camera through doors and along passages when he was shooting *Tartuffe* and *The Last Laugh*, both for Murnau, and to see him balancing his enormous bottom on the tiny saddle of his machine while he operated the camera, was unforgettable. He had come to England to join Ludwig Blattner, a promoter of genius with far-seeing ideas about technical developments in Sound and Colour. Blattner had bought the small Ideal Studios, a bunch of brick buildings in the middle of an Elstree field, and with him from Germany he had brought the patent rights to the Stille (steel tape) sound recording process and the rights to a French invention, the Keller Dorian colour film, a lenticular process by which dozens of small lenses were indented on each frame of black and white film, producing instant and accurate colour in projection through a prism. With these two inventions, Blattner reasonably expected to make his fortune, but he needed a film as a showcase, and he commissioned Freund, whose name and reputation was known world-wide, to make a sound film in colour, using the two processes.

Karl turned to Lee Planskoy for advice in finding a story, and Lee, when I returned from Chamonix, turned to me. I don't remember whose idea it

was, but by the middle of the summer I found myself with the travel writer
Rosita Forbes as a companion, rattling across Europe to the Italian port of
Bari, there to take ship for Albania, where we were to do research and write
a film script about a blood feud between two families. As the family of King
Zog of Albania was presently at daggers drawn with Ras Touelli, the King
of the Mountains, and we had already decided to visit him, it was evident
that there would be plenty of realism in the screenplay.

Rosita Forbes (this was her pen-name, her married name was Lady
McGrath) was a well-known writer, traveller and romantic figure of the
twenties. She was tall, loose-limbed, curly-haired, with large, liquid eyes
and an attractive smile. She had done all the right things: crossed the Gobi
Desert and discovered the sources of all the most fashionable rivers. Her
amatory exploits with various public figures were felt, somehow, to be
right. She was rather put out when she discovered that I had never heard
of her.

We were met at Tiranë, then the name of the capital of Albania, by
Colonel Stirling, who had been with Lawrence in Arabia and was now
head of the police in Albania, don't ask me why. After a World War, the
British have a way of popping up in all sorts of strange positions. His
authority in the country was concentrated in his walking-stick, which he
gripped firmly at all times. He was weather-beaten and pessimistic. I liked
him. He had heard of Rosita Forbes, which raised her morale a bit. Tiranë
is in the plain between the mountains and the sea. Not far away is
Argirokastro and the Greek border, where guerrilla fighting between the
two countries was still going on. We got our papers and moved up the
coast. Among our party was a young man called Stroud Read. If he had any
other name, I never heard it. He was along for the ride. Something to do
with London University. Or perhaps not.

It was proposed that we march up into the interior, using the pack-
horse tracks which were styled "roads". I suggested horses, and saw to
it that I had a good one. It was years since I had been on a horse, but once
a horseman, always a horseman. I let my animal pick his own way on the
hair-raising paths we had to follow for three days. Rosita Forbes, who was
not a horsewoman, fell off and broke her collarbone. She was quite good
about it.

We arrived in the high country where Prince Ras Touelli had his castle.
It was quite a strong place, a crusader castle with steep ramps and towers
and lavatories in the corner towers, where if you felt inclined you could
watch your shit fall away to the foot of the towers. We stayed two days.
The prince's two sons were home for the holidays. They were at school in
Italy. Italy, or rather Mussolini, had designs on Albania.

At noon we heard the wolves howling in the high hills. It was a weird
sound, like a finger rubbed around a wine-glass. They weren't hungry, they

were just singing. They come down in the winter in packs of three or four hundred. They had cleaned out a police post the winter before. Somebody left a door or window open and the pack got in. The man who found the post in the morning was with us. He went grey as he described it. It had been a shambles: blood over the walls and roof, bones and clothing mixed with the bodies of wolves, not a scrap of flesh left on the bones.

I took a few black and white stills of our journey, but I can't find any of them. Albania is not a scenic country, but the men are magnificent and the few women that we saw – we were in Muslim country – were handsome. None of the men on the coast would accompany us into the mountains, but the mountaineers were not averse to escorting us down to the coast, armed to the teeth. They were very tall, lean men wearing a costume which was a mixture between Italian and Montenegrin, topped with a round brimless hat. They had excellent lungs. They put their fingers in their ears and shouted from hilltop to hilltop, in voices of extraordinary carrying power. I suppose they stopped their ears to keep from bursting the drums, and to concentrate the sound on the distant point.

I had worked out a story with Rosita Forbes, openly stolen from Prosper Mérimée. She was going on to Athens to stay at the embassy and send back a few articles to London. I took the boat back to Bari, which I forgot to explain is a port on the Adriatic coast, near to Brindisi, but less of an international port. The town is prosperous, friendly and dignified. I was burnt as brown as a nut and wore my khaki shirt, riding breeches and boots with a bit of a swagger. I suddenly found I had made an impression on two Italian girls on board and they were not backward in making it clear. The prettier one had olive skin and dark eyes, with small white teeth in a mouth with a downward curve. We got into conversation. We talked French, as my Italian was *brutto*, to say the least. Our eyes made up for the lack of words. By the time the ship docked we were holding hands. Their parents were waving from the dock. Suddenly I felt a piece of paper thrust into my hand, a kiss on my cheek and they were gone, looking back over their shoulders. There was an address on the piece of paper.

A reconnaissance, an open window, and a parting at dawn seemed to be called for, but the plain fact was that after reconnoitering their house, I saw the whole family, *en paseo*, as they promenaded through the main street in company with all the other respectable families in the town. The girls pointed me out. Their parents looked. The girls smiled. I bowed, they bowed. I followed them at a distance to their house in a quiet street. They went in. I passed by slowly. The heavy outside door was not closed, and my lovely girl suddenly appeared. We rushed into each other's arms. I can never forget that moment. It was exquisite. It was romantic. It lasted ten seconds and has lasted fifty years. Do you remember, I wonder, warm-hearted, lovely old lady in Bari? She tore herself away, pressed another note into my hand and disappeared. The door shut. I looked at the single sentence under a street lamp. *"Papa a beaucoup admiré votre courage."*

In the morning I took the train back to Milan and London.

Our story of a blood feud was never filmed. Disaster had befallen Blattner's plans. In America, the giant firms of RCA and Western Electric were fighting between themselves to become the dominant sound system in Hollywood. Warner Brothers had their own system, Vitaphone. In Germany, Klangfilm-Tobis had their own steel tape process. The American giants soon took over Britain, leaving no room for Blattner. His colour process was excellent, but too excellent for its competitors, like Kodak, Technicolor and Agfacolour. They bought up the Keller-Dorian system and shelved it. Disillusioned, temperamental and despairing, Ludwig Blattner committed suicide. His son, Gerald, carried the Blattner name on in the business. The studios were bought by Joe Rock, another American showman-comedian, who had come to Elstree to establish himself as a producer.

Karl Freund decided to go to Hollywood, where MGM wanted him. His ambition was to direct, and America was to be the centre of the movie business for the next ten years. He tried to get Lee to go with him. He was interested in Lee's experiments in trick work and promised him the technical camera department of Culver City to play with. But Lee didn't want to go to America; he had succeeded in interesting Jerry Jackson in his ideas and Jerry was ready to back his experiments. So Karl Freund went and I was out of a job.

By now *Blackmail* was finished and distributed, publicised as "The First British Talkie". It was a smash hit and put Hitch on top of the heap. It had all the atmosphere and suspense of *The Lodger*, plus a few clever tricks with sound, like the repetition of the word "knife . . . knife . . . knife!" rising to a hysterical scream from the girl as she relives the moment of the murder. And the film *talked*! Charles Bennett's dialogue (not to mention mine and Hitch's) was spare and taut. The film had all the visual appeal of a silent film and a suspense which mounted steadily to our British Museum climax. John Longden as the detective, Anny as the girl, Donald Calthrop as the blackmailer, underplaying every scene so that he walked away with the film, were all good. When the film reached Hollywood, Hitch was deluged with offers. But he wasn't ready to go. Yet.

Meanwhile, for others less gifted, less famous, there was a slump in London. Only the distributors of American films were making money. Elstree was converting slowly to Sound. Harry Lachman was preparing to shoot a sound version of Thomas Hardy's *Under the Greenwood Tree*, with lengthy sequences of the village choir and the village orchestra playing country songs and dances. The other studios, which were mostly scattered around the suburbs of London, were shuttered or looking for finance to convert. Hundreds of technicians were out of work. Lee had his small back room, financed by Jerry Jackson, where he could spend the days glaring through a spectrophotometer. I was on the beach.

Organised by Lee, we took three dingy apartments, one on top of the other, in a terraced house with basement in Bryanston Street, near Marble Arch. The house has gone and no blue plaque or marble slab commemorates our tenancy. I had the ground floor flat, Lee had the one above, and Merrill Hoxie, an American who worked for RCA as an engineer, occupied the top floor. The manager of the apartments lived next door in a similar house. With due notice he was prepared to serve meals on trays. Girls came and went as they do around any unattached bachelors.

Many years later, in 1971, I had an office at 4 Albemarle Street, in an eighteenth-century building opposite to the publisher John Murray, and the fascinating shop of Captain Watts, known to all small-boat sailors. Our building was owned by Agnew's, the picture dealers, whose premises went through the block into Bond Street. On our other side was the Marlborough Gallery, the National Book League and the Folio Society. It was an exclusive quarter.

One day, when I was abroad, an angel visited us. At least that was how Bill Paton described her. "A tall lissome lady, a blonde, with cheeks like roses. She said you had been friends together in the early days, when you still had your way to make. She must be all of fifty, if that's the case, but she didna look it." It was Muriel Angelus! "She said ye'd mind her." Mind her!

My heart turned over. Of course I remembered Muriel, of the golden hair, the blue eyes with eyelashes that needed no mascara, and a skin that would make rose petals seem abrasive. How generous, frank and undemanding she had been during our love affair. No lucky, young, penniless student in Murger's *Scènes de la Vie de Bohème* was so lucky as I. She had a mouth made for love.

"Didn't she leave a number? An address?"

"No. She said that if you had been there, it would have been nice to talk over old times. But as you weren't, I was to say she had hoped to see you."

So Muriel still had her sense of theatre, her sense of mystery! How smart she had been to leave no follow-up, to have passed like an angel! I was tormented with curiosity and hoped fervently that she would reappear, for I concluded that she was on a visit to London and, as I had never heard news of her before, that she had probably married an American and lived in the USA, a guess which proved to be correct.

Providence intervened. In November 1980, the Museum of Modern Art held a retrospective of my films and the *New York Times* wrote me up generously. An angel wrote from Wilton, Connecticut. It was Muriel. "It's a lovely warm feeling to reach across the years to an old-time beloved friend," she wrote. Proust didn't put it half so well.

She enclosed colour snaps of her house at Belden Hill under snow, of her grandson Brian (fifteen months) and of a tall, slim, confident woman in unpretentious smock and blue jeans. "I have not gone completely to seed, but neither am I the beautiful angel you remember. I have just grown in wisdom and understanding. No face lift or dyed hair. Just me."

How beautiful love is when we allow it room to grow and to become part of our lives. How little we understand it when it happens to us. How comforting it is to realise that an image of yourself, that you have perhaps forgotten, or never recognised, exists in the heart of someone who loved, who perhaps still loves you after half a century has passed.

It's all been said before, but these are things you have to find out for yourself, without the help of poets.

Shall we ever meet again? I am at the age when you count the days rather than the years. I have always loved each day. *Carpe diem!* "Seize the day," the Latin proverb that the Reverend H. V. Tower translated as "Make hay while the sun shines." It will serve as my motto. I am reckless rather than brave. In 1929, Muriel was a burst of sunlight in a fog of despair.

It is a bitter experience to be out of work when you love your job; when you realise that the profession you have given yourself to, can get along without you. It has happened to me three times: the winter of 1929–30; the summer of 1937; and the years between 1970 and 1979.

You may wonder why, in 1929, I didn't use my friends who were working; why I didn't ask Hitch or Harry Lachman to help me to a job. I think it was partly pride in my profession. I knew that I had a grasp of every department of the business, the sort of knowledge that takes years to acquire if you are not so lucky as I had been. I knew very little of life, and all of it from books, but I held exalted views of movies as a storytelling medium and had a high opinion of the intelligence of our audiences. Hitchcock had made a talkie of Sean O'Casey's *Juno and the Paycock*, and in spite of erratic casting he had shown what could be done with tragedy in the new medium. His camera-work was as mobile as ever, because he insisted on it.

I suppose that my diffidence in not asking for work was due partly to pride and partly to the fact that I had been mollycoddled from the beginning. I had never had to fight for myself. My father had got Harry to take me, and Harry had been my guiding star with Rex, Harry had kidnapped me from MGM and taken me to England, Hitchcock had been my Elstree sponsor, with Lee a sort of Mephistopheles appearing and disappearing in puffs of smoke, half-admiring, half contemptuous of my encyclopaedic knowledge and cheerful willingness to tackle anything – and then it had all come to a stop! Just when I should have been learning to use the new talkie medium, I was outside the gates. The American Jerry

Jackson and the showbiz newspaper *Variety*, were my only contacts with Hollywood and New York. With the British film industry I had no contacts at all. Or so I thought.

Unknown to me, Jerry had ambitions to be a producer, and he listened to Lee when that authority assured him that I was capable of any job in the movies. He often came to see us, bringing magnificent presents of wine and food from Fortnum and Mason, and Lee was already working for him on the Planskoy Process. But Jerry was still with United Artists and Nick Schenck, and he had to be careful how he used Wardour Street, and all the people in film distribution that he knew, to further his own ambitions.

By Christmas, I could hold out no longer and I went home to Mother.

My amazing mother welcomed me with open arms. I had visited her at Turling Farm during my two years at Elstree, but only for lightning visits, as when, for instance, I was scouting locations in the West Country with Hitch. I still poured out my experiences to her in letters. In the summer of 1928, I had even joined my mother again for a few days at "The Look Out", the hut at Sandbanks where we had spent the last holiday with my brother John, and had trailed my glamorous coat-tails around Ringwood; and had even looked in benevolently on old acquaintances at the three banks. I don't remember that my mother and I ever had a conversation about my idiot marriage, which could very easily have spoilt two lives. She was not a believer in inquests. There was always too much to do in the present.

Now here I was slinking back home to Mother's after being, according to my account, the Toast of Europe. The confident and casual frequenter of those mysterious concrete barns called film studios was outside the gates. For five years I had had free run of the men and the mechanics that transformed lights, sets, magic and performers into that incredible piece of extravagance, the feature film. I had a smattering of half a dozen crafts, and was expert at none. I only knew that I was a film director, was born to be a film director, and would never be satisfied with any other job but a film director's.

Turling Farm was situated at the upper end of Poole Harbour, where the train to Wareham and Weymouth crosses the narrows on an iron bridge. It was as remote as it was possible to be in coastal Dorset. The farmhouse was a small brick cottage with a slate roof and small windows. With the help of a local young man called Roy, my mother was already transforming it. There were a few outbuildings: nothing so grand as a barn, but there was a henhouse and piggeries and a row of home-made hutches for the rabbits that were intended to make my mother's fortune. There was also Jane.

Jane was a Sealyham bitch and had already given birth to four daughters, named, naturally Meg, Jo, Beth and Amy. Later on she was to achieve a litter of four sons, named Roly, Poly, Gammon and Spinach. Jane was a splendid mother. Over the next ten years she shared my mother's wanderings and adventures.

My mother had learnt to drive and had bought a battered open tourer made by Wolseley. By driving it to and fro between the house and the piggeries, I learnt, too. Greatly daring, I took it out on the rough track which led across the moor to the main railway line, where there was a locked gate to which we had a key. In those days there were no driving tests and there was nothing to stop me crossing the lines and driving into Poole. But even my confidence failed before such a piece of folly. Driving a car in England has never been the natural thing it is to every American, particularly to people of my generation between the two World Wars, who were whisked violently into the twentieth century, as Judy Garland was whisked into Oz by the twister.

There was no telephone on that lonely moor and we went into Poole once a week for the mail and the marketing. I discovered the delights of harpooning sand-dabs in the shallow waters of the harbour, and I started to make a platform of bricks where we could sit and have meals when the days got longer. Trust my mother to have created a large vegetable garden, and when the spring came, and the summer, I took all our surplus vegetables and fruit to market, supplemented our slender income and got books from the Free Library. I remember picking about ten pounds of green gooseberries and selling them for a good price to the Sandbanks Hotel.

An occasional postcard from Lee kept me in touch with his work, then one day in June a letter arrived with a money order: "Jerry has got some sucker to back him to make a talkie. It's a play by T. W. Robertson called *Caste*. Get it, read it and wire him what you think of it." I rushed to the Public Library, drew out the copy of the play, read it and wired to Jerry at his flat at 106 Hallam Street: "Where did you get this old fossil? You can't be serious." A boy from the post office trudged over the moor with the reply. "It is not an old fossil it is an English classic come at once Jerry." I kissed my mother and caught the next train.

It was Ideal Films, owned by the Rowson brothers, who had bought Harry Lachman's *Travelaughs*, that was backing this bright young American lawyer, who talked big about his New York film connections, and who could summon out of the blue experienced technicians who had worked with Rex Ingram and Hitchcock, and who were acquainted with the latest techniques. It was brave of this little firm, after a lifetime of silent films, to tangle with a talkie. Harry Rowson was a burly, short-sighted man with grey curls, and he was of a generation that made it understandable how, for a talkie subject, he would turn to a play that had thrilled him and amused him in his youth. *Caste* was about caste, that is to say about class, the bane of England now as it was then. I was to write the script and work beside the director throughout the production. He was not a technician, he was an actor named Campbell Gullan. Through being in a play on Broadway when *The Jazz Singer* broke, he had had the luck to be whisked to Hollywood as a dialogue director on the early talkies. He had returned to London, where he was known and liked as a first-rate character actor, with an aura of glamour and Hollywood experience around him, and could now take his pick of offers. Luckily for me, he turned out to be an enchanting old pro with a lifetime of experience on the stage and an infallible ear for a line. He was a Scotsman, as his name would indicate.

Lee met me at Waterloo Station and we joined Jerry at his flat off Portland Place. Campbell Gullan was there too. Jerry had furnished his flat by going to Maples and pointing at an enormous divan and armchairs in the red Venetian style, with tassels and crimson fringes and enough thick cushions for a dozen orgies. It was the sort of decor to make a female visitor run for her life, or roll over with her paws in the air.

I had given a few seconds' thought to the writing of a script from this boring play. Improvising, as I usually do at script conferences, I described a scene in a pub where the customers hear a military band accompanying marching troops down the street and realise that England is at war (probably an actual memory of my boyhood, for I had decided to transport the period of the play from the time of the Boer War to the 1914–18 War, which was within my experience). Campbell Gullan liked my ideas and approved the updating. He was a spare, bony, intelligent body (in the Scottish sense) with remarkable dark eyes. (If you ever catch up with a print of *The Red Ensign* at some retrospective of my films, you will recognise him at once as the secretary of Leslie Banks's ship-building company.) He was a sociable men with a fund of professional anecdotes, and was desperately keen to learn about this new medium, the talkies; for in Hollywood his functions had been limited to dialogue directing and making screen tests of actors from the legitimate theatre. Jerry asked me how long I needed for a first draft, and I said three weeks. What studio would we use? I was hoping to return to Elstree in triumph. But Lee had been nosing about and had discovered the Nettlefold Studios at Walton-on-Thames, which were owned by Guest, Keen and Nettlefold, the engineering firm. They had efficiently sound-proofed their one big stage and equipped it with the latest sound system and camera. At Elstree, we would have had to stand in line for services. At Nettlefold, we would be the bosses.

Originally the Walton-on-Thames studios had been the cradle of the infant British film industry. The very first British film to make an impact had been made there in 1905 by Cecil M. Hepworth, entitled *Rescued by Rover*. The studio was located on the banks of the Thames. All around were typical sedate Surrey fields and woods where, many years later, Richard Greene, as Robin Hood, would draw a very long bow. These charming little studios were to be my studio for the next five years.

We drove down to Walton-on-Thames the next day. Jerry was nervous about saying the wrong thing and betraying his ignorance. Lee was an engineer and knew what questions to ask. I was aloof and silent, as befitted a big studio man of vast experience, a friend of the great and famous. The studio studied us in the way that rental studios do study their customers, particularly when they are extending credit until delivery to the distributor of the finished negative, as they were doing for Jerry.

They had a little reception on the sound stage and we were introduced to the heads of departments. Among them I particularly noticed a tall, soldierly-looking man in his thirties with an observant twinkle in his eye. When introduced as John Seabourne, head of the cutting room, he seized my hand before I offered it and shook it vigorously, as if greeting an old friend, but without the slightest trace of familiarity. I also noticed that he knew all our names and even pronounced Lee Planskoy's properly. Since I knew the important part that the cutting room played in the making of a film, I felt that I had met a friend and ally.

Being owned by Nettlefold, the studios were, technically, in good shape. Everything was new. There was a permanent staff, paid every Friday, and it was up to the studio manager to get clients to meet his wage bills. The charges were probably cost plus 20 per cent. We were aiming at an eighty-minute talkie. The budget was £8,000. The shooting schedule was four weeks.

Although I was actually co-director of the film, Gullie deferring to me in everything to do with the camera, I don't remember that I was credited with anything but the screenplay. Anyone less amicable than Campbell Gullan would have taken offence at the high-handed way I took charge of the film. I remember insisting upon rehearsals with the cast in London, which was an unheard of thing with English talkies, but judged necessary by both Gullie and me because *Caste*, do what I could, was a talky talkie.

When we came to the scene in the pub, I learnt from Gullie. He knew all the good bit-part actors in London and he had cast every character with care. It was ensemble acting but an ensemble where every face, movement and line of dialogue counted. I made sure that they registered and, remembering Rex's passion for modelling, I encouraged Geoff Faithfull, the resident Nettlefold cameraman, to light each face to bring out its character. This was old stuff in silent movies, but new in talkies, where dialogue directors, not knowing what else to do, tended to line actors up in stage positions and stage moves. I relied on cutting between close-ups, and John Seabourne, who, luckily for me had assigned himself to our film, at once saw what I was after. I daresay that the technique looks primitive now, if a print exists. But it was new then.

Sebastian Shaw (who played the upper-class hero) was a stagey actor and about as lively as a cigar-store Indian. He was always getting himself in profile, in spite of all I could do. I was to wrestle with him later when we were both under contract to Alexander Korda on *The Spy in Black*. The immensely tall Alan Napier (who played his languid friend) strolled through his part, as he was to stroll through his life, with complete detachment. Eddie Chapman (as the proletarian underdog) overacted. "Totie" Baddeley (his girlfriend Polly) delighted me. She was a totally modern actress, already an outspoken and outrageous personality who owned every last bit of herself. She ran the most popular nightclub in London, the Gargoyle. Nora Swinburne (the blonde heroine) was lit by me with a loving care which was totally at variance with a realistic subject. But I couldn't resist her perfect mouth and slender cheekbones. By the time we finished the film, both Jerry and I were in love with our leading ladies, which was as it should be. Where Nora and I were concerned, this went no further than a sisterly kiss. How Jerry and Totie celebrated the end of the film, I have no way of knowing.

During the shooting, Gullie begged a morning off. It was because of an occasion he "couldn'a, just simply couldn'a, miss": a theatrical wedding between the daughter of one of the most famous West End theatre families and one of the most glamorous of rising young actors, whom Hollywood was already paging. Everybody would be there, and Gullie was, of course, invited. Had he not played the cynical, worldly wise friend of Gerald du Maurier in *Cynara* with Gladys Cooper and young Celia Johnson? And had he not played it on Broadway too? How many times had he run through his lines for me, so that I could admire his timing, his pauses, his delivery? How could Gullie not be present at the wedding of Jill Esmond and Laurence Olivier?

That morning at nine Jerry was watching on the sidelines when I sat down in the director's chair and said: "Well, let's go." It was the first time I had been in complete charge. I thought, If only Hitch could see me! It was a scene involving all five principals, and we had left off in the middle of it the evening before. I said, "Let's run the first half of the scene, which is already in the can, and pick up from there." This was not because I had any particular plan – it was just to give me time to think. I continued flipping over the pages of the script, which I knew by heart, while the actors took up their positions.

"All ready, Micky," said an assistant.

I said in an off-hand voice to Sebastian Shaw, "Buster, make your entrance a bit quicker and don't stop and gape in the doorway. Action!"

The mimes went through their paces.

I said, "Cut! Fine. We pick up from there with a closeup on the two young lovers – Nora's point of view."

Someone tripped over a lamp. It was John Seabourne come to lend support. He gave me the thumbs-up sign.

Geoff Faithfull asked, "Do you want to see the shot, Micky?"

I said, "No. But don't line them up side by side. Have Miss Baddeley peep around Ted's shoulder."

By now the set was an orderly bustle. Jerry drifted away to his office. The show went on.

By lunchtime we had five shots in the can. Gullie reappeared in a sweat of sentimentality.

"The darlings! They looked pairrfect together." (Gullie skidded into Scots burr when emotional.) "Eva was wonderful!" (That was Eva Moore, star in her own right and wife to H. V. Esmond, the actor-manager.) "Och, I am so grateful to you, Michael! I wouldn't have missed it for anything."

In those days, before Hollywood's raids on Europe, a theatrical marriage between two families meant a lot. A stage alliance led, usually, to actor-management. The Terrys, the Wyndhams, the Bancrofts, Gerald du Maurier, had accustomed their contemporaries to look to them for leadership and employment. But with the sweeping impact of the talkies, all that was to melt away like sand castles before the Pacific rollers on Santa Monica beach.

I reluctantly handed the reins back to Gullie on his return, and started to worry about my future. I had tasted blood – nobody would ever keep me outside the studio walls again. I was prepared to sleep in John Seabourne's cutting room if necessary. We already knew each other's mettle.

The great advantage of the editor's job on a film is that when everybody else gets laid off at the end of shooting, his work is just beginning, and as I was scriptwriter, co-director, and co-editor, I was able to keep rivals at bay and look around for another job. It came. Another script.

For a long time after sound took over the international movie business panic reigned. The Americans had the lead on every nation, except Germany, where Klangfilm sound on tape was already adopted as the national film norm. England capitulated to the Americans and took second place in everything, while begging on our knees for the new techniques. It was to happen again with colour, with 3-D, with CinemaScope, and with 70-millimetre. The British distributors lived from distributing American movies in their original language, which bore a distinct resemblance to English "as she is spoke". It needed a certain amount of mental translation, but no sub-titling or dubbing. So the Americans called the tune. British theatres and British studios had a sort of local sound system which was installed by a few patriots, and was known cheerfully to the trade as British

Mumblephone. But ninety per cent of the showmen signed contracts that were highly profitable for Western Electric and RCA, and were content to stand in line, having no other choice but to follow the enormous investments by American capital in the talking picture.

European cinema didn't take this lying down. Talkies had damaged, if not destroyed, their foreign markets and ruined a lot of big names, but the proud national cinema industries of the major European countries still existed, and they saw at once that co-production was one of the answers. Alert showmen were already forming companies to make multi-lingual versions of the same film. One of these companies planned to make a film simultaneously in English, French and Spanish, to be distributed by United Artists, and to be made at the Nettlefold Studios. I was on the spot and was known to be a friend of Hitchcock's and a European know-it-all. My credits were minimal, but I got the job to write the shooting script. It was called 77 *Park Lane*, a play by Walter Hackett. I was to be paid £300.

As soon as I read it, I realised that this was the big time. A rich and debonair young man returns from abroad with a friend, goes to his town house and finds that, in his absence, a bunch of crooks have rented it and are running a gambling club there. All the action took place in the house at 77 Park Lane. The situation gave scope for misunderstandings, comedy, thrills, fights, glamour, lovely clothes, stolen jewels, and suspense. I licked my lips. This was better than dusting off old fossils.

I had kept my eyes open during my time on the Riviera, and with memories of the hot-house glamour of the Grand Hotel at Folkestone reckoned I could make a pretty good shot at sophistication. I was only twenty-five, remember. It was nice to know that everyone in the studio was anxiously waiting to read the script.

My mother was as thrilled for me as I was. I think she had been afraid I might vanish to Hollywood. I had talked of going there. She found me a dingy little flat in Bayswater: Salem Mansions, off Moscow Road. She stayed with me for a bit, "to see me in". She had all the dogs with her and used to walk several hundred yards further west so that she could take them into Kensington Gardens by – you've guessed it – Bark Place. You would have liked my mother.

I started work before my twenty-fifth birthday and completed the script in about six weeks. I worked all day and every day. It was my first real talkie script. *Caste* didn't count. The old play had just one situation and half a dozen characters. But 77 *Park Lane* had lots of good parts and unexpected situations. I had learnt from Hitchock about starting a scene in the middle of the action: I opened the film with the two leading men in top hat and tails, pleasantly drunk, arriving at the house in Park Lane about midnight on a hansom-cab. I write on, instead of in, because that was where I put them: on the roof. Nobody objected, so I took the bit between my teeth and liberties with the story. I knew how to lay out a script and how an important screenplay should look, and I was so well prepared to defend my script, that when we all met at Nettlefold Studios for a conference, Laurence Irving, who was designing the film, suggested that I direct it: a suggestion that was not well received by the appointed director, Albert de Courville.

De Courville was a famous West End showman who had had his name on the marquee of several successful musical shows, although that didn't make him a good film director. But he was good enough: he knew actors and acting, he was good at casting and he got on with the job. We could have done a lot worse. In show business there is always a reason for everything, and it's usually a family reason. All the early showmen of Hollywood were either related, or came from Odessa, or from the Russian pale. Thirty years later, when sitting on the terrace of the Ruhl Hotel in Nice, with my wife, and Albert de Courville and his wife, and Arthur Kelly and his wife, I learnt why: de Courville was married to Arthur Kelly's sister. Arthur and his sister had been bosom friends of Charlie Chaplin in the early vaudeville days. Arthur was Chaplin's representative on the Board of United Artists. UA was distributing 77 Park Lane. De Courville got the job.

He was an interesting man, cultivated and temperamental, with a sweet smile and a cigar perpetually clenched in his teeth. He had a sharp profile, pale skin, and beautiful eyes, with heavy lids. He was something of an invalid, and like so many invalids was as strong as a horse. I had hoped to be at his elbow during production, to co-direct as I had with Campbell Gullan. Albert made it clear that he would be delighted to profit by my experience – in the cutting room.

I had been embarrassed by Irving's airy suggestion, thrown out at random and although I was certain that I could direct any assignment, this was a big job and I knew it was better to learn from other people's mistakes, rather than from my own. Besides, in the editing rooms, John Seabourne had become a major attraction.

John was the most talkative, lovable and generous man I have ever known. By now, I knew the whole story of his life. He had been a regular soldier before the 1914 War, but, disliking garrison duty at Dover, he deserted, joined the gunners under another name, and was posted to Alderney in the Channel Islands, where he remained as a bombardier until the outbreak of war. He went through the whole war in France, becoming quartermaster sergeant as soon as he could wangle it, as befitted a regular soldier who knows where the real authority lies. Because he was still officially posted in the Army lists as a deserter, he continued to use his assumed name of Seabourne for the rest of his working life. His baptised name was rumoured to be Alfred and his surname possibly Diss. In hospital he married his nurse and begat two sons, John and Peter. He got into the movie business as a stagehand, but having the gift of gab he soon talked himself into a job as one of the director-editors of the weekly *Gaumont Film Magazine*, shown worldwide with the feature film, a compendium of items of interest, strange handicrafts, odd characters, news events, interviews with the famous and so forth, all of which John took in his stride, for he delighted in oddities, whether human or otherwise. A better training ground for an editor or director couldn't be imagined, and his experience of people, his impish humour and his large heart were to be at my service for many years. Lucky the young, arrogant director that has a John Seabourne at his elbow.

By November, the three casts of 77 *Park Lane* – British, French and Spanish – were assembled in London and rehearsals started. The plan was to have them all on call and to rehearse an ensemble scene using English extras and bit-players. In other words, the master shot was in English and was used whenever possible, in all three versions. When the scene was in the can, the close-ups of all three nationalities were filmed, each actor stepping into the shoes of the one before him. This was particularly fascinating to watch, because the actor of each nationality had his own way of handling the scene and his own personality to put over, and I sneaked onto the stage a great deal to observe them. Sometimes the French actor, or actress, would be the most inventive, sometimes the Spanish or the British.

The Continentals, who all acted as naturally as they ate or slept with each other, were more realistic than our actors. We were a stagey lot. Our leading man was Dennis Neilson Terry, from a famous theatrical family. He had the Terry charm, a small head with classic profile and a long, lean body. He handled himself well, but he was not quite real. His companion on top of the cab, Roland Culver, was, however, a great talent, an inspired comedian and a unique personality. I have never, ever, seen a drunk man acted with such inventiveness and charm. He was just at the beginning of a long and successful career, and I longed to work one day with actors of that calibre.

The girl was Betty Stockfield, an enormously beautiful and beautifully enormous young woman, who had suddenly become the rage of Europe by appearing with the singer Jan Kiepura in a talkie-singie shot in Rome by Carmine Gallone entitled *City of Song*. She looked impressive stalking about Rome's Seven Hills while being serenaded by the tenor from the Roman Baths, but she was altogether too big for *Park Lane*. It was like having Minerva for supper at the Ritz.

The young actor who played her brother in the film was however a real find. He was a sulky, handsome young man with a mane of black hair and magnetic eyes. He was almost too romantically handsome to be true. Then one day I saw him giggling with one of the sound engineers and I realized that it was all a pose and he had a sense of humour. He was not tall, but I felt he had star potential. He was a protégé of de Courville's, who had starred him in an experimental play, *The Unknown Soldier*. His name was Esmond Knight. In an effective but dangerous fight with the heavies in the film, in which they hurled soda-water syphons at each other, Esmond managed to cut his own hand to the bone.

Our art director, Laurence Irving, was a revelation to me. He was a true designer as understood in Europe. It was the first time I had worked closely with an orderly, imaginative mind, a trained artist, a good draftsman, whose action sketches, on which the sets were based, were the sort of interpretation of the movie which Hitch would have liked to make, if Hitch could have drawn. I seem to remember that Laurence had already had Hollywood experience. He was an especial object of interest to me because he lived in the old black windmill in the seaside town of Whitstable, where the oysters come from. The windmill had long been converted into a house and I had wished to visit it as a child. Laurence was grandson of the great Henry Irving and son of H. B. Irving. After the next war, he was to write his grandfather's biography, and create a masterpiece. He was tall, and as beautiful as an angel, with the eyes of a visionary. I looked over his shoulder with awe and learnt something for every hour he shared with me. He looked as I imagine Peter Abelard looked.

I moved between the art department and the cutting room, which are the nerve-centres of production, and I hardly missed the hurly-burly of the studio floor. I wouldn't have enjoyed it even if I had been welcome. De Courville knew what he wanted, but his direction was theatrical – he was an onlooker, not a participator – and when he directed action it was from the eighth row of the stalls, instead of getting his camera in the line of fire.

Besides, *Caste* had been shown and judged acceptable for a British effort, although I can't help suspecting that the public shared my view of the old fossil. Still, nobody had lost money and Jerry Jackson had talked Ideal Films into financing another low-budget film, with him as producer and me as *sole* director this time! He then proceeded to lay off the odds by screwing a contract out of Fox British Films to make yet another short feature.

"What's the budget?" I asked.

He gulped, "A pound a foot."

This was the normal visible cash payment by the American distributors to independent British producers. My stomach dropped away from me. There was a big difference between working on a £30,000 top-of-the-bill feature like *77 Park Lane*, and a fifty-minute "quota-quickie" designed to fill the bottom of the bill.

This was a very important step in my career; but it was a step down, rather than a step up. However, a young director cannot afford to give himself airs – he has to make the best of what he's given and I was very conscious that I owed the rebirth of my career in movies to Jerry Jackson.

I was tempted to go it alone. One more job successfully accomplished like 77 *Park Lane*, and I would have been in the big time – I would have been in the same league as Hitchcock. We would have been running level for the job of directing the next big talkie. But the prospect of directing not only one, but two films in the next two months led me to make the wrong decision and sent me up the wrong track for the best part of five years.

By the time we had edited 77 *Park Lane*, I was in love again, with an enchanting Cockney kitten of a girl whom I had met as an extra. She was a pleasantly naughty and sexy girl, with a lively sense of humour, and was a virgin. When she lost it on the floor in front of my gas-fire, I remember her saying, after stretching herself, "Is that all?"—which is as good a comment on the sexual act as any I can remember. But a Cockney is always quotable. She was a natural comic. Her observation was acute and lively, and she turned it into words and music when she became a star of London cabaret. She had a wonderful gift of intimacy in putting over her songs, and her face was lively and human rather than pretty or funny (although she was both).

All the same, my darling Cockney sparrow wasn't in the very first film I ever directed on my own: *Two Crowded Hours*, the "quota-quickie" for the Fox Film Corporation. I had better explain what a quota-quickie is.

When movies became talkies, the British Parliament passed a law to protect the baby British talkie from being thrown out with the bathwater by the all-conquering Yanks. It compelled a British exhibitor (which name applies equally to the manager of one palatial link in a super-cinema chain as to the owner of a flea-pit) to show a certain percentage of British-made products, whether the public (who couldn't care less) screamed for them or not. The aim was to keep the British film industry, which was always in trouble financially because of the overwhelming American competition, solvent by filling the lower half of a double-feature bill, in the hope that British talkies would creep up and up and eventually compete on equal terms and billing with the eight hundred films that Hollywood was pouring every year into Europe in the years between 1931 and 1942. In the event this pious hope became a fact, against all expectations, thanks to people like Michael Balcon, Basil Dean, Alexander Korda, Lady Yule, Victor Saville, and dozens of other struggling British film-makers. The tide had turned even before the Second World War. The quota had risen from ten per cent to twenty per cent and good British films were actually being supported by the British public, who asked for more. But in 1931, the only people interested in backing quota films were the big American companies who had hundreds of films to unload and couldn't, unless they shared the bill with a British film. To achieve this they were prepared to finance second features made in England. They drove a hard bargain, and the going rate for the intrepid producers and financiers of these quota-quickies was one pound sterling per foot of film, cash on the table.

So *Two Crowded Hours*, my first film as a director, entered the history of the motion picture as a quota-quickie for Fox. The basic idea was to involve a comic taxidriver in a murder mystery. One of his fares is mysteriously murdered in his cab and the pursuit and capture of the murderer follows. Jefferson Farjeon, a good dialogue-writer and a member of a famous literary and theatre family, wrote the story and script and worked with me through the two weeks of shooting. The contract was for a forty-minute film. Allowing for trims and editing, that meant shooting four minutes of finished film a day for twelve days, for which we were to be paid a pound a foot on delivery. Naturally it was Jerry's ambition to turn out the films for less than a pound a foot, for that would be the only profit he would ever see.

I could perform miracles, and on my first film I did, because I had two first-class actors: Jerry Verno, who played the taxidriver (you see him as the stage-door keeper at Covent Garden every time that *The Red Shoes* comes up on the box), and my old acquaintance John Longden, who had played the detective lover of Anny Ondra in Hitchcock's *Blackmail*. It is his voice that you hear as the narrator: "This is the universe. Big isn't it?" in the opening sequences of *A Matter of Life and Death*. These were professionals for whom Take One was OK.

When I look back at my first days as a film director, I am amused at my presumption. I was in my twenty-sixth year. I had never had the slightest doubt that I was born to be a film director, and I didn't have any doubts then, on that morning in London in April, 1931. The schedule of the first day's work read: "EXTERIORS IN LONDON – Refer to Mr Powell. Standby shots at Nettlefold Studios to be confirmed." I had picked all the locations myself, noting the time of day when the light would be good for each shot – and there were sometimes only twenty minutes to grab it. This is an essential part of moviemaking. I had learnt the technique from Tomatis in the South of France when he and I used to go about with a watch and a compass, picking locations for Rex Ingram or Harry Lachman in the narrow streets of Marseille or Villefranche, where the sun comes and goes in twenty minutes. I had picked the location for the taxi-cabmen's shelter in North London, where an impressive railway viaduct crosses the road. Shooting was to start at 9:00 a.m. and at 10:00 a.m. we had wrapped up that shot and we were on our way to our next location, Upper Rathbone Place in Soho, north of Oxford Street, where I had timed the scenes for 11:30 a.m. At 11:30 we were shooting. I had not worked with the great Rex Ingram and Johnny Seitz for nothing. I knew the script and I could make up my mind quickly. I already had the knack of convincing technicians and actors that they were carrying out their own ideas.

If you want to know what Upper Rathbone Place looks like, you can see it in the opening shots of *Peeping Tom* (1959). There is a narrow, arched passage – Newman Passage – leading through to Newman Street, that gives you gooseflesh just to look at it: they say it is associated with Jack the Ripper. The newsagent's shop at one end of Upper Rathbone Place, where Mark goes to make his porno photographs in *Peeping Tom*, is still there, and the other end of the Place leads you back into Charlotte Street. When I picked this location for *Two Crowded Hours* there was an old-fashioned lamppost standing on the corner, and two dirty little girls (for the poor were dirty in 1931, remember?), had attached a cord to the lamppost as high up as they could reach so that when they took a bit of a run and hurled themselves into the air, they whirled around the lamppost a couple of times before crash-landing into the gutter. The post had been worn as smooth as a bottle by the game. When we arrived with the crew there were no kids swinging on the lamppost, but the property man soon fixed that. I shot exactly what I needed with the actors and no more.

"What next?" asked the assistant. It was 12:30.

"Lunch," I said, "then back to the studio to pick up the rest of the sequence. The taxi can go ahead."

"Shouldn't you cover yourself a bit more, Micky?"

"Why?" This must have been that deadpan "Why?" David Lean has made so famous in his stories about working with me as my editor.

Anyway, it satisfied the assistant, who bawled: "Lunch!" Then: "Back to the studio, ready to shoot at three."

I telephoned Jerry, who was in Wardour Street, and said we were up to schedule. Inwardly I was as proud as a peacock. Another thing made that day memorable. Opposite the entrance to Upper Rathbone Street, I had noticed a typical Soho restaurant, painted blue and white, geraniums in window-boxes and a menu in a brass frame outside the door. It was the Restaurant de l'Etoile. I had never been there. I couldn't afford to dine out, and if Jerry Jackson stood me a dinner it would be at one of the famous theatre restaurants where you saw the headliners, places like The Ivy in St Martin's Lane and Rule's in Maiden Lane. But I knew the spot because it had been pointed out to me as the restaurant where Charles Laughton and Elsa Lanchester always dined copiously and well, paying handsomely when they were working, running up a tremendous bill when they were not. My informant said that they had a bed-sitting room on the upper floor and that was why they always ate in the restaurant. But I had seen Charles, with a napkin tucked beneath his chin, wading into the minestrone in cheap Soho restaurants and I knew that the food at The Etoile must be exceptionally good for him to dine there every night. So when John Longden suggested that he buy me lunch, I accepted with indecent haste. We only had an hour. We crossed the road and went in to cries of "*V'là Monsieur Longden!*"

John probably thought that he was doing this infant director a favour by buying him lunch at an exclusive little Soho restaurant known only to a few connoisseurs. So he was considerably taken aback when I turned out to be an old friend of the management. The long narrow room was clean and charming in the best bourgeois style. It presaged excellent bourgeois cooking, even without the delicious smells that wafted up the dumb-waiter from the kitchen below. Frank Rossi, the son of the owner, a tall, bespectacled youth, was making a great fuss of John Longden. It seemed to me that I had met him somewhere before. Then I heard an unmistakable Niçois voice yelling an order to the cook: "*Chef! Deux pasta chouta.*" And what's more a voice I knew. It was Nino Cauvin, whom I had last seen as barman at the Golf Club on Mont Agel above Monte Carlo, the mountainous golf course where you drive off your tee into the clouds and some holes are so short and steep you only need a putter to hole out in one. Nino had stood me many a long orange squash there in the early twenties. We fell into each other's arms, talking Niçois. And Frank? I thought I knew him? Of course I knew him. Frank was his brother-in-law, and he had been barman at Caressa, the famous bar in Nice. And here was Lola, Frank's sister and Nino's pretty wife, presiding over the cashdesk with her mother.

"*Merde alors! C'est le fils du Capitaine Powell de la Voile d'Or, à St Jean . . . ! Bien, voyons!* What are you doing in London, Michael?"

"I'm directing that film out there – I'm a film director."

"*Sans blague!*"

"And Mr Longden is the star of my film."

The attention shifted to John and it was about time. He was looking and feeling distinctly neglected.

We were back at the Nettlefold Studios at 3:00 p.m. and shot the rest of the sequence, with the body of the murdered man falling out of the taxi and onto the road – the dead end street leading to the studio. By 4:30 we were inside it, lining up the heroine's apartment. She was the first of my red-headed heroines, Jane Welsh. By now the crew were getting into their stride, and used to my way of working. They said, "What's next, Micky?" with tails wagging, and I knew what was next and I told them. They were not used to associating high quality with high speed, and they liked it. We were shooting four minutes of screen time a day, remember. John Seabourne appeared on the floor from time to time, held murmured colloquies with the script-girl, then vanished back to his cutting-room. This was the pattern of the working day.

We finished the first day ahead of schedule, and finished the picture on time. Within a week I was directing my second feature *Rynox* by Philip

MacDonald – a different kind of thriller. I had a little more time and a little more money to spend on it, but not much. The small studio was humming with excitement. I have always encouraged the crew to come and see the dailies (on their own time, of course!), and the executives of the studio had seen them as part of their job, and there was a new spirit in the studio. In the days not so long ago of Cecil M. Hepworth, the Walton-on-Thames studio had produced silent films that went all over the world, and now here was a new generation that babbled of talkies as one of the fine arts. The fact that we didn't have much money didn't matter. Their whole attitude changed.

By the time we finished shooting *Rynox*, John Seabourne had completed the editing of *Two Crowded Hours* and was standing waiting, sharpening his scissors, saying: "Bring on the next one." These two little films are forgotten, except by the film historians, and the negative has been junked, although there may be a print or two somewhere. I have often tried to analyse the great success of these first two pictures that I directed, and ask myself why they made such a stir on the British talkie scene. For, let's not kid ourselves, these were competently made B-pictures, what Hollywood called poverty-row productions. The first one, *Two Crowded Hours*, for the great Fox Film Corporation, was a real quota-quickie, handed over the counter in return for one pound a foot, and actually costing us, its makers, seventeen shillings and sixpence. The second film, *Rynox*, was not a quota-quickie production. It was a British feature, financed and distributed by Ideal Films, a respectable and respected English film-maker, which had financed the production of *Caste* that had brought me back from the boondocks. It cost £8000. The two films were quite different, but both had good stories and were written by professionals.

Two Crowded Hours was obviously influenced by Continental films. There were lots of clever angles and quick-cutting, but it was also obvious that the director meant to entertain first and foremost. The shocks and suspense were of the most primitive kind, but they worked. There was plenty of good observation, but no scene to bring a blush to a maiden's cheek. (In 1931, maidens still used the blush as a gambit, but it hadn't got long to go.) In its detachment about the plot, in its interest in people, it was like the films of H. G. Clouzot after the war: *Quai des Orfèvres* and *The Wages of Fear*. The climax of the film comes when the villain tries to murder the heroine, who is rescued by John Longden in the nick of time. The villain runs out into the road and is run down and killed by Jerry Verno's taxi. John Seabourne and I, working hand in hand, achieved a bang-up finish with a kaleidoscopic montage of images inspired by the Soviet cinema.

Rynox, on the other hand, was much more like a Hollywood film. There were two reasons for the change of style. One was that the screenplay of *Rynox* was adapted from a book. *Two Crowded Hours* had been an action picture, a director's picture. I had to create the scene. But *Rynox* could just as easily have been a stage play as a film, and was more of a talkie. The plot was ingenious; it had a clever twist in it, and lots of suspense. There was a certain slickness about the script that nagged me. I got away with it by good casting.

All the same, there is no doubt in my mind that the success of our first two films was due to good scripts. We had had plenty of time to write them and rewrite them. Standing behind the lights watching some other fellow misdirect an actor is excellent training for the moment when you pick up the megaphone yourself. Never again would Jerry and I give such loving enthusiasm to every word of dialogue and every stage direction.

I am speaking in 1986 about talkies that I was directing in 1931. Fifty-five years – a long time in movies? Perhaps. But it is certainly a long time in art. The Impressionist movement, the Pre-Raphaelite movement, the Romantic movement, came and went in less than fifty years. But in the movies, nothing has changed. People go into films in this day and age to make money. And so long as money is the only yardstick, there will be no advance in any art. There will only be the surge of the wave on the pebbles on the shore, which sounds very impressive, until you realise the tide is going out.

We turned *Two Crowded Hours* over to Fox, and they showed it to the trade at a lovely old theatre, the Palace Theatre in Cambridge Circus, where Alfred Butt had presented Anna Pavlova in 1910. Because of the angle of the projection from the back of the Upper Circle it was not an ideal movie theatre, but it served. For me it was associated with one afternoon, ten years before, when I escaped from Dulwich College to spend the afternoon leaning over the rails of the Upper Circle of the Palace, watching Douglas Fairbanks in his silent masterpiece *The Mark of Zorro*, presented with full orchestra and sound-effects.

Each of the big American companies were turning out twenty to thirty talkies a year in 1931, and as they were bound by law to have a censor certificate and to have a public tradeshow, it had become the custom to show one of the quota-quickies before the glossy American feature, which in this case was the *The Affairs of Annabel*, starring Jeanette MacDonald. *Two Crowded Hours* came on first, so a lot of the professional audience arrived halfway through. They must have thought they had come to the wrong house. People were roaring with laughter, or tensely quiet, and even clapping in the middle. Before we came to the dazzling montage at the end, we knew we had a surprise hit. They put the house lights up. Jerry and Lee were embracing each other. They even embraced me. Half the people gathered around us and the other half left, leaving very few people to see Annabel's predictable affairs. I stayed, because it was free and one can always learn something.

A week or two later, Ideal showed *Rynox*. The house was packed. We could hardly believe it, but we had another smash hit. We were riding high. The great ladies of the Sunday newspapers, C. A. Lejeune and Dilys Powell, film critics of the *Observer* and the *Sunday Times*, respectively, came to see *Rynox* and wrote it up. They had missed *Two Crowded Hours* but they knew all about it. Miss Lejeune said that I was a "red-hot talent shot molten into the world". Lee and Jerry were delighted, and never tired of asking me how my red-hot talent was that morning. She also said that there were only three film directors worthy of the name working in England: Anthony Asquith, Alfred Hitchcock and Michael Powell. I was staggered. So I was level pegging with Hitchcock! But to make thrillers, however ingenious, was not my goal. And I kept my eyes and ears open for "the big subject".

In that same year, this *annus mirabilis* of 1931, my eye was caught by the following item in one of the Sunday newspapers:

During the evacuation of the entire population of the island of St. Kilda, who are returning to the mainland, it was found impossible to evacuate most of their sheep. They had never been sheared and had been allowed to run wild so long, that they were as active as goats and nobody could catch them, and when dogs were brought in to help, the sheep turned on the dogs and bit them.

Mr Gladstone has gone on record as saying that there is nothing so frightening as a mad sheep. But even he could not have expected that they would be quite so mad as that. The story should have been headed: "Sheep Bites Dog."

I knew nothing about the evacuation of St Kilda, and only vaguely recalled that the island was one of the Hebrides, which lie to the west of Scotland. But the depopulation of a wild and remote island was an epic subject, and I cut out the newspaper item and dropped it into a file I always had with me, labelled "Ideas".

My life was changing. Jerry Jackson had a warm heart and an impulsive nature, and he had no intention of letting his nursling be snapped up by some other hungry producer. Urged on by Lee, who was as thrilled as any of us, he proposed that we found a company, and make a series of films in which we would share the credit: "Produced by Jerry Jackson, Directed by Michael Powell." As the production company for *Two Crowded Hours*, Jerry had used a little company, the Film Engineering Company, which financed Lee's experiments in trick-work. *Rynox* was financed and produced by Ideal Films, with whom we had a service contract. But now, with our two successes, we were in a position to form our own company and raise money. We decided to call our company Westminster Films –

"Westminster Films Presents" – and it was unanimously decided that our trademark should be Big Ben. I am sure that both Jerry and I secretly thought that our trademark would become as famous as Paramount's snow-capped mountain, or MGM's Leo the Lion, who, since talkies, had started to roar. Very well, *we* would have chimes! I knew that Vernon Campbell Sewell, a member of the sound department, whom I had noticed at the Nettlefold Studios because he wore the tie of a famous school, plus an eyeglass, was a veritable Admirable Crichton. We had become friends. He was a trained engineer, but he could also put his hand to anything, and I discussed our trademark with him. In two days he had made a model of Big Ben for our logo. Before we began filming it, it started to lean a little, but you can't have everything. None of us could agree what time it should be on the clock face. I forget who won, but that trademark fronted our films for the next two years, until Alex Korda arrived in England and quite unwittingly stole our trademark for his "London Films Presents". He didn't care what time it was.

The trade press had been very generous with their praise, and to my delight one of the reviews was written by that very same W. A. Williamson who ten years before had written the article about location shooting in England which decided me to make the movies my life and my career. Meanwhile Jerry was going up and down Wardour Street, boring his friends at United Artists, most of whom were New Yorkers like himself, by reading them juicy bits from our reviews. He had asked me to come and share his flat. He had a spare room. I could furnish it, and pay a nominal rent and a share in the current expenses. We would live, work and play together. The idea suited me. The offer would bind me to him, but I was already fond of Jerry. I knew we could live together and I accepted with gratitude.

For four years we were inseparable. We were like brothers, or, if you prefer, like the wild animals that young men are. Working, playing, hunting girls, gossiping, biting, scratching, creating, going to the Plaza Cinema every Sunday to see the new Paramount movie, eating at all the best restaurants, going to all the hit shows, patronising the best tailors, buying hats from Locke's and shirts from Cole's, shoes from Lobb, ties from Washington Tremlett in Conduit Street, going to Ciro's or the 400 or the Berkeley after the show, tolerantly applauding the cabaret stars of the Thirties, listening to wits like the Honourable Richard Norton and Jack Dunfee capping each other's stories in the little room at the Berkeley, just off the main dining room (which we all liked, because you didn't have to dress), stealing ideas, stealing one another's girls.

Weekends we often spent in the country, accompanied by various ladies, staying at old inns like the Spreadeagle at Midhurst in West Sussex, or the Bear at Burford, a typical Cotswold town and inn, where the river flowing under the bridge is beautifully named the Windrush; or at the Drove Hotel at Singleton, a chalk and flint village in the heart of the West Sussex Downs, where high in the air majestic Trundle Hill carries Goodwood racecourse on his shoulders. We explored the Downs on horseback, and let the horses have their heads when we galloped along the crest of Cocking Down. Sometimes, we would stay on the river (the River Thames), perhaps at Sonning, where the two bridges link the road with the island in the middle of the weedy river, or perhaps at Maidenhead, or Bray-on-Thames, where we rode in Windsor Great Park. Sometimes we went as far as the Branksome Towers Hotel on the sandy cliffs above Sandbanks, and rode our horses along the beach to Bournemouth. Jerry was mad about riding and mad about the English countryside: his joy and energy were so infectious he was a marvellous companion. Such a lovely man should not have died so young.

Jerry and I made three more films that year – three quota-quickies in a row. They couldn't all of them be good and they weren't. *My Friend the King*, another Jerry Verno taxicab thriller, was a flop. *Rasp*, a Philip MacDonald thriller refused to become a film and remained a book. *Star Reporter* with an original screenplay by Philip MacDonald, and starring Harold French in the title role was fun and I was not ashamed of it. Harold French was a real pro. He understood comedy timing and I learned from him every day. *Star Reporter* played as the bottom half of the bill with Frank Capra's *Platinum Blonde*. I felt really complimented when one of the critics wrote that *Star Reporter* scarcely had the polish of *Platinum Blonde*. My film cost £3700, the Columbia Film $600,000.

For most of that incredible year, when I was not directing films, I spent my time with John Seabourne in the editing rooms at Nettlefold Studios, cutting them. I dined off snacks or with John and his family. By the time winter came I had already moved into Jerry's apartment, but at Christmas, when Jerry always took a boat back to New York to spend the season with his family, I suddenly found myself alone and without any plans. I think that my mother must have despaired of trying to tie me down to a promise and had gone to spend the holiday with her sisters. Anyway, England's popular and successful young film director was alone on New Year's Eve and decided to have dinner at the Etoile, for it was now within reach of my purse. I walked through the gloomy backstreets off Great Portland Street and came out in Fitzroy Square (one of the great squares of London, associated forever for me with Ford Madox Ford and his Pre-Raphaelite relatives) and walked down Charlotte Street, past the Scala Theatre (which was playing *Peter Pan*) to the Etoile. It was lit up, and there was noise and music, laughter, the popping of corks and the rich smell of garlic and basil used with understanding and discretion. It augured well, but the door was locked. I knocked, at first softly, then louder, and a waiter opened the door.

"Very sorry, sir, it is a private party." By now I was loaded with self-pity and nostalgia. It would have taken Cruikshank or Daumier to picture me as I stood on the step and glimpsed the festive scene inside. Seeing that I wouldn't go away, the waiter said: "I'll fetch Mr Frank." The son of the house appeared wearing a paper hat. Frank was sympathetic. He explained that it was a party of the whole staff, of the Rossi family and friends. I turned away feeling dreadful. I had gone a few steps when the door opened again and Frank reappeared, followed by Nino and Lola. She looked lovely and out of breath, flushed from wine and dancing, in a short black frock.

"Mr Powell! Michael! Michael!"

I stopped. It was too good to be true.

"Frank told us. Of course we remember you! Of course you must stay! It is family, you understand! But we would love you to join us. You are alone? On New Year's Eve! What's the matter with you?"

Protesting insincerely, I was bustled back. The heat of the big room and the garlic-scented warmth of everybody's welcome hit me like a blow. We had a wonderful night. I, who seldom dance, danced madly, nay, passionately, with Lola. We twined together like two grape vines. Nino was roaring drunk and the Master of Ceremonies. It was three o'clock in the morning as I weaved my way home to Hallam Street. Most of all, I remember Mrs Rossi, in handsome black, her grey hair beautifully arranged, presiding over the party and counting the bottles.

Over the period 1931–36, I directed anything that Jerry put in front of me. I directed nineteen films. They were of varying lengths, and had various sponsors. They were mostly made in, or from, the Nettlefold Studios at Walton-on-Thames. Two of them were shot at the Wembley Studios. We had made Nettlefold so popular that there was no room for us, but we edited the films there, for I couldn't imagine any other editor so quick yet so imaginative as John Seabourne. I remember that while we were shooting the music hall sequence of *Born Lucky*, we shared the sound stage at Wembley with Alexander Korda, who was noisily directing his first production for his own London Films, *Wedding Rehearsal*, a society comedy that had half of Mayfair in the cast, including Joan Gardner, Gertrude Musgrove and Merle Oberon, all of whom married Kordas. For those interested in who was who: Zoli married Joan Gardner, Gertrude Musgrove married Vincent, and Merle Oberon, after a courtship as protracted as that of Elizabeth I with Philip II of Spain, placed her little hand in Alex's.

We made four eighty-minute features for Michael Balcon, who was production head of the newly refurbished Gaumont-British Studios at Lime Grove, Shepherd's Bush, now occupied by the BBC. It was one of Mickey Balcon's several heroic attempts to place the unstable British film industry on a firm foundation. The year was 1933. In Germany, Hitler had become Chancellor of the Third Reich and writers, actors, directors and artists generally were in fear of their lives and careers. Those who could, got out to Paris or to London. For many of them London was only a stepping stone to New York and Hollywood. But some of the most talented preferred London and brought first-class technical experience with them. They joined Michael Balcon and the sleepy British film industry woke up when he announced a programme of twelve to fifteen British features a year. The money for all this had been found by the Ostrer Brothers, of whom Isidore, the eldest, was a genius. He had written a book, *The Conquest of Gold*, which I took the trouble to read, as I thought he was a stayer. But although films amused him and he had a daughter, Pamela, who was more than amused, he soon lost interest in his plaything and went to live in South Africa. It was left to Arthur Rank, a Yorkshire miller and a Methodist, who was already sponsoring some small religious films, to make the real breakthrough for British films when the war came.

Jerry and I were pretty excited by Mickey Balcon's invitation. At least, Jerry was. I had begun to realise that I had missed the creative bus. When C. A. Lejeune had made her celebrated pronouncement that there were only three British directors, I should have gone for broke, for the real movies that Hitchcock and Asquith were making. With our first two pictures to show, we could have found backers, American or English, or even from the Continent. I knew far more about European films than Jerry did, and Hitchcock himself had started in Germany, making a modest little film that put him at once in the first league back in his own country. Instead, we had grabbed at the first offers to make more cut-price films, and for two years went on quite happily and thoughtlessly, as if poverty-row productions were the be-all and end-all of film-making. The films that we were making were just footage. Some of them were downright bad. Jerry was perfectly happy with this sort of hit-and-miss existence; but films were my life, my art, my mistress, my religion. And I was betraying all of them by making potboilers. But I had a dream and the dream was of the Hebrides. I am a great browser among second-hand bookstalls. And one day my eye was caught by a title: *The Last Days of St. Kilda*, by Alasdair Alpin MacGregor. I had never forgotten the newspaper item about the St Kildan sheep, and when my mother had asked me what book I wanted for my birthday, I had told her *Islands of the West* by Seton Gordon. It was a beautiful book with good photographs in it taken by the author and a chapter on St Kilda, which I learnt for the first time, lies some fifty miles further west than the rest of the Hebrides, and is, except for the rock called Rockall, the most westerly point of land in the British Isles. I had started to collect books about the Isles, so I was able to appreciate MacGregor's book all the more. Here was the full story of the death of an island, of the evacuation of St Kilda, by a writer (who had acted as the *Times* correspondent covering the actual evacuation) who had lived for a month or two on the island before the evacuation, and who had taken the trouble to see how the islanders fared afterwards, on the mainland, and how men who had never seen a tree in their lives, had reacted to their new occupation – forestry. It was an odd book, but appealing. The author was full of prejudices, loves and hates, and he stated them loud and clear. But it was an honest book, and a piece of good reporting, and valuable to me because it confirmed me in my belief that here was a story worth telling, a film worth making. I didn't see why this folk epic should cost any more per foot than the trash I was canning.

So Mickey Balcon's offer came at a good time for me. I knew that Hitchcock had joined him and I could always get on with Hitch. Perhaps he could give me a hand up into the big league. I knew that Günther Stapenhorst, one of Erich Pommer's best producers, was moving to England and was going to make *The Great Barrier*, a film about the building of the Canadian-Pacific Railroad. His wife was Jewish. I knew that Lothar Mendes was already in London, preparing to make a film from Feuchtwanger's book *Jew Süss*, starring the great Conrad Veidt as the Jew. Berthold Viertel was there, preparing to make *Little Friend*, with an English girl in the title role, Nova Pilbeam; Basil Dean was going to make a film of Margaret Kennedy's *The Constant Nymph*, and was going to follow it up with Ivor Novello in tantalising Tyrolean shorts in *Autumn Crocus*; and of course we had seen *Rome Express*, Michael Balcon's opening production, with an all-star cast including Conrad Veidt, and directed by Walter Forde. It was a smash hit.

Of course there was a hidden hook in Michael Balcon's invitation. First of all, our total budgets were not to exceed £12,500. Balcon would present the film; Jackson and Powell would write, produce and direct. All the studio services, all the contract artists, all the technicians, were available to us at cost. Also, all the contents of the story department. When I heard the terms, I whistled. Obviously it would pay us to write all our own stories and scripts, at a nominal cost. All the money that we saved could go towards the other costs of production. But at that kind of a budget, I was not going to be able to give Hollywood sleepless nights. I was sure that Alfred Hitchcock was being given four times as much. He was making *Waltzes from Vienna*, a film about Johann Strauss starring Esmond Knight as the Waltz King. It was like asking Picasso to design greeting cards. I tracked him down in the labyrinth of stages which was Lime Grove. He was shooting a sequence in a bakery, with the loaves being raked out of the oven and thrown into a basket in waltz time. He seemed pleased to see me, but cooled rather when I explained my mission. He cooled still further when I ventured to remark that prerecording music and synchronising it with action had been done so brilliantly by Erik Charell in *Congress Dances* that it was a waste of time to copy it.

Anxious to improve the atmosphere, I asked him what script he was preparing. He cheered up, saying it was *The Thirty-nine Steps* by John Buchan. "Hurray!" I cried. "Of course! The best thriller ever written. A real dime novel. Who's going to play Richard Hannay?"

"Robert Donat." I knew he was one of Christopher Mann's clients, and I had seen him in the theatre in *A Sleeping Clergyman* by James Bridie, and in a small part in *The Rose Without a Thorn*, a play about Henry VIII and Catherine Howard, in which Donald Wolfit also had a small part.

"And the girl is Madeleine Carroll."

"The girl? What girl? There's no girl in the book."

"There is in the film." I was stopped in my tracks. Hitch was right. There was no reason why there should not be a girl in the film.

"And the secret service man at the beginning? A wonderful part! The man who is always afraid, but goes on until he gets killed? Who plays him?"

Hitch gave one of his smiles. "Shall we tell him, Alma?" Alma nodded, watching my face. "Lucie Mannheim."

I gaped at him. She was one of the best actresses in Germany, now a fugitive from Hitler and living in London. This was the Hitchcock who liked to bewilder you, to turn things topsy-turvy. The Hitch who cast Peter Lorre as the hairless Mexican, when he was neither hairless nor a Mexican.

I left them to their waltzes and went in search of the editing department at the top of the building which resembled a four-storey car park. With so many co-producers, associate producers, and just plain producers on his plate, Mickey Balcon had decided to run his studios by the Hollywood method, which meant nearly autonomous departments, with a head of department who reported directly to him. Alfred Junge, the great German designer who knew more about making films than anybody in the building, was head of the art department, with half a dozen ordinary art directors and a dozen draughtsmen working under him. The sound department and camera department each had their responsible heads, and the head of the editing department was Ian Dalrymple. You either liked Ian Dalrymple at first sight or you never did. I did. He knew all about me, of course, but we had never met. Ian is one of the great men of the British cinema. As editor, writer, producer and teacher, he has had an enormous influence. At the moment, all I saw was a big, bulky young man with an air of one who did not suffer fools gladly, curt to the point of rudeness, while in his eyes there lurked an unidentifiable something – could it be a sense of humour? He was shy, I could tell that and I didn't mind his brusqueness. With him was a tall, good-looking, rather lantern-jawed young man, obviously a bosom friend of Dalrymple's, who was introduced as the man most likely to cut my first picture for Gaumont-British – Derek Twist. Derek had charm, and we were soon talking movies as only movie buffs can talk. My chief worry

over leaving John Seabourne behind melted away. These were not only my
equals, but my superiors. As collaborators I couldn't ask for anything
better.

My next port of call was Alfred Junge's art department. It was a daring
act to enter here without an appointment, and for social reasons. Alfred
was a Prussian, a great disciplinarian as well as a great organiser. He hadn't
a second to waste, but restrained his impatience and was cordial when I
reminded him of the splendid work he had done for E. A. Dupont when all
of us were at Elstree and I was shooting stills for Hitchcock. The great
designer was now in his late forties or early fifties. He was a handsome man
of medium height, rigid and powerfully built. I knew the directors he had
worked with, and yearned to work on something with him myself, but on
something big and spacious. How cramped this man, who had been trained
at the UFA Studios at Neuebabelsberg, and in the big spaces of the exterior
lot at Elstree, must find himself in this jigsaw puzzle of a studio, where sets
had to be built in the carpenter's shop, then taken apart and put in big
elevators, which took them up two or three floors to a stage where they
were reassembled. By now, a queue of chiefs of construction, master
painters, master plasterers, and art directors were waiting to see the great
man, and he saw me go with relief.

I had told all my friends that Jerry Jackson and I were contemporary
film-makers, we were not interested in talky-talkies or costume dramas; we
expected our stories to come from today's headlines. This theory of
opening the tabloids to see what film you were going to make that morning
was a bare-faced steal from Darryl F. Zanuck, the erstwhile whiz kid of
Warner Brothers, who was said to go around the studio lot with a typewriter hung around his neck. Lee Planskoy who was pro-American in every
way and should have gone to Hollywood, had convinced me that so long as
I was tied to such low budgets, the only chance I had to get attention and
audience acclaim was to make contemporary subjects. Jerry needed no
convincing.

That spring I met Frankie. When Jerry was away, Lee and I often hunted in
couples. We had gone to a fashion show at Olympia. Lee had some girl who
was a model, and he was mad about model girls anyway – quite rightly
because they are more beautiful, more original, and more hard-working
than a girl has a right to be. Lee's girl – or she may have been mine –
anyway she was called Lorna, brought another girl to our table. She was
quite literally the most beautiful girl I had, or have, ever seen. She was tall,
with a model's figure, wonderful shoulders and legs – a natural blonde with
hazel eyes that were twice the size of any ordinary girl's, fringed with long

lashes, and with the most wonderful serene expression in them. She wore some outrageous outfit and was completely successful in conveying that she had forgotten all about it. She downed two huge whiskies without batting an eyelid, and when I admired her performance she said that her father had told her that whisky was the most healthy drink, provided that you drank only whisky. Her name, she said, was Frankie Reidy.

Reidy is an Irish name; her family came from the West of Ireland, although she had been born in Whitechapel, in London's East End. Her father had been a surgeon at the London Hospital at the same time as Frederick Treves, the discoverer of the Elephant Man. So when she said in her light, detached voice that her name was Frankie Reidy, I thought it was a joke from the way it rhymed, and she had to write it down for me before I would believe it. I also asked her to write down her telephone number, but she shook her head like a mutinous pony, and had another whisky.

I was desperate that I would lose track of her, although I had found out that she was a famous photo model and had done the fur catalogue for Bradley's. Lorna told us that they were going over to the White City at Shepherd's Bush to do a hat show that evening. We were there. Frankie was marvellous with hats. Everything seemed to suit her. She would take the most absurd creation and put it on and it no longer looked absurd, it looked right. Everything she did was right. On that evening she must have shown twenty hats, each one more absurd than the last, and by the tenth hat I was a goner.

I got her telephone number – but she wouldn't let me see her home.

After a day or two, I invited her to go riding with Jerry and me in Windsor Great Park. She came along. She wore an old pair of jodhpurs, a tweed jacket, and a shirt with a pin, and looked as if she had ridden all her life. They were her brother's jodhpurs. She had never had her legs over a horse's back, but she never said a word. We rode as recklessly as usual, galloping, cantering – she did everything we did. She was the most monosyllabic beautiful girl that we had, either of us, ever seen. She never even murmured "Thanks." Lee called her La Belle Dame Sans Merci.

We went down to Goodwood and rode there on these terrifying steep sides of Trundle Hill. We came to the wood behind the grandstand. Frankie's horse stopped abruptly and she fell off on her head. I was surprised. I caught her horse's rein, jumped off and picked her up.

"What happened?" I asked.

"He stopped."

"Is that any reason for falling off?"

No answer.

"You were riding with too slack a rein. And you must keep your knees in to your horse's side."

"Must I?"

"Look here, you've ridden before, haven't you?"

"Not before I met you."

I proposed to her on the spot.

Imagine what she had been through. That beautiful poker face fronted for a dauntless heart and a brain like her surgeon father's.

I could think of nothing but marriage. But I was already married.

Until now this had never bothered my conscience for a moment. The whole experience in Nice had been unreal. Now, suddenly, it was a wall between me and having a family. And Frankie was a Catholic, like all her family, although her beautiful mother was from the North and was a convert.

I had been married in France and I must get a divorce from France. It took two years. And by that time we were literally at the edge of the world.

The Fire Raisers was to be our first production for Gaumont-British, produced by Jerry Jackson and directed by Michael Powell with an original story and script by both of us. The story was suggested by the activities of one Leopold Harris, an insurance assessor of repute in the City, who was arrested and convicted of arson in the course of his daily duties. The newspapers had coined the word "fire raisers" for these villains and gave us our title and our plot.

The hero-villain of our script was played by Leslie Banks. It was the first time that I had worked with a great actor – a West End and a Broadway star, who had made a sensational debut in Hollywood as the villainous Count in The Hounds of Zaroff. He was an actor's actor. He had speed and he created magic. (Did you see Laurence Olivier's Henry V? Well, Leslie Banks played Chorus. See what I mean?)

When I had so grandiloquently claimed to Ian Dalrymple et les autres that Jerry and I were only interested in contemporary subjects, I had reckoned without Mickey Balcon. He played us a trick. Jerry and I were happily making up our story, which mostly consisted of ideas stolen from the latest American smash hit, and writing our script with an eye on our slender budget, when Michael Balcon sent for us. He said he was in a jam. Someone had let him down. The studio would be empty for four weeks. Could we go into production right away with Fire Raisers? No, we couldn't. Well then, would we take on another assignment to fill the gap, and follow it up with Fire Raisers? He had a script all ready to go. It was on his desk, and he pushed it towards us. Jerry pounced on it. I looked at it with an appraising eye. It was one of those talkie scripts. At least a hundred pages. Mickey went on: it was intended for an all-star cast; there was a good part for Leslie Banks; we could have any actors from the contract list we liked. It was called *Murder Party*.

It was clever of Mickey Balcon to dangle an all-star cast before my eyes, because the script was a stinker. It was the work of two English playwrights, who had often collaborated, who had written it as a play and then collaborated on the screenplay. We have all seen this sort of film in the past, and I am sure we shall see it tomorrow. You cannot imagine the awfulness of it, in out-of-touch Old England, in 1933. As we read it, I could hardly believe it. How did Mickey dare to try to get this piece of shit off his plate and onto ours?

"Well," said Jerry, "what do you think? Are you willing to take it on?"

I hesitated. To tell the truth, I was flattered, and there was a big trial scene at the Old Bailey, which I thought I could make something of. Pretty, charming Jane Baxter was to play the juvenile lead and the other girl would be played by Viola Keats, a redhead. Both ladies were my type. There were a number of good parts for men. I could have Ian Hunter, Malcolm Keen, Ernest Thesiger, all good West End actors, and I could still have Leslie Banks, although his part couldn't be compared with the part we were writing especially for him in *The Fire Raisers*. I groaned.

"I'll make it a separate deal," said Jerry. "We've got him over a barrel."

"Oh-h-h . . . all right," I said. But it was not Mickey we had over a barrel, it was me.

"What on earth made you let Mickey Balcon sell you *Murder Party*!?" Ian Dalrymple was very cross. "It's a phony. A lot of worthless people gathered together, the men in black tie and women in evening dress, like *Dear Brutus*, without J. M. Barrie. Mickey's been trying to find a sucker for it for years. I thought you and your partner were all for social realism. You walked right into that one, didn't you?" I nodded and he relented.

"Well, how is your own script going, *The Fire Raisers*?" he asked. "I see that you start in a month."

I asked him if he would read it, and he and Derek Twist made some good suggestions. "Derek is going to be your editor," said Ian. "Believe it or not, he asked for you." I looked at Derek and he grinned and nodded. I felt a little better. I had friends in my corner.

During the shooting of *The Night of the Party*, which is what we ended up calling this piece of junk, I had been mentally kicking myself. Had I escaped from quota-quickies to make polite society dramas about non-existent people? Even the love affair that I had started with dear Jane Baxter went wrong when Frankie saw us together at Ciro's. I was so afraid of losing Frankie that I dropped poor Jane like a hot potato, even though I wasn't sure that Frankie had seen us. Of course she had. Frankie saw everything, and knew everything, but never said anything.

Although the lessons I learnt from *Night of the Party* were minuses, however, there was one plus. A piece of advice from Glen McWilliam, the cameraman, a dry, bespectacled American with a twinkle in his eye. He was highly professional. I had been used to doing everything for myself and pushing the unit around at top speed, afraid I wouldn't get what I wanted. We fell over each other several times on the first day. Finally, he caught me by the arm as I rampaged by.

"Micky! I want a word with you," he said.

A word? And lose five seconds? I visibly champed at the bit.

He looked at me quizzically. "We've both got a job to do and we don't want to get in each other's way. OK?"

I saw his point. I said it was OK. I was in a different league. I had learnt my lesson.

Like all Europeans of my generation, I loved and admired America and the Americans. We loved their Constitution, their generosity, and their success in creating a real democracy, owned by the people themselves. If we were interested in the arts, we admired their journalism, from Mark Twain to H. L. Mencken, and we inhaled with eagerness the oxygen that Ernest Hemingway and others were breathing into tired old English prose. I had felt this myself when I was nothing but a schoolboy and a bank clerk. It was intensified and clarified by my deep interest in movies, and I had had it all confirmed when I moved to France and joined an American film unit, and worked alongside men like Frank Scully, Howard Strickling and Willis Goldbeck. I suppose that it is this strong predilection and admiration for everything American in the lively arts that makes the English critics and literary ladies and gents, suspicious of me. And yet I never wanted to go to America and make their pictures for them. I wanted to make English ones. I was English to the core, as English as a Cox's Orange Pippin, as English as a Worcester Pearmain.

Feeling as I did about England's cottage industry – the film business – a feeling shared by Alfred Hitchcock – it was a wonder that I never emigrated to Hollywood. I knew that I had friends there – I read of them from time to time in the pages of *Variety* and other showbiz papers – and if I had chosen to follow them up, I would have found that Walter Strohm, for instance, was high up in the production department of MGM and could give me a dozen introductions; or that Howard Strickling was now personal publicity representative to Louis B. Mayer; and there was Grant Whytock, who had taught me how to handle film in the cutting room, and who was now supervising editor for Edward Small at the old Harold Lloyd Studios. But I had no money saved and I hate asking favours. Hitch managed it much better. Of course, from the beginning, his budgets were much bigger than mine. The worldwide success of *The Thirty-nine Steps* brought him Hollywood offers, but he continued to make his wonderful London thrillers – his best work, in my opinion. He had everything he wanted for the present. He was content to wait until the right offer came along, which it did, and we lost him to David O. Selznick and Hollywood.

We went straight on to *The Fire Raisers*, which was a success. *The Night of the Party* sank without a trace. Leslie Banks enjoyed himself and we started at once to plan and write another film together. Derek Twist and I got on famously. I encouraged him to come on the floor a good deal, which was not the custom at Mickey's studio. "Divide and rule", was his motto. The cast was good, and there was an especially charming performance by Jack Anderson, the father of Michael Anderson the director. But my big discovery was Carol Goodner, who played the secretary to Leslie Banks's crooked assessor. She was an American actress, and I first saw her when she was playing in the West End in some American importation, I think it might have been the play of Vicki Baum's *Grand Hotel*. (If it was, then she was playing the part that Joan Crawford played in the film.) She hadn't got much of a figure, but she had expressive eyes and a quiet intensity that was quite unforgettable. In addition she was highly professional. I decided that what I liked about American actresses was that they were not content with speaking a lot of words: they knew that there was a real woman hidden somewhere amongst all that verbiage and they were trying to find her.

Our next picture was *The Red Ensign*. "That's more like it," said Ian Dalrymple after reading it. He came of Scottish stock, and the picture was set on Clydeside. But it was the semi-documentary approach to the fine art of shipbuilding that he savoured. Leslie Banks's part was his best yet, that of a Glasgow shipbuilder and shipowner who has to fight his board every step of the way over building a new type of cargo carrier which will bring work to the shipyards and prosperity to the Clyde. Once again, we got the idea from a newspaper article. I had seen Leslie play a young Scot in Norman Macowan's play *The Infinite Shoeblack*, and knew that that Scottish burr would bring warmth to his part. I surrounded him with good Scottish actors in the small parts, and when he came on the set to play his first scene and saw all those authentic Scottish actors looking at him he nearly broke up. One was Campbell Gullan, my co-director on *Caste*. Another was John Laurie, who scored a memorable hit in *The Thirty-nine Steps*.

People just didn't know what to make of *The Red Ensign*. (By the way, is there anyone who doesn't know that the red ensign is the flag of the British Merchant Navy, and that "ensign" rhymes with "tocsin"?) The elaborate staging of the shipyard, the big, sweeping exteriors, the high standard of performance and the sincerity of the actors, the overall seriousness of my approach to directing our story, made them run for cover. I met Joan Maude in Oxford Street. She was the red-headed daughter of Nancy

Price, with spectacular good looks and a fine, intelligent approach to her work.

"Michael," she said, "I have never seen a film like yours. I don't know why I like it, but I do."

"It's like when you see the Indian rope trick for the first time," I explained kindly. "You don't expect to see it, and then you see it and it's very disconcerting. And you're quite wrong when you say you haven't seen films like that before. Every year there are half a dozen films made on the Continent with serious social subjects as their theme."

Carol Goodner was in this one too. She was half of our sedate, but somehow moving, love story.

About this time, late in 1934, I got a telephone call from, of all people, Gordon Avil. Do you remember Gordon Avil? – the tall, blond, bony, lanky Yankee camera assistant to Johnny Seitz on *Mare Nostrum*, who was so kind to the clumsy English apprentice who dropped all those glass photographic plates on the threshold of his career? He was in London, staying at the Piccadilly Hotel, and wanted to see me. I was as excited as a girl at her second date. I met him in the bar. He looked just the same.

"Hey, Micky," he said, "you've put on weight." He explained that he was in town for Metro. He had to shoot some backgrounds and some matching shots for King Vidor, and he wanted me to organise it. I never asked him if Walter Strohm had put him on to me. And I forgot to ask Walter Strohm in Hollywood, forty-seven years later. But I expect it was a plot of the old *Mare Nostrum* companions. We have so few friends in this shiftless, world-wide-flung business that we cling to those friends we've got. I was immensely touched that Gordon had thought of me. He was a professional, he was an American, he was on his way to the top of his profession. He had broken fresh ground with his photography for King Vidor on *Hallelujah*. And his first thought on coming to England had been of me!

"Gordon," I said, in the tone of one confessing to syphilis, "I'm a director."

"Well, what of?"

"A movie director," I said, rather miffed, in spite of myself, that he hadn't been more impressed. "I got my chance two years ago, and I've made about a dozen since. They're only poverty-row productions," I hastened to add, "not like yours." Gordon's delight and surprise that little Micky Powell should become a director, was so genuine that I was all the more sorry that I couldn't help him with his project – not because of my rise through the ranks, but because my partner and I were under contract with Gaumont-British to make one more film for them: *The Phantom Light*.

We gossiped for hours, and I arranged that he should use our office and our facilities while he was getting his small unit together. Gordon had so much to tell me about the progress they had made in Hollywood, freeing the camera from the tyranny of sound. He told me how the new directors from Broadway were pressing for colour. What was the use, they would say, of planning elaborate routines and effects for musicals in black and white?

All sorts of colour processes were being marketed, but King Vidor was quite sure that Technicolor was the answer. Technicolor three-strip, Gordon hastened to add, not two-strip. The most interesting of the new directors, and the one who talked the loudest for Technicolor, was Rouben Mamoulian. But Gordon worshipped King Vidor, as I did. As a silent director, as a talkie director, he was without a peer.

I asked about Rex. Was it true that he refused to make any more films? Gordon looked embarrassed. It was more the reverse. Rex's demands were so imperious and sweeping that he got no offers. Several times it had looked as if Louis B. Mayer and he, who had parted over *Ben-Hur*, would agree on a subject worthy of them both. But it always fell apart. Rex would not beg, and Louis B. would not entreat. I was shocked. Was this the way to treat one of the great Hollywood film directors, one of the few directors who had a personal style, who understood what was meant by the grand manner? Rex, Alan Crosland, Erich von Stroheim, were great stylists, great men. Louis B. was not an idiot; surely he must understand that? But Gordon shook his head and looked sad. This was the other side of the Hollywood mirror.

We parted long after midnight and I never saw him again. He died suddenly. I know nothing of the circumstances of his death, but I still miss him. He was my first friend in films.

I left all of the business side of our partnership to Jerry. So, I am not sure whether our much-touted "films from tomorrow's headlines" were box-office successes or not. *The Fire Raisers* and *Red Ensign* cost about £12,000 apiece, plus studio charges, probably about 20 per cent on top of cost. So they could hardly have lost money at that price. I can't remember who suggested my fourth and final film with Gaumont-British. I fancy that it was Jerry, anxious that I should direct a box-office picture, and one that would give me more scope, for I was already badgering him about the St Kilda film, making remarks about the art of the cinema, comparing quota-quickies to comic strips and dragging him, with Lee on the other side to back me up, to see the latest Continental films in arty flea-pits, which was, for Jerry, a fate worse than death. I had accused him of being a film producer because it was glamorous showbiz, with girls standing in line to get laid. There was some truth in this, but it wasn't the whole story. He really was one of us, and it was admirable the way he strained his own resources to back Lee's optical experiments without really comprehending their value. *The Phantom Light* starred Gordon Harker as a lighthouse keeper. I am a sucker for lighthouses. The lonelier and more inaccessible, the better. And I love comedy-thrillers. I said 'yes' to this one right away, and never regretted it. I enjoyed every minute. The less said about the plot the better.

Gordon Harker was one of those naturals that every country has – a face to remember: in France Fernandel, in Mexico Cantinflas, in Italy Alberto Sordi, in America Humphrey Bogart, in Ireland Victor McLaglen, in Germany Conrad Veidt, and in England Gordon Harker. He was one of Hitch's favourite faces, and Hitch had helped to make him into a star. He had one of those flat, disillusioned Cockney faces, half-fish, half-Simian, with an eye like a dead mackerel. In one of Hitch's first successes, *The Ring*, a boxing picture, Gordon Harker had played one of the hero's seconds and nearly stole the picture. He was wonderful in silent films, but even better in talkies. He got his effects with all sorts of strange sounds, and to my delight he could hold a pause as long as any actor I had known. Close-ups were made for him, and we both took full advantage of it.

Of course, I said that I had to visit all the most inaccessible lighthouses before starting the picture, and I remember that Frankie went with me to the Eddystone Light, and was very sick coming back in the supply ship. And, of course, I had to go and see the Chance Brothers, in Birmingham, who made all the lenses for all the lights. The light in the film is at Hartland Point, North Devon, but that was only for the light itself. There were other lighthouses in the film as well.

I had a major disappointment over casting. This was my first experience of being overridden by the front office and I didn't like it. I had seen Roger Livesey at the Old Vic and had been very impressed by this broad-shouldered, golden-haired Viking. I made a test of Roger as the naval hero of the film and introduced Roger and the test to Mickey Balcon. Mickey was very conventional, not to say suburban, and he didn't like Roger's lovely, husky voice. Because he said nothing, and just stared at the screen, his opinion was obvious. So when the lights went up, Roger turned around and applauded himself with an amiable grin. That settled it. I got Ian Hunter, a contract artist, instead. But I vowed to myself that one day I would make Roger's husky voice beloved all over the world. And I did.

On the whole, I didn't enjoy my year with the Gaumont-British Film Corporation, and I don't suppose they enjoyed it either. I had made friends in the editing department. Alfred Junge had come down on the set of *Night of the Party* and made one or two suggestions in my early days. But he soon realised that the kind of films I was making were of little interest to him personally, and we never saw him again, although we got good service from his underlings. Nobody could foresee the future of British films, and Mickey Balcon was not an exciting leader.

In the editing periods of our films, the only person I could find to talk to was Robert Flaherty, who, with assistance from John Goldman, was editing his Irish film, *Man of Aran*, while I was making my four films. He was cutting when I arrived, and recutting when I left. He had the room at the end of the hall when we were cutting *Night of the Party*, and each time that I returned, for *The Fire Raisers,* for *Red Ensign*, for *The Phantom Light*, he had taken over yet another cutting room for his miles of film, and film billowed out of the doors and spilled out of the bins and hung from the hat-racks and you had to wade through film to find him. I disapprove of waste, but he was a lovely man. He was like an Irish bishop who had turned gangster, and he could sell the flies off the wall if you didn't see him coming first. The man who could sell the Hudson's Bay Company on the idea of making a little documentary about their trading with the Eskimos, and who then disappeared for two years to return with *Nanook of the North*, the first feature documentary; the man who could persuade F. W. Murnau, the great German film director, to go with him to the South Seas and make *Tabu*; who persuaded Korda to back *Elephant Boy*, and discovered Sabu; and who persuaded Mickey Balcon to send him to the West of Ireland for two years to make *Man of Aran* – this was no ordinary salesman. This was a salesman of genius, in spite of the fact that when in production he was quite uncontrollable, vanishing into the blue, shooting millions of feet of film, and usually having to have someone else finish it. The whole editing department of Gaumont-British was under his spell. Mickey Balcon, protesting feebly, was as helpless as the Wedding Guest with the Ancient Mariner. This wonderful man, talking, always talking, would drift from one cutting room to another, leaving behind him young heads dreaming of jungles and coral reefs, wrecking Ian Dalrymple's schedules and leaving his theatre bookings in a shambles.

I had told Flaherty about St Kilda, and we had endless arguments about the way to film such a wonderful event. He would strike the cutting room table with his great fist, sending everything falling into the bin and roar: " 'Tis God's pity, Michael, that you were not there with even a Kodak on the day the event took place. 'Tis a crime!"

I agreed, of course, but I told him that my film would have a story. It would be about the people of the island whose lives were changed for ever – some for the better, some for the worse.

"A story? What kind of a story, Michael?" I would make up a different one each time we had the argument, and he would listen and shake his massive curly head. "Facts are facts, you cannot beat Nature. You can't invent the evacuation of an island, you can't ignore the death of a people! Ya' should have been there when it happened! With half a dozen cameras."

By this time, half the editing staff had joined in the argument: fact against fiction, the eternal argument between the liar and the journalist, between "I was there", and "this is how it must have been". Until finally Ian broke us up and we all went back to our little hutches.

My cameraman on *The Phantom Light* was Roy Kellino. He was in his early twenties and he did a good job. He was a romantic, sullen-looking boy and was married to Pamela Ostrer, the daughter of Isidore. He was a good boy, always playing pranks and taking risks. Pamela Ostrer was ambitious, and presently the two of them formed a company with James Mason, a young actor with the same sullen good looks as Roy. They made one film and not long after, Roy Kellino died. Pamela married James Mason.

We had fun shooting *The Phantom Light*, but I had had two films forced on me and collaborated with Jerry on two others that were just not good enough. Jerry was quite happy with them, but I was not. They were American B-pictures without the slickness and confidence that genuine American B's have got. Mickey Balcon had a Programme, and when as a film-maker you have a Programme, you have lost your soul. He only got it back again when he took over the Ealing Studios, surrounded himself with real film-makers, and produced film after film that delighted the world. Who that saw the Ealing comedies did not become a fan for life of Alec Guinness, T. E. B. Clarke, Robert Hamer, Charles Frend, Sandy Mackendrick and a dozen others?

The quota-quickies that I made during the last months of my purgatory for the American Irving Asher at Warner Brothers' British Studios at Teddington, were a damn sight more honest and more entertaining, because they were not trying to be anything but what they were, and they were tailored from first-class scripts. Irving had the run of the Warner Brothers' library in Hollywood. He had to make about twenty films a year to fulfil his British quota and keep the Warner Brothers' Teddington Studios running. He went back to California each year with the head of his scenario department, raided the story department at Burbank and came back to Teddington with perhaps fifty scripts that had already been turned into films by those satanic mills and were already playing at Palaces and flea-pits all around the world, many of them with big stars like Bette Davis, Edward G. Robinson and James Cagney. Everything was run like a machine at Burbank and the average length of a script was eighty pages. Darryl Zanuck used to tear twenty pages of dialogue out of a verbose script with his own hands, fling them in the writer's face and say: "Get on with the story." All that Irving had to do was hand the script to his story department, who cut it down to fifty pages and handed it over to a director like me. This was how tight little dramas like my *Crown v Stevens*, or comedies like *Something Always Happens* or *Someday*, co-starring Esmond Knight and Margaret Lockwood, arrived on the British screen. I made six or seven of these for Irving, slotting them in between other assignments. Jerry and he, both young Americans both in the quota-quickie business, were good friends. They carved me up between them, dovetailing their schedules so that I could work for both of them.

Irving Asher was a Hollywood baby, born into the business. He had married one of the early blonde screen charmers, Laura La Plante, an all-American girl. Laura had no particular ambitions to be an actress, and partially retired as soon as she was married. Irving had good connections in Hollywood, and when Warner Brothers decided to produce quota-quickies in England, Irving got the job. I liked Irving. What he knew, he knew, but he didn't know very much. On the other hand, he didn't pretend that he did. Our relations were always happy. His job was to run a studio and mine was to direct as many films as I could fit in. He had a good staff, including a cameraman who was a wizard, Basil Emmott, and, more important to me, he also had Poppa Day under contract.

Poppa was the greatest trick photographer and double-exposure merchant that the movies have ever seen. He had started as a boy in 1905 with the great Georges Méliès in Paris, the inventor of screen wizardry, and he was saving Irving a fortune on set construction costs by painting ceilings and chandeliers, and even landscapes, on glass, which he then superimposed over the long shots that Basil Emmett had lit and photographed. Later, he was to use this process when he brought the Himalayas into the studio for me on *Black Narcissus*. I was always dropping into Poppa Day's studio. It was like chatting with Jules Verne.

Irving Asher had been getting offers from the newly emerging studios at Denham and Pinewood to produce feature films and was looking for someone to co-produce with him at Teddington and eventually take over. Jerry was the obvious choice and he was in no position to say no, for he was married!

Yes! Jerry Jackson, the Wolf of Hallam Street, the toast of the Embassy Club and the Kit-Kat and of the Little Room at the Berkeley, cornered, lassoed and hog-tied by an enchantingly pretty and sweet girl! It was all over in a flash. Jerry had given up his flat in London, and was already living with Peggy in an imitation Tudor manorhouse near Maidenhead. Too late – too late – Jerry's family, his mother and sister from New York's Upper West Side, descended upon them, for Jerry had married a non-Jewess, and there was wailing in the land. I gathered from Peggy that they sat side by side on the largest sofa and glared at her. Remarks were made like "Jerry, you remember Irene Morowitz? She still has the high school ring you gave her." There were interminable days in the kitchen, where Peggy was being instructed how to make particular Jewish delicacies.

Most marriages would have been a bit rocked by such an invasion, but Jerry and Peggy were very much in love. They survived it. After all, we all survive each other's families, don't we?

My mother, of course, was delighted at my being thrown out of Hallam Street on to the open market. Sowing wild oats was all very well and no doubt necessary for young men, but it was quite time that I too found a nice girl and settled down. And if Frankie and I were not going to get hitched, then Mother was bent on finding a substitute. She sold her farm in Dorset and rented a cottage in Chalfont St Peter, a village in Buckinghamshire, which was only two or three miles from Denham and Pinewood Studios. So I was back under my mother's wing, although when I was actually making a film I usually took a room in town.

By this time Denham Studios were in operation, and a great modern laboratory was rising beside it. I used to cast longing glances at the great white stages as I drove by on my way to yet another quota-quickie.

I knew all about the exciting and glamorous films that were being made behind those towering walls. I, poor outcast, was working at a one-stage studio at Beaconsfield, uneasily sound-proofed by its owner.

When I look back on those turbulent years which led our generation up a stairway, not to Heaven, but to Armageddon, I marvel at my good luck. I was old enough to have seen the flowering of European cinema and the finest works of titans like Abel Gance, Eisenstein, Fritz Lang, Henry King, Chaplin, Griffith, Lubitsch, Sjöstrom, Pastrone, von Stroheim, Ingram, Raymond Bernard, Jean Renoir, René Clair, Hitchcock. They dazzled me with images that I carry with me in that great head of mine, whose memory box is so much more reliable than any computer, of which I have, perhaps, used not more than a tenth of its potential. Only those thousands of people who have recently had the privilege of seeing a great European silent film in the 1980's, like *Napoleon*, can perhaps get a glimpse of what I mean and what I carried with me all through those pedestrian years in England, when I was learning my profession at a pound sterling a foot.

Lee was sometimes puzzled, because of his superior outlook and high standards, and would protest. "Micky!" (he would always pronounce my name "Meeky"), "why do you make a piece of crap like this?"

"This" was a thriller made for the Joe Rock Studios, called *The Man Behind the Mask*, with Hugh Williams, Jane Baxter and Maurice Schwartz, a famous actor from the New York Yiddish Theatre, who happened to be in London.

Lee persisted: "Why? What for?"

"For a thousand pounds," I answered.

He shrugged. We were outside the Palace Theatre after the trade show. "It can only do you harm."

"On the contrary, it has done me good. Joe Rock has read my story about the evacuation of St Kilda and he wants to back me to do it."

It was the early spring of 1936. My long, patient apprenticeship was nearly over.

Joe Rock was an American. Like many small-time Hollywood producers, he had learnt the business in vaudeville. He was ambitious and, finding the Hollywood walls too hard to climb, he had come to England, found a backer and bought the old Ideal Studios in Elstree, which had once belong to Blattner. In his Hollywood days, Joe Rock had sponsored a famous film called *Krakatoa*, about the blowing up of an entire South Pacific island in a vast, volcanic explosion. Joe Rock believed in the off-beat picture; and, undeterred by the cool reception afforded to our *Man Behind the Mask* (or perhaps because of it), he wanted to back me to make my island story.

By now, I had found a title for it – *The Edge of the World*. It came from a book about the early European navigators who sailed up the west coast of Europe as far north as the Orkneys. Beyond that, reported the Roman general Agricola, was nothing but hairy Vikings and shocking weather, which he dismissed as *Ultima Thule*, the last landfall, the edge of the world.

Joe Rock had read my outline: two families at loggerheads over whether they should leave the island, and a love story involving the girl of one family with the boy of the other. I had written it in self-defence, because nobody could understand why I wanted to go off to make a film on an island when I was in demand for making thrillers.

"Oh, it's going to be like *Man of Aran*, is it?" they all asked helpfully.

I was livid. "No, not at all like Flaherty's picture. He hasn't got a story, just a lot of waves and seaweed and pretty pictures. This is a *Drama*! an *Epic*! About people!! I want to dramatise it and use actors mixed with real people."

"Like *Pêcheur d'Islande*," Lee added, referring to Léon Poirier's film, which had started a vogue among Paris intellectuals.

"No! Not like Poirier's film," I spluttered. We were having a steak and kidney pudding dinner with Jerry, and all talking at once. "You've got no imagination. I don't want to make a documentary. Documentaries are for disappointed feature film-makers or out-of-work poets." (The GPO had recently sponsored *Night Mail*, with W. H. Auden's words and Benjamin Britten's music.) I said, "I see I'll have to write it," and I did.

Now that I had moved into the £1000 a picture class, I felt that I needed an agent, or, more accurately, agents felt they needed me. Christopher Mann was an old acquaintance. You may remember that he was managing Madeleine Carroll when I first met him; he was now managing me. Chris got me £2,000 for the job, and I did get half that. I had a room at that time in Bloomsbury, at 46 Bloomsbury Street, just by Bedford Square, in the heart of Woolf country, where you couldn't throw a slim volume of poems at a stray cat without hitting a publisher's reader. I had a cat, as a matter of fact, who may have had a practical acquaintance with T. S. Eliot. His name was J. Alfred Prufrock, for obvious reasons ("Shall I wear my trousers rolled?") and with more than a nodding acquaintance with the wasteland between Bloomsbury Street and Russell Square.

As soon as the money was agreed, and without waiting for an advance, for it was May already, I sat down to dictate a script. Or rather, I stood up and walked about. The typist sat and typed. I had never dictated a script before, but it proved easy and quick. A lot of a writer's time on a film script is spent on technical directions, shooting instructions and scene numbers. I never take long over a script when it's something already churning around in that head of mine. We did this one in eight days.

I think I have mentioned that when I first arrived at the Nettlefold Studios at Walton-on-Thames six years before, I had made a friend in the sound department, named Vernon Campbell Sewell. This friendship had prospered. Vernon had got his job at the studio through nepotism, but he retained it by sheer competence. He is the most competent man I have ever known. When consulted about an estimate for anything from the model of Big Ben to the interior of a submarine, Vernon snorts: "Ridiculous! Daylight robbery!", tears up the estimate and does the job himself. His hobby is boats – from steam to diesel to outboard – but he never keeps a boat long. He does it up, masses all the controls under his eye on the bridge, installs all the comforts, designs heads that actually work, reduces the necessary crew from four to two, and then sells it and buys another wreck.

Men such as Vernon are invaluable around a film studio. There are no mysteries for them; they are at home in all departments. Vernon was totally unlike me; for one thing he was always going to see films, while I would be at the theatre, or walking around England. But I had confidence in him. I gave him lots of responsible things to do, and when he finally directed an important film, *The Silver Fleet*, it was the success I knew it would be.

I have a habit of surrounding myself with people whom I like and admire, and of dragging them with me into an adventure. I look on my films the way an explorer surveys an empty portion of the map and vows to fill it.

At my call, John Seabourne left his cutting room at Nettlefold and joined my war council at Rock Studios, Elstree. Vernon Sewell no sooner realised that I destined him to be captain of our supply ship than he was at my side. Monty Berman, a young cameraman who had done outstanding work on two of my films at Warner Brothers' Teddington Studios, was to be lighting cameraman. Syd Streeter, whom I had noticed as an exceptional man as stage carpenter at Rock Studios, was to be chief of construction which meant he would have to build the base camp in addition to the normal work of a stage carpenter.

Gerry Blattner, whom I had met as a boy in his late father's day, was now studio manager at Rock's. He announced: "Now, Michael! We have been over your lists and we would like you to keep the number of personnel you take to the island down to twenty."

"Including actors?"

"Including actors."

We compromised with twenty-three personnel – including a house-keeper when we finally realised just how big a pioneer job we were taking on.

I set about casting. The story involved two families. There were important parts for a father and son, and at first I had set my heart on Malcolm Keen and his son Geoffrey, who at eighteen or so was already a promising actor. I thought it would give something to play a real father and son; I only realized, twenty years later, when I made *The Queen's Guards* with Raymond Massey and his son, Dan, that a father and son are about the last parts that a father and son would want to play.

Anyway, Malcolm had other plans, and turned it down. John Laurie had become a name since *The Thirty-nine Steps* and he had worked with me on a couple of quickies. I admired his sharp quickness, his active brain, his outspokenness, and I knew enough of his career (he had played a very young Hamlet at Stratford) to realize that he had the potential of a great actor. He saw the possibilities of the part and took it.

The head of the other family was played by Finlay Currie, who cast himself in the part and by doing so added a third career to the two he had already made in America, in England and in Australia. He was a trouper – a Scotsman from Caithness, an actor so true and so natural, so rugged and so powerful, so modest and so lovable that, like a French actor, he didn't play a part, he lived it and breathed it. His great stature – he was over six feet tall – and his heavy frame, which appeared as clumsy as an elephant's and which, like an elephant, he moved with ponderous grace – made him unforgettable on the screen. His slightest move registered, because he always thought of the scene and of the other actors in the scene, never of himself. I loved him and admired him and put him in my personal pantheon with John Seabourne. I can't put him higher than that.

A new name in British films, the Yorkshire Methodist and flour-miller named Arthur Rank, who had been sponsoring short religious films to be shown in chapels and churches, had finally given way to the urging of his team of film-makers and financed a feature film, *The Turn of the Tide*. Two young Irish people had thrust themselves into it: Geraldine Fitzgerald, one of the sweetest women to take Broadway by storm, and Niall MacGinnis, who, with his grace and powerful frame and musical Irish voice, could have had Hollywood at his feet, but went his own way instead. Niall, who was to play Finlay Currie's son, joined us, with a slow smile, but Geraldine had a job, and I tested several girls at Elstree before deciding to cast Belle Chrystall, a Lancashire lass from Fleetwood, who plays the girl in the other family, headed by John Laurie. I hesitated a long time over one of the girls we tested. She had a baby face, but I sensed a passionate nature and a strong character. Her name was Joyce Redman.

The only other part that couldn't be cast in Scotland better than in England was the son of Peter Manson (John Laurie) and with some hesitation I cast Eric Berry, a young West End actor with imagination and brains, to emphasise the contrast between him and Niall. You can see Eric as a Nazi radio-announcer in *49th Parallel*, and as Dmitri, the confidential secretary of Lermontov, in *The Red Shoes*. Eric made his later career in America, was impressive in the Broadway production of Albee's *Tiny Alice*, and now is imposingly stout. He had no chance to get stout on Foula.

Yes, on Foula, for the film was not made on St Kilda in the Hebrides, after all, but on Foula, in the Shetlands. When all our preparations were at their height, a message came from Lord Dumfries, the owner of the island, refusing permission for the film company to land on St Kilda. The island was now a bird sanctuary, and the birds were not to be disturbed. This was disconcerting to say the least. Vernon had a friend, Niall Rankin, the nature writer and photographer, who knew Dumfries. He telephoned him and arranged an appointment on a Sunday morning at Cumnock, in the Scottish Lowlands.

I drove up. Something warned me to be mobile. I arranged for Vernon to meet me at Kilmarnock station.

Dumfries's home was very fine: a big, square, white eighteenth-century house, designed and put together by the brothers Adam, seconded by a joiner and cabinet-maker, an Englishman called Chippendale, who carved some of the panelling too. The young lord was cordial but adamant. He had bought the island as a bird sanctuary and as a home for the Soay sheep which he intended to develop. His plans would be disrupted by the invasion of a film company. I said we were prepared to pay for our tenancy. This had some effect. I also said that the evacuation of St Kilda was an historical event which had the effect of contracting the area of Scotland by forty miles and it should be recorded. This had no effect. It was agreed that we would meet next day in Glasgow at his solicitor's office, but this was mere face-saving. I had dreamed of St Kilda for five years, I had sold St Kilda to Joe Rock, and it was becoming obvious that I couldn't have St Kilda. I must find another island. And quickly.

As I expected, the Glasgow meeting was pointless. Our offer was refused. St Kilda was out. We drove to Edinburgh after talking to J. W. Herries, the chief reporter of *The Scotsman*, on the telephone. He was sympathetic. He would see us as soon as we arrived in the capital. It was about two hours' drive between the two cities. He would locate John Mathieson of the Scottish Geographical Survey. Mathieson had done the latest survey of St Kilda. He would know a similar island if anybody did. Herries would assign us one of his cub reporters for the job. His name was Forsyth Hardy.

During the next twenty-four hours, I learnt about Scottish hospitality. People dropped everything to help. Edinburgh is a great city, but its citizens have time for the stranger. The chief reporter of *The Scotsman* took me himself to see John Mathieson, a small, rosy man who could have been a lay-brother in a monastery. It was he who suggested Foula, two hundred miles further north than St Kilda. He had done the survey of both islands. Foula lay solitary, out in the Atlantic, about twenty miles from what Shetlanders call the Mainland. The cliffs, the birds, and the isolation were very like St Kilda.

But who owned Foula? We flung ourselves into the files of *The Scotsman*. Towards one in the morning we found an item on Foula. It was an obituary of the late owner, the Reverend Ian Stoughton Holbourn (no Scottish name that!), and it described the island briefly. Holbourn had left a widow and three sons, Alasdair, Hylas and Philistos. Their address was given as Penkaet Castle, Pencaitland, East Lothian.

"You're in luck, Mr Powell," said Hardy. "It's a bare twenty miles away. You go by Musselburgh and Portobello."

Next day I drove out and, after some difficulty, found the house, which was one of the most beautiful old manorhouses I had ever seen, built of grey stone with a turret stairway three storeys high and latticed windows sunk deep in the walls. Penkaet means the "head of the wood", and I found it by following a track through the trees. Only Alasdair Holbourn was at home, and he was refreshingly simple. I offered him £200 for permission to make our film on their island. His brothers were at Oxford, but he said he would telephone them that night. They agreed, provided that Alasdair went with us on the expedition. I agreed, and asked what they had actually said. He chuckled and said: "Pennies from heaven."

This is the true story of why the evacuation of St Kilda was not filmed on St Kilda in the Hebrides, but on Foula, in the Shetlands, where they talk Norse not Gaelic. It was a blessing in disguise. First of all, I had a populated island and didn't need to bring and feed islanders for the film. The men of Foula were either members of the mailboat team responsible for the supply and communications of the island, or they were deep-sea fishermen, or merchant seamen, away at sea all winter, who returned to cultivate their fields and collect sea-birds and their eggs in the spring. The island was more rugged and inhospitable even than St Kilda, where Village Bay was a good harbour used regularly by trawlers and Admiralty patrols. Foula only had a jetty and a harbour which dried out at low tide. It was just deep enough to float our supply vessel at high tide. Both St Kilda and Foula claimed to have the highest cliff in Britain. John Mathieson gave the palm to St Kilda, whose cliffs were over 1,300 feet sheer to the sea, but there was very little in it.

Joe Rock listened with delight to my tale when I returned to Elstree. He was romantic. It was a shame that he never came north with us. It was agreed that an advance party consisting of myself, Syd Streeter, John Seabourne and Alasdair Holbourn should land on the island and start things moving. At this stage Joe preferred to have no publicity. An off-beat subject, he said, created its own publicity. He had no idea how right he was.

Every schoolboy – and every schoolgirl, I hasten to add – knows what the British Isles look like on the map. But hardly anyone has ever really looked at them. They have been around such a long time. Half the world looks on Britain as "home", even if they've never been there, possibly because of the magnificent indifference shown to them by their mother country. Even so, they would be hard put to name the parallels of latitude which Piccadilly Circus, the Four Courts in Dublin, and Holyrood House in Edinburgh, lie on. A New Zealander, or even a New Yorker, knows that Land's End is in Cornwall and John o' Groat's is the most northerly point of Scotland, but when I tell them that north of Scotland are the Orkney Islands and north of them Fair Isle, and even further north the Shetland Islands, where the most northerly lighthouse in the British Isles, Muckle Flugga – a splendid Norse name – stands more than 800 miles from London, England, they are impressed and interested, while politely stifling a yawn.

The Shetlanders are proud of their Norse ancestry and like to run themselves. They are crofters, and fishermen, and deep-sea men, who know the seven seas as well as you know your village pastor. The women are great knitters, for Shetland sheep carry the longest and finest wool in the world on their backs. They are never sheared. At the right time the wool is pulled off them. In 1935 the main export of the islands was fish and woollen goods. Today it is oil. North Sea oil.

The capital of the islands is Lerwick, a fascinating up-and-down town with a harbour which can take the whole fishing fleet at the height of the season. It is situated on the largest island in the group, which is character-istically called by the Shetlanders the Mainland.

Lerwick's great day, when it celebrates the Norse traditions of the Shetlands and Orkneys, is a Viking festival called "Up Helly Aa" held in January each year. It is a pagan affair. The whole town is involved, and the celebration lasts just as long as the whisky bottles have a dram left in them. The climax is always the burning of a Viking long-ship and the casting of flaming spears into the hull. It's a grand party.

There are more than a hundred islands in the Shetlands, most of them uninhabited, most of them within hailing or sighting distance of each other. Although Lerwick is the only town, there are good roads on the

Mainland, and there is always someone to row over to see how their neighbour is getting on on his island. To all this Foula was an exception.

Foula has no neighbours, except the deadly reefs between it and the Mainland, which are such a danger to shipping. Twenty miles out into the open Atlantic, the top of a great mountain rears itself up out of the sea, 1,300 feet above sea level. The high cliffs on the west slope down to the sea on the east, where there was a jetty and an apology for a harbour and the house of the Laird – the Haa. There was no village, only isolated crofts and one road which ran north and south for about three miles. The situation of the crofts depended upon natural things like freshwater springs, or good peat cuttings, for the peat cut in summer and burnt in winter was the natural fuel of the islands, where there are no trees, for like all of Shetland, Foula lies above the tree-line.

It is difficult to believe today, with short-wave radio and television, the BBC, and even an air-strip on which light aircraft can land, how isolated Foula was before the last war. Letters and newspapers, cigarettes and other luxuries, came by the mailboat. Sometimes it was storm-bound for three weeks. The lives of eight able-bodied seamen could mean the life and death of the island. Ham Geo, the so-called harbour, dried out at low tide. A constant watch had to be kept on the boat and on the weather, night and day. Until our arrival, the islanders were waiting philosophically for conditions to improve. A lot of money was needed. The Mainland would not contribute because Foula was a privately owned island. The Laird could not.

The late and Reverend Ian B. Stoughton Holbourn, father of Hylas, Alasdair and Philistos, was a romantic man. He told his three sons on his deathbed that he had left them the most beautiful house and the most beautiful island in the northern hemisphere. That was true, but he had nothing else to leave them. This is not an uncommon story. The British Isles are strewn with gazebos, follies, monuments, landscapes by Capability Brown, hothouses, icehouses, lime-walks, beech-hedges, mazes, houses great and small, ornamental cottages, castles, watchtowers, stone circles, herb gardens and arboreta – visible tributes to the originality and imagination of their creators, and an embarrassment to their descendants. The Holbourns were a case in point. Young men have to be educated, young men have to earn a living. A beautiful house like Penkaet, not too far from a great city, can be let or can make a home for young men who work in that city. But what can they do with a romantic island, sparsely populated, difficult of access, two days' journey to the north, producing nothing but a few bales of wool and some knitted goods? What use can such an island be to them, or they to the island? The island needed money spent on it, not taken out of it. The breed of sheep needed to be improved, and there was grazing for hundreds more. The houses were maintained by the crofters themselves and there was need of improvements. Above all, a new harbour was necessary if the islanders were to purchase and run a modern fishing vessel. The answer to all this was probably a cooperative society, run and owned by the islanders themselves, with help from the Laird. But there was no Laird, only three puzzled young men with no capital, lots of good will and rather shakily claiming to be the owners of Foula by udal tenure (held for the Chief by right of possession).

We went north by train as far as Aberdeen, then flew to Shetland and landed at Sumburgh Head in an ordinary field. Our flight was the first commercial flight between Scotland and the Islands. We flew over the Orkneys and saw several units of the Fleet exercising off Scapa Flow. Fair Isle lies in the middle of the empty seas between Orkney and Shetland, and our pilot, a small brown man in battered hat and overcoat, took us obligingly around this fascinating island. It is small and green, has only one one possible access from the sea, and is now a bird sanctuary, with a hutted camp where birdwatchers can stay. We stayed that night in Lerwick, which then was a seasonal fishing-port, and at this time of the year the home port for hundreds of trawlers and drifters, who would move south with the herring as the summer drew by.

We temporized with the local press, remembering Joe Rock's injunction, for we planned to be on Foula for only twenty-four hours, and the next day drove to Scalloway, the port nearest to Foula, on the west coast of the Mainland. The Foula mailboat was waiting for us. We had a lot to arrange and we didn't get under way in the big, half-decked launch until half-past six. Her top speed was about four knots, and we didn't reach the island until moonrise. The sun never sets at that time of the year; it just touches the horizon, then starts to climb into the sky again. So my first view of Foula was with the sun and the moon shining on the surrounding sea. It had a poetic craziness about it.

In the summer, in the islands, nobody goes to bed at any fixed time, and if a man starts milking the cow at two in the morning, neither the cow nor his wife is surprised. We had a crate of provisions with us, and John Seabourne was cooking eggs and bacon over a black and greasy stove half an hour after we landed. We all found beds in various crofts and turned in.

Next day, we made a tour of the island. It was a tough walk – Alasdair saw to that: the honour of his island was at stake and were we not a band of townspeople, soft, ignorant Sassenachs (foreigners)? But I matched him, though my lungs were bursting on the cliffs and my brogue-clad feet were sore from walking on the steep slopes of short, slippery grass. The great cliffs were terrifying, and it was a dizzy sight to see the fulmars dropping away from us as we lay on the edge of the Kame, down, down, a quarter of a mile to where the Atlantic surges creamed on the ledges. The sea is never still there. The next land westward is North America and the depth of the sea a few yards out from the cliffs is 500 fathoms. The Atlantic swells that break at the foot of the Kame or of Wester Hoevdi may have come from Greenland, or have been started by some great ocean liner. On calm days, when a daring fisherman rounds the South Ness and casts his lines, he watches that he doesn't drift too near to the cliffs. The Atlantic never sleeps.

Alasdair Holbourn loved his island, but his idea of inspiring similar love in us, the invaders, was a peculiar one: he wanted to make our flesh creep. He told us tales of death and disaster, of shipwrecks and drownings, that would have made Robert Louis Stevenson (who came from a family of Scottish lighthouse engineers) envious. There was a terrible reef between Foula and the Mainland named the Hoevdi Grund, and as soon as the swells started to break there, Alasdair was off, with his tales of the wreck of the *Oceanic* and the bodies of drowned seamen that were washed ashore at his feet as regularly as clockwork. That was all very well, but Jemima crooned a different song:

A bonny place is Foula, in the soft summer weather. The work is hard and there's little enough to carry us through the winter, but all around there's beauty and there's things to see if you have a mind to see them. They say this will be a lightsome summer. Ay! A bonny place is Foula!

Jemima Gear was a remarkable person. But then all women have something remarkable about them, and island women and sailors' wives, sisters and mothers, more than most. She was slender, she had big eyes, her hands and her face were worn and she moved with a natural grace in her old shoes. She wore her shawl, black, home-knitted and as fine as lace, around her shoulders, crossed over her breasts and tucked into her waist in a way which was most becoming. She was light on her feet and her mouth had a humorous twist to it. It was she who told us about the bonxies.

"The what?"

"The bonxies. Skuas their proper name is, but we call them bonxies. There's the Great Skua and the Allen Richardson Skua. I have seen a man with his head bruised and bleeding and his eye blackened because he did not heed them."

There was a rush of wings and a heavy brown bird, with a wing-span as big as an eagle, roared over our heads like a bomber. We all ducked.

"Do you no hear them calling their name?" We listened.

"Skua! Skua!"

She was right.

"There was a time there was only two pair in the world and them on Foula, but Mr Holbourn let them be and now there's too many."

We soon found that the safe way to walk the bonxie territory was with a stick held high over your head. They would still dive down on you, but would sheer away at the last second. Without that aid you were liable for a ding on the back of the head, for they always attacked from behind. One of the crew went one better. He had a funny woollen hat with a coiled piece of stiff rope on top of it, the kind of headgear you see otherwise staid people wearing at Blackpool or Atlantic City. When uncoiled the stiff piece of material stood up perpendicularly like a tom-cat's tail. It baffled the bonxies, and George Black was able to bring in some of their eggs, as large as a hen's, olive with brown markings.

The wind changed in the night and there was a gale warning on the radio. We had planned to leave the next day with the island mailboat, but would have to wait till the gale dropped. Syd had chosen the site for our base camp and decided on sectional huts, held down with wire cables, as the only things for local weather conditions, where winds got up to ninety miles an hour overnight, in spite of Alasdair croaking: "Wire will never hold them. Never!" We were already islanders and were cooking kippers that evening in the squat cottage so grandly named the Haa, the local name for the Holbourns' house, when John dropped a kipper in the fire. The radio news announcer was saying: "From the Shetland Islands we hear that three film technicians from Elstree are marooned by a gale on the lonely island of Foula, twenty miles out in the Atlantic. It is not known whether they are safe or whether they have provisions with them. There is no means of communicating with Foula and the gale is still raging."

John retrieved his kipper and dusted it off. "If we're near starvation," he remarked, "we may need it."

So much for Joe's "no publicity" policy, I thought. It will be in all the Sunday papers. There was no other news that weekend, so it was. But no film producer, whatever he says, can resist publicity. He forgave us.

The gale blew itself out, and on the following day we left the island. There was no time to be lost, and without consulting the front office at the studio, I asked John Seabourne to remain behind, to his great content, to mobilize the islanders, and ordered Syd to make his base at Lerwick until he had all the materials for the base camp ready to be ferried across from Scalloway to the island. I went to London, leaving him in charge, completely confident that he would make his dates. He did, with twenty-four hours to spare. I planned to return in ten days and shoot first in Lerwick, while the fishing fleet was in, and then move to Foula with the whole unit. Vernon had been commissioned by me to find and buy a supply ship while we were "down north". He would command. We were going to use the steamer in the evacuation sequence, so it would figure in the budget under "special props" and could be resold when we came south. After some searching, he found *Vedra*, an ugly pilot-boat lying at Sunderland, and was also able to acquire one of her officers, Bill White, who didn't love her but knew her foibles. She rolled. She rolled in calm or stormy seas. But she only drew six feet of water and she was solidly built about the bilges. Without our own supply ship, we would have been at the mercy of the longshoremen and middlemen. Some of the unit said we were equally at Vernon's mercy. But she did the job and saved us from being marooned in the end, and she was Vernon's first command in steam, the joy of his heart and soul. Nothing in his war service that was to come would equal his supreme command – the *Vedra*.

On June 22, 1936, *Vedra* left the port of Aberdeen on the tide, bound for Lerwick. I and my unit, and some of the actors – trust Niall MacGinnis to be on board – had joined ship there. The two girls – Frankie and Belle Chrystall – were to fly north next day. They were, I hoped, steaming out of King's Cross on the night sleeper to Aberdeen. The camera crew were already ahead of us, in Lerwick with the cameras. John and Syd, the base camp nearly completed, were on Foula. With them was Buddy Farr, a staunch friend of Vernon's and jack-of-all-trades.

In Elstree, Joe Rock put down the telephone, turned to Gerry Blattner, and smacked his lips. "It's OK. They sailed on the tide."

"And on schedule," amplified Gerry, marking the fact on his chart.

After the past five years' arguing, struggling, begging, pleading, shouting, raving, persuading, I was at last going to make the film that I myself wanted to make: all the others had been chosen for me and I had to try to make entertainment out of them. I was still innocent enough to believe that the film-maker should choose what he wanted to do and that he is the best judge of how it should be done. With freedom of choice, however, goes responsibility to the financial backers of the film. This was the philosophy we were to work out with Arthur Rank, personally, in the fullness of time and in the middle of a war for survival for everybody, not only for artists.

In the days I am writing about, talkies were pouring out of America at the rate of twelve expertly manufactured pieces of entertainment a week, 600 a year. For film-makers in Europe it was like painting a watercolour in a millrace. It was a question of survival. I had no illusions about the value of the potboilers I had made, nor did I make the slightest attempt to preserve them, or to record their success or failure. They were not what I was in films for. I was a sorcerer's apprentice, and I was going to follow and put on record my master's teaching or bust. It was not a thirst for glory, but the love of the art which I served. And when I showed little *Edge of the World* at the Santa Fe Film Festival in 1980, forty-five years later, and it received a standing ovation for the film, not for me, I felt that my love had been justified.

Frankie came on the expedition because I asked her to. There had to be a female companion for Belle Chrystall – one who had common sense and was afraid of nothing, even mice and spiders. (The Foula Mouse by the way, has exceptionally large feet, as you will find in the text-books. Frankie and Belle used to complain that from the row they made, they not only had large feet but wore sea boots as well. This is not mentioned in the textbooks.) Frankie also appeared in the Prologue of the film.

I was a monstrously silly and serious young man. ("Young!" you say. "Why, you were thirty in September 1935." You misunderstand me. The emphasis is on the word "silly".)

We had been both happy and unhappy for the three years we had been together. Happy because we were both busy at our work and were good at it; happy because we loved; unhappy because we both wanted to marry and have children, and my early marriage stood in the way. I had found out the French legal position, I had good advice, obtained through my father, it was only a matter of time before I would be free, but I wasn't free yet. Foula suddenly became a fact, after years of talking about St Kilda. I was going to be away for months. I couldn't bear the idea of separation. I was selfish and asked her to come with me. She was unselfish and said she would. Then, when I had got everything that I wanted, I became a complete moron. I was jealous of her.

I was jealous of her being there. I was jealous of every member of the crew. I was jealous of her beauty, her friendliness, her popularity, finally of her being there. When I saw that lovely young woman walking down the quays at Lerwick looking for us (for we were abroad early, the fishing fleet was coming in) and then she saw us and waved "good morning", I realised that I had put her in a difficult position. And to make matters worse, I stuck my nose in the air (it's not much of a nose) and didn't wave back. Fool! What a fool! I saw her smile die and her face change, and she turned away in her white dress, with every man on the jetty looking at her. Fool! Idiot! Film director!

Nobody who worked on *The Edge of the World* will ever forget it. We were a band of brothers. We had started out as an ordinary film unit, light-hearted, irreverent, some of us hand-picked, others along almost by chance. When they were introduced by Syd Streeter and me to the huts where they would have to live for the next three months, some laughed, some swore, one went home. But led by men like Niall MacGinnis, Ernie Palmer and Syd, the rest dug in. It was a rehearsal, without knowing it, for 1939 and the war.

Within a short time each hut had its distinctive character. There were five in all. The girls slept in Alasdair Holbourn's home, the Haa. No. 1 hut was artistic – the actors and me. No. 2 was the old soldiers who knew how to scrounge: Finlay Currie and John Seabourne. No. 3 was the camera crew and all their vitally important gear; No. 4 the sound crew; No. 5 property department and Bob the dog. There was rivalry between the huts which sometimes broke out into open war!

When Syd planned the camp he forgot baths, assuming that showers would do. But there is nothing like stewing in a hot bath after a day on the cliffs in a tearing gale, so five zinc baths were ordered from the Mainland, like coffins in shape and size. Water was heated in buckets over primus stoves. It was the ultimate luxury. I remember doing the rounds one stormy night, then entering No. 1 hut to find Niall MacGinnis's hairy great body covered in soap and steam as he sat smiling in his tub. I helped him empty it outside, then fell asleep while I was taking my boots off.

We had our teething troubles. When we sent our first week's work to the laboratory at Elstree, a message came back from Gerry at the studio: "Your rushes received and viewed. Sound inaudible. Picture invisible. Is this intentional? Blattner."

The cameraman returned home, and Ernie Palmer, who had worked with me on the *Mask* thriller, took his place. There was no further trouble from the camera department, but to even things up John Laurie tried to copy me jumping over a gate and broke his collarbone. It meant shooting for four weeks without him, and I was left with half a dozen important sequences to finish with him after he rejoined us. Meanwhile we worked on the cliff climb, which involved the island women as well as the men.

This cliff climb by the two young men, carried out by Niall MacGinnis and Eric Berry in the film, was one of the two crescendos that I had planned for my film. The second one was the great gale, which made it impossible to reach or leave the island for several weeks. This was part of the structure of the story, and perhaps I had better explain the story that I had invented to lead up to the scenes of the evacuation of the island.

I called the island Hirta, which is the name of the principal island in the St Kilda group. My island had a population of about a hundred souls, and the two leading families were the Grays and the Mansons. Robbie Manson (Eric Berry) is a marine engineer who works for the winter months on the trawlers that fish around the island. His father, Peter Manson (John Laurie), looks on the trawlermen as enemies and is bitterly opposed to his son working for them. The population of the island is shrinking. There are fewer children at the village school. If the island is to survive, it will need every single able-bodied man. Peter wants to hear no talk of evacuation. Robbie's sister Ruth (Belle Chrystall) is in love with Andrew Gray (Niall MacGinnis), whose father, James Gray (Finlay Currie), is in favour of a planned and orderly evacuation. By this scheme the main conflicts are set up. A meeting of all the men on the island is called and there is a key scene in which they discuss the pros and cons of the evacuation and the desperate plight of the islands around Scotland. Andrew challenges Robbie to a race up the precipitous cliffs on the west side. Whoever wins will decide the fate of the island. Ruth tries to stop the two young men but fails.

The women of the island gather on the cliffs to watch the race. Andrew Gray wins the race, but Robbie Manson is killed taking a short cut. The issue of evacuation is shelved for the time being, and the two families become deadly enemies. Secretly, Andrew and Ruth have become lovers. Andrew decides to go to the mainland, make a place for himself, and come back for Ruth.

He is away some time and it becomes clear that Ruth is going to have his child. Andrew is on a deep-sea voyage and she has the child without him. The baby helps to reconcile the two families. A storm comes up and blows for several weeks, making it impossible to leave the island when the baby becomes ill. Messages attached to floats are sent out in the old-fashioned way, and Andrew picks up one of them. At the height of the storm he comes back to the island on a trawler and rescues Ruth and the baby. The last scene depicts the evacuation of the island by the whole population and their animals. Peter Manson meets his death on the cliffs.

I added a framework for the main story, partly because I like flashbacks when they are well done, and partly to introduce Hugh Roberton's wonderful music sung by the Glasgow Orpheus Choir, which he conducted. I had heard their work in Glasgow. Some of the choir members appear again in the ceilidh scene in *I Know Where I'm Going*. On *The Edge of the World*, with my small budget, I couldn't afford to hire the whole choir, so Sir Hugh Roberton arranged the music for women's voices only. In the flashback you see a yacht arriving with three people on board: a man and a woman, both English, and a local seaman. The local seaman is Andrew Gray, and he tells them the story of the island. Frankie and I played the two visitors on the yacht. Alasdair loaned us his own boat for the occasion.

The geographical definition of an island is a piece of land entirely surrounded by water. Please notice the adverb; "entirely" – what a difficult word to live up to. But every true island does, and that is its fascination. I collect islands, I admit it. I have only to see, or smell, or hear of a piece of land surrounded by water and unknown to me, to want to visit it. Do you remember J. M. Barrie's play *Mary Rose*? Alfred Hitchcock always said that he wanted to make a film of it, but he never did. In the play there is an island "that likes to be visited". It's true. Barrie was a Scot and he knew. Islands do like to be visited.

How much more does an island like Foula, which presents such an unwelcoming face to the intruder. Like Alasdair, her one-third-of-a-Laird, she wanted to be loved, but wouldn't make the first move. And goodness me, how difficult she made it for us. All the best locations for the film were a three-mile tramp from the base camp, and we carried all the equipment, using stretchers and wheelbarrows. Later, much later, we imported Shetland ponies, and Alasdair, who was built rather like one, was appointed pony master.

The film unit landed on Foula before the end of June and we were pulled off, still shooting, towards the end of October. As the days shortened and the weather turned against us, I became quietly desperate. There was a whole string of close-ups needed of the men in the boats when Andrew and Robbie raced one another in the cliff climb. The camera had to be in the boats with the men. The coast of Foula is inhospitable. There is no shelter. The sea is never still. The rise and fall of the tide, surging from the open Atlantic, is never less than twenty feet. That doesn't sound much? Try trans-shipping camera, actors and crew under those savage cliffs! Day after day we tried and failed, and the days were drawing in. For the first time, I was facing failure.

The equinoctial gales had cut off all communications for about two weeks. Food supplies were running low and there was a cigarette famine. Joe Rock got anxious and it was decided to evacuate us, whether I agreed or not. There were still the boat shots of the men watching the cliff climb to be done, and I decided to take half a dozen of the leading islanders with us and shoot them at Lerwick. The girls went first and reaped a harvest of publicity, for we had been in the news for six days. Frankie was described as "a tall blonde in heavy tweeds", much to her family's amusement. The rest of the evacuation followed in batches. It was time. It was getting late in the year for those latitudes. We got the missing shots on the very last day before the boat sailed for Aberdeen. There was no sunshine anywhere else in the British Isles on that October 26, but there was sunshine at Lerwick.

Thirty-seven shots in small boats in a choppy sea, with the cast and the men of Foula working as one unit! We all knew what had to be got, and the island's mailboat crew, Walter Ratter and Dodie Isbister, and the Gears and the Mansons knew as well as we did how vital for the film those shots would be. We worked together, with hardly an order given, changing the camera, at sea, from one boat to another, and then ashore on the rocks. We were brothers in the work and in our dedication to it.

Why didn't I trick these shots in the studio? It was the faces. Islanders have an inner strength and repose that other men and women do not have, and it shows in their faces. The smaller and more remote the island, the greater the individuality. The men of Lerwick, although they were Shetlanders and were possibly related, did not have eyes like the men of Foula, with whom we had worked for four months. There is something lacking in the townsmen: gravity, self-possession? When I showed Bill Paton my photographs of the Cretan mountain folk, after I had walked across the island in 1951, he studied them closely, then said: "Ye can see that they're all islanders."

I have not mentioned Bill Paton before. He is a Shetlander from Lerwick and is built like and was intended to be a professional footballer. But he injured his knee and decided to become a baker and confectioner, a profession of power and authority in Scotland, particularly if you've got a light hand with the scones. This brought him into contact with Mrs Rutherford, our housekeeper on the island, who was looking for an assistant cook and could pay well. Bill joined us and very soon distinguished himself from the mob by carrying an iron pot of potatoes to the location on the other side of the island and boiling them to go with the cold lamb every day. Bill's a good mixer and he was soon an active member of the unit and taking part in the Foula Reel danced in the film. He was a tower of strength, a simile which really is accurate if you knew Bill. I know a good man when I see him and we became friends. Later on he was to come south and join me as my friend and my right and left hand for more than thirty years.

My last days on the island were saddened by the absence of John Seabourne. He more than anyone was responsible for the friendly cooperation of the islanders. He became a buddy of Finlay Currie's, and the two tall men together were irresistible. Whenever there was a gathering, or a party or a crowd scene, these two were in the thick of it, joking, persuading even the most sullen and solitary islander, man or woman, to take part. They taught our city-bred film unit "a man's a man for a' that", and I shall always remember the lessons I learnt from them in handling people. But in spite of his energy and his apparent health, John had been plagued with duodenal ulcers ever since he left the army. He would go on for months, apparently cured, then a sudden violent haemorrhage would lay him low and he would be at death's door. When we came to Foula he was just recovering from such a seizure and I had doubts about bringing him, but he pleaded so hard that I gave way and let him come, for I needed him badly and he was to cut the film.

"Don't worry about my dying, Micky," he said. "I'd sooner die on Foula than miss the film." His wife, Margaret, said: "Yes, let him go." And for a few months, he was the mainstay of the film. Then he started to spit blood, all his splendid strength melted away, and he had to be shipped out as a stretcher case.

He clasped my hand as he was hoisted on board the Vedra. "Bill Paton and Finlay have all my notes and the names of all the crofters. You'll manage all right without me. God bless you for bringing me, Micky."

And that was the last I saw of him for weeks. But it was not by any means to be the last time we worked and played together. By no manner of means.

Before we left the island to the storms of the coming winter we had a farewell gathering at the camp with every able-bodied man or woman on the island. The population was about one hundred in 1936, and a lot of them were old age pensioners, carefully nurtured like hothouse plants, as John Seabourne cheerily stated, for the sake of their valuable pensions. Some of the more solitary islanders never took part in the film at all. Their daily routine of survival was all they could manage. But there were others, like Robbie Isbister (the Archdeacon as John named him), whose large family took part in everything from the funeral sequence in the film to the mock evacuation of the island, when children and animals, sticks of furniture and bundles of belongings all had to be brought miles to the harbour, some of the wild Foula sheep hogtied in wheelbarrows, for they would come in no other way. Anyway, the final gathering at the Haa was a great party. Walter Ratter, skipper of the mailboat, made a speech; I made a speech; Finlay made a speech and there were presentations on both sides. We were leaving the huts as a gift to the island and the remaining stores were divided up. It finished with a concert at which Syd Streeter sang "Trees" and Maude, Finlay's American wife, sang, by special request, the song that she had created and made famous on Broadway, more years ago than any of us could imagine: "You Are My Honeysuckle, I Am the Bee." It's a good song and when Maude cried "Now, all together! Follow me!" we fairly lifted the roof off.

Back in the studio we had a few pick-up shots to make, like the interior of the trawler cabin in the storm and the doctor operating on the dying child. There were a few close-ups too. But, by and large, we had completed that film on the island and we had saved the film by that eventful day's shooting at Lerwick.

When we shot the cabin scenes at Elstree, Syd asked me whether I wanted a platform extended from the floor of the set to carry the camera. It was a small cabin, with one entrance from the top like a well, but of course, we built it three-sided. I asked if the cabin was on rockers.

"Of course. That's why I thought you would want the camera to rock with it, as it would in the real trawler."

I shook my head. "I want the camera on the studio floor, the set and the actors must rock. The camera must be stationary."

Syd was puzzled. "But that won't be real."

"No. But it will look real."

John Seabourne was still in hospital, so the resident editor at Joe Rock's Studio made an assembly of the film. By an assembly, I mean he strung all the scenes together in rough continuity, or what he assumed to be continuity. It was pretty rough. Hundreds of shots had been improvised during shooting, or had no notes. We had no script-girl on the island, so there were only my own daily notes to go on, and, of course, the camera

sheets kept by one of the camera crew. After a month, John was able
to return to work and we set about identifying shots and getting reels in
some sort of order. There was no dispute, of course, about the story
scenes and the dialogue scenes on the trawler or the cliff climb by the
two boys. It was the sequences like the rooing of the sheep (the Shetland
name for the method of plucking wool from the live sheep without
using shears), the scenes of the gathering storm, the final Wagnerian
sequence of John and Finlay climbing through the clouds to the high
seacliffs, which had to be built up shot by shot. But we knew the film
too well.

It sounds queer, but when you have waited week after week then
month after month for a particular shot, you cannot be detached about it.
We loved our baby and were blind to its faults.

After a talk with John, I went to Joe and said: "We need an editor." His
eyes bulged. "You fellows have been editing the picture for two months.
And now you want an editor?"

"Yes. I want Derek Twist. We're too close to it, Joe. We need an editor
with the eye of a hawk, the memory of an Indian and a heart of granite. I
want Derek Twist."

Joe had the makings of a great producer. He was hard up for money,
but he took my word for it and we borrowed Derek from Gaumont-British.
It was he who made sense out of our ravings. The final cut of the film is his.
He proved, as I knew he would, extraordinarily sympathetic to our ideas,
and particularly to the final sequences of the evacuation of the island and
Peter Manson's climb, step by step, to his death on the cliffs. A lot of scenes
were shot to Smetana's *Moldau*, a record of which I played on my portable
hand-cranked gramophone. It must have been a weird sight to see John
Laurie or Finlay Currie, followed by Bob the dog, striding through the
mist, while perched on a drystone wall, a muffled hobgoblin of a director
nursed a battered machine in his arms, which was churning out a recording
by the Prague Symphony Orchestra, so scratched and distorted that their
conductor would have disowned it.

Fortunately none of this was known by Bill Williamson, who was
orchestrating the Scottish tunes which had already been recorded by the
Glasgow Orpheus Choir. Using only women's voices as Sir Hugh had
suggested was a great success. Their attack was splendid and the purity and
freshness of their voices is memorable. Their voices again, in the lament for
Robbie Manson's funeral and the scene in the churchyard, were wonderfully moving and had the true note of tragedy. Bill Williamson took all
these tunes and orchestrated them for passages in the film; he invented
sprightly music for the rounding up of the sheep and for the love scenes;
and when it came to the final sequences and I explained what I wanted,
how the audience must slowly become aware that they are witnessing,

through the death of one man, the death of a whole community, he took the bit between his teeth and composed ten minutes of opera without the voices.

The Edge of the World was a turning point of my life in art, and I found it impossible to return to the world of cheap thrillers. Jerry Jackson was no longer an independent producer. He was holding down Irving Asher's late job at Warner Brothers' Teddington Studios, on the Thames. He could only offer me the same quota-quickies. He had ambitious plans for bigger pictures, and he had been promised a long-term contract by Warner Brothers, but the American companies were getting alarmed by the European situation, and when Jerry pressed for his contract they stalled him off.

Joe Rock had run out of funds for production and was sitting tight at Elstree waiting for *The Edge of the World* to come out. He had nothing to offer. Alfred Hitchcock was still making his wonderful series of London thrillers, but was about to succumb to Hollywood and accept an offer from David O. Selznick to direct *Rebecca*.

MGM, my old company, were making some splendid pictures at Denham, using Korda's facilities and Korda's stars, but pictures like *The Citadel* (with Robert Donat) or *A Yank at Oxford* (with Robert Taylor and Vivien Leigh) were out of my class at that time. I knew I could make films as good as that and better than that, but nobody else did. The best I could hope for in the big time was a job as second-unit director. I had friends at Denham, among them Victor Saville, who was producing *Goodbye Mr Chips*, with Robert Donat, and on my way to Elstree I would sometimes stop at the gates of Denham, and get the porter to ring the production office and get me a pass.

I was no longer living in London. My mother had not been idle all this while, although much to her annoyance she never landed on Foula. She had moved from Red Leaf Cottage, Chalfont St Peter, Bucks, accompanied by Jane and her latest batch of puppies, to Orchard Cottage, Bramley, Surrey, thinking by this means to save me hours of driving through the foggy mornings and dark nights of the Thames Valley. It was here that, jobless, I settled down to write the book about the making of my film. One year later, I would be working at Denham, within two miles of Red Leaf Cottage, which we had just vacated.

But the most important thing that happened to me in 1937 was a spiritual experience. I rediscovered art.

Since 1925, twelve years before, I had been passionately devoted to the cinema. I have already described how all the greatest artists in Europe –

writers, painters, theatrical directors – were just as passionately interested as I was in this new medium of silent film. When a great American director like Rex Ingram decided to make Europe his home and his base in Provence, he was visited and surrounded by many of the most interesting artists of his time. But they didn't talk painting and writing and acting and dancing and singing. They talked movies. Artists have always been fascinated by motion. And the movies moved. We were all fascinated by the direct approach of the camera to character; by the huge emotion that could be aroused by a close-up. Moviemakers with a theatrical flair, like Ingram and Seitz, his cameraman, loved a big sweeping effect, a combination of theatre and film. But around the corner were the real children of the cinema, Buñuel, Dali, Renoir, Cavalcanti, the real moviemakers. These were the men who ate the cinema, who gobbled it down and spat it or shat it out.

I carried these ideas and ideals with me to England until the coming of talkies left me and hundreds of others without a job. When I finally managed to scratch my way back into the film business with the help of Jerry Jackson and Lee Planskoy, I was only too glad to gnaw at any bone that was thrown to me, and to tell story after story in the simplest possible way, using what amounted to a pulp medium.

It was at an exhibition of eighteenth and nineteenth century French drawings at the Royal Academy, that I received the friendly kick up the bottom from my particular benevolent goddess, which led to my eyes being opened to the meaning of art. I love eighteenth century France, and I knew there would be lots of good Fragonards and Chardins in the exhibition. Then I saw a drawing in a corner: a family – father, mother, baby – eating soup. Armed with great spoons, the parents were bent over their plates, although whether the curve of their shoulders was from greed or hunger, or whether they were naturally bowed from constant toil in the fields, was difficult to tell. You could feel that it was the big meal of the day. One great breast hung out of the woman's dress and the baby hung on the breast. You could feel the soup flowing in a warm tide up from the plates and through their bodies. Father, mother, baby. I felt that I had never seen – really seen – anything before. The powerful composition showed the parents full length, as they were seated at the wooden table on wooden benches. I could hear that soup, I could see that soup, I could smell, taste that soup. The drawing was called *La Soupe*, and it couldn't possibly be called anything else. The artist was Honoré Daumier.

I love every one of Daumier's drawings and paintings, and especially the self-portrait, standing at his easel. But I have never loved any Daumier as I loved this one at first sight. I have always loved soup and making soup, and that wonderful soup of Daumier's warms my guts whenever I think of it.

From that day on I returned to my allegiance. "Art is all one", as a greater writer than I shall ever be has written. Art is merciless observation, sympathy, imagination, and a sense of detachment that is almost cruelty. Art is *La Soupe*.

By the summer of 1937, *The Edge of the World* was ready for presentation and my book was ready too. I had planned it while I was still on the island, I was so sure of the permanent nature of what I had done. For the honour of my profession, I wanted our achievement to be on record. I was lucky in having one of the best publishers in England for my book (*200,000 Feet on Foula*, by Michael Powell, Faber & Faber, 1937) and they gave me an editor who was tactful and saved me from my worst excesses.

The film opened at the New Gallery Cinema in Regent Street, now the London headquarters of the Seventh Day Adventists, but then a rather classy movie theatre. The critics gave it cautious reviews. But my old admirer, C. A. Lejeune, writing in *The Observer* knew the difference between a lyric drama and a documentary, and said: "I hope everyone who can will make a point of seeing *The Edge of The World*. In some obscure judgment day, when these things are measured, I have a feeling it will come up somewhere near the top of the English classics."

And Basil Wright trumpeted in the *Cinema*: "If *The Edge of the World* achieves the success it so well deserves, it will be yet another reminder that vast production costs, exotic casts, and cosmopolitan scenarios are perhaps not the ultimate plan for the British Cinema."

The *Era*, a showbiz newspaper now defunct, was enthusiastic. The editor, George Atkinson, was a film critic. He invited me to use the front page of his paper to answer my critics and I did, starting my guerrilla war with the London press, who resented the fact that a director who up till now had given birth to quota-quickies should suddenly be big with art.

At the same time, Alasdair Alpin MacGregor, who had never forgiven me for not making the film on St Kilda, which would have benefited him and his book (for I suppose he would have taken the place of expert advisor that the other Alasdair took on Foula), started a suit against me for plagiarism. He thought that the film company would settle, but as he sued me personally, he lost his case. But the Arbitrator, taking pity on him for a nut, awarded him costs. So in the end I didn't make any money out of *The Edge of the World*.

After a week at the New Gallery, the film moved to Studio One (where Disney films always played) for a week, and then it was distributed by a new group of exhibitors, mostly North Country theatre owners who were looking for British products. Their head was Jack Prendergast, a fine showman. He and his friends loved the film, but their brave venture failed for lack of other films to show, and my film vanished from circulation.

Joe Rock, who was fighting for the film, had sent a copy to New York to a small distributor, who submitted it to the National Board of Review film critics, and they chose it as one of the best foreign films of the year, which gave me a wonderful lift. I felt a refreshing stream of sympathy flowing between me and America, its people, its language, its literature and its films. I still was passionately English and had no wish to leave England, but I saw no chance of making anything but second features so long as I stayed in my own country. I decided to go to Hollywood.

I was fed up with English film-makers who seemed to think that they were automatically entitled to have a film industry. They didn't seem to realise that if you made English-speaking films you had to succeed in the American market and make films which would appeal to audiences on both sides of the Atlantic.

Hollywood-bound, I had booked a passage on a banana-boat, destination Los Angeles. I had told nobody of my intentions except my long-suffering mother, who saw herself cast loose on the world again if I were to follow my star to Hollywood. I don't think that I had even told Christopher Mann, my agent, who by this time had begun to take me seriously. One evening (he sat up late to receive the Hollywood calls, which came into London between six in the evening and two in the morning, and consequently he never surfaced early) Chris rang me. "Is that you, Mick?" he said. "Korda has seen *Edge of the World* and wants to see you. I think he may give you a contract."

Alexander Korda's name was by now a legend, and it had all happened in a very few years. When in 1931 talkies had stripped France, Italy and Spain of their talent, and had silenced Soviet Russia, some of the big American companies had gone seriously into multi-language co-production in an attempt to retain their foreign markets. Paramount established a production mill at Paris, where dozens of European directors, Hungarian, German, Italian, Polish, French, ground out foreign-language versions which kept a number of refugees from Hitler from starving. One of these in 1933 was Alexander Korda, a clever Hungarian journalist turned film director, who had previously been invited to Hollywood with his actress wife to make the silent version of John Erskine's *The Private Life of Helen of Troy*. He had not been a success in Hollywood, where his intelligence, intolerance, independence and, in particular, his culture, had made his name anathema to the studio production heads. He returned to Europe and was given the job of directing as a talkie the French version of *Marius*, the first play in Marcel Pagnol's immortal trilogy. He had the original French cast of the play, and the collaboration of Pagnol himself, who fell under Alex's spell immediately and became a lifelong friend. The film was a smash-hit, and in his usual regal way Alex took all the credit. He was able to do this when it suited him because he was equally generous in giving credit to others. He was then sent to London by Paramount to make a typical Central European comedy of manners entitled *Service for Ladies*. The hero was a head waiter and was played by Leslie Howard.

Korda was a perceptive genius. He saw that there was a vacuum to fill in the British film business, and he proceeded to fill it. He was directing a lavish, polished comedy about high society and he had in embryo all the talents and personalities which, fused by his genius and charm, were to make him an instant success.

Korda had charm. He could charm the birds out of the trees and, as Emeric Pressburger later remarked, the birds loved it. London society took him to its heart. He was tall, ugly and elegant, spoke all European languages with a Hungarian accent, smoked nothing but large Coronas, ate at all the best restaurants, lived at the Savoy. He was sociable, cultivated and generous. In any assembly, because of his height, his personality and his tailor, for he had learnt from Leslie how important it is, in England, to go to the right tailor, he was always the outstanding figure. He realised that the English were snobs and proud of it. He was a snob himself.

Sooner or later, everyone wanted to know Korda, and Korda knew everybody. Never was there such a success. In England, if you are amusing, all doors are open to you. In no time Korda was established in London and was making a film about the London society which he was exploiting, *Wedding Rehearsal*, a frothy comedy whipped up by Lajos Biro, his old friend and scenario writer, with parts for the daughters of all his new society friends. In no time a company, London Films, was formed, financed by the Prudential Assurance Company to the tune of £6 million sterling, and Denham Studios was on the drawing boards as the largest planned studio in Europe.

In the early days of talkies, there was an American comedian called Jack Oakie who was much loved by us all. He made a more than lifesize reappearance in *Around the World in Eighty Days*, when he was long past his prime, but if you had seen him teamed with Bing Crosby in a song and dance, you would never forget him. I always had a fantasy that it was really he who designed Denham Studios, not the American architect Jack Okey, who is credited with the layout. Jack Okey, if it were indeed he, was from Hollywood, where things like stars and studios "just growed". Burbank, where Warner Brothers produced their films, started out as one studio, then went on expanding laterally away from the front offices and the service area, until there were twenty stages in a straight line, like a Western set in the movies; and since this was presumably the only kind of layout with which the comedian – sorry! not the comedian, the architect – was familiar, that was the way he built Denham: a long row of huge stages, with a covered walk for pedestrians, stretching alongside it for about 600 yards. The machine shops and the carpenters' shop, which are in constant daily service for film productions, were tucked away somewhere in the rear, and all the long footage on the Denham by-pass contained dressing rooms and offices so numerous that Jeffrey Dell was inspired by them to write a fantasy called *Nobody Ordered Wolves*, in which a pair of wolves were ordered for a jungle film and left, forgotten, in a dressing room, until by natural selection, they developed into a pack. However, when the men from the Prudential came to find out how their money had been invested and saw all those acres of concrete, inspected the new bridge over the River Colne, and ate sumptuously in the studio restaurant, whose manager was a graduate of the Savoy kitchens, they felt that they had their money's worth.

But five years later, in 1937, the year after Foula, the future of Denham looked almost as hopeless as the future of Czechoslovakia. In the scant five years that Korda had been producing films in England he had imported stars and directors from all over the world to make international films and so many Hungarians had rallied around him, mostly uninvited, that the Colne had been rechristened the Danube. Alex himself, who had a lovely light hand as a director, had made London Films' biggest success with Charles Laughton in *The Private Life of Henry VIII*, and their biggest failure with Douglas Fairbanks in *The Private Life of Don Juan*. (*The Private Life of the Gannet*, a sensationally beautiful film made on the island of Grassholm by Professor Julian Huxley, was a small masterpiece.) Above all, Korda had discovered the British Empire, and with *Sanders of the River* in West Africa, *The Four Feathers* in Egypt and the Sudan, *Elephant Boy* and *The Drum* in India, he had a noble list of titles to his credit.

But perhaps his greatest contribution to the British film industry and to his adopted country, was the friendship he formed with Winston Churchill and with Robert Vansittart, both implacable enemies of Hitler and his gang, who were in the inner circles of English political power. Churchill, of course, was not in office, although everyone knew that there was nobody else to rally the people of England and the Empire if war came. Korda admired Winston, and knowing that his income was small, and that he had no chance of regaining power and office so long as the British believed in appeasement, he inspired Two Cities Films to buy the rights to his biography of his ancestor, the first Duke of Marlborough (published in four volumes) and commissioned him to write a screenplay. Their friendship, for they soon became friends, with a similar taste in Coronas and brandy, was to have important consequences for British films and for the war effort.

Alexander Korda was the eldest of three brothers and they soon became as well known as the Marx Brothers, to whom they were affectionately compared by their friends and collaborators. Vincent Korda was a painter and was living happily in Paris when his elder brother peremptorily summoned him to London to head the Denham art department and design films. Zoltan Korda was a film editor, destined by Alex to be a film director of vast epics of the British Empire, which Alex dreamed up but had no intention of directing himself. He got his results mainly by entrusting his brothers with the execution of his imaginative and extravagant dreams, and then bawling them out when the results of their titanic labours didn't measure up to his expectations:

"Zoli! I have seen the African scenes. They are nothing like Africa."

"They were shot in Africa, Alex. On the locations that Edgar Wallace said were the right ones."

"You should have seen as soon as you got there that they were not suitable, Zolikan. They must be retaken."

"Where, Alex? There is no more money."

"There is a very good river at Shepperton Studios. I have seen photographs. It is just like Africa. You will reshoot the scenes there."

"Yes, Alex."

And they were reshot, canoes and all, with Paul Robeson singing and Nina Mae McKinney bringing a touch of Harlem to West Africa.

The sleepy old cottage industry of British films, which was all that remained after Hollywood had swooped down and picked the ripe plums of our talent, scoffed at Alex Korda's flamboyance and extravagance, but the cottagers certainly took note. Efficient and independent producer-directors like Victor Saville were not too proud to work for Korda. The leading actors of the London stage flocked to his banner. Even Irving Asher in 1937 left his safe berth as head of Warner Brothers' Teddington operation for the more exposed position of one of Alex's co-producers. He was to make four films for release by Columbia, using Denham Studios, and all Alex's contract stars: Laurence Olivier, Vivien Leigh, Ralph Richardson, Conrad Veidt, Valerie Hobson. Of all this, I was kept informed by Jerry Jackson, who had remained a true and faithful friend.

As I have told you, but it is worth telling again, the Kordas had also married, or been married by, the first English or English-speaking girls who could throw a mean lasso over them. Alex's two younger brothers, carried away by England's stately charm, fell victim to two young actresses in the cast of *Wedding Rehearsal*. Vincent married Gertrude Musgrove, a delightful woman and charming comedienne, a mating which produced Michael Korda, the author of *Charmed Lives* (Random House, 1979). Zoli married Joan Gardner, who, forty-six years later, is one of the best looking women in Hollywood. Alex was preserved from immediate capture by the existence of Maria Corda, who still persisted in spelling her married name in her own way, partly out of cussedness to annoy Alex. Alex was in love with Merle Oberon and was planning a great career for her, commissioning scripts right and left, including an original story about a ballet dancer from one of his contract writers.

I drove out to Denham with Chris in his car. I had sold my old car – it was a De Soto with a fabric body and a sliding roof – before I went to Foula. Chris drove carefully and with no fuss, as he did everything. He had become even more dapper and was living with a beautiful young actress, tall and blonde, of course, like Madeleine Carroll, but in all other ways quite unlike her. He briefed me as he drove westward through the green belt which encircles London, through the foresight of urban planners. Meanwhile I studied Korda's Olympian letter.

September 28th 1937

My dear Mr Powell,

I have just seen your picture "THE EDGE OF THE WORLD" and I would like to congratulate you on having produced a really magnificent film. I enjoyed every minute of it – much more than I have any picture for a very long time.

I hope we shall meet very soon, as I should be glad if we could come to some agreement between my Company and yourself.

Yours sincerely,
Alexander Korda

Chris avoided a cat bent on suicide.

"Korda has had a print of your film to look at for some time. I telephoned Cunynghame every week until he saw it. He's planning some low budget features to keep Denham turning over while he prepares some of his big productions. You would be one of a creative group. He will probably offer you a year's contract. With options. What do you say?"

A year's contract! With options! I had nothing to say. Such a thing as a year's contract had never entered my head. Films were my wife, my love, my life. They were, in part, my creation. For them I feared no responsibility. In life I was an innocent, an infant. In movies I was a veteran. I saw the whole mad movie business from a mountaintop as I do today. When people paid me a fee to do what I loved best in the world, I pocketed it absent-mindedly, for my head, that great domed head, was already busy, full of images, crammed with dreams waiting to be made visible and enchanting. At the first glimmer of a chance, I had grabbed it until I reached the top of my little world of B-movies and saw before me the chasm which separated A from B. Now this god, this Korda, was going to offer me a year's contract: he was going to save me from the mills of Hollywood.

"What will he pay?"

"I shall ask for a hundred a week," said my amazing agent, without a quaver in his voice.

"Too much money." Korda shook his head and laid his burning cigar carefully on top of a silver ash-tray so that the inch or so of ash was undisturbed. He took off his thick glasses and wiped them with a white lawn handkerchief that he extracted from the breast pocket of his suit. It was made by a good tailor. He beamed vaguely in my direction to show that there was nothing personal about his qualifications. We were both film-makers, we were both cultivated gentlemen, we understood one another. I was already under the spell of his charm. Chris and I had parked the car and walked along Denham's endless corridors to the executive offices to be told that Mr Korda was in his room at the Old House. We left the crowded corridors behind and crossed the lawn of carefully rolled and mown grass that sloped down to the bright little River Colne which spread out here in clear gravel beds and where trout lurked among the water plants. A comfortably ugly red brick house stood on the bank, the original home of the keen fisherman who had once lived there. Here Alex had a room, as well as some favoured beings, like David Cunynghame, his personal assistant and member of the board of London Films; or Miklos Rosza, the composer who was already working on themes for an Arabian Nights fantasy that was one of Korda's favourite projects.

The stages of Denham stood in a formidable row along the new road, which would one day be one of the main link roads around London. At present it swept grandly up to Denham Studios and petered out on the other side of the hill, where the huge beech trees of Buckinghamshire marched down to the river and the elephants had danced for Sabu, the Elephant Boy. There were two huge stages, about 200 feet square, so large that I couldn't imagine how to control them, little anticipating that in five years' time I would be creating Heaven and Earth within those giant concrete walls. I had caught a glimpse of the machine shop and the carpenters' shops and the electrical stores. This was how a film studio should be! A box of tricks out of which to create marvels.

A watchful commissionaire in full uniform received us at the entrance to the Old House, which still remained a semi-private residence. He took us to David Cunynghame.

David was a cultivated, bright-eyed, eager young man, with a slight stammer and beautiful manners. He was also tough to have survived, as he did, so many years with Alex. He had a rather boyish face, with a high colour and the black hair that goes with it. He had a slight stoop – he was tall – and never forgot anything or anybody, although it sometimes suited Alex to pretend that he did. I found him sympathetic and was to become very fond of him. He spoke on the intercom. There was a pause. Presently, a door opened and a tall, bony young actor, draped in tweeds and carrying a thick script, backed out of the doorway. He was addressing an invisible presence and was obviously in great awe of him. I recognised Ralph Richardson. He was stammering, "Alex! I really must make a decision about this play. They won't wait for me much longer. What have you and Irving decided about the film?"

A tall, elegant figure edged him out into the outer office. "Conning-ham" (that was how Alex always pronounced the historic name of Cunynghame), "what has been decided about Ralph's film?"

The question obviously caught Cunynghame between wind and water. He stammered: "Decided, Alex? I thought you said . . . we thought . . . we . . . you . . . I . . ."

Korda cut him short. "Nothing has been decided, Ralph. Leave it to me. Come and see me on Thorsday." (This was a famous dismissal line of Korda's that both Ralph Richardson and Laurence Olivier could imitate to improve on the original.)

The door closed. Richardson and Sir David Cunynghame, for David was a baronet (of course), exchanged a look, a smile, a shrug. Ralph nodded to Chris – "Ah, Christopher!" – and looked courteously in my direction in order to acknowledge my existence, picked up his hat and stick and made an impeccable exit. Cunynghame vanished inside for a minute or two, then reappeared and nodded to Chris, leaving the door open. We went in. I let Chris lead the way.

In this autumn of 1937, the position of Denham and of London Films was critical. Korda had planned grandly and spent nobly. He had built Denham and brought artists and craftsmen from all over the world to make its films. He had persuaded one of the two major literary prophets of our time to make *Things to Come*. He had made Henry VIII into a sex symbol, and his daughter, Queen Elizabeth, incarnated by Flora Robson, into an anti-Hitler spokesman ("I have the body of a weak and feeble woman, but I have the spirit of a King – ay! and of a King of England, too!"). He had glorified the British Empire in its decline. He had made a world star of a little Hindu boy. He had borrowed from France two great directors: René Clair, to make *The Ghost Goes West*, and Jacques Feyder to direct James Hilton's *Knight Without Armour*. He had starred great Continental actors like Elisabeth Bergner, Marlene Dietrich, Harry Baur, in spectacular productions. He had convinced men in power in England of the importance of an independent British film industry. However, making films was one thing and selling them in the world market was quite another.

He had bought control of United Artists, the company founded in 1921 by D. W. Griffith, Charlie Chaplin, Douglas Fairbanks and Mary Pickford. Here were giants, but ageing giants; and although the giants were tiring, they were the right size for Korda; and the company, known everywhere as U.A., stood for the kind of quality that Korda understood. Yet still the American market eluded him; and without the American market it was impossible for the kind of films that Korda created to make money. The

American film-makers had too long a start in the race. By the time Korda brought sophisticated Hungarian irreverence to his treatment of the much-married Henry VIII, the Americans had monopolised the talkies for more than five years. American voices, American music, American morals, had delighted and democratised the world. All other English-speaking voices were inaudible, incomprehensible and unmarketable, according to the film salesmen, who, for the most part, themselves spoke English through a thick Central European accent you could cut with a knife. These expressed opinions were all the more offensive to the Korda brothers because they never bothered to learn to speak English properly themselves, and lapsed into Hungarian whenever a crisis loomed, either in their films or in their private lives, as so hilariously described by Michael Korda. By 1937, the year of my despair for British films, Hollywood and New York between them were turning out something like 600 films a year, including shorts and second features to make up the cinema's programmes. All the big companies were buying up theatres and vying with each other for a piece of the market. There was simply no room for Korda and his films.

You wouldn't have thought he had a care in the world as we filed in. He rose and came to meet us, shook hands and waved us, with a Corona, to our seats. The furnishing of the room was civilised, by which I mean it was full of books in five European languages. My fingers itched to browse among them. There was a painting of Merle on an easel. Ever since her famous close-up as Anne Boleyn, with her slender neck bared for the executioner's axe, she had been a legend. There were some good French paintings, probably chosen by Vincent, for Alex liked paintings, but liked their investment possibilities even more. There was a picture by Vincent himself, very well framed, an oil of a large fat man, planted in his chair and staring at the painter, a typical Parisian bourgeois out for a day's fishing on Sunday. I liked it. If Alex had not summoned his younger brother to help him create London Films, Vincent might have been a considerable painter. He was already a considerable draughtsmen.

Chris said the usual things and looked expectantly at me. Alex said he had seen *The Edge of the World*. He asked a few questions about it. He liked the use of music, then he said: "I would like you to join us here at Denham. It is a good studio, one of the best in the world, but we need more film-makers who can tell a story simply and well. We have a lot of good actors, we have writers, we need directors who can be depended upon to bring in a film within the budget."

I said I had done nothing else for the past seven years. He asked what I was doing now. I said bluntly that I had a ticket for Hollywood, where I had friends. I no longer believed in a British film industry.

Those wild words may have been decisive. He said: "We have powerful friends. War is coming. Who knows? There may be a part for British films to play. Stay a year and then if you want to go to Hollywood, go!"

I said I only wanted to make films.

"You can make them here. We will give you a year's contract."

Chris cleared his throat. "A hundred a week?"

A wave of the cigar.

"Too much money."

"Eighty?"

"Too much money."

We settled for sixty pounds a week.

For fifty-two weeks! Open Sesame! Alex Korda might be going broke, but a year at sixty pounds a week stretched before me like deserts of vast eternity, deserts that blossom like the rose.

I was a Denham man. I was on the staff. The concerns of the studio were my concerns. Alex Korda's cause was my cause. I had access to him . . . on Thorsdays. I was a potential director for London Films. The story department was open to me. I knew only too well the sterility of story departments that spend their days negotiating for properties that will never be filmed and their nights in trying over dinner at expensive bars to interest a director in their pet project, when he already has a pet project of his own. No matter! Korda wanted me! I was one of the leaders, not an employee.

Carol Goodner, who had acted in two of my Michael Balcon films, had rented and decorated a little cottage at Uxbridge, two miles away across the watermeadows, while she was working on a film and a play. I took over the lease and on January 1 Bill Paton and I moved in. The windows looked west, across the valley to the white walls of the studios. My studios!

Carol Goodner, besides being one of the best actresses I ever worked with, was an enchanting woman, deep and quiet, a woman of many loves. She came of German stock, I believe, and had all the qualities of a German *Hausfrau*. When they saw Carol trudging about shopping, fifteen pounds overweight, happy, blowsy and laden down with purchases of sausages and liver, cabbage and potatoes, casting directors knew it was no good putting her up for a glamorous part. Carol was in love and was cooking for her man. Then one day you would meet her – slim, blonde, elegant, sparkling with diamonds, at all the right places, turning down offers right and left. Carol was her own woman again. Until the next time. So the cottage at Uxbridge was for rent and soon became known to a number of young ladies.

I bought a car, an Auburn Six, a green two-seater convertible with a spacious rumble seat at the back. It was a splendid car, ample and beautiful (like Carol Goodner). When I took it out for the first time and called for Frankie at the flat she shared with Vera in Knightsbridge, her great eyes opened even wider. It was the only time she had allowed me to see her impressed.

When Bill and I had set up our ménage in Uxbridge, I invited Nino and Lola from the Etoile to lunch on Sunday for the express purpose of teaching us the art of cooking spaghetti *al dente* and of making a sauce bolognese. For there is a mystery in every simple dish. As the months went by, we repeated the experiment and drank astounding quantities of wine. Nino had a good palate and we sprang surprises on each other.

It should be plain by now that although I am slim, I am not indifferent to food. Eating is one of the great pleasures of life, but cooking is, for me, almost as great a pleasure. To serve a classic dish properly and correctly gives me as much pleasure as eating it. Several hours spent planning and giving a good dinner to good friends is time well spent. I am with Dr Johnson when Boswell remonstrated with him for grumbling about the dinner they had just eaten with friends.

"But surely, Sir, it was a passable enough dinner?"

To which the great man answered, "Yes, Sir, a passable enough dinner, but not a dinner to ask a man to."

Meanwhile, I was bombarding poor Korda with projects. I hadn't enough political sense to smell out the situation and the policy of the company, and I didn't have the common sense to look at the contract list and make friends and influence people. I loathe talking shop, and if I started a conversation in the studio restaurant, it was likely to be about books and paintings. Young directors are boringly single-minded. Dozens of interesting men and women were in and out of Denham every day, but all I thought about was my film, my plans, my contract. I think I was genuinely perturbed that Alex was paying me sixty pounds every Friday and getting nothing for it. One day I was sent for by David Cunynghame.

"Powell! Alex would like you to do a little job for him." He got no further.

"All right, what is it?"

He looked reproving. "I was going to tell you. We have a contract with one or two selected firms to do their cinema advertising for them. We use our contract players, you understand. This is some tea or something. You can have Flora Robson and Ralph Richardson. Alex told me to tell you that you needn't do it if you don't want to."

"Of course I want to, if Robert Benchley and Pete Smith can make commercials for MGM." He'd never heard of them.

At last I met some of my colleagues. I think Robert Krasker was lighting. I don't think it was the great Georges Périnal, who had been René Clair's cameraman and whom I was longing to meet. It was a tea-table setting, dumped down in the middle of the vast, dark, empty No. 4 stage. There is not much that anybody but Luis Buñuel can do with two people sitting at a tea-table, but I managed by cross-cutting to make a scene out of it. I would love to see it now. Flora was an amiable girl, but her thoughts were far away. Ralph and I started talking about books and he told me that he bound his favourite books himself: he had been apprenticed to a book-binder when a young man in his teens. Seeing I was interested, he went to get a book from his dressing room. Later on he said to Alex: "That's a queer young director you've signed up. He's read a book." Alex replied that I had not only read a book, but had written one. Alex had read everything.

Alex's chief worry, which soon became mine, was to find a subject for Conrad Veidt. This great actor and legendary personality (who could ever forget his madman in *The Cabinet of Dr Caligari*, or the student in *The Student of Prague*, or Metternich in *Congress Dances*?) had been signed up by Korda after his successful debut in English films in Walter Forde's *Rome Express*. Korda was probably paying Veidt about £50,000 a year and in the normal course of production such an investment would easily be worked off in a year, and would even show a profit. London Films was finding it difficult to raise finance from its backers, and a box-office subject had to be found. The case of Sabu, the Elephant Boy, was similar. In his first films he was paid a living wage and glad of it. But when be became a star, he was quick to know his value. A film called *The Drum* had been thrown together by A. E. W. Mason from one of Kipling's stories. It starred Sabu and the boy actor Desmond Tester as the two drummer boys on the North-West Frontier, with Roger Livesey and Valerie Hobson as the stiff-upper-lip representatives of the British Raj, and Raymond Massey as a gorgeously camp raja.

The obvious solution, given two such exotic and expensive actors as Veidt and Sabu, was to star them together, and Korda had already commissioned Mason to develop an idea entitled *The Conjuror*. In all this, of course, I was neither consulted nor informed, but I had been longing to get my hands on Conrad Veidt ever since he came to England. He was such an overpowering personality that directors were afraid of him. He was tall, over six feet two inches, lean and bony. He had magnetic blue eyes, black hair and eyebrows, beautiful, strong hands, and a mouth with sardonic, not to say satanic, lines to it. He used an eye-glass. He was the show-off of all time. In private life, as I was to discover, he was the sweetest and most easy of human beings.

Because of the fear he inspired, and the admiration that his gifts awakened in his English directors, they let him get away with mispronunciations and false readings of key words that made his English unintelligible. He gave a superbly realistic performance in *Under the Red Robe*, a great old swashbuckling story by Stanley Weyman, but although he had our sympathy, you couldn't understand a word he said. I vowed that I would change all that and bided my time.

The Lions Starve in Naples is associated in my mind with the first time Korda's dilemma was brought to my notice. It was a book, a translation of a foreign novel, published by Gollancz, which had a certain vogue. It was snapped up by the story department as a possible vehicle for Veidt and Sabu. It was about a circus stranded in Naples for lack of funds. I was asked to make a report on it. I never lose an opportunity of saying that I have a lifelong hatred of circuses. Of course, actors love them, but audiences don't. Even Chaplin's *The Circus* had been a comparative failure because of its gritty realism, but I tackled the job with enthusiasm and probably asked for the front office to book me a sleeper to Naples. The chief part intended for Veidt was the lion tamer, and I must say that I should have liked to see the lion that could, or would, return the stare of those eyes. But it was not to be. I produced synopses, story-board sketches, memos by the dozen, and even a few written sequences. But Korda was not interested. It was not the big thing that he smelt was around the corner for his two stars.

All of a sudden, I had a call from Alex. We were now Micky and Alex. He was a genuinely affectionate person and inspired affection in others.

"Micky! Come and pick up a book that I shall give you by Edward Thompson. I want you to read it at once and meet Edward Thompson with me – on Thorsday."

I raced across the lot, picked up the book from Cunynghame's office and retired growling to my den. One glance at the book told me that it was a distinguished piece of writing, but that was to be expected from the poet who wrote the war memoir about the Middle East *These Men Thy Friends*. I knew Thompson as a poet and knew vaguely that he had been trained as a medical missionary. I looked him up in *Who's Who*. He was a Fellow of Oriel.

I settled down to read the book. After two pages I was gripped: by a writer, by a style, and by a story. In two hours I had read it. It was called *Burmese Silver*.

Edward Thompson came to the meeting with his wife. He was a gentle, cultured individual, like the senior civil servant in the book. His wife was perfectly cast as the devoted and practical wife of a medical missionary. They were like the Lugards or the Barings or the Kingsleys, missionaries who went out to teach and heal and end up by adding a new burden to the overloaded shoulders of the British Empire. They were gentle but inflexible, cultivated but with the common touch. Neither threats of torture nor bedpans could dismay them.

I knew that Alex was genuinely interested in this story or he would never have asked me to meet them. He wanted to know my reaction.

"If we buy your story, my dear Thompson, Mr Powell will direct the film," he said.

Thompson observed that it was a good omen that the hero of his novel was called Powell. He asked me if I knew the East, India or Burma.

"No," I said. "But one of my uncles was in the Indian Civil Service – Geoffrey Corbett. And another uncle on my father's side was an Irrawaddy River pilot."

"Sir Geoffrey Corbett. Of course. I knew him well. He died in Egypt, I heard."

(My uncle had been summoned out of retirement and a teaching job at Oxford to sort out Egypt's tangled finances (which even the Pharaohs could never do) and he died on the job. He suffered from high blood pressure.)

"And is your other uncle still in Burma?"

"No, he's back home now." I made a mental note to look him up and pump him dry.

Alex was getting bored with this chit-chat. He could see that we got on like a house on fire.

"Micky, I have asked Sir Robert Vansittart to read the book. He will write a screenplay. Now, why don't you take Mr and Mrs Thompson down to the restaurant and give them luncheon and we will all meet again in a few days' time."

I took the hint and we made ourselves scarce. The Thompsons were charmed by Alex, by his authority, by his wide knowledge of the world and by his powerful friends among the men and women who made the sluggish wheels of rich old easy-going England turn a little faster.

"I didn't know Robert Vansittart was a screenwriter," volunteered Thompson. "Of course, I knew he was a bit of a versifier. He published a book of Fleckerish lyrics when he was still at Oxford. *The Singing Caravan*. It was rather charming."

I held my peace. If Alex chose to spend time and money on commissioning a screenplay from the Permanent Under Secretary of State for His Majesty's Foreign Affairs, it was none of my business.

I asked the Thompsons if they had noticed the big, square, red-brick Georgian house, Denham Place, where Vansittart lived. The Colne had been dammed to make an ornamental lake, and there were some fine trees and an impressive entrance gate at the western end of the pretty little village – all this just on the other side of the railway line which took you up to London via St Pancras Station. I had never travelled by it, but I was to get to know it well later on.

"Hm!" said Thompson to his wife. "He's a neighbour of Korda's. That explains a lot."

I had too much respect for my own jugular vein to get between two warring poets. I had a chit from Cunynghame to pay for the lunch, and I was going to make sure that the Thompsons left Denham anxious to return. Meanwhile I questioned Thompson about Burma.

"*The Soul of the People*," said Mrs Thompson. "*The Soul of the People* by Fielding Hall. If you want to know the Burmese, that's the book to read."

I made a note of it.

The story of *Burmese Silver* was the story of a quest. It takes place around the turn of the century, when the men who ruled India, and who had just added Burma to the Indian Civil Service, were all-powerful, governing provinces that were as large and as rich as other people's kingdoms and treating with rajas and nizams of the native states on equal terms. India was far away from Whitehall, six weeks by P and O steamer, and it took a long time for authority to catch up with any misdemeanour in government. The record of the ICS is high, but the memory of Robert Clive, the great soldier and governor, and some say great thief, was still green and there were administrators who looked on their appointment to a high post as the time to fill their pockets. Certainly no Indian would expect otherwise. Edward Thompson's anti-hero was one of these ruthless men who had "shaken the pagoda-tree" as the phrase went, and shaken it to such purpose that gold and silver, gems, elephants, golden howdahs, and women hung with strings of pearls were his for the taking. He took. And when his regal behaviour could no longer be hushed, and when a court of inquiry, headed by no less a personage than the attorney general, was making its slow way to Bombay, he skipped to Burma, to Rangoon, where he was greeted and treated as the great proconsul that he undoubtedly was. He then vanished up country in the direction of China, taking his vast booty with him.

This was freebooting on a grand scale and was obviously a part for Conrad Veidt, who could annex empires without moving a muscle in his face. But where did Sabu come in?

Thompson's story concerns a high official of the Indian Civil Service, a man who "has had his whack" of power and authority, and who is under sentence of death by his doctor. He can live so long if he goes home and takes care of himself; he can live a much shorter time if he continues an active life in the East. He is a contemporary and a friend, an admirer of the impeached official. Over the past twenty years, word has filtered down to Mandalay and Rangoon of a white raja, Raja Gabriel, who has carved out a kingdom for himself in the debatable land between the Chinese and the Burmese borders and the frontier of Assam, known as the Triangle. There was no border, only a shifting authority. This is Raja Gabriel's territory. To root him out, to send a punitive expedition up into the Naga territory, would cost money and annoy China, who like an amiable lunatic claims jurisdiction over all the countries adjacent to her borders. Even to acknowledge the existence of Raja Gabriel would be an embarrassment to Rangoon. So they pigeonhole him and hope for the best – or the least worst.

Clive Powell – for that is the name of Thompson's seeker after an old friendship – decides to spend his last years, or months, looking for this mysterious white raja. He knows it will be a long and difficult journey, he knows that Raja Gabriel may not be his lost friend but some other adventurer, and he knows that the Administration will not approve of his journey and will do nothing to help him. But he feels he must go. And when his colleagues see him off, it is eastward that he is going, not westward and home to die in an English bed.

The central part of the book is an account of his journey and the clues which lead him eventually to Raja Gabriel's country. On the way he picks up a companion, a half-caste Burmese called Gussie, and I saw at once that Alex had glimpsed the nucleus of a part for Sabu in the fast-talking, entertaining character. They go up the Irrawaddy to Bhamo, cross to the Chindwin and follow it for days into the territory of the Nagas, an independent nation, tall and slim, like American Indians, with shaven heads and scalplocks, headhunters and handhunters. There Raja Gabriel's daughter comes to meet them, a beautiful Eurasian girl (what a part for Merle!), for whose sake Raja Gabriel has allowed them to come so far. For the news has spread that this territory that nobody wants contains a mountain of silver, with veins of ore so rich that all the great powers are moving in, including a representative of the British Government. It is the situation and his love for his daughter that decides Raja Gabriel to fight or sue for peace. For he does indeed turn out to be Clive's old friend and chief.

Thompson was no novelist, and I seem to remember that his wife had a good deal to do with the development of the book. But he was a writer of style and was good at local colour and atmosphere. His characters were painted people on a wall, his scenes and riverscapes – for Burma is a land of rivers – were full of life and colour. But if this were to become a film of high adventure for Merle Oberon, Conrad Veidt, Sabu and another (for a lover would be needed and the gentle, half-dead civil servant was not he), then a first-rate dramatist would be needed on the screenplay, and I felt strongly that the Right Honourable Sir Robert Vansittart, a member of His Majesty's Privy Council, a Knight Commander of the Victorian Order, etc., etc., was not he either. But I did not pass on these thoughts to the Thompsons, who were counting their chickens.

I had met Vansittart at one of the get-togethers Alex held to stimulate the Prudential and encourage his distributors and I had been fascinated by the man while remaining cool about the artist. He was attractive to men and to women. It was said of him that his present marriage was the outcome of a stormy love affair and hushed-up scandal. He had ridden the storm and come out of it more romantic than ever. He was tall and broad-shouldered, built like an athlete, and had observant, humorous eyes with an Oriental slant to them. Perhaps there was colonial Dutch blood in his family tree and this accounted for the Asiatic cast of his brown, mobile face. An attractive man. I knew he had been writing some lyrics for Alex's projected Arabian Nights fantasy and that Miklos Rozsa had found tunes for them. He had a good ear, but a conventional outlook, was my opinion.

But I could forgive Vansittart anything for his courage – social and political. The man who wasn't afraid to risk his career by running away with another man's wife was not the man to fear his enemies, inside and outside the Foreign Office.

Vansittart was writing a script, based on the book by Edward Thompson. How could I contribute anything unless I knew Burma? I decided to go there and asked poor Cunynghame to arrange it.

The sheer audacity of the proposal carried me through. Cunynghame, of course, refused point-blank. That was his job. The purchase of the book was being negotiated by Biro; a price had been agreed, but there was no appropriation for the film, and, of course, no budget. Veidt's and Sabu's weekly salary would be charged against *Burmese Silver*, instead of *The Lions Starve in Naples*. That was all the accounts department knew. As for me, I was just a pain in the ass of the chief accountant. I demanded to see Alex. By this time I had read Fielding Hall's book, and books about the Nagas and the Shan States, and I learnt from Ian Campbell Gray that Peter Fleming was travelling in those parts of the country, accompanied by the indomitable and enchanting Celia Johnson. Living off the country in the unmapped, unsurveyed, unadministered territory between Burma and China needs a stout heart and an iron constitution, said Thompson. This only made me more anxious to go. I dumped all my books on Alex's desk and made the point that Burma was not India, with its many religions and cultures. It was essentially a Buddhist country, whose people had a national identity. Alex fingered the books and asked me what I proposed to do.

"Fly out there. Pick up a native servant. Go up the Irrawaddy and the Chindwin, just like Powell in the book. Collect costumes and props and send them back. Establish a chain of contacts who would be useful when the main unit comes out. Bang the drum a bit about London films."

Alex lit another Corona. "Conning-ham! What will Micky's journey cost?"

"About £2,000, Alex. He would fly by Imperial Airways to Calcutta, where our people would meet him and outfit him. Then on to Rangoon. And from then on it will be up to him." He added nastily: "If he goes up the Chindwin, there's no telling when he'll get back. He may run into the monsoon."

I had discussed this with Thompson. "The monsoon is on now," I said with authority, "and on the whole it makes travelling easier, except for the leeches."

Alex puffed a beautiful smoke ring. "Let Micky go, Conning-ham. It is not too much money for a reconnaisance. It will pay for itself."

I said: "Thank you, Alex," before anybody else could speak.

He looked at me benevolently. "Are you taking any books with you?"

"Yes, Alex, Boswell."

"The great Doctor? Do you remember what he said about travel?"

"Of course: 'If I had no responsibilities and no fears for the future, I would spend my life driving fast in a post-chaise with a pretty woman.'" Alex blew another smoke ring. "Shall you write a book, Micky?"

"No, Alex. But I'll send you cables and reports."

"And keep in touch with the office," added Cunynghame with memories of Zoli Korda in West Africa.

I flew to Burma in a boat – A boat? Yes, a real boat with mahogany rails and brass fittings and a splendid great bow-wave. And it flew. It was a flying-boat.

In those far-off days before the Englishman's world was destroyed for the second time, the British Lion's paw was extended, protectively or offensively, over the East, Far East and Middle East, and Imperial Airways in that year before the Second World War exploded, had established a service of flying boats from Southampton to Singapore to create a waterborne line of communication within the British Empire. There were few established airports in those far-off days. To land on water was the solution. No better way of globe-trotting has ever been invented.

The flying boat is what the name says, a boat that flies, but no words can prepare you for the delightful adventure. First, it is so very much a boat, solidly built by Messrs Short of Sunderland, roomy, plenty of head and leg room. But it was sometimes not easy to remember that it was a boat. There was a certain Minister for Air who had been a pilot in the Royal Naval Air Service in the 1914 War. He was inspecting Portsmouth, saw the Sunderlands and asked if he could take one up. He still had his pilot's ticket, and after all he was Minister, so after some hesitation and crossing of fingers, they let him do it. He flew the heavy boat with great skill, then handed over to her pilot for the landing on the Solent. As they stood chatting on the float, waiting for the launch to take them ashore, the pilot said to the Minister: "You flew very low over the airfield as you came in, sir. For a moment. I thought you were going to land on the runway. That was why I jogged your elbow. I thought you had forgotten she was a boat."

"What an absurd idea," said the Minister, laughing heartily and stepping off the float into the water.

The beauty of a flying-boat is that you land on water. There seems to be a lot of it, and you don't have to cover it with thousands of acres of concrete as you do with good farmland; nor do you need vast administrative offices and hangars. All you need is a lake, or a river, or a sea, or even a reservoir at a pinch, some caravans, a punkah wallah or two, a dog, and of course a cat to arch its back at new arrivals. Then, of course, you have the enthusiastic local populace, black, brown or yellow (and in 1938, respectful), some fast launches to run races with, rafts and buoys and coloured floats, rockets, ropes, cables and other toys – and you are ready to go!

My journey out by flying boat remains one of my happiest memories of travel. We averaged about 2,000 miles a day and saw sights enough to fill my head with dreams for the rest of my life. What does the modern traveller see? Nothing but concrete – acres, miles of concrete. Istanbul? Concrete! Samarakand? Concrete. Mandalay? Add corrugated iron. In a modern jet we fly at 35,000 feet, at which height the world of men, with all its beauties and horrors, its triumphs and failures, is only "an objective." We flying boatmen fly low looking for lakes and rivers on which to splash down. Splash down! What a lovely phrase, reminiscent of childhood. How thrilling the great bow-wave, roaring past the portholes as we splashed down or took off! How fascinating to meet the watermen of all shapes and colours who dashed, dived, and swam out to meet you! To alight in extinct volcanoes, on sacred lakes, and swirling rivers that reminded you that this huge airborne creature was also a boat, straining at its cables. "Bring back the flying boats!" is my cry. Splash down to Adventure!

I devoured my itinerary and smacked my lips. We would be leaving from Southampton, putting down (weather permitting) on the River Saône where it joins the Rhône in Central France; at Marignane, Marseille, where one of my great heroes, Saint-Exupéry, spent so much of his short life; on Lake Bracciano in Fascist-dominated Rome; at Alexandria; on the Sea of Galilee; at Lake Habbaniya, an RAF station in Iraq; at Sharjah on the Persian Gulf; in Baluchistan; on private lakes as we crossed India, by gracious permission of native princes and rajas; on the Jumna, on the Hooghly, on the Irrawaddy (monsoon permitting) – and all of these romantic and beautiful spots were subject to change without notice. It was pure Jules Verne, and I was living it.

JULY 11, 1937
TIBERIAS, PALESTINE
POWELL TO CUNYNGHAME, LONDON FILMS
SPLASHED DOWN SEA OF GALILEE. NOBODY FISHING.
MICKY

It seemed an enormity to be taxiing and gathering speed on the Sea of Galilee.

We flew on over the desert, crossed the gorges of the Euphrates and turned south to Basra. Whitey (one of a bunch of American oil engineers) sat beside me and talked about the Persian Gulf. He had been here before, but the other Americans were out for the first time. I tagged them all with the names of Hollywood actors (when talkies were new, every American used to act like one of those familiar faces and voices on our screens), and I had dubbed him as Barton MacLane. The others were Ned Sparks, Wallace Beery, Richard Arlen and Slim Summerville.

We came down on Basra long after dark, but our skipper made a perfect landing on the river, in spite of all the flares and rockets. He was a bulky, fair-moustached, indignant man, with china-blue eyes and very short shorts depending on one small button to keep them from a spectacular collapse. He walked amusingly like Charles Laughton, he had the same short swing of the arms, and he pushed his belly before him, with the same intolerant air: "Damn you! Yes. I'm fat. And I like it! Damn you!"

He was eating a most enormous breakfast at Basra as I looked over his shoulder in awe. He absorbed five illustrated papers, grapefruit, a couple of newspapers, haddock, reports from the flight officer, bacon, sausage, and a heap of fried tomato, marmalade, toast, iced coffee and a bunch of grapes damn you.

We slept at Basra, which means I spent a wakeful night lying under the punkah with a towel over my vital organs. This keeps one's stomach happy and full of confidence in you. The heat was torrid, the hotel first-class. I heard a good deal about Sir John Ward, the British Resident, and his wife, who matched him. He seemed to be the uncrowned King of Iraq, and the hotel, which was splendid, was his latest achievement.

At Bahrain, our next stop, Whitey and the rest of the Americans left us. They were going "up-country", destination unrevealed. I missed them. We had been warned not to expect home comforts that night at Sharjah and Dubai, two Arab cities on the Gulf, with natural harbours scooped out of the sand by the movement of the tides. We landed inland on a lagoon, presided over by a fort.

As we circled around, we saw the westward-bound flying boat ready to take off from the lagoon.

JULY 13, 1937
SHARJAH EMIRATE
POWELL TO KORDA

COULD YOU IMAGINE WHOLE PERSIAN GULF TO CHOOSE FROM COLLIDED SHARJAH WITH WESTBOUND FLYING BOAT. AWAITING REPLACEMENT FROM KARACHI.

MICKY

On our way again we stopped for fuel at Juinli. It was like a scene from the Arabian Nights. The sea was a violet indigo, there was a great bare beach, and the altogether uninhabitable interior was altogether uninhabited. It was a new fuelling post – the old one was at Gwadar – and both of them were on the marshy coast of Baluchistan. The whole coast there was a chain of salt-lakes with a sand-bar between them and the Indian Ocean, which came roaring in, in splendid long surf-rollers. The post had been established only two weeks previously and was pretty crude. Two engineers, who expected to be picked up by us yesterday, had had to spend the night there and were disgruntled. They were both huge young men in shorts, with enormous hairy buttocks, and they sweated absolute gulf-streams all the time and didn't speak to anyone.

Tribesmen appeared from nowhere in scarlet turbans and scanty loincloths and climbed on our floats. The leading Baluchi jumped into the sea with the mooring rope and swam to the mooring buoy, while his friends screamed their encouragement. When he had tied it, he climbed on top and squatted there grinning. The others flew to the job (which for them was fun, not work) of pumping petrol and pouring cans.

I sometimes think, and smile as I do so, of all the obscure corners of the world that were illuminated, held briefly in the spotlight and then allowed to lapse back into obscurity again. Lonely rivers, sacred lakes that had been left to the birds and beasts for hundreds of years, were to hear the thunder of marine engines and some native prince would dream of international airports. Then suddenly one morning a better landing-place was found, his lake was downgraded to "Emergency Landing Only" and the sleep of centuries resumed.

We splashed down across India from Karachi to Calcutta, sometimes flying several thousand feet up, sometimes at nought feet, below the clouds, stampeding buffalo, with villagers shaking their fists at us. Our first stop was at Udaipur, on a sacred lake full of crocodiles that we fed with ham sandwiches. All around were little hills, each one crowned with a shrine. On the biggest hill was the white fortress palace of the raja. The town of Udaipur was about twelve miles away and we saw it from the air. The reigning raja was air-minded and planned to spend four lakhs of rupees on developing an airfield. Meanwhile, he let Imperial Airways use his lake, although littering and swimming were forbidden. The last prohibition was hardly necessary after one look at the crocodiles.

We refuelled at Shaipur, a town of white marble and at Gwalior, where the citadel, its cliffs several hundred feet high, dwarfed everything else. At Allahabad we landed on the Jumna, sending ripples over the pilgrims washing their sins away in the sacred river. Calcutta, next stop! We climbed above the monsoon ceiling to 15,000 feet. Just imagine! Three miles high in a boat. How Jules Verne would have revelled in it!

At last the Hooghly came in sight and we swooped down over jute mills and landed above the Willingdon Bridge. Hartley, the local representative of United Artists, met me at the landing stage and whisked me through customs and away. This was one of the excitements of working for Alexander Korda. Neither he nor one of his representatives must be kept waiting.

JULY 17, 1937
CALCUTTA
POWELL TO CUNYNGHAME
    STOPPING CALCUTTA OVERNIGHT. RANGOON NEXT. YIPPEE.
                                                    MICKY

To my delight, when I rejoined my beloved flying boat to Rangoon, the captain was the same, bulky, Charles Laughtonish figure who had marooned us at Sharjah, damn you! He ignored me. We flew low over a most fascinating archipelago: hundreds of tiny islands, each with its shy, retiring house on stilts and a white beach on which the sea was lazily breaking. I went and got my big map and spread it out on the floor of the flying boat, and even the navigator came to have a look. I had ordered it from Stanford's, the map people in Long Acre, as soon as I knew I was definitely going. It was on a scale of 1:2,000,000, which is about thirty miles to the inch, which resulted in a map four and a half feet long and two and a half feet wide. An impressive instrument. No such map had ever been seen outside the office of the government surveyors. It created a sensation wherever I went – among men, I mean. It is one of the minor griefs of my life that women don't like looking at maps. I have tried to point out the beauty of a place by indicating it on a map, and I have seen a glazed look come into their eyes. I don't really think women care where they are so long as they are with the right man and have enough clothes to make do in an emergency.

Burma has its head in the Himalayan snows and one foot in the Bay of Bengal. The other leg is long and trailing and shares a peninsula with its neighbour Siam. To the west of this long coastline are the Andaman Islands, once upon a time convict islands of British India, whose name will always be familiar to fans of Dr Watson and Sherlock Holmes from that masterwork of Arthur Conan Doyle's – The Sign of Four.

Burma is a country where water is king. Three great rivers descend it and divide it from north to south: the Irrawaddy, the Chindwin and the Salween. The Irrawaddy, over 1,000 miles long, is the main artery of the country. At Mandalay, 500 miles up-country, the river is still half a mile wide. Until the railway was built, the great river took all the traffic in the country. The Chindwin, which rises in the wild, northern hills, served all that part of Burma, which was virtually roadless and joined the Irrawaddy below Mandalay. The Chindwin was my ultimate destination, but I kept quiet about this because the country at the head of the river had only recently come under administration, and I would need approval to get into what sounded like Raja Gabriel country, where the mysterious Nagas had their villages. The Salween was swift and spectacular, running through tremendous gorges, with rapids so deep and so long that only the timber rafts dared to tackle them. The gorges of the Salween have been the goal of many an ambitious canoeist, or his grave.

Burma in those days was the private preserve of ambitious Scotsmen. The country was run by big companies who all had head offices in Glasgow. After Calcutta it was a refreshing change. The businessmen had made this rich country richer, and the Indian Civil Service was teaching the Burmese to run their own affairs. Everybody seemed to have time, or make time, to help me. Films, and especially film-makers like Alex, whose name was known world-wide as a maker of great British epics, are a passport to people's hearts. Soldiers, policemen, civil servants, teak wallahs, elephant trappers, riverboat captains, dropped everything when they heard the magic word "movie". I often think of them all, and wonder how they survived the war and the Japanese invasion that swept through Burma three years later.

My new friends took me to a tropical outfitter. In practically no time at all I was in khaki shirt and shorts, showing white knees, unfortunately.

"And you'll need puttees in the jungle, Mr Powell!"

And a solar topee. When I had a riding switch dangling from my fingers, I was saluted by everybody and constantly asked if I were rejoining my regiment.

"You will need a boy, Mr Powell, who can talk Hindustani."

Inquiries were made and in due course a servant appeared.

He was not a Burman, nor a Mohammedan, he was a Madrasi, from the faraway south-eastern coast of India, whose men make good soldiers, servants and sailors. He was tall and slim for a Madrasi, not very dark and he wore a toothbrush moustache. His eyes were melancholy. He was dressed in spotless white.

He said his name was John. There was something motherly about him.

"Are you married?" I asked.

"Yes, sir. Four children."

"Can you get away? I am going up-country."

"Excuse me, sir. Are you working for Government?"

"No. I'm a film director, I am here to prepare things. The others will come after the monsoon. I shall want you for five weeks now, and much longer when I come back."

"My wife will be excited. She loves the movies."

"That's settled then. We take the train tomorrow, to Mandalay."

"We must pack tonight, sir. The train leaves at 8:00 a.m."

Instead of charging up the Chindwin like a bull at a gate, my new friends, who knew something of the difficulties I might encounter – such as the rains, the river in flood, jungles full of leeches, and above all, the favour or disfavour of overworked district commissioners in a newly pacified territory – had worked out an itinerary which would take me first to Mandalay, which everyone recommended as a base for the production. From there the steam train from Rangoon to Mandalay took about twenty hours. The Burmese were very proud of it. It left one morning and got in the next. I was warned that it was dirty and rackety, but it got you there. The alternative was six days in a river boat. I took the train.

JULY 21, 1937
RANGOON
POWELL TO KORDA
  ON THE ROAD TO MANDALAY
  WHERE THE FLYING FISHES PLAY
  AND THE DAWN COMES UP LIKE THUNDER
  OUT OF CHINA CROSS THE BAY
    THANK YOU ALEX.
          MICKY

We arrived in Mandalay early next morning, cross, hot and dirty. It is an abominable trip at that time of the year. John proved to be an excellent travelling companion.

Mandalay came up to expectations. The Palace of King Thibaw is outrageous. The whole country must have been mobilized to build it. Forests of teak must have been felled for the floors and staircases, and they say that workmen were still carving precious woods and sticking mirrors on the ceilings when Thibaw was already a prisoner of the British. The Palace is surrounded by an immense fort about a mile square, which is itself surrounded by a moat. As I drove by, people were washing in it or filling jars. The fort has twelve gates and five bridges – a little too large for my Raja Gabriel, I thought. Mandalay is not flat, like Rangoon, but hilly and almost every hill is crowned with a pagoda.

I decided to go by boat and rail up the Irrawaddy to Bhamo and Myitkyina. Beyond there was "the Triangle" and the mountains where the elephants lived. Debatable land. This could be where Raja Gabriel had established his kingdom. The railroad had only recently been completed – the advance of civilization and all that. Nobody quite knew what was going on in "the Triangle".

July 22, 1937
Mandalay
Powell to Cunynghame
If necessary contact me through Major Learmond
Military police HQ Mandalay. Going up country.
Micky

During the next eight days I covered a lot of ground – and water. I saw a lot of people, learnt a lot, and as a film director I was disappointed. The biggest disappointment was Bhamo. It was a frontier town all right, with an astonishing mixture of races, but predominantly Chinese. It was also a garrison town and there was a Sikh regiment and a Punjabi regiment stationed there. The place was overcrowded and smelt to high heavens. So far as *Burmese Silver* was concerned, Bhamo was out.

John wrinkled his nose. For him too, Bhamo was out.

I stuck to my plan of making several detours into the hills.

I found Mogok fascinating. It was high up in a volcanic crater on the Chinese border, and was the greatest source in the world of rubies, also topaz. There were dozens and dozens of small mines that had been worked by the Chinese for centuries. The valleys were honeycombed with mines in the red earth, and with deep stone-lined watercourses to wash the stones out of that soil. Bamboo troughs distributed the water over the heads of the miners onto the stone platforms. All the systems used were as old as China, and as effective. All the hills were incredibly rich in semi-precious stones and in Chinese jade and soapstone.

But the finest jewel in Mogok was Nichols. He was beyond rubies. He owned the electric power company, had an Anglo-Burman wife and a daughter whom he adored, always spoke as if a forty-mile-an-hour gale were blowing, and addressed me as "old fellow". He claimed to know the jungle around there better than the natives, who were mostly Li-Chaws with huge blue turbans, and he settled my destiny, so far as Mogok was concerned, in about four thousand ear-splitting words.

"Well, you saw what you wanted to see and what did you see after all, man? Nothing down there you couldn't do a bloody sight better at home, eh? Oh, it's nothing at all, man! Waterfalls and bamboo and little hills and bloody great slabs of rock! What? Oh, I agree with you. Mud and slush and flies and leeches and what do you gain by it all? Nothing at all, man! What's that you say? Villages on hills and streams with pagodas on hills above them? You ought to go up the valley and over that hill. There you've got Palaung villages on every hill and pagodas and all you want. But not in monsoon weather, man! It's one in five, and climb all the time and dodging bloody great elephants. December's the time, man! Oh, they don't mean to hurt you, but they're big and they get frightened and then they stampede, and then they go right through you. Tusks through your back and two feet out of your chest. That's how my old father got killed, and they almost got me, man! Bloody great bull! And I had two mules and a pony. He got them all and I got behind a bamboo clump and when he came back looking for me, I dropped him. Five hundred chips I had to pay, man, and I knew that when I shot him; but I thought, if 500 chips were all I had to pay for my life, I never made a better bloody bargain. What's that you say, man? Li-Chaws? Oh, ay, you get them the other way, over Chaung-yi way. There's your jungle for you, man! See those bison, there, you'll see something. Six feet at the shoulder they stand, and a china blue eye as big as my fist. Goah, they call them. But mind you see them first! Herds of thirty or forty, but it's the old bulls you've got to watch for. They'll be through you like a dose of salts, man. Go for you in a minute. Wicked great buggers! See them coming for you, you'll see something, man. A .470 bullet will hardly stop them and it will stop an elephant! Necks two feet thick, like the American bison, but the American bison is *small*, man. Terrible great buggers these are! Go for you like an express train. Old bulls they are, lie up in canebrakes all day by themselves and if you come by, they're after you! Run? I've never run from elephant, but I've run like hell from goah, man. Two are worse! Brothers, you see – twins! They're the worst of all. Destructive buggers, all over the country, killing tame buffalo, tearing down houses and telegraph poles. What? Just for pure devilment, I suppose. Seen him do it. Get his great arse against an iron telegraph pole, over she goes and down goes the wire and off he goes. You'll see them on the road. See them tonight if you're lucky. Ask the driver. He knows all about them. The other day, coming up from Thabbeikkyin, there was a bull in front for half a mile. Honk! Honk! Honk! There he stayed in front of them. All of a sudden he turns and puts his horn through the radiator. Right through, man. But the steam and the boiling water went all over him and he cleared off. But two days later, another car came along and he was waiting for them. Tore it to bits, man. Kicked it down the gully and the men in it were up the banks and running all over the counrty. Nasty great buggers, they are. I've got that radiator now, man, show it to visitors when they come here. But not in the dry season. You see what we've got here. Godforsaken spot . . . just a few white men and howling great jungle country. I was born in Leeds, but they're all dead. I shall live and die here and I might do worse. Came here for a year and I've been here twenty-three. Shan, Burmese, Chin – I speak 'em all. It's the only way I can understand some of the men that come up here. Scotsmen now. Never a bloody word could I understand of my Scots engineer till he learnt to speak Burmese. Then we understood each other and then he goes and blows his brains out. So I have to do his job. And then the manager commits suicide, so I do *his* job. And then they send someone out to help and he can't stand it and clears off, and now I do all three jobs and I own the companies. Ruby Mines, Ltd., that was, and the power company, that's my lights you burn up at the bungalow. Cheap? Fifteen rupees a month, man. That's all I charge and it's all I want. Cheap enough, isn't it? But you come back in December, I'll help you all I can. Give you men that know the country, take you easy, see good things, no need to have a bloody sweat, man, what's the good of that? Fever and leeches is all you get. But come in December and I'll do all I can for you. And if you want anything sent, wire me, I'll do it up and hand it over to Thomas Cook, they'll send it to you. But come back in December, you can have fine shooting then. You like shooting? You don't shoot, man? Well, I don't any more myself. Used to shoot a lot, but I shot a little deer up the valley, wounded it and it cried and I've not shot a thing since, man. Pathetic it was. But look out for those buggers of buffalo; I've got a .333 – the only one in the country, a bullet as long as your finger. It goes right through them and never stops them or an elephant, but a .470 in the shoulder, that will do the business. Goodbye man, don't forget: 'Nichols, Mogok' will find me."

JULY 29, 1937
MOGOK
POWELL TO ALEXANDER KORDA
   RUBY MINES TERRIFIC. BOUGHT YOU SOME JADE. RETURNING
   MANDALAY.
                RAJA POWELL

"Sahib! Do we stop one day in Mandalay so that I can get your shirts and second pair of sheets to the dhobie?"

"Yes, John. Don't be so domestic."

By now Major Learmond of the Military Police, known universally as "Tarzan Sahib" had taken control of my destiny. The Civil Powers were not keen on my plan to go up the Chindwin, but Tarzan was a soldier. He pooh-poohed the warning and demanded to see my itinerary, and scrutinized it with a general's eye.

He dashed off half a dozen letters, chits, and telegrams to the head official at each place. He seemed to be on Christian name terms with everybody. Burma, compared with India, is a delightfully small country, and everyone knew everyone else, and had worked in their district at one time or another. We worked out a very ingenious itinerary which would take me up the Chindwin, round the Somra Tract on foot, returning to Mandalay by the downstream steamer in about two weeks.

I and my servant would go by train to the river port of Monywa that afternoon and sleep on board the steamer, so Tarzan dashed off another wire to the Police Post, telling them to meet the train and deliver Sahib right side at up the wharf, for there had been rumours of some trouble there. Of a retiring nature, I viewed these orders with misgiving and asked who would meet me.

"Oh, the Jemadar or Subadar."

"How will I know him?"

"He'll be a Sikh."

"What shall I say to him? Does he speak English?"

"Probably not. Say: 'Salaam, Subadar Sahib. I don't speak Hindustani, but my boy does.' At which I expect he will say: 'Very good!'"

"And a Jemadar has one star and a Subadar two?"

"Correct. I'm off now. Call for what you want. You know how to work the fan. Lunch at quarter to one."

I spent the morning writing letters while John packed.

The distance to Monywa was fifty-five miles and the train did it in four hours. At last, about 7:15 p.m. we loafed into Monywa and my carriage window was instantly besieged by a dozen anxious faces, touts for coolies and gharries. But I ignored them haughtily and was justified, for as the train stopped an enormous, black-bearded figure, in spotless khaki and Sam Browne belt, with knees like the roots of an oak and sparkling black eyes, stepped swiftly up to my window, glared up, sprang to the salute and poured out a volume of consonants, while behind him a thin, anxious looking Havildar snapped a file of men to attention and everyone saluted again and stared hopefully at me for a speech.

I cleared my throat and got off my line ("Salaam, Subadar Sahib") without a fluff. But it was too good. Before I could proceed, I was washed away with another flood of Hindustani. Fortunately John turned up with the luggage and saved the situation and in no time each man had seized a portion of my baggage, searched the compartment thoroughly under the keen eye of the Subadar himself, and swept me out of the station, where several gharries having been rejected, one was found suitable for the body of the Heaven-Born, whose luggage was piled into an ox-cart, which lumbered off under escort.

AUGUST 3, 1937
CUNYNGHAME TO POWELL
C/O TARZAN SAHIB, MANDALAY
    UNDERSTAND THERE IS SOME TROUBLE IN THE BAZAARS.
    ALEX SUGGESTS YOU MAY WISH TO RETURN. WHERE ARE YOU
    ANYWAY?

AUGUST 3, 1937
POWELL TO CUNYNGHAME
    UP YOUR CHINDWIN

                                      MICKY

The Chindwin was navigable, but was smaller than the Irrawaddy, muddier and swifter. The deep-water channel veered impulsively from bank to bank in a way which would have been impossible for the big paddle-wheel steamers of the Irrawaddy Flotilla. So Scottish engineers had designed a stern-wheel steamer for service on the Chindwin. They were not beautiful, but they did the job. The *Saga* was one of these. She had a large noisy paddle wheel up her rear, but John and I loved her. She was very comfortable.

All life in Burma centres around the rivers, and as soon as we sailed we became part of it. The *Saga* and her sister ships were popular because they not only looked like a floating bazaar, but had one on the lower deck, which was stocked up before each trip. Her engines were wood-burning, which meant frequent stops at woodpiles in the jungle. Sometimes the village was visible, sometimes not. The village headman acted as con-tractee. I remember coming to a woodpile one evening. It was late, there was no sign of a village, but there were about a hundred girls sitting on the logs in silence, swinging their legs and smoking their cheroots, which glowed in the darkness. Gradually, I made out a number of young men lounging about in groups. Nobody spoke, nobody moved as the ship edged into the bank. At the rattle of the gangplank touching the dock, there was pandemonium. The girls did all the loading, bearing the logs on their heads and shoulders. Each group would take four or five logs between them, drop them on the deck and then run back chattering and laughing for more. The boys did nothing. They had done the cutting and considered that that was where their job ended. In ten minutes two tons of logs were on the deck of the steamer, at the cost of eleven rupees, forty annas. The boys went shopping on the lower deck and bought presents for the girls, and soon the whole of the money was back in the Skipper's pocket, minus the headman's commission.

I had a plan, and I had no plan, like the Powell in the book: unless it was to keep going until I got, like him, to the back of beyond. Thanks to Tarzan Sahib, I had friends and friendly officials all the way up the river as far as Tamanthi, the gateway to the Somra Tract, and to the villages of the mysterious, headhunting, handhunting Nagas, who insisted on privacy and were prepared to fight for it.

Meanwhile on the *Saga*, I was living the life of a slug. After the frantic activity of the past two weeks, John and I enjoyed lounging on the upper deck eating four meals a day and complaining if they were late. I found that I was putting on weight alarmingly.

"Never mind," I said to my stomach. "We shall sweat these pounds off in the jungle."

I never spoke truer words.

Cut to: EXTERIOR JUNGLE PATH. It is raining. Half a dozen porters,

Chins or Kachins, are strung out along the narrow path, talking and laughing as their toes grip for the holes in the slippery sandstone. The leading porter, chattering nineteen to the dozen, is a woman whom I call the Merry Widow. The boys march better with her in the lead, like the bulls on a French merry-go-round, following the one solitary cow. The porters carry their loads on bamboo poles between two men, or else in wicker-work baskets on their backs, balanced with a tumpline across the forehead, like the Merry Widow.

John comes next, carrying his precious tea-basket and his umbrella. The boy in front of him has my bedroll, and the man in front of *him* carries all the comforts of home, including a bottle of whisky, and a protesting fowl destined for my dinner. When they stop, John stops. He has no intention of letting them get behind him and come straggling in at midnight like they did last night. Our progress is slow. Thud! There goes the Merry Widow down on her backside. She roars with laughter and all the boys help her up.

I come next, moodily slapping at my bare knees with a little bag of salt, intended to make the leeches drop off – in theory. These little beasts sit on the top of the bamboo leaves with their mouths open, waiting for me to come abreast of them. They take a bold leap and fasten their teeth in my delicate flesh. That's where the saltbag comes in handy. I carry nothing but my camera and a stick and a look of importance, for word has come back from Layshi, our destination, that Tamanthi has flashed a message that I am a captain in the Burma Rifles on a secret mission.

Last of all comes the rear-guard, Private Darra-Kwe, a sepoy with a rifle and fifteen rounds of ammunition. The District Commissioner thought we ought to have a sepoy with us, "just in case". He has been told to keep well back since I discovered his rifle was loaded. I always thought the term "sepoy" as applied to Indian soldiers went out with the Indian Mutiny, but apparently not. He is cheerful, tireless, and last night he went back two miles to bring in the stragglers.

Every twelve miles, there is a Public Works Department (PWD) bungalow, with a local dirwan, or butler, supposedly in charge, with fuel in the kitchen and water in the bathroom, and, if you are lucky, a dozen eggs and a pessimistic chicken. But nobody expects you to travel in the rains, unless you are a mad dog or an Englishman. John was very indignant about the lack of hospitality: "Sir, this is very jungly place."

The first two nights we have to fend for ourselves. By then the news had spread through the jungle that a Sahib of great wealth and power was on his way to the Somra Tract, and Government said they'd better look out. From then on, chickens and eggs were forced into our pockets, and John, who had been sulking at our lack of face, cheered up and made some fudge out of a tin of condensed milk which he found at the bottom of a bag.

On the fifth day, the sky cleared at last and a most splendid view was unrolled below us to the east. At the same time we met our first Nagas. There were three of them and they stood by the side of the path and murmured "Salaam." Evidently pacified. They were all over six feet tall, broad-shouldered, with very slim hips. They carried spears eight feet long, covered with goat's hair except for the grip; the blade was triangular in shape and very broad. Their eyes were large and lustrous like an animal's, and the brain behind them was watchful like an animal's. They wore a thin patterned blanket knotted around one shoulder, and a sporran, or apron, of plaited grass to cover their privates. Their ears were pierced and two of them wore brass cartridges in the holes. They were nothing like Burmans, they were more like American Indians than anything. Although polite, they kept their distance. As they went on down the trail, I saw how they used their tall spears in walking on the slippery path. I was very impressed by my first Nagas, and I had the feeling that they were not at all impressed with me.

The path wound around the shoulder of a big, bare hill, and we could see perhaps eighty miles. For four days we had been trudging along jungle paths with only brief glimpses of the sky, taking our destination on trust, sweating for hours through mountainous jungle for no other reason than that the path took us there, only to find ourselves slithering down another thousand feet into a water-soaked gorge. Suddenly we could see all the way to Tamanthi. Hearing an exclamation from one of the men, I turned and looked north. The clouds parted and we saw range after range of high mountains and, for a moment, the dome of Saramati, Burma's tallest mountain, 13,000 feet high. Soon after, the Merry Widow shouted: "Layshi!", and there it was across the valley.

MESSAGE BY HELIOGRAPH FROM LAYSHI MILITARY POST, SOMRA TRACT:
LEAVE TOMORROW FOR HEADHUNTER VILLAGES.

TRADER MICK

There are two kinds of Nagas in the Somra Tract: the Para-Nagas and the Tongkhul-Nagas. The Tongkhuls are the most picturesque. Their villages are always sited on slopes so that each family has ample room to clear a platform and surround it with a stockade. This gives them plenty of notice should friend or enemy drop in. They erect carved sacrificial poles outside their houses, and the size and number show the importance of the owner. They hang the skulls of animals along the eaves of their houses: buffaloes with curved horn, and mithun (wild sheep) with long straight ones. At all angles above the village, there are long bamboo poles with tufts of feathers or bunches of grass attached to them, swaying in the wind. These symbols of wealth and respectability have taken the place of the heads and hands recorded by Cartmel thirteen years before.

I began to get excited. There was a wonderful atmosphere about these windswept villages, nearly all located on deep gorges. I had found what I was looking for. A strange and interesting tribe of people, warriors and headhunters, who could bar the way to Raja Gabriel's secret kingdom. His fortress-palace, in an impregnable position, could be shot elsewhere, perhaps in the Shan States.

We saw very few men in our tour of the villages and as our little military escort approached them, the women and children silently withdrew. But there was no unfriendliness, only an aloofness and dignity which I personally found fascinating. After umpiring a football match at the fort, and inspecting the troops, which I had no earthly right to do, we retraced our steps through the jungle and caught the steamer down river.

We displayed our trophies. By now I had the complete kit of a Naga warrior:

> yellow and red bamboo plaited helmet with crest of red goat's hair, red and white striped waistcloth, red and white striped blanket, red and yellow bamboo shin-guards, murderous dah (long-handled sword) in wooden sheath, murderous axe, also in wooden sheath, two ornamental spears covered with coloured goat's hair, except for the grip.

(Come to think of it, this was practically the costume worn by a Highland gentleman in the time of Macbeth, if you add a broad-sword, a murderous dagger, and a cowskin shield.) I didn't bring a hunting spear, because it is an ordinary seven-foot hunting spear, neither more nor less, with a large diamond-shaped blade.

How different was my descent of the Chindwin, compared with the ascent of it only a week or two ago. I had a Naga blanket, recently washed, for the Skipper, and he spread it proudly on his bed. The rest of my trophies were laid out on the afterdeck, and at every whistle stop I invited distinguished guests to a private view. They looked at me with new respect. They really began to believe that there might be a Technicolor adventure filmed on the Chindwin. Their Chindwin. I had gone up the river babbling of Nagas, and now here I was, returning with trophies from the back of beyond. I had seen Saramati and spoke of "sunny domes and caves of ice".

I telephoned Tarzan. "I'm back."

"I know. I heard about it. Now listen. Your boss is recalling you. He wants you home as soon as possible."

"How do you know?"

"You had two cables in the last three days. One is from your Mr Korda, the other is from some fellow called Cunynghame."

"That's Korda's right-hand man."

"Well, he can't spell his own name."

"He's a baronet."

"Oh, that explains it. One of that lot of Cunynghames. Well, what are you going to do?"

"I don't know. The Chindwin was great and so were the Nagas."

"Will they do your job?"

"I think so."

"So what do you want to do about Korda?"

"I'll have to go, but I must see the Inle Lake and the Shan States first."

"Exactly. Here are your marching orders. You will proceed with escort, by automobile, across Burma to Kalaw. Your contact there is Major Peffers of the Burma Rifles. You cross the Rangoon road at Myktila, where you will have tiffin and drop your military escort, who will return home. You will come back that way, so leave your laundry at Myktila. You can pick it up on the way back. On August 20, Peffers will drive you to Yawn-ghwe in the Shan States, where an interview has been arranged for you with the Sawbwa. The Sawbwas owe fealty to Burma, but consider themselves independent princes. Like a Highland chieftain, so treat him as one of us. If all goes well, you proceed to Inle Lake and spend the night there in the guesthouse on the lake. Next day, August 30th, return Mandalay. I'll tell Korda you can't be reached until then. Don't be late for dinner."

At Kalaw Major Peffers came to breakfast. He was Scottish, slow of speech, but by no means dumb. We left at ten, Peffers driving. He had never been to the Inle Lake.

Yawn-ghwe was a modern town and not very picturesque, but the Sawbwa's palace, called a Haw, was a fine big building with a lovely pagoda and shrine to the north of it, surrounded by a high wall. It is here that the famous Hpuungdaw-U image is brought and housed for two days of festival, which is one of the reasons why we were there, with Peffers to lend weight to my appearance. We entered the great hall, which was divided into many offices full of clerks by partitions made of strips of wood about three inches apart. In the centre was one of iron bars, with several mysterious chests in it. This was the strongroom of the Sawbwa.

The Shan Sawbwas were absolute rulers, spiritual and temporal, held powers of imprisonment and death and used them. They exacted instant obedience from their people, and if you carried the Sawbwa's seal in the state which he ruled, nothing was too good for you and all payment was refused. In the case of Yawn-ghwe, which had a neighbouring commissioner at Taunggyi, an appeal could be made, but in point of fact seldom was, for the Sawbwas were usually just princes. In any case, unless there was flagrant injustice, the Sawbwa's judgment would be upheld. The Sawbwas had nothing to do with the Burmese Government, and treated only with the King of England through the Governor of Burma himself. Shans considered themselves to be superior to Burmans, although they copied a lot of their customs and dress. Their language was quite different, and their country was known as the Federated Shan States. Theirs was an alliance and in return England protected them from any trouble.

We saw a secretary. Presently there was a stir in the inner office and we were loosed in. The Sawbwa sat at his office desk, behind him a long red screen. He was a smallish man with a quick, lively expression, clean-shaven, about thirty-five, Chinese in countenance, with very clever eyes and hair cut *en brosse*. When at ease, he laughed a great deal. He was extremely intelligent and spoke English with a heavy accent, but fluently, was very quick in the uptake and when he issued an order, his people jumped to it.

I had written to him already and he had a boat arranged and the guesthouse open. He was interested in my proposals for photographing the lake, the leg-rowers and the Golden Boat Festival, particularly when I said it would be in colour. I told him that I wanted to survey the exact course of the processions and to erect bamboo platforms in the lake for the cameras. He proposed lending me his motorboat to switch cameras quickly, which I would need to do, summoned a nephew and put us in his care. He was interested at hearing that I was flying back; his little son was just going to school in England, where his elder brother was already, but he had decided to send him by boat. I asked what school and was told the King's School, Canterbury. I told him it was a very good school. My school.

We then moved off through the town, down to the landing stages – ramshackle buildings on piles amongst the reeds. Waterways cut through the reeds led off in all directions; houses, monasteries and even farms were on piles or floating islands, and everywhere the long black boats slid to and fro, propelled by upright, beautifully balanced figures, standing like a stork on one leg, while they paddled with the other. The lake people were Inthas, and nowhere else in the world did people propel their boats so fast, so accurately or so strangely. Their paddles were long, with a big handle at the end and a short blade. Their leg was wrapped round it, and leverage obtained with their toes. Up went their leg and the paddle, and over went their body as they balanced sideways. Then the paddle dipped down through the water with a strong stroke, out and up again, till the sight of the jerky, bowing figure became hypnotic. From a distance, the motion was quite fantastic. Some rowers varied it by bringing the leg up and back with the paddle only as it dipped in the water and then let the paddle alone complete the stroke. When passing through the reed waterways they alternately punted and leg-rowed, and on the open lake they used a crazy sail. But whichever way they went, they moved fast, a good five miles an hour at least, and they never got tired.

Our boat was about sixty feet long and about three at its widest beam.

The freeboard, when loaded, was two inches, yet I have never felt safer in a boat. Even when a storm came up on the lake, it was as seaworthy as a Shetland boat. In the centre a bamboo-mat cabin had been placed, with bamboo seats. All our baggage was piled in and covered with mats, the Major and I took our seats and we were off, the nephew instructing the three boatmen.

For an hour we passed through the channels, gliding along past monasteries, shelters, fishermen hauling up their basket traps, children picking great red lotuses and twining their long stems around their bodies, solemn cranes fishing, women cutting boatfuls of the lake-grass to take home and dry in hanks for house roofs – all of them on, or in, or moving over crystal-clear water or pushing their way through reeds, shouting a greeting and questions to our boatmen and roaring with laughter when someone's hat got swept off by the rushes or when I tried my hand at leg-rowing and nearly fell in. The Major smiled paternally at my delight, my activity and my photographs, but I think, beneath the granite exterior, he was enjoying himself.

The channel, which was not the common canal to the open lake, was overgrown with great masses of a pestilent weed whose roots seemed made of india-rubber. All this would be cleared for the great day. A Shan would work like a beaver if there was a big festival in view, but seldom at any other time. The royal barge would consist of three great boats lashed together, covered with a bamboo platform and rowed by sixty leg-rowers. It would be covered with ornamentation in the shape of a golden swan and surmounted by a golden pyathat or palanquin. Behind it would follow everyone who had a boat that would float, about five hundred of them, every person in their best clothes and biggest turbans – even the children would have some clothes on. This whole procession, banging gongs and blowing trumpets, would sweep out of the reeds onto the open lake from the north while, from the south, another procession, brilliant with the orange and yellow robes of monks, advanced to meet them, bearing in their boat the sacred golden image of the Buddha, the Hpuungdaw-U – the Buddha of the Royal Boat. To the east, the hills rose sheer out of the water in black, jagged peaks against the morning sun; to the west they were lower and more rounded; in the south the open water stretched as far as I could see; while out of the northern reeds, the boats continued to pour, until the surface of the lake was covered with them.

This was the scene I wanted to have in the film, and can you blame me?

In the centre of the lake, not far from the guesthouse, the two processions would meet and the image would be transferred to the royal barge, in which it would be borne back in triumph to be placed in the Sawbwa's own shrine, where it would be adored by the people until the third day, when, with the same ceremonial, it would be brought back and restored to the care of the monks, until the next year came round again.

The guesthouse was approaching rapidly now, for the sail was up and there was a good breeze. The lake was choppy and we shipped water. We were passing rows of floating islands, each one "anchored" to the bottom by a long bamboo, stuck right through it. The fishermen laid their traps below these islands and used them for shelter against sudden storms. The bigger ones were even cultivated and vegetables grew like mad on them. Behind the resthouse, about fifty yards away, the dirwan's house was surrounded by quite a big weed raft, on which chickens strolled quite happily and his children played.

The guesthouse was built on piles in the centre of the lake. It was all bamboo, except the floor and pillars, which were wood. There was a spacious verandah and four little rooms with a wide passage between, and little gangways around the outside, like a ship. The kitchen and outhouses were separate. The water was so clear that you could see all the fishes swimming beneath and the grasses waving. The greatest depth of the lake was twenty feet and the average must have been ten or less. We explored everything and got settled in. Then, while John prepared dinner, I went over the side and had a swim, watched indulgently by the Major. At dinner, which was good, with the mountains looking very romantic, he suddenly became quite talkative, and it was then, for the first time, that I found he was enjoying himself.

It grew quite cold in the night, and there was a storm which made the water lap so loudly it was like being on a boat. John woke me at five but I had already been awakened by the dirwan's cock crowing lustily. It was queer to hear it out in the middle of the lake. And when I saw the grey, windswept lake, I shirked going in again. We were off at 6:30, with a following wind, and back at Yawn-ghwe in two hours. We returned by the main canal, which was prettier and shorter. There was a little carved rest-house about half-way. Some men were having their meal as we passed. The drivers were ready, for a wonder, and we got off at once to Kalaw.

While Peffers snored, I sat back and relaxed for the first time in six weeks, and dreamt of the glorious film I was going to make.

LONDON FILMS PRESENTS
BURMESE SILVER
from the book by
Edward Thompson, etc., etc.
Photographed by Georges Périnal
and Osmond Borrondaile, of course.
Designed by Vincent Korda, etc., etc.
Music by Miklos Rosza

I could hardly wait for the final glorious credit:

Directed by Michael Powell

Then there were the stars and co-stars, some of them over the main title, others under it. Let's see . . .

MERLE OBERON   CONRAD VEIDT

SABU

Leslie Howard perhaps? And I hoped Roger Livesey, whom I envisaged as my special discovery.

And then I imagined the film itself. I heard the opening music written by Miki Rozsa: gongs, fireworks, brazen horns . . . Conrad Veidt in his palanquin, a silk and tinsel umbrella held over him . . . Sabu commanding an elephant stampede . . . Leslie Howard as the dying but faithful friend of the Raja Gabriel in love scenes with the young Princess, Merle Oberon . . . other love scenes, less disembodied, with Roger as the young soldier sent in by the British Government . . . great Chinese and Indian and Burmese actors in scenes especially written for them . . . the NAGAS barring the way to the Lake Castle of Raja Gabriel . . . and the procession of boats that would open and close the film, the meeting of the Buddha and the Swan . . . the spectacular death of Conrad Veidt . . . I imagined it all . . . we must hurry! I must be back by Christmas! Thank goodness Alex was in a hurry too . . .

"Sir! Soon we are at Mektila. Can I have the money for the dhobie?"

Mektila already! And it was only three in the afternoon. By six o'clock, in spite of hundreds of bullock-carts on the crown of the road, we were in Mandalay and I was telling everybody at the Club that twelve hours ago I was in the middle of the Inle Lake. Nobody believed me. I hardly believed it myself.

AUGUST 31, 1937
CUNYNGHAME TO POWELL
RETURN AT ONCE. WHERE ARE YOU?

I opened the door of his office.

"I'm back."

While I was talking to Cunynghame in his outer office, Alex came out of his room with a few people.

"Ah, there you are Micky. Welcome back. We are going to run Eisenstein's *Alexander Nevsky*. Come and see it with us."

He pressed off, followed by his wave of adherents and guests, and I followed. There was nothing I less wanted to see than Teutonic knights plunging through the ice into the black waters of the lake, but it meant keeping close to Alex, so I followed. We saw about an hour of Eisenstein's slow-motion epic, and even for Alex that was enough. We left the little projection room which, with the cutting rooms, had been built close to the Old House for Alex's convenience. Alex was deep in consultation with Bill Hornbeck, the American who was his chief editor, for whom I had a considerable admiration. Besides being a good cutter, he was a grand organizer. Nevertheless, Alex had time to say to me: "Micky, come and see me. On Thorsday."

I went over to the scenario department and demanded a script of *Burmese Silver*. I had been promised that it would be ready for me on my return. The story department had no truck with directors: they reported to Alex direct, and they got their orders from him. Someone telephoned to Cunynghame and he okayed my request. Lajos Biro himself handed me the slim typescript. It credited Edward Thompson, the author of the book, but not Robert Vansittart, the author of the screenplay.

"This script is confidential, Mr Powell. Alex says you are to read it and discuss it with him on Thursday."

I read it.

As it happened, that afternoon was the usual monthly get-together with the press by the stars, artists under contract, actors and resident geniuses working at Denham. Vansittart was there with his beautiful wife. He saw me, and waved to me to come over.

"Well, how did you like Burma?"

"Very much."

"And my script?"

"Not very much."

He made the sort of face which the French call a *moue*, and skipping any further conversation with this formidable character I moved diplomatically away. I had not been kind. But if amateur lion-tamers stick their head in the lion's jaws, they have nobody to blame but themselves if it gets bitten off. The Robert Vansittart I knew and admired was afraid of nothing and nobody – a fascinating and complex personality, a charming man, a neglected prophet who, like Winston Churchill, had been ignored and driven into the wilderness by little men. If Alex, for his own good reasons, had commissioned and paid Robert Vansittart a large sum of money to write the screenplay of *Burmese Silver*, as well as some heady little lovesongs for a projected Arabian Nights film, it was Alex's business, not mine, and I looked forward with interest to Thursday.

I had assumed that Vansittart would be there and was expecting a battle. But, as usual, Alex took the wind out of my sails. There was nobody with him in the big room with the windows looking on the lush valley of the little River Colne.

"Micky, I have read your Burmese diary and enjoyed it very much. Thank you for taking so much trouble."

Oh God, what author could resist such an opening? I was putty in those masterful hands.

"Now, we shall not make *Burmese Silver* immediately."

My heart sank.

"The political situation is very serious, as you know, and nobody knows whether there will be war this autumn or not. It is too big a risk to send a film unit to India or Burma, Micky."

His voice was very sympathetic. I was staring at him dumbly. Was all my research to be wasted? Were all the props and costumes that I had collected and sent back to be mothballed? Remember, it was my first picture after months of waiting. Alex's voice was very sympathetic. A craftsman himself, who had struggled to make his first picture and to get the money for them, he understood how I felt.

"Be patient, Micky. We will make *Burmese Silver*. But meanwhile, I want you to make another film for us."

My head came up. Another film? What film? Nobody had even spoken to me about another film! When Alex delivered his sentence on all my work in Burma, I had assumed that my contract would be allowed to run out, and that I would be once more facing the future of an independent film director, in a market where everyone was too scared of Adolf Hitler to back a feature film. Alex picked up a script from his desk and handed it to me. I took it and glanced at the title. It was *The Spy in Black*.

The intercom telephone buzzed. I am sure that Alex had a button under his desk which he pressed with his foot when he thought an interview had gone on long enough. He picked up the telephone.

"Yes, Conning-ham? Yes, Micky is leaving."

He switched off and looked at me benevolently.

"You know that our company, London Films, has made a contract with Columbia to make four feature films for them, using our facilities and our contract stars."

Of course I knew nothing of the sort.

"Irving Asher is producing them for me. He's an old friend of yours, is he not?"

I nodded.

"You will have Conrad Veidt and Valerie Hobson as your stars. The script is adapted from a famous book by a Scottish writer called Storer Clouston. The story takes place somewhere in Scotland, so you will be quite at home. Read it, and come and see me . . . next Thorsday."

Of course I knew who J. Storer Clouston was. I knew who everybody was in the literary world, thanks to my Aunt Ethel and *The Times Literary Supplement*. Storer Clouston was one of *Blackwood*'s authors – the famous Scottish magazine *Blackwood*, known affectionately to the initiated as "Maga". It was published in Edinburgh and impeccably produced. John Buchan and Robert Louis Stevenson had cut their literary teeth on "Maga". Storer Clouston had made his name by a short novel entitled *The Lunatic at Large*. I went through Cunynghame's office with my nose in the script, came out of the Old House, turned right and took the Elephant Walk, where Zoli Korda had shot all the pick-up shots of the elephants dancing in *Elephant Boy*. There were hundred-year-old beeches all the way along the right bank of the Colne, and the path went nearly a mile to the end of the lot, which finished in gravel and cement and a telephone kiosk and all the barrenness of a studio lot which had not been used since *The Ghost Goes West*. The life-sized ship which had been created for *Fire Over England*, made of wood and plaster and firmly bedded in concrete, was still sailing among the rushes of the Colne.

By the time I returned to the studio, I had read the whole script. It was awful: wordy and quite obviously adapted from a novel. By now I knew the way Alex worked, and guessed that he had something up his sleeve. This script had Irving Asher's name on it as producer, so presumably he had accepted it for better or worse. It was written by a member of a famous English theatrical family, who knew all about writing for the theatre and nothing about writing for films. I had crossed swords with him once before and the result had been disastrous. The script had lots of pleasant dialogue scenes, but pleasant British dialogue scenes do not make a pleasant film. The screenwriter had followed the original story fairly closely, so there wasn't even a good part for Conrad Veidt. The best thing about the script was the title *The Spy in Black*, which he'd had the sense to keep. As for Valerie Hobson, a crisp young beauty whom I had admired from a distance, she was being asked to play the usual brainless, nerveless, boneless English heroine. Yes. Alex certainly must have a scheme. And we would know . . . "next Thorsday".

I sought out Irving Asher. When Irving had taken over the running of Warner Brothers' English studios, he had given me lots of work and I was only too glad to get it. But I soon outgrew Warners' quota factory, and Irving and I had several differences of opinion before I went to make *The Edge of the World*. It might be thought that I would be nervous about working with Irving again, and would be tactful about it. On the contrary, I now felt that I was on my home ground and he was the incomer, also employed by London Films.

I found him in the studio restaurant, and got down to brass tacks. "Irving, I believe I am assigned to direct your picture *The Spy in Black*, and I have the impression that I am just about the last person you would want to do it."

He couldn't have been nicer. "No, Micky, don't get me wrong. This is just the subject for you, and I couldn't want anybody better for it. What did you think of the script?"

I'd hoped he wouldn't ask. "There's too much dialogue for a ninety-minute picture," I said. "What does Alex think of it?"

"I don't think he's read it yet."

Yes. Alex certainly must have some scheme up his sleeve.

We foregathered on Thursday, in the ante-room outside Alex's office. It was usually crowded, but today there was only a small man making notes on a piece of paper. Irving arrived, accompanied by the author of the screen-play. We nodded to each other. The author was bristling: he had obviously heard something to his disadvantage. Irving was ready to fight for the script too, but looked a bit uncertain, like a champion who doesn't know from which direction the attack is coming. Alex had this effect on people.

Irving said to me: "Have you ever heard of Emeric Pressburger?"

I said that I hadn't. As a matter of fact, I had seen the name on a screen treatment of Tolstoy's *Kreutzer Sonata*. I had been asked to read it, and had reported favourably, and had remembered the name.

"He's one of Alex's contract writers," Irving went on.

Of course, in a large organization like London Films, with many hundreds of people working there, it was perfectly possible for two people under contract not to know each other.

At this point the character in the corner, who had continued making notes unnoticed by any of us, stood up and introduced himself. "Excuse me, I am Pressburger." He made a little bow. We shook hands all around.

With perfect timing, the door opened and Cunynghame put his head out. "Alex will see you now, gentlemen." We trooped in.

Alex sat at the head of a long table, with Cunynghame at his left hand, and in front of him a lot of books, folios, and so on. I took the seat next to Cunynghame. Irving sat on Korda's right hand, with his writer on his right hand, who was still bristling and looked more than ever like an honest English cricketer going out to defend his wicket in a test match. Pressburger took a seat a little further down the table, leaving a tactful gap between himself and the screenwriter and giving himself a fairly unrestricted view of Alex and the rest of us.

Irving said: "Alex, I . . ."

Alex said: "Irving, will you stay after the meeting. I want to ask your advice about something."

Irving shut up – but not without glancing around the table to see if we were impressed by the fact that Alex wanted to ask his advice, not he Alex's.

Alex began to doodle and said to no one in particular: "Well now, I have asked Emeric to read the script, and he has things to say to us."

He continued to doodle with great concentration, while Emeric produced a very small piece of rolled-up paper, and addressed the meeting. I listened, spellbound.

Since talkies took over the movies, I had worked with some good writers, but I had never met anything like this. In the silent days, the top screenwriters were technicians rather than dramatists. They knew that things had to move and they moved them. In the America of those days, only the screenplays of D. W. Griffith indicated a wide theatrical knowledge and a general culture, both in the images on the screen, and in the titles which accompanied the silent film and involved the spectator in the action. I was familiar with all this from my years in France, for the European cinema remained highly literate and each country, conscious of its separate culture and literature, strove to outdo the other. All this was changed by the talkies. America, with its enormous wealth and enthusiasm and its technical resources, waved the big stick. Films must talk! And they must talk American. Famous writers and dramatists all over the world, from Nobel Prize winners to Edgar Wallace, were hurried to Hollywood, put into rabbit hutches and told to write dialogue. Three years of confusion and agony followed, at the end of which eight men in Hollywood and New York had the whole world's film market in their pockets. The European film no longer existed. The national film was a thing of the past, or existed only on sufferance, or because Paris is a nice place to live. Only the great German film business was prepared to fight the American monopoly, and Dr Goebbels soon put a stop to that in 1933. But the day that Emeric walked out of his flat, leaving the key in the door to save the storm-troopers the trouble of breaking it down, was the worst day's work that the clever doctor ever did for his country's reputation, as he was very soon to find out. As I said, I listened spellbound to this small Hungarian wizard, as Emeric unfolded his notes, until they were at least six inches long. He had stood Storer Clouston's plot on its head and completely restructured the film.

The action of The Spy in Black took place during the 1914–18 war, and the place was the anchorage of Scapa Flow, which was still, in 1938, the base for the British North Sea Fleet. It is in the Orkneys, not more than fifty miles from Foula, as the gannet flies! Emeric praised the atmosphere, but pointed out that the object of the exercise was to provide a stunning part for a great star, Conrad Veidt, and in the present script no such part existed. It was also necessary to provide an intriguing part for Miss Hobson, who was no dummy. No such part existed, and so long as we were bound to the iron rails of Storer Clouston's plot, it would never exist. Emeric threw it out and invented a new one. He brought action which had taken place off-stage in the book and in the existing script onto the screen.

Instead of the shadowy, conventional spy figures that were usual in British thrillers of this kind, he invented a whole gallery of masculine types, led by the magnificent Conrad Veidt as a gallant U-boat commander who, acting under sealed orders, risked his command and his own person on a secret mission to sink half the British fleet.

In the original story, the "spy in black" had been a Scottish minister of religion whose black cloth had been a symbol of his respectability and anonymity. (In the weeks to come, we racked our brains, and turned the studio wardrobe inside out, to find various ways to clothe the gallant Captain Hardt in black.)

Emeric went placidly on with his exposition, looking neither to right nor to left. I glanced across the table at Irving and his unfortunate screenwriter. They were sitting with their mouths open. Nobody had ever told them that when you buy the rights to a famous book which turns out to be useless for a screenwriter's purpose, you keep the title and throw away the book. That lesson had been learnt many times by Alex and Emeric in Germany in the past. I looked at Alex. His doodle was assuming fantastically complicated proportions.

As for Miss Valerie Hobson, Emeric had turned her into a double agent, which had two advantages: she could play love scenes with Conrad Veidt as the supposed German agent, but she could also play love scenes with Sebastian Shaw, who was one of the most interesting actors on Alex's contract list. London Films had a number of expensive artists under contract, and Emeric had obviously been briefed by Alex to use them. I knew Shaw because he had played the lead in Jerry Jackson's production of *Caste*, but I had lost touch with him since then. In *The Spy in Black*, he was to play an ornament of the British Navy, an apparent traitor who turns out to be a double agent as well. In order to introduce our new heroine properly, Emeric had thrown in a kidnapping and a murder, which would provide a very nice little part as a schoolmistress for young June Duprez, the baby on Alex's contract list, who was reputed to be as dumb as she was beautiful.

At this point, Alex had completed his doodle and bestirred himself. Before anybody else could speak, he spoke. "Well now, Micky and Emeric, that all sounds very nice. So why don't you go away and find Conrad Veidt and Valerie and work out the rest of the script with them?"

He rose to his feet and we automatically rose too. Irving's screenwriter seemed on the verge of an apoplectic fit. Irving's eyes bulged slightly. He was not used to having command of the script transferred from himself to the people who were actually going to make the film. But we presented a solid Denham front and he was an intruder.

We made for the door and he followed us, but Alex was by no means willing to let him escape and possibly sow dissension in our ranks.

"Irving," he said. "Please wait. You remember I wanted to speak to you. I have been talking with Larry and Ralph" (Laurence Olivier and Ralph Richardson were two of Alex's favourite contract artists) "about the film you are making with them. They are not very happy about certain aspects of the script." (The film was *Q-Planes*.)

Irving gave up the struggle and remained behind with Alex and Cunynghame. Outside the door, the screenwriter paused and sat down. He was obviously going to wait for Irving in order to make his complaint. I searched in my mind for some form of farewell which would be relevant and came up with "Chin, chin", which seemed to me to be about his age group. Emeric and I then made a beeline for the studio restaurant.

Now I am as sure as I am sure of anything that this whole conference had been foreseen and manipulated by Alex, but how cleverly he had done it. He and Imre Pressburger (Imre was Emeric's Hungarian Christian name) and Lajos Biro, the head of the scenario department, three ingenious Hungarians, must have had a meeting and decided all the changes which were necessary, both from the entertainment point of view and for the maximum employment of the London Film contract artists. The rest was then left to Pressburger and me. Alex, of course, and Biro would only appear in their official capacities, which nobody dared to question. In the same way, Alex had ensured the outcome of the revisions of the script, by linking Emeric and me with the two biggest stars in the studio. He didn't tell Irving Asher to keep out of it. He merely made it impossible for him to get into it. To use a fine Goldwynism, he included him out. The writer and the director of the new film were left in the most enviable of positions: to work out the new script in company with two highly intelligent and experienced actors, who were to play the principal parts.

A script conference which could have gone on all day, and left the participants floundering and divided, was over in a quarter of an hour. A story which consisted of nothing more than a situation and an anecdote, had been turned into an efficient and entertaining little thriller. The part of Captain Hardt, as interpreted by Conrad Veidt, was to measure up to some of his best performances.

Conrad Veidt was seated alone at a table by the window drinking coffee when Emeric and I arrived at the studio restaurant. Emeric and I exchanged a glance. This magnificent animal was reserved for us. Then we looked at each other. I saw a short, compact man, with beautiful and observant eyes, and a broad intellectual forehead, formally and neatly dressed. He was a Hungarian Jew, which meant that he was witty, ingenious, creative and sports-loving. I learnt later that he had been a runner himself, over a distance of 440 metres. He had also been a professional violinist and had played in theatre orchestras. Although small in stature, he looked well made and strong, both in person and in his convictions. And he obviously feared nobody, not even Alex Korda.

Emeric saw a young lean Englishman (for the Burmese trip had brought me down to about 148 pounds and the sun had burnt me black), with a toothbrush moustache and piercing blue eyes. At the moment, they had a look of veneration in them. They had seen a marvel: a screenwriter who could really write. I was not going to let him get away in a hurry. I had always dreamt of this phenomenon: a screenwriter with the heart and mind of a novelist, who would be interested in the medium of film, and who would have wonderful ideas, which I would turn into even more wonderful images, and who only used dialogue to make a joke or to clarify the plot. I congratulated him on the conjuring trick he had pulled with poor Storer Clouston's plot.

"Let's talk to Connie Veidt before Irving gets at him," I said. I was learning rapidly from the Hungarians. Emeric, like me, looked upon Conrad Veidt as a legendary figure. For us, he *was* the great German cinema. For us, he was invention, control, imagination, irony and elegance. He was the master technician of the camera, who knew where every light was placed. Only in the English language did he lose his magnificent authority, walking like a tongue-tied Samson amongst the Philistines. I went over and stood at his table. He looked up and I got the full impact of those deep blue eyes under black brows.

I said: "Mr Veidt, my name is Michael Powell. Alexander Korda has told me that we are to work together on *The Spy in Black*."

He said: "Ye-e-e-s." Pumas purr like that.

"May I sit down?" A thin smile gave me permission. I sat down and looked at him across the table. "I imagine that Alexander Korda has discussed with you the changes that Pressburger is making in the script. But I know your work, and the theme as I see it, is about a man who is completely devoted to his duty."

I wouldn't say that he relaxed, but a slight thaw set in. He fetched a monocle from some recess and a handkerchief from his breast-pocket, polished the monocle, put it in his eye and looked at me with attention. "Proceed," he said. I waved across the crowded restaurant to Emeric to come and join us.

The Old House at Denham was a Hungarian enclave transported to Buckinghamshire. There Alex had his office and a suite of rooms. The office in the main block was only for state occasions. His brother Zoli had an office there too, when he was not plowing through Congo swamps making *Sanders of the River*, or frying in the Sudan to make *The Four Feathers*. Vincent Korda had his studio there. Lajos Biro had his scenario department there. Miklos Rozsa had his piano in one of the rooms, and the room above him and the room below him shared in the composition of his

themes, whether they liked it or not. Now, for three weeks, the four of us –
Conrad Veidt, Valerie Hobson, Michael Powell and Emeric Pressburger –
had a room there too. It was right up in the roof of the red-brick Old
House, and it was sparsely furnished with four chairs and a table. But what
did we care! We were creating a film!

Emeric! Do you remember those wonderful days when we were
working with an actor we venerated: one of the greatest names in
European cinema, one of the most romantic and magnetic men alive. Best
of all, we were not working with him on some historical personage. We
were creating a real man with a man's appetites and resourcefulness.
Valerie was a tall, strong, intelligent girl with glorious eyes and a quick wit
(too quick a wit, some people thought, but I had suffered too many English
ladies to complain about that). Emeric would arrive every morning with
the scenes roughed out and we would tear into them as if we were making
home movies. It was great. Connie and Valerie were both serious,
dedicated artists, but we were all more often laughing than we were crying.
They would act the scenes out in front of us and we would watch, eager and
excited, chipping in with our comments or suggestions in the middle of the
scene, scribbling down ideas to be debated afterwards, while up from the
floor below came the sound of Rozsa's piano as he composed themes for
pictures yet unborn, including *The Thief of Bagdad*.

In this way Alex, in the years just before the war, had begun to dream
up his films and make his truly personal ones. At the start, with the
foundation of London Films, it had all been an exciting adventure. Alex's
first support came from the important men and women whom he had met
in London. His company was truly named London Films. The kind of rich
and aristocratic people who enjoyed Alex, and whom Alex enjoyed, and
who were amused to play with this new toy the talkie, were also amused to
challenge Hollywood on its own ground, attending premières of big, lush,
star-studded films full of English accents, even though, quite often, the
English was ornamented with the baroque accents of Central Europe. In
this, Alex only imitated Hollywood. He gathered together at Denham all
the available big names and hurled them into costume pictures. He hired
great European directors, and also many not-so-great American directors.
But, unheard and unseen, the young British cinema was learning from these
old hams. Alex himself was learning. He had become as English as the
English at seeing a joke against themselves. *The Private Life of Henry VIII*
not only satirized a whole decade of film-making, including Alex's own,
but started off the true British modern cinema.

At the same time, Alex had made the British film what it should be: a
power in the land, a mirror for England. The kind of men who backed him
and befriended him were well-read, only semi-educated, but representatives of a great past and a great tradition. A hint or two across the dining

table from men like these, and from their clever and beautiful wives, had been enough to set Alex off on rediscovering the British Empire. The fathers and grandfathers of these men and women had casually created it. Great epic films of British triumphs and disasters in Africa and India followed. Zoli Korda vanished for a year or two and *Sanders of the River* and *The Four Feathers* were the result. These were magnificent achievements, and there were many others, as well as many spectacular failures. With the help of the American distributors Alex could have won through, but the Hollywood men were too blind to see that this healthy competition from London was as good for them as it was good for England. Only MGM seemed to be taking advantage of the lessons which Alex was giving the world in developing British talents, which had been unsuspected until now, for the world cinema. Valiant fighters like Mickey Balcon, who had all his life tried to make big films with small resources, took courage from Alex's daring and success. By the time I joined Alex, these great days were over, Hitler was growing more and more powerful, a Continental war was becoming more and more certain, and the great Denham Studios ceased to be an instrument in the hands of Alex and his friends and was becoming a liability. I just got in under the wire.

Alex turned to politics and politicians, for the reasons so beautifully and aptly described by Rudyard Kipling as "the ties of common funk". He was a Hungarian national, surrounded by family, friends and fellow film-makers who would all be enemy aliens when the war was declared, which, with Central European clear-sightedness, they knew it would be. He set about safeguarding his own and their positions. Alex didn't have to go round about to ask favours. All doors were open to him, even Ribbentrop's. By taking steps to safeguard his Denham kingdom, Alex also saved the British film industry from disappearing.

Alex had been a lavish host and an unfailing friend to many men who were now moving into power as the shadow of Hitler darkened Europe. They had told him their secrets and fears. He had talked of the speed and power of the cinema as a weapon of propaganda. He was only repeating what Dr Goebbels had already shown the world, but the British leaders were impressed. Over the cigars and brandy one evening, he promised Churchill and Vansittart that he would turn all the resources of Denham Studios to making a big anti-Nazi propaganda film on the day war was declared. In return, he asked that the British film industry, as it existed in 1938, full of young, experienced, enthusiastic film-makers (who had learned their job from the great international film-makers who had been working all these years principally at Denham and Pinewood), should be regarded and used as an essential war weapon, which could go immediately into action against the enemy, and which, when the Ministry of Information was inevitably formed to control the press and propaganda, would be one of its main weapons. He got his agreement. I believe it was a verbal one. Without it, the British film industry might have vanished as completely and totally as it did under the pressure of the 1914–18 war, and there would have been no basis and encouragement in the early days for planning and making films like *The Lion Has Wings* and *49th Parallel* and *London Can Take It*.

Leningrad, March 6, 1982

I am looking back at those months before the 1939 war and dictating these words to my micro-cassette tape recorder, sitting in a bleak and efficient box which is nowadays called a hotel bedroom. It is not very cold, only a few degrees below zero and the Neva is only half-frozen over. The Pavlova film unit have just left for location, two hours beyond the city limits on a frozen lake, where they are staging a party with sleighs and troikas and the inevitable gypsies dancing and singing. I think the reason that Tsarist Russia always seemed to be putting on parties in films, is because the Russians themselves adore parties. Emil Louteanou's eyes sparkle as he exclaims: "And he holds out the bottle of champagne to Anna Pavlova! Real champagne!"

Two weeks ago, we were in Cuba at the Paso de Caballos, with the smoke drifting over the shuttered houses and the unburied corpses of that particular sequence of the film. Films are a greater plaything than ever, and for extravagance and innocence, it would be hard to beat the Russians. Well, they've earned their right to a little fun, but who would have thought that I would be lending them my advice and experience forty-four years after The Spy in Black *and those happy, creative days in the old house at Denham Studios.*

Today I had a flare-up of all the muscles in my body. At least the doctors call it a flare-up, but it is more like a rust-up. Apparently, it comes from thinking that your body will last forever, and thanks to my dear mother, I always thought it would. I think I must have been using it particularly hard towards the end of last year, and it suddenly made me a Christmas present of this. Six months before I had been capering about Hollywood for the benefit of the Arena Programme for the BBC. Now, overnight I couldn't bend down, stand up, or walk. The eternal juvenile, I have become a character actor and an over-played one at that. The doctors have given me tablets which will, they hope, melt the fire in my bones.

I don't know what has been the overriding motive for this new breed of men whom we call film directors. Arrogance, money and women, I suppose. My own motive has been to learn – to learn and travel widely at every opportunity. *Burmese Silver* sent me to Burma, in spite of the fretful frowns of Cunynghame, so when the new script of *The Spy in Black* was approved, and we all met again in Alex's office, I announced that I was going to the Orkneys.

"What for?" demanded Irving, who detested location work and suffered agonies when any of his chickens were off the lot for more than two hours at a time.

"Because Scapa Flow is in the Orkneys, and I've never been to the Orkneys and I'm going to make a film about the Orkneys," I said in an unnecessarily truculent tone.

"You made that film in the Hebrides . . ." Irving went on.

"In the Shetlands," I snarled.

"All those northern islands are the same."

This offended one of my dearest principles. "Every island is different from the other," I explained. "Anyway, I can't make a film about the Orkneys unless I go there."

"Let the boy go," said Alex dreamily. Irving growled something and we left that night on the night train to Aberdeen.

All four of us were "Foula Regulars". The Powell legend was being created. From now on, no project, however big, however small, would be initiated by me without some veteran to keep the tradition going. I did this instinctively. I was not a loner. I had been taught by Rex Ingram, and had rapidly learnt the lesson, that the best way to make a work of art was to surround yourself with a band of brothers, master craftsmen, who would give you of their best, and who would expect you to lead them to triumph. The memory of those golden days in France supported me through the lean years in England. I never gave up on my ideas, I never gave up my ideals. I was an uncomfortable person to have about.

On this reconnaissance (for I had promised to be back within three days for a conference with Vincent Korda over the sets) I was accompanied by Vernon Campbell Sewell (lately skipper of the supply ship *Vedra*), Buddy Farr (Vernon's right arm) and, of course, Bill Paton. We were a formidable party. We had speed and stamina, and Vernon's eyeglass gave us class.

On our arrival at Kirkwall, the executive capital of the islands, my first act was to go to the local hotel and find out where Storer Clouston, the author of the story, lived. He had a house on the shores of Scapa Flow, looking southward, and he was at home. I hired a car, and in twenty minutes we were marching up to his front door, demanding a cup of tea, a technique I had learned from John Seabourne. It has two advantages. It puts your host under an obligation to you for assuming his hospitality, and you get a cup of tea.

Storer Clouston and his wife, family and animals were thrilled at our arrival. They had, of course, no idea that the film was on the point of being

made. The rights had been sold some time ago, and they had given up hope
of ever seeing it. But they had all seen *The Edge of the World*. Now here
was the maker of that film announcing that within three weeks *The Spy in
Black* would be in production. Clouston was a nice, tweedy, bookish man
who had lived in the Orkneys for years and had the answer to most of our
questions. Most of the islands and places in his story were there before our
eyes. It was a lovely, pale, calm, northern day. The waters of Scapa Flow
lapped at our feet. The great humpy island of Hoy, the only really high
island in the Orkneys, reared up to the southwest, and we vowed to stand
on top of it that very afternoon. I had brought maps and charts in the town
on arrival, and armed with these we pelted Clouston with questions, and
left him as flat as a gutted herring.

By three o'clock, we were in a hired motorboat, crossing the sound to
Hoy. The island was a sheep-run and uninhabited, but it had some
interesting Iron Age monuments and we were pledged to stand on the top
and look down at the Old Man of Hoy, a famous rock stack, or pillar,
which is a landmark for seamen and a dangerous goal for rock climbers. I
had read about it in the *North Sea Pilot* and had determined to use it in the
film as the secret landing point for Conrad Veidt, commander of the
German U-boat, after it has penetrated the mine defences of the islands. We
were soon lying on the short turf on the edge of the cliff which looks down
on the Old Man. He is an impressive figure, about 600 feet high and
completely detached from the island, having been created by the howling
winds and thirsty seas which never cease to surge around his feet. Only the
great stacks of St Kilda can be compared with the Old Man for grandeur.
And he's dangerous. His sides are rotten with grass and moss and the litter
of sea birds. The chimney is full of loose stones. His shape is slightly crazy.
He is a sinister old man.

I could hardly be dragged away from the cliff by the others. I was
fascinated. We ran down to the harbour and crossed in the motorboat to
Stromness. We already knew Kirkwall, and I planned to stay in Stromness
that night and explore the new town that evening.

My rough plan was to use this survey as a briefing for Vernon and
Buddy. I intended them to operate beyond the clutches and control of
Irving Asher. There was no question of my being able to return to the
islands again: I had too much to do already in preparation and casting.
As for coming with a second unit to pick up essential shots with doubles,
we simply couldn't afford it. It wasn't on. But I knew I could screw a few
hundred pounds out of the budget to keep my wildcat film unit going until
they had got all the atmospheric and establishing shots, using local doubles
for the principals in the story. They could both operate a camera, and
Vernon, of course, was mad about the Navy and was also a marine
engineer and a highly ingenious handyman capable of camouflaging

anything and everything. He was also a qualified sound engineer and, although not a cameraman, understood the principles of photography. I consulted nobody about this, of course – least of all Irving, who would have felt bound to inform the unions, and the studio departments that would normally be involved. Upon our return I labelled it as a reconnaissance and research unit trip of two people, which sounded routine and got them their money.

We had a brief and rather secret conference with Poppa Day, who was now in charge of all trick-shots and special effects at Denham and who, it may be recalled, was an old friend of mine from Teddington and Gaumont-British. Poppa was the greatest trick-man and film wizard that I've ever known. Like all wizards, he was highly practical as well. He looked like a wizard, for he used to wear lightweight floppy suits draped over a very thin body, so that you felt there was hardly anything there, and he had big round spectacles, which he wore over his nose, and a hat which he was continually dancing on in frustration. His manner was jerky and impatient, and as he thought about a thousand times quicker than anybody else, that was rather natural. He was one of the greatest moviemakers that I have ever known. I told him what we were up to, and that our little unit would pick up all sorts of photographs of the island in the 1914–18 war, so that he could use them as a basis for his matte shots. We talked this over with Hugh Stewart, who was going to be the editor of the film, and swore him to secrecy about the establishing shots we were going to get for him without benefit of chapel so to speak. It might seem strange to the reader to hear how much work went into concealing the fact that we were doing our best to improve the quality of the film, but that is normal in the film business. If you know what you want and are determined to get it, there are always people who are determined to get in on the act, turn it to their own advantage and increase the cost of the picture. My aim was simple. I had been jumped into a picture which was looked on as another studio thriller, without any opportunity to do proper research and preparation, and with no apparent possibility of having the sort of establishing shots which are necessary in creating atmosphere. The producer wasn't interested. It was just another studio picture off his plate. It was up to me to get what I wanted in my own way.

On returning to the studio, I found an ally in an unexpected quarter – Vincent Korda. Vincent was the only one of the three Korda brothers who was an artist. He was a painter and was living happily in Paris when Alex invaded England, built Denham Studios and brought Vincent over to be head of the art department. If you had seen the brothers casually, you might have written down Alex, with his intelligently ugly face, bifocal glasses, his elegant suits, and the elegant way he smelt, as a newspaper tycoon. Zoli was obviously a man of the City and probably a journalist.

Vincent was equally obviously a peasant. He was rather good-looking, but looked as if somebody had sketched him in pastel and then crumpled the portrait carelessly before throwing it away. He moved in an aura of bohemianism, which was almost visible around him. He had a tousled, curly mop of hair, with a hat perched on top. He wore clothes until they fell off him.

He had crafty, observant eyes: a peasant's eyes – a painter's eyes. He was usually smiling, but his eyes gave him away. There was always something going on in the brain behind those eyes. When Emeric and I were writing the script, we met him on the lot. He was accompanied by his dog, Nuisance.

"Micky and Emeric, why do you not write a part for Nuisance in your film?"

"What kind of part, Vincent?"

Vincent shrugged. "A dog's part." I think that Nuisance got into the ferryboat scene.

We discussed using revamps of sets already standing on the lot. In some cases I agreed, but in most cases I didn't. I explained that the scale was entirely different in the islands, because of poverty, because of primitive materials, because of the terrible winds in winter. The houses hug the ground. The rooms are tiny, and a man of six feet two like Conrad Veidt should look like a black giant in the white box-like interiors. Vincent understood at once, and I found him most sympathetic to my demands. With his painter's imagination he visualized at once a world totally different from the fake-Tudor and warming pans of the average British art department. We decided that the submarine scenes, which were night shots, would be done in the big open-air tank on the lot. Vernon would sketch and supervise the cramped interior of the submarine and supply most of the gadgets. The rest would be stock shots from the library.

I was thrilled by this unconventional collaboration, this willingness of Vincent's to throw away stock doors and windows and create a new scale of things for the actors to move and act in. I showed him photographs of Scottish crofts and Scottish manses and Vernon returned with a boxful of photographs of the 1914–18 war in Scapa Flow and a portfolio of photographs and sketches upon which Poppa Day pounced. Vincent was one of the few people that Poppa liked around Denham, and together they planned some beautiful shots, recreating Stromness as it was in 1915 and filling Scapa Flow, as seen through the window of the schoolhouse, with the whole British North Sea Fleet at anchor.

A detached historian, Thucydides for instance, would have observed with amusement the enthusiasm with which we all rushed into making this film about a heroic German *Unterseeboot* commander penetrating the defences of Scapa Flow with the worst intentions. With the Munich

Agreement only weeks behind us, and the prospect of a major war with Germany in 1939 almost a dead certainty, what made the humour of it even grimmer was the fact that Scapa Flow was still the main anchorage of the North Sea Fleet, and its defences, land, sea and air, were ridiculously out of date. Moreover, there was no secrecy, as we had amply proved by our lightning tour of the islands. The area was open to anybody, and maps and charts could be bought anywhere. Calculating the odds, Thucydides would have concluded that the picture, if made, would never be shown to the public, and if it were shown we would all be shot as traitors and saboteurs. Thucydides, however, would have been wrong.

Irving Asher was fortunately kept too busy by Ralph Richardson and Larry Olivier and Tim Whelan on *Q-Planes* (a comedy-thriller which the stars and director were happily rewriting and making up as they went along) to be able to take more than a token interest in preparations for *The Spy in Black*. We kicked off with a conventional little sequence featuring lovely June Duprez as the good schoolteacher leaving her simple island home for the first time. By encouraging June to underplay, and by leaving the camera on those ruby lips and Babylonian eyes, I made quite an impression on the Old Guard with my dailies. They started to wonder why they had told Alex that she was nothing but a beautiful dummy. I completed the kidnapping sequence in the studio with some very phoney process shots. But then the fun started. For the next ten days I was to play out most of the main drama and love story of the film in the cramped quarters of the schoolhouse. Vincent had created a delightful doll's house, and Conrad Veidt in black leather, dwarfed the sets. As it was a suspense picture and I had to shoot it in about five weeks, I was shooting mainly in close-ups, with one eye on the cutting rooms. Even with Conrad Veidt in the close-ups, this was not the way to impress producers. After a couple of days of this, Jerry Jackson at Teddington Studios got a ring from Irving, asking him to come over. Irving met him at the screening room. He was looking bombastic, which is the way a weak character looks when he is about to make a strong decision.

"I think I shall have to take Micky off the picture," he told Jerry. "He's been on it nearly ten days and I don't understand a word of it."

Jerry's heart sank. He loved me and could see my head rolling.

"What's wrong?" he asked, settling into his seat in the theatre.

"I'll show you the last three days' work," was all that Irving said. The dailies had not been broken down, and Jerry saw them just as they had come from being assembled in the cutting-room.

When the lights went up Irving looked at him. "Well," he said, "what do you think?"

"I think you ought to have your head examined," said Jerry.

"What do you mean?" asked Irving, half-relieved, and at the same time half-regretting his proposed massacre of the innocents. Jerry had been watching the schoolhouse sequences between Conrad Veidt and Valerie Hobson on the night of his arrival, and I had shot it all for cutting, mostly in close-up, using unusual angles and foreshortenings to emphasize the smallness of the set, and the enforced intimacy of the scenes between the two principals. There was no room for tracking or panning or clever camerawork here. What mattered was what the principals were thinking. Of course, Irving was used to seeing master shots, that is to say long explanatory shots with dialogue as long as possible, so that the people who sit there chewing their cigars can get a rough idea of what the story is all about. I detest master shots. I hardly ever make master shots; they're a waste of time and money. They are just an excuse for a director to make up his own mind about how he is actually going to tell the sequence that morning. Quite often, half the day will be taken up with a so-called master shot.

"Well," said Jerry, getting up, "you're going to get one hell of a picture. I've never seen Conrad Veidt so good, I've never heard him speak such good dialogue, and Hobson is more beautiful than I've ever seen her look. Let's go down to the studio and tell Micky to get on with the good work!" It was only a month or two later that Jerry told me how nearly I had been out on my ass.

We had a tight budget and schedule and as this is a history, I shall have to be accurate about that. I think the schedule was five weeks of five and three-quarter days (Saturday then was a three-quarter day), and the budget, excluding the contract stars, of course, was about £17,000. The total cost of my private location unit and its work was about £350 and was much appreciated by Hugh Stewart, the editor, who could always find a little realistic cut to drop in when he needed it. Needless to say, Vernon doubled all the parts himself, including, I believe, Miss Hobson. We had started the film in the late autumn and so it was full winter when we did the night shots on the tank. It was very cold and wet and the studio lamps showed up against the fog. By then, Captain Hardt, his officers and crew, among them the young Marius Goring and Torin Thatcher, were old pals, and a great deal of whisky and rum was consumed as the night wore on and we waited for the fog to clear or for the wind machines to blow it in the right direction. By the time the fog had lifted, the gallant Captain and his crew could hardly stand, and were lined up on the deck of the submarine singing "Silent Night, Holy Night". Nobody could row the dinghy against the wind machine except Bill Paton, who as a genuine Islesman treated wind machines with contempt. He knew the real thing.

I had hardly seen Alex since I had started work on The Spy in Black, and I hadn't expected to. I knew he had his own troubles. I don't even know if he ever saw the dailies. I doubt it. He had put us on the right road and he let us go our own way. Emeric came to see all the dailies and we were very close. We were already planning to do other films together if Denham were to close its doors. I no longer believed in the possibility of *Burmese Silver*. It was common knowledge that the Prudential Assurance Company were no longer prepared to finance Alex. All around us, people were asking what would happen when the current productions were wrapped up. All the same it was a shock to be dropped at the end of the year.

I was no longer under contract to London Films. There has been so much yapping over the years about the film director, the film *auteur* – Ingmar Bergman, Rossellini, Fellini, Visconti, Old Uncle John Huston and all – that it is very difficult for the general public, and even for the informed public, to realize that making a film is an industrial process and it is perfectly possible to edit, alter, present and have a resounding success without the director having anything more to do with the film from the moment he stops shouting at the actors. These are hard words for the new crop of movie brats, but they are true words. Rex Ingram didn't like going into the cutting room and he avoided it as much as possible. Grant Whytock told me the other day: "We never allowed directors into the cutting room." Even David Lean, who in my opinion is the greatest editor since D. W. Griffith, would prefer not to do the first cut on one of his own great films. In my own case, with this little film, which was no more than an expanded quota-quickie except for the exceptional talent on the acting side, and the quality of the thinking and of the dialogue, I was perfectly content to leave it in the hands of Irving Asher and Hugh Stewart. I could trust them to do a good piece of finishing and presentation. I had made *la soupe*. It was up to them to dish it out.

At that time Emeric was living in London, in Grove End Road, St John's Wood. It is a charming part of London, quite unlike anywhere else, and I think he was never happier than when he was there. I can't remember where I was living. I suppose it was when I went to Burma that Bill and I gave up Carol Goodner's house at Uxbridge – not without a certain number of complaints about damage which was alleged to have been caused by the bachelors involved. The only close friends that Frankie and I had at that time were the Stewarts, David and Bobbie, whose daughter, Gail, was to be a close link through my mother when the war flung us all over the map. When I came back from Burma, Bill and I took a house on the spectacular ridge which overlooks the valley of the Colne and runs from Uxbridge to Harefield. It was an ugly, flimsy, draughty house with a gift for conserving the cold which would excite envy in a Frigidaire. I don't remember that we ever spent much time in it. The main thing that I remember is that one of my early heroes, Maurice Elvey, the director who had arrived in Nice with Victor Saville to wrap up the sequences of *Roses of Picardy*, the director who had done one of the first important British talking pictures *High Treason*, and who had directed perhaps fifty to a hundred British features, lived next door. He had a theatre background, was widely read and never did a shoddy piece of work. He had a charming girlfriend who was a very good cook.

Jerry Jackson, who kept in touch with Irving and had probably seen the rough cut of *The Spy in Black*, came to us with a proposition. His own position with Warner Brothers at Teddington was a bit shaky. His contract hadn't been confirmed, and although he was in charge, and Warners hadn't decided their production policy, in actual fact they were scared stiff of the international situation and were thinking of pulling out of England. In that case they would probably offer Jerry the option of going to Hollywood. No American company wanted to know about the war with Hitler, and their answer to any international incident would be to hightail it back to New York, for which we couldn't blame them. But I for one could see that if the Americans cleared out, the field would be wide open for anybody with ambitions. Jerry saw this, but his employers were not so enthusiastic. Jerry decided to try and develop a couple of medium budget pictures on the same lines as Alex. He came to us and offered us a contract to write them and develop them. I think he offered us £500 apiece – take it or leave it. We were very glad to take it.

That winter I was introduced to Emeric's cooking, which is on the epic scale: whole turkeys, a nine-pound piece of boiled beef, boiled in the same juice as the chicken, mounds of sausages, mountains of noodles. Hungarian stomachs like to have these little snacks handy. Now that he was in the money – comparatively – Emeric was regularly visited by a poor countryman of his who sold tinned Hungarian delicacies on commission: breasts of goose, whole goose livers, goulash. Emeric could never refuse his friend and the tins piled up in the cupboard, and we were very glad of them later. My friend and collaborator had no use for vegetables, except with boiled beef. Nor had he any use for stuffings, garnishes and other gew gaws. He liked meat, and it was quite common for us in those days to demolish an eight-pound turkey between us.

Emeric had been one of the highest paid screenwriters working for the great UFA company at Neuebabelsberg Studios, Berlin, before he took it on the lam ahead of the Nazis. He often talked to me of those great days under Erich Pommer. This producer and businessman of genius had got together a group of creative people who surpassed Hollywood in wit, imagination and fun. Emeric had been supporting himself – well, barely – by making one cup of coffee last the whole morning in a Berlin café while writing short stories on the café note paper (with a clever twist in their ending) for submission to the newspapers. It was one of these that attracted the attention of the UFA story department. On one of his first assignments, Emeric was to work with the famous actor and director Rheinhold Schunzel. Schunzel's attitude to films was typical of those Berlin days. It was winter.

Schunzel said: "How do, Pressburger. We leave tomorrow for Monte Carlo to do research and get local colour."

Emeric said: "But Mr Schunzel, the story is not set in Monte Carlo."

Schunzel shrugged. "It will be by the time we finish with it."

It was at one of these junketings, during which a great deal of work was written, argued and declaimed, and a great deal of food and drink was consumed, that Emeric acquired his vast capacity for eating. He blames it on Bad Ischl, the Austrian spa where people go to lose weight and put it on. Bad Ischl is famous for its hotels and restaurants, for its rich Austrian food, and particularly for its fabulous desserts. Emeric's stomach was never quite the same afterwards, he claims. "Something happened. I think my stomach must have changed shape. I was always hungry after that."

This Falstaffian love of beer and beef — for Emeric was a student at Prague, and holds that there is no other beer but that of Pilsen — has undoubtedly stoked the fires of his energy and imagination. It also carried him into his eighties without ever being seriously ill.

But I was talking of the winter of 1938–39. The two scripts that Jerry Jackson had selected from the heap of non-starters at Warner Brothers were, respectively, a book about the Cunard Line, and a play.

The Cunard Line book covered the hundred-year development of Atlantic passenger traffic and the rivalry between the Cunard Line and the White Star Line for the blue riband of the Atlantic. It was an ambitious subject.

The play was *Caesar's Wife* by W. Somerset Maugham. I have never been lucky with Maugham, nor he with me. It was one of Maugham's 1911–12 successes and was about a British proconsul and his wife, and his troubles with the natives he was supposed to be governing. Presumably it was the success of Korda's Empire films that had made Jerry think it might have a chance. It had starred, originally, C. Aubrey Smith, whose craggy countenance decorated many a Hollywood film as well as *The Four Feathers*, and who was famous later on as the Grand Old Man of the Hollywood-British cricket team. The play had been set by Maugham in the Egypt of the Sirdars. Emeric moved it to Afghanistan.

Unfortunately, I was not able to leave immediately for Afghanistan. Warner Brothers' budgets didn't run to that sort of research. We had to do our research in the British Museum Reading Room and in the columns of *The Times*. Emeric had been fascinated by the accounts of King Amanullah's attempt to modernize his country, which included putting his highly picturesque parliament into frock-coats and bowler hats. He thought that this new setting would give some zip to what was otherwise a polite domestic intrigue in an official setting. I agreed, provided that we were allowed to go there. I contributed childhood memories of the famous painting *The Remnant of an Army*, depicting the lone survivor of the British Expeditionary Force which had been sent out of Kabul from Kandahar. I managed with some trouble to track down a print of the picture, probably from Ackermans in Bond Street.

Liverpool was nearer than Kabul, and Jerry allowed us to go there to research the Cunard film. Liverpool had been where it all started. Samuel Cunard, the American entrepreneur of genius, had started the transatlantic passenger traffic early in the nineteenth century and founded the Cunard Line. The heroes of our story were the members of the McIver family, and their great rivals were, as I have said, the people who created and ran the White Star Line. The main story covered about a hundred years of exciting and dramatic incidents. We found many relics of the period in the magnificent, solid businessmen's houses, and estates and offices. It would be fascinating to make a graph of the ups and downs of the two companies, how the fortunes of one of them rose as the other fell. We decided that in these family sagas, success seemed to skip a generation every now and then. We made this the theme of our film. I remember one lovely scene that Emeric described to me as we walked about the wet streets of Liverpool. McIver has just returned from America and is met by his faithful manservant and boyhood friend. It is a foggy night and so, instead of travelling in his carriage, they both walk at the horses' heads, leading them. Hector McIver is excited at the prospect of seeing his newborn son, who is, of course, going to be the heir and owner of all that McIver has created. Quite casually, before they arrive at the house, he learns that his servant has also had a son. It is this boy, and not Hector McIver's son, whom we destined to be the engineering genius who will bring the company back to prosperity in the future. We called the film *Fathers and Sons*.

I rather wish we had made that film. I don't regret *Caesar's Wife*, but I do regret Afghanistan.

Of course, although Emeric and I were no longer under contract to London Films, we kept our ears to the *pustza* (the Hungarian "grapevine"). Hugh Stewart, the editor of *The Spy in Black*, kept me informed of progress. I saw the first rough cut, of course, and the fine cut, and one day he asked me to come down especially to see some magnificent stock shots he had discovered of depth charges being exploded in pursuit of enemy submarines. They were splendid shots with very satisfying big explosions and fountains of water going up, and made a marvellous climax to the film, even though we knew that all our favourite character actors were being blown up in the submarine with them. This is the kind of thing that an editor can bring to a film in which he's interested. His artistic sense feels that the long patient effort to arrive at the climax should be rewarded with equally spectacular sound and picture.

We had by no means lost contact with Conrad Veidt either. He was far too shrewd a person and far too good an artist not to know what we had done for him. He had seen all the dailies and had spent quite a lot of time in the cutting room, chatting and seeing rough-cut sequences with Hugh Stewart. We had a young cameraman on *The Spy in Black*, Bernard Browne, and I believe it was his first film. I didn't know him, he was a Denham man, and he was lost quite early in the war. As lighting masters he had had Georges Périnal, René Clair's legendary cameraman, and Bob Krasker who, like Périnal, was as great a master in colour as he was in black and white. I had made no concessions to Bernard Browne's inexperience and gave him a hard time, and he had responded magnificently. There were effects shots and close-ups of Conrad Veidt that were as good as any of the German Expressionist films. Veidt knew how to use the muscles of his face and eyes, and I knew how to photograph them. In all this Veidt had collaborated and he had noted the result.

Miklos Rozsa was another sure source of information. He was a friend of Emeric's. He had composed the music for *The Spy in Black* and Muir Mathieson had conducted it. It was Mickey Rozsa who told Emeric that Alex was making a last gigantic effort to get enough money together to start making *The Thief of Bagdad* in Technicolor.

Conrad Veidt was equally well informed, and although there was no script (there never was) he knew that the part of the villainous magician Jaffar was being planned for him. Sabu, the little elephant boy, was to play the thief. "Connie" had rented a house on the hill at Denham, only a stone's throw from the studios. We went there several times for lunch on Sundays. Lillie Veidt and her sister were a great attraction. They were tall, intelligent, handsome girls who had started a nightclub in Berlin in the days when Berlin was Bert Brecht and Kurt Weill and Billy Wilder. To everybody's surprise, Conrad Veidt, at the height of his career as the great screen lover, married Lillie and lived happily ever after. The sisters were Hungarian Jews, and had to leave Berlin when the purges started, and of course Connie Veidt left with them. This greatly upset Dr Goebbels, who looked on Veidt as one of Germany's assets. He made many efforts to tempt him back. Veidt went back once or twice, but finally settled in England. His marriage was one of the happiest I have ever known.

Spring came early and Chris Mann telephoned: "Korda wants to see you. He says he has a job for you."

My heart leapt. Could it be *Burmese Silver*? Only the other day I had received a sad little letter from John, my Madrasi servant and companion on my Burmese march:

4 Guru Street
West Myenigon Cantonment
Rangoon

Dear Sir,

I am sorry to tell you that my dear wife expired on 31st October. I going to take my children to the Convent at Mandalay or Toungoo. I got to do the matter before you come. Please let me know the date you arriving in Rangoon. I wrote a letter to you last month. I never receive any letter from you since the first letter. The 15th November I will finish the death ceremony. After that I will take the Children to Convent before 20th November. I hope you will write and tell me yours coming date.

Yours obediantly
C. M. V. John (Butler)

There we were around the familiar table again: Cunynghame shuffling his papers, Alex puffing his cigar. Opposite to me was seated a pale, bulky man with powerful spectacles and wispy hair. He looked like a Continental professor and regarded me with some suspicion.

"Micky, this is Dr Ludwig Berger. You know who he is, of course."

Of course I knew. He was a famous German theatre director who had turned from the theatre to films and created an enchanting black and white fairy tale film, *Cinderella*. He was a learned, pedantic, patient, professorial talent. What on earth was Alex doing with someone like this?

"Dr Berger is going to direct *The Thief of Bagdad*, and is working with us on the designs and the script. He has made some very beautiful tests with Sabu and John Justin, who is going to play the Prince in the story. I'd like you to see all of this with him."

What was coming now? Dr Berger was looking across the table at my youth and Englishness with a startled eye. Evidently, I was not his idea of the kind of collaborator that could bring much to a German academic.

Alex continued in his most soothing voice: "We are a little worried that we are late in starting the film and that there is a great deal to prepare here at Denham."

Vincent, who was sitting at the other end of the table surrounded with sketches and plans, grunted his agreement. He was doing some action sketches of the Jinnee on his blotting pad.

Alex continued: "As you know, Miki Rozsa is composing the music, and there are a thousand decisions for which I need Dr Berger here with me. Now, I would like you, Micky, to take Sabu and a film unit down to Cornwall and start making the film there."

This was the only briefing that I ever received from Alex Korda about the making of *The Thief of Bagdad*. I consider it the greatest compliment ever paid me.

I spent the day with Vincent and Dr Berger. All Vincent's sketches were in black and white and they were magnificent, but the picture was to be in Technicolor. I fancy that this may have been where Alex and Dr Berger parted company artistically. He had signed the German director in a fit of enthusiasm, and then as Vincent developed the ideas Alex had taken more and more interest in the production and, being a great showman, had decided to take the picture out into the open air and build great fantastic colourful sets on the lot. I saw the tests made by Berger, and they were delightful. He handled the two beautiful young men brilliantly (all curves and arabesques). Sabu, whom I had not had much chance to meet up till then, was about fifteen at the time, all juvenile high spirits and open movements. John Justin, slim, with broad shoulders and a noble head, was quite simply one of the most beautiful young men I had ever seen. He had an excellent voice. I showered compliments on the Doctor, who was pleased.

"Mr Powell, I do not quite understand what Alex wants you to do in Cornwall."

Neither did I. "I suppose Alex wants to show something to his backers. It's the sequence with Sabu, the bottle and the Jinnee. All I need is Sabu and the bottle," I said.

"You'll need a great deal more than that, Mr Powell."

I was sorry for him. Whatever Alex had thought of him at the beginning (and he had given him complete control of the film in his contract), they were no longer soulmates. Alex was not going to sit in his office and let Dr Berger make a stylishly directed, modishly black and white, decorated film. As his mind cleared and crystallized under the influence of Vincent's magnificent designs, he realized that what he wanted was a great, big colourful extravaganza, and he was determined to get it. Dr Berger didn't want colour, particularly Technicolor. Dr Berger didn't want Miklos Rozsa to write the music; he had his own man working on the score in Germany. Dr Berger wanted to create an Oriental fantasy in the studio, under his iron control. Very well, Alex would fix Dr Berger!

I stood with Vincent, both of us looking gloomily at the huge ship built at the far end of the exterior lot, fixed immovably in concrete, sailing along by the River Colne.

"What do you think, Micky? Do we use this ship?" asked Vincent hopefully. Nuisance raced up and placed a large stone on his owner's toe and shook himself all over us.

"Sure, Vincent," I said confidently. "It just needs rerigging, and I'll have them paint a bloody great eye on the prow, like they do on all the Arab ships."

"What kind of eye?"

"A big, open eye. They've got to see where they're going."

We trudged back and looked down on a tangled mass of tubular scaffolding and flat-bottomed boats on the Colne.

He pulled a crumpled sketch from his satchel, showing the port of Basra. "We make entrance of Connie Veidt, Micky, right? No?"

"Do we have Connie Veidt in the foreground?" I suggested.

"If you want." A huge open space was being cleared near the stages. "Here we make the marketplace."

"What are you going to do about the backgrounds?"

"Maybe we make foreground miniatures. You think good?"

"Why not, you get the sun all day here."

Gradually, the basic shape of the film in a series of studio-built exteriors was becoming clear to me – the marketplace, the palaces, the harbour, the gardens and the ships. And all the rest could be done on the great Denham sound stages. My heart leapt at the prospect. Summer around the corner and we would have hours of daylight for these gorgeous conceptions. Once and for all, I decided that the only way to do a big show was to plan it and execute it in a first-rate film studio. Where else could you work such miracles?

The next day I left for Sennen Cove in Cornwall with an astonished film unit, Sabu and a bottle.

My cameraman was Osmond Borrodaile, one of the great pioneers of exterior photography. He had done miraculous work on *Elephant Boy*, and ever since then he had been off on many expeditions for London Films, always coming back with the most superb material. I remember particularly some of his shots on *The Drum*, which gave the picture a style which the interiors conspicuously lacked. He was an old hand at Technicolor. Alex had, of course, produced several films in colour, notably *The Four Feathers*, but I don't think he had ever been personally stirred until Vincent's sketches for *The Thief of Bagdad* got him going.

I think Alex had suddenly realized that he should throw all his chips on the table, and muster around him all the amazing talent which he had gathered together at Denham over the years, and make *The Thief of Bagdad*, if it was to be the last film he made at Denham, the best one.

Nobody can follow with certainty the subtle twists of Alex's mind, although Michael Korda has done better than anybody else in that direction. But I think that his reasons for hiring me and sending me off to Cornwall with his chief star are not beyond conjecture. First of all, it got Sabu out of range of Dr Berger's disturbing Continental influence. Sabu was at an impressionable age, and very shrewd. He was bound to play off his producer against his director. Alex knew exactly how good those tests were which I had seen. They were not in the style of the picture that he now intended to make. I was unknown and afraid of nothing. If Alex had asked me to take over the whole picture, I would have said "Certainly" and got down to it. But he didn't do that. He made it sound like a harmless second-unit expedition: "Why don't you go down to Cornwall and start making the picture with Sabu?"

How innocent he made it sound! It sapped Dr Berger's authority, and once he had agreed, the way was open for other directors to sneak in. Alex, for instance, between cigars. Or Tim Whelan, still under contract and who was particularly good at action comedy scenes. Or Zoli, who was in America, but could be available. Alex knew that I couldn't do much good in Cornwall without proper preparation, but I was in the position of a valuable guerrilla leader, on the payroll, and ready to jump in anywhere and at any time at the head of an experienced unit. And in glorious Technicolor, and in full naturalism, not in the style of the deliciously erotic Arabian Nights entertainment of Dr Berger's dreams.

Sennen Cove is a delightful little spot, a smugglers' haunt on the south coast of Cornwall. It was unsuitable in every way. It was chosen as a location for the shots we had in mind because Geoff Boothby, Alex's most trusted assistant director, knew it was there. What we needed for the encounter between Sabu and the Jinnee was a landscape and seascape like the Persian Gulf, like Sharjah where I had been stranded on my way out to Burma: vast quantities of sand and sea, with plenty of room for a forty-foot-high Jinnee to move around in; and that was what we finally settled for on the coast of Pembrokeshire, South Wales. What I found at Sennen Cove was a picturesque natural landing between low cliffs, where the tide came right up to the steps and where there was only a beach of golden sand when the tide receded, leaving deep, clear rock pools full of colourful sea anemones. After a quick look around on the evening of my arrival, I decided to stay at the pub on the location. The unit were booked into some big hotel not far away. I like to live on the job, talk to the locals and see where the sun rises and sets.

In the morning, Sabu and I met for the first time. His last picture had been *The Drum*. Since then, he had been going to school and making personal appearances – not a very exciting regime for a high-spirited boy. He came to me with a reputation for being difficult. I found him enchanting. In *The Drum*, he had co-starred with Desmond Tester, who had been an angelic child star and who was now a teenage wolf. Desmond played the drummer boy in the film and must certainly have taught Sabu a thing or two about raising the roof as well as beating the drum.

Sabu was my friend until his wickedly premature death at the age of forty-two. He was kind, direct, strong and intelligent. He never had the slightest bit of star fever about him. He said: "I and my family are eating well and sleeping well and that's all that matters to me."

Marilyn, his lovely American wife, adored him. His two children by her, Paul and Jasmine, talk of him as if he were still alive. He always will be for we who loved him; and for the children in the world, so long as there is a print of *The Thief of Bagdad* which holds together long enough to be projected. We had such an occasion the other day at Francis Coppola's Zoetrope Studios in Hollywood. The projection theatre was jammed with children sitting on the floor right up to the screen, and the great opening sequence of the Magician's arrival at the seaport, which Vincent and I and Alex had dreamed up together, left them with their mouths open. Halfway through the film, after the scene between Sabu and the Jinnee, one little boy of my acquaintance, Jesse Law, rushed through the other children to where I was standing at the back (there were no seats available), clasped me firmly around my knees and said: "*Did you make that movie?*"

"I had something to do with it," I said truthfully.

He said, still clinging to my leg: "It's the best movie I've ever seen!" and then rushed back to his seat right in front of the screen. A lot of grown-up children, even today, share this view, including Francis Coppola and his elder brother August.

It is true that my name is on the picture, as one of the directors, together with poor dear Dr Berger, who was still hovering about Denham, puzzled and perplexed, when the film was nine-tenths finished. But the film is really the swan-song of the Korda brothers – Alex, Vincent and Zoli. I don't remember that Zoli shot much of the film, except, of course, the Hollywood sequences. But Vincent's masterful hand and his eye for colour were visible throughout the film. As for Alex, in those days he was everywhere at once. Over the past years, they had built up together, with no specific intention, but by results, a tradition of exotic and magnificent productions which filled the studio with strange props and costumes. Every department of the studio had experts who were the envy of other studios. These men were used to dealing with great productions where everything had to be invented. The Denham pattern-shop was better than any in Hollywood. For H. G. Wells's *The Shape of Things to Come*, which had been one of Alex's greatest commercial failures, and also one of his greatest technical triumphs, he had brought a host of trick-men of every kind from America and from Europe to work on it, and he brought the best of them back again to work on *The Thief of Bagdad*. Georges Périnal, certainly the greatest cameraman alive at that time, a mystic of the cinema, with a face like a weary Spanish saint, was the lighting cameraman in charge of the whole production. Miklos Rozsa's great musical themes had at last come into their own, even when he was saddled with such banal lyrics. But these are minor matters. The power and beauty and mystery of a great studio with a great tradition was behind the production from beginning to end. And the Korda brothers had created this mystique. Confident that everything was possible, the rest of us got on with the job of making it happen.

But the triumph of the film and the reason for its perennial success is Sabu. It was a stroke of genius on Korda's part to buy from Douglas Fairbanks the rights to his original production of *The Thief of Bagdad* and remake it with a child. For a boy there is no future and no past – only the present. He speaks the truth or tells lies with equal facility, according to circumstances. His reactions to danger are immediate and unsubtle. All this is in Sabu's performance as the little thief, and he is kind and wise and just, and would certainly make a good warrior king for his people, only – he just wants one more adventure first.

All this was discussed by Sabu and myself while we lay on the cliffs among the daisies of Sennen Cove. We also did some work – that is to say, we played. It was soft Cornish spring weather. About all that we knew of the script at this point was that Sabu's boat had been wrecked in a storm and he had been washed ashore. All right, that was common enough on the Cornish coast. We shot it. Meanwhile, I had had the prop-men construct an ingenious sort of fishing contraption, faintly resembling what I had seen being used in the Persian Gulf. It was a fishing pole and net mounted on a big bamboo tripod. We lowered the net into those shining pools at low tide and brought up treasures. The coast there is full of beautiful stones, shells and shellfish, and wonderful sea anemones of every colour. We constructed numerous bottles of different sizes, covered in barnacles and sealed at the mouth with mysterious emblems, and hoped they would bear the scrutiny of Vincent's eye. We staked out a location for Sabu's possible opening of the bottle and meeting with the Jinnee, which showed how impossible it was in such a cramped location. Amazingly, there were some of the Sennen Cove shots in the final cut of the film, thanks to Bordie's photography.

I had made friends with the rest of the unit, particularly the electricians, led by their gaffer, Bill Wall. Bill was a bit of a genius. He had an instinctive understanding of photography, and knew more about lighting than most cameramen. He was Périnal's favourite gaffer. His boys were rough, tough, competent men, with nicknames like Popeye and Wimpy. Nobody knew who I was or what we were doing there, but they looked at me with new respect because some of them had seen a sneak preview of *The Spy in Black* and the buzz was on about it. Also it looked as if I was one of Alex's boys, or Sabu wouldn't be down there with me. I reported to Cunynghame that there was very little more we could do and we were recalled.

By this time, Sabu and I were firm friends. We trusted one another. He had thought a lot about this marvellous position he had arrived at, from being one of the elephant boys in the stables of the Maharajah of Mysore, to being an international star with enough money in the bank to keep him for the rest of his life. He had no illusions about his career as a boy wonder. He knew that it must come to an end some time, and that he would have to come to terms with life. We discussed the future. I told him that I believed Alex would take the film to America to be finished because the war was coming almost any month now. I advised him to go to America. He would be out of the war and America was a better land for a boy to be growing up in at that time than Europe. Sabu's brother was his business manager and was always talking about dollars and cents. Sabu thought about what a man was, and is.

I fancy that Connie Veidt put in a word or two about me as soon as he learned what Korda's intentions were with regard to Dr Berger. He had seen the fine-cut of *The Spy in Black* and he knew that he had never been directed and photographed like that since he made *The Last Column* in Germany. Also, here was a sympathetic side to the famous Conrad Veidt menace. Connie had always been a master of sardonic humour. Emeric and I gave him lightness and charm. I never forgot that I was dealing with a great star who knew where the camera was as well as I did.

I had never directed a colour film, but I found the crossover easy. "Make the colour work for you, don't start working for the colour," I said to myself.

And when Natalie Kalmus was firing off her clichés at a grumbling Vincent Korda as she stalked about the big sets on the lot, I said to myself: "We are not making coloured picture postcards for Technicolor."

Mrs Kalmus, naturally, went by the book. She was not an artist, and the sight of one of Matisse's canvases of that period would probably have sent her to bed for a week. Alex knew even less about painting, although he pretended he did, and Vincent had bought him a Manet to hang on one of his walls. I have been with him and Vincent and Nuisance and Frank Walker, the chief of construction, as they walked around the huge pink set of the marketplace and looked at the elaborate foreground miniatures of the city on the hill which were being put in place. Alex, on principle, was never content with anything his brothers did, and he would grumble: "Vincent! What do you think this set is supposed to be?"

"It is the palace, Alex."

"It's a piece of shit. Tear it down and rebuild it four times as big and paint it blue."

"Pink, Alex."

"Pink, then!"

Vincent would shrug and grumble and turn away, followed by Nuisance and me and Frank Walker, who would be saying: "Mr Korda, Mr Korda. I must have your order about the palace set. We ought to have started it yesterday."

Vincent would say to me: "Carpenters, carpenters, they always want to knock the nail in the wood."

Yet, somehow, everything got done and was, one day, ready.

We had a host of prop-men, prop-makers and art directors working for us in all sorts of obscure corners. Even the great Alfred Junge was available to work on a sequence or two. MGM were no longer producing their great pictures, all of which he designed and more or less masterminded, so far as the studio was concerned, and he was looking for a job. I had had my eye on him ever since he worked with E. A. Dupont at Elstree and then took over the art department at Gaumont-British as I have described. I felt that one day we would work together and do great things. I think the sequence that we worked on (but which was never shot) involved Bengal tigers. That's all I remember about it. But I am sure that if my little friend Jesse Law had known that there could have been a scene between Sabu and Bengal tigers, he would never have forgiven me for not shooting it.

The trouble with so many cooks enriching the broth was to know when you were ready. Alex taught me that you were ready when he said you were. By this time, I had three complex sequences under my command, in exterior sets, strung all along the valley of the Colne, right up to the studio gates. There was the sequence with the ship and the arrival of the magician, Jaffar. There was the sequence in the harbour where Sabu swims ashore and turns back from a dog into a boy. There was the sequence of the raid on the marketplace by the archers of the Khaliph, and the procession of the Princess passing by on her pink elephant as seen by John Justin and Sabu. I had rehearsed all three of these sequences for days, and stolen most of the principal props myself. I had a troop of daring horsemen under my command, and I surreptitiously increased them from half a dozen to about eighteen. They were led by a fiery and foul-mouthed ex-captain of cavalry. Nearly all the horsemen were actually girls, whom he treated abominably and whom he cursed continually. Of course they loved it and him. I had a magnificent-looking champion archer with a forearm that would have given Praxiteles something to think about, and who stood by me, ready to send an arrow to within an inch of where I wanted it. One day, Alex strolled down to the ship set at the far end of the lot, where for the fifteenth time slaves were unrolling a red carpet which I had removed from one of the palace sets that morning, while Sammy Lee's stunt men were all aloft, furling the sails and sliding down ropes, and Conrad Veidt, magnificent in red turban and gold scimitar, stepped ashore to meet his slavegirl Mary Morris, whom I had last directed as the Nazi chauffeuse in *The Spy in Black*.

Alex cocked an eye at all these capers. "That all seems very nice, Micky. Why do you not shoot it?"

"Well, Alex, um, the light will be better in about an hour or two, and I'm waiting for a stuntman to – "

"Shoot it, Micky. It will not be any better for one more stuntman." We shot it.

The next day we had to prepare the ship and all around it for the storm scenes, which entailed firemen and hoses and wind machines and God knows what. Or perhaps I should say God knows but we thought we knew better. I moved my combat team up to the port of Basra set and started to rehearse with Sabu and the dog. (I suppose that dog lovers will want to know whether Nuisance auditioned for this dog, but I must tell them that Nuisance did not, and I chose the dog who did play the part for his alertness and beauty and strange resemblance in close-ups, somehow, to Sabu himself. He was a most unpleasant dog and bit everybody.) It was a big scene with hundreds of people in colourful costumes, and I had just got everthing working perfectly for about the first time when Alex appeared again, dressed immaculately, his hat over his eyes, a long scarf around his neck, and a long Corona between his long fingers.

"How did you like that, Alex? It's our first real rehearsal."

"Very good, Micky. Shoot it. It will never be any better if you rehearse it for a week." We shot it.

Connie Veidt, who was in the next sequence, was standing nearby. "Alex, did you see the dailies of the scenes with June?" he asked.

June Duprez had got the part of the Princess in the picture, and a picture she made of the part. An enthusiastic visitor said to me: "Until now, I have always had to *imagine* the Princess in the fairy tale wearing diaphanous trousers, sitting on silk cushions, eating Turkish Delight between tumbles." (I paraphrase his actual words.)

Alex said: "Yes, Connie, they were very good."

"Don't you think, Alex, that I was overacting in my close-up a little bit?"

"My dear Connie, you are supposed to be a magician in a Technicolor film. Nobody minds if a magician overacts. A little bit."

And all the while the drums of Hitler were beating louder and louder across the Channel, and the banners were waving as the harvest came in. All the weight of Dr Goebbels's propaganda was directed against England and America, to warn them to keep out while Germany decided who was to be the next victim, Poland or the USSR. Mussolini yapped away in his corner of Europe, and tried to make it sound like the roaring of an African lion. The British people had decided that war was inevitable, and that is not a thing that happens every day in England, as Dr Goebbels should have known. And we at Denham were making fairy tales.

I was living in a caravan all that summer. Bill and I hated the bleak windy house on the ridge which we had rented, and we got out of it as soon as spring came. When I answered Alex's call to action, I had first proposed to Bill that we live on the location, but he ruled that out, pointing out that we were far from any shops for stocking up, a practical consideration which had not occurred to me. Bill was great on two things: stocking up and frying up. He couldn't be faulted on either of them. Frank Wells, H. G.'s younger son, who had been my art director in the quota-quickie days and was now part of the Denham ensemble, had always been a caravan buff and offered to rent me one of his. We finally installed it in a field along the valley of the Colne, near Rickmansworth, where there was an open-air swimming pool as well. It was on a little farm where they reared pheasants and had the advantage of being "near the shops" and near the swimming pool, while being quite isolated from anybody but the tenant farmer.

I had accumulated a cat, as usual, in this case a marmalade cat called Chivers. The spaniels used to go to work with us, but Chivers stayed behind to mind the house and was always to be seen on top of the caravan, scanning the horizon, when we returned. She would then jump down and come leaping through the long grass to give her news, which usually included a fieldmouse or two. The spaniels, pretending to be exhausted and lying in a tangled heap, would tell her about their terrible day directing all those people.

Suddenly, in September, there was the Blitzkrieg on Poland, Churchill returned to the British Cabinet, and Neville Chamberlain told us that we were at war with Germany.

A week earlier, Alex had summoned a meeting of all his principal contract people – people he could depend upon and who depended upon him. I remember that Merle was there, proud, beautiful and nervous, recently returned from Hollywood, where she had been making *Wuthering Heights*, co-starring with Laurence Olivier, for Samuel Goldwyn. Among the actors present were Anthony Bushell, an attractive and enigmatic personality with pale hair and pale blue eyes, a potential director. Ralph Richardson was there, filling his eternal pipe, and also Brian Desmond Hurst, the brilliant Irish director, a follower of Renoir, with a gift for poetic realism. He was later to show that he could put on romance too in the grand manner when he made *Dangerous Moonlight*, famous for its Warsaw Concerto.

Alex explained his personal agreement with Churchill, and how it affected us all. Britian was preparing for war. Denham was already a classified area. Now came our orders. When war was declared, filming on *The Thief of Bagdad* would stop. The next day, everybody at Denham would start working on a feature propaganda film which Alex had promised Churchill would be ready in one month. During this month, Alex guaranteed the salaries of all his contract people. All he asked of us was that we would go with heart, mind and soul into making his new picture, and work with whomever we were assigned to. The coordinator of the whole production was to be Ian Dalrymple, my old friend from Gaumont-British days, who was now one of Korda's associate producers. Dalrymple's brief was to build the main case against Hitler as a warmonger and butcher of his fellow men, to show Britain's potential for men and munitions in the coming struggle, and above all, to star the Royal Air Force. The film was to be called *The Lion Has Wings*. I looked with affection at Ian's bulky figure as he stood, as usual, among a crowd of other people, inconspicuous, one hand in his old tweed jacket, the other fiddling with a cigarette in a long holder, his kind, clever eyes dreaming behind his spectacles. He was completely unmoved by the magnitude of his task, and I thought that no better man could have been chosen for the job.

You, the instructed reader, whom Virginia Woolf in her essays called "The Common Reader" are also, I hope, the common moviegoer, interested enough in the history of your country to visit the British Film Institute from time to time, to see a film of particular interest to yourself. So I don't intend to go into great detail about the content of the films I worked on during the war years. One thing led to another in those days and I was in the thick of it, so I am giving you a peek behind the scenes. During the next ten years, Emeric and I worked to a consistent pattern, but nobody was aware of it. It was only forty years later, in 1980 to be exact, that the BBC showed the main body of our work, in its proper order. The present generation, who only knew our work by hearsay, or piecemeal, awoke to the realization that two observant children had been in their midst, taking notes.

    You will be relieved to hear that I don't propose to rescreen *The Lion Has Wings*, and then give you a blow-by-blow description of it. It was a hodgepodge. A good third of it was a brilliant reconstruction by Ian Dalrymple and E. V. H. Emmett, commentator of the British Movietone News of the way Europe in the last five years had crawled to lick Hitler's boots. England, the great appeaser, was as much to blame as anybody, and Ian and Emmett poured scorn on our policy makers. Another important section was the industrial section, which showed the Midlands swinging into war production. It was mostly done by clever montage technique, and was mostly lies. Our war production and war preparation was completely illusory. We could still talk about and show our glorious British Navy, although most of the ships were without air cover. Our bigger battleships were already outclassed by the German pocket battleships and by the huge new German submarine fleet, which was already going into service. The only arm of the services which was near parity with the Germans was the Royal Air Force. One day, in the last week of peace, I was shooting some scenes of Sabu on the flying carpet when Cunynghame came onto the set, bringing with him a smart young Air Force officer, looking about him with smiling curiosity.

"Micky, this is Squadron Leader Wright of the Royal Air Force. He will be seconded to us in due course. He wants to talk to you."

I really can't remember how Dalrymple and his mixed bag of directors made the decision as to who would do what, but apparently it was settled that I was the best person to do all the flying sequences in the picture. There was no script and no information available. Everything was, of course, top secret. We had heard about the Spitfire and heard rumours of the Hurricane, but nobody knew what these aircraft were like or how they worked, or how they were ordered into the air and commanded when there. We had to present a picture of an impregnable Britain, capable of defence and attack through its Air Force. But that was all we knew. Squadron Leader Wright had come to chat about this.

"Flying carpets?" he said. "We'll have you flying on something better than this before you're finished, Mr Powell."

I confessed my entire ignorance of aircraft and of combat aircraft in particular.

"No problem," he said over lunch in the canteen. "You'll have to see for yourself. You ought to see everything, and know everything and go there with me. I am your surety against wrathful station commanders, who shoot at sight. Your Jinnee," he added with a grin. He had evidently been on Stage 4, where Rex Ingram, the black actor, was playing a Jinnee forty feet high.

We were all working at Denham on *The Thief of Bagdad* on the Sunday morning when Chamberlain came on the air to announce that Britain was at war. None of us knew what war meant, except our Central European friends, who were shaking in their shoes, and I don't blame them. War might mean bombs immediately falling on London. War might mean the immediate blocking of the Channel by the German High Sea Fleet, the invasion of England within a few weeks.

Are you old enough to remember the air raid warning which we heard for the first time as Neville Chamberlain finished speaking? At Denham, we had all gathered in one of the big concrete coalbunkers to listen to the broadcast, and I remember John Justin, and June Duprez, Conrad Veidt and Sabu and Miles Malleson in his wonderful white whiskers as the gadget-mad Sultan, whispering together, their extravagant costumes somehow making the whole drab scene more menacing and final. Alex and his brothers were there, and Merle, who was holding Alex's hand and crying. Alex was smoking one of his Coronas, as usual, and he took a deep breath and sent a perfect smoke ring into the air. We waited for the All Clear and then trooped back to our fairy tale. And that was my last day on *The Thief of Bagdad* at Denham Studios.

During the day a priority message arrived for me from the Air Ministry: "Please meet me Monday morning 9 a.m. Denham Golf Course Club House. Warm clothing. Signed Wright, Squadron Leader."

I did not take my clubs.

Wright was walking up and down as I parked the Auburn near the professional's hut.

"Nice car," he said running his eye over the convertible lines. "Auburn 6, isn't it?"

We talked for a moment about that great engineering genius, Cord of Indiana.

"My bus is down by the sixteenth tee."

He looked very smart and alert as we walked together down to where a neat little three-seater aeroplane had been parked on the fairway. Wright had blunt features, with sensitive eyes and mouth, and looked as game as a terrier. He looked me over.

"Well, we're off at last," he said. "This is your flying carpet. Nice little bus, isn't she?"

"Where are we going?"

"I thought we'd fly over the barrage balloons – they're all up this morning, give you a view of London as a target and give you a rough idea of how we propose to defend her – and then drop in at some of the east coast stations which will be in the first line of attack."

"Bombers or fighters?" I asked.

"Both. Fasten your seat belt tight. It's a steep take-off."

It was almost vertical.

"A nice little emergency landing place, Denham Golf Course," he observed as we shaved the tall elm trees on the edge of the lane. The studio cartwheeled beneath us, the great white stages dwindling to match-boxes as we soared up above the valley of the Colne. We crossed the water-meadows that the spaniels loved in a flash, skimmed over watery Uxbridge, crossed Hounslow Heath, and found the Thames near Richmond. As we followed the river eastwards across London it was impossible to think of these twenty million people in the Thames Valley and the Home Counties as a future target for Hitler's bombs. They were as defenceless as sheep. The Thames was full of shipping heading for home, anxious to escape delay or worse. We were over Galleons Reach. On our left hand the barrage balloons raised a gossamer wall of defence against the bombers of Hermann Goering's Luftwaffe. There were hundreds of them, shining white and silver in the sun.

"Pretty, aren't they?" shouted Wright as he skimmed up and over the shimmering, dancing wall of tethered balloons.

"Damn sight more dangerous for our young chaps than the Jerries," he observed. "But good for civilian morale." We turned northwards.

"That's Hornchurch. It's a fighter station. One of the best. We will drop in on them on the way back if we have time."

"Where are we headed for?"

"Mildenhall. One of the best. Bombers. But there are fighters stationed there too."

Mildenhall! It's a name that must evoke many emotional memories among the men and women who served there over the next twenty years, both British and American. To many American and European freedom fighters, those rolling meadows and those short, brimming rivers of Norfolk and Suffolk are more familiar than their own countryside. Mildenhall! Twice it would be in the very centre of attack and counter-attack. At the height of the Battle of Britain there was hardly a serviceable aircraft left on the tarmac. Two years later, it was black with American Flying Fortresses. Mildenhall! A name to conjure with. Like Camelot.

Security was already very tight, but we were expected. I had brought with me my 35mm Eyemo hand camera, and I was allowed to use it. Nobody knew at that time what was officially secret and what was not. The answer was either everything or nothing. There was nothing much to see, but I had a lot to learn and of course I was interested in these men who were going to be the first Englishmen into battle. We were having a beer with Wing Commander Harris, a big blond man, when a message came to him.

"Sorry, I'm off!" He put down his beer hastily, leaving it rocking and slopping on the bar, and vanished.

"What's up?" I asked. Wright was already circulating around the room and had got the news. He came back to me.

"Kiel," he said.

Kiel! The location of the opening sequence of *The Spy in Black*! I seized my Eyemo camera and rushed out. They were bombing up what I think were Wellingtons.

I was wild with excitement. "Can we go with them?" I asked Wright.

He hesitated. "Would be rather a scoop. I'll ask the Station Commander."

Of course the request was refused. I persisted. The only high-ranking RAF officer I knew was Sholto Douglas. He had been in love with Frankie for years. As an Air Vice Marshal and head of Fighter Command, he had other things on his mind, but for a wonder he accepted my phone call.

"Sholto, could you fix it so I can go on this raid to Kiel? They are leaving in ten minutes."

"Micky, what on earth are you doing in Mildenhall! Go home at once."

"But it would be the first operation of the war! It's for *The Lion Has Wings*. I have a movie camera and there's nobody here but me. Don't you understand?"

"Give me your liaison, Squadron Leader Wright." I handed over the telephone to Wright.

"Wright!"

"Yes, sir."

"Take Micky Powell back to Denham and drop him there without a parachute."

"Yes, Air Vice Marshal!"

I don't know who gave the order for this impudent attack, but I was told they went in at low level and the Germans were doing their laundry. Harris's squadron got rid of their bombs without much harm to anybody and flew back home. It *would* have been a scoop! After all, it was Britain's declaration of intent, if nothing else.

At that time, radar was the topmost of top secrets. The boffins were working hard on it, but it did not come into operation until the Battle of Britain. I got on the thread of it while we were spending two freezing nights at Hornchurch, the fighter station nearest to London and uncomfortably near to the barrage balloons for take-offs. On the outbreak of war, all aircraft had been ousted from their cozy hangars and dispatched to remote dispersal points all round the perimeter of their airfields in case of enemy action, and no proper arrangements had been made for the comfort of the men. There were no telephones or privies, and worst of all no hot tea. As old hands at this sort of thing, Bill and I were shocked, and we mobilized hot food and Thermos and whisky to mitigate the Essex fog. There was a squadron of Spitfires stationed there and the Squadron Commander was called Tracey, I think. A young idealistic boy, a magnificent pilot. I remember him with great admiration and affection. He was full of gallantry and ideals, but didn't know how to make himself comfortable.

When I wanted to find out more about radar, Wright felt it would be difficult to get over to the film audience. But as soon as I realized that it was a system for zoning in on the approaching enemy from different angles and blowing him out of the sky before he could see you, I decided to use it in the film. By cross-examining fighter pilots, including the celebrated "Catseye" Cunningham, who was a friend of Frankie's, I learnt enough about how the system worked to put on a show. The system was not in operation, but very soon would be. No reason why it should be "top secret". Night fighting up to that time had been a matter of who had the sharpest eyes and quickest wit. If we could make Jerry think that we could already shoot his pilots down before they sighted ours, we would shake his nerve. I told Dalrymple that I was going to exploit this magical radar thing in the flying sequences in the film.

We decided that my sequences in the film were to show how an all-out attack by Nazi bombers, supported by fighters, was completely wrecked by the use of radar by the fighter squadrons of the RAF (as actually happened nine months later). Of course, it wasn't known as radar then, nor did I explain it. It was this "new thing" – "this electric eye". Squadron Leader Wright managed to give me the fuselage of a crashed Spitfire, plus two odd wings from some other station, and we brought the lot back to Denham and set it up on one of the big stages with lots of room around it. I surrounded it with wind machines and sound machines and arranged with the engineering department so that the whole thing was on a platform that could be tipped and turned and made to do all sorts of things, including dips and swings against a night background.

One of Korda's young contract actors, who had a particularly fine-drawn face and a brutal passivity which rivalled Jean Gabin, was selected by me as the prototype of the "First of the Few". His name was Brian Worth. We chose some mock-up aircraft for the invading Nazis (anything would do for them, they were going to be sitting ducks for the RAF anyway). I cast two or three dastardly Luftwaffe pilots to be shot down in flames. I then went to work in the studio with lighting effects, sound effects, playbacks, back projection, recordings of shells exploding, and machine gun fire, prop-men throwing firecrackers – the works in fact – and had a really high old time. I didn't make the mistake of making the radar work all the time, but it worked well enough to blow the Luftwaffe out of the sky and give Goering something to think about.

Other directors on the team making *The Lion Has Wings* were grabbing their chances as Dalrymple made them available, and he himself, and his superlative team of editors, among them Hugh Stewart and Derek Twist, were hauling the whole thing together. It was an incredible job and a justification of all that Denham stood for in Alex's vision. It was all shop-made, edited and directed in less than a month. The labs worked day and night and the film was playing in about sixty countries all over the world a week or ten days later. It was an outrageous piece of propaganda, full of half-truths and half-lies, with some stagy episodes which were rather embarrassing and with actual facts which were highly distorted; but the will to fight was there, and I think *The Lion Has Wings* can claim to have caused a lot of people all over the world, who were inclined to support the Axis, to stop and think again. The making of this piece of popular propaganda also saved the British film industry from eclipse.

Added to that was the commercial success of *The Spy in Black*. It had opened at the Odeon Leicester Square, the flagship of Oscar Deutsch's fleet of Odeons, the week that war was declared. It was a smash hit. It was booked in for a week, ran a month, and could have run another four weeks with ease if they hadn't had a queue of pictures waiting. England was at war and the public wanted to see war pictures, and *The Spy in Black* was a war picture. It didn't matter that it was the 1914–18 war. It didn't matter that the hero was a heroic German. It didn't matter that all the values and sympathies of the story were in direct contradiction to the current course of events. It was a war picture, all about submarines and spies, full of action and suspense, looking authentic. The British Navy triumphs in the end and it was all lovely! Columbia, the American distributors, with a completely unexpected hit on their hands, whipped it over to America, retitled it *U-Boat 29*, and made a fortune with it.

I said to Emeric: "We ought to follow that up. How about it? With no films being made we ought to get Connie Veidt and Valerie Hobson for another picture for peanuts."

He said he'd think about it. I had an invitation to go to the Isle of Skye. I thought I could do with a change, I needed a holiday, so I went there.

Skye is a large rugged island off the coast of Scotland, and the Seton Gordons lived at the northwest corner of it, on the Bay of Wick. Seton was a naturalist and field observer, perhaps the most famous since W. H. Hudson. His wife, Audrey, had been inspired by *The Edge of the World* to write a film story which was interesting enough for me to have thanked her and written her a letter about it a year or so before. Now, with my name in the papers as the director of another Scottish film (this time the Orkneys), she invited me to come up and stay for a few days and see Skye for myself.

The journey to Skye is leisurely and John Buchanish. You take the night train from London to Inverness, breakfast at the stately Station Hotel, board the little local train and trundle along the shores of the loch and down the Great Glen. After about two and a half hours and innumerable stops, you arrive at the end of the line at Lochalsh, where the ferryboat takes you over the sea to Skye. It's a beautiful and wild spot. The Cuillin Hills, with their black, menacing, granite peaks, fill the western sky. Across the Kyle is the little whitewashed town of Portree, shining under the rolling heather-covered hills of the island. Northward, the narrow passage opens out and it is a wonderful sail up to Applecross, where you can look at the Quirang, the strange spiky hills which dress the north end of Skye. The Kyle of Lochalsh is only a few hundred yards wide and the tide runs strongly at the full, so it is not always possible to cross when you want to. All this was Johnson and Boswell country and I had a pocket copy of *A Journey to the Western Islands* with me.

It was about noon when the ferryboat landed me at Portree. Audrey and Seton Gordon and Dara, Seton's black and white Highland collie, were waiting for me in their open car. We shook paws all round and Audrey explained that we were driving about twenty-five miles to their house, where her two daughters were preparing a meal. It was Seton Gordon's book *Islands of the West* which had first confirmed my interest in the evacuation of St Kilda in 1931. He wrote beautifully and unpretentiously, and took lovely old-fashioned photographs. He had done one of the standard books on the Scottish red deer and had also written *Highways and Byways in the Highlands and Islands.* Seton was to remain one of my best friends for many years. I suppose he was about twenty years older than me, and was very tall and stately. He was a hairy man with a large dark moustache, and busy eyebrows over large, observant eyes. He stooped slightly because of his height, and always had a half-smile on his lips. He wore the kilt, and it suited him. No other Highlander that I knew could wear it so well, and he was never without his shooting glass, his camera, and his long walking stick whose length was just the height of his shoulder, as it should be. On his head, he wore either a battered old Highland bonnet, or an equally battered deerstalker. He loved bright colours and they suited him. Nothing that moved on the hill escaped his attention. To walk with him, or climb with him, or to stalk with him, was an education. Every sound and sight was interpreted by him immediately. As soon as we reached the top, he would stop and take out his glass, using his stick as a firm support. He would scan the heather-covered slopes all around, and of course everything that moved stopped. Now that he has gone, I feel, when I am on the hills, deaf, dumb and blind.

He was a great judge of piping and was often in demand at Highland Games. He was a good piper himself, and it was a sight to see him walking up and down with his long stride as he played a pibroch. For a nature lover and judge of piping, Seton was surprisingly hard of hearing and was rather deaf to ordinary conversation, and I can see now his gentle, inquiring face, with his hand cupped round his ear, as he listened to what you were saying. Perhaps his hardness of hearing for ordinary conversation was mainly diplomatic.

In his youth Seton had studied nature and gained his spurs as a field naturalist in the Cairngorms and the forest of Braemar. One of his proudest possessions was the stalking glass which the then Prince of Wales, later Edward VII, had given him after many a successful stalk together. It was perhaps these early years which had given him his courtly, simple manners.

Caitriona and Bridie had a grand tea waiting for us, with hot scones, eggs, whisky and innumerable cups of tea out of a huge teapot. They had expected somebody truculent and awe-inspiring, but they looked me over and decided I would do. I returned the compliment.

Audrey's story had a mystic thread running through it. It was not really strong enough for the kind of film I was about to make, and in any case it was not a film to make during a national emergency, although she could hardly be expected to appreciate that. Skye was not yet the closed area that it became when the submarine war increased. The war seemed very far away. But the story had fascinating things and people in it, and we talked it over while we toured the island in the next three days. I gazed in awe at the Cuillin, where Caitriona and Seton had had many a scramble together. She was her father's constant companion on the hills, together with Dara. We drove sixty miles down to Talisker in the south of the island, where they make one of the best whiskies in the world. We climbed the great square tableland which is called MacLeod's Table (when it is covered with snow, they say that MacLeod has spread his table cloth), and of course we paid a visit to historic Dunvegan Castle, hereditary home of the MacLeods. And then it was time to go back to London.

Emeric had not only thought about a story, but had half written it. He needed me. I left next morning in pitch darkness to a murmured farewell from the girls from their bedroom window.

In twenty-four hours I was back in London and having breakfast with Emeric. His story was no great shakes, but it served its purpose, which was to provide two stunning parts for Conrad Veidt and Valerie Hobson which they simply could not refuse, even if England were to be invaded next morning. It was called *Contraband*. Of equal importance were the glimpses provided of England preparing for war. It explained how the Contraband Control was being operated against neutrals, and why the Royal Navy had set up the control at Ramsgate, on the east coast of Kent, and the first twenty minutes of the film would be acted out in the thick of it, or at sea. Then the action moved to London in the blackout.

The newspapers had told us that there were already hundreds of ships at anchor off the Goodwin Sands, always one of England's most vital nerve centres in time of war. You would have to go back to the Napoleonic Wars, or even the Dutch and Spanish Wars, to find a parallel for the situation which was developing in the English Channel. I thrilled to my Kentish toes at the prospect of showing how my country, with her long and vulnerable seacoast and her defenceless harbours, was already taking the war against Hitler into what he had the cheek to call "the German ocean". We both saw a chance to prove once more that films can be a weapon of war. In *The Lion Has Wings*, we had told Herr Hitler's fat friend what would happen to his Luftwaffe pilots if he sent them to attack London. Now in this new film we were going to tell Admiral Doenitz, who commanded the huge fleet of German U-boats, that, in spite of his protection, any neutral ship bringing vital supplies to Germany or her neighbours would be arrested and interned and her cargo confiscated. This was swaggering with a vengeance, but Emeric had been impressed by the high hand that I had shown with radar, and by the other outrageous lies that the other directors had contributed to *The Lion Has Wings*, and he had decided to do a little sabre-rattling himself on behalf of the Royal Navy and the Royal Naval Volunteer Reserve (the RNVR), most of them private yachtsmen, who were already flying the blue ensign at their stern, and the burgee of their yacht club at the truck.

Conrad Veidt's part was again that of a sea captain – Captain Andersen – this time not of a German U-boat, but of a Danish merchant vessel, a freighter that also carried passengers. His home port was Copenhagen, and he was bound for Rotterdam, at that time a neutral port. His cargo was valuable chemicals, and if it fell into enemy hands it could be used in a very unfriendly manner. The other explosive element in his cargo was a passenger – a Mrs Sørensen, an elegant Danish lady who refused to wear a lifebelt at breakfast – Valerie Hobson, of course.

So far, it was a conventional beginning to an obvious romance between two attractive principals. Only the novel and up-to-date setting of a detained neutral ship in Ramsgate Roads, and the charisma of the actor and actress, saved the scenes between them from banality. Obviously, I would find the details of the Contraband Control fascinating, and when Captain Andersen is told by two bland young yachtsmen in uniform that his ship will be held for twenty-four hours and may be confiscated, and then two of his passengers vanish ashore (one of them Miss Hobson, the other Esmond Knight), and Captain Andersen has to follow them to London in the blackout, things start to perk up. From then on, Emeric was concocting an amusing thriller in a wartime setting. We were on familiar ground here, and we made the conditions of London, blacked out but still getting on with its night life and private life, so interesting and so fascinating that they called the film *Blackout* when it was released in America, and I wish we had too. With its double meaning, it's a much better title for the story.

It was a spy story, of course, with Raymond Lovell as the master spy, Valerie Hobson and Esmond as counter-espionage agents, and Conrad Veidt coming to the rescue with a bunch of waiters from a Danish restaurant called the Three Vikings. I particularly remember Hay Petrie as twin brothers, and Denis Arundell as a creepy-crawly, inaudible and almost invisible German agent who acted everybody else off the screen. The film was full of restaurants and nightclubs, in one of which Paddy Browne was doing her stuff. There was also an adorable little cigarette girl in another nightclub, all lovely liquid eyes and nice long legs, who had a tiny scene with Conrad Veidt that ended up on the cutting-room floor. Pity I didn't keep the clipping, because it was Deborah Kerr's first appearance on any screen. I have said enough, I think, to indicate our showmanlike approach to our first genuine wartime picture. In fact, it was the first genuine wartime picture made anywhere.

The anti-climax to the story was a shoot-out in a warehouse stacked with ghostly white plaster busts of Neville Chamberlain, bullets shattering his sad, drooping moustaches. And in the climax next morning, they are all back at Ramsgate, where Captain Andersen and his Danish ship are allowed to clear, leaving the two principals free to drop their lifebelts on the deck and go into the final clinch. It was all pure corn, but corn served up by professionals, and it worked.

Naturally we had planned to make the film at Denham. But where was the money coming from? Alex had vanished to America with the unfinished *Thief of Bagdad*, to arrange to finish the film there in Hollywood. All the Americans had upped stakes and gone home. Irving Asher and family had gone. Even Jerry Jackson and his wife, Peggy, who was expecting a baby, had gone. I went to Chris Mann, and Chris Mann arranged a meeting at Denham, on our home ground with John Corfield, production supervisor for Lady Yule, the widow of the banker who had founded the private Yule-Catto Bank. Lady Yule was a racehorse owner, and she also owned a film studio at Elstree, and she was partly responsible for the financing of Pinewood Studios, which are still active.

John Corfield was one of those men who are scared to death by every decision they make, but can't resist making them. He came to see Emeric and me at Denham, practically wringing his hands at our announcement that we would make the film at Denham Studios and nowhere else.

"Of course, I know that you two are Denham men," he wailed, "but can't I persuade you to make the film at Elstree, where we have a perfectly good studio standing empty, with a permanent staff eating their heads off?"

But I was adamant. Yes, we were Denham men and we were not going to give up that proud title without a struggle. We had already announced our very popular decision to the other technicians at Denham, who were only looking for someone to give them a lead. In the end, the great name of Denham, and the watchword of quality, and maybe the fact that *The Spy in Black* and *The Lion Has Wings* both had my name prominently on them, and were making fortunes at the box-office, had something to do with Corfield's decision. We had the script finished and the production ready to go by the end of October. And nobody could believe it. How was it possible, they asked, to get an original story with two big stars going in such a short time? It was possible, I answered, because we were technicians, and we had the best technicians in England with us. We knew how to make films and we knew when to say yes and when to say no. As for the story and script, we wrote it ourselves. All they had to do was pay up and shut up. This willingness to take responsibility for our own decisions carried us right through the war and into the peace that followed.

As for the technicians, we skimmed off the very top of the *crème de la crème*. Fred Young was chief cameraman, and you can be sure that his camera crew was the best in the business. Alfred Junge was designer and art director. At last I had got my hands on this Prussian genius. He was taking orders from me. With him he brought an art department second to none, draftsmen, sketch artists, costume designers, prop-men – of all these, Uncle Alfred had the finest and the best. When he said "Jump" his staff beat the record. John Seabourne was my editor. My sound recordist was the best man at Denham, C. C. Stevens. My composer of music was Richard Addinsell. My chief lighting gaffer was Bill Wall. I knew and loved and admired them all. They were the very cream off the top.

Emeric wrote and was credited with the original story. We wrote the shooting script together, as we had on *The Spy in Black*, laughing and fighting, biting and scratching, with frequent consultations with Valerie and Connie. It wasn't nearly such a difficult job as *The Spy in Black* had been. It was basically a chase in the blackout.

I had my first serious difference of opinion with Emeric over the music. Miklos Rozsa, the composer of the original musical score for *The Thief of Bagdad*, who was Hungarian like Alex and Emeric, had also written the music for *The Spy in Black*. Emeric naturally supposed that I would want his friend and compatriot to write the score of *Contraband*, and had assured him of the job. But I felt that we needed more English contributors. Miklos Rozsa's future was already assured in Hollywood, and it was time to give an English composer a chance. My decision caused an understandable coolness between Emeric and myself, but I stood firm.

East Kent was not yet a closed area. Later on, of course, it was the most restricted zone in England, but though war had been declared, it was still wide open for a film unit. The Admiralty read our script, laughed a great deal, and gave us their blessing. The county police followed suit. I left the obtaining of permits to the people at London Films, who had lots of experience in this sort of line, and we had all the cases marked in letters six inches high: LONDON FILMS PRODUCTIONS, DENHAM STUDIOS, CONRAD VEIDT, VALERIE HOBSON, care of the best hotel in Ramsgate, right on the seafront. And I had a stencil made – CONTRABAND in big letters – and we used it extensively on all the boxes, cases and mysterious pieces of equipment that a big film unit carries about with it. This particular gag delighted the real Contraband Controllers at Ramsgate, and they insisted on stencilling our crates with their own provocative stencils, like EXPLOSIVES, EXAMINED, CONDEMNED.

That evening, at the Ramsgate Hotel, I could hardly believe my eyes as I looked around the crowded lounge. The bar was doing a brisk business, and our crew, including Conrad Veidt and Valerie Hobson and Esmond, were hobnobbing with the Royal Navy, the Royal Naval Reserve, and the Royal Volunteer Reserve, all very much on deck. Connie and Valerie had the biggest crowd around them, asking what it was like to be a film star, and telling them what a wonderful job they had done in *The Spy in Black*. Connie had been granted British citizenship the year before, but here in another group was Alfred Junge, an enemy alien (for although he had been in England continuously for fifteen years, he had never taken out naturalization papers). Yet here he was, holding forth to a circle of admiring senior officers on how you design a motion picture, and asking searching questions about Ramsgate and Contraband Control, which should have got him interned for the rest of the war. Emeric, another enemy alien, was seated at a table with the Chief Constable of the county, expounding the script and explaining how we cut between studio and real exteriors. I rubbed my eyes and marvelled. The mighty names of London Films and Alexander Korda had helped, of course, and everyone here had seen *The Lion Has Wings* and *The Spy in Black*. But it couldn't possibly last. Such openness and enthusiasm, and such innocence! And I decided that the sooner we shot the essential scenes the better, and we should get out as soon as possible, taking our booty with us, before anyone high up mentioned the word "Security".

Just then, there was a burst of laughter from the biggest circle of all, around John Seabourne, who was giving them a rundown on the script, describing how Captain Andersen, a friendly neutral, outwits the Contraband Control and gets ashore in spite of the Ramsgate Coastal Watchers, mixed with reminiscences of his own escape from Dover Castle as a deserter from the army in the other world war.

A week later, we were shooting the scenes on board Captain Andersen's ship in Denham Studios. We were up to schedule and John Corfield had calmed down. After our first day's work, I thought he would cut his throat. It was a very atmospheric scene in the Contraband Control, with lots of movement and technical jargon. We had experts from the Admiralty with us, and anyway we had all the jargon on the tip of our tongues. The scene ran four minutes, and after consulting with Fred Young we decided to shoot it in one continuous tracking shot, rehearsing it and speeding it up until we had cut about a minute out. This took all day and nothing was in the can at five o'clock.

John Corfield was going crazy, walking up and down with his watch in his hand, saying to anybody who would listen to him: "Is he always like this? Does he always work like that? What's he doing, I don't understand! There are seven scene numbers to be covered. The schedule says so!"

John Seabourne calmed him down. "It's all right, John, he's covering all seven numbers in one shot. He's whipping the actors up. He doesn't want the tempo to drop for one second. You'll see."

"But why doesn't he shoot something?"

At twenty past five, we started shooting and got it in the third take.

I said: "That's it. Home boys," and Bill Wall started to put the lights out.

John Corfield was still bleating: "Mr Seabourne, isn't he going to cover himself? Doesn't he want some close-ups? Don't *you* want some close-ups, Mr Seabourne?"

"Three minutes and twenty-two seconds of finished film on the first day," replied John. He picked up the cans of exposed negative and weighed them in his hand. They were all taped, ready to go to the laboratory, marked CONTRABAND on the white tape with black pencil.

"That's about three to one, John," he said. "You can't do much better than that. Micky hates wasting film."

We had a studio schedule of six weeks, and we finished on December 16. We turned the camera unit over to John Seabourne to direct the letters, signs and inanimate objects so dear to an editor's heart, and so boring for the unit on the floor. Then we had a terrific party, which John Corfield paid for. The picture looked like being about £8,000 under budget. I believe the total cost was finally about £47,000.

Alfred Junge had done us proud on the art direction. As the headquarters of the spy circus, Emeric had asked for a modern office building with a lot of action around the elevator. Freddie and I were perfectly prepared to trick this with moving shadows, etc., but Alfred pooh-poohed this and gave us a full working elevator, from basement to ground floor, and the unit never tired of using it. He had a large number of sets to build and he was always on time and always ready. He finished the picture under budget. Alfred Junge is always under budget. Hitler could have used him for the invasion of England.

It is not generally recognised by the public that the most genuinely creative member of a film unit, if the author of the original story and screenplay is excluded, is the art director. In the legitimate theatre, his creative authority is recognized and "costumes and decor by so-and so" are given the credit and importance they they should have; but in the film world the producer and director and cameraman are so full of themselves that it is not sufficiently acknowledged that the art director is the creator of those miraculous images up there on the big screen, and that besides being a painter and an architect, this miracle man has to be an engineer as well.

Before we stopped working on *The Thief of Bagdad*, I had realized that Bill and I would have to move into London. We found a little mews house in Belgravia, 65A Chester Square. It is on the corner of Eaton Mews South and Eccleston Street, only a couple of hundred yards from Victoria Station. Miraculously, it is still there. It was a doll's house, with three storeys and a room and a half on each storey. It was about as bombproof as a packet of cigarette papers. I was very happy there all through the war. It was comforting to know that if a bomb did hit you, you would never know it.

During the shooting of *Contraband*, I had noticed a constant visitor to the set. This was rare for me, because my system of direction is to make myself the storm centre of anything that is happening on the stage that morning or afternoon. From the moment I step on the floor, I am immersed in the creation of a film, and see nothing outside that. I come out of the whirlwind, briefly but definitively, for lunch, which Bill usually prepared in the caravan. Alex gone, we had pitched it on the lawn, where it remained for the whole of the war. It was somewhere between the studio restaurant and the Old House, a good spot to keep on eye on things. Bill would retail gossip while I ate.

One day he said: "Yon felly, him we called the Skipper, him that helped us with the launch at Ramsgate, and had a master's ticket in sail . . ."

"Oh, George Mills . . . yes?"

"He's coming out tomorrow for the day. I told him he could come with us."

"OK."

Bill was standing in the corner polishing a cup and clucked disapprovingly as he saw someone coming from the Old House. "There's that felly again."

"What felly?"

"He's a friend of that Cunynghame's." Bill had no time for chair polishers. "He's been hanging around to see you for days. I had to head him off. He said maybe he could see you at lunchtime, and I told him he could not."

I squinted out of the window. It was John Sutro, one of the directors of London Films. He was the son, or grandson, of the famous playwright Alfred Sutro, one of a group of very successful London playwrights in the early years of the century. I only knew him by sight. He was about my age. He was ugly in the way that a bulldog or bullfrog is ugly, yet very endearing. George MacDonald thought that ugliness in a human being was the animal inside, trying to get out. John was a bit of a clown, and I remember seeming some dailies from, I think, *The Divorce of Lady X*, in which John played a waiter with a loaded tray who got into difficulties with ·a swing door. He had very good taste, was an amateur in the arts, and mad about films.

As he crossed the lawn he called out: "Micky, can I see you? Are you there?"

Seeing there was no hope for it, Bill stepped outside saying to me: "You'll need all your time," a dark saying of his. I heard him say to John outside: "He's due back on the floor in six minutes."

John sidled in with his disarming bulldog grin.

"Have a cup of tea?" I inquired. He made a vague gesture of assent and I poured it out.

"Milk?"

"Yes . . . I mean no."

I nodded. "Sugar?"

"No . . . I mean yes."

"Lemon?"

He shook his head impatiently. "I've been wanting to talk to you. Oh! Congratulations, by the way!"

"Congratulations? For what?"

"For everything." He made a complimentary gesture. "For carrying on."

This was nice, for he obviously meant it.

"Thanks," I said.

He waved his hand again. "Duff Cooper is going to be the Minister."

"Minister of what?"

"Minister of Information."

"Will he be good?"

Another gesture, impatient this time. "That's not the point. Duff's an artist, a writer. He's a great friend of Churchill's. He's one of us – he understands the importance of films."

I digested this. This strange young man was obviously very well informed – better informed than I was.

John went on: "The film department of the Ministry of Information is going to be very important. The Government wants the film industry to pull its weight in the war. It's going to be a separate department, reporting only to the Minister."

Even I could understand that this was big news. "Who's going to be the head of it?" I asked.

"Kenneth Clark."

I stared. "The Director of the National Gallery?"

"Yes."

I wisecracked: "Well, at least he knows something about pictures."

But John was very much in earnest. "Micky, I want you to come with me and see Clark."

The meeting with Kenneth Clark took place about two months later. The "phoney war" was on, and the appeasers still hoped that an honourable peace could be made with Hitler. Not so the Jews, the Poles, the Czechs, and most definitely not Churchill. That Naval Personage was at the Admiralty biding his time and preparing for total war.

Contraband had opened at the Odeon Leicester Square, and was a smash hit. Like *The Spy in Black*, it ran for four weeks, four times a day, at this enormous cinema, before going out and cleaning up in the country. Oscar Deutsch, the chairman of the Odeon circuit, who had created this chain of super-cinemas with the help of an industrious accountant, John Davis, had publicly announced his belief in the future of British films. Other producers, getting over their fright, or stirring in their sleep, were starting to announce plans. Gabriel Pascal, who before the war had produced a highly successful *Pygmalion*, directed by Anthony Asquith and edited by David Lean, announced that he would personally direct a film of Shaw's *Major Barbara*, with a starry English cast. It was difficult to see what that could do for the war effort, but perhaps Gabby had been impressed by the Salvation Army lass's military title. It kept together a group of top technicians, including David Lean as co-director and Fred Young as lighting cameraman, and that was all to the good. Among my close friends, Vernon Sewell had joined the Navy and was in command of a little ship, a coastal defence vessel, and was stationed at the Isle of Wight. He had persuaded Esmond Knight to join the Navy (with dire consequences to his later career), and he nearly got me in too. The interviewing officer said that I had nice blue eyes, real seaman's eyes. But although I went for the interview and got registered, I had other plans for my eyes.

The Ministry of Information had taken over the buildings of London University in Bloomsbury, and it was there that John Sutro and I went to see Kenneth Clark, Knight Commander of the Bath and Director Designate of the Films Division. He was brilliant and likeable, though physically he created a curious impression, because the head on his body seemed to belong to some other man. He had written a very entertaining book, *The Gothic Revival*, while still at university. He had then become a pupil of Bernhard Berenson, which opened the door to the world of art for him while he was still a young man. Back in England, he was made Keeper of the King's Pictures, and then Director of the National Gallery and a KCB. He saw John Sutro and me at the Ministry, alone except for an elderly female secretary who took notes in the shadows. Such a clever man was bound to be a film fan, and he was.

"I've seen all your films, and I must congratulate you," he said. "The main work of this Division will be to sponsor and encourage documentary films and information films, but it is also part of our policy to encourage feature-film makers, provided that we approve the script."

"When you say encourage, do you mean with money?" I asked. John Sutro waved his hand deprecatingly.

Clark hesitated. "This has been discussed, but has not yet been decided. We understand that a feature film can cost anywhere from £20,000 to £50,000."

"Or more," I suggested.

"Or more," he agreed.

I said slowly: "The difficult part of making a film is the development money. That is the money to buy the rights or an option on the rights of a book or a play, or an idea, and to commission a script, plus the necessary overheads to keep the producer going for perhaps six months or a year. This would be a very small percentage of the total cost, but it's the most valuable part of the financing because otherwise the film will never get going without a script that people can read."

He was listening attentively. "Is that how you and Mr Pressburger would like to proceed?"

I said cautiously: "We might. If the film had the approval and backing of the Ministry, and a good script, it should not be very difficult to raise the rest of the finance. Don't you think so, John?"

John nodded vigorously, got half way up from his chair, sat down again, wreathed his hands and beamed. Things were going well. He obviously felt like a lion-tamer who had just brought off a difficult trick with two new lions.

Clark said: "Would you be interested in making a film about mine-sweeping, and the way we are handling the anti-submarine war?"

"No, I wouldn't," I said.

The typist looked up from her notes. The others looked at me expectantly.

I opened my briefcase and produced a folded newspaper. It was a page from the *Daily Express*. I unfolded it, placed it under Clark's nose and said:

"I want to make a film in Canada." I had not rehearsed this, and I suddenly felt that this short speech was one of the most important in my life.

Clark said: "Why Canada?"

"Because Canada is in the war already as a member of the British Commonwealth and is no more ready than we are to deal with Hitler. Sooner or later, their coast will be attacked and their ships sunk, and that will bring America into the war. I want to make a film in Canada to scare the pants off the Americans, and bring them into the war sooner."

Clark started to read the article. John Sutro sidled round the desk, bent over his shoulder, and started to read it too. It was an article by A. Beverly Baxter, a Canadian journalist, and was reprinted in a Beaverbrook paper from *Maclean's* of Toronto. It was a brilliant piece of journalism. The writer knew his facts. I had only read it the day before, and it cured me of insularity. I suddenly understood what Churchill had seen years ago. This was going to be a global war, a war of survival, a shift in world politics that would affect communications all over the world. Without that article, I would never have said anything so positive as "I want to make a film in Canada."

The idea went up to the Minister and in due course came back to us approved. Clark asked me what was our next step? What was our story to be? What had we got in mind?

I said: "How can we tell, when we've never been to Canada? We shall have to go there at once, and write it."

Sutro suggested that the Treasury put up some money, say £5,000, to pay for me and Pressburger to go to Canada. The Treasury didn't like the idea. The Treasury didn't like films. The Treasury didn't like us. Clark was firm and they had to reach down into their Whitehall jeans and pull out

£5,000 for our estimated expenses. Then there was a hitch over getting the appropriation signed by the appropriate official, and so on, and so on. Finally, Leigh Ashton, from the Victoria and Albert Museum, and one of Clark's close friends and associates, who was also working for the Ministry and acting as his deputy, was persuaded to sign it. I remember that he did so in the tiny office he occupied next to Clark, almost completely filled by himself. He was a bulky man. There was a small table and chair and a huge image of some Asiatic god or other, with incense smoking in front of it. He signed the paper with a quill pen, which he sharpened carefully with a penknife.

Emeric and I had seen Connie Veidt off to America on the *Queen Mary*, together with Lillie and her sister, only a week or two before, wishing him luck with the submarines, and we were now to follow him on one of the Canadian lines, for we had decided that the sooner we went Canadian, the better. We were booked on the *Duchess of Bedford*, one of the famous "Drunken Duchesses". We were the only first-class passengers on board, and lived on great spoonfuls of caviare and champagne for the whole six days. We ransacked the ship's library for books on Canada. True to her reputation, the dear *Duchess* rolled drunkenly all the way across the Atlantic. But champagne and caviare made us proof against seasickness. The *Duchess* and her sisters served gallantly through the first years of the war, and I believe they were all lost at sea – war casualties, torpedoed or bombed. By the time we arrived at Halifax, Nova Scotia, Emeric had produced an idea. I listened and said: "Yes, I think I can sell that."

I must remark to the student of motives that all this was neither planned nor calculated. I was just following my daemon. I had been preparing for a leading part in my profession for thirteen years, and I was ready for it. One thing followed another. I was offered opportunity after opportunity and took them with both hands. *The Spy in Black*, coupled with the reports of Vincent Korda and Connie Veidt, had put me in solid with Alexander Korda. He had needed a co-director for *The Thief of Bagdad* and sent for me. *The Thief of Bagdad* led to *The Lion Has Wings*. Both films encouraged me to deal with masses of men and materials and to try out new techniques. The creative partnership with Emeric led naturally to *Contraband*. The success of all four films, and the prestige of *The Thief of Bagdad*, made me in six months the most impressive figure in British films. I had no notion of this. One thing followed another, and I followed my star.

Halifax was the main port on the eastern seaboard of Canada, for it never froze up in winter. As soon as we landed, we booked our tickets for Ottawa and mounted the magnificent coaches of the Canadian National Railway with great respect. I suppose that the chief impression of the United States and Canada that had been made upon the European filmgoers of the twenties and thirties was of the magnificent trains: the great engines, with their enormous wheels and their bells tolling across the prairie; the coloured Pullman car porters; the sleeping cars with their bunks and green baize curtains. The Canadian National and the Canadian Pacific Railway had all this and more. We had neither of us been to the North American continent, not even to the Western Hemisphere, and although our profession was an international one and had familiarised us with America, we enjoyed every minute of our experience in an atmosphere of high romance, and delighted in the confirmation of all our imaginings.

It was good to be rolling through this rich and unhurried land, across Nova Scotia, New Brunswick, Quebec, through Montreal to Ottawa, the federal capital and seat of Parliament. We were beginning to appreciate the majestic simplicity and enormous size of Canada. The snow was melting and the ice had lost its grip on the land. The train took us into the heart of Ottawa, where the railway station and the CPR hotel formed a group with the Parliamentary buildings. Everything was within easy reach. We walked across to the hotel and booked a suite. We were accredited to the Department of External Affairs, which corresponds roughly to our Foreign Office. We were recommended to H. L. Keenlyside. We had read his book in the ship's library on Canadian-American relations. He sent somebody to fetch us over.

With him in his office, stretched out on two or three chairs, was a long, lean, handsome man with reddish curly hair and extraordinary bright eyes. He was obviously crippled and tortured by arthritis, and wore a very expensive suit which was crumpled and covered in cigar ash. This was Leonard Brockington, intimate of the Prime Minister's, man of leisure, wit, raconteur and bon viveur. He was always in pain and always prepared to help others. He was just the kind of experienced, civilised, knowledgeable man who knows and knew everybody that we needed to meet at that particular moment. Keenlyside was keen, hospitable and ready to help.

I told them that we had come prepared to talk about our project and would like a meeting with all the Ministers concerned. This sounds perhaps a tall order, but they didn't seem to think so. They opened the Parliamentary telephone directory, which had the numbers of the extensions of all the Ministries, and using two telephones they rang up everybody they could think of who might be useful for a meeting that afternoon at three. In most cases the Minister answered the telephone himself. With my limited experience of British governmental departments, this was something new. Keenlyside told them that they should come; and Leonard Brockington told them they had to come. They were all there that afternoon, from the Prime Minister's secretary and Head of the Privy Council, to the Minister of Woods and Forests. Keenlyside chaired the meeting; Leonard Brockington put in an occasional suggestion.

I explained who we were and what we were doing in Canada, and that the British Treasury supported the venture. There were one or two incredulous looks and whistles at this statement. I said that the first purpose of the film was propaganda to counter the extremely able Nazi propaganda that had been threatening and frightening the North American continent for years. They sat up at that. I said that our second aim was to bring America into the war with us, and this got a cheer. I said that as long as the frontier between the United States and Canada remained open, this was unlikely to happen. The object of our film was to get it closed, or at least patrolled and surveyed. I said that the whole vast Atlantic seaboard of the Dominion was vulnerable to enemy attack and that it would take several years to set up a network of defence and communication to guard it. It would not be long, I said, before citizens of Eastern Canada would be able to see torpedoed vessels sinking off their coasts. If America remained neutral, and if the German pocket battleships and super-submarines had command of the North Atlantic, it would not be long before the Germans would be grabbing bases in Iceland and Greenland and threatening the coast of Canada. I said that it was our idea that a big feature film that took cognizance of all these facts, and had the courage to face up to them, could do a lot to shake Nazi confidence during the next eighteen months. This I was only quoting from my experience on *The Lion Has Wings*. I then introduced Emeric formally as the writer on the project. They had seen our films, of course. Every scrap of information that came from the Old Country about wartime conditions there had been eagerly gobbled up long ago. I told them Emeric's idea.

It was *The Ten Little Indians*. We were going to show a Nazi submarine sinking vessels within sight of the American shore, pursued northward into Hudson Bay and sunk there by the Canadian Air Force (loud guffaws from the others at the expense of the Air Minister). There would be six survivors whose one aim would be to escape westward to the Pacific and so home, or at worst southward into internment in the neutral United States. One by one, they would be killed or captured. It was propaganda at its subtlest. They would look like heroes at first. Only when they started murdering, lying and thieving and coming up against the peaceful citizens of Canada would their actual nature and beliefs be revealed.

We proposed to let the facts speak for themselves, and to do no sermonising until the big final scene when the lone survivor comes up against a typical Canadian. We proposed to follow their possible route west and south and asked for letters of introduction to all the provinces we would have to visit, as far as the Pacific coast and back again.

I was talking very big and pushing a great big country around as if it was no bigger than England, but they didn't seem to mind. Canada is a big country and these were big men.

"When you say a big feature film," interjected Leonard Brockington, "how big do you mean?"

"As big as they come," I said firmly. "Emeric thinks that the six Nazis should be young men, each of them typifying a certain aspect of Nazi teaching or personality. There are all kinds of Nazis: courageous, cruel, resourceful, brutal. One of them might be a very decent fellow. But they are all Nazis, and they all come to a sticky end. Emeric's idea is that in their trip across Canada, they come up against typical Canadians in different surroundings and circumstances, and these would all be played by big names so that the audience, following the adventures of the heroes/ villains or villains/heroes, whatever you like to call them, would always be expecting one of these stars to turn up and confront the escaping Nazis."

"Have you any particular stars in mind?" asked Leonard, obviously a born showman. I looked at Emeric.

"Vell," said Emeric, "obviously the Nazis should meet some Canadian citizens who are of German origin. For this we shall play actors like Anton Walbrook and Elisabeth Bergner."

"I'm sure we could get Laurence Olivier," I said. "He's working in Hollywood now for Korda, with Vivien Leigh on *That Hamilton Woman*. I know he's coming back to join the Fleet Air Arm at the end of the year. He could play one of these parts before the Navy gets him."

"Leslie Howard would be a good bet," said somebody. "He could pass as English or Canadian."

"And Raymond Massey," I said. "I know that Americans think he's Abraham Lincoln, but he's Canadian and he'd hate to be left out of something like this."

"Ray Massey is back in the Canadian Army," observed Brockington. "We'll soon have him out of that."

They were all talking enthusiastically now! We seemed to have carried the motion unanimously.

Before we started on our Canadian lightning tour, we did a naughty thing, because it wasn't in our brief from the Treasury. We went to New York. We just couldn't resist it. There we were just a few hundred miles from the fantastic dream city of all Europeans. We decided to play hooky and see a play on Broadway. The Lunts, Alfred Lunt and Lynn Fontanne, were playing in Robert Sherwood's play *There Shall Be No Night*, about the vicious war between mighty Russia and tiny Finland which made the Russians respect the Finns for ever, and treat them as equals. It seems like a dream to me now, but I know we did it. I don't even remember whether we flew down or whether we went by train. I know we arrived in New York in the afternoon, walked around marvelling, went to the theatre that night, ate at Schraffts and got a bed somewhere (I think the price was seven dollars a night), and returned surfeited to Ottawa next day. Like that O. Henry story of how Ikey Sniggle Fritz shook the hand of the Big Boss, we had seen New York and were no longer from the boondocks.

In less than three weeks, spent constantly on the move, Emeric and I absorbed the Dominion of Canada, digested it and incorporated it in our script. The giant provinces were linked not by road, but by railroad: by the Canadian Pacific Railway and by the Canadian National Railway, which was publicly owned. In 1940, Trans-Canada Airways linked the provinces as well, mostly with small aircraft, twenty- or thirty-seaters, and flown by bush pilots. We switched impartially from railroad to automobile, from aircraft to horseback. We crossed the vast prairies by air, reducing 2,000 miles to a few hours, and we crossed the Rockies through Banff and down the Red River Valley to Vancouver in luxurious CPR coaches, crawling down to the Pacific Coast by the famous seventeen hairpin turns. We made sudden sallies into the country north of Winnipeg, or south of Calgary, and in Vancouver we crossed the bay to Vancouver Island, where the capital Victoria stands. Osmond Borrodaile, my cameraman on the first shots of *The Thief of Bagdad*, was in Vancouver. He had shot most of *Elephant Boy* and the great panoramic scenes of *The Four Feathers* in the Sudan, and loved adventure. He came from Vancouver and had returned there when the war broke out. We went to look for him. He took us in a light aircraft into the great mountains at the head of Vancouver Sound and we arranged with him to shoot the opening shots of the picture there (they are in the film under the main title and as a heroic background to the names of the stars). In the Rockies we saw Banff and Lake Louise, and couldn't decide between the two, so wonderful was the setting of both of them. And it was at Banff that I found out about Lake O'Hara, a jewel of a location, above the 10,000-foot-line in grizzly country. And we learned there about the Blackfoot Indians and their yearly parade on Indian Day.

We visited the German-speaking Hutterites at their settlements near Winnipeg, and we picked a lake in the woods and farmlands for the crash of the stolen aircraft (for, of course, the Nazis would have to steal an aircraft in order to get them from Hudson Bay to the centre of Canada). We marvelled at Toronto's ugliness (now it is a much changed and strikingly modern city), and the twin cultures of Montreal. And we made trips to Quebec and Trois Rivières because we intended to use French-Canadian separatism and cultural independence as one of the sore points the Nazis would try to exploit once they had a foot in the Dominion. Everywhere we went, we bought pamphlets, books, maps, poems, posters, advertisements, until our luggage had doubled in weight. Finally we reported to Leonard Brockington in Ottawa that we were through. We were talking to him on the telephone in Montreal, from the Hotel Windsor, which was to be our base when making the film. We were taking the next Drunken Duchess back to London. We had finished our research and were heading home to write the script and have our showdown with the Treasury. Perhaps I sounded a bit too cocky. There was a long pause and then his voice drawled: "Have you heard the latest news? France has surrendered."

As we rolled back to England we pushed and pulled and sweated our story into an outline of about twenty pages. It was typical of two moviemakers like us, that although we were returning to a country under immediate threat of invasion and bombardment by air, by sea and by land, where the "phoney war" was over and the remnants of our army were gathering at Dunkirk, all that interested us was our story, our plans and our film. It was one thing for me, who was English, to be so nonchalant about returning to my country in the middle of a disaster, and quite another for Emeric, who was an enemy alien, an artist, a journalist, a writer who had come to England for a haven from Hitler after an uneasy passage through Prague, Berlin and Paris. Yet here he was, planning with me how we would proceed with our divided responsibilities, sharing my confidence that we would get the approval of the Minister and the money from Whitehall to make our picture, discussing with me what writer he could work with in collaboration over the English dialogue, agreeing that he should stay in England for the present, while I would gather up my unit and the actors that we needed on location and return as soon as possible to Canada to start shooting the picture before it got too late in the year, for the harvest was near and we had already got a deadline for our activities in the far north. We planned that he was to return to Canada in September, for the final rewrite of the Raymond Massey sequence, which was to be shot in a tiny film studio belonging to the CPR in Montreal, although he knew as well as anyone that by *that* time the Atlantic would be alive with U-boats and the chances of any vessel reaching port were evens. As I have said, it was one thing for me, for whom defeat was inconceivable, and who shared the attitude of any Englishman worth his salt, putting down his pint or his pipe and saying "Well, suppose we've got to do something about Herr Hitler" before he signed up for military service, and quite another for Emeric, who had escaped from Hitler's SS by the skin of his teeth, and who knew that writers who can influence public opinion are the first victims on the list of those in power when they have got the wind up.

Dunkirk was on, but in spite of that we had our appointment with the Minister without delay. Duff Cooper was a handsome and attractive man. He wore a dark suit, but looked like a soldier. He had won his MC in the First World War. He wore an Old Etonian tie. He was signing some papers and talking in low tones to a secretary. A small group of Treasury officials were lurking in the shadows. "The enemy," John Sutro murmured.

Clark introduced me as the spokesman for our group, and Duff Cooper settled back in his chair to listen.

I said: "Minister, may I introduce Emeric Pressburger, the author of this story, which we propose to call *49th Parallel*."

The Minister stood up, Emeric stepped forward, and they shook hands. Then I unfolded my map of Canada and spread it out on the Minister's desk.

"This is a propaganda picture in which the only good Nazi is a dead Nazi," I began. "But as that kind of propaganda can be self-defeating, we have started out by making them human beings. There are all kinds of Nazis, as there are all kinds of human beings. Our group of seven are a composite of the Nazi character and creed. Emeric's story is about seven little Nazis, who are survivors of a German U-boat's crew, which has been operating off the coast of Canada, sinking defenceless vessels. Their ship is tracked down and destroyed by the Canadian Navy and Air Force. The commandant is killed. He was a foolish great bullock of a man, unthinking, obedient, an executioner. The six survivors are left in a desperate position next to a Hudson's Bay post, where they meet their first two Canadians, a French-Canadian trapper and the factor of the post. This is the start of their trail of thefts and murders in an attempt to escape across Canada. One by one they are captured or killed. The first to go is the youngest of them, Jahner. He has been a Nazi since he was twelve. Murder and violence is his way of life. He is shot by an Eskimo. Then there are five in a stolen seaplane. They fly across Canada until the gas gives out. They crash land in a shallow lake near Winnipeg, and Kuhnecke, the engineer officer, is killed. He is the kind of Nazi who has been, since the beginning, a high-ranking officer in the Party. He had to be given a job, whether he was competent or not. He proves his competency by breaking his neck. Now there are four. They are in the heartland of Canada. A group of German-born immigrants, Christian communists of German descent (they call themselves Hutterites), take them in without knowing who they are. Deceived by the kindness they have received, their leader, Lieutenant Hirth, second-in-command of the U-boat, makes a typical Nazi speech claiming them as brothers. A young girl whose father and mother have been killed by the Nazis threatens to denounce them. One of the Nazis, Vogel, is a decent fellow and wants to stay and become one of these friendly farmers. He is a baker by trade. Lieutenant Hirth orders the others to arrest him, and after a brief trial one of them executes him as a traitor to the Führer. Now there are three."

In spite of themselves, the Treasury men were listening intently. However much they disapproved of us, they wanted to know what happened next. I caught Clark's eye. He nodded. John Sutro was listening with all his ears. Emeric was like a graven image. I went on:

"These three murder and rob their way across Canada to the West. They thumb a ride, kill the driver and steal his car and his money. They ditch the car and go on by railroad. They arrive at Banff in the Rockies on Indian Day. Now they are surrounded by people. The Mounties are looking for them, and are hot on their trail. Even the tourists at Banff are pressed into service. The nerve of one of the three remaining cold-blooded murderers breaks, and he is captured and nearly lynched by the mob. Now there are two. They escape into the high Rockies. They are not far from the border with America now – the 49th Parallel. This is, if I may remind you, Minister, the title of our film. They are given shelter in his camp, by a rich and easy-going writer. He seems to be a sitting duck for the ruthless Nazis. But when they become violent, it rebounds on them. Lohrman, the gunman of the group, tries to shoot his way out and is captured by the man he despises. Now there is only one, Lieutenant Hirth, the zealot, the fanatic, the devotee, the dyed-in-the-wool Nazi. He doubles back across Canada. The final scene between him and a Canadian soldier who has overstayed his leave takes place in a boxcar which will take them across the border into neutral America, by the suspension bridge below Niagara Falls. These two, the fanatical Nazi and the Canadian soldier, end the film with a showdown of their very different beliefs and creeds."

The big room was very quiet. Duff Cooper hesitated. It was time to play my trumps.

"We are taking the actors who play the Nazis with us. They are cheap and we can get authentic scenes with them in Canada. The big parts are star parts which will be filmed here later in England. A Canadian trapper, Johnny, who is murdered by the Nazis at the Hudson's Bay post; the Hudson's Bay factor; the leader of the German-Canadian settlers; the charming, easy-going ethnologist in the Rockies; and finally, the Canadian soldier. There is only one woman's part in the story, the Hutterite girl who threatens to denounce them and causes the death of the young Nazi who has fallen in love with her. This part will be played by Elisabeth Bergner. The leader of the Hutterites will be played by Anton Walbrook. Leslie Howard has agreed to play the charming escapist gentleman in the Rockies. Raymond Massey has agreed to play the Canadian soldier, provided that his part can be filmed in Montreal, as he has rejoined the Canadian Army. Laurence Olivier hopes to be able to play the French-Canadian trapper, Johnny. We have contacted all these actors, and we have no reason to believe that they will go back on their promises. They have all agreed to work for the same flat fee."

Duff Cooper had been talking to Clark. He turned to the Treasury officials and said rapidly and almost inaudibly: "Finance must not stand in the way of this project."

He then left the room by a small door. The Ministry officials looked glum, and St John Bamford, their leader, started to put away papers in his briefcase and the others followed suit.

I said to Clark: "What happened?"

He said: "You've got your money."

I had told John Sutro to ask for £50,000 as it was obviously the ceiling figure in the discussions that had so far been held between the Minister and his Films Division. We had made a guess at a budget, and it looked as if we might conceivably come within the target. The main charge, of course, would be transporting, feeding and sleeping the cast and crew all over the Dominion of Canada during the next two months. But we knew all the figures and these were predictable. The budget included the fees for the actors who were to go to Canada – they were getting a round sum for the job. It wasn't a very round sum, but it was a question of take it or leave it, and they took it, even Finlay Currie and Eric Portman – Finlay philosophically, Eric ungratefully.

Did I utter the name, Finlay Currie? He was the first of the "Foula Regulars" to sign on the dotted line for this new adventure. Bill Paton was already packing his bags – and mine. Niall MacGinnis was to play Vogel, the young Nazi engineer whose struggles with his conscience at the Hutterite settlement lead to his death at the hands of his fellow Nazis. Syd Streeter left the Rock Studios at my command and joined us as chief of construction. It was a big jump from building small studio sets to building a life-size replica of a German U-boat which could be handled at sea but he made it. Skeets Kelly joined us as operating cameraman, making five "Foula Regulars" in all. But, of course, one "Foula Regular" is worth three other men.

Fred Young was to be our lighting cameraman. During *Contraband*, we had become devoted friends and admirers of each other's technical resource. We had sworn to work together again, but of course nobody at that time knew what was around the corner. For me it was John Sutro and Canada, for Fred, Gabby Pascal and *Major Barbara*. It was a prestige picture, full of big names, Rex Harrison, Robert Morley, Wendy Hiller (whom Gabby had made famous as his Eliza in the film of Shaw's *Pygmalion*). That film had been directed by Anthony Asquith and Leslie Howard, but Gabby always spoke of it as *his* film. Gabby was presumed to be a Hungarian exile like Alex Korda, but was unlike Alex in every other particular. He and Alex couldn't stand each other. Gabby was built like a bull, with a sulky expression and large magnetic eyes. Heaven knows if he were really Hungarian. He claimed to have been a cavalry officer in the Hungarian army and rattled a phantom sabre. There was a touch of the gypsy in his makeup. But his big talk didn't impress Freddie Young, who was thirsting for action. He was somewhat comforted by the fact that David Lean, whom he admired and liked, was going to be co-director with Pascal. But he yearned to know more about *49th Parallel*. It was in black and white, of course, and I wanted to give it a rough appearance, as if it were a real war picture, shot off the cuff. I wanted the compositions to look accidental and sometimes almost as if they had been grabbed by a hand camera in the middle of the action. I wanted to vary the exposures and speeds of the cameras. We would be shooting in the far North in Hudson Strait as late as September, when there would be only just enough exposure for the speed of the film. We would be shooting wide open and the wild scenery would look grainy and realistic. Freddie caught on to this idea at once, and could have cut his throat to think that he was missing such a chance, and with such stars too! I let the mischief work, and one morning in my little London house (I was ill in bed with bronchitis), I heard Freddie's voice below, Bill answering it, the thunder of feet on the staircase, and Freddie burst into the bedroom, his hair standing on end, his eyes, gleaming behind his spectacles, and exclaiming "I'm yours!" as he plonked down out of breath at the end of the bed. I didn't bother to ask him how he had obtained his freedom, but threw him one of the story outlines with which the bed was littered. And Bill brought tea.

What days those were! Although there was a clampdown on all publicity, the news soon got about, and we were the white hope of the British film industry. That a young man who a year before had been earning sixty pounds a week as a Korda contract director, should be producing and directing a picture of this size, in the middle of the war, astonished people and gave them new hope. In spite of *The Lion Has Wings*, in spite of Dunkirk, not everybody believed, like us, in the impregnability of the British Isles, yet here we were casting and preparing a big picture, taking a number of actors and technicians out of the country at a time of national crisis, and proposing to bring them back again by a specific date in November. Everyone had to agree to this – it was in their letters of engagement. Gradually, the news leaked out to the press, although there was no official press release, and when they got no information from the Ministry of Information they naturally came to us, who gave them even less. I was to pay for this later.

The actors playing the Nazi sailors were to be a permanent part of the expedition. I needed them all with me because I had to be prepared to switch plans if the weather changed or if some location was no longer available. After all, it was their adventures in Canada that I was improvising and the scenes with the principals would be shot all in the studio, either in Montreal or back at Denham, with one exception. Elisabeth Bergner agreed to appear in exterior scenes at the Hutterite colony at Winnipeg. The support cast were all actors whom I had worked with before or seen in theatre productions outside the West End. Raymond Lovell had played the Nazi spy in *Contraband*. In the new film, he was to play Kuhnecke, the engineer officer. John Chandos, who would play Lohrman, had done good work at Marie Rambert's little Mercury Theatre in Notting Hill Gate, where later on Moira Shearer was to dance *Swan Lake* in *The Red Shoes*. (The fact that it is raining in that scene in the film is a reminiscence, because it always seemed to be raining when one queued up for Madame Rambert's productions.) Peter Moore I had seen in some Sunday performance, trying out a new play. Basil Appleby came from the stage also. I didn't want people whose faces were familiar to the film-going public. Richard George, who played the Commandant, I had seen as Ajax in a production at the Westminster Theatre of *Troilus and Cressida*. By and large, they were all new faces except Eric Portman, who played Lieutenant Hirth.

From the moment of Hirth's creation by Emeric, I had planned that this fanatical Nazi, second-in-command on board the U-boat, should be played by Esmond Knight. I have already mentioned that he had become a close friend, and I had met his family and his uncle, Captain Knight, who had tamed and trained and then toured the world with his famous golden eagle, Mr Ramshaw. Captain Knight was a great falconer and animal trainer, and Esmond had taken part in some of his expeditions. Later on, in 1944, when I made *I Know Where I'm Going* on the island of Mull, both Ramshaw and his trainer took part in the film, to the annoyance of Esmond, who detested amateur actors and claimed that he could play his uncle much better than his uncle. But it was his performance as the Angel in Tolstoy's *What Men Live By*, the little film that I wrote for Vernon Sewell in 1937, that convinced me that he had that extra something that a good actor needs to dominate the screen. It only needed a good part to bring it out, and here, at last, I had it for him. To my dismay, when I returned from Canada, I found that he had joined the Royal Navy at the urging of Vernon Sewell, which was all very well for Vernon, with his sea experience in small ships, but quite another for Esmond, who would get his training in big ships. I tried to postpone his enrolment until the film was made, but the times were too desperate for that kind of arrangement.

So I found myself suddenly in the position of having to find another actor of star quality, comparatively unknown and at the right price. I do all my casting direct by personal interview. In an important part there has to be a sympathy between the actor and the director. This is established right away or not at all. I had seen Eric Portman in a play starring a new Irish actress called Barbara Mullen. It was called *Jeannie*, and was a real smiling-through-the-tears comedy. It could have been a vehicle for Mary Pickford in the old days. Eric Portman played the sympathetic Yorkshire foreman of the factory where Jeannie works, and between them they worked up a very moving and believable relationship. Eric Portman was particularly good at showing, without words, the inner workings of this simple, intelligent, practical man. As to his authentic Yorkshire accent and attitudes, I learnt later that he hailed from Halifax. I argued to myself that anyone who could be so good at conveying his feelings without words would be very good at using them when he poured out his long Hitler tirades with the conviction and sincerity of an acolyte serving an archbishop.

I was right. There was a wonderful moment in the scene in the Hudson's Bay factor's house in *49th Parallel*, which may have been missed by a lot of people. In the course of a conversation between the invading Nazi and the French-Canadian trapper, while discussing their different ideologies, the trapper says: "I know my Bible. That's enough for me."

To which the German answers, laying his hand on the copy of Hitler's *Mein Kampf* from which he has been quoting: "This is the bible."

The deep religious sincerity of Lieutenant Hirth, as played by Eric Portman in this scene, is quite frightening.

It was this purity, this sincerity, which explains why Raymond Massey was so impressed with Portman's performance that he started a campaign with the other stars of the film to give him co-star billing. Besides being a great actor, Eric was a proud and suspicious human being, and in the initial stages of the picture he was quite convinced that I was a ruthless, sadistic Boy Scout leader, intent on submitting the actors to all kinds of hardships and indignities, which were not really necessary – to show that I had them in my power, and on starvation wages too. He knew very little about films, and what he did know he didn't like. He had only played in a few films before, and certainly not in an important part. He felt that his suspicions were justified when I started to improvise scenes for which there was no script, and for which there never would be a script until we returned to London. He fought me every step of the way and we both enjoyed it. He is dead now, and his many films are grinding through the television mill, but his performance in *49th Parallel* will never be forgotten.

I have come so far, have listed the names of the actors, have discussed my fellow technicians, and have not yet mentioned David Rawnsley. I don't know who introduced him to me, or where he came from, but he was the sort of young man that you wanted to be shipwrecked with on a desert island. When you met him, you thought that he could have been an actor, except that his charm and good manners were real and not assumed. He was tall, broad-shouldered, good-looking, considerate of others – in fact, too good to be true. Then you discovered that he was an architect and an engineer of genius and imagination. When you add to all these qualities the gifts of tact, diplomacy, patience, pertinacity and a love of his fellow men, you will agree that I should have mentioned him earlier. Every now and then, in our extraordinary, heart-breaking, back-breaking business, a man or woman appears or disappears upon whom you look back with regret, because they were made of too fine a material to be wasted on ordinary storytelling. David Rawnsley was one of these. He was to be our designer and art director, and he and Syd, recognising the craftsman in each other, fell into each other's arms. What a team they made!

We believed in treating our crews well, particularly in wartime, so everyone was travelling first-class, as the new and even more drunken *Duchess* rolled us from Liverpool to Halifax, Nova Scotia. I spent most of the voyage in the ship's library, dictating letters, memoranda, schedules, and tentative action sequences to Betty Curtis. David and Syd joined us, annexed the big table, spread out all their paper, slide-rules, T-squares, and all the paraphernalia of architects and spent the whole voyage calculating the coefficients of wood and steel. Syd had a mysterious little book which he always carried in his left-hand outside jacket pocket, and which was brought into play whenever some particularly hazardous camera position was suggested by me on Foula. Watched with reverence by the rest of us, he would whip it out and go into a conference with his slide-rule, until he finally pronounced what had to be done in order to suspend the camera and its operator over a thousand-foot precipice. He would then proceed to build this massive contraption, and nobody in the camera crew doubted for a moment that he would be as safe as on the studio floor. This little book went with us to Canada and was always the final arbiter – even with David Rawnsley. He and Syd would appeal to me from time to time, for confirmation of what I wanted. And their plans became more and more ambitious until, in the end, they had designed, and were going to build in Halifax Naval Dockyard a full-size mock-up, 120 feet long, of a German U-boat capable of a speed of five knots on the surface of the sea. It was not self-propelled. They planned to use two tugs. It was built in four parts, with a steel keel (I particularly remember the steel keel, because I was appealed to about it, and said "Certainly," without reflecting for one moment on what I was saying), which was cut into sections for transportation, each piece with a locking device at each end, so that the entire submarine could be reassembled at the chosen location. This was not to be in the Gulf of St Lawrence, where we could be a danger to shipping, but off the southwest coast of Newfoundland. I had already decided that the ship bringing us from the far North, after shooting the Hudson Bay sequence in September, would rendezvous with the submarine at a little town called Cornerbrook, operated by a paper company. It had wharves, cranes and auxiliary vessels, all of which would come in handy for our naval operation. Even I, who did not shrink from filling the executive offices at Lime Grove with water from my fire hoses in the cause of art, was shy about blowing up a submarine in full view of half a dozen neutrals scurrying for home.

There are two more names on my Roll of Honour: Henty Creer and Betty Curtis. Henty was the second cameraman, and was a protégé of Fred Young's. He was the hero of a famous occasion at Denham when Merle Oberon, directed by Joe von Sternberg, took a bath in the nude. Every technician in Denham wanted to be on the set of *I, Claudius* that day and the final successful candidates were a hand-picked lot. It was even rumoured that the three Kordas were there in disguise. Henty was known for his courtly manners, and when the lady came out of the bath and towards the camera, stepped on a cake of soap and did a pratfall, he instinctively – like a perfect gentle knight – rushed to her rescue meeting the lady face to – well, face to face, and realising the awfulness of his position, turned in terror to escape, skidded on the same cake of soap and joined her on the marble floor. The heroine of this piece of slapstick, completely unperturbed said: "Thank you, Henty," and, with the use of Henty's shoulder, rose to her feet, saying to two eager prop men: "My towel, please."

Henty came from a distinguished and creative family and he would certainly have become a film director if he had survived the war. He was sandy in colour and observant – he reminded me of an inquisitive bird. He was no respecter of persons, and yet was a hero-worshipper too. As one of the Technicolor camera operators he had been with me in some tight corners during the filming of action sequences on *The Thief of Bagdad*. Fred had suggested him because we might need some pick-up shots, which a second camera unit could do while we moved on to beat the weather. This is, in fact, what happened. We left him and Bill Paton behind at Lake O'Hara, while we moved on to the Hutterite settlement to get the harvest scenes.

Henty's experience, until then, had been with big films like *Knight Without Armour* and *The Ghost Goes West*, and with directors like Jacques Feyder and René Clair – great European masters. He was a bit irked by the lack of secrecy and the informal way I had of handling the unit, but eventually he decided he liked it. He became a particular pal of Bill's. Perhaps it was the salt sea in their blood.

Betty Curtis was one half of the firm of Curtis & Page. They were a typing agency and they were the best little firm in Swiss Cottage. As soon as I could afford them, they had typed all my scripts, including my precious little *Edge of The World*. Joan Page was the one with the sense of humour. Betty Curtis was desperately sincere. She broke her heart half a dozen times a day. She also bred golden cocker spaniels from her bitch Tupenny of Ware, and promised me two boys. In due course they arrived at my apartment in Bloomsbury, in a shoebox, and tumbled out stepping upon each other's ears: Erik and Spangle. They were destined for fame in four of my movies. They appeared first in *Contraband* in 1940, and their final performance was in the *camera obscura* sequence in *A Matter of Life and Death* in 1945. I received a fan letter of inquiry about them, in 1984. Very few actors can boast of having such a devoted fan.

Betty Curtis was a girl in a million. She would be the sort of a wife that Howard Keel was singing about in *Seven Brides for Seven Brothers*. I didn't marry her, but somebody else did. In England in 1940, everything was in a turmoil, except me and my unit. We knew what we had to do and we were going to do it. We were lucky. Small firms like Curtis & Page would vanish and the girls would be called up. I got in first by offering Betty the job of my confidential secretary and script-girl for the non-existent script. No extra money for doing the two jobs. It would mean a twelve-hour day, I warned her. I was wrong. It was often a fifteen- or sixteen-hour day.

Emeric and I both had a nodding acquaintance with Laurence Olivier. I had directed him when he was playing the juvenile in Gloria Swanson's European production, *Perfect Understanding*, and we had all three been contractees of Alex's at Denham. He was in Hollywood now, but had casually agreed with us on the transatlantic telephone to play Trapper Johnny in *49th Parallel*, when and if he returned to England to join the Fleet Air Arm at the beginning of 1941. But he had become such a big star now, after Hitchcock's *Rebecca* followed by *Wuthering Heights*, and now Lord Nelson in Alex's production of *That Hamilton Woman* – coupled with his romance with Vivien Leigh, that both he and she were besieged by tempting offers. We privately decided that it might be a good idea for me to fly down to Hollywood, see Larry in person, and get a firm commitment from him before I started work on our film in the Western Rockies. We could now name a date when his presence would be required at Denham.

It seemed to me that we should have a second card up our sleeve, and I arranged to see Charles Boyer as well at his home in Hollywood. I sent the unit off on the three-day railway journey to Edmonton, Alberta – the gateway to the Rockies – where I would rejoin them to begin shooting scenes on the observation car as it arrived at Banff. We established the headquarters of the film at the Hotel Windsor in Montreal, and I took off for Los Angeles.

In those days the Pacific Coast aircraft stopped at every major city, and at one of these, I think it may have been Portland, Oregon, I got out to stretch my legs and found Herbert Wilcox and Anna Neagle shooting *No, No, Nanette*, or some similar title. They were as surprised to see me there as I was to see them.

At Los Angeles, the airport was at Burbank in the San Fernando Valley. They sent a car to meet me and it wasn't far to Charles Boyer's house. It was luxurious, with maids and butlers and all that, but being French he was not embarrassed. We conversed in that language. We got on well, but as soon as he learnt that he would have to go to England to shoot his studio sequences at Denham, he started talking English. He shared the view of most European expatriates in Hollywood, that gallant little England would last about three weeks. With his own country on her knees you could hardly blame him. But after all it was his war as well as ours. I asked if I could use his telephone and rang Larry: I was in Hollywood for twenty-four hours and would come to see him at the General Service Studios in the morning. I forget where I stayed the night, but it wasn't with

Boyer. The whole flying visit is now like a dream. War is a great leveller and suddenly doors were opened to me that were shut three months earlier, because my country was on the verge of annihilation. The position that I was now in, and the demands that I was making, joined with England's danger and obvious intention to fight to the finish, invested me with a queer authority.

Next morning I went to the studio on Santa Monica Boulevard where Alex had completed *The Thief of Bagdad* and was now producing and directing the film about Nelson and Lady Hamilton. I didn't want to see Alex or any old friends. I wanted to get back to my unit in the Canadian Rockies. Larry came out to see me in his Nelson suit, black patch over his eye, empty sleeve, cocked hat, the lot. He repeated his promise to play the trapper if the navy agreed. I could have kissed him; maybe I did. Because of the war, this was the first time I had heard about Vivien Leigh, David Selznick, Scarlett O'Hara, and *Gone With the Wind*. I asked Larry to give Alex my love. What was his schedule like?

Larry grimaced: "Six weeks. Alex is shooting four minutes a day. You know how he hates directing."

I started to laugh. "How's he behaving?"

"Just the same. Saturday I did my big scene with Viv: 'Goodbye, my darling. I go to win Trafalgar and come back to you on my shield.' That sort of thing. It was a long scene, nearly six minutes, on a terrace in Naples with flowers all around and the old volcano smoking in the background, big stuff. I was terrible. I dried up twice and had to fling myself about to cover up, got my scabbard caught in my cloak. At the end of the scene Alex said: 'OK, cut. Next shot.' I went off the deep end. I really exploded. 'Alex!' I said. 'You must be mad! Can't I have another take? It's the worst acting I've ever done in my life! I must have another go at it.' And do you know what that bastard said?"

I said: "Yes. 'Larry, my dear boy, you know nothing about making pictures. Sometimes there must be bad acting. Next shot.'"

Larry stared at me. "You're absolutely right!"

Of course, Korda had meant: "Larry, dear boy, I am directing the picture, not you. That was a master shot of the scene between you and Vivien, and we shan't use much of it, if at all. There are other shots favouring you and more shots favouring Vivien, in which you can act your heads off, if I let you. If I let an actor have another take of a scene just because he wants to, we would never finish the film. Next shot" – lighting a Corona.

Larry confirmed his intention to return to England in January and do his part of the film before he joined the Fleet Air Arm. We put our arms around each other, remembering that we might never see each other again. Forty years later, in 1981, we stood on the identical spot in the same studio with our arms around each other while a photographer took our picture. Larry was wearing a yamulka. He was playing the father in *The Jazz Singer*. "They're paying me so much money that I can afford to buy a condominium for Torquil, who is going to UCLA," he confided in me. He was still acting, still a star. I was Senior Director in Residence, according to Francis Coppola, who now owned the studio. England must have won the war after all.

Back in the Dominion of Canada, Betty Curtis was writing her diary:

"The unit consists of twenty-four men (seven of whom are actors) and myself, and although my letter of identification from the Royal Canadian Mounted Police describes me tersely as 'Continuity Clerk' I am also personal secretary to Michael Powell, the Director of the picture and leader of the expedition. It was as secretary that I had my introduction to Canada: two days after we landed at Montreal (two days during which I literally hardly left my typewriter) I went with Mr Powell to Ottawa to take notes of a meeting at which the chiefs of various Government Departments – headed by the First Secretary of the Department for External Affairs – were to give official blessing to the expedition.

"We were in Ottawa only one night, and less than a week after I had walked into the Parliament Buildings dressed in my most 'secretarial' outfit complete with hat, gloves and briefcase, I was riding up the trail on horseback clad in cotton dungarees and a 'slicker' (a kind of enormous yellow oilskin) with my typewriter travelling behind me on a pack horse – no longer a private secretary, but a continuity girl on location in the Rockies! The long, tedious journey (two days and three nights in the train) ended in a burst of activity as the first scenes were to be shot actually on the train. At a station in the foothills early on the last morning we picked up an open flat truck which was hitched on behind the observation car and the camera rigged up on it. On this, yelling at one another to make ourselves heard against the noise of the train, filthy from the smuts and buffeted by the wind, the director, cameraman, camera operators, two of the actors and myself swayed and jolted our triumphant way into the Rockies. During our two weeks in the West we spent part of the time in Banff itself and then moved up into the mountains to a lakeside camp, and it was not long before the unit began to assume a faintly 'Western' appearance: grey flannels and windcheaters gave way to blue jeans, gaily coloured shirts and cowboy hats; we talked glibly of horse-wranglers and teepees, and leapt on and off our horses as though we had ridden to work every day of our lives – though we only learnt how to sit well down in a western saddle after painful experience!"

Thanks, Betty, I'll need you again. Stand by.

We finished shooting the Leslie Howard sequence at Lake O'Hara with a local fly-fisherman doubling for Leslie, and ran helter-skelter down the

Rockies to the wheatfields of Manitoba. We were in a hurry. We were shooting from west to east and the days were getting shorter. At the Hutterite village near Winnipeg they had held back the harvest for us, and as soon as we advised them we were on our way, they started the big combines. From Winnipeg we rushed north to Lac du Bonnet where we shot Elisabeth Bergner's scenes on a farm near the lake. We crashed the stolen airplane in the lake and nearly drowned Raymond Lovell with, as Eric Portman claimed, malice aforethought. We rushed back to Winnipeg. It was already August. I left John Seabourne with the second unit to pick up the scenes in the big cities, using doubles for principals. I and my unit boarded the "Muskeg Express", the unofficial name for the Canadian National Express which runs to The Pas, junction for Flin Flon – a copper-mining town in the wilderness of 10,000 people. At The Pas we changed to the Hudson's Bay Company's private railway to Churchill, where polar bears come down in the main street on their yearly migration. There was very little time left before the ice would close the bay. Duff Cooper little knew what he had started.

At Churchill we were met by polar beards grown by Dick George, Finlay Currie and Basil Appleby while they were waiting for us. Why had they been waiting for us? Because we were shooting the story of the film back to front and they were already dead according to the script. Their big scenes were now going to be shot in Arctic waters: Dick George, blown up with his U-boat; Basil Appleby shot by an Eskimo marksman; while Finlay Currie's Hudson's Bay Post, of which he was factor, was to be our first port-of-call – Wolstenholme – on Hudson Strait.

The three actors were already old inhabitants of the town and anxious to show us around. They were worn out from Churchill's hospitality. The Excursion train had been there the previous week and then the *Nascopie*, the Hudson's Bay supply ship, and the town had thrown a dance on each occasion. They proposed to have one that night for us – there had never been such a constant whirl of gaiety in Churchill. The ship we had chartered, a trawler called the *Continent*, lay alongside the pier by the huge grain elevator. Captain Halfyard came from St. John's and was youngish and Scottish. The ship was a pretty one. The unit's quarters, which had been constructed in the hold, were not pretty, but very serviceable. At first there were dismayed looks and loud complaints, but they soon shook down. An army hut was not very appetising either, I reminded Eric, who was particularly outspoken. He annexed the Captain's cabin, the owner saying philosophically that he would be on the bridge most of the time anyway. Betty was assigned the mate's cabin, and I had the Chief Engineer's.

My "Foula Regulars" had no complaints. Everyone was busy all day buying last minute things. You would have thought we were going for six months if you had seen the parkas and mukluks and moccasins. Fred bought caribou hide and canvas and wool waste and sail needles and said he was going to make a sound blimp for the Mitchell camera, which would only weigh a few pounds instead of three hundredweight. Oscar was aiding and abetting. Oscar was three years at sea, he told us, as well as everywhere else he'd been.

The dance was a great success.

In the morning there were queries about insurance on the ship and the waiver demanded by the owners. A full-dress meeting, with the Captain present, straightened this out and we sailed at 3:30. The Captain was very interested by our democratic form of government and struck by the youth of all concerned.

By this time our troupe was as various and motley as a Shakespearean production:

DOWN NORTH

Dramatis Personae

Betty Curtis, Continuity Clerk and Sole
Representative of Female Species

Eric Portman, actor

Raymond Lovell, Actor

Richard George, Actor

John Chandos, Actor

Peter Moore, Actor

Basil Appleby, Actor, the baby of the troupe

Niall MacGinnis, Actor, Foula Regular

Finlay Currie, Actor, Foula Regular

Bill Paton, strong and silent, Foula Regular

Syd Streeter, chief of construction, Foula Regular

Fred Govan, carpenter from Montreal, and Syd's shadow

George Brown, production manager, will a dollar do?

Jack Hynes, still photographer and anything once

George Blackler, Arctic makeup a specialty

Fred Young, Cameraman, the bearded wonder

Skeets Kelly, two yards of trouble, Foula Regular

Henty Creer, second cameraman

David Mason, camera assistant and focus king

Leslie Falardeau, grip enlisted at Winnipeg

Oscar Paulin, aforementioned camera grip, recruited from taxi in Winnipeg

Walter Darling and Dex Harrison, sound engineers and cross-talk artists, recruited at Montreal

Captain Halfyard, Master of the *Continent*; the Mate of the *Continent*; the Crew of the *Continent*; Cyril, our Steward; Ken, our Cook.

Abraham Bloomfield, hunter and Eskimo interpreter

and Me.

Abe Bloomfield, our interpreter, joined us at Churchill. He was a short, broad, amiable, brown, squeaky-voiced, kind-hearted individual in sealskin boots bearing a letter "from the Honourable the Hudson's Bay Company (J. W. Anderson, District Manager) announcing by these presents that Abraham Bloomfield would act as Eskimo interpreter for our party, that Mr Bloomfield was returning to Labrador that summer after many years of service with the Company, and that he had planned to connect with the Company's sailing-ship *Fort Garry* at Port Burwell, but was willing to avail himself of any other arrangements we might make." We inspected Abe, liked him and found him invaluable. However recondite or technical the request, Abe could find an Eskimo phrase to express it. He was always cheerful, a desperate cribbage player and had three rifles, also wrapped in sealskin. For some years he was the interpreter and companion of Donald B. MacMillan, the American explorer.

Each member of the unit as they came on board was handed a copy of the script by Betty. It was the first result of the collaboration between Emeric and Rodney Ackland in London and covered the whole action in Hudson's Bay up to and including the escape of the Nazis by sea-plane.

Betty records: "August 23. Work began for me at ten next morning as we had a script reading of the scenes that were to be made on this trip. A calm sunny day changed early to fog and the little ship heaved and rolled in an oily sea. Below decks in the tiny saloon I sat near the only porthole and longed for the meeting to come to an end! From the moment we had started work in Montreal I had made it a matter of personal honour to take whatever was coming to me as though to the manner born. So on the *Continent* though she heaved and rolled I put in an appearance, however brief, at every meal and learnt how to keep my fingers on the right row of keys even when my typewriter lurched away from me as we rose to a wave, and I nipped in and out of boats and clambered up and down rope ladders as nimbly as my impedimenta of typewriter, note book, pencils and stop watch would allow!"

Over to me, Betty. It was interesting to see the actors begin to assume their parts. First readings are always interesting. Eric gave nothing away. Finlay was already deep in the part of the Hudson's Bay factor. He growled his lines like a polar bear and was most impressive. For weeks the actors had followed my direction blindly without any text to help them. Now they snapped at the typewritten pages like hungry wolves.

Months later, when we were back at Denham, Eric told me that it was at this reading on board the ship, heading north into Arctic waters, that he first realised what a wonderful part he had, and what a splendid project this was. I think it was during the exchange between the invading Nazi Lieutenant Hirth, and the Hudson's Bay factor, when Hirth demands

Canadian money to help them escape. The following dialogue takes place:

> "There is none."
> "Don't lie to me. You buy furs from the trappers."
> "Not for money. It's exchange. Barter."

These gritty syllables, ground out from between Finlay's teeth, gave Eric an inkling of the quality of Emeric's dialogue. About me, he reserved judgement.

It took us two days to steam across Hudson Bay, and we arrived at the Eskimo village at Ivugivik on the morning of August 25th. We groped our way into the anchorage in dense fog. Presently a rough boat with four little Eskimo boys in it came creeping from the invisible village. Abe Bloomfield talked to them. One boy in a white koolyatuk was the spokesman. The other three, in dirty canvas and duffle, rowed and stared. They had a red splash of colour high on their cheekbones, making them look like delightful Dutch dolls. Eric called them "little woodenfaces". They told us all the people had gone to Wolstenholme to see us.

At 1.00 p.m. we reached Wolstenholme and put in – like Henry Hudson and Robert Flaherty before us. A smart schooner put out to meet us. It belonged to Dimmot, the factor from Dorset Island. Melton, the Wolstenholme factor, was aboard, also Dimmot's young wife, Walter, a big, good-looking fellow from Lake Harbour and an Eskimo crew from Dorset. After suitably formal greetings, they took us all ashore. The little white red-roofed buildings stood in line. A great valley rose behind, carpeted by the broad shallow river and the hills were covered thickly with great snowpatches. A crowd of fifty Eskimos came down from their tents and beamed a welcome. We asked a hundred questions, bought things at the store, ordered costumes for Finlay, ordered sealskin boots for ourselves, held social conversation with Mrs Melton, a nice apple-cheeked Leicestershire woman, climbed to the top of the big hill above the village looking for the location, got all the gear ashore into an empty house and returned to the ship.

The next day was fair and windy. We shot all the scenes around the trading post, then the police arriving after the massacre. The Eskimos worked in all these scenes and were splendid. They very much enjoyed rushing about shouting, and when told to lie down on the beach and pretend to be dead, they promptly went to sleep and never moved. Jack Hynes and Leslie played the two aviators.

The next day it blew a gale rising to fifty miles an hour in gusts, which kept us from going ashore. There was a certain amount of tension in the unit, for which work was the only remedy. Fred Young now had five sealskins to cover his blimp. He and Oscar were making caribou mitts. For those who have followed Fred Young's splendid career, it may be hard for them to imagine the great autocratic lighting cameraman of *Lawrence of*

Arabia and *Doctor Zhivago* as simply a good companion and a resourceful technician, but there are several Fred Youngs.

During the night the storm blew out. We steamed outside into the open sea and got a few periscope shots, got the shots of the landing party led by Lt Hirth on the lonely beach, transferred to the *Nanak*, the Eskimo boat, to go ashore and ran aground three times. George's control of the crowd of busy Eskimos worked very well to signals, but we had arranged no signal for "lunch!", and it took our united efforts to make them understand it. Finally Oscar chalked it on our camera cover and we held it outstretched. Then George got it and, to his credit, laughed, for he had been rushing up and down the beach trying everything else.

After lunch we completed the massacre scene. The Eskimos were very cheerful and intelligent and seemed to enjoy acting in scenes very much, down to the last "little woodenface". I even got a shot of a mother playing dead with a crying baby in her hood. We broke at intervals for acid drops, or awful sticky sweets, for which they loved to scramble. The shots completed, we told them to pack up their encampment, and return in their kayaks to Ivugivik, where we would rendezvous with them next morning.

That night at supper Abe told us that the Eskimos had names for each one of us. We extracted some of the less personal ones: Niall was "The Big One with the Wild Hair"; Eric was "The One Who Carries the Revolver"; Walter and Dex were "The Ones Who Listen to Voices"; George Brown was "The One Who Puts People in Places"; Betty was "The Lady Who Writes Down Everything"; Jack Hynes was "The One Who Plays Dead" (in his role as the aviator); Oscar was "The Hairless One on Top"; Michael Powell was "The Boss" (very dull); Freddie was "The One Whose Beard Does Not Cover His Mouth" (very fascinating).

We went ashore next morning at Ivugivik and enlisted the whole village. By now they were old hands at this game and practically directed themselves. They built fires and walked about and chatted, and came rushing out of their tents down to the beach and pointed at aeroplanes; and they fled in panic and returned drawn by curiosity; and one really good actor with a bullet head and a forelock like a Shetland pony, proved perfect as the seal hunter who shoots the boy, Jahner. He hurled himself down, watched with an eye like a polar bear and when he got his Nazi he grinned from ear to ear. He also rushed out of his tent, pretended he saw the seaplane approaching and yelled, "Timyut! Timyut!" to his family, who all rushed down to meet it – one take only!

After lunch the day cleared, but a breeze sprang up. It stiffened all the time we were shooting the kayak scenes and by the time the great moment came for lowering the seaplane, it was very stiff indeed. But the scene had to be got now or never. We towed the seaplane in to the beach. It floated magnificently without ballast on the most even of keels. Henty and Bill took charge of it and treated it like their own child, to Syd's relief. He had had enough work nursing and patching and assembling it without having to drown with it. We anchored it some two hundred yards off the village in fifteen feet of water. We had a bit of shelter from the low land, but it was about as unpleasant a situation as could be found. The tide was running at about six knots, and anything let go for a moment promptly vanished out to sea in a cloud of spray. The sun was sinking rapidly, the spray blew all over Skeets, Fred and the camera, but in spite of it all we just managed to get the two shots, and to see the six kayaks come flying out in the spray, with the silver streamlined seaplane in the foreground, was an unforgettable experience.

What a wind! It blew and it rose and it rose and it blew until by midnight it was a gale and a howler! It was no use anchoring at Wolstenholme, we had to ride it out, to and fro between Erik Cove and the Cape. I was on the bridge at midnight. The air was full of the crash of wind and water; the dim shape of the land lay to the south, great black cliffs and a starry sky, the sea a whirlpool of contrary gusts and tides, a pattern of black and white; "Five miles east, hard-a-port, five miles west, hard-a-starboard", and so on till daylight and the usual abrupt magic calm.

This was the real end of our great adventure "down north". I could make your flesh creep with accounts of how the *Continent*'s engines broke down amongst a pack of icebergs, how Abe shot three polar bears, how we steamed by night and by day down the coast of Labrador to the Strait of Belle Isle to our rendezvous with David Rawnsley and the submarine he and Syd had built, and which was waiting for us at Corner Brook, Newfoundland, but I won't.

Instead I shall quote from Betty's diary:

"Though we found the sun as we sailed down the coast of Labrador, we were still cold because there were so many icebergs about. The blast of cold air when you pass near them seems nearly to take the skin off your nose! We saw hundreds of bergs in the eight days that it took us to reach our next anchorage and at night the Northern Lights hung in the sky like curtains, changing as you watch from lemon yellow to jade green and again to dark red.

"One morning we woke to find ourselves once more in the Strait of Belle Isle. The temperature of 60° seemed almost sultry after weeks of 35° and gradually suits and ties began to make their appearance – and I remembered I had a skirt. As we sailed up the beautiful wooded inlet to Corner Brook in the Bay of Islands we marvelled at green fields and neat little towns after weeks of barren rocky coast and grey seas."

Thank you, Betty, I'll take over now.

The unit were visibly enchanted by the colours and signs of a civilisation where eggs and butter and milk no longer came out of a can, and where a hot bath was not just a fond memory. Everyone was cheerfully resurrecting suits and hats and ties and the other forgotten worries of civilisation. Eric was resplendent in lounge suit, overcoat, soft felt hat and spotted white scarf. The Captain brought the *Continent* in to her wharf in a masterly fashion, and the "Down North Expedition" was ended. About five thousand miles had been covered. Much was still to happen, but the voyage *With Powell to the Arctic* was over. A loud cheer rang out as the side of the *Continent* gently rubbed the wharf. Eric put on his hat.

Important news awaited me. During my absence down north, Elisabeth Bergner had taken it on the lam. One of the five stars who had committed themselves to the film, and the only woman in the cast, she had elected to come with us to do her own exteriors, saying that she didn't like to be doubled. She completed her work in the sequence at the Hutterite settlement near Winnipeg, after which she was to return to Montreal and London. Whatever had been her intentions when she signed the agreements, now, with the German blitz on London, she had no intention of returning to England to complete her part in the studio. She refused a ticket to London and went to join her husband, Paul Czinner, in Hollywood. This was exactly the sort of thing that the press had said would happen, but which I and John Sutro had denied vehemently. Insinuations had been made about escapees and a bunch of young men being in the film, obviously avoiding military service, and the stage was set for a monumental row when I returned to London.

It was my birthday – September 30, 1940 – when we arrived at Corner Brook. David and Syd came aboard the *Continent* with long faces. They had planned to give me a submarine for my birthday, but the Customs and Excise of Newfoundland had spoilt their plans. They had seized the submarine and demanded payment of duty. When I had decided upon the rendezvous in Newfoundland, I had completely overlooked the fact that Newfoundland was a crown colony. It was not part of Canada, it was a separate country, with a British Governor. Our front office in Montreal at the Hotel Windsor had blithely followed my lead and made all the arrangements without realising their implications. David and Syd had enough to do in Halifax, nursing their enormous baby, assembling her, disassembling her and reassembling her, until they were sure that all would be ready for me when I arrived on the day. They were at Corner Brook with their submarine three days ahead of schedule. The whole town – in fact the whole island – was abuzz and everyone was ready to help when the Customs pounced.

At first I thought it was a joke and could be settled in a few hours. The British Empire was at war, this film was part of the war effort and was sponsored by the British Government. But I had not reckoned on the jealousy of one of England's oldest crown colonies (and one of its poorest) for the rich and expanding Dominion of Canada. The Newfoundland Customs had put one of their best men on to us, and he came down to see me at the harbourmaster's office, a wooden hut on the quays. They gave me tea as strong as tannin, with four spoonfuls of sugar in the mug. They saw my point, they pitied my ignorance, but we had brought a Canadian object into Newfoundland and duty was payable upon said object at an estimated price of $22,000. Right was on their side and it was going to remain on their side as far as they were concerned. We were the biggest fish that had so far tumbled into their net. I had only just learnt from our office in Montreal that our accounts were $30,000 overdrawn at the Canadian Bank of Commerce. That trusting institution didn't seem particularly worried about it, yet. I saw that it was useless to argue with Customs. It was always useless to argue with Customs. It was time for the big guns. I went to the Corner Brook post office and composed a telegram to the Governor of Newfoundland at St John's, that evoked the total admiration of the postmaster and all his buddies. I wish I had a copy of it. It was not conciliatory. It was definitely high-handed. I implied that the Customs and Excise of Newfoundland were in league with Dr Goebbels, and unless they released my submarine immediately, the war would be lost. Anyway, it worked. The head of the Customs himself came down to the quay where I was standing with Syd and David, expressing my doubt of the strength of the steel hawsers that were to tow the submarine. He bore no malice, he was grinning all over his face.

"You win," he said.

"You mean we can go ahead?"

"Sure. I'll be out there with my launch to pick up any salvage."

In the film this opening sequence looks efficient and realistic, but there was plenty of excitement behind the scenes. We were shooting a mile or two off-shore in deep water, and nobody quite knew how the submarine would behave when she was taken under tow by the two tugs we had hired for that purpose. The camera crew, Freddie and myself were on a fast launch which could quickly lay us alongside the submarine when necessary. The actors had to be coaxed to go on board the sub, but after a few rehearsals were skipping about like trained submariners. The order of shooting was first the scenes of the survivors from the ship torpedoed by the submarine being questioned by Hirth and photographed by Kuhnecke and then pushed off and left to sink or swim when the submarine submerges. Second, there were scenes of the submarine underway on the surface, and third was the attack and sinking of the submarine by the Canadian Air Force. For the victims of the submarine, we were using local actors and very good they were; we had all the close shots in the can by lunchtime, and prepared to shoot the scenes of the submarine moving. This was quite another kettle of fish.

There was an anxious moment when the tugs took the dead weight of the submarine under tow and the submarine refused to move for a very long second or two. Syd and David, standing beside me, were trembling with anxiety. Something would have to give if their baby didn't get a move on. Then, slowly, she got underway and there was a cheer from the onlookers.

"Start rolling," I said to Freddie. Almost immediately the steel hawsers towing the submarine rose out of the water glistening like two monsters of the deep.

"I can see the hawsers, Michael," reported Henty Creer, who was shooting the second camera.

"Try to keep them in the sound-track," I replied absently. "Nobody's going to notice them anyway."

I had already rehearsed all the action by numbers with our control ship tied up to this gigantic prop made of canvas, wood and steel. Eric Portman, who was still highly suspicious of me, obeyed every suggestion under visible protest. He remembered only too well the sequence we had shot in the lake near Winnipeg, where the Nazis' escaping aircraft crashdives into the lake and Raymond Lovell nearly got drowned, trapped inside the fuselage. The submarine, with its four sections, began a sort of snake-like motion, as I'd always said it would.

I seized the loud-hailer and roared: "Action Sequence One!" By now, the submarine was travelling at four or five knots and our launch was closing on her rapidly. The actors did their stuff. As the submarine gathered speed it started to shudder. So now we had a sort of shuddering snake cutting through the water at maximum speed. I knew the motion wouldn't show, but the actors didn't. They were having difficulty keeping their feet.

"Action Sequence Two!" I roared. We were only 300 feet from the sub.

"Try not to run her down," I advised our helmsman. He winked.

By now Eric was seriously alarmed. He kept on with the action, speaking to the survivors in the water through a loud-hailer, but in fact yelling at me: "Michael, are you completely mad?! You're going to drown us all!"

David Lean, who had access to all the guide-tracks and sound-tracks when he was editing the film, dines out on what happened next. Amid a crossfire of orders and recriminations, he imitates Eric's panic-stricken yell of "You bastard, you'll kill us all for your damn movie!" echoing over the water. And then a little voice just beside the camera saying: "Keep rolling."

What Eric fortunately did not know was that the ship on which he was dancing contained deep in her hull explosives the equivalent of three 1,000-pound bombs, a gift from the Canadian Air Force to be used in the final sequence of the destruction of the submarine. About 3:00 p.m. we took the actors off, placed a few dummies around the machine-guns and prepared for the big bang. At 4:05 the Canadian Air Force was sending over three aircraft (which incidently was the entire strength of the Canadian Air Force at that moment), with instructions to circle around the submarine and then get home before their fuel ran out. They would be at the extent of their range. The explosives expert had connected up the leads and brought Syd Streeter, standing proudly beside me, the control panel. The script called for two or three near misses, bringing up fountains of water near the ship, and then a series of direct hits, the last one to be the biggest of all. Right on time we heard the hum of the aircraft approaching. By this time about fifty launches, rowing boats and sailing ships filled with salvage hunters were ringing the submarine. They all raised a cheer at the sight of the Canadian bombers.

"Turn over camera! Sound! OK, Syd!"

Fountains of water sprang up on both sides of the submarine as the bombers swooped overhead.

"OK, Syd. Give it the works." Syd drew a deep breath and pressed the button. One after the other, three direct hits tore the vessel apart. The huge construction of steel and wood disintegrated before our eyes.

I shouted over the loud-hailer: "All clear! The show's over!" From all corners the boats swooped in, and I have no doubt the Customs and Excise launch led all the rest.

Two days later, the whole of Corner Brook gave us a huge sendoff, as the *Continent* sailed with us for Sydney, Nova Scotia, on the south shore of the St Lawrence. We made a landfall about midnight and I remember the shock that I got when I came on deck and saw the lights twinkling all round the horizon. England had been under blackout for more than a year. Our ship was rising and falling in a big black swell as high as the mast. We slept one more night in the *Continent* and left without regret in the morning.

Two days later I was in Montreal and shaking hands with Emeric, who, at my request and with the help of the Ministry of Information, had crossed the Atlantic for the third time, bringing with him an unheard of luxury – a complete script. He had seen everything I had shot and had had some surprises, but was now incorporating my scenes in a rewrite. The main purpose of his visit was to meet Raymond Massey and prepare the final sequence of the film, the confrontation between Lieutenant Hirth and a Canadian soldier played by Massey. A draft of the scene had already been read by Massey, who had declared himself by no means satisfied, and he arrived next day in Montreal in a high state of agitation, supported by his wife, Dorothy Whitney; they made a formidable team. It really looked for a time as if the whole Niagara sequence would blow up in our faces.

Ray, when excited, has often been compared by his wife to one of the famous Canadian whooping cranes. As he wanted to change practically every line in the scene, Emeric began to do a little whooping himself, and the whole story conference nearly ended in a brawl. Then, suddenly, we started to understand one another. It was followed by love at second sight, and we finished up with our arms around each other singing "Oh, Canada!" – which was pretty good for Dorothy Whitney, who was a Daughter of the American Revolution.

We were now, for the first time, tackling the scene with the most vivid dialogue. The scene in the boxcar in *49th Parallel* sums up all that we have learnt about Nazism and democracy. There are only four characters in the sequence: the fugitive Lieutenant Hirth, the AWOL Canadian soldier, the American Customs official, and his Canadian counterpart. For Eric Portman it was a great moment in his professional career. The scene was a duel of words and ideas between the Nazi and the Canadian soldier, and although there was some violence, force didn't come into it. The opponents were of equal stature, but different creeds. Raymond Massey had been at the top of his profession for more than ten years, in London and in New York. He had been the most memorable Abraham Lincoln of his generation. He had starred for Korda at Denham in *Things to Come* and *The Scarlet Pimpernel*. He was rich and well-connected. His elder brother was the High Commissioner for Canada and would one day become its first Canadian Governor-General. From the very first scene between them, Massey recognised Eric's mettle and they locked horns with relish. For Emeric and myself it was a thrilling experience. The whole sequence took three days, and by the end of the scene Ray was trumpeting to anyone who would listen that Eric must be co-starred in the picture along with the other stars, or he would know the reason why.

We shot the sequence in a tiny studio built and used by the Canadian Pacific Railway for their documentary and advertising films. It was the only film studio available in Montreal. The manager of the studio was in a panic.

"We can't give you what you're used to at Denham, Mr Powell. We haven't any back projection."

"I don't want it."

"I suppose you'll use matte shots?"

"No."

"We can build a replica to scale of a boxcar, but we haven't got carriage springs big enough to simulate the movement of a train, and if we did have them, the squeaking and creaking they make would make recording dialogue impossible."

"What do you say to that, David?"

"Easy, Micky, we'll hang the whole thing on chains. A couple of stagehands at each end, we'll swing it about. It'll look great – and be quite silent."

"What'll we do about moving background, Freddie?"

"Well, Micky, it's night, isn't it? We'll need one or two extra Sparks to pan the lights and I'll have a drum made in case we catch sight of something through the windows."

And that was how we did it.

I had one memorable lesson while shooting this sequence. It sounds naive, but I had always imagined that American actors didn't have to act, they just opened their mouths and it came out that way. For ten years, we had been watching American talkies and hearing American voices and had been quite stunned by the pointed, well-paced delivery of even the smallest bit-player. I had come to believe that it just came naturally, that there was no art in it. Then in the middle of the boxcar scene, something rattled the experienced old American actor playing the American Customs officer and his timing went to pieces, and I had to call a halt for a smoke and a breath of air before we proceeded. I realised with relief that I had been wrong about American acting – there was art in it after all.

With the certain knowledge that we had a great finish to a great picture, we returned by drunken *Duchess* to England. It was the height of the Blitz, and on landing in Liverpool Emeric was immediately arrested as an enemy alien. It was too late to get to the right people, and in spite of all his letters and papers proving what his mission had been, it looked as if he would have to spend a night in jail. However, as I refused to be parted from him except by force, we eventually got somebody to see reason. I believe we had to stay in Liverpool that night. Next day our grateful country let us in. Emeric had the usual warnings, of course, that he must report to the police every week, and so on. Hungarians can see humour in most things, but I doubt if Emeric ever saw the point of this joke, particularly when most of his friends were already behind bars, being screened in British concentration camps, or exiled by slow boat to Australia or Canada.

We had a warm welcome awaiting us in London from our loved ones, our not so loved ones, and the press. They all felt, perhaps justifiably, that they'd been kept in the dark about the making of *49th Parallel*, and they said so. On the home front we could hardly fight back, with the smoking ruins of fire-bombed London all around us. All the members of our crew had to run a gauntlet.

The press, who had got on to the Bergner story, were in a particularly apocalyptic mood, and I called a conference the day after we arrived back. I think it was at the Odeon Leicester Square, but I can't be sure. Anyway, there was a big attendance, because the new editors obviously thought there was a story there. The Ministry of Information's Film Division was functioning by now, so I made a brief statement, explaining how we had jumped the gun with ministerial approval and the help of the Canadian Government. I brandished the names of Leslie Howard, Anton Walbrook, and Laurence Olivier, and disclosed that Raymond Massey's part in the final episode of the film was already in the can.

How much of the taxpayer's money had the Ministry put up, asked my accusers. I answered £50,000, and hoped that no smart-aleck reporter had got on to the £30,000 I had overspent, by courtesy of the Canadian Bank of Commerce. Nobody had, and the atmosphere was rapidly changing from accusation and criticism to open interest and excitement. This was a showbiz story and a big one, not a news story. There was one last attempt to raise the Bergner issue and lay the blame for it on somebody.

Wasn't it true that Elisabeth Bergner had agreed to play an important part in the film, a German girl who, after being orphaned by the Nazis, had joined a group of German refugees in Canada and after completing her location scenes had skipped to Hollywood, and had refused to return and complete her part at Denham?

"Quite true," I said. This revived a little interest.

What did I propose to do about it?

"We will cast Glynis Johns, the teenage daughter of Mervyn Johns, in Elisabeth Bergner's part," I answered. "By careful editing we shall use most of Miss Bergner's exterior scenes in the film. The only difference will be that instead of playing the part herself, she will be doubling for Glynis Johns."

It was only fair, I added sweetly, that a big star who had made her reputation playing cute teenagers well into her forties, should be replaced by a cute teenager who was also a bit of a character. And that was that. They all went off to file their stories and interview Glynis Johns.

It occurred to me that I had not yet consulted Glynis or her father. Mervyn Johns was as Welsh as a Corgi and very like one, small and sturdy. Glynis ditto. Both were battlers. Mervyn was considerably startled when I told him that his young daughter was going to step into Bergner's shoes and co-star with you-know-who. Like many West End actors, he was puzzled as to how I knew all about him and his performances while he knew nothing about me. (So far as Mervyn was concerned, I had appeared from nowhere, and many other actors had the same impression. But during the years of obscurity, when I couldn't afford the actors of the calibre I wanted, I had done all my casting myself, and had been to see all the plays and made my notes on what I considered good performances. I still have all my theatre programmes, and it is interesting to see how certain names come up again and again with one, two or three ticks against them, and how, years later, they appear in the casts of my films.)

His daughter I had seen in the London production of Elmer Rice's *Judgement Day*. She had a great outburst on the witness stand. I had heard that Mervyn had coached her in the part, and they had fought tooth and nail over every line and every move.

Meanwhile, that November of 1940, London was burning. Everybody who could be evacuated from London had gone, and with only three million people left in the city we survivors were beginning to enjoy the empty streets at night. There weren't many people still living in the lordly squares and crescents of Belgravia, behind which our little mews cottage jumped and trembled at the fall of every bomb. Pat Bingham, who lived in Eaton Square, was our air-raid warden, and his house became a rendezvous for me, my father and Bobby Helpmann, who were his resident fire-watchers. Our job was to wander about the roofs of these stately terraces, armed with a shovel and a tin hat, and when the fire bombs showered down we were supposed to shovel them smartly into the street.

There were no private cars, so Bill and I went to Denham every day by steam train from St Pancras Station on the other side of London. We came back after dark by the same excruciating route. When there was an alert, the train would stop and try to look like something else. The journey would take anything up to three hours. Strangely enough, there were still taxis about, mostly driven by old age pensioners who took not the slightest notice of air raids, and only spoke when grumbling about a favourite through street being closed.

After a conference with my team, I had decided to wait for Larry Olivier's arrival in January before starting to shoot the interiors of the film at Denham. There was a lot to prepare, and I just carried on as if I had all the money in the world, and told John Sutro to find it. With all those stars' names over the title, it shouldn't be too difficult. The Treasury was anxious that we should buy them out, leaving the film a totally commercial proposition, and in the end this was done by a joint agreement between Columbia Pictures of America and General Film Distributors in London. J. Arthur Rank had only just started on the buying spree which, when it was over, left him head of one of the most powerful combinations of film production, distribution and exhibition in the world. At present he had just bought control of General Film Distributors, whose chairman was Charles Woolf. Rank also had his eye on Korda's Denham Studios and was negotiating with the Prudential Assurance Company to buy them. He was already wooing Oscar Deutsch and his chief accountant, John Davis, hoping to buy control of the huge Odeon circuit of Super-cinemas. A film of the size of the *49th Parallel*, which he would wholly own in his own territories, was just what he needed.

In Canada, I had shot so many bits and pieces of different sequences that I felt the need now to shoot the interiors in continuity. We had an immense amount of material and it was necessary to get it in order while we planned the studio sequences. We needed an editor. I had intended that John Seabourne should edit the film, and he had been the second-unit director as well. But on his return to London, he had collapsed with his old trouble of duodenal ulcers and was no longer available.

At this crisis point, Harold Vauxhall came to see me. We were old friends. He had been general production manager with Mickey Balcon and knew the business through and through.

"Micky, I want you to agree to let me put David Lean on the film," he said.

David Lean! I was staggered. Somehow it had never occurred to me that I could now command the services of a craftsman like David Lean. My rise had been meteoric, and nothing was too big for me to tackle, but I was still at heart the same little eager beaver who had persuaded Joe Rock to let me make *The Edge of the World*. A load dropped from my shoulders. I realised what it would mean for the film to have a cutter, an editor like David Lean to review and pass sentence on those thousands of feet of film.

"Is he free?" I asked, still doubting my good luck.

"He finished on *Major Barbara* last week. Fred Young has been telling him how wonderful the stuff is you shot in Canada. He is the man for you, Micky."

Of course, I said yes.

Forty-four years later, David Lean was addressing the Directors' Guild of America in Los Angeles, and in reply to a question about his editing of *The Invaders*, the title under which *49th Parallel* was released in America, he grinned and said it was an eight-hour film when he started work on it. I think he exaggerates. I hope he exaggerates, because I recognise that he was the best editor I ever worked with – or should I say, worked for. And three weeks ago, for I am writing on St. Valentine's Day, 1985, I received on David's behalf, at a dinner at Sardi's, the New York Film Critics' Award for the Best Director of 1984 for the film which he wrote, edited and directed: *A Passage to India*. The sense of continuity that this event gave me was almost overwhelming. "Films are the folklore of the twentieth century" – yes. But they are also an ephemeral and perishable art, and I can assure you that in 1940 nobody thought of a film's life as more than half a dozen years. Alas, too many masterpieces had already disappeared without it being noticed. Yet half a century after it was made, *49th Parallel* was being redistributed to a new public on video-cassette. And David had triumphed in his first film in thirteen years.

What shall I say of David Lean, except that we share the same exalted view of our craft, and that he has never compromised. On *49th Parallel*, I gave David *carte blanche*, and he dived into that sea of film like Johnny Weissmuller into a jungle pool full of crocodiles. We had spent countless hours and dollars on night sequences in the Canadian Pacific marshalling yards showing the escaping Nazis on the run. Out it all went, neck and crop. The back projection plates for Leslie Howard's scene in the canoe were shot from the wrong angle if they were to cut with the exterior scenes.

"Were there any others?" David asked, squinting down at his moviola, concentrating on the film and ignoring the trembling director. No? Then he would find some in the London Films library, something out of *Sanders of the River*, perhaps? We needed close-ups of the U-boat crew ransacking the Hudson's Bay Company store, stealing arms, ammunition, food and clothing. Had we shot these? No? Then he would shoot them – with my permission, of course. He would talk to David Rawnsley and they would only shoot exactly what was needed. The U-boat sequence was great stuff, but it needed an opening scene of a submarine surfacing in Canadian waters. He thought he had seen, in some captured German film at the Ministry, the sort of shot that we needed. He would check whether this could be used. This became the shot of the German U-boat surfacing from the depths, accompanied by Ralph Vaughan Williams's powerful chords of music which lift the audience out of their seats. We would also need a shot of the cargo ship sinking, seen through a binocular matte, to match the close shot of the U-boat commander in the conning tower of the submarine that we had filmed at Corner Brook. The Denham tricks department would make the matte, and Denham labs the combined print. He hoped that I didn't mind that he had asked the tricks department to check for steadiness all the back projection plates we had made on exterior. They had reported that they were all very good, he added casually. I was relieved that something was good. I began to dread David zoning in on me with a list of questions in his hand.

I had been saved by some good editors, but never on this scale. I felt as a general with an unprotected rear must feel when he learns that some insubordinate young commander has arrived with reinforcements. I turned my attention to our actors.

It was January 1941, with Larry due to arrive and report to the Admiralty at any moment, and Vivien now and forever Scarlett O'Hara. Larry had asked for a few days to work on his French-Canadian accent with a corporal from the French Canadian Army, and then we would kick off with the scenes in the Hudson's Bay factor's house. The Hutterite sequences starring Anton Walbrook and Glynis Johns would follow, and then the Leslie Howard sequence in the Rockies, for which we had shot exteriors at Lake O'Hara way back in late July of the previous year.

Since receiving such generous treatment from Raymond Massey and his co-stars, Eric Portman had stopped blowing raspberries in my direction and had become our greatest trumpeter. He stalked the corridors of Denham proclaiming that *49th Parallel* was going to be a masterpiece. The first scene in the studio was the one in which Finlay Currie bursts in on a naked Larry Olivier having a bath. Next morning the projectionist who showed our dailies was besieged with questions. "Terrific!" was all he would say, which did us no harm.

During the days which followed, Finlay achieved the full stature of humanity in his part, the performance which caused David Lean to call for him when he was looking for someone to play the convict Magwitch in *Great Expectations*. But the greatest sensation of all was when Eric Portman made his Adolf Hitler speech in the crowded Hutterite dining hall after the evening meal. There were about a hundred men, women and children seated on long wooden benches at the long wooden tables, and we had picked every face. More than half of them were Germans and German Jews, refugees from Hitler. We ran a rehearsal several times with Eric mouthing his part, but occasionally his voice rang out as he reached a peroration or a climax. You could feel the temperature in the room rising as these victims of Hitler's oppression realised what we were attempting to do and say, with the added knowledge that Hitler's soldiers and airmen were massing only a few miles away for the invasion of England. Every word of the long speech that Eric and Emeric had worked out together rang true, the minted gold of liberty. I don't know how these things happen, but before we had run the rehearsal twice people were filtering in from the other stages and surrounding the big set to listen to the performance. As usual, when I have a big emotional scene to direct, and particularly in this performance of Eric's, which was sheer witchcraft, I planned to shoot it in one continuous take and let the pauses come naturally with the emotion. I think that Eric's speech ran about four and a half minutes, and by the time we came to the take everyone on that huge No. 4 Stage (where later on I was to shoot the Court of Heaven in *A Matter of Life and Death*) – actors, extras and onlookers – shared in the emotion and identified with the reaction to it. When Eric's voice rang out with the appeal "Brothers! *Germans!!*" with that peculiar brazen insolence that was a speciality of the Nazi orators, and of their leader, our flesh tingled and the palms of our hands grew moist, and when at the climax Eric shouted "*Heil Hitler!*" and his four companions leapt to their feet with the Nazi salute, I could feel all those hundreds of people take the insult like a blow. I yelled "Cut!" and started clapping, and everyone on the set and around it joined in a roar of applause. After that, the film's reputation was made.

All of us, Fred Young, David Lean, Emeric and myself, had discussed and analysed Anton Walbrook's speech in reply, wondering whether it would ever be possible to top Eric's superb ranting. But we need not have worried. Anton's gentle, New Testament reply, "No, we are not your brothers," was the perfect answer to the Nazi lunacy, just as Glynis Johns's emotional outburst, threatening the Nazis with exposure, brought us back with a jolt into this story of suspense and violence.

It will be clear by now to readers of this book, that when I identify with one of my actors, I love him. It is an unselfish love; I ask nothing in return. As I understand it, loving is giving. I suppose that my love for actors like David Farrar, Roger Livesey, Eric Portman and Marius Goring is the love that the painter feels for his painting. The love, for instance, that Constable felt for his subjects. But there was no love lost between me and Leslie Howard. We were both quick, febrile, impatient and rude. His charm, which had an instant effect upon people, including me, was entirely artificial. There was no contact between him and me at all. He acted as if he were playing a solo musical instrument. I frankly don't think he liked acting. His timing was impeccable, and I had no fault to find with him as a worker. He had the fastest brain and the quickest movements of any actor I have worked with. Watching him as an onlooker on his set when he was acting and directing *The First of the Few*, I have seen him get up from his chair, cross the room, open the door and go out of the room at a speed that seemed impossible to photograph. Yet when I saw the scene in the finished picture, it looked a perfectly normal movement. He must have known instinctively, for he was no camera technician, that twenty-four frames per second (the normal camera speed for a synchronised sound film) slows everything down. His brittle, insolent comedy amused me, but I did not love him.

It was a solemn experience for myself and Emeric, who had planned all this nearly a year before, to watch all these great sequences of the film slowly coming together like ice floes in a frozen river, pushing and grinding each other and changing in importance as the current sweeps them remorsely on towards the open sea.

49th Parallel was the first film on which either Emeric or myself had ever had a percentage of the producer's share of the profits. At that time it was unusual, to say the least, for the creative people on a film to receive any royalties, as is customary for the author or illustrator of a book or a play. The market was competitive, the fees for an original story or screenplay were high, and the gross potential of a successful film was still unguessed. In show business, the rewards are very small or very large. There is no in-between, and the producer is reluctant to part with slices of the cake when, by paying a high fee to the members of his creative team, he can keep the cake for himself. In this way, writer, producer and director were all satisfied. Emeric and I had started to make *49th Parallel* without a written agreement, and although we must have drawn some money for ourselves it can't have been very much, perhaps a couple of thousand pounds. We were at war and the film was our contribution to the war effort. I have already explained how we made an off-the-cuff agreement with the principal actors: that they should each give us two weeks' work for £2,000 net, tax-free. Agreement was by exchange of letters and they had all agreed, even Miss Bergner. But now the film had become a commercial enterprise, with big distributors financing it, and Christopher Mann had negotiated a proper contract for the two of us, which gave 5 per cent of the profits to Emeric and 10 per cent to me. We disclosed these new agreements to the stars, in view of the special concessions that they and their agents were making. Larry and Ray Massey replied that they were satisfied with the present arrangement. Anton Walbrook had already given half of his fee to the Red Cross. But Leslie Howard took violent exception to our 15 per cent, and insisted on sharing it, which left Emeric, the author of the original story, in possession of the smallest royalty. He never let me forget it. And in return I have never let Emeric forget that Leslie Howard, the archetypical English gentleman, was in fact Hungarian-born.

I must say that I was rather shocked that Leslie should turn on us like this, practically accusing us of taking advantage of his innocent patriotism. But it must be remembered that at this stage he was already a producer and director, with his own company. And producers are notoriously sensitive about percentages. As for Emeric and me, we had all the courage in the world, but we were far too innocent to take advantage of anybody.

49th Parallel runs for two hours and eight minutes, thanks to David Lean, and there is not a bit of fat on it. My favourite criticism of it is that of the man who sat behind Frankie the third time she went to see the film. He said to the girl next to him: "Golly! What a tough picture!" As for America, we had made the film to convert the isolationists, and the fact that Emeric got the Oscar that year for the best original story was good enough for us.

We finished the interior sequences of *49th Parallel* and settled down admiringly to watch David Lean sewing our picture together. (He always cuts on the silent head of a moviola, because he doesn't want to be distracted by what the actors are saying. How good for the actors to know that!) We, in England, were facing a new situation. It was true that France had fallen, and that the Germans had occupied the whole of Europe, but the Battle of Britain had been won and there was a growing feeling that we could hold the Germans until the Americans came in. Meanwhile President Roosevelt was sending us every help short of a declaration of war.

The Ministry of Information was a great success, and its Films Division was one of its triumphs. Churchill had need of Duff Cooper elsewhere, and Brendan Bracken, a dynamic journalist, had taken his place as Minister. In charge of the Films Division was Jack Beddington, one of the most unjustly forgotten men of the war. He had been chief of advertising and publicity for Shell: it was he who sponsored the superb Shell Guides to the English counties, employing all the leading artists and craftsmen of the day in their compilation and decoration. His knowledge was wide and his taste faultless. He was diplomatic, evasive and cunning – just the man for the job. We got on with him famously throughout the war. It must be understood that the way the Ministry of Information worked with commercial film-makers was that Beddington would send for one of the well-known film-makers to discuss an idea that the Ministry wanted dramatised, or else we would come to Beddington with ideas of our own. We would discuss this with him and the idea would either be approved or not. In our case, because of the unique nature of our creative partnership, it usually was. The point was that these films were financed commercially after having obtained the Ministry's approval of the themes and the general content. They would then help us get actors, perhaps out of the Service Departments, get permits to go to prohibited areas, obtain the services of technicians who had been drafted, and so on, and they also kept us in touch with what other people were doing, including the Germans. The film industry had become a war weapon. Under Ian Dalrymple, the great documentary film-maker of the war, films were made, both feature and short, which were more directly sponsored by the Ministry. That was how *Desert Victory* and *Western Approaches* were made. But I am telling the story of our feature films and the way we worked with the Ministry as far as our original stories were concerned. It is sometimes forgotten, or never appreciated, that all the Powell-Pressburger wartime films were original stories, written for the screen, keeping pace with events and trying to put into action what people were thinking and saying at the time.

All remarks about my "escapist" film unit and my enemy alien scriptwriter vanished when *49th Parallel* opened triumphantly in London (at the Odeon Leicester Square, of course – we were beginning to think we owned it), followed by a huge banquet at Claridge's, jointly hosted by Oscar Deutsch and J. Arthur Rank. I made a short speech. I had been sitting next to Mrs Rank, and as the party was breaking up Arthur came over and asked me what we were doing next. I said we were working on a script and that it was only in outline form so far – about twenty pages of typescript. He asked if he could read it and introduced me and Emeric to C. M. Woolf, the head of General Film Distributors. We were not very keen on showing outlines or synopses. No dramatist is. But we believed in our idea, and in the general euphoria we agreed to send it to them next day.

After I returned from Canada and I had time again to listen to the nine o'clock news of the BBC, I had become fascinated by a phrase which occurred only too often: "One of our aircraft failed to return." Although Britain had not yet moved over to the full offensive, the raids on military targets in enemy-occupied Europe were mounting steadily, and every night the inhabitants of the eastern counties and the Channel area could hear the roar as the bomber squadrons of the RAF swept across the Channel towards targets in the Rhineland, the Ruhr and occupied France. Emeric liked the idea, and after the usual pause for digestion and secretion, he suggested that we tell the story of a typical British bomber crew, who are forced to abandon their aircraft and parachute into enemy occupied territory. This would give us an opportunity to show how people in the Low Countries and France were risking their necks every night to help such crews get back to their own country. After several narrow escapes, the six-man crew would succeed in crossing the Channel to return home and fight again. It was the obverse of the Canadian adventure, and I marvelled at its simplicity and the ingenuity with which Emeric worked out the suspense and told the story.

We had confided our idea to Jack Beddington, who was delighted with it, and he had put us in touch with the Dutch Government in Exile. They in turn had put us in touch with one Meyer Sluyser, a Dutch publicist and journalist, who seized on the idea with enthusiasm and brought us invaluable material. We consulted him on every twist and turn in the story and on the districts that the RAF men would have to cross, and the way they might be able to secure a boat and escape across the Channel and he was never at a loss. (After the war he wrote a book about the Jews of Amsterdam during the German occupation and died shortly thereafter. We remember him with affection.) This research was briefly set out in the twenty pages we had hammered out so far.

Until now, married by Korda, Emeric and I had marched up the British Film Industry together. I was a director, he was a writer; I led and he followed. In fact, though, I consulted him at every turn. After the mediocre minds I had had to make pictures with in the great gap which yawned in my career between Alfred Hitchcock and Alexander Korda, it was a relief to talk to somebody who knew what you were driving at almost before you said it. (Emeric very handsomely paid me the same compliment forty years later in the *Arena* programme for the BBC.) Credits on the screen were another matter. I was busy grabbing titles to get as much power and prestige in my hands as possible. We all know how important credits are in our highly competitive business. On *The Spy in Black* it was: "Directed by Michael Powell" on a solo card in the final position on the screen immediately before the action started. This was considered the director's position in an important film, a concession which kept him happy and stopped him from asking awkward questions about profits. On *The Thief of Bagdad* and *The Lion Has Wings*, I received co-director credit from Alex in the same advantageous position right before the action. Although Alex, and later Zoli, had directed several sequences of *The Thief*, they never received any screen credit for it. London Films presented – that was all that Alex cared about – and the profits. On *Contraband*, Emeric received credit for the original story as well as for the screenplay. I forget who his collaborator was on the screenplay – maybe it was me, as well as Connie Veidt and Valerie Hobson, as before. Once again "Directed by Michael Powell" appeared at the end of the credits. I think that John Corfield was credited as the producer. It meant that he had found Lady Yule's money for us, and had stood by with a watch in his hand while we made the picture.

49th Parallel had a stupendous list of big names, which included all our superstars and the name of Ralph Vaughan Williams as composer of the music. I had also persuaded Ray Massey's brother, Vincent Massey, the Canadian High Commissioner in London, to speak the prologue which explained what the 49th Parallel was. He was very glad to do it without credit, remarking that he didn't need credit as much as his actor brother did, and that he, Vincent, was a better actor anyway. All the title cards were overprinted on spectacular Canadian scenes, ending with my own title: "Produced and Directed by Michael Powell". You couldn't very well have a better position than that. Emeric received a separate credit for the original story and a shared credit, with Rodney Ackland, for the screenplay.

Now that we were to receive some small percentage of the profits in our future films, Emeric suggested that we form a company of our own, for which we would work and which would receive our fees. Until now, we had always worked for a salary or a fee, and other people had become rich and famous from the exhibition and distribution of our films. This was all right, but we didn't see why we shouldn't have a slice of the cake. Obviously we were not going to get more than a working salary during the war, but Arthur Rank and others were planning for the worldwide distribution of British films in the future and they would be prepared to give us a percentage of their hopes.

I went to see Chris Mann, who was all for our forming a company. He got out his little pencil and asked how the company would be owned and managed.

"Fifty-fifty," I said.

He was appalled. "You worked all these years to become a director and producer in your own right, and now you want to give away half of that to a writer who is perfectly satisfied with the credits and opportunities that you have already given him?"

Of course he was right, but this was a case of love at first sight. I was not to be shaken. "Fifty-fifty," I insisted.

Seeing that I was adamant, Chris Mann suddenly became enthusiastic and went out and acquired Emeric as a client.

"Another thing," I said. "We are going to pool our talents and show the film industry we know where the priorities are. We are going to share the final title in the credits, and it is going to read 'Written, Produced and Directed by Michael Powell and Emeric Pressburger'."

"What do you mean by priorities?" he asked.

"It's in the title," I replied. "The story and script are the most important thing. Then we have to find the money and boss the show – that's the 'produced by' bit – and then I have to direct it."

"Will Emeric be on the floor too?" inquired Chris, now prepared for anything.

"Only when he wants to be," I answered. "When I get going, I wouldn't know whether he was there or not. Of course we share all major decisions together and that's where the co-producer comes in. Personally, I think it's extremely generous of Emeric to share with me the title of original story writer and screenwriter."

"You won't get many people in the business to agree with you," said Chris grimly, making another note. "You'll have to have a trademark. Have you thought of anything?"

Now I don't know who first suggested the famous target, but I think the seed may have germinated in Denham on *The Thief of Bagdad*, when I watched my champion archer send arrow after arrow into his chosen target. One day, I pointed out to Emeric a little pastiche poem that the drama critic James Agate had dashed off:

> The arrow was pure gold
> But somehow missed the target.
> But as all Golden Arrow trippers know
> 'Tis better to miss Naples than hit Margate.

Emeric liked the conceit and we adopted the target as our trademark with *A Production of The Archers* overprinted.

"And the arrow thudding into the gold," I said enthusiastically.

"Vell," said Emeric quietly, "somewhere near the gold."

The critics, generally, raved about *49th Parallel*, and it was doing standing room only business at the Odeon, while the reports from Columbia in America were equally encouraging. Our friends in Canada wrote to us that the effect on their public and upon the American public had been everything we had hoped. Columbia's press campaign had included a gigantic coloured drawing of three heroic Canadians, Raymond Massey, Laurence Olivier and Leslie Howard (Larry casually carrying a tiny Glynis Johns in his arms as if she were a bag of groceries – they never met in the film, of course). They were confronting the advance of the armed Nazi hordes and looked pretty alarmed about it. This was the stuff!, and we had proved that propaganda that people paid to see was the only propaganda worth talking about. So in the circumstances, it was embarrassing for J. Arthur Rank to come back to us with a turndown of our bomber project after discussing it with C. M. Woolf.

I still had my caravan on the lawn at Denham, but I had an office as well, and that's where Arthur Rank came to see me. He placed our outline on the desk and stood there looking rather embarrassed, jingling the money in his pockets like he always did. He was just about to buy Denham

Film Studios from the Prudential, and possibly he would have to cross their palms with a piece of silver.

"I'm afraid C.M. doesn't like your story," he said. "He thinks it is a defeatist picture. He doesn't think it will be box-office."

"Oh! Doesn't he?" I said.

"You understand, Michael, that we are just as anxious as ever to get a picture from you and Emeric, but not this one. Could you give us some other idea?"

"Mr Rank, I'll tell you what we'll do," I said. "We'll go to some other backer for our money, and we'll make the picture and it will be a big success. And when it's a big success, you'll come back to us and say, 'Now what do you want to do next?' And we'll tell you. We are not film distributors, nor film exhibitors, we are film-makers, and we are the best judges of what we shall do next. We are reserved by the Ministry of Information to make films for the war effort, and the way things are going we are more likely to be right than C. M. Woolf. Is it a bet?"

He looked at me thoughtfully with his dark, serious eyes and then gave a half-smile. "It's a bet," he said.

So it was back to John Corfield and Lady Yule, who leapt into the breach without consulting their distributor. You might say they did it with enthusiasm. Our screenplay, which was half-finished, was entitled *One of Our Aircraft Is Missing*. We were never too proud to take a tip from distributors, and we saw that the original title, *One of Our Aircraft Failed to Return*, although evocative and euphonious, was downbeat. Probably C.M. Woolf never read more than the title. Later on, when we got to know him well, we liked him; he had a mischievous sense of humour. His two sons, John and Jimmy, with their companies Romulus and Remus, were to make a remarkable series of quality productions after the war.

I have described the script of *One of Our Aircraft Is Missing* as half-finished, and half-finished it remained for most of the production. There was so much to find out. It was an all-star production, which in film language was a no-star production. The first thing to decide was the type of bomber, because that would settle the number of leading men in the film. We settled for a Wellington, with a crew of six.

Then there was the topography of the Netherlands to be sorted out with Sluyser, and Dutch actors, or Dutch-looking or Dutch-speaking actors, to be found. Most of the picture would of necessity be shot on exteriors, and Jack Beddington quipped: "I suppose you two will go to Holland for them, ha, ha, ha!"

We said the Fens would do. I went with John Seabourne – he came from Diss in Norfolk – to scout out our own Low Countries in East Anglia, and found perfect Dutch locations in King's Lynn and Boston, and, of course, the Wash in Lincolnshire. Since the Dutch Wars, in the early eighteenth century, trade had been brisk between these two proud and rich old ports and the Netherlands. They were full of houses built by traders who intermarried between families and between the two countries. Then there were the Fens, reclaimed sea marshes, which stretched for miles and dated back six hundred years. They were full of lock gates and canals and windmills and roads raised high against the tide. We only had to change the appearance of the windmills.

I had decided on complete naturalism. There would be no music. There would only be the natural sounds of a country at war. It was not a documentary; it was a detached narrative, told from the inside, of what it is like to be a pawn in the game of total war. First, you are a well trained member of a unit and have a skipper from whom you take orders. Then suddenly you are on your own and a decision can mean internment or death. Your survival depends upon the local people, upon their friendliness or their potential for treachery. Sluyser had many stories of both. He told us how Netherlanders had been tortured or shot for helping or hiding RAF officers who turned out to be Gestapo men in disguise. In our story, when the crew of our bomber, "B For Bertie" were collected by the villagers and brought to a central point, they would have to be interrogated by somebody intelligent. Were they what they said they were, or were they part of a cruel deception? Out of these games of life and death, Emeric and I had to construct the story which C.M. Woolf did not think would be box-office. One of Emeric's very best ideas was to hear Germans everywhere, but only see them in the distance, if at all. We picked all the dozens and dozens of voices carefully, whether they were making jokes as they signed civilian passes, or barking orders. The audience saw military vehicles packed with soldiers careering along with their klaxons blaring, but we never got close to a German in the whole film, except in the sequence in the church. It was one of those inspirations that are worth their weight in gold. The Dutch language was, of course, used throughout and very carefully supervised and written and rewritten by Sluyser, to give authenticity. When it was necessary for an English actor playing a Netherlander to speak English, we had to find a reason for it. I had some big ensemble scenes of women all talking Dutch together, and held auditions for them. It was extraordinary how many Jewish or German-Jewish actresses discovered they had Dutch ancestors or relatives. I remember that Lilli Palmer's family, who were numerous, all learned to speak Dutch in about twenty-four hours.

The most knotty problem was how to get our gang of heroes back to England to fight again. Of course, it was being done every day by the European underground, but involved a whole network of arrangements, including the crossing of France and Spain – a film in itself. A nice escape boat from one of the smaller Dutch ports is easy to stage and arrange, but the English Channel was too wide at that point to cross in the hours of darkness. From dawn onwards, German patrol planes met their English counterparts over the Channel and our heroes would undoubtedly be shot to pieces. The Ministry records could not help us. We consulted the Services, and suddenly we learnt from the Admiralty that a number of floating steel platforms were going to be anchored out in the North Sea, some of them as much as ten miles from the English coast, as a refuge for airmen who had been shot down and had taken to their life-rafts. If they reached one of these sweaty, plunging, smelly boxes they had a fair chance of survival, because there were rations, stimulants, and first-aid necessities in the cabin below, which had two bunks. It was the ideal solution for us. If we could get our bomber crew, one of whom was wounded, to one of these lobster pots, as the Navy already called them, we could have them all picked up by the fast patrol boats which visited them regularly. The question was, would we be allowed by the powers-that-be to mention them, and would we be allowed to send a camera unit out to one of them to take establishing shots with doubles? To settle this, I sent John Seabourne down to Dover, where he had once started his career in the regular army as a drummer boy; and being John Seabourne, he wangled a trip out to one of the lobster pots in a patrol boat. From the moment that he leapt dangerously onto the slippery steel deck of the lobster pots, he was seasick until the moment he jumped off again, but he reported enthusiastically that as a solution to our problem it was ideal; and in due course he directed the shots himself, in ideal conditions with patches of raw sunlight and an uneasy sea. They were some of the most atmospheric shots in the picture. The Ministry helped us to get permission to use the lobster pots and our main difficulty was solved.

We now had all the makings of a screenplay: "authentic" Dutch locations, Dutch-speaking villagers, lots of suspense and a spectacular climax. It was time to think of "B For Bertie's" mission: the bombing of factories in Stuttgart, and how to make the raid as authentic as everything else. We thought that the long run up to Stuttgart, the raid itself, the injury to the aircraft by enemy flak, the attempt to limp home on one engine, and the eventual bailing out of all six members of the crew, would take about twenty-five minutes. How were we to make the bombing of the great city as authentic as everything else? The answer lay partly with Emeric, as he had completed his academic career in Stuttgart.

David Rawnsley, who was again our art director, and whose ideas were as big as himself, pooh-poohed the difficulties. Give him one big studio stage to himself for one month, and he would guarantee to lay out such a stupendous model that nobody would know it was a model. Nobody did. He would install overhead railways for the bomber's approach, and he demanded a cameraman of his own to work exclusively on the model.

Ronnie Neame, who was to be lighting cameraman, agreed enthusiastically. There were no stages free at Denham at that time, apart from the one we had already got earmarked for the film, so we hired the Riverside Studios near Hammersmith Bridge and shot all the model scenes there. You can imagine what an immense model it was, for it covered the whole studio floor and it was all wired for explosions and lighting effects, and flak coming up towards the camera, and you name it. It was a boy's dream come true. If only my brother John could have lived to see it. I went down once or twice when they were working on it, and was appalled by the ingenuity and complexity of the whole set-up. The devoted cameraman, who spent ten hours every day lying stretched on his stomach in the roof of the studio, was Freddie Ford who had always wanted to get into the big time. "Mind it, Guv'nor? I just love it!" he said.

Back at Denham, the RAF got us the complete shell of a Wellington bomber and we wired it up so that the gun turrets worked and all the essential parts moved. We had a lot of dialogue between the individual members of the crew and decided to use intercom throughout. Every sound was to be authentic, and as I have said there was to be no music. When I announced this, Emeric asked me what sound I imagined would be over the credit titles, which usually come at the beginning of the film. I said I supposed the drone of aircraft engines. This gave Emeric the idea of an opening sequence in which "B For Bertie" flies home pilotless, abandoned by its crew, like the famous abandoned ship *Mary Celeste*, only to crash into an electric pylon and come down in flames. It made a smashing opening to the film Arthur Rank had rejected.

It was now time to think about casting, and I begged Emeric to write some decent parts for women. He obliged. The interrogator at the first village, who was to grill the crew so mercilessly, was to be the local schoolmistress and was played by Pamela Brown. The daughter of the mayor of the town where they were taken on their journey back to the coast was played by Joyce Redman. Jo de Vries, the woman who concealed them in her house in the small port until they could escape by night, was played by Googie Withers.

Of the three only Googie Withers had ever made a film before: I had discovered her in quota quickies. But she was still relatively unknown, and like many actors during the national crisis, she was hard up and at her wit's end. She broke down and cried when I gave her the part. She had never played anything but comedy, but she had Dutch blood, her mother was Dutch, and I knew she could do it.

Joyce had been one of the girls I had tested for the part in *The Edge of the World* which was eventually played by Belle Chrystall. She was straight from the bogs of Mayo. She was only five feet tall, but it was five feet of dynamite. Later on, in 1943, she was a member of the Old Vic Company led by Laurence Olivier and Ralph Richardson, in that historic season at London's New Theatre.

Pamela was already being talked about. She had won the Gold Medal at RADA and had played Juliet at Stratford. I first saw her in an appalling comedy called *The Disappearing Wife*, at the little Torch Theatre just off Knightsbridge. It held about sixty seats, and they were most of them empty. I think that I had come at the request of Julie Mars, who played her maid. But it was the mistress I fell in love with.

The inspiration of our film came from the BBC's recurring announcement, but the plot came from a statement made by Sir Arnold Wilson in Parliament when France fell, to the effect that he for one did not propose to shelter behind the bodies of young men, but was joining the Royal Air Force to be trained as a rear gunner at the age of fifty-one. Sir Arnold was a genuine British eccentric, a hero of the last war, an explorer, a writer, a troubleshooter and a troublemaker. When sent by *The Times* to areas like southwest Persia, he would write a book about it which would start a new war.

"Here is our hero," said Emeric. "Just imagine, Michael, what a bore such an old gentleman must seem to the young men who make up the bomber's crew. They would want to get rid of him. They would think he should be grounded, and yet such a man, when they are trying to find their way home through enemy-occupied territory, would be invaluable. Airborne, *they* are the professionals. On the ground, *he* is. For them, it is a new and frightening experience. But he is an old soldier. He has been lost before, sometimes alone, sometimes with a scouting party, perhaps with a whole regiment. What do you think, Michael? Shall we make him the hero and ask Ralph Richardson to play the part?"

I agreed enthusiastically. But, alas, Ralph was in the Fleet Air Arm, learning to fly and mad about it. I had once ridden pillion behind him on his giant motorbike after a naval party consisting of broadsides of gin and water, and I could imagine with what joy he took to the air, and with what horror his instructor sat beside him gripping the seat with his eyes closed. Sir Arnold Wilson could have played himself very well, but that old hero had been posted missing over the Low Countries. Godfrey Tearle played the part.

Godfrey was a stage (and stagy) actor who had been a matinée idol in his youth. I used to egg him on to show me his stills of when he acted with Tree and Irving and Sir George Alexander. They were wonderful romantic poses which his dresser used to sell at the stage door. You can't imagine what they were like.

I would split my sides laughing and cry: "What were you doing, Godfrey? What were you thinking of? How could you act such terrible stuff?"

To which he would reply, quite unperturbed: "Act, my dear boy? I didn't need to act in those days. I just shook my hair at them."

He was still a magnificent presence, and it amused me to see how our bunch of younger, more modern actors reacted uneasily to him until they got used to him and got to like him, just like the young men in the film.

It must be remembered that most of the public had no idea what a bombing mission was like, or what the individual members of a bomber's crew did. These things had never been seen on the screen, so before the actual story of "B for Bertie" and its crew started, we had the members of the crew introduce themselves and their jobs, playing directly to the camera, with the name of the actor who played the part superimposed on the film. Here they are, all six of them:

HUGH BURDEN
"John Glyn Haggard, Skipper"
HUGH WILLIAMS
"Frank Shelley, navigator"
EMRYS JONES
"Bob Ashley, wireless op"
BERNARD MILES
"Geoff Hickman, front gunner"
GODFREY TEARLE
"Sir George Corbett, rear gunner"
ERIC PORTMAN
"Tom Earnshaw, co-pilot"

We had invited Eric Portman to play Tom Earnshaw, the Yorkshire businessman who was co-pilot of the aircraft, never thinking he would take it. Although it was a good warm part, it hadn't got any opportunity for his genius, but he liked working with us and he took it.

Hugh Burden was suggested by Frankie for the pilot and captain of the aircraft. These *Wunderkind* of World War II, these knights of the air who had revived the ideal of personal combat, seldom looked the part. I had met many of them at London nightclubs, and most were still wet behind the ears and looked appallingly young. I'm sure that Hugh won't mind if I say that he suited the part to a T.

"Tam" Williams, one of our most elegant, sensitive actors (he was a memorable Darcy opposite Celia Johnson in *Pride and Prejudice*), played Frank Shelley, an actor in civilian life. Amongst his fellow actors "Tam" had a reputation for sarcasm and the kind of wit that kills. Actually, his closest friends knew he was a warm-hearted and idealistic young Welshman, intensely patriotic, who had joined the Army Reserve at the time of the

Munich crisis, so that he was called up the moment war was declared and spent the next nine months, penniless, guarding a bridge. He was flat broke and working for ENSA (Entertainments National Service Association) when I asked him to call at my house and offered him the part, but typically he arrived to see me in dinner jacket and black tie, as if he had just dropped in on his way to a party.

Emrys Jones was cast as the wireless operator, who had been an international soccer player in civilian life. Emeric was a soccer fanatic, and his idea was to reunite the members of the bomber's crew with their missing wireless op by means of a soccer match. I'm afraid I disappointed him. I despise all games and made no effort to understand this one.

Bernard Miles (later Lord Miles of the Mermaid Theatre, Puddle Dock, City of London) was not an actor, he was a preacher. He absorbed culture in large sticky slabs. He played small parts in some of my early films and was always trying to educate me. He reminded me of our cook Nora on the farm, who took a plate of fish to my pet heron that I was nursing over a broken wing, and stuffed fish down the unfortunate bird's throat until it expired. Bernard had made a bit of a name for himself with a couple of comic monologues at the little Players' Theatre, but this was the first time that he had worked on equal terms with leading West End actors. During the inevitable waits between scenes, he was always backing his victims into a corner to discuss Art, with particular reference to the career of Bernard Miles.

Bernard Miles was an original. An original *what*, nobody has quite decided. There are many varying opinions. He is an original, let's leave it at that. He was a character, but the kind of character that alarms other actors more conventional, less intelligent, and less inclined to throw things up and make trouble. Perhaps it will convey the power of his personality best, and the kind of actor that he was, when I say that he was a wonderful Iago. But above all, he was a monologuist. One night, he appeared on the stage of the Players' Theatre with a new act. He was a working member of a seedy provincial theatre orchestra, and his only prop was an immense brass wind instrument which he continually fingered and continually prepared to play, and on which he finally blew one fart as a climax to the act. It was a good monologue. It contained all the stories about working musicians which have been circulated, mostly by Sir Thomas Beecham. He delivered them straight at the audience, his big, earnest eyes gazing sorrowfully down his long bony nose, deadly serious, like the proper clown he was and is. There are very few clowns, just as there are very few poets, and I mean this as a high compliment.

Anyone looking at the cast list of *One of Our Aircraft* today must get a slightly topsy-turvy feeling. The supporting cast are now all well-known names, while of the six members of the bomber crew only a vapour trail remains. I have already dealt with the ladies, and as for the rest they were all personal friends of mine who were working their way up into big show business. They were Alec Clunes, Robert Helpmann, and Peter Ustinov. For all of them it was their first film.

Alec Clunes I had always admired very much. I had seen him often at the Sadler's Wells Theatre in revivals of classic plays like *Peer Gynt* or *Boris Godunov*. Alec had a beautiful star-crossed face, the kind of face that delighted Leonardo. He ran the little Arts Theatre for many years and did some memorable work there, including the first production of Christopher Fry's *The Lady's Not for Burning*, in which he played the Soldier of Fortune. In our film, he is the organist who plays the Dutch national anthem in the church scene.

Peter Ustinov came of a theatrical family, and how! His mother was Nadia Benois, the designer daughter of Alexandre Benois, the St Petersburg designer who created the first big Diaghilev ballets. The family had lived for several generations in St Petersburg, and had associations with big theatres all over Europe. Peter was a wonderful mimic and had a cruel sense of the grotesque. He had been delighting us for years at the Players' Theatre with imitations of his numerous relations. He played the part of a priest in *One of Our Aircraft Is Missing*.

Robert Helpmann had been the principal dancer of the Sadler's Wells Ballet under the administration of Ninette de Valois. She was an Irishwoman who had worked with Diaghilev and absorbed the traditions of the Russian Imperial Ballet. Bobby was the brilliant partner of Margot Fonteyn, but I only got to know him well when I was living in the little house in Chester Square. He had a mews flat only fifty yards away, and recognising each other, we became more intimate. He told me his plan to take the play of *Hamlet* and compress it into a short ballet of lust, murder and revenge, and then to follow it up with a performance of *Hamlet* itself, which Michael Benthall would direct. Few people, except Michael, believed that Bobby could play Hamlet. But I did. In our film, he played a Dutch traitor, a quisling, and did a splendid piece of overacting which shocked the other, less naked and more reserved actors. I encouraged it. I loved Bobby's overacting. I spoke to him the other day as he passed through New York, although I am writing these lines in Leningrad in 1981. He told me he had been in London restaging the ballet of *Hamlet*, and it had been as big a success as ever.

All in all, not many films have had so many potential stars in the supporting cast.

For the final sequence on board the lobster pot, I had set my heart on the gay and nonchalant Roland Culver, whom I had so much admired as the inspired comedy drunk in *77 Park Lane* ten years before, and who was now an established West End actor. John Corfield came to me white-faced.

"Do you know how much Culver wants for a day's work?" he asked. "Fifty pounds!"

I was shaken – I think the budget was thirty pounds. I said: "If necessary, I'll pay the difference myself."

"But suppose it goes two days!" wailed Corfield. I said I would see that it didn't. It didn't.

Oh! I forgot to mention that I repaid my debt to Stewart Rome, that fine actor who played the dual role in *Rynox*, my second talking picture and had helped to make it a small triumph. He had retired in 1941, but I insisted on dragging him out of retirement, and he plays the station commander in one of the opening sequences in *One of Our Aircraft Is Missing*.

Our story told how six individuals became united as a crew, to the point where the five younger members were prepared to risk their lives and liberty to save the crusty old bastard who up till then had been a pain in the neck to them. Unlike *49th Parallel*, in which the U-boat crew dropped out one by one, this story depended upon keeping the crew together, and this led to many ensemble scenes. It was both amusing and instructive to see how those polished and inventive actors would manoeuvre to get even the tiniest advantage. I could see how they were all racking their brains as to how to stand out from the ruck when Pamela Brown, as the local schoolmistress, entered the room. "Tam" Williams came over to me and muttered in my ear: "Micky, can I turn the collar of my jacket up?" I nodded. "Good idea. Tell the script-girl." Bernard Miles chose to sit astride a chair facing the door. Godfrey kept watch at the window. Eric stood centre, his stillness showing that he was ready for anything. Hugh Burden listened to the noisy argument in Dutch next door.

So you can imagine what happened when we moved from the village to the Dutch town and increased these ensemble scenes with the addition of Peter Ustinov and Robert Helpmann, and Hay Petrie as the burgomaster. Things got to such a pitch, as Peter Ustinov relates in his autobiography *Dear Me*, that he decided to play it very cool as it was his first film.

"Tam" Williams came over to him. "Here you, Ustinov. What are you going to do in this scene?"

"Well," said Peter, "I thought I would do nothing."

"Oh no you don't!" said Tam. "I'm the one who's doing nothing in this scene."

The picture was finished on schedule. Our editing and post-production budget was small, but we made up for it with ideas. We followed one stunning effect with another. The public were thrilled by the sound of the bomber's engines as they sent the titles flying over their heads. The long quiet sequence of the airborne bomber abandoned by its crew was shattered by the explosion as the aircraft hit the power lines and blew up.

Then followed the sequence with each member of the crew introducing himself, and we were into the story.

Nobody could edit such a long opening sequence so casually, and with such feeling, as David Lean, and we had him again as editor. It was he who brought Ronnie Neame to us as cameraman, and David Rawnsley was watching every detail. Noël Coward was visiting all the studios at the time, asking questions and watching film units at work. He was planning to make a film about the battle of Crete and the dive-bombing and sinking of the HMS *Kelly*, the destroyer commanded by Lord Louis Mountbatten, and as a large part of the action consisted of the destroyer turning turtle after being repeatedly hit, he needed the most expert crew of technicians he could get. He visited us one day near the end of the film, when we were all working in close harmony, and watched us stage and wrap up a sequence which was quite elaborate in about two hours. He took over the whole of my unit and together they made *In Which We Serve*.

We showed *One of Our Aircraft Is Missing* to Jack Beddington and members of his Ministry in private. It had certain weaknesses – there were inconsistencies of style – but we thought we had a hit. Sluyser was there, of course, and was very enthusiastic. He arranged a showing for his Government in Exile, and got their official approval.

Wardour Street still thought that *One of Our Aircraft Is Missing* must be a feature documentary and not their cup of tea, so the trade show and press shows were a surprise. Oscar Deutsch, although he was a sick man by now, demanded to see the film himself. It was booked to go at once into the Odeon Leicester Square for a guaranteed four-week run and then out on general release. The total cost of the film had been about £70,000, a big increase over *Contraband*. But Lady Yule and John Corfield seemed quite happy about it, and had the honour of presenting the first production of the Archers: the first to show the target on the screen. It was, of course, in black and white. Our next production was to be in Technicolor and I well remember the panic at the final editing of that picture when we realised that we had an epic in Technicolor, but no Archers' target in glorious three-strip to precede it. This post-production crisis fathered a mystique around the target and we always shot a new target for each Archers' picture. There was no logic in them. Sometimes there were as many as nine arrows in the target, sometimes only one, and not always in the gold – a silent comment by the Archers on the accuracy of their aim.

The day after the trade show Arthur Rank rang up and asked if we could have a meeting. I can't remember whether John Davis was there, but he probably was. We had been introduced to him at the *49th Parallel* luncheon at Claridges. This brilliant young accountant, who had been the right hand of Oscar Deutsch, was to become the right hand man of Arthur Rank. Rank was acquiring control of the Odeon circuit, which consisted of more than two hundred super-cinemas in good positions all over the country. But although regarded as a self-contained circuit, each one of the cinemas had been financed locally and was formed and owned as a separate company, although they looked for their product to a central booking office. This device had outlived its usefulness and Rank and Davis then set about consolidating the circuit. Oscar's health was failing and the situation was urgent. Arthur had already bought Denham Film Studios and was now prepared to relieve Lady Yule of Pinewood. He would then have the best producing facilities in England, the best distribution company, General Film Distributors, later to be Rank Film Distributors, and the biggest, most profitable and most modern circuit of cinemas. Arthur was a big man, and his father, old Joe Rank, the miller, had taught him to think big. It was an empire of entertainment, instruction and communication and was only rivalled by the BBC for the rest of the war. In the enforced absence of the Americans, who were already preparing for war, Rank and Davis were the men of the hour. But I shall never forget that the survival of the British film industry was due to the little private talk between Winston Churchill and Alexander Korda, in that convivial hour after dinner when the cigar smoke mounts and clings to the curtains and the golden brandy splashes into big-bellied glasses; and how they made two promises to each other and how they were kept.

Arthur made no bones about the success of *One of Our Aircraft Is Missing* and was the picture of smiling cordiality.

"Well, you were right and we were wrong," he said. "Tell us what you want us to do. We would like you to join us. Would you like a long-term contract?"

"I don't think that we want a long-term contract," I said. "We would rather be in the position of making one film for you at a time, but, of course, we are looking for finance and we would be perfectly prepared to give you first refusal of our next film – subject to terms, of course."

"What is your next film?" he inquired eagerly.

I suppose he had expected us to say *One of Our Submarines Is Missing*, or *One of Our Regiments Is Missing*. God knows, they were all made at one time or another during the war, or after it. So everyone looked a bit blank when I said it was about Colonel Blimp.

David Low, the left-wing New Zealand-born cartoonist, had invented the gallant Colonel to hammer his betters with. Low was well-informed, disrespectful and delightful. He was also a great draughtsman, a man of high ideals, and absolutely fearless. Although his politics ran counter to those of Lord Beaverbrook, for whom he worked, the Beaver gave him a free hand. Low's slashing indictments of Chamberlain and his gang of appeasers were only equalled by his treatment of Hitler and his gang of thugs and murderers. He alternately ridiculed or disembowelled. Colonel

Blimp had been invented by Low as a typical member of the Services establishment, who was given to making contradictory statements which revealed the cloudy insecurity of the military mind. He was usually depicted in a Turkish bath, a walrus-like figure haranguing a cowering David Low, wrapped in a skimpy towel, sometimes with a bowler hat on, and sometimes not, while the gallant Colonel held forth amid clouds of steam, one bulging finger like a banana held aloft, while his white sealion's moustache drooped in the heat.

The genesis of this new film was a scene between Godfrey Tearle and Hugh Burden in *One of Our Aircraft Is Missing* which depicted the conflict between intolerant youth and experienced age. The young pilot is thinking of the wit and courage of the Dutch schoolmistress who has helped them, and whom they have now left behind, and is astonished to be approached by his elderly rear gunner with the remark "Nice girl, wasn't she?"

The old man goes on to tell him that they are very much alike. They are two editions of the same man. Sir George was just like this young idealist when he was in his twenties, and John will be an old Blimp like him when he is in his fifties. David Lean persuaded us to drop the scene from the final cut, arguing: "It's got nothing to do with the plot. It's the sort of idea you could make a whole film about." So we did.

To announce a film called *Colonel Blimp* was a challenging step to take in 1942. Everybody knew that a great upheaval was due in the High Command and in the War Office. To make a hard-hitting film which lampooned the military mind and said we must pull our socks up if we were going to win the war, at a time when we were losing it hand-over-fist, was a bold enterprise. We went to see David Low.

At first he couldn't believe that there was a film in his Colonel Blimp – after all, a cartoon character is more two-dimensional than most – but when he heard Emeric's scheme he changed his mind. Emeric proposed to open the film in the present day – early in 1942. In the course of a war game, a callous young commando leader captures Blimp and his whole staff in a Turkish bath, by using Hitler's strategy of attacking before war was officially declared. After a violent argument between the young soldier and the old one about the ethics of total war, we would go back to the year 1902, when our Blimp was an enthusiastic, ruthless soldier himself. Our film would then retrace his life over the past forty years, ending up in the present day again, when after a night of doubts and self-torture he admits that there is no longer such a thing as a gentleman's war, and that we have to fight dirty if we are to beat the Nazis. It was a classic comedy Emeric was sketching out and very timely, but even Low, the arch iconoclast, could foresee how difficult it would be to get such a theme through the Ministry of Information, and after them the War Office. He admired our courage and said he would give us all the help he could. He asked us whom we had in mind for Colonel Blimp, and I told him "Laurence Olivier."

This calls for a digression. During the making of *One of Our Aircraft Is Missing*, I got very pally with the cast. They were all members of the legitimate theatre – the theatre was their father, their mother and a constant topic of conversation. I had always adored the theatre, and since becoming a director I had haunted the Fringe and the experimental theatres like the Everyman in Hampstead, the New Lindsey in Notting Hill Gate and the Mercury, run by Ashley Dukes and his wife, Marie Rambert, where good work was being done. These were all very modest enterprises in those days but were a hive of talent. I had many actor acquaintances, but few friends – Ralph Richardson was becoming one of them – and I found it delightful to exchange ideas with our compact little group of legitimate actors, and particularly to talk about the theatre and the possibility of doing something in it.

It was becoming clear, even to Emeric and myself, that we couldn't expect to make more than three films in two years, which in our palmy days meant having one in preparation, one in production and one in post-production, simultaneously. You might think that was enough to satisfy most people, but I was anxious to do more. There were so many themes and subjects struggling to get out of me, and since there was a limit to how many films we could make I wanted to produce a play.

Emeric disapproved of these legitimate aspirations. We were doing very nicely. We now had a source of finance – it looked like an unlimited source – and we had already agreed to do another Dutch Resistance film starring Ralph Richardson, Googie Withers and Esmond Knight, which we would produce but I would not direct. I had been persuaded into this by Sluyser, who was a wonderful salesman, and who offered us all kinds of help in the making of it. It was called *The Silver Fleet* and Vernon Sewell would direct it. Emeric was to supervise the writing of the script, but he would not be directly involved except as co-producer.

At about this time, Lieutenant Commander Ralph Richardson, pilot in the Fleet Air Arm, came to Denham Studios to see us by appointment. Some high-ups in the Admiralty had decided that they were not getting enough recruits for this particular arm of the service, and had sent for him:

"Richardson, you know all these film people, don't you?"

"Yes, sir. I'm still under contract to Sir Alexander Korda." (Alex had been knighted at Winston Churchill's insistent recommendation. He had a print of *That Hamilton Woman* in his concrete dugout beneath the Admiralty.)

"Good show, Richardson. Does it pay for your gin?"

"Just about, sir."

"Ha, ha! Where was I? Ah! I want you to get your friends to make a film to stimulate recruiting to the Fleet Air Arm. The Army and the Air Force have made all the running up till now. They're turnin' them away by hundreds because of all these films. We need a film, Richardson. See what you can do about it."

Emeric was a particular friend of Ralph's and in a weak moment agreed to produce a semi-documentary about the Fleet Air Arm.

"Emeric, what is a semi-documentary?" I asked. "I have never made a documentary in my life. The thought of a semi-documentary scares the shit out of me."

Originally, Ralph never proposed to appear in this hybrid, and I never wanted to direct it. We were being drawn into it by Emeric's glittering eye. It had to have a title, so we called it *The Volunteer*. I said it sounded like a Restoration comedy, but was overruled.

And all this time we were developing, writing and preparing what was to prove the most beautiful screenplay of Emeric's career, and one of the most romantic and remarkable love stories we ever made, and Larry was involved through "Tam" Williams.

"Tam" Williams had always been one of my heroes. He was so Welsh and so arrogant, so sultry and so elegant. I had first seen him in David Selznick's production of *David Copperfield*, in which he played Steerforth. It was an impeccable performance. He went on to do other Hollywood films and played Cathy's wild brother in *Wuthering Heights*. He couldn't come to terms with Hollywood: he was too fastidious and had too sensitive an ear. He told me once that on one of his first nights in Hollywood he took out the most beautiful, ravishing girl, ready to be ravished, and he was going absolutely splendidly until he put cream in his coffee after dinner. She said: "Cream in a demi-tasse! tsk, tsk, tsk." He took her straight home, rang the bell, and left her on the mat.

He had worked with me on two second-feature films on his return to England, and we had become, distantly, friends, although he was not easy to make a friend of. However, during the making of *One of Our Aircraft Is Missing*, Tam and Bernard Miles struck up a friendship. Now that Tam was out on leave from the Territorials, he didn't want to go back in a hurry. He wanted to get into the theatre. Bernard Miles had a project to form a theatre and put on a performance in the London West End of *Henry V* in battle dress. It was a perfect propaganda piece for wartime and there would be a part for everybody. I would direct it. Bernard suggested we sell the idea to Larry and get him out of the Fleet Air Arm to play the king.

It was a great idea, but Larry didn't go for it. Larry only likes ideas of his own. But we had a great reunion, and a great party discussing it. As I have said, Larry and Ralph had both joined the Fleet Air Arm. It had welcomed them with open arms for the sake of the publicity which their names brought to the service. But their service chiefs had become noticeably colder towards the idea of Larry and Ralph being airborne as they crashed plane after plane. Larry was stationed at Worthy Down in Hampshire, and was eating his heart out there. He was madly jealous of Ralph, who had already got leave and was working with us, but he couldn't see Henry V in battle dress on the stage, and then about the third bottle of whisky, I mentioned our project *Colonel Blimp*.

Larry stooped like a hawk. Born with a golden spoon in his mouth, related to big theatrical families, he had suffered as a cog in the wheel at Worthy Down. Larry is, above all, an inventive actor who has to find the secret passkey which makes a character work for him. He had created the leading part in *Journey's End* on the stage. He had played Lord Nelson on film. But these ten years were nothing compared with what he knew he had to do. What bitter, burning satire he could bring to bear from his own experience in his portrait of a diehard Blimp as he ticks off the century at St James's Palace, and strides along thinking to himself: "After all, nothing's so good as being a jolly good soldier."

Of course, I was delighted with the idea of working with Larry again, and on such an important picture, where we would be spending big money for the first time and would need a star name. How we got home that night I can't remember. It must have been a hired car, for none of us were running a car during the war. But before I left the others, I had promised to give Larry a first sight of the script.

Arthur Rank and the others were impressed. A film from the Archers about Low's Colonel Blimp was one thing. A film about Colonel Blimp starring Laurence Olivier was quite another. They gave it their approval, provided we got the theme and the title through the Ministry, whose approval would be necessary to get Larry out of the service. Already the future progress of the film was conditional on his name. Already the name of a star was considered as important as the names of the writers, producers and the directors who were making the film.

This was a dangerous decision, particularly in wartime, when genuine box-office stars were in short supply. Alex never let the shortage of big box-office names stop him from making big pictures. He created his own stars like Charlie Laughton and Sabu, and Merle Oberon. Emeric and I had never made a failure, but we still didn't have that kind of charisma. This optimistic situation didn't last long. Approved by the Ministry of Information, the script went up to Sir James Grigg, the Minister of War, who had to approve our borrowing of Army material: uniforms, guns, transport, etc. I don't know whether he himself actually read the script, but he must have had a scathing report from touchy underlings. He turned our request down point blank, and sent a memo to Churchill and to Brendan Bracken, the Minister of Information, telling them what he thought of it. The fat was in the fire.

Emeric's story was about the friendship that existed for over forty years between an English regular soldier and a German one. This alone scandalised the Establishment when the two countries were at war. But what really put the cat among the pigeons, so far as Grigg and Churchill were concerned, was the climactic scene between the two old friends in 1942, the very year in which we were making the film, in which it is the German, now a refugee from Hitler, who tells his English friend that war is no longer a blood sport for gentlemen, but a fight to the finish against the most devilish racism ever invented, and that if he goes on treating it as a gentleman's war he's going to lose it.

The Ministry were a little startled at Grigg's choleric memo, which smacked rather too much of one of the scenes in the film. They sent for us and told us Grigg's reaction, and said that if we couldn't get War Office support we couldn't have Laurence Olivier in the film. This was a facer, but I had feared as much and was prepared for it.

"Do you forbid us to make the film?" I asked the Minister and Jack Beddington.

"Oh, my dear fellow, after all, we are a democracy, aren't we? You know we can't forbid you to do anything, but don't make it, because everyone will be really cross, and the Old Man will be *very* cross and you'll never get a knighthood."

We stood outside the gaunt building in Bloomsbury. Emeric looked at me.

"Well, Michael, what do we do now?" Emeric had the heart of a lion, but he was a little bewildered by all the double talk.

"Do?" I said. "We make the film."

"Good," said Emeric, and we walked straight to Wardour Street, where Arthur Rank and C.M. Woolf were sitting biting their nails and waiting for us to come back from what might be our Dunkirk.

"They won't stop us making the film," I reported. "But they won't help us either. They won't release Laurence Olivier from the Fleet Air Arm."

Rank and C. M. looked at each other. "But who would you play?" they asked.

A little daemon (as in the case of Elisabeth Bergner and Glynis Johns) inspired me to reply: "We'll play Roger Livesey in the part."

Emeric looked at me, but said nothing. Of course he remembered Roger Livesey as one of the broad-shouldered scarlet-uniformed figures that thronged the corridors of Denham in Alex's Empire-building days, but he had no idea of his real quality, nor of my secret vow to prove to Mickey Balcon that Roger's husky voice was no bar to stardom. His name was vaguely familiar to the others, but they weren't too sure who he was or what films he had appeared in already.

Rank asked: "Is he in the Services?"

"No, he's working in an aircraft factory, and we can get him out."

Such was their relief and confidence in my instinct that they gave us leave to go ahead. I had already taken the precaution of finding out where Roger was. It was a very different Blimp we had now. Instead of his lips dripping corrosive acid, they dripped saccharine. Larry was very upset to lose the part, and the golden opportunity to get out of the Services and stay out, but Providence, in the person of Filippo Del Giudice, was already working on his side. Del, the chairman of Two Cities Films, had marked down Larry and Vivien as his potential stars in Alex's absence in America and had already started to pull strings to get them. Larry and Roger Livesey were old friends and friendly rivals, and Roger and his lovely actress wife, Ursula Jeans, were members of the group known by the collective phrase "Keeping up with the Oliviers".

Roger and I had an affinity for one another, as people have who know they are going to be important to each other one day. I don't think I had seen him since the Denham days, but I knew he had been directed into industrial war work and knew how to find him. It was probably one of the happiest inspirations I have ever had. So Colonel Blimp was settled. What about Colonel Blimp's love life? It was Emeric's answer to this which made the film his favourite of all our films. My own favourite has always been *A Matter of Life and Death*, although I have personal reasons for loving *The Life and Death of Colonel Blimp*. It was a very personal film for both of us.

We decided that our hero's military career should span forty years and three wars: the Boer War in 1902, in which young Blimp wins the Victoria Cross; the First World War, in which he is a Brigadier and in which his German friend is made a prisoner of the British; and the Second World War, which brings Blimp out of retirement, and his German friend to England again, this time as a refugee from Hitler. The opening sequences of the film would be the commando raid on the Turkish baths, already described, climaxed by Blimp's sealion-like roar of: "How do you know what I was like forty years ago?" followed by a giant SPLASH! as both men fall into the swimming pool.

The scene shifts back to 1902, and shows Blimp as a hot-headed young soldier fresh from the South African war where he has won the VC, trying to persuade the War Office to let him go to Berlin and counter the anti-British propaganda rampant there. His request is turned down. Encouraged by a letter that a friend receives from Edith Hunter, a young English governess working in Berlin, he disobeys and goes to Berlin anyway. He meets Edith and they go on the warpath together. In the course of their adventures, he insults the whole German Army and has to fight a duel with a German officer picked by lot as the Army's champion. This officer, Theodor Kretschmar-Schuldorff, becomes his lifelong friend.

The duel is fought under the strictest German rules of duelling.

Burrowing in the British Museum, Emeric had discovered a little book in German on the etiquette of duelling. It contained every one of the points which we used so effectively in the debate between the seconds before the duel. It is grimly funny, and we went to town on it. Both parties are wounded in the duel, honour is satisfied, and they end up recuperating in the same nursing home, where their friendship begins.

Clive – for I had settled Blimp's name as Clive Candy, known to the Army as "Sugar Candy, VC", and to his friends as "Suggie" – falls in love with Edith Hunter, but thinks he has plenty of time to tell her so when they return to London together. Theo, his new German friend, also loves Edith, and with Continental directness pops the question when he learns that she is leaving Berlin. Caught between two fires and confused by Clive's backwardness, Edith chooses Theo. Clive only discovers that his heart is broken when he reaches London.

Clive never gets over it. Edith remains his ideal woman, and he spends the rest of his life looking for her in the intervals between big game hunting. Now a brigadier, he finds that ideal again during the First World War, in the shape of a young English Red Cross nurse. With typical Blimp persistence, he tracks her down after the war and marries her. It is a love match, but after a few years' happiness he loses her in an accident. He finds his ideal woman again in the third act of the comedy when he picks her out of three hundred candidates to be his driver in World War II. The plan was for the same actress to play all three parts, and the actress we chose for the job was Wendy Hiller.

The career of Clive's friend Theo follows the unhappy road taken by so many of his fellow German officers. First an officer in one of the crack regiments of Uhlans, and married to a beautiful Englishwoman who gives him two sons, he is captured early in the 1914 War, and spends bitter years as a prisoner of war in England. When Clive seeks him out, he refuses to shake hands. He returns to a Germany devastated by war and turning towards demagogues like Adolf Hitler for leadership. His wife Edith dies, and his two sons join the Nazi Party. He comes to England as a refugee, and only escapes being interned due to the intervention of Clive, now the familiar Blimpish figure, who is back on the active list. They renew their friendship, and Theo is able to comfort Clive when he is put out to grass for the second time after the BBC has cancelled a speech he was about to make exhorting the English to fight fair, whatever Hitler did. Clive's driver Angela encourages him to join the Home Guard, which is being formed to defend Britain. Clive plans an exercise for the defence of London; it is scheduled to start at midnight, but one of Angela's boyfriends, who is taking part in the exercise on the "enemy" side, profits by some careless talk on her part and attacks at 6:00 p.m., capturing Blimp and his whole staff in the Turkish bath. Clive accepts that he has to hand over to the new generation, and takes the salute with Theo and Angela standing beside him. The part of Theo was written by us for Anton Walbrook.

Rank and his associates may have had some doubts about the wisdom of our choice of subject, and our decision to go on with it after the cold douche we had received, not only from the Ministry, but from the Old Man himself. Of course, they all knew, including James Grigg, that we were going ahead with the film in spite of their expressed distaste for it, a number of official minutes were flying to and fro between Churchill, and Brendan Bracken, and James Grigg. These minutes were only discovered when Ian Christie of the British Film Institute was going through the war files for the BFI booklet on Powell and Pressburger, and they were gleefully used by the compilers. It caused a mild sensation both in England and America, because it was quite obvious that Churchill would have stopped the film if he could, and when it was made he tried to stop it being sent abroad. "Is this democracy?" we were asked. The answer is "yes". It's a free country, and you can express your opinion. He did and we did.

I have often been asked how we managed to obtain military vehicles, military uniforms, weapons and all the fixings after being refused help by the War Office and the Ministry of Information. The answer is quite simple: we stole them. Any prop man worth his salt – and we had one of the best – would laugh at the question. There may have been one or two forged passes too. Who knows? It was all part of the war effort. The Archers were famous now, and we had friends in all sorts of quarters, high and low. We didn't sneak around the by-streets with our Army trucks either, but came careering into London, down Western Avenue, through and round Marble Arch to Berkeley Square. Our commandos jumped out of their trucks and ran into the Royal Bathers' Club, watched benevolently by a single policeman. The Royal Bathers' Club was the name I had given to Blimp's own club. We should have made James Grigg a member.

By now our backers could see that this was going to be an unusual and spectacular film, and they were as enthusiastic about it as we were. It was budgeted at about £200,000. I had decided to make it in colour, first of all because I had never directed a feature film in colour on my own. Secondly, Technicolor film stock, laboratory and technicians were still available and Georges Périnal, whose lighting on *The Thief of Bagdad* had staggered the Americans and the Technicolor Company itself, was available too. It was a film of many episodes, all of them in sharply differentiated locations, each one full of its special atmosphere. But it was the question of how to present the three heroines that decided me to use colour. Wendy Hiller, who was going to play all three women, and had good clothes sense, would be going through the most sensational period of transformation of women's bodies since the Garden of Eden. It was like an escape from prison.

The beginning of the century saw the hourglass figure, the heavy material of the dresses and skirts, the enormous hats and all the paraphernalia to make a woman feel decorative and useless. The 1914 war freed a woman's body from corsets, which went into the dustbin. It was a time of ugly, serviceable clothes, drab colours, cloche hats, skimpy skirts, and low heels. Finally, there was the Second World War with women in uniform beside their men.

Then there was the question of make-up. Technicolor insisted on supervising the make-up, because of the pigments already in the skins of the actors and actresses. Their make-up reduced the faces of all actresses to a deadly conformity: sticky, cherry-coloured lips, all character in the face smoothed out by the dreaded use of pancake, rouged cheeks, and eyes staring hopefully through a thick fringe of mascara. In my opinion, make-up was the province of artists, not make-up artists. Alfred Junge, recently released from an internment camp, which he and his crew had so successfully camouflaged that nobody could find him, was screened and summoned back to design films. He was now a British citizen. I put him in complete charge of the art department, that is to say all the art direction, the sets and props and also all costumes and accessories, including make-up. I had learnt from Vincent Korda on *The Thief of Bagdad* the value of a painter's eye, and I was determined to go one better than Alex. Georges Périnal, our cameraman, a law unto himself, subscribed to this.

Roger Livesey had as big a problem as the actress who was going to play his three sweethearts. In 1902 he was to appear as an upstanding, chestnut-haired young soldier who had recently won the VC in South Africa. In 1918 he was a kindly, conservative Brigadier in his forties with thinning hair and a moustache. In 1942 he was Colonel Blimp, by gad, Sir! For Roger, the solution to turn himself into Blimp was to shave his head. Leaving the scene in the Turkish bath to be done at the end of the film, we planned to shoot in sequence, from 1902 to 1940, and then off would go that wonderful thatch of hair. Ursula screamed, but Roger was adamant.

But what were we to do in the Turkish bath, where he was to appear half naked – a tub of lard. How could we construct a Blimp torso and how would Roger be able to act in it. I ruled that the solution lay in doubles: in cutting from an actor who had a body like the apocryphal Colonel to Roger's close-up with his shaven head and vast moustache. This is mainly what we did. The art department insisted on working out a sort of carapace in two halves which would fit together like a suit of armour around Roger's torso. The only problem was what would they do with the join at the neck. Goodness knows how many man-hours were wasted upon this idea, which may have appeared once on the screen. Anyway, the real answer came down to acting, as it always will do. In some magical way, Roger was able to blow up his face, heighten his colour and put plastics inside his mouth, until he looked like a streaming volcano ready to explode. We made numerous tests of this make-up, because once Roger shaved off his hair we were all committed.

These problems all came up again in 1979, when Martin Scorsese began making *Raging Bull*, starring Robert De Niro. The hero of the film, Jake LaMotta, had to put on thirty or forty pounds when he retired from the ring, and De Niro was set on doing the job himself without help from the make-up department. His solution was to eat Italian pasta, morning, noon, and night. Martin, who was a great admirer of our film, suggested consulting me, and there were many discussions as well as strange cables flying to and fro across the Atlantic, before Bob De Niro finally put his foot down and started on the pasta. Of course, they had to hold the film up for about three months while he put on the required poundage. He was horrifyingly successful in turning the body of a superb athlete into that of a slob. It was a risky procedure, and I hope he won't do it again.

We were scheduled for twelve weeks, the longest schedule I had ever been allowed. But our weeks were only five and a half days long, because of transport difficulties, and a great deal of our time was spent travelling to and fro to Denham by rail, or sitting in immobilised carriages while an air raid alert was on. It was the grim period of "London can take it", and the contrast with Alfred Junge's gay, colourful and fantastic sets was very striking. We used to rush whooping into the studio, like children returning to their newly decorated nursery.

One day, when we were in full preparation for production, and other actors were visiting our sets and the wardrobe to sigh with envy over the period costumes and props, we went to have a coffee in the studio restaurant, and seeing Deborah Kerr, I sat down at her table. She was now a rising young screen actress, and had already attracted the attention of theatrical producers as well. She was shy. She told me afterwards that she remembered our first meeting in the office of her agent, John Glidden, and how I said quickly and dismissively: "She's too young for this part, but she'll be a star in a couple of years." Glidden had been impressed by my remark, and was even more impressed when it came true.

She was going to stand up, but I sat down quickly and saved her the embarrassment. We talked, and as I recounted the plot of *Colonel Blimp*'s three leading ladies, I felt the same mysterious affinity between us that I had felt for Roger years before. Deborah had a sensitive, expressive face. She was intelligent. She was all actress. I found myself wondering, had we perhaps made a mistake? Wasn't this the right girl to play Blimp's three sweethearts? I suddenly felt unsure. But I said nothing about it to her, or to anybody else.

Then, a few weeks before production started, a mine exploded under us. Wendy Hiller, who was married to Ronald Gow, the playwright, was going to have a baby. There was no question of postponing our production, except for a week or two. Everyone looked at me. What were we to do? Should we send to America for a leading lady? Should we offer Greer Garson the part? Even wilder suggestions were made. I kept my head and told Emeric that I thought Deborah Kerr, although only twenty, had the character for the part, and, of course, our wonderful art department and technical crew would help her through the three transformations.

In the two years since we had cut her out of *Contraband*, she had played Robert Newton's girlfriend in *Major Barbara* and the part of the girl in love in *Love on the Dole*, which Wendy Hiller had created on the stage. These were quality performances. She had just finished a run-of-the-mill Resistance film in Norway, playing opposite a lot of Heavy Water.

"Would a French company," I asked, "start yelling to America for a star, when one of their own girls has a little mishap like this? They wouldn't. They have confidence in their girls, and would find an even better girl for the part." Emeric agreed. I went on: "If we had more time, we'd look around, but we haven't. Let me talk to Deborah. If I think she can do it, I'll offer her the part." Emeric agreed.

She was living in London at the English Speaking Union in Charles Street, Mayfair. It was a fine morning and she walked over to see me in Chester Square. She was bare-headed, and I remember her hair shining in the sun like burnished copper. No. 65A Chester Square has a little bay window with a window seat, which looks out into the street. We sat there and talked. We looked at the bulky script together and I watched the subtle transformations that passed over her face as I made suggestions about the script. Again I felt that mysterious affinity, as between an artist and his model, which is one of the most inexplicable of the sensual sensations. I made up my mind. I said that frankly we had no time to lose. So long as her agent agreed to our terms, she had the part. She stopped breathing and looked at me. She has told me since that I was already thinking of something else. I said absently: "All right then, see you at the studio," and she took her leave.

I remember standing at the lattice window and watching Deborah walk away up the street to Belgrave Square and noticing how straight her back was and how high she held her head.

Ten days later we started making the film. It was an unforgettable experience for everybody. It is difficult for me to explain what it feels like in a work of art to be borne along on the wings of inspiration. Emeric's screenplay for *Colonel Blimp* should be in every film archive, in every film library. The actors grew and discovered themselves with every line that they spoke. We averaged three minutes of finished film per day. We shot over six hundred set-ups. John Seabourne, who was once again my editor, used to come running from the cutting-room to the stage to tell me how excited he was with each day's work. We all depended upon one another, we all learnt from one another. I was not the only director. There were four directors. I learnt from Anton what an artist is. I learnt from Roger what a man is. I learnt from Deborah what love is.

In those days before the pill there were still virgins in the land, and even in the film business, although the actresses who chose that particular form of expression must have known that they wouldn't be virgins long. The power that a film director has over his star was already a legend. But it was a complete surprise to me to find that I was falling in love with an actress. I had never used my craft to woo a girl. I had had brief encounters that sprang from the world I worked in, as I might have had if I had worked in any other canning factory – a bit of slap and tickle on an outing. But these had not affected my love for Frankie, which had remained constant for nearly ten years. I had never confused my art with love or lust. Was there no sensuality in my work? Not much. Not until now.

I was fundamentally a serious little boy. I am fundamentally a serious little man. I had grown up with a keen appreciation of the art of writing, and when I chose film-making as my medium of expression I brought the same ideals to it that I had already brought to literature. I had carried this to ridiculous lengths. But now I was caught. It was thoroughly confusing and annoying, exciting and ridiculous.

I had never thought that I could marry an actress, nor a girl sixteen years younger than I was. Besides, I was in love with Frankie. We had always meant to marry, but the moment passed, my career faltered, Frankie had a host of admirers, and then the war was upon us. Frankie, being the daughter of a doctor with consulting rooms in Harley Street, was in the thick of it. She should have been a surgeon. She never lets me forget that at the height of the Blitz, with buildings blowing up all around Portland Place, with ambulance calls night and day, and with nothing to give the casualties but cups of tea, she received a cable I had sent from Canada after our trip to Hudson Bay. It read: "Safe and well". As she was laughing, the house that was back-to-back with 148 Harley Street fell down.

Here are two memories of those days at Denham. We had rigged up a very small set, two easy chairs and a fireplace, in one of the big, empty, echoing Denham stages, for an intimate scene between Roger and Deborah. It followed the dinner party attended by Theo after being a prisoner of war in England. When the party is over, Clive's wife comes home from the theatre, and there is a lovely domestic scene of the two of them, plus my two spaniels Eric and Spangle, by the fireside.

Clive tells his wife what he has said to Theo: "I told him: 'Don't worry, old man, we'll soon have Germany on her feet again.'"

"Did he believe it?" she asks.

He answers: "I think so, hope so."

But the scene was a little short, and besides I wanted something more intimate for the last glimpse of Clive Candy's beloved wife. Deborah in the firelight, in a shimmering evening dress and a bit of tulle, looked good enough to eat. I invented a bit of business which scandalised Emeric – the anti-feminist.

Clive starts to hum the tune from the opera *Mignon*, which is one of the themes of the film.

After a moment, she says: "Darling . . . don't hum."

He stirs and looks inquiringly at her. "Was I humming?"

She nods and smiles: "It's a little habit you've got."

He takes it beautifully and makes a face and says: "Mmmmm." Then after a pause: "But what will I do if I don't hum?"

She laughs and loves him and stretches out her arms to him and he takes her in his arms. The spaniels snore at their feet.

As I was shooting this scene, I felt the presence of two or three strangers behind me. I glanced round and saw that they were wearing American uniforms. One of them smiled and nodded at me. It was William Wyler, the great Hollywood director of countless thirties films produced by Samuel Goldwyn. I knew that he and other leading directors were already in uniform, having to make combat films. He crept up behind me and I could feel his breath on my neck as I said "OK. Cut!" He gave me the thumbs up sign and vanished with his aides as silently as he had arrived. I shall never forget that moment. To receive Wyler's accolade for such a delicate love scene, of which he had directed many, was a great experience. A moment later, Alex Korda was standing there, as immaculate as ever. He had obviously arrived with the delegation from MGM and in company with Wyler and the other directors. We walked together to the exit door from the stage.

"Meekey," he said reproachfully, "why do you play an unknown girl in such an important picture?"

The second memory is of the long corridor at the studio. It no longer exists, but I can see it still. It served all of Denham's great stages, and it had service doors which were always swinging and banging. It had parallel bands of colour running along the wall, to indicate the way to particular departments. Because of the fall in the ground there was every now and then a rather nasty jink in the concrete, and as I was always running up or down this corridor (I was always in a hurry), I once or twice had a bad fall. But not such a fall as I had that night.

Deborah and I had worked in delightful harmony throughout the picture, and I knew that we had made a new star. Roger and Anton shared my opinion and showed her they did. We were four happy colleagues creating something good, with never a second to spare apart from that. Uncle Alfred was the greatest organiser and disciplinarian that I have ever known, and the film ran as smoothly as oil. There was never time for anything except eating, sleeping and working. As soon as the whistle blew for the end of work, the actors hurried away to change their costumes, and everyone else made a beeline for home in case there should be an air raid warning before they got there. But that night we must have quit early, for I was walking with Deborah up the long corridor, tired, but happy with the day's work, and chatting about the next day's. My office was about halfway up and she went on to her dressing room at the top end. I watched her go. She opened the swing door, then she turned and looked back. That was the moment. That was the *coup de foudre*.

September 30, 1942, was to be Deborah's twenty-first birthday. It was my birthday too. I would be thirty-seven. We were up to schedule on the film, so we thought we could afford to give Deborah a surprise party. Although we were not approved of by the War Office, we did have a Military Adviser: General Brownrigg. His military experience had covered the whole of the years of our Colonel Blimp's military career. And I had used his souvenir book and scrapbook as one of the essential props for showing the passing years in Clive Candy's life after his happy marriage. The souvenir sequence cuts off abruptly when his wife dies. And although he still turns the pages, they are blank until he goes big game hunting again. General Brownrigg was mobilised once more to present a bouquet of twenty-one roses to our young star and a courtly job he made of it. That night I took Deborah to dinner at the Martinez Spanish restaurant in Swallow Street and told her that it was my birthday too. We were born on the same day. I asked her to marry me. As far as I remember, we just sat there, our hands clasped, as dumb as two oysters.

Of course, I had to tell Frankie, and there was a hell of a row. Perhaps it was tactless of me to tell her when we were in bed. I had always had doubts about whether Frankie wanted to marry me, but apparently she had no doubts at all; she just hadn't got around to it. Diamond engagement rings were hurled into the gutters of Harley Street and Ebury Street – the Ebury Street one was never found – and there were some very painful conversations between the two ladies, mostly on the telephone. The trouble was, each appreciated the quality of the other. Of course, Scottish Deborah was no match for Irish Frankie, in an exchange of sentiment. It was no good telling myself that I should marry one or the other dear charmer. It was no good telling myself that instead of jumping into bed with Deborah, I should feel myself bound to Frankie. With her independent spirit, she would have regarded this as an insult. Whatever I did I would hurt one of the two people I loved most in the world. Frankie had shared my life for nearly ten years; Deborah for as many weeks – but what weeks they'd been, and what years lay ahead of us! All my very real prejudices against mixing my profession with my private life had vanished.

I realised that Deborah was both the ideal and the flesh-and-blood woman whom I had been searching for ever since I had discovered that I had been born to be a teller of tales and a creator of dreams.

At this point, the crisis was postponed by two jobs of work that had to be done: H. M. Tennant, the leading West End theatrical company, offered Deborah the part of Ellie Dunn in their production of *Heartbreak House*, a play of Shaw's which they were reviving that winter at the Cambridge Theatre. I was sent to Gibraltar, a disgruntled Volunteer.

I have mentioned that Emeric and I took on the production of two other films at the time I was directing *Colonel Blimp*: *The Silver Fleet*, and *The Volunteer*, both of them in close creative association with Ralph Richardson, although he had no credits on the films other than as an actor.

The Silver Fleet got its title from a legendary Dutch hero called Piet Hein, who sank the Spanish silver fleet in the Bay of Matanzas on the northwest coast of Cuba in 1628. There is a Dutch folksong with the refrain: "Piet Hein, Piet Hein / He sank the Silver Fleet," and there was a very nice scene in the film in which a young schoolteacher tells her pupils, while their country is under occupation by the Germans, the story of Piet Hein and his resistance to the oppressors. The young actress who played the schoolteacher had a dreamy voice and great eyes like a lynx. Her name was Kathleen Byron, of whom more later.

Vernon Sewell directed the film. We got him out of the Navy to do it. He had served two and a half years in small ships and that was enough. He did a fine job. It was very much Emeric's production, for I was busy on *Blimp*, and at first they didn't get on, because Emeric fancied that Vernon had snubbed him, not realising that Vernon had literally not seen him. His eyesight had never been first-rate, and during his naval service, he received a nasty head injury on board his ship, which took him to hospital for several months. When he was directing Esmond Knight in the film, he said it was the blind leading the blind, for Esmond was at that time totally blind. He had lost his sight as a result of a direct hit on his gun turret on board the *Prince of Wales*, in which he was serving during the pursuit of the German pocket battleship *Bismarck*. I remember he wrote to me from hospital a typical letter saying that while he was wallowing around on the floor of the turret in blood and guts and oil, he heartily regretted that he had not accepted my offer of the part of Lieutenant Hirth, in *49th Parallel* played by Eric Portman. When Esmond came out of hospital, his fellow actors gave him a magnificent benefit performance which collected a few thousand pounds for him, and thought: "Well, that was Esmond." They could not have been more wrong. In a few months he was back with us, playing a big part as an SS officer in *The Silver Fleet*, and he has been with us on and off ever since. A little annoyance like blindness only made Esmond's torch shine brighter.

I knew Vernon would get on with Ralph Richardson because they were both oddballs. We were shooting concurrently and on adjacent stages at Denham, and I used to run in there occasionally from the *Blimp* set to see how they were getting on. They didn't need me. I remember hearing a burst of laughter one day as I came through the sound-proof door. It was caused by Esmond winning a bet that he would end up on his marks, in the right position on the set. He finished on his marks all right, but facing the wrong way. It had the Nelson Touch, I thought. Googie Withers, as Ralph's wife in the film, had her first real co-starring role, and she was fine. At last people realised what I had known all along, that her beauty had an erotic quality, strange and provocative. It was delightful to learn that she had a keen sense of humour. She had a deep chuckle when she was amused that was irresistible. There had been a lot of pressure from the Rank publicity people that she should change her crazy name now that she was a dramatic actress. "Of course not," said Googie. "Googie means crazy. I'll always be Googie, and I'll always be crazy." There was no answer to that.

The Silver Fleet was our first production that Emeric didn't write and I didn't direct. It was a success, and opened up the way for other associate productions. More importantly, it led to the formation of the production company to be known as Independent Producers.

Our two Dutch films had an important effect upon me, at any rate, for thanks to them Emeric and I met Jan de Hartog. We had been to the Ministry for a briefing. I think we had seen a remarkable colour film about blood transfusions, or it may have been the even more remarkable film that was made about plastic surgery, particularly on the faces of pilots who had been burnt in the Battle of Britain. We also saw some German propaganda films, and after they were over we were introduced to the newest arrival from the occupied countries: a self-styled actor, author and dramatist. He was about thirty, had long blond hair, a merry eye and a merry wit, and he himself claims that he is one of the biggest liars you could hope to be entertained by. He addressed the group.

He had been a pupil in the drama class that had been conducted by Dr Ludwig Berger during the years he was in exile in Holland. At the mention of this illustrious name, I sat up. Jan de Hartog had been one of Berger's best pupils. He had written an anti-Nazi play, an underground play called *Skipper Next to God*. Jan de Hartog, playing the part of the Skipper himself, had performed this in many underground cellars and other strange places in occupied Holland, before having to take off with the Nazis at his heels. He had then crossed France and Spain by the underground railway, and eventually reached England where, as far as I can remember, he had landed in the middle of a field, and been instantly arrested. He described this episode with great enjoyment. Apparently, he had walked to meet his English hosts with enthusiasm, telling them how he had escaped from

Holland, across France and Spain, and how glad he was to be in England. He told them what a terrible time he had had, and what narrow escapes. The officer in charge said "Did you really?" and shut him up in the local police station for the next twenty-four hours, until he was passed on to somewhere else for a fortnight's screening. He was now released and declared speakable, and was very impressed by the nonchalant efficiency of the British. He was an excellent mimic. He spoke English fluently and well, with an accent that hovered about half a mile north of Marble Arch. It reminded you of Evelyn Waugh's characters in *A Handful of Dust*: Sussex Gardens, with a whiff of Paddington.

But with all these mountebank qualities, which Jan would be the last to deny, he was impressive, and I remember Emeric whispering to me, as we sat listening to his answers to some tricky question from the audience: "What a fine mind he has." Emeric was right, and yet his assessment wasn't completely accurate. Jan had a lightning mind – he could see a point, make a connection in a flash – but he was also the actor, the jester with the cap and bells. I loved him on sight, and I love him still. Since then, he has written and staged many plays, he has written many books, he has delighted the world, and the world has paid him back handsomely, although never as handsomely as a Dutch author expects to be paid. Maybe I shall see him and Marjorie again this week, for I am on my way by jumbo jet to New York, forty years later. It would be pleasant to hear Jan's outrageous lies and stentorian laugh again.

Jan has the face and puzzled expression of a child, but his eyes give him away. They are watchful, worried, thoughtful and tragic. He tells you a story and rolls about roaring with laughter, but his eyes have seen the sins of the world. Lord have mercy upon us. This is perhaps what has made him so popular in America. Americans love a club sandwich, a three-decker, and Captain Jan de Hartog, Skipper Next to God, is a three-decker of a man.

We gave Jan free run of Denham, and he spent a lot of time on our set and in the cutting room. He saw at once how Emeric was handling the propaganda in our film and was enormously impressed. We always encouraged the editor, or cutter (the terms are synonymous) to keep up with the shooting, and it was rare that John Seabourne was more than three or four days behind us with his first assembly of the film. I needed to know what he thought of the scenes and whether he needed retakes or extra shots to complete sequences, while the sets were still standing in the studio.

"Micky, are you going to shoot close-ups on the actor who plays the bandmaster?" he might ask.

"Denis Arundell? Why?"

"I need them."

"OK, looking which way?"

"Both ways. To left of camera for Roger and Deborah and right of camera for Kaunitz. And do them to playback, won't you?"

"Sure, come and direct it yourself."

"No. I've got real work to do."

This question of which side of the camera to look is a nightmare which haunts actors in films. Too often the director himself is not sure. If there is a master shot, which covers most of the action on the set, of course, it is much simpler: the point of view of the camera moving and following the actors is the focal point of the scene. But when you are shooting a picture off the cuff, as Hitchcock and I often were, with a pattern of shots, an exchange of looks, a violent piece of action, or a shot filmed mainly in close shot, or cutting around all over the set, then it is possible, unless you are a master like Hitch, to find when the sequence is assembled in the cutting room that your two main actors are looking two different ways. I have seen a director and his camera crew – not mine, I hasten to add – completely baffled by this and all squatting around the camera, drawing chalk marks on the floor to prove their point, while some bored actor waits for their verdict. I have often longed to ask David Lean, who has been known to say caustic things about my choice of camera angles, whether he ever got into such a jam himself on his own pictures, but I know the way David looks down that beautiful, thin, delicate nose of his, and I didn't dare.

Since we are talking of that great director and precise technician, I'm sure he won't mind my telling how he came to me for advice in the early stages of his directorial career. I believe it was when he was directing *Blithe Spirit*. Noël Coward and my team of technicians from *One of Our Aircraft Is Missing*, which also included Sydney Streeter, had made *In Which We Serve* into a stunning production and a big success for Noël personally, in the triple threat of actor, director and writer. Like Emeric and me, they had banded together to form Cineguild Films, and since there was a demand for Noël Coward films they had understandably gone on to make more, including *This Happy Breed*, *Blithe Spirit*, and *Brief Encounter*. Fortunately for them, and for all of us, they then decided that an exclusive diet of Noël Coward plums would result in the colly-wobbles. Noël went back to the theatre, where he belonged, and the boys at Cineguild, having recruited John Bryan as their designer, turned their attention to Charles Dickens, which gives some indication of how difficult it is for young and inexperienced producers to choose a subject which is both commercial and valid. Anyway, it is to this that we owe *Great Expectations*, with Finlay Currie's unforgettable performance as Magwitch the convict, and the superb David Lean and Alec Guinness *Oliver Twist*.

On the occasion mentioned, David came to me in a great state. His forehead is always wrinkled by thought and concentration, and on this day it looked as if all the railway lines from *Brief Encounter* had met in the middle of it.

"Micky, I must have your advice. It's terribly urgent."

"What's the matter?"

"I'm talking to you in strictest confidence. Promise me you won't tell anybody."

"I promise." (And I've kept that promise until today.)

David took a deep breath. "I have completely misunderstood what Noël was driving at in the sequence which I'm shooting now."

"That's nothing. I often don't understand what Emeric's driving at, until the preview of the picture."

"No, no, Micky, this is serious. We have been shooting for two days, and I realise now that it's all wrong. What am I to do?"

"Do? Go back and reshoot it."

"How do you mean?"

"Scrap it. You are the boss."

This was a new idea to David. He considered it. Like all of us, he had been brought up on a strict diet of mean budgets and tight schedules. A day's work in the studio was an enormous investment to us. Retakes were as rare and unattainable as wild strawberries, and then there was his craftsman's pride.

"You think that I should call a meeting and tell the others that I've made a mistake and we've got to retake two days' work? They'll never forgive me."

"Don't call a meeting. Do it in the projection room, at the end of the dailies. They're going to wait to hear what you're going to say anyway."

He gave a hollow laugh. "You don't know Ronnie and John. And Tony." (Anthony Havelock-Allan, a far-sighted and imaginative young producer, who was married at the time to Valerie Hobson, was the fourth member of the Cineguild team.) "They would never respect me again."

"Oh yes they will. We are all fallible. They will respect you for realising what you were doing and they'll respect you for saying so. And then they'll respect you for having the cheek to say you're going to retake it. You've got a 10 per cent contingency in the budget that will take care of that."

He groaned and said he would try. Cineguild weathered its first great crisis. I'm telling this little anecdote to show how strictly we had been trained and how proud we were of our direct responsibility to our profession. We had all worked on big films and now it was our own show. Arthur Rank had asked Emeric and me to invite other creative producers to join our group and we had at once invited Cineguild. They were followed by Frank Launder and Sidney Gilliat, two brilliant and experienced screenwriters who had written for Hitchcock and Carol Reed, and many other comedies and thrillers, and now had come together as a writer-producer-director team. The next recruit was Ian Dalrymple, fresh from his triumphs with the Crown Film Unit. I think I proposed him, but he was voted in unanimously.

Rank and Davis were delighted. Here was a group of producers who could guarantee that the stages of Denham and Pinewood were kept busy after the war was over. The new group was to be called Independent Producers Ltd, and we told Arthur Rank that he had to be our chairman whether he liked it or not. In his speech of acceptance, he told us that we should have a managing director. He didn't want to interfere with our independence, but we were too undisciplined a bunch to be able to run ourselves and also plan ahead. It was a new concept to us: by forming a group that was necessarily dependent on a single source for finance, had we walked into a trap? We debated this openly with Rank and Davis, and safeguards were suggested and accepted. Looking back now, I marvel at their patience. However, when the new managing director turned out to be George Archibald – later Lord Archibald – I began to see that there was merit in the idea, and started to unload a lot of work onto George's thin but willing shoulders. But independence is a heady thing. I'm afraid George sometimes found us too hot to handle.

I have drifted downstream a year or two, and must somehow pole back with you against the current of the winter of my discontent – 1942–43. *Blimp* is in the editing stages, Allan Gray is composing the musical score, and to our amazement the final cut of the film runs two hours and forty-eight minutes. We had never planned this. We could not have planned it, because it was our first experience of working together on an epic subject full of character studies and period touches, with full-length portraits of men and women over a period of years. Emeric's beautiful scheme of Colonel Blimp's love for his three wives – the one he had lost, the one he found and lost, and the one he will lose to a younger man – had inspired me. If you have read the early part of these memoirs, you will know how deeply I had steeped myself in the period which covered Blimp's career: 1892–1942 (and now here I am myself, forty years later in 1982, writing about it and I, like Blimp, still haven't changed!). From the ordinary talk of my grandfather, my mother and my father, I was familiar with the events and personalities of the first half of the twentieth century. I remember when Noël Coward wrote and produced his play *Cavalcade*, a patriotic family saga which covered very much the same period as our film, there was a cartoon in *Punch* showing an observant baby with the face of young Mr Coward, looking out of its perambulator, taking note of the celebrations over the Relief of Mafeking. A case of sour grapes on the part of the cartoonist, perhaps. This gift of curiosity about the world we are born into and in which we grow up, is a rare and wonderful one. All artists have it, and wish to pass it on to others. So, working on the final version of the script with Emeric, I would pull out of this ragbag of reminiscence enough coloured patches in Blimp's life to make a crazy quilt of Technicolor. Emeric would query some allusion. I would explain it, and he would embroider it. And so the script grew until it had all the beautiful inconsequence of the life and death of a typical English gentleman.

Even then, when he realised that he had a three-hour show on his hands, with no intermission, and which could not fit into any of the normal distribution patterns, Rank was not dismayed. On the contrary, he was thrilled by the film. I remember that we had a meeting with him around the middle of the winter, when we were discussing the formation of Independent Producers Ltd, and we asked him what kind of film he was looking for, and at what price, in order to compete with the Americans in the enormous international world market, and after reflection he answered quite simply and seriously: "Like *Colonel Blimp*." And that was at a time when the general public had not seen the film, and when the dark clouds of displeasure engendered by the War Office and laced with thunderbolts from the Old Man at No. 10 Downing Street were still threatening the film and its future.

Meanwhile, *The Volunteer* had gone into production and was a pain in the ass from start to finish. We undertook this piece of recruiting for the Fleet Air Arm at the suggestion of Ralph Richardson who, since he was already serving in the Fleet Air Arm, was to be our liaison officer, and would also appear in the film as himself. Emeric's idea was to make Ralph the narrator and the story he has to tell concerns his dresser in the theatre. The young man decides to join up and his mother gives him some advice: "Join the Army, son. If you join the Air Force, ten to one they shoot you down in flames. If you join the Navy you have every chance of being drowned. Join the Army and be safe." The boy confides in Ralph: "I don't want to be safer than anyone else, I'm going to join the Fleet Air Arm." On this simple premise Emeric built up his structure.

Because Ralph, the narrator, was an actor as well as a naval officer, I had opened the film with a few scenes taken at Denham Studios: glimpses of famous people. There is a brief glimpse of Larry Olivier imitating a goldfish, and another of Ralph himself as a Beefeater, proclaiming some lines about "the wooden walls of England". And in the last shot of the film, taken outside Buckingham Palace, there's a brief glimpse of me, one of my few appearances in my own films. I was a photographer this time. It was that sort of film: innocent, interesting, but scrappy.

In the film, Ralph is playing Othello at the New Theatre in St Martin's Lane, where he and Larry were later to create two memorable seasons. We see him in his dressing room and from the wings on stage. There was a scene at the stage door with autograph hunters, and Emeric couldn't resist the classic joke that, for an actor, the only thing worse than fans waiting at the stage door is to have no fans waiting at the stage door. After these preliminaries, both Ralph and his dresser join the Fleet Air Arm, and the film gets more interesting as we follow their respective careers.

At the suggestion of the Admiralty, we established a pattern of cooperation which was to serve us well many years later in the *Graf Spee* film. The Lords of the Admiralty laid it on the line as follows: "Dear Powell and Pressburger, if you ask for what you want when you want it, you can't have it. Or if you could have it, it would cost you an astronomical fee. Do as we say, tell us exactly what you want, and when it is possible to give it to you, we'll tell you to come and get it, and it won't cost you or the taxpayer a penny."

The British Navy and their lordships are like that: direct, helpful, cogent, logical and speaking basic English. It was a pleasure to deal with them after a bout with the War Office.

I had cast one of the boys from the commando troop from *Colonel Blimp*, Pat McGrath, as Ralph's dresser, and we had a small camera unit standing by, led by Freddie Ford, who you may remember spent hours on his stomach shooting the bombing raid over Stuttgart for *One of Our Aircraft Is Missing*.

We joined the training ship, a famous old aircraft carrier at Liverpool and spent some days crashing around the Irish Sea. She was far too old and too slow for up-to-date operations, but she was ideal for training and for the kind of camera work, by night and by day, we were planning. Nearly all the shots of the interior of the ship in the film were made in her, and when Emeric was planning the script, he landed on her, piloted by Ralph.

Dear Ralph! On October 11, 1983, all the lights in the London theatres were switched off to mourn the passing of a great actor – Ralph Richardson. He had been working with the National Theatre up to a week before his last illness. You could say that he died on the boards, and he would have been proud to hear me say so. He was as much loved in the business as he was by audiences, and he left behind him a staggering record of performances in theatre, radio, television and film. He had a gift of fantasy and a sense that the world was mad, though not as mad as he. There must have been many people weeping when they heard the news on the radio. But anyone passing down the lane outside Lee Cottages in the Cotswolds would have heard nothing but laughter. For I was talking on the telephone to Emeric at Shoemaker's Cottage, Debenham, Suffolk, on the other side of England, who was recounting his experiences on the research trip for *The Volunteer* when, piloted by Ralph, they dropped in on an aircraft carrier for the first time.

I was incredulous. "Do you mean you actually flew with Ralph? You got in a plane with him?"

At the other end of the line, Emeric was giggling. "I hadn't any choice. I had gone to Worthy Down to ask him questions for the script, and he said: 'Look here, Emeric, the best thing to do is go and see for yourself. Let's go and find her.' Find what? I naturally asked him, because he was already struggling into his flying gear, and I could see by the faces of the ground staff around me that they thought I was as mad as he. There was a ground fog, I remember, but I didn't like to point this out, and they were already bringing me a flying suit – you know, a Mae West and an intercom – and I saw, with horror, a sergeant hurrying up with two parachutes."

By now I, at my end of the line, was rolling on the ground in hysterics. "Weren't you frightened?"

"I was scared shitless," replied Emeric sedately, "but I didn't dare say so. We climbed into a small two-passenger aircraft, and they put plugs in all the holes and showed me how the parachute worked, and where the release catches were, and how to use the intercom, until I felt there was no hope for me. Ralph was snorting and humming in the way he had. He was looking at some very dirty, creased maps, and pushed them into my hands. 'Here, Emeric, you be navigator.' He stabbed vaguely at the chart. 'Course 300, got that? She's somewhere about here.' He stabbed again at the map, which resented the treatment by falling in a puddle of water. We were soon ready. Too soon for me. I still couldn't believe that I was trusting my life to Ralph. Then we were off."

"In the fog?" I asked spluttering.

"In the fog," replied Emeric's voice. "I made some remark about it, and Ralph said: 'Oh, don't worry, Dormouse, we'll be out of it in a jiffy.' And we were. We taxied down the runway and took off after about a hundred yards, straight up. 'Like an elevator,' I roared. He answered: 'Yes, just like an express elevator.' We passed very close over some warehouses, but Ralph didn't seem to mind. He said something on the intercom that I did not understand. He said: 'These bloody things never work. Take it off. When I have anything to say, I'll shout. That's the Isle of Wight over there. Now we're on course. You can follow it on the map. We're supposed to keep wireless silence, but if we do that, we'll never find the carrier.' 'What carrier, Ralph?' This was the first time I had heard of a carrier. Ralph shushed me mysteriously: 'Our training ship. We'll land on her and spend the night.'"

Thelma looked in from the kitchen. Tears were running down my face. I gasped: "What happened next?"

"Vell, I realised I was done for. We couldn't find the carrier and were running short of gas. I realised then that airmen are not brave, they're just crazy. Ralph was very good. He was talking to the carrier and flying low over the sea to get under the fog, and at the same struggling out of his parachute. He yelled: 'Don't worry about your parachute, Emeric. They never work anyway.' Then we saw the carrier dead ahead."

"How did he land on it?" was all I had strength to say.

"Perfectly."

I recovered my voice. " 'Take him for all and all / We ne'er shall look upon his like again.' "

While shooting in home waters, we had kept in touch with the Admiralty in general, and the Fleet Air Arm in particular, and we had all decided that we had to have a sequence or two on board one of the great big modern aircraft carriers. They were all, of course, at sea, either in the Med, or off the coast of Europe. Then suddenly we got a signal that room could be made for me and my unit to travel down to Gibraltar on a troopship taking several hundred service personnel to the Mediterranean area. It was the beginning of the preparations for the North African landings, but, of course, we didn't know that. Ralph would go with us as liaison officer. At Gibraltar, we would be taken care of by the garrison of the Rock, who would see to it that we met the Captain of HMS *Indomitable*, which was at that time the largest and fastest of our aircraft carriers, and recently equipped with new defensive armour. When the Captain had learnt what we wanted, he would decide whether we could sail with him or not. Under service conditions, space was at a premium. We had to bunk where and how we were directed. Finally, we were warned that our presence in *Indomitable* was at the discretion of the Captain. It was not a very encouraging prospect, but troop ship *Letitia* was ready to leave and we had to join her within twenty-four hours.

It must have been the early spring of 1943 – what do you mean it must have been – this is supposed to be an autobiography? Was it early Spring or wasn't it? You should know . . . yes I should, but believe it or not I was still confused and amazed.

Two of the most beautiful women in England were in love with me and I with them, and I didn't know what to do about it. Frankie was still running things in Harley Street, and Deborah was playing Ellie Dunn to Robert Donat's Captain Shotover at the Cambridge Theatre. The press show and trade show of the film *Colonel Blimp* was to be in about three weeks' time. Nobody, not even David Low who had his ear to the Beaver Dam, knew what Grigg or Churchill would do about our defiance of their expressed wish. The film was scheduled to go directly into the Odeon Leicester Square, by now our favourite cinema, and nobody knew whether it would be allowed to open there or not. It was the biggest artistic crisis the Archers had had to face so far, and it was a relief to have the other decision thrust upon me. I took off for the Med, leaving Emeric holding the bag.

When France fell in 1940, like many other optimists during the phoney war – P. G. Wodehouse, Somerset Maugham – my father sat tight at Cap Ferrat, leaving the Normans to hold the manor house in Chantilly. When the crunch came and it was a question of staying or going, he never hesitated. He went. He was no collaborator, but his heart was in France. He was in the west of France at St-Jean-de-Luz, and I have never been able to discover whether he had gone there to play golf, as he often did, or whether he was there ready to take off. The SS *Arandora Star* was full up with refugees and he and Somerset Maugham, his immediate neighbour at Cap Ferrat, decided to sail with her.

My father left his car at the golf club, parked it and took the key, but he never saw it again. Later on, he never lamented the loss of the car, but couldn't get over the stupidity of leaving his golf clubs, particularly one favourite driver. My little house in Chester Square was open to him, and he at once re-established his connections with the Royal Automobile Club in Pall Mall, of which he had been a member since the foundation. So long as my father had a club where he could play bridge, he was all right.

I had two farewells to make, and although I had risked my life scores of times for the fun of it, there is always a distinct possibility in wartime that you are saying goodbye for keeps. Frankie's "Godspeed" was characteristic: "I don't care if you never come back, but take care of yourself." And Deborah said: "Goodbye, Michael. I know you are running away from both of us, but I don't blame you."

We sailed in convoy from an unnamed port, which proved to be Glasgow. I and my unit went up by sleeper train and Emeric saw me off. We shook hands. I said: "Good luck, old horse." And he said: "Good luck, young horse."

Ralph met me on arrival with the words: "I've got bad news for you. It's a dry ship."

"Why?"

"It's a troopship, you see. We're carrying eight hundred Army, Navy and Air Force personnel. The ship is requisitioned. The crew are all civilians – Merchant Marine. They just sail the ship and get us there, if we're lucky. We're sailing at . . . mustn't say when. Come and have a snort."

We joined our ship at Greenock, and sailed after dark, joining up with other ships from Belfast and Liverpool as we crossed the Irish Sea. Our escort was waiting for us off Cape Clear, and from then on we proceeded in convoy. After breakfast, Ralph and I were sent for by the military commander who was responsible for the troops on board. He had nothing to do with the sailing of the ship, but was responsible for the morale and safety of his personnel.

"Ah, Richardson," he said, looking doubtfully at Ralph's civilian companion. "I understand that you and Mr . . . hmm . . ."

"Powell," I suggested.

"Ah . . . Powell, yes. I understand that you've got a film crew on board. Can you give us a show?"

I looked respectfully at Ralph, who explained our mission. We were not there to give film shows, but to make a recruiting film.

"Yes, that's all very well, Richardson, but I'm told you're an actor in private life, and Mr . . . hmm . . . is a film director. You both know something about show business, what?"

We admitted the charge.

"Well then, I want you to get together and put on a show for the troops. You can have any of the military personnel on board to help."

Ralph looked at me blandly. "We'll be a bit short on materials," I suggested, "but I understand there are two hundred Wrens on board, and there must be some talent available. We'll hold auditions."

That was enough for the Commandant, who said: "Get on with it, please," and dived into a sea of paper.

Outside the door of the cabin, I looked at Ralph and Ralph looked at me.

"The audition bit sounds all right," I suggested.

"But what are they going to say?" asked Ralph mournfully.

"For God's sake, Ralph, you've been in enough plays. You must know scores of scenes by heart."

"Not now, dear boy. As soon as I finish a part, I haven't the slightest idea what I've been saying. And anyway, I'd have to have someone to play to. Oh, dear, what an ass that dear man is."

"Why not play him?" I suggested.

"Who?" queried Ralph. I jerked my thumb at the closed door. "The Commandant. We can build the show around you as the Commandant of the ship and give you lots of props, like W. C. Fields."

Ralph brightened. That great mind was working. Like all good clowns, he adored vaudeville. "I'd need a feed, Micky. A straight man."

It was by no means my idea to appear in the show, but I could see I would be roped in. Ralph was again bemoaning our lack of material. "You and I can improvise the bit in the Commandant's office, but what about all these girls? I've never been in a musical comedy. Do you know anything about making a chorus line, Micky?"

I said no, but it was pretty basic, as long as we had a piano. "And I've got a copy of John Donne's poems," I added helpfully. Ralph was interested. "Really? The Dean of St. Paul's? I've never had time to read him. He never wrote a play, did he?"

"No. But he wrote some pretty sexy poems." I handed him "To His Mistress on Going to Bed":

To teach thee I am naked first, why then
Why needst thou other covering, than a man.

Ralph liked this. "Mmm, 'Why needst thou other covering . . .' than a Wren, eh?" John Donne was in. I also sold Ralph on "The Flea".

This flea sucked me and now sucks thee
And in this flea our two bloods mingled be.

Ralph liked that too. You would have loved to have seen him with his great height, plucking the flea from the plump, rounded arm of a young Wren, who had smuggled an off-the-shoulder gown into her kit. We called it "The Shipshape Show." By this time we knew by heart the Commandant's nightly broadcasts which were meant to boost our morale and Ralph found a rich source of material in them.

We held auditions on the first day out and went into rehearsal as we crossed the Bay of Biscay. Although it was mid-winter, we had a smooth passage. I don't remember that we lost any ships from the convoy. There were tinfish around, but Jerry was too busy trying to figure out when and where the invasion was coming from and had concentrated his main U-boat fleet in the Med. The night of our premiere there was standing room only. We gave three performances on the first night, as the dining room only held 250 at a time. Number 15 on the programme was entitled:

"You Lucky People"
With Lt Comm Ralph Richardson
Loudly Supported by Michael Powell

I tried to hush this up for forty years for fear that some of my actor friends would get wind of it – but murder will out.

(*The scene is in the O.C.'s Cabin.*)

The O.C. is discovered in his dressing-gown; a towel is wrapped turban-wise around his massive head, he has his back to the audience and his legs straddled, he is shaving. Enter his adjutant, LIEUT. NIGEL FITZURSE, carrying a cup of tea in his left hand. He comes smartly to a halt about half a pace from the O.C. After a moment he salutes.

FITZURSE (*bellows*): Your broadcast, sir!

O.C. (*gives a volcanic start and turns, his heart beating violently*): You ass, Fitzurse! Don't shout like that! What is it? What do you want?

F.(*extending wrist*): Time for your broadcast, sir.

O.C.: 1710? So it is! So it is! (*He turns, ruminating*): Ah!

F. (*putting down teacup carefully on table, salutes, screaming*): And your tea, sir! (*Exits smartly*)

O.C. (*reacting with ferocity, picks up the tin waste-paper box and hurls it after his Adjutant*): Noisy brute! (*Fumbles for a while*) Let me see! (*shouts*) Fitzurse! (*F. entering inquiringly*) Bring me the rough notes for my broadcast.

F. (*salutes smartly*): Yessah! (*Exits.*)

O.C. (*upsets his cup of tea, then calms himself by a puff on his pipe*).

F. (*staggering in with two packing cases full of paper*): Your rough notes, sir!

O.C. (*testily*): Put them down, then, put them down!

F.: Yessah! (*Puts boxes on the table.*)

O.C. (*aiming a wild kick at him*): And gettout!

F. (*salutes*): Yessah! (*Exits.*)

O.C. (*dives into his boxes, gets tangled up*): Fitzurse, you ass!

F. (*entering*): Sir?

O.C. (*furious*): Get me out of this! These aren't my notes! These are last year's quiz questions.

F.: Really, sir? Sorry, sir! (*Extracts the O.C. from the foam of papers and boxes which has somehow formed around him, indicates second box*) Here, sir! (*Exits.*)

O.C. (*aiming a kick at him*): You ass, Fitzurse! (*Fumbles around, lathers his face with shaving brush, broods, switches on microphone.*) This is Tuesday, the 25th May! Black-out will be from 1066 to the Fall of the Roman Empire! (*Consults notes*) Many of you in this ship do not realize how lucky you are. On my last voyage we embarked 40,000 troops and on the way out we were becalmed for two years! During that time we ate the Adjutant! What a tough guy! You on this ship are fortunate in having a particularly *tender* specimen of Adjutant! After the calm came the wind: it blew and blew and blew, it blew blue murder! And we'd eaten everything except our tropical kit – you lucky people! (*He turns aside and picks up a military cap.*) Now I wish to address myself individually to the people on board. To the Army (*putting on cap*) I say: Keep fit. (*Takes off military hat and picks up a naval one.*) To the Navy (*putting on cap*) I say: Keep wet! (*Takes off naval cap and puts on cloth cap*) To the civilians (*putting on cap*) I say: Keep out! (*Then putting on all three caps at once*) You lucky people!

Next about whales! The greatest peril you are likely to encounter in these waters on which we sail is the peril of whales. Against this peril I have devised a special warning on the alarm bell – two long and one short. For the purpose of exercise only I will now demonstrate the wall whaling – the whale walling – the wailing wall – the – the wooly will – the whirling . . . (*bellows for help*) Fitzarse, you urse! (*F. enters hurriedly. O.C. addresses him in despair.*) Get me out of this! Quick! What *do* I mean?

F. (*salutes and answers with bell-like clarity*): Whale warning, sir!

O.C. (*throwing something at him*): Whale warning! I will now demonstrate the whale warning! Two longs and one short! Fitzurse, you ass! (*F. salutes, demonstrates with bell-push two longs, one short. Then he puts the bell-push down on the table, where the O.C. promptly puts his elbow on it. It rings deafeningly. F. reacts, so does the O.C., who is just saying*) That is satisfactory. (*O.C. menaces Fitzurse, then announces*) Once again I will demonstrate the whale warning – two longs and one short. (*F. demonstrates the whale warning, two longs and one short, but this time the bell sticks and goes on ringing to the visible horror of F., who shakes it, tries to stop it. Finally the O.C. kicks him and the bell stops at once.*)

O.C. (*trembling with rage*): For the last time (*whisper*) – You ass, Fitzurse! – I will demonstrate the whale warning – two longs and one short! (*This time all goes well, but the over-anxious Fitzurse puts the bell out of the way on the O.C.'s chair, where he promptly sits on it. It rings violently. Fitzurse hastily exits. The O.C. leaps up, chokes, throws the bell after his Adjutant, collapses in despair.*) In future the whale warning will be one long wail!

O.C. (*he consults his notes*): Finally, I must speak of the rats on board this ship. You will understand that I mean the concert party! During one of my midnight prowls (*he prowls violently round and round the table*) I discovered the members of the concert party on the forward hatch. I can only hope that what was taking place was only a rehearsal. One last word! (*He lathers his shaving brush in the shaving water.*) One final word which I must always tell you – about water! Don't waste it! You lucky people! (*He absent-mindedly gulps down his shaving water with immediate results – quick exit.*)

As to what may, or may not have taken place at rehearsals on the forward hatch, I received on the occasion of the BBC celebrating my eightieth birthday, a letter recalling those sweet, shared moments, signed: "A Wren called Bobbin".

It took our stagehands nearly the whole interval to clear the stage after Ralph had done his stuff. The real Commandant sat in the middle of the front row and enjoyed every performance. The girls were lovely, although our chorus line was a bit shaky when dancing the hornpipe out of Noël Coward's *Red Peppers*:

> Has anybody seen our ship?
> The HMS Disgusting?

One morning we awoke and we were at Gibraltar, that thorn in the flesh of General Franco. The Rock was a busy place in those days. It had been even busier during the Siege of Malta. Ever since Mussolini had brought Italy reluctantly into the war, the Rock had been under constant threat. Spain,

Franco's Spain, was pro-Fascist, but neutral. Portugal was neutral with the great and beautiful port of Lisbon as a secret battleground for agents on both sides. For hundreds of days Valetta, the port of Malta, and Gibraltar were the only ports left to us in the Mediterranean. The loss of men, ships and aircraft in keeping Malta supplied with food and ammunition had been terrible. But now the Americans were coming, the tide had turned.

HMS *Indomitable* was at sea, making a routine sweep of the Eastern Mediterranean, part of the operation of our Mediterranean fleet that was keeping Mussolini's ships bottled up in harbour. She was expected back shortly. For a wonder, all our papers seemed to be in order, but as there were a lot of other civilians about the Rock we didn't feel too conspicuous. We parked the unit at the Rock Hotel and Ralph and I went to call on the Governor. His smart and efficient ADC looked familiar. It was Anthony Quayle.

I had met him several times with Ralph at a pub in Belgravia, near Eaton Place. He was mad about the theatre. He was an earnest young man, with a round, moon-shaped face that belied his quick wit. He had extremely shrewd and observant eyes. He was tall and powerfully built and obviously extremely strong. He was deferential to Ralph, who accepted the homage with a mild amusement, referring to "this young man's enthusiasm for the theatre". But Tony was tactful, patient, and cunning as well as a good listener, and I couldn't help noticing how intently he listened to everything Ralph threw out, questioning him casually and almost apologetically, and how he stored it all away for future use. At that stage, I'm not sure whether Tony had done any professional acting, but he must have done a great deal at his university. His knowledge of the theatre and of its personalities and of the literature of the theatre was extensive – not only the English theatre, but the European theatre as well. I couldn't help noticing how high he was aiming, and my heart warmed to him. Here was a man who believed in the highest and the best, who loved the classics and adored Shakespeare, and dreamed of seeing that great poet and dramatist approached with reverence and understanding in his own country. I envied him his dreams of revolutionising and rebuilding the musty old Memorial Theatre at Stratford-on-Avon, and making the Old Vic Theatre in the Waterloo Road, which Lillian Baylis and Tyrone Guthrie had created, into a showcase for English genius in acting and production. I liked the fact that he was never embarrassed by his own fire and enthusiasm, and so did Ralph, I think, although he sometimes made fun of Tony in the way a professional makes fun of an amateur, but always gently and tenderly. Ralph had a habit of talking to the air, his large eyes turned dreamily away from us, as he sipped his disgusting gin and water, trying to hide that he was just as much committed to the theatre as his young friend.

Now here was Captain Anthony Quayle, standing at the Governor's elbow, a very smart soldier indeed, and playing the part to perfection, the only difference being that he was no longer an amateur, but a professional.

I felt once more that curious affinity to someone, that feeling that one day we should do something worthwhile together, that I had experienced before on several occasions. I felt that after the war, two people with such a faith in their chosen profession would be bound to meet and be of use to each other, and I filed him away in my memory in the same way I had filed away Cyril Cusack after seeing him play the part of Dubedat opposite Vivien Leigh, in an elaborate production of Shaw's *The Doctor's Dilemma* before the war. Being an Irishman, a Catholic, and a patriot, Cyril had retired to Ireland for the duration of the war. But I never forgot him. I knew that we were destined to work together.

As far as I remember, the Governor was not too keen on idle civilians, particularly with movie cameras in their fists, hanging around his Rock, and because of this he was glad to cooperate in handing us over to the Royal Navy. His ADC would make the arrangements. I noticed how tactful and shrewd Tony was, and that there was a streak of ruthlessness in his character that I hadn't suspected. He acted as if he had never seen us before. And Ralph took the cue. He took us off with him to the Mess. Once we were there, Captain Quayle vanished and Tony reappeared. He revealed, to Ralph's delight, that he was running the garrison theatre at Gibraltar, and had reorganised it on professional lines. He was already planning a series of productions in which he would play all the parts he had always wanted to play – as a star, of course. I seem to remember that he had just done, or was about to do, *Noah* by André Obey, playing Noah of course. This was delightful and I thoroughly approved of it. I liked to think of rows of garrison soldiers sitting there scratching their heads over the performance of parts which I had last seen played in Paris by the Pitöeffs. I telephoned Freddie Ford and the others to go ahead and eat, and we stayed to lunch with Tony. We went to his office and made all the necessary arrangements and signals. I gathered that *Indomitable* would be coming in during the night hours and there would be a turn-around of possibly two days before she sailed again.

Tony was mad about Gibraltar and spoke with awe about the new galleries and gun emplacements which had been recently blasted through the Rock. I asked if we could have a tour, but it didn't seem to be on. That week, Gibraltar was just about the top security spot of Europe. Tony said comfortingly that we could go swimming off the beach which everybody used on the south side of the Rock, beneath the towering face of this extraordinary fortress which frowned across the Strait to Tangiers. The last thing we had expected was to get some swimming, except involuntarily. We spent the next two days sunbathing and scuba diving along the underwater cliffs of the Rock. After being cooped up in London it was heaven. We knew that something was on, but we couldn't guess that it was the biggest operation planned by amphibian force since Rome destroyed Carthage.

I think that the Admiral commanding the Western Mediterranean Fleet was flying his flag in *Indomitable* when we joined her, but neither he nor her Captain made any objection to us accompanying them, except to remark that "It would be a 'bit of a squeeze'." Since the full company of His Majesty's aircraft carrier *Indomitable* was 820 men, you might think that seven more wouldn't make much difference. You would be wrong. At sea and in wartime, everyone bunks or slings their hammock wherever they can, and we were never sure what corner we would curl up in. But we were offered the hospitality of the Warrant Officers' Mess, as well as that of the Ward Room, and soon got into the habit, when at sea, of seizing some vacant corner and curling up in it for a nap. When we first appeared on the Flight Deck in the strange miscellany of clothes which a film unit affects, and started to set up our cameras and lay out our gear, an order came down from the Commander on the bridge:

"Master at Arms! Collect the members of the film unit on the flight deck, take them to the slop chest, and have them fitted out in Mediterranean Whites."

We were soon indistinguishable from the rest of the ship's company in our white canvas shoes, white socks, white shorts and singlets. Only our mixture of hats, berets and caps gave us away, for the sun was keen. I went without a hat, as I usually do, behaving as if I were at home at Cap Ferrat, but I had underestimated the strength of the sun at sea, and got the top of my bald head burnt crimson. The next day, the Captain's voice came over the loud speaker from the bridge:

"Ship's company, attention! Your Captain speaking! You may have noticed a group of civilians with cameras busy about the flight deck. This is a film company from England. They are here to make a documentary about the Fleet Air Arm. Please give them all the help you can. The one with the pink head is the director."

This got us an embarrassing lot of attention, and everybody wanted to be in the picture. Needless to say there was no hanging about. The Petty Officers and Warrant Officers saw to that. The ship was like a great humming steel beehive, with every man fully occupied for each one of the twenty-four hours. At first, we were a little shy of staging enemy attacks upon a ship which was liable to be attacked by the enemy at any moment, but nobody else seemed to be embarrassed so we got on with it. Pat McGrath, in particular, who had struck up friendships with half the lower deck, was enjoying his hero's role. Our story required us to stage an attack on *Indomitable* by enemy fighters. They would be engaged by our own fighters taking off from the flight deck and forced to keep their distance by intense anti-aircraft fire from the ship. It was the first time we had seen the new pom-pom guns in action. They were firing cannon shells at the rate of about 240 rounds a minute, and the ejecting cases bounced down like hail upon the deck. There were other, more secret, weapons which I was not allowed to photograph, but which I supposed were radar controlled. We staged an incident on the flight deck with a plane on fire, and the pilot injured and rescued by Pat, and still there was no sign of a threat from the real enemy. We had been steaming on an easterly course for two days. I always watched the sun and suddenly I realised we had altered course ninety degrees and were steaming south – towards the coast of Africa, Algiers, and Vichy France! We had made a friend of the Commander of the ship and dashed to see him, and learnt that the North African landings were on.

To anybody who loved France, and knew the Mediterranean as well as I did, this was tremendous news. The partitioning of France by the Germans, the collaboration of the forces of Vichy France with the occupying Germans, the sinking of the French fleet at anchor and Mussolini's decision to link his fate with that of Hitler's, had been bitter pills to swallow. But now the moment of reckoning had come. So long as the balance of desert victory had swung from Montgomery to Rommel and back again, Admiral Darlan, in Algiers, had been hotly collaborationist. It was notorious that he hated the British for their ruthless sinking of the French ships that had failed to surrender. Algiers, not Vichy itself, was the key to Vichy France and it was to be expected that the fighting there would be bitter. It looked as if we had a scoop for me and for my film crew. I rushed back and told them, and they agreed to have a go. I got the Admiral's secretary to fudge up some passes accrediting us as news cameramen attached to *Indomitable*. At the same time, the Admiral informed us that he was perfectly willing to land us at Algiers when we arrived in harbour, but after that we were on our own. I cannot remember how our party was financed, and how much money we had with us, or whether we had any money at all, but we received the news calmly. In those days, one took things as they came.

But there was no bombardment of Algiers. The mighty flotilla of transports and fighting ships that had been assembled, the clouds of aircraft that darkened the sky that morning, the landing crafts and the paratroops that seized all the important points, paralysed resistance. Within two days the whole North African coast was occupied by the Allied Forces. Never was an operation so well planned and so humanely planned. From the moment that the operation started, the French were informed what was happening, and told not to resist their friends. They could, with honour, lay down their arms. The moment that they did so, they could take them up again to fight against the common tyrant, the Germans. The plan worked. There were some tragedies, notably at Oran. There some hot-headed commanders, with mistaken loyalty to Vichy France, had fought to the death. Some American troops, betrayed by false information, fell into a trap. But resistance lasted for only a matter of hours, and Algiers and Oran, the two keys to the coast and the two best harbours, surrendered. My memory now of the whole exciting time is confused. I remember setting up my cameras in the streets of Algiers and photographing cars sweeping by containing Admiral Darlan; then later on Churchill and de Gaulle. What a moment it must have been for de Gaulle to arrive back in Algiers, which was of course at that time part of Metropolitan France. How we got to Oran I can't remember, but it must have been in *Indomitable*. Probably we landed at Algiers and managed to cling on to our parent ship, and went with her when she moved west to Oran. I think Ralph stayed on board. All I can remember now is that we were finally landed on the beach at Oran, with all our kit and cameras dumped around us, and that was it. How were we going to get back to Gibraltar and the white cliffs of England, I inquired of the Royal Navy? The Royal Navy couldn't care less. It had got its beloved Mediterranean back again, thanks to Ike, and was ridin' high. We too, we unhappy few, also had the Americans to thank for getting us home.

When the Americans go to war, they do it in the same efficient and extravagant fashion that they do everything else. They are not niggardly. Where the British say cautiously, will thirty transport aircraft do, to service an unknown number of operational airfields strung out along an inhospitable coast, the Americans say, better be on the safe side and take three hundred. I had been informed that the Americans were running the transport system back up the coast. I abandoned my orphans on the beach, and walking up into the town I commandeered a taxi. The driver was drunk and happy – he was not Vichy French. When I told him to drive me to the airport, he got out of his cab, stood to attention, saluted and we sang the "Marseillaise" together. We couldn't remember the words, but that didn't matter. The sentiments were the thing. I told him I had no money, but he just said: "Je m'en fous."

There was a curfew in Oran, and although it was still daylight the streets were empty. We stopped at several cafés to celebrate on the way to the airport, which was near the foothills as I remember. I was still wearing my naval kit and I had "borrowed" a cap which has some gold braid on it. Anyway, I was admitted to the airport at Oran without question. Big transport aircraft were shuttling in and out like buses in Piccadilly Circus. A young American was in charge. This was Oran, mind you, on the fourth day of the invasion, with everything popping around us.

I said to him without any hope of being listened to: "Got a film unit here. We've been working with the British Navy. Want to get them back to Gibraltar. Can you help me?"

"Sure," he said. "How many are you?"

I couldn't believe my ears. "Seven and myself," I told him.

"Where are you all?"

"On the beach."

"Well, get them up here as soon as you can, and we'll have you out on the next plane."

I just stared at him. I couldn't believe I had heard the words. They made sense – not the kind of sense I had been listening to in Britain for so long. I said: "Can you give me a three-ton truck to go and get them?"

"Sure," he said, and scribbled a chit. "Take this to the transport officer, he'll fix you up."

I did, and he did. I realised that the war had taken a new turn. It was no longer a gentleman's war. It was a people's war.

That same night, when I was on the beach at Oran, *Colonel Blimp* had a very unusual première before a very unusual but distinguished audience. In my absence Emeric was the host at a terrifying private view for Churchill, James Grigg, Brendan Bracken and their aides at the Odeon Leicester Square, before the film opened to the public the next day. By the special request of the Ministry of Information, Emeric had been asked to attend and to receive the Odeon's distinguished guests. I rely on him entirely for his account of this amusing, hair-raising and secret première of the film. He was left to deal with his guests alone, while Rank and John Davis kept out of the way, probably wisely. He tells me he remembers waiting, shivering, for the arrival of the political party, and that he was greatly disturbed by the fact that the usual cleaners of the cinema went about their work quite unperturbed by the subversive events that were taking place on the screen that night: they were used to having special shows after the usual performance. Producers are always very sensitive about the general atmosphere whenever they show any of their films in private for the first time, and Emeric was very conscious of these vacuum cleaner ladies in the background. As soon as the visitors settled into their seats, the projection started and the distinguished audience became absorbed – but not Emeric. In spite of the action on the screen, he could only hear the action behind him in the theatre. Finally he could bear it no longer, and rushed back to the cinema manager, who was in control of the sound for this special showing.

"Mr Thornton, can't we stop your ladies from working? They're making such a banging with the seats that I can't hear the dialogue."

"Mr Pressburger, it's not the banging of the seats that you are hearing, it's an air raid that's been on for some time. Those are sticks of bombs you are hearing fall, not the seats." At the end of the showing the VIPs departed in silence and fast cars.

The next day the doors were opened to the public and there were lines all around the block – until the next air raid. We were told privately by the M of I that there would be no official banning of the film, but that pressure would be brought upon Rank to persuade him not to export the film. Meanwhile in the provinces, the cinemas were advertising: "Come and See the Banned Film!", and Rank had his first big hit to compare with *49th Parallel.*

At about the same time in Oran, I was unloading my truck, still without believing what was happening. We were all walking into an enormous American transport plane, half full of men and materials, but with plenty of room for us. Nothing in *The Thief of Bagdad* had prepared me for this miracle which the young transport officer seemed to take as a matter of course. He handed me a piece of paper, I signed it, and we were on our way. The aircraft was stripped of all comforts, of course – no seats, no heating – but what did that matter? Gibraltar! Gibraltar here we come! What kind of welcome we would get when we got there was another can of beans.

Churchill, typically, was in North Africa to see for himself right after the landings, accompanied by de Gaulle, whom he hadn't always treated quite so handsomely. But he was statesman enough and poet enough to realise what this, the first step in the reconquest of France, meant to de Gaulle. He had flown into Africa straight across Europe in a specially prepared high-speed aircraft. The Nazis knew all about it and they knew about his presence in North Africa, and the value it had for the Allies particularly the Americans. Naturally, they were gunning for him, the biggest of big game. Spies and agents all over the Mediterranean area were alerted to pinpoint the presence of Churchill. He was reported to be still in Algiers (which he was) or perhaps in Oran (which he wasn't). Then he was reported to be in Gibraltar (this was about the time of the tragic accident to the aircraft which killed General Sikorski, the Polish Prime Minister). Then suddenly, Churchill was reported to be in neutral Lisbon.

Typical of that city in wartime was the aircraft, the blacked-out aircraft, which flew every evening from Lisbon to an airfield in the West of England. This rather sinister blacked-out aircraft took off every day and flew out to sea to a certain point in the Atlantic and then in again to another point off the British coast, where it landed. Everybody knew of the existence of this aircraft. Everybody knew, more or less, who the passengers were. The Germans knew of it, of course. It suited their book not to interfere with it, and it probably had some of their double agents on it. Anyway, there was a gentleman's agreement about it and as far as I know, this was never breached, except on one occasion.

Leslie Howard, since I had launched him into British wartime films with his part in *49th Parallel,* had created a unique place for himself in wartime England as a film producer on his own account. He had made a film about the designer of the Spitfire aircraft, called *The First of the Few*, and had himself played the part of R. J. Mitchell, the inventor who had not lived to see his aircraft win the Battle of Britain. It was a success, and Leslie showed very quickly and efficiently that he had grasped the ideas which we had first promoted with the Ministry of Information, of making popular feature films which reflected the changing conditions of the war in England. He worked at Denham as before and we saw a lot of each other.

In his group he had a lawyer called Chenhalls, who looked very like Churchill, except that he was taller, and he played on the resemblance. He used to wear the same sort of clothes and hats and smoked the same cigars. At the time we were shooting in the Med, Leslie and his company were working on a subject which required the cooperation of people on the spot. It was probably a film about Gibraltar. Anyway, it required a visit from them to the Mediterranean area, and Leslie and Chenhalls had both been in Gibraltar the week before we arrived there. They had been spotted. Leslie Howard, of course, was known by everyone, including the Nazis, and Chenhalls was reported as his companion. They went on to Lisbon, and were there only twenty-four hours before embarking on the blacked-out aircraft to return home. The whole world knew that Churchill had been in North Africa and would be returning to Parliament, but nobody knew how he had got there and how he would return, but Chenhalls, who resembled him, was noted in Lisbon, and duly reported, and what must have happened is that somebody fairly high up said: "Don't take a chance. Leslie Howard we know, and we've nothing against him, but if there is the slightest chance that the other fellow is Churchill, don't hesitate!" Three Focke-Wulfs came out of the sky and blew the unfortunate aircraft to pieces. We received the news on our arrival in Lisbon. We were to fly back to England by the same route the next night.

Lisbon was an extraordinary sight to anybody coming from wartime Europe, with its blacked-out cities and empty shops. The beautiful city on the Tagus blazed with light, smelled of money, and reeked of the Black Market. Every second person was an agent, every third a double agent. All the embassies spied on each other. The German Embassy was, of course, the biggest and busiest; the British embassy, the quietest and most inconspicuous. The night life was terrific. Nobody ever went to bed to sleep. Every cellar called itself a nightclub or cabaret. There were more call girls than there were telephones. No major writer has done justice to Lisbon in World War II. Casablanca? Pooh! The city on the Tagus could deal aces and spades to Casablanca and still take the jackpot.

I was all for staying a while. *Colonel Blimp* was packing them in in London, and there seemed no reason for my presence there, except for the fact that Deborah had also opened in *Heartbreak House* and got good notices. Then it was a moot point which was the safest and surest thing to do: to assume that the Nazi attack on the Lisbon aircraft had been a regrettable incident, unlikely to be repeated, or alternatively that some new broom of a Nazi general had been appointed to the Western Approaches, who was determined to shoot up the Lisbon Express until further notice. On the whole, I thought the first choice was the safer one and we booked our seats that night. The representative of Associated Press had told me that the British and German ham radio operators, who were always in touch with each other, had already expressed and received condolences for what was evidently a blunder: "Sorry about Leslie Howard. We liked him so much as the Scarlet Pimpernel." It was a long, dreary, unheated and uncomfortable flight, but without incident. We landed back in the West Country on a rainy morning. My film unit looked a little bit the worse for wear, so I gave them two days off and ordered them to report to me at Denham – "On Thorsday".

That night I went to the Cambridge Theatre in Seven Dials and saw *Heartbreak House*. Deborah wasn't very good, nor was Robert. But I went round afterwards and sent my name up. I had difficulty getting past the stage door. The Cambridge Theatre had the worst dressing rooms in London. When they built the theatre, they forgot the dressing rooms. When this was pointed out by some more than usually bold actor, the dressing rooms were designed and glued to the side of the building, in much the same way that a swallow's nest is glued to the eaves. As there were a lot of H.M. Tennant regulars in the glossy cast of this production, I seem to remember that Deborah's dressing room was about as big as a broom cupboard, and very badly lit. Maybe there was no telephone – I don't remember the details – but she told me later that she had determined not to see me and then I appeared, thin, brown, and blue-eyed, and her heart melted and she fell into my arms.

It was on again. We had it worse than ever.

We looked for a house outside London in the country. She ordered the wedding dress from one of the dressmakers in the wardrobe department at Denham Studios. We were the most unworldly sweethearts. We were so glad to have found each other again, that we thought life was made up of kisses. We didn't plan our lives together. We didn't talk about our careers. Her performance in *Colonel Blimp*, coupled with the West End reviews of the play, put her at the top. Alex Korda was already paging the "unknown girl" whom he had blamed me for playing in *Colonel Blimp*. He wanted her for Robert Donat's leading lady in the film he was directing for MGM – *Perfect Strangers*. With the worldwide success of *Colonel Blimp*, I had had seven big successes in a row without one failure. I don't believe that I regarded this as extraordinary. I certainly didn't believe in luck. We had known what we had to do, and with the backing of our financial partners we had done it. We were already planning our next film, and the gods were already smiling. We were planning our first failure.

The theme of *A Canterbury Tale* had grown organically in our minds, but it was not understood, or even enjoyed, until some thirty-odd years later. When we made the film, in the summer and autumn of 1943, the theme seemed to us to be an important one. In 1940, with *49th Parallel*, we had told the Americans that we were fighting their war as well as ours. In 1941, with *One of Our Aircraft Is Missing*, we had told the world that Europe would never be conquered. In 1942, with *Colonel Blimp*, we had said that Britain would never be conquered. In 1943, with *A Canterbury Tale*, we were explaining to the Americans, and to our own people, the spiritual values and the traditions we were fighting for.

To say what we had to say, we invented the character of an American soldier who was training in England for D-Day. In this way, he would encounter the English with all their prides and prejudices. I don't know which of us first used the phrase "a modern pilgrim"; but I am certain it was I, who had walked the Pilgrims' Way many times, who suggested that he should be a pilgrim to Canterbury, and with a nod to Chaucer we proposed to call the film *A Canterbury Tale*.

I had never made a film in the orchards and chestnut woods of East Kent, where I was born, and I couldn't resist it. Could I have some scenes with Chaucer's fourteenth-century pilgrims, I inquired: the Knight with the falcon on his wrist, the Friar, the bawdy Wife of Bath . . . and suddenly in Emeric's agile mind the Knight's falcon soared into the air and turned into a Spitfire. Modern characters crowded in on us, pleading to be noticed and used. There was a loony English squire, who was so anxious to preserve Britain's traditional virtues that he poured glue on girls' hair when they went out at night with soldiers. This traditionalist had to be given a good old English name, and we called him Thomas Colpepper. The modern pilgrims to Canterbury were three: a young British soldier, in civilian life a cinema organist, a virtuoso on the Wurlitzer, who combined ruthless materialism with sensitive musicianship; an observant young American soldier from a lumber town in Oregon; a young land-girl, one of the Women's Corps mobilised to take over fighting men's jobs on the farm, and who is trying to forget a tragic love affair. The rest of the characters all marched solidly onto the screen. Didn't I know them well? Hadn't I heard them talking and seen them working when I was a child? Wasn't every lane around Canterbury and every stone in Canterbury itself familiar to me? An artist often hesitates to use material that is too familiar to him, too near home, but now I had this feeling no longer. I was looking forward to the great swags of the laden hop-vines, to the dusty lanes with the dogrose in the hedges, to the sharp Kentish voices. Deborah, of course, was to play the land-girl, and Roger would play Mr Colpepper.

A *Canterbury Tale* looked on the surface conventional, but it was filled with subversive material. Emeric's story, worthy of de Maupassant, was too Continental for Rank and Davis. But we were so sublimely confident, so sure of ourselves, that nobody dared to say out loud what they were thinking, and they obediently put up the money for it. We had never had a failure.

Deborah may have had her doubts, but she was too loyal to express them. We had found a house at Bratton Fleming in North Devon, on the edge of Exmoor. The situation was remote and romantic, but it was a modern house built in the 1920s. There used to be a small-gauge railway running between Barnstaple and Lynton and Lynmouth on the North Devon Coast. It was a real mountain railway, and it must have been a problem to maintain in the heavy Devon rains. Anyway, it was derelict by the time we bought the house, which was built on the side of the Devon Combe, which dropped five or six hundred feet almost directly into a trout stream at the bottom of the valley. The old station house was about fifty yards below us. Everything went straight off into the air. The place was a wilderness of rhododendrons – a plant which I have always hated: it has filthy habits, which it cloaks with glorious blooms. Two buzzards, birds of prey with a wingspread equal to an eagle's, with the same palmate spread of the feathers, lived in the combe and used to rise and fall on the warm air currents flowing up from the valley. They would rise up, hardly moving their wings, and float level with the windows of the house, give us a sharp look, and then sink away again into the valley. There were one or two strange features about the house – for instance, a gallery with an organ loft at one end. One of the previous owners used to perform there to a sleepy audience of his dependants. On the other hand, there may have been nameless orgies performed while he pulled out all the stops. We both looked on the house as our first house, but primarily as a refuge from the flying bombs which were just starting. I planned to move my father down here and he was enthusiastic about the idea. He had already got fed up with his London bridge partners, and was looking forward to organising the Home Guard in North Devon.

At this point, the whole of my present and future life blew up in my face. Gabriel Pascal had a weakness for redheads and an eye for talent, and it happened that the most talented actresses in England in those years were Greer Garson, Deborah Kerr, and Pamela Brown, all redheads. He had tried to put them all under an option contract, paying them only a nominal fee per year, but which gave him the right to have first call on their services, and when he had the money, to take up the contract for its full value. With the first two he succeeded, and Greer Garson was accordingly shipped off to Metro-Goldwyn-Mayer in Hollywood. She became one of their greatest stars. Gabby, of course, cashed in on the transfer, because MGM would naturally want an exclusive five- or seven-year contract. Pamela wasn't having any truck with long or short contracts with Gabby, and had smilingly bowed out; but Deborah remained under option until I brought her into the limelight with her performance in *Colonel Blimp*. In giving Deborah her first chance, I had cut my own throat. Gabby advised her he was taking up the option, and was selling her contract also to MGM. I discovered this when I rang her agent to discuss the terms for her part in *A Canterbury Tale*, and was told out of the blue the news of Deborah's future plans. Until then, I had never heard of any option contract.

Emeric and I were not flesh peddlers. We hadn't got the capital to put actors under contract, even though it meant paying five times as much when we wanted them to work with us again. We weren't in that sort of business. We had spotlighted many actors and actresses during our partnership: Glynis Johns, Eric Portman, Pamela Brown, Joyce Redman, Googie Withers, Roger Livesey, Deborah Kerr (Anton Walbrook was a star already, although his three parts for us certainly completed the job), and the public confirmed our good taste by making them stars. But we were so intent on getting the right actors for every part, (there are no big or little parts in films – there are only short or long ones), that it never occurred to us to make money out of the people we were making famous. Still less had it occurred to me that other people might be waiting to do so. In the middle of this great war, in the middle of this great industry that we and Arthur Rank had created, it seemed inconceivable that anybody would be interested in Hollywood. I rang Deborah and asked her to meet me in Hyde Park at our usual place. It was near where she lived. I asked her if it were true that MGM were taking up her contract from Gabby Pascal. She said that they were.

"What on earth made you do a thing like that?" I asked. "You surely don't want to go to Hollywood in wartime? Hollywood is a runaway express running into a dead end. This is where the action is. This is where you have to be."

"They say they don't want me for the present," she said helplessly.

"Of course they don't," I said. "They don't want you taking the shine off Mrs Miniver."

"They want me to stay here for the present and play in Korda's film," she whimpered.

"But you're playing in *A Canterbury Tale*," I shouted. "Now look here, this is all nonsense. This is what we have to do. We get married at once. That's half the battle. We can plead wartime conditions and get you out of the contract. They can't hold you to it in wartime. Particularly if you are Mrs Michael Powell."

She looked at me, and I could see that she wanted the Hollywood contract. My heart turned over.

"If you go to Hollywood," I said, "you can go without me. I'm not going to be Mr Deborah Kerr, either in Hollywood or at Denham. Marry me, and tell them to go to hell. Or go to hell yourself."

She cried and pleaded. I swore and raved. Dear Deborah! Is this how you remember this scene at the Achilles statue? You, who were so gentle, and couldn't believe that anybody could be as cruel as I was? Did you think I would come round eventually? I had made the British film industry after my own image, and I gloried in it. I wouldn't have given it up for anything in the world. Not even for you.

For a few days I soared and plunged between hope and misery. Then I rang her agent, and he told me the contract with MGM was signed. The next day I telephoned Frankie and we met. The day after that we went together to Marylebone Registry Office, with Belle Chrystall and Emeric as witnesses, and were married. It was July 1, 1943. I never regretted the decision, but it has lived with me for a long while – until I die or the end of Volume II, whichever comes first.

Frankie always complained that she never had a proper honeymoon. I would reply that we had had at least nine improper honeymoons including Foula but apparently that didn't count. This honeymoon we spent on the night sleeper to Glasgow. *Colonel Blimp* was opening there, at one of the biggest cinemas, and Jackie Robertson was masterminding the event. We stayed at the Central Hotel and had a marvellous time, thanks to Scottish hospitality, which is the most homely and best in the world. But I can't really believe that Frankie enjoyed seeing the film again with three different images of her unsuccessful rival. We returned to London, to 65A Chester Square and to *A Canterbury Tale*.

Emeric had been following, as well as he could, my knockdown and dragout contest with Deborah, and he was worried about it – and rightly, for there was now no question of her doing the film. Roger Livesey had read and refused the part of Culpepper, so at one blow the romantic combination that we had created through *Colonel Blimp* was divorced. These things happen. Students of films who have seen both *Colonel Blimp* and *A Canterbury Tale* will realise how much Roger could have brought to the part of the sentimental squire, and how much Deborah could have given to the part of the land-girl, and her passionate love for the landscape where she had lost her virginity. Their relationship in *Blimp*, a love story, which everyone had seen, would have made their mystic relationship in *A Canterbury Tale* more believable. Roger didn't understand the part; and because he didn't understand it, he found it distasteful. I knew this was a forewarning of what the critics' reception of the film might be; but I thought I could carry it off, and did not communicate my doubt to Emeric – the first and only time I did not fully confide in him. It became quite clear to us that we had lost Deborah to *Perfect Strangers*. We decided to offer the part of Culpepper to Eric Portman, who did understand it, and accepted it. He gave an extraordinarily perceptive performance. His Colpepper had the face of a medieval ascetic, which could quite easily have been torn out of a monkish manuscript.

At about that time, at a party given by Brian Desmond Hurst in his studio, I had met two enchanting young people, deeply in love, and who looked as if they had just burst out of an enormous egg, like the character in the final act of Shaw's *Back to Methuselah*. They spoke when they were spoken to and an air of innocence and freshness seemed to cradle them. I offered the part of the land-girl to the female of this enchanted couple. Her name was Sheila Sim. His was Richard Attenborough.

Some months before, I had been to the Arts Theatre to see a production of a Jean Jacques Bernard play in which Mary Hinton, one of my favourite actresses, and a most beloved woman, played a countess, or something. A tall slim young man played the other important part; he was somebody quite new to me, and I determined to give him a break in films if I could find the right part for him. I found out that his name was Dennis Price, that his father was a general, that he himself had been in the Army and had been invalided out. He had charm and elegance and a long, good-looking oval face with a long, sensitive upper lip. He was impudently well-mannered. I gave him the part of the British soldier, the organist in our film.

The only remaining major part was that of the American soldier and it was, in its way, one of the most important parts. He had to be rather unusual – a film matinée idol and a kind of soldier the Americans would like to see representing them over here in Europe, and which we would like to think represented the typical American soldier. Emeric had conceived it and written it as a country boy, not a townsman, and I agreed. I was a country boy myself, and I was looking forward to marrying the American experience with the British. There was no question of going to Hollywood to cast the part, because half of Hollywood was already in uniform over here. I was sure we could find the man we wanted in the Forces. Of course, it would depend upon the authorities whether he could be released from duty to work with us. The M of I, as the Ministry of Information was now familiarly called, advised us that there was a superior production by the U.S.O. of Thornton Wilder's *Our Town* going around the camps and that it was being brought to London to give a few performances at the Old Playhouse Theatre, Gladys Cooper's old theatre, where Campbell Gullan had played with Gladys and Gerald Du Maurier and Celia Johnson in *Cynara*, from which he used to quote all his best lines to me, while we were working together on the production of "that old fossil" *Caste*. As a serving soldier, Sergeant John Sweet was playing the part of the storekeeper who also acts as commentator throughout the play on the lives and deaths of the other members of his town. I went. It is a great play, almost foolproof to any cast, but made particularly moving on this occasion by the fact that all the parts were being played by young servicemen and -women, in the middle of a war from which many of them would never return.

John Sweet was homely, honest and a natural actor, with a very good speaking voice. There was no doubt he would be wonderful as our American soldier. At the end of the play, there is a scene in the little graveyard, where the dead people sit around on their gravestones and talk about the weather and the local events and the young bride in the story is buried and the young husband is left alone and lying above her on the freshly turned earth. In the middle of this scene I started to cry and I couldn't stop. I cried my heart out. I lost my breath, I gulped for air. I went on crying. All the emotion of the past months seemed to be concentrated in that one moment. I truly loved both Deborah and Frankie. I had torn myself in half to make one of them happy. It was suddenly revealed to me that I had been more unfair to Frankie than I had been to Deborah. It had been no basis for the kind of marriage a woman of her grace and intelligence and beauty had a right to expect. And yet I knew I could never have been a Hollywood husband and that my marriage with Deborah would have drowned in the great gulf that would separate Hollywood from Pinewood after the war. All this bitterness, all this realisation, all the truth of my situation welled up in me, summoned and made clear to me by Thornton Wilder's vision. I cried and cried. I was still gasping for breath when the lights went up. I saw with relief that other people were crying or at least wiping away tears.

The Army agreed to lend us Sergeant John Sweet for four months to make the film, after which he would return to his unit. Our cast was complete.

When I worked at the Rock Studios on the horrific thriller (I mean horrifically bad, not horrifically good) called *The Man Behind the Mask*, Ernest Palmer, who was with me on *The Edge of the World*, photographed it; but operating the camera and influencing every angle and every lighting effect was an almost insanely enthusiastic young man called Erwin Hillier. He was always dreaming up new angles, new points of view for the camera to explore, new movements for the camera to make, which would intensify the atmosphere and the action. He approved of me, because I had seen all the Continental films that he had grown up with. We both knew in our hearts that nothing could be done with the appalling story and screenplay with which we had been furnished, but we both behaved as if we were working on a Fritz Lang super-production. We were destined, however, to meet again at Denham, where Erwin reappeared as camera operator on *The Spy in Black* and had a ball. We made him chief lighting cameraman on *The Silver Fleet*, which was a black and white picture. He got on with Vernon and did a good job. We had just been told by the Ministry of Information that no more Technicolor would be available for feature productions for the duration of the war because all the Technicolor stock was needed for training films. We would have to go back to black and white and make the best of it. I decided that this might be the chance that Erwin was waiting for, and gave him the job of lighting cameraman on *A Canterbury Tale*. He proved to be a master. With this one film, he sprang into the front rank of lighting cameramen. He had a keen eye for effect and texture and I gave him ample opportunity to use it. Whether in the studio or on location, we decided to go for complete realism, and he never let me down. The only thing he was a bit loony about was clouds in the sky. He detested a clear sky, and it sometimes seemed to me that he forgot about the story and the actors in order to gratify this passion.

"Meekee, Meekee, please wait another few minutes," he would plead. "There is a little cloud over there and it is coming our way, I'm sure it is."

"Oh, for God's sake, Erwin! It won't make the slightest difference to the actors' performance."

"Meekee, Meekee, please just five more minutes, please!"

This would go on all day. I admired his dedication.

We had scheduled about six weeks on location, for more than half the film was to be shot out of doors. I put the unit in Canterbury and went myself to a small pub on the River Stour at Fordwych, familiar to me from childhood, for it was only about half a mile beyond the eastern boundary of my father's farm. It was a comfortable pub run by three sisters, and had a room over the bar where I could hear all the chat while I read *The History of British Civilisation*. There I licked my wounds. Bert Woodcock, my driver, came for me every morning at about eight o'clock in an enormous hired car. I think it was a Daimler, and I would go to wherever the call sheet directed me. It was a hermit's life and it suited my mood.

I have said already that Deborah and I had found a house in a North Devon combe. We had been down to inspect it and decided to buy it, and I had started negotiations immediately. The price was about £3,000. I saw no reason to cancel negotiations along with the wedding dress, particularly as the buzz bombs had started and there was a new evacuation from London of everybody who could and would go. I had handed the furnishing of the house over to Frankie, who had swung into action immediately. Before I went to Canterbury my father had moved in, and he was soon joined by Emeric and his wife, Wendy, and their baby daughter, Angela. Percy Sillitoe, the Chief Constable of Kent, had refused Emeric permission to accompany me, or even visit me on location. Kent was an area prohibited to enemy aliens, and Sir Percy stood pat on that. We pulled every string we could, but he was not to be moved. He had recently been Chief Constable of Glasgow, which probably explains his toughness. Anyway, Frankie and I were only too glad to extend our hospitality to the evacuees; and as for my father, he drilled the local Home Guard and used to spend hours walking on Exmoor, straining his eyes towards the south in the hope that he might catch some indication in the atmosphere of the presence of the coast of France, which I suppose was about 150 miles away to the south. He was once overheard by Emeric and Wendy talking to Angela as she lay gurgling in her cot on the terrace, enjoying the sunshine. "Angela!" he said commandingly, pointing southward, "there is France!" He was always a single-minded man.

In 1943 the whole of England was on the move. D-Day was in preparation, and, after my grandfather died, my mother had sold her Berkshire house and taken off for Scotland. Frederick Corbett had continued his journalistic work and his visits to the British Museum Library until the blitz on London when he had joined my mother in the country. He left me a memory of what old age should be like. I can see his eyes twinkling behind his steel-rimmed spectacles, full of humour under bushy eyebrows, clean and sweet and in full possession of his senses. He was ninety-eight when he died of a slight cold, or perhaps it was a from a sense of humour. Mother sold the house and left for Scotland.

Bobby Stewart, who had been a neighbour of ours when my mother was living at Red Leaf Cottage, Chalfont St Peter, always kept in touch with my mother before and after the birth of her daughter, Gail. When the war came and her husband, David, joined the Army, Bobbie and Gail were evacuated to the Lowlands of Scotland, where David had a sister married to a hill farmer, Jim Gourley. They lived at a comfortable farmhouse, the Ford, in the shadow of the Dun, the famous old fort that overlooks the valley of the River Nith as it rushes out of the hills to pass through Dumfries on its way to the Solway Firth. Of course, this is all romantic Border country, and above all Robert Burns country. It is one of the most beautiful and fertile parts of Scotland. Bobbie and Gail were living at the Manse of Tynron, a tiny village in a steep-sided valley with a brawling stream running down it. From the Manse, which stood at the edge of the stream, a dirt track ran down the valley to the Ford, and about halfway there was a fault in the rock and a spectacularly beautiful waterfall, called by its Scottish name of the Linn. Above the Linn was a shepherd's cottage, and this was offered to my mother and the five Sealyhams on condition that she would take in and look after the series of Land-Girls who would come up to help with the farm. My mother was not only delighted to have a bit of war work to do, but the situation of the Linn – remote, inconvenient, down a road where nobody went, overhung by giant cliffs and enormous hills, with a roaring torrent at the front door – made it exactly the kind of house she would have spent several years looking for.

Remote though the situation was, it was by no means un-get-at-able. The nightly Scottish express from London to Glasgow steamed up to Carlisle during the night, stopping only at important junctions, and from there on stopped at Annan and Dumfries. The next railway station, Thornhill, was a request stop. The countryside around there belonged to the Duke of Buccleuch. His great-grandfather had allowed the railway over his land when it was first built, and he had retained the right to insist that anybody wishing to descend at Thornhill should inform the guard so the express would then stop there. I took advantage of this, and always made sure that the engine driver was informed not later than Annan. It was two miles' walk to Penpont and another mile and a half to Tynron, after which you had another half-mile "doon the Glen". If I was bringing a lot of stuff, I would try and get a taxi; but what I liked was getting out of a train early in the morning and walking along the road with the Dun towering in front of me. I would stop at the Manse to see Mr and Mrs McWilliam (he was from Northern Ireland, an Ulsterman), and tell Bobbie and Gail that I had arrived, and then on down the road past the house called Milnton (the stream ran by just on the other side of the garden, so I expect there was a mill there in the olden days) and on along the lane and up through hazelwoods and rowans to the gate which closed off the field, and by that time there would be barking Sealyhams everywhere and my mother would come rushing out with whatever she had in her hand, to welcome me home. This break from London to the Lowlands was so precious to me that I would often do it when I had only twenty-four hours to turn around in. I would catch the sleeping car express from London at nine o'clock at night and arrive at the Linn for breakfast next morning, spend the whole day in the open air and then get a car into Dumfries to catch the express back to London the next night. Sometimes I would go earlier to Dumfries and drop in for tea with John Laurie's two sisters, who kept a clothier's and haberdashery shop on the Square. They were delighted with his performance as Murdock in *Colonel Blimp*, but of course, being his sisters, they couldn't understand why he hadn't been offered the leading role. I would usually return home with a haggis or a black pudding tucked away somewhere in my rucksack.

You will remember Bill Paton. I had hung on to him as long as I possibly could, but he was too valuable a seaman to escape conscription. Of course he went into the Navy, and in a very short time indeed found himself a pretty good berth on board a service vessel on the west coast of Scotland, on which, according to his accounts, he was acting captain, acting mate and acting bosun, and it was only due to him that the vessel was still afloat. I never quite understood what they did, but it seemed to involve hawsers and anchors and harbour booms, and heaving masses of chains about, which was just Bill's cup of tea. Chris Challis, a Technicolor technician who was no weakling himself, said Bill was about the strongest man he had ever known. Bill was good-looking and shrewd, and he had a way of standing on the earth which made one wonder what possible earthquake could topple him. He was outspoken and quick in attack. No opponent ever saw Bill's back. As a consequence, the two of us never got into serious trouble: I was heedless; he was prudent.

His room in London would be kept for him, and he would appear at intervals and dive back into the world of film as if he had never left it. I missed him sorely. A personal assistant who has no loyalty to anybody else but you, can save a film director hours of time and worry, besides saving him from a breakdown or from going mad. On the pictures we were making, where every decision, however large, however small, would be made by Emeric and me and eventually by me alone, a man like Bill was beyond price.

When looking for locations for *A Canterbury Tale*, one of our requirements was a smithy and a wheelwright's shop, for a blacksmith and a wheelwright have gone together ever since the invention of the wheel. At Shottenden, they were even closer, for they were brothers, the brothers Horton: Benjamin and Neville. Benjamin was the wheelwright and Neville was the blacksmith. When I found the place and the Hortons, I just couldn't believe my luck. Between Chilham, with its castle and the valley of the River Stour, which is deservedly famous, and the main coastal road which runs through chestnuts and hazelwoods to Whitstable and Margate, there is a maze of little valleys with leafy deep lanes which turn and twist out of them, and which lead you, or in many cases don't lead you, to the ridge-roads which run along the top, east and west. Shottenden, embowered in apple orchards, dozes on one of these lanes. It has one pub. It has a few farms, but mostly it has cottages. It has several narrow lanes which turn and twist abruptly for no apparent reason, for which G. K. Chesterton offers an explanation in his fantasy "The Flying Inn":

> Before the Roman came to Rye
> Or out to Severn strode
> The reeling, English drunkard
> Made the rolling English road.

The Hortons lived cheek by jowl on one of these lanes, sheltered from intruders by hedgerows full of honeysuckle, foxgloves and columbine. The smithy was a tarred open shed, and there was a pit outside for the great big cartwheels to lie in while the iron tyres were bound on. The wheelwright's shop was close at hand. It was a prop-man's dream. Over the years, every conceivable sort of woodworking instrument had been collected by Mr Horton, and the hand of any do-it-yourself man would start itching at the sight of those benches, wrenches, clamps and tools. The sunlight poured in through the dusty panes. It was a heavenly place. We arranged to shoot there on a certain date and it happened to coincide with a week that Bill was on leave from the Navy, so he came down to spend it with us. It also happened to be the week that Neville's daughter Myrtle was home on leave from her duties as a matron in a hospital. A spark was struck from the smithy. The link was forged. Myrtle was tall and slender, quick and intelligent. One glance at Bill's clear steady gaze, his mighty torso, was enough for Myrtle, and Bill evidently felt the same about her, because six months later they were married at Chilham.

The principal scene that we had to shoot at Shottenden was between John Sweet, our American actor, and Edward Rigby, the old actor who had told me the stories about working with Jack Conway on *A Yank at Oxford*. The character played by John Sweet had been born and brought up in the lumber business in Oregon, and Emeric had written the scene in Kent to show how two craftsmen understand each other's methods, even though they are from opposite sides of the earth. The wheelwright's yard was full of timber, most of it sawn into planks which were then stacked so that the air circulated around them, and this gave a lot to the scene. At the end of it Allison, the land-girl, arrives to collect her farm cart and she and the Yank go off together. George Merrit played the smith in the sequence, and both the Horton brothers participated. Neville the blacksmith proved to be an exceptionally good actor.

In spite of Emeric's valiant attempts to turn it into a detective thriller, the story of *A Canterbury Tale* remained a frail and unconvincing structure. It was motivated by an encounter in the blackout which covered all of England in those days, between Allison and the Glueman, who is terrorising the district by pouring glue on girls' hair when they are out with their escorts. Allison is accompanied at the time of the incident by an English and an American soldier. For different reasons they have all alighted from the train in the dark at the little village of Chillingbourne. The English soldier is training there, Allison is going to work at a farm there, and the American thought it was Canterbury. They all chase the Glueman, but he escapes and they decide to spend the weekend hunting him down. Suspicion falls upon the eccentric squire of the neighbourhood, Thomas Culpepper. To liven things up, I recruited a gang of local boys to help in the detective work, and we had some fun with them, but essentially the film is a morality play in which three modern pilgrims to Canterbury receive their blessings. The last thirty minutes of the film are very fine. All the story and characters are rounded out in a masterly manner. Only the lonely squire, who proves to be the puritanically minded Glueman, receives no blessing. He has tried to play God, and the part of God is a lonely one.

The scene where the hard-bitten cinema organist achieves his secret ambition to play the great organ of Canterbury Cathedral, by playing "Onward Christian Soldiers" at a farewell service for his regiment which is going overseas, always brings a lump to my throat. The way that Allan Gray's theme music mixes with the sound of the Canterbury bells, taking over from the old hymn, is a triumph of sound and imagination.

Three little items for the record:

During the war Canterbury Cathedral organ was dismantled for safe-keeping, and we recorded the organ music for the sound track at St Albans.

The scene in the nave of the Cathedral was filmed at Stage 4 at Denham. Alfred Junge built it in perspective and it was one of his triumphs. We are sometimes asked why we didn't shoot our scene in the real nave. People forget that during the war the priceless stained-glass had been taken out piece by piece and the windows boarded up. They were back in their original glory when I walked up the nave in my scarlet robes to receive my honorary doctorate from the University of Kent, in July 1984.

For the peal of the bells in Canterbury's Bell Harry Tower, it was not possible to shoot the real bells because the design of the shot I wanted called for the camera to track up to the bells and through them. We did it in the studio. Alfred Junge's art department constructed the bells in miniature out of fibreglass and to scale with the real ones, and then hung them with the advice of experts. Allan Gray selected the notes of the peal to mix with his music at the beginning and end of the film. This peal was recorded on play-back. When all was ready, a team of expert bell-ringers came to the studio, the recorded peal was played back over the loudspeaker for them to follow, and they rang the peal on the miniature bells, using the finger and thumb to pull the tiny ropes. This was the kind of lark that the Archers were always getting up to in those days. It was the right way to do the shot, but who else would have taken the trouble to work it out and do it? It was problems like the bells of Canterbury, the whirlpool of Corryvreckan in *I Know Where I'm Going*, and Dr Reeves's camera obscura in *A Matter of Life and Death*, that made people want to work with us.

September 30, Deborah's and my birthday, arrived while I was still living my hermit life in the Fordwych pub. Deborah and I were both just as much in love as ever. We have always been in love, although our jobs have kept us thousands of miles apart. There are some loves like a precious jewel, that you carry about with you all your life, but are shy to wear in public. Mingled with this was the respect of one first-class craftsman for another. I had been in the film business for seventeen years before we worked together on *Blimp*, she only three years; but she was so quick at learning, and so inventive, that I dreamed that she knew as much as I did. We could have done anything together. We showed a little of what we could do in *Black Narcissus*, where Deborah pleased me with her authority and imagination. Yes. We could have done anything. We were fools, but ambitious and headstrong fools, and we both were "hard as the nether stone".

We had seen each other since my marriage, not once, but several times. Not to make love, but to torture one another. On the day after my wedding day, if you can apply such an evocative phrase to the stark reality of a registry office, I had asked Deborah to meet me again at the Achilles statue and had told her that I was married. I have never heard such a moan from a human creature, and I was the cause of it. If she had screamed or shouted at me, I had a hundred bitter things to say. If she had caught hold of me, hit me or run away from me, I think I would have welcomed it, my heart was so full of bitterness. But she just sat there on the park bench holding my hand, while the bitter reality sank in. Our hands and our hearts grew colder. While great tears welled up in her eyes and splashed on the dusty grass, I could only sit there dumbly and look at the ravages I had caused. She did not reproach me. She did not ask questions. She knew. I don't think she had thought for a moment that I could not be won round to her way of thinking. She must have thought that time and an MGM contract can work wonders. It is quite possible that Alex Korda may have had something to do with it. Since Alex had returned to Denham as MGM's chief producer, he may have promised Deborah that she and I would make a film together after *Perfect Strangers*. I know that they had bought Nevil Shute's *Pastoral* and were scripting it for her. It never occurred to me at the time – why should it? – but looking back to 1943, it does seem possible. Deborah and I had never talked about our mutual careers. We were too much in love for that. She knew that I had a sentimental attachment to MGM because of my years with Rex Ingram and the friends I had made in that great company. But that was long ago, and I was my own master now, and a contract to MGM meant as little to me as it did to Alex Korda, who shook off the yoke as soon as he found some finance.

The sun was sinking behind the trees that lined the Row. At last we stood up and, still handfasted, we walked like old people back to Charles Street. I felt as if I had been beaten all over, and I think she felt the same.

"But, Michael, we're going to see each other again?"

"I don't see how we can."

"We must – we must!"

"What's the good?"

"We can't part like this, we can't, we can't."

I knew then what heartbreak means. I hurried away.

We did meet again several times, as if there was some talisman in the touching of our hands and bodies. But we never made love again. Our sorrow was too deep for that. I had hurt myself as much as I had hurt Deborah. I had broken the mystic link that had bound our fates together ever since we met in that agent's office. We sat, silent and suffering, beside the corpse of our dead love, half hoping for a miracle, but knowing it would not happen. Then I went away to Canterbury and didn't see Deborah for several weeks.

September 30, our shared birthday, meant so much to us that there was no doubt in both our minds that we had to meet on the day after Michaelmas Day. Canterbury is fifty-six miles from London by the road that pilgrims have always followed, and wartime Kent was blacked out, and the trains could not be depended upon. Air raid alerts were constant. Assuming that I reached London, the certainty of getting back the same night was slim if I depended upon public transport. Bert Woodcock had ways and means of getting extra petrol, and I made a bargain with him to drive me up after the day's work, wait there and then bring me back. Deborah had left the English Speaking Union Club and was living in an ugly apartment in one of those fantastic red-brick and red-tiled tall houses in Duke Street, Mayfair. They are still there, and as I live at the Savile Club when I'm in London, in Brook Street, around the corner from Duke Street, I think of her every time I walk past.

The drive up to London was without incident, and took about two hours. It was ten o'clock when we got there and already dark. London was blacked out and eerily quiet. I think we came the length of Oxford Street and only saw a handful of air raid wardens. The entrance to the Duke Street apartment was around the corner, and without a torch it would have been difficult to find the bell. Of course, the efficient Woodcock had a torch. Deborah came down and let me in. She had been working all day at the studio and had made some rather desperate attempts at getting a few goodies together for a birthday treat. Neither of us ate or drank much. Neither of us spoke much, except about the day's work. Both knew that this was the real farewell. The end of our shared love. We sat with our arms around each other without speaking until the front door bell buzzed. We took our cue like well-drilled actors, and she saw me down the stairs to the imitation Gothic front door.

"Bert, this is Deborah Kerr."

"Good evening, Miss." He looked with respectful admiration at the tall, beautiful woman in the shimmering dress.

"How do you do, Mr Woodcock. Take care of him. I know how difficult it is driving in the blackout."

We were stopped once or twice at roadblocks on the drive back, but Bert got me to my pub at Fordwych at 2 a.m.

Sheila Sim, now Lady Attenborough, who was landed with the job of playing a part which had already been written for Deborah Kerr, made it entirely her own. At the time it was impossible for me to be fair about her Allison, because I was always seeing Deborah in the part. I recognise today the depth and sincerity of her performance.

John Sweet was fine as the carpenter from Oregon. He was Sweet by name and sweet by nature – and he was a true artist. He came to the retrospective showing of our films at the Museum of Modern Art in New York in November 1980, surrounded by wife and friends and children. He had not made acting a career. He went back to teaching: he felt that was where he belonged. At any other time but in that climactic year of 1944, his performance would have been recognised in Hollywood and he might have had a very different life – and who knows – been far less happy.

Dennis Price – who died far too young, in 1973 – was put under contract by the new and growing J. Arthur Rank Organisation. He became their brightest star. There was nobody like him for style, looks and polish. He gave many good performances and many remarkable ones, such as the murderous protagonist of Robert Hamer's *Kind Hearts and Coronets*. I sometimes blame myself for pushing him into the limelight. Then I think how his charm and intelligence would have been instantly recognised once the war was over. It was the luck of the game. For all three of our modern pilgrims, it was their first film: and I think of them with affection when I remember how much they brought of love and dedication and enthusiasm.

But it was our first failure. The story and the premise of the film failed to hold the audiences. The Americans were already overseas, fighting their way through Sicily and up Italy. The centre of interest had shifted to the Continent. The values that we tried to discuss in the film were already "old hat", and if you weren't interested in the theme of the film, there was something unnecessary and even unpleasant about the activities of Mr Culpepper. We felt this at once when we showed the film in a private session to Arthur Rank and John Davis. They were both immensely moved by the last third of the film, but doubted whether it was commercial. We had been so often right, and they had been so often wrong, that they mistrusted their own judgment for a while, and we all did our best to put the film over. But the audiences wouldn't have it.

The magic of the Archers' name and their trademark, the target as the arrow thudded into the gold (for we were less modest now), made audiences less inclined to forgive us for a failure. We all had to admit that we had misjudged this one. It was not until thirty-three years later, at the retrospective of our films organised by the British Film Institute in 1977, that it was recognised as one of our most original, iconoclastic and

entertaining films. We had been on the defensive about *A Canterbury Tale*
for so long that even we were surprised. After all, what's thirty-three years?
André Chenier had to wait almost eighty years after his execution by the
Jacobins before the Bibliothèque Nationale admitted his manuscripts, and
at least Emeric and I didn't lose our heads.

Thank goodness I'm writing this story of my life at the end of my life,
not in the middle, as seems to be the case with so many clever men anxious,
perhaps, to point out to their public what a treat they're missing. When
Emeric and I were young, films were looked upon as an ephemeral art. The
life of a film, so far as the public was concerned, was a year or two –
perhaps, for a classic, five years. Nobody gave a thought to film
preservation, to film historians, film libraries, film institutes and film
archives, which now proliferate in every forward looking country. When
television took over, all but the most far-seeing film-makers looked upon it
as an enemy. Times have changed. Suddenly it was the BBC that combined
with the British Film Institute to pay for a reconstituted *Colonel Blimp* to
be shown in its entirety for the first time since that memorable showing
before Winston Churchill. We have been privileged to live to see films
which, forty years ago, we hoped, modestly, would be considered good,
hailed as masterpieces. That's long enough.

Having succeeded in making a failure, through failing to follow my
instincts, I now proceeded on my own to produce a theatrical flop. It was
not my first play, it was my second, but it was my first try for the West End.
The first had been Jan de Hartog's *Skipper Next to God*, which I put on at
the Theatre Royal, Windsor. The Windsor theatre had a policy of try-outs,
and quite often they were transferred to the West End, for they had high
standards. They were prepared to let a distinguished amateur from another
branch of the profession have a go. I loved the theatre, but at that time I
didn't understand it. Above all, I didn't understand its technique. I didn't
realise how easy it is to do simple tricks to hold an audience's attention,
provided that you have something worth saying. Jan had something worth
saying, and as he was playing the Skipper himself, in a wonderful sort of
London School of Economics English, he didn't have much spare time to
give me advice. The play was set in the captain's cabin in a big Dutch
freighter. The cargo he was trying to land was three hundred Jews escaping
from Hitler. The plot concerned his repeated attempts to land them in
countries that didn't want them. Alternatively, he could take them back to
the port from which he had shipped them, probably Hamburg, where they
would undoubtedly have been sent to the gas chambers. Being a Christian
and an obstinate Dutchman, he decides to cruise the high seas, until he can
find a country to receive his cargo.

I went to see Jan and Marjorie the other day at their home in New
Jersey, and we talked about those days. As I have said, Jan is a liar, and

although he reminded me of many incidents and people I had forgotten, I found it hard to believe that, at his first entrance, he found the cabin door to the bridge was jammed, so that he had to make his entrance through the clothes closet. The production needed simple tricks of lighting and sound effects, and perhaps music, of which I was not yet the master, and it also needed an authority which I had not yet got. But the play was far from a failure. The sincerity and genuine theatrical skill of Jan's text brought people in, and held them while they were there. We all felt it had been worthwhile. We ended the week with a loss of about one or two hundred pounds.

My second attempt was more ambitious, and nearly bankrupted the Archers. Ernest Hemingway's works had been rather prematurely collected into an omnibus version by Jonathan Cape, and among the short stories, short novels and other pieces there was a three-act play entitled *The Fifth Column*. The setting was the siege of Madrid in 1938, and the main scene was the battered Palace Hotel, where the war correspondents were staying to see it out. The chief characters were a war correspondent who is a Communist sympathiser, based upon Hemingway himself, and a maddeningly lovely and maddeningly stupid lady, whose contribution to Communism is to get the correspondent into bed. Hemingway only wrote one play, and I thought and think that it is a magnificent one. His dialogue is meant to be spoken, and I only wish that Hemingway could have heard how Roger Livesey and Margaret Johnston spoke it. Hemingway had an infallible ear and so had they, and there were feverish love scenes worthy of Jacobean drama. I tried to give it a rich production, with sound effects and music all recorded beforehand, and all the small parts were very well played. Peter Copley, Pamela Brown's husband, whom I had met when they came to the Archers' Christmas party, played one of them, and Pamela came up with him for the opening night in Glasgow. Frankie did too. The key part of Max, the Communist Commissar, was played by Frederick Valk, the Czech actor, with a face like one of those broken-nosed ivory busts so beloved of collectors. It was a beautiful performance, understanding and tender, that brought the Communist/Fascist tragedy very near.

But our sets were a disaster. Alfred Junge was now established as the Archers' art director, and naturally I asked him to design the sets, but I hadn't realised that he didn't really understand the theatre, or had forgotten what he did understand. The sets he designed were colourful, effective, imaginative, but they couldn't be changed. They were film sets. They were solid and heavy with plaster and props. The wait between the first and second acts in Glasgow was about half an hour. The wait between the second and third, more like forty minutes, and by that time most of the audience had left, except Bill Paton, whose ship happened to be in Glasgow that night. It was entirely my fault. I hadn't seen it coming. I had assumed

that everything would roll on and off, fly up and down, and I left it entirely
to Alfred.

During the three weeks that followed, while we toured, we worked
and lightened the whole production. But it really needed to be recalled
and redesigned. We were a very happy company. Everybody loved the
atmosphere, and loved their parts. I had two stars playing as if they were
inspired. The fact that it was a disaster was all my fault. I had put some of
my own money into it, and some of the Archers', but we soon realised that
if we went on touring as we were doing, we would run out of money. We
had to close and never came into town.

It was the only time that Alfred ever let me down. And it was really my
fault for asking him to do it. The person most disappointed by the play not
coming into town was Al Parker.

Al Parker was a Broadway actor from the days when Hollywood was
only a collection of greenhouses. He was a friend and fellow actor of stars
who were really stars, like Douglas Fairbanks and John Barrymore. He
knew the theatre and the theatre knew him. When these great gorgeous
hams were called to Hollywood, Al was in their train. He acted with them,
managed them and, in due time, directed them. He was one of the first
important silent film directors. He confessed it was all done on nerve. One
of the most important films that he directed was *Eyes of Youth*, starring
Clara Kimball Young, and made at one of the New York studios. The most
important film he directed on the West Coast was *The Black Pirate*,
Douglas Fairbanks's first film in colour. It was two-strip Technicolor and
they designed for it. Until *The Thief of Bagdad* came along, it was the best
colour ever seen. Doug was a great producer. Talk about Samuel Goldwyn.
Phooey! Sam Goldwyn bought established Broadway successes, spent a lot
of money on them, and presented a highly polished production. He was a
cabinet-maker. Doug was an artist. That was my opinion, but it was Al
Parker's too.

Al and I had been rivals in the days of quota-quickies. Al had been one
of the first to see that cheap English pictures would employ good English
actors, and when they were seen they would be offered Hollywood
contracts that he would negotiate. He also directed most of these pictures.
Quite often, we were in competition for particular jobs, but he soon saw
where the money was and became an agent. When we started to make our
big films, he woke up and realised I was not just a hot breath on the back of
his neck. I was a film-maker and a film lover. We became bosom friends.
We bored our women friends by swapping memories and anecdotes of
the early days. I met lovely Maggie Johnston through him. She was an
Australian girl, and had had quite a bit of experience in the theatre. She had
the looks and the legs for the part of Hemingway's girlfriend in *The Fifth
Column*, and also the intelligence and the voice. I gave her the part, and Al

was in front every night. I really think that at one point he was about to offer to finance the production to come into London, but he remembered in time that he was an agent, and didn't.

So far as Roger and I were concerned, *The Fifth Column* strengthened our friendship. He admired my courage in tackling the play. He loved the part. He was only sorry that my lack of experience had been against success. He and Maggie loved every minute of the scenes they played together. Hemingway had written in his stage directions that various pieces of Chopin's music should be heard, played on a portable gramophone, throughout the love scenes. We followed his instructions, but the scenes between Roger and Maggie didn't need Chopin. They were all naked tenderness and earthy lovemaking.

After *A Canterbury Tale*, neither Emeric nor I was quite sure what our next film would be. We had taken such a tumble over Mr Culpepper and his little game that we were not quite sure where we were going. It was quite clear that the Allies were winning the war, but nobody knew how long it was going to take. Meanwhile, the Normandy landings were in preparation. Suddenly, we got a call from Jack Beddington at the M of I. He not only wanted to see us, but he invited us for lunch – not that the M of I's executive canteen was anything to boast about. We countered by inviting him to lunch with us at the Etoile, which in the miraculous manner known only to good restaurant owners had continued to function all through the war: I know that Frank was often out in the very early hours, returning with ten dozen trout or a hundredweight of rabbits. You don't know how to cook *lapin à la moutarde*? I pity you.

My old friend Nino was interned on the Isle of Man. He was a passionately patriotic Italian and planned, when he retired, to return to Italy and become the Mayor of Ventimiglia, which name suggests it is situated 20,000 Roman paces from the border between France and Italy, on the road which runs along the Mediterranean coast. Nino had inflammatory opinions, so when he was screened by patient officials from the Aliens' Branch, he was deemed too loquacious and too intelligent to be at large, and was interned for the duration. Frank Rossi, his brother-in-law, carried on with his mother. He still had a couple of bottles of good Tavel *rosé*, and Jack Beddington, whose expression was normally that of a pessimistic basset hound, became quite cheerful, even optimistic.

He was a shrewd, jerky conversationalist who liked to throw a bomb into a discussion and then wait for it to explode. He was a great listener. He saw his job as a creative one, and he was quite right. He had immense power and he used it wisely. He understood artists and treated them with tact. He had a devoted staff, and they worked for him as they worked for nobody else.

He looked across the table at us with his mournful, bloodshot eyes and said: "Now listen, you two, I have asked you to lunch and have a talk, because I'm seriously worried."

"It's our lunch," said Emeric, wounded to the quick by this attempt to usurp our hospitality. Emeric likes to be a host, not a guest.

"All right, have it your own way. I know it'll be a good one if you order it, but the Ministry will pay for it."

I think I said: "If we pay for the lunch it means something. If the Ministry pays for the lunch, it means nothing. So shut up and pass the black olives."

He took about a dozen before passing them on. "Very well. Before America came into the war, our relations with them were excellent. After Pearl Harbor, we were one people. Their war was our war and vice versa. But now that we are winning the war, all that has changed. The top people are already planning strategy in terms of spheres of influence, spheres of business. There's a danger that the ordinary man and woman in the Services will forget what they have learnt about each other. The old jealousies, misunderstandings and distrusts will return."

"Jack," said Emeric, "we have already said all this for you with *49th Parallel*, *One of Our Aircraft Is Missing*, *Colonel Blimp*, and *A Canterbury Tale*. Are you suggesting that we make a fifth film to prove to the Americans and the British how much they love each other?"

Jack sighed. "Yes." He neatly decapitated his trout. "It really would be a worthwhile thing to do. I know that if you two fellows can find a way of doing it, that it will be a big film. And we need a big film. It really is a most important thing. When Europe falls apart, there is going to be a most awful lot of bickering and skullduggery. You fellows don't make ordinary films, after all. In a way, they're sort of sermons . . ."

"Thank you very much."

"No – you know what I mean. You know how to put these things the way that people understand without understanding, if you follow me. And if you make it, it'll be a big film and it has got to appeal to the Yanks as much as to the British. Look at the way *49th Parallel* is still going around and making money."

"For whom?" I said nastily.

Jack flapped his hand dismissively. "Well, will you have a go?"

"We will think about it," said Emeric, carefully demolishing a *tête de veau vinaigrette*.

"It's a tall order," I said reflectively, although I knew very well that Emeric already had at least four ideas in his files and was selecting one of them carefully. "You wish us to write a story which will make the English and Americans love each other, with a mixed American and English cast, with one or two big names in it, and it obviously has to be a comedy, and spectacular, and imaginative, and you want it to be a success on both sides of the Atlantic, and you want it to go on playing to audiences for the next fifty years."

"Thirty years will do," said Jack, his mouth full.

"We will think about it," repeated Emeric, settling down to a large plate of *ravioli à la Romagna*. If the war had to be fought, we had no intention of fighting it on an empty stomach.

A few days later we settled down to the final mix of *A Canterbury Tale*. In the normal way of things, the effects and dialogue of the film are all completed and laid on the track before the composer takes over. The last sound to be recorded is usually the music. In our case it nearly always was, because we worked very closely with the composer and he with us, so a week after recording the music of *A Canterbury Tale*, we settled down to mixing sound, music, effects and dialogue for the final edition. There are always little adjustments to make, and discoveries also to make when you come to the final mix so there is plenty of free time for other discussion.

Emeric said to me in one of these pauses: "How do you feel about making a fantasy?"

"All our films are fantasies," I said firmly. "Allan! That piece of music starts too early, can you do something about it?"

Allan Gray, who was always nervous during music sessions, fizzed like a badly corked soda water bottle. "Do you think so?"

"What do you think, Desmond?"

Desmond Dew, who mixed most of our pictures towards the end of the war, and at the beginning of the peace, blinked amiably. He was rather like a Cheshire cat. "Yes, perhaps."

"John, will you have a look at that with Allan?"

John Seabourne, who had been lying on his shoulderblades in a comfortable chair enjoying the film, jumped to attention. "Aye, aye, sir! Come on, Allan." And they went off to the cutting room.

I looked at Emeric and repeated: "All our films are fantasies."

Emeric looked at me solemnly. "Michael, you're never serious. I mean a real fantasy with supernatural beings."

"Period? Or modern?"

"Well, in a way both. A kind of surrealism."

"All films are surrealist." This was a favourite theme of mine which I was prepared to demonstrate with half a dozen examples at the drop of a hat.

Emeric sighed. "Very well. I think that to do what Jack Beddington wants in a realistic way, would be hard for us to control. In a way we have done a sketch for what he wants in *A Canterbury Tale*, but now he wants an epic film about two great nations, full of colour and larger than life, with parts for good actors and full of jokes about America and England. For this a fantasy is best."

This was basic Hungarian dramatists' thinking. They like to treat serious themes lightly. They like to keep tragedy in reserve as the hidden weapon of comedy. They like to think that it is they who control the audience, not the actors. I thought of *Liliom* (a play), and of how beautifully life and death were blended in that love story.

"What's your idea?" I asked.

Emeric, contented with my reaction, purred: "I will tell you in a day or two."

The next day he said to me: "We would need Technicolor."

"Would we?"

"There are two worlds, the one we know and another in my story."

"I see. And the other world is in colour?"

"No, I don't think so. After all, we know this world, or think we do. And it's in colour."

"True."

"So I think it is the other world that is in black and white. We move to and fro between the two worlds."

"Hmm! Yes. Shoot part of it in colour and part of it in black and white. That's been done."

"Of course. Everything has been done. It's the way you do it."

"But I don't think we can get Technicolor now, at this stage in the war. It's all being used for training films."

"For my story, Technicolor would be necessary."

"What is your story?"

Emeric looked very solemn. He always does when he has to share one of his long-cherished ideas with the vulgar herd. "Do you remember reading in the newspaper about that English pilot who jumped from his aircraft and the parachute failed to open and he survived?"

"Yes, I seem to remember reading something. Nobody could explain his survival, least of all the pilot."

"That's my story."

During the next few weeks, while we were waiting for the answer print of *A Canterbury Tale*, we both did research in our various ways. Frankie's brother, Joe Reidy, is a plastic surgeon, and went right through the war as one of McIndoo's team of plastic surgeons who were giving burnt pilots back their faces.

"Hallucinations," he said. "You don't need drugs to have hallucinations. Pressure on the brain will do it, if the brain is good enough. Here! Take this pamphlet."

I read that "pressure on the brain can produce highly organised hallucinations, comparable to an experience of actual life, and which took place in space, but not in time".

Emeric was in the British Museum reading up on American Revolutionary history.

"Michael, do you know who Abraham Farlan was?" he asked me one day.

"It sounds as if he invented something. Did he?"

"He was a schoolteacher, Michael. He was the first American to be killed by an English bullet in the Revolutionary War."

"Did *you* know that the olfactory nerve is one of the signals that the brain uses to predict a hallucination?" I asked him.

"How does it predict it?"

"By recalling some smell to the owner of the nerve. A familiar, easily identifiable smell, like fried onions, for instance."

We were just getting into our stride when the Ministry of Information informed us that it was absolutely impossible to get us Technicolor for a year or more. Jack was very apologetic about it. We had told him roughly what our scheme was, and he was enthusiastic about it. But there was no getting around the hard fact that Technicolor was important for the war effort, and Technicolor wouldn't be available, and we couldn't make our story without Technicolor. It was a hard decision to make, but we had to make it. We left our two lovers, June and Peter, in Purgatory, drifting in space between this world and the next, for a whole year, and turned our attention to finding a new story, a new hero and a new heroine. One of the strengths of the Archers' films was that each one grew organically from the other. But after a few weeks, no follow-up to the themes of *A Canterbury Tale* had suggested itself, and Emeric said to me one day:

"I have always wanted to make a film about a girl who wants to get to an island. At the end of her journey she is so near that she can see the people clearly on the island, but a storm stops her from getting there, and by the time the storm has died down she no longer wants to go there, because her life has changed quite suddenly in the way that girls' lives do."

"Why does she want to go to the island in the first place?" I asked reasonably, as I thought.

Emeric smiled one of his mysterious smiles. "Let's make the film and find out."

I Know Where I'm Going was given its title by Frankie, who was travelling with me on the Number 9 bus to Piccadilly Circus. I told her Emeric's story between Hyde Park Corner and Green Park.

"You ought to call it *I Know Where I'm Going*," she said, standing up to get off at Piccadilly.

"Why?"

"Because of the song," and standing there in the swaying bus, she sang it:

> I know where I'm going
> And I know who goes with me
> I know whom I love
> But the dear knows whom I'll marry.

We were opposite Fortnum and Mason. I said, fascinated: "Is there any more of it?"

She nodded.

> Some say he's black,
> But I say he's bonny,
> The fairest of them all,
> My handsome, winsome Johnny.

She nodded to me, jumped off the bus and vanished in the crowd. Frankie's always like that – never wastes time or words.

There was no doubt that Frankie was right. Emeric liked the title. Everyone liked the title, even Allan Gray, who would have to write orchestrations for the little Irish song. But for the purposes of communication between the insiders, the title was telescoped to *IKWIG*, and by this title it is known to the initiated today.

We were all down at the house in Devon when Emeric started to write the story. He wrote it in five days. When I reminded him of this the other day, he said: "As soon as I realised that there was not one love story but two love stories, then it wrote itself." Anyway, it was a *tour de force* on his part, and his story stood up nobly to all the local colour and huge production that I heaped onto its slender framework.

While Emeric was writing, I went off to look for the island. The reader may think that I know enough islands already, and it is strange how islands, and the sea, and even submarines, have turned up again and again at a significant point in my movie career. I was thinking about this only the other day. The first film I worked on, Rex Ingram's *Mare Nostrum*, had its climax in a battle to the death between a merchant skipper and a German U-boat. My first film for Korda, *The Spy in Black*, had as its hero the captain of a U-boat. The Archers' first big international success, *49th Parallel*, opened with the sinking of a U-boat and then recounted the adventures of the survivors. Our first co-production, *The Silver Fleet*, had as its hero a submariner and naval engineer, played by Ralph Richardson, who scuttled his ship, taking himself and half a dozen high-ranking Nazis to the bottom with him. Sea warfare crops up again in our films with the

Graf Spee film and in *Ill Met By Moonlight*. I don't seem to have managed
to get a submarine into *The Red Shoes*, but its reappearance in so many of
my films makes me want to quote the famous clerihew by E. C. Bentley:

> Cecil B. De Mille,
> Greatly against his will,
> Was persuaded to leave Moses
> Out of the War of the Roses.

I ransacked the west coast of England and even visited the east coast to see
the Farne Islands and Holy Island, which was later used for most unholy
purposes by Roman Polanski for his film *Cul de Sac*. I had great hopes for
Bardsey Island off the Welsh coast, but it didn't suit the story. I stormed up
the west coast, arriving at all sorts of jumping-off places usually on foot,
sometimes by bus, sometimes by steamer. I finally set my sights on Argyll
and the Western Isles. Frankie needed a holiday and joined me in Glasgow.
It shows how secure we felt in our island at this stage of the war, that I was
able to buy all the maps of Scotland at the scale of two inches to the mile, as
well as Admiralty publications like *The West Coast Pilot* and any charts
that I might need. Neither of us had been to the west coast of Scotland, and
were very thrilled. It was as if we were visiting a foreign country after being
penned down for years. We had friends in Glasgow who could check for us
the sailing of the MacBrayne steamers, and next morning we took a train
down the River Clyde to Greenock, where we sailed on the SS *Lochinvar*.
The little steamer was crowded with sheep and cattle, as well as people.
The weather was fair, and we had a fine sail to the Isle of Arran, and then on
through the narrows to Lochgilphead, finally stopping at Tarbert on
Kintyre. Tarbert is a fishing port and almost landlocked. We were
delighted with it, but not for our story. Here Frankie and I parted
company. Our little ship carried passengers who were going on to Islay and
Jura. They had to cross the peninsula by bus to West Loch Tarbert, where
another little steamer was waiting for them. I had planned for Frankie to go
by the same route to Islay, and from there by bus across the island to Port
Askaig, where there was supposed to be a decent hotel, and which was the
port of embarkation for the island of Colonsay. The position of Colonsay
on the map looked very promising for our story, lying as it did between the
great jaws of Jura and the island of Mull.

I myself proposed to take a bus up to Crinan, where there is a yacht
basin at the end of the short canal which connects with Lochgilphead. Of
course, in wartime, there were no yachts, but I would try to get a local man
to take me over to the north end of Jura, where there was a jetty. Once
there, I would find somewhere to sleep, and next day walk over the island
to the south end, where I would be in hailing distance of Frankie's hotel

across the Sound of Jura, and she could send a boat for me. The sound at
that point is only a few hundred yards across.

"There's always someone with a boat in the isles," I said optimistically.

Frankie received this hail of directions with her usual poker face.
"What do I do if you never turn up?" she inquired.

"It's a perfectly practical plan. Look, I'll show you on the map."

"Maps give me a headache," said Frankie firmly. She would never have
any truck with maps. "Well, try not to get shot for a German spy."

I ran to my bus and just caught it. At Crinan I was in luck. There is a fine
hotel there standing four-square on the quay with its feet in the sea defying
the western weather. A lot of young naval sub-lieutenants were playing
with boats. The hotel put me on to a local man who for five pounds took me
over to Jura and landed me on the jetty, which was badly in need of repair.
The roof of a fair-sized house was visible among the trees, and I shouldered
my rucksack and set off towards it. People who live on islands have
extrasensory antennae, and a man and a woman were already strolling
down to meet me. As they approached, I had the feeling that they were
reluctant to meet me, but as we got nearer and they realised I was a
stranger, their manner changed and they bade me welcome. I said who
I was and what I was doing there. They had seen all my films and asked me
to stay the night. There was no one else at the house and there were plenty
of beds. I had liked them immediately, so I accepted, and we set about
making tea in a huge Highland kitchen. We had a lovely evening. There
was a radiance about them as if they were counting the hours that
they were together and wanted to make the most of them. They became
more and more confiding, and at one point he asked me what I thought
of them, alone in this house without a third person to make it right. I
said we were at war and that one of the by-products of war was to banish
conventions. I was drinking dram after dram of malt whisky and felt
that I loved everybody. They kept on asking my advice, and I kept on
refusing to give it, except to say that he is a fool who hesitates in love
or war.

My new friend offered to go with me in the morning. There was only
the one road on the island and it ran from the Laird's house in the north to
the jetty in the south. About halfway along, there was a stalker's road
which led to the top of the Paps of Jura, the two rounded eminences about
3,000 feet high that dominated the island. There he would leave me and I
could find my way down the rough mountainside to the shores of the
Sound.

I got up early in the morning and saw smoke coming from the stalker's
cottage. It was a modest house with a slate roof, a hundred yards along the
shore. I mentioned it at breakfast.

"It's let," said my hostess merrily, "in case you are thinking of renting it for the film. He's a writer. People come and go there, but none of them seem to have any idea of looking after themselves."

"Does he stay there all year round?" I asked incredulously.

"Yes, he's got it for the duration. Of course, in winter time it's pretty bleak, but at least it's out of the war."

I was curious. "What's his name?"

"Blair."

I shot in the dark. "Not Eric Blair?"

"Yes. Do you know him?"

"No, but he's a great writer."

"Really! We hardly ever see him. He's so shy."

"Writers usually are as neighbours. But one day your stalker's cottage will be a place of literary pilgrimage."

"It'll need a new roof by then."

I parted from my friend on the top of the Paps of Jura at about two in the afternoon. The hillside was very rough and it took me three hours to get down opposite to Port Askaig. A man riding a bike along the white, dusty road promised to telephone the hotel and send a boat for me. The tide had turned and was running at about ten knots. The Sound of Jura is narrow and many fathoms deep, and it is an impressive sight to see the tide racing along, silent and menacing between these two great underwater cliffs. The boatman from Islay will never make it, I thought, but he did. He crossed the tide diagonally, and landed almost at my feet.

"You'll be Mr Powell," he said. "I was watching for you."

Frankie was reading a book in the hotel lounge. "Hello, Mikibum," she said. "Did you have a nice walk? Did you meet some nice people?"

I said that I had nearly met George Orwell.

Islay is famous for its peaty waters and there are perhaps a dozen distilleries around the shores of the rocky island. Their names, revered by malt whisky drinkers, are painted on the roofs of the distilleries and the rocks of the shore. It's a solemn thing to sail around the coast of Islay and see waves breaking over names like Islay Mist and the fabulous Laphroaig. Malt whisky needs plenty of peaty Highland water, and as the burns are short, the distilleries have their feet in the sea. That evening I sampled Islay Mist, which is a blend of malt whisky, and was clubbed by Laphroaig – a heavy, treacly, straight malt.

The weekly steamer for Colonsay was leaving in the morning, but after the long day I couldn't sleep. You know how it is. Frankie was sleeping. You'll never guess what I did. I got out of bed, went down to the hotel lounge, found some notepaper and wrote a long letter to Deborah, describing the day's doings. There was a full moon outside, but when it came to a description of the Sound, I went outside to see the shape of the twin mountains towering into the sky across the water. When I came back

Frankie was standing there in her silk nightdress reading the letter. It was like a punch in the kidneys.

I said: "That's a private letter. You had no right to read it."

She said: "I have read it and you're a shit."

She crushed it into a ball, threw it at me and stormed out, leaving me with egg on my face. I was still furious at my stupidity in leaving the letter around, and by her reading it, although I don't see now what else she could have done. I followed her to the bedroom – she hadn't locked the door – and approached the bed.

"Frankie . . ." I began. She shot up in bed like a queen cobra and hissed: "Shit! Shit! Shit! Get out!"

There were other people staying there, so I got.

In the morning she said: "I'm going back to London."

I said: "Don't."

She said: "Why?"

I said: "Because it's the obvious thing to do."

Her mouth twitched. She said: "Micky, you're a shit."

I said: "Oh Christ! Set it to music. There wasn't a word about love in my letter."

She said: "You still love her," and burst into tears. After a while we were in each other's arms and I convinced her she was wrong. We were late for breakfast.

About eleven o'clock we sailed, and we arrived off Colonsay in about an hour. It is only when you are abreast of the island that you realise that there are two islands, Oronsay and Colonsay, separated by a shallow ford, which dries out at slack water. The islands had no jetty, and sent a boat out to meet the steamer. There was a comfortable little hotel, and we soon scrambled to the highest point of the island, which is only about 300 feet above sea level. From here the whole glorious panorama from Iona to Kintyre lay before us, and I shouted out that this wonderful land and seascape could be the only setting for our story. If I could only get a film unit up here, and somehow feed them and lodge them, I knew that we would bring back a wonderful film. It wasn't just the scenery, it was the feel of the place.

I had made a film in the Shetlands on the sixtieth parallel, I had made a film in the Orkneys a hundred miles further south; now I was in the Western Isles, the fabled Hebrides ("as we in dreams behold the Hebrides"), and I was already bewitched by the magic of the Isles. I had Seton Gordon's *Highways and By-ways in the Western Isles*, and I read it as I travelled. Mull, of course, is full of legends and sagas, and my notebook filled with names and phrases, but very few of the stories dealt with the sea and the dangerous races – what the Norwegians call *rösts* – which make it necessary to know the tides and the time of day before you go sailing in this wild area. Our heroine in the story was determined to get to an island, but natural forces prevented her, or if you like, mystical forces stopped her from making a fatal mistake. In Emeric's story, which he had sketched for me, bad weather kept her chained to her rock. Bad weather – what does that mean to a film director who can part the Red Sea if he likes? I read in *The West Coast Pilot* that these passages between the islands of Jura, Scarba and Mull are dangerous and the currents amazingly swift. Only the Lofoten Islands in Northern Norway could compare with the tidal races which roared around the island of Scarba. I woke up. Was not my favourite story in the world, almost, *A Descent into the Maelstrom* by Edgar Allan Poe, and was not the setting of the story the Lofoten Islands? Now here were the Admiralty, or at any rate their surveyor, nudging me in the ribs to point out that this area was not only the most beautiful in the northern hemisphere, but one of the most dangerous for small boats as well.

This is how Emeric and I always worked together. He invented a situation and I followed it through to the end. Authors think of a storm, wind and waves and a stormy sea. A director personalises the conflict, in the same way that Edgar Allan Poe did. He had never been to the Lofoten Islands, but he had heard of the great and awesome Maelstrom. What a name! What a sound! I decided to take a tip from Poe – no writer should be ashamed to do that – and create my own fearsome whirlpool off the island of Scarba. This had to be the real thing and a very genuine danger. Also the whole construction of the film depended upon it. Once Emeric had manoeuvred his people into a situation where they were committed to try to reach the island, it was up to me to create about twenty-five minutes of spectacular action to prevent them doing so. It was the difference between an ordinary love story and a saga, in which the elements play their part. In addition, it was necessary to bring onto the screen a whole new world, full of people with their own standards and judgments, dependent upon one another, feudal, democratic and totally devoid of materialism. These virtues could not be displayed by talking about them, they had to be shown.

Corryvreckan is the name given to the tidal race which roars around Scarba, and *The West Coast Pilot* advises all mariners to give it a wide berth, whatever size their ship is:

There is an overfall close to the Island of Scarba where the sea bed suddenly drops several hundred feet and creates a disturbance.

I should jolly well think it would!

With a strong motorboat and by keeping close to the shore of the island, it is possible to creep up to the edges and observe this phenomenon at close hand.

It is possible, but it's rather more exciting than he makes out in his description.

The main race is further out, and when the wind is against the tide, the passage should not be attempted by any vessel under 100 tons, and even then it is not recommended. A small boat would be lucky to survive in the seas that are encountered.

But we managed to get a boat through just the same.

When the tidal and climatic conditions are as described, a whirlpool is formed close to the steep side of Scarba, which is capable of engulfing a small vessel. The surface of the sea here is very disturbed and frequently very large boils arise up for no apparent reason, and can be dangerous to a motor boat.

They are and they do, but by lashing myself to the mast of our motorboat, I managed to photograph one.

So great is the volume of water trying to get out through this narrow passage, that when the tide is running it is possible to note a difference of several feet in the level of the sea.

So much for the official description of Corryvreckan. According to Seton Gordon and other authorities, here is how it got its name. There was a prince of Norway called Breacan, who came courting the local earl's daughter. She looked favourably on him and told him he would have to prove his courage by anchoring his ship for three days and nights in the tidal passage which runs between Scarba and Jura. He went and had a look at the race when it was running at the full, and then returned to Norway, where he consulted the wise women. They advised him to have three ropes specially woven: the first of hemp, the second of flax, and the third made of the hair of maidens who had been faithful to their lovers. With these three ropes he returned to Scotland and announced he was ready for the trial. On the first night the hemp rope broke, on the second night the flax rope broke, but the third rope held fast. But one of the maidens had been unfaithful to her lover, and on the third night her hair broke; and when it broke, all the other hairs broke with it, and the prince was drowned. He and his ship, with everyone on it, were sucked down into the dreaded whirlpool.

This was the legend of Corryvreckan that I brought back to Emeric. He said: "We need a Curse."

"Do we?"

"Yes. We do. Wouldn't you like to know why she goes to the island?"

"Yes, of course I would."

"Then shut up and listen. I have written it all while you've been away. I've never known a story to write itself so easily as this one."

We were sitting in the long window seat at Bratton Fleming in North Devon. I have described how the house and garden were laid out on platforms hacked out of the side of the combe, like the Rajah's Palace in *Black Narcissus*. We were sitting on the long window seat that looks out over the rhododendrons into the empty air. As we talked the two buzzards came lazily sailing up on the currents of warm air from the valley 500 feet below. They hung in the air, observing every detail with their wonderful telescopic eyes, and then they trimmed sail and glided down and out of sight to rise again in about ten minutes' time.

We were a full house. Frankie had invited my mother to spend her short holiday with us, and she was actually living under the same roof as Thomas William Powell, her lawful spouse. It gave me quite a queer feeling to see my parents together again, but they seemed to take it all for granted, and chatted away like two magpies. Seton Gordon had come by invitation to see the buzzards, and to take gigantic walks over Exmoor with me. Knowing he liked a long walking stick, I lent him the shepherd's crook made on the Isle of Skye which he had given me on my first visit. It's a beautiful hazel rod, and it had a finely carved crook with an eyehole in it. I had always meant to mount a magnifying glass in the eyehole to look at flowers: but to Seton's mortification, as we crossed the stony moor, he struck the stick sharply on the ground, and the crook snapped off. There must have been a fault in the wood. Seton was inconsolable, but I assured him it didn't matter. I have the stick still, forty-three years later, and it is still my favourite stick; while Seton, whose lean bony form seemed as indestructible as a Balmoral pine, has gone to the special heather-covered Heaven that awaits field naturalists for whom every sound and sight and smell on the hill is an open book.

Emeric writes his stories – or he did then – with thick pencil in longhand into a quarto-size ringed notebook which accompanied him everywhere, nestling down comfortably in the big saddle-stitched brief-cases that we both used, and which, besides scripts and maps, usually contained a bottle of some firewater and a couple of salami sausages. We believed in being prepared at all times, and there is nothing like a stout Hungarian or Polish sausage to give you confidence. When he has written "The End", he takes the script out of the rings, numbers the pages, and staples them together at one corner of the manuscript. Only then am I allowed to read it – sometimes. There were occasions when he read me the first draft himself, but on the whole he preferred me to read it. He said that when he read it, I was always interrupting or asking questions, or guessing what was coming – all of which put him out. And Emeric put out by the preception of one of his stories, could be as sour as a quince. But on this occasion, he did read aloud the adventures of Joan Webster, otherwise known as "The Island Story", and had an attentive and fascinated audience.

After congratulations, I asked: "What gave you the idea of having a Curse in the story?"

"Sir Walter Scott. His stories always have a Curse in them. People will expect it."

I decided he was quite right. In order to top Corryvreckan we had to have a terribly strong Curse.

"One thing is a great relief," I said.

"Only one thing, Michael?"

"Only one really important thing. We started out with an idea that was purely entertainment – frivolous if you like. I couldn't see how the new film would fit into the logical pattern of our war work. We may have come a cropper over *A Canterbury Tale*, but the value of its theme was never disputed, and the film we are going to make after this one looks like being the most important film we will ever make."

"Oh, Michael, how can you say such a thing? *Colonel Blimp* is the best film we have made and ever will make."

"Have it your own way. But I couldn't see how the love story of Joan Webster could justify its inclusion in the body of our work, but now I do. We have been at war so long, that we are beginning to forget fundamental truths. It is time they were restated."

"Yes, Michael."

We sat silent for a moment or two. Then Emeric said in his wise, gentle voice: "Kindness rules the world. Not money."

The next day we started work on the script. Emeric sat thinking beside Angela on the terrace in the sunshine. Occasionally he scribbled a note. I was in "another part of the forest", writing away for dear life with my big Parker pen. According to our usual plan of work, my job was to add to and change the location sequences, bringing in all I had learnt of the authentic dialogue, atmosphere and names of the Western Isles. I ransacked Monty McKenzie's pot-boiling novels for Gaelic phrases and idioms. As soon as I had completed the first few sequences, and numbered them with regular script numbers, I turned them over to Emeric for him to agree or disagree, or to point out to me that I had entirely missed the point of the scene.

Meanwhile I was rewriting the next batch of sequences and so on. By the end of the three weeks, we had the first complete draft of the script for our collaborators to work on and for us to discuss with prospective actors and actresses. This was a sore point. Of course, the part of Joan Webster would have been an ideal one for Deborah. She was rising twenty-three and was already astonishing her directors by her quickness and her willingness to learn. Talent and beauty she had already. I cursed my fate – and hers – and ours. Emeric was a truly wonderful friend to me in those days. He never brought up her name for the part. Once he asked me very tenderly whether I ever saw her, and I answered no. But that led us to the solution which we had both been thinking about. In *Colonel Blimp*, Wendy Hiller had lost the part to Deborah. Wasn't it the obvious solution, a gift of the gods, to give the part in *I Know Where I'm Going* to Wendy? She was a few years older than Deborah, but she had a lovely body and lovely legs, a real-life down-to-earth personality and an impudent face. What started as logic became enthusiasm; and as everyone knows who has seen that much-loved film, she made the part her own.

Perhaps now I should sketch the story.

Joan Webster knows where she's going. She has known it ever since she could crawl. Now she is going to marry her boss, Sir Robert Bellinger, chairman of Imperial Chemicals, a widower, a millionaire, and old enough to be her father. This worries Joan's father, but it doesn't worry Joan. She knows where she's going. Money isn't everything, but Joan reckons it's a good substitute, and that's good enough for her.

In spite of wartime restrictions, Sir Robert has a hideout, an island in the Western Isles of Scotland, called Kiloran. It is remote and beautiful and they are going to be married there. The Bellinger organisation is set in motion and an itinerary is prepared down to the last detail. Joan is met and cushioned at every point by representatives of the organisation over the 500-mile journey. The Bellinger organisation can control everything but the weather: Highland weather is beyond even their powers. A thick fog comes rolling in, and when Joan arrives at the boat harbour for Kiloran, there is no motorboat waiting. There is, however, another passenger – a young naval officer on leave, who is also disappointed at not being able to get to the island. He announces that he is staying with his cousin at the local big house and tells Joan that he is quite sure she will put her up too. But confident of Sir Robert's omnipotence, Joan refuses. She still believes that she knows where she's going.

At the end of an hour, cold and forlorn, she gives in and takes refuge at the house, where her hostess is Caitriona Maclaine, one of the Maclaine's of Lochbuie, who is married to an Englishman called Potts, and who breeds Irish wolfhounds. Her husband is away at the wars. Joan meets the naval officer again, whose name is apparently Torquil. There is also an eccentric colonel who trains falcons and hunts rabbits with a golden eagle from his wrist. It is clear that Caitriona and Torquil have been brought up together and run wild in the Western Highlands. They have been childhood sweethearts. It is also clear to both Joan and Caitriona that Torquil is strongly attracted to Joan and he is not the kind of man to let the grass grow under his feet. Joan, resentful of anything that may interfere with her plans, tries to head Torquil off by telling him that she's going to the island to be married. But he says he has a permit from the owner of the island and intends to cross with her in the morning.

That night Joan does something she hasn't done for some time. She prays. She prays that the wind will get up and blow away the fog for the morning. In the morning, a gale is raging. She has overdone it. It is just as impossible to get to the island in a storm as it would have been in a fog.

The weather forecast is bad. Torquil suggests that they catch the bus to Tobermory, the chief port and town on the island of Mull. From there Joan can talk to her fiancé on the short-wave radio telephone. And they will be more comfortable at the Western Isles Hotel than at Caitriona's, where the Irish wolfhounds take all the best beds, chairs and sofas.

On the way to the bus-stop, they pass the ruined keep of a castle. Joan has been told that the Clan Maclaine have put a Curse on the Lairds of Kiloran if they should ever cross its threshold. She announces her intention of exploring the castle, and since she will soon be the wife of the Laird of Kiloran, she is presumably included in the Curse. She dares Torquil to come with her.

He refuses, saying: "I had better introduce myself. I am MacNeil of Kiloran. And I am the Laird of Kiloran. Sir Robert is only the tenant for the duration of the war."

Joan digests this information. It is not very palatable. He tries to make it easier for her. "It's all the same. It's Bellinger's for the duration."

But it is not the same, and they both know it. And as he stands there in his kilt with those dark hills behind him, looking her straight in the eye, she feels something stirring within her which is very disturbing to a girl who knows where she's going.

They catch the local bus and in the general conversation there is some criticism of the rich man on Kiloran for his lavishness and for what he spends his money on. He is building a swimming pool on the island, and he has salmon sent from the mainland. Joan defends her fiancé to Torquil, who with impenetrable politeness refuses to be drawn.

At the post office at Tobermory, they talk to the island on the short-wave radio telephone. Joan gets a shock when she hears Robert's throaty managing director voice. She has already become used to the soft voices of the islanders – perhaps also to Torquil's gentle manly voice. Sir Robert has arranged for his fiancée to stay with some good friends of his "top hole people", who live in another castle on Mull.

He asks if Mr MacNeil is with her, because his factor on the island wants to speak to him. "What's he doing here? I thought he was in the Army?"

Joan finds herself answering: "Yes, Robert. He's here and he's in the Navy."

In the post office, there is a dusty, framed engraving of the legend of Corryvreckan, showing the heroic Norwegian prince defying the whirl-pool. Torquil tells Joan the legend, but is interrupted before the third rope breaks. Joan and Torquil go off to the Western Isles Hotel to book rooms. At her suggestion they sit at separate tables.

He says: "I think you are the most proper young woman I have ever met."

She answers in a flash: "I take that for a compliment."

That night Joan prays harder than ever, but in the morning the gale is still blowing.

She spends the next day with Robert's rich friends, and in the afternoon they go over to play bridge and have tea with Rebecca Crozier, who belongs to one of the oldest families on Mull. Torquil turns up as a fellow guest. Rebecca tells Joan something about life in the Highlands and kindles the girl's natural romantic enthusiasm. When the company starts to play bridge, it turns out that Joan doesn't play and of course Torquil says he doesn't either.

The golden wedding of the chief stalker and his wife is being celebrated that evening in the big barn. Music is provided by three pipers – they had been ordered by the rich man of Kiloran to play at his wedding, but because of the storm they can't get there. The party is tremendous fun – dancing and singing, and mountains of scones. The pipers play "The Nutbrown Maiden" and Torquil seizes his opportunity to declare: "You're the maid for me." Then he sweeps her into a Highland reel, saying: "Cheer up! They are your pipers!"

As she finds herself dancing the reel, Joan realises that she no longer knows where she is going.

The next day they go back to the boat harbour, but conditions are worse than ever. Rory, the boatman, refuses to take Joan to the island, and forbids his boy, Kenny, to take the boat out either. They go up to the house. In desperation Joan turns to Torquil for help. Caitriona watches the two lovers with a jealous eye and a breaking heart. Of course, Torquil refuses to take Joan and tries to convince her that there is real danger out there.

While Torquil is absent on the hill with the colonel, who has lost his golden eagle, he sees through his spy-glass that the boat is getting ready to go out. Joan has bribed Kenny with twenty pounds to take her to the island. Torquil dashes down and is in time to catch her and have a blazing row. Finally, he tells her to go to the devil.

Caitriona, at last, takes a hand. "Torquil! She'll never make it."

"She's as stubborn as a mule."

Caitriona makes a sacrifice. "She's running away from you!"

Torquil runs down to the harbour and takes command of the boat. They set sail for Kiloran in the storm – Joan, Torquil and Kenny, in an open motorboat. There follow twenty-five minutes of battling with the elements. At one point they are drifting with a drowned-out motor towards the whirlpool of Corryvreckan. But even while Torquil is cleaning spark plugs with a toothbrush, he has time to tell Joan the rest of the legend.

"The third rope held. There's nothing stronger than love."

Joan agrees in a faint, seasick voice: "No, nothing."

Torquil continues: "One of the maidens had been false, and when her hair broke, all the other hairs broke with it."

At this moment the engine sparks and roars into life. They pull away from the whirlpool, into the eddy, and make their way home. They are back where they started. Caitriona is waiting for them and gives Joan her bed. The two girls have a talk. They use simple words, but the theme is love and money.

"I thought you and Torquil and Rebecca Crozier were happy to live here?"

"What else can we do?"

"Well . . . you could sell Erraig and Rebecca could sell Achnacroish and Torquil could sell Kiloran. Then you could live where you like."

Caitriona with her wise eyes considers this. "Yes. But money isn't everything."

In the morning it is a beautiful day. The sea is calm and the ferryboat is coming from Kiloran. Torquil's leave is up. He has to go back to the war. Joan, the perfect little lady, goes down to meet her fiancé. Joan and Torquil part on the hill.

Torquil says: "Will you do something for me?"

"It depends."

"When the pipers play at your wedding, will you ask them to play 'The Nutbrown Maiden'?"

"It might be done, and will you do something for me?"

"Anything."

"I want you to kiss me."

He takes her in his arms and they kiss. Then she goes off down the hill to the harbour and he goes up the hill. He gets to the castle and stops. He no longer believes or cares about the Curse. He opens the door and crosses the threshold.

The Curse of the Maclaines had been put upon the MacNeils because of an actual incident in the fifteenth century. It is a typical Highland legend involving love, revenge and massacre. It has been handed down for generations to end with our modern Torquil. He finds the Curse engraved on the stone of the rampart:

This is the Curse of Caitriona Maclaine of Erraig on MacNeil of Kiloran . . .

But what is that he hears? Pipes playing "The Nutbrown Maiden"! He rushes to the ramparts and looks over. Joan is marching up the road escorted by three pipers. He runs down the steps and they fall into each other's arms. As they go up the road hand in hand, we read the rest of the curse:

Never shall he leave this Castle a free man. He shall be chained to a woman until the end of his days and he shall die in his chains!

Poor Sir Robert! Poor Caitriona! Poor Arthur Rank! Joan and Torquil, their arms around each other, march up the hill. They know where they're going and so do we.

This was the script we took back to London with us. Time was getting on. We would have to start shooting in the Western Isles not later than September. We had our Joan. Captain Knight, Esmond Knight's uncle, was enlisted to play the colonel and bring his famous tame eagle Mr Ramshaw, who was in good feather, with him. But where was our Caitriona, where was our Torquil? Since I had met a few Highland chatelaines, I saw Caitriona as half witch, half debutante, the sort of woman who could turn her hand to anything, from running a Highland castle to skinning a rabbit. The mournful great Irish wolfhounds with which I surrounded her kept loneliness and despair at bay. It seemed to me that I had at last found a part worthy of Pamela Brown. Her deep voice and commanding way of speaking would blend mysteriously with the black rocks and the tortured oak trees of the Glen of Erraig. Emeric didn't agree. He thought her hideously ugly, and what was worse, hideously intelligent. Hungarian woman do not wear their brains in their head. The fact that I thought Pamela's great face and haunting eyes were something I could do wonders with on the screen, did not weigh with him at all. He just thought I was mad. I forget whom Emeric wanted for the part. He was a good judge of an actress in the conventional sense, but in this case originality won and Pamela got the part.

Of course there had to be parts for Finlay Currie and John Laurie. And George Carney gave a lovely performance as Joan's bank manager father. There was a nice little part for a young girl in Caitriona's household. She is Kenny's sweetheart and is the reason why he takes the boat out, in spite of his fear of the wrath of Rory Mor. I gave her the name of Bridie. It was the name of Seton Gordon's second daughter, so now we had Caitriona and Bridie both in the same film. There remained only Torquil MacNeil of Kiloran.

About ten years ago, a few years before his death, Nigel Balchin described to me his first sight of James Mason, when they were both undergraduates at Oxford. It was down at the boats. Nigel described a tall, black-haired, magnificently built man in white rowing shorts and singlet which modelled the graceful shape of his muscular limbs. Nigel was a master of words and phrases, and in that moment I saw that wonderful young man exactly as Nigel had seen him on that sunshiny morning. I also realised that Nigel had been in love with James all their lives, and I thought with tenderness and understanding, how beautiful the love of one man for another can be.

This dark young god had come to London expecting to find it at his feet, and he was very soon noticed in, I think, a play at the Arts Theatre. This was London of the thirties, and his contemporaries and rivals were John Gielgud, Michael Redgrave, Laurence Olivier, Brian Aherne, George Sanders, Ralph Richardson, Alec Clunes and William Devlin, and they had all got their foot in the door ahead of James. Pamela Brown told me that she met him once in the King's Road, and they talked over a coffee, as actors will, of how hard it was to "get in".

"They don't want me," he said bitterly and talked of going to Hollywood to try his luck there, although he longed to play the great parts and was physically and mentally equipped to do so. He had a voice and bearing second to none. He found a readier reception in films, and when the war broke out he had already made a British reputation. At this time, Pamela Ostrer's marriage with Roy Kellino had broken up, and Pamela had married James. This certainly helped his career, for she was clever and active as a wasp. James went from film to film, and by the time we were looking for Torquil MacNeil he was the obvious candidate. We had only met once before, when I was considering him for the part of Spud in *Colonel Blimp*. In the course of these new negotiations, I was invited to lunch at their house at Beaconsfield, Bucks. I found it an oppressive meal and I fancy they did too. Three more aggressive personalities surely never met before around an unsteady gate-legged table. They were suspicious and I was enigmatic. They were suspicious of everything. I can see their anxious faces now as they pelted me with questions, the answers to which became shorter and shorter. James's questions were mostly about the part. He had read the script, of course, and wanted to know how I proposed to do this, that and the other. Such questions always irk me. I loved the movies and had been in them long enough to know that everything can be done. One of my grievances against scriptwriters was that they didn't demand more and more miracles. I and my associates were miracle workers by taste and we loved to be set some new and apparently impossible problem. When I described how Mr Ramshaw, Colonel Knight's golden eagle, swooped down from his perch on the top of the bookcase to land on the dead dog-fox held up for him by his master, I was only describing something I had seen; but when I described the open motorboat with its three passengers leaving the safety of the little harbour and meeting the first chop and roll off the cliffs, and then getting further out into the big sea of the Sound, where every wave is a problem; then told how a black squall of wind and rain swoops down on them, half blinding and half drowning them, filling the boat with water and drowning out the engine so they have to drift at the mercy of the seas; how they hear the roar of the whirlpool of Corryvreckan getting nearer and nearer, while Torquil works desperately to get the engine working again, and how Joan no longer cares about her wedding dress floating away and only thinks of survival; and how they enter the Race and drift nearer and nearer to Corryvreckan, while Torquil is calmly coaxing the engine into action again, and how the motor springs into life just when they are reaching the edge of the whirlpool, and how they pull away from the deadly suction and head triumphantly for home – well, then I was describing what I hoped to see. I hadn't any doubt that I could get it on the screen, and that the whole spectacular sequence would be made up of shots of the real thing, involving the actors or doubles for the actors, intercut with studio scenes against back projection, tank shots using the great Denham tank, and model shots of various sizes. But how we would get the final shots of the boat pulling away from the whirlpool I had no idea. I was quite confident that it could be done, however, so when James and his wife, who had heard stories about *49th Parallel*, and rumours that I considered actors expendable, plied me with questions and insisted on specific answers, I was airy in my replies and evasive in my explanations, and left them with the impression that I was going to do it all for real and probably succeed in drowning us all. So when, a little later, Emeric and I and Erwin Hillier had made a reconnaissance of Mull and made our plans, and when we had found the House of Carsaig (called Erraig in the film), which had been commandeered and recently evacuated by the RAF, and which would make a splendid base camp for the film unit, where we could do our own catering and be on the job from dawn until dusk, and wrote James an enthusiastic letter about it all, he replied – or I suspect she replied – with a curt telegram saying that he didn't propose to play Boy Scouts for anybody, and would expect first-class transportation and accommodation, as in his contract, which fortunately had not been signed. I was in the Western Isles when I received his message, and as soon as I got to the nearest telegraph office I sent him a wire firing him and left the lawyers and agents to work it out. It was a pity, because we both wanted to work with each other, and James would have been darkly romantic in the part. It was twenty-six years later before we got together on a film on the great barrier reef in Australia, *Age of Consent*.

So James was out and Roger Livesey was in, for he had read the script and had been pestering me to let him play the part.

"You're too old, you can't play a young naval lieutenant," I said.

"Nonsense, I'll take off ten or twelve pounds," he retorted, and he did.

"You're in a West End hit [Peter Ustinov's *Banbury Nose*]. They won't release you."

"You can double me on location," he replied. "Go on, Micky, you can do anything, I know."

"You're thinner, but you still don't look under thirty," I said critically.

"I'll bleach my hair and then you'll see!"

The effect was amazing: he lost a few more years and was now definitely on the right side of thirty. His whole manner changed, even his physical make-up. He moved quickly and energetically. Losing weight had brought back his eagle-like profile. He was almost the young Roger Livesey whom I had tested so many years ago for Michael Balcon. Actors like Roger and Larry are wizards when they come to creating a new person; they can change their walk, their voice, their shape. Emeric and I were convinced. But Roger couldn't get out of the play, and now came the greatest conjuring trick of all.

Roger Livesey, playing Torquil MacNeil in *I Know Where I'm Going*, never came within five hundred miles of the Western Isles. I know that those of you who have seen the film won't believe it, but it's true.

I'm not sure, but I think it is one of the cleverest things I ever did in movies. Of course, in quota-quickies you were always doubling somebody, and in *49th Parallel* I doubled about half a dozen well-known personalities, but to double the leading man in all the exterior scenes of the film and intercut them with studio close-ups with such a distinctive person as Roger Livesey, was a miracle. We tested twenty young men before we found one who had Roger's height and could copy his walk, which was very distinctive. Roger came to the studio and took endless trouble teaching him to walk and run and hardest of all, stand still. Then there was the little matter of wearing the kilt. No two men walk the same way in a kilt. We had six weeks of exteriors in front of us and Torquil MacNeil was in all of them. The secret of doubling an actor is not to run away from the camera or turn your back on it; on the contrary, you walk straight up to it. The camera is just as easily fooled by calm assurance as people are. Erwin Hillier and I would work out the scene and rehearse it, and the script-girl would make notes of the places where we proposed later to cut-in medium shots and close-ups of Roger filmed in the studio. Then we would shoot the scene exactly as if Roger were playing the part. Of course, there were all sorts of tricks: sudden cuts and turns and masking pieces in the foreground, which we used to help the editor of the film. But so perfect is the illusion that I couldn't tell myself, now, which is Roger and which is his double in certain scenes.

What a pity that James Mason didn't trust me more. He need never have gone on location at all, and the rest of us could have played Boy Scouts to our hearts' content. In the weeks that I had been travelling around, I had read everything I could lay my hands on about the Western Isles. I was determined to make the film as authentic as possible in every detail. Every face was chosen by me, and every voice. I persuaded Malcolm MacKellaig of Morar, where the sands are as white as the sands of Kiloran are golden, that he had to come and be my Gaelic dialogue director and he came, besides playing a small part in the film. I engaged Ian MacKenzie and his powerful great diesel motorboat to be with us permanently throughout the film, so that I could always be sure of transport, or of taking advantage of a change in the weather. Ian had his big motorboat undecked, because he used it in the spring for transporting cattle to the uninhabited isles, for instance the Isles of the Sea; he left them there all summer to get fat on the good grazing, and then fetched them in September for the markets, fattened up at no expense to himself. He knew the islands and the cliffs and the currents and the tides, and was not afraid to go anywhere. I could never have got half the shots without him. Once, when we had been shooting all day at Lochbuie Castle a few miles along the coast of Mull, he brought the whole unit back in his boat, cameras and all. I remember how, as we sailed up the coast, the wind got up and became a strong headwind. We were so heavily laden that there was very little freeboard, and I began to wonder what would happen if the wind got stronger and the big open boat ran under. I stood up by the foremast, and every now and then glanced back at Ian. He was completely unmoved. A tall, lean, handsome man with eyes like a deer's, he always wore the kilt and a battered old mackintosh, and an even more battered Highland bonnet. He was a man you could trust. He had a wicked sense of humour.

From the first shot until the last – there were about 780 in the film – Erwin and I had our usual love/hate relationship. We both of us thought we knew all there was to know about black and white cinematography, and this was very likely true, with the proviso that poor Erwin had to actually do the job, while I was cast in the role of impatient critic.

"Come on, Erwin, for Christ's sake. We've got to be down at the boat by 4:30."

"I'm waiting for that little cloud, Meekey. It will be here in five minutes, I promise."

"Five minutes, my foot! It's October, Erwin, and the sun is sinking. Those clouds are going to disappear!"

"Oh, Meekey, just one more minute, please."

Of course, Erwin knew that I knew what he was talking about, although I pretended not to. The black and white cinematography on *I Know Where I'm Going* was inventive, poetic, miraculous. Only Johnny Seitz, Rex Ingram's cameraman, who taught me to appreciate romantic photography, was his equal. Erwin has done many wonderful films since then, but his work on *A Canterbury Tale* and *I Know Where I'm Going* was original and unforgettable.

Alfred Junge was again our art director and spent a week or two with the film unit when we started shooting the Isles. He was now known to one and all as Uncle Alfred, and blossomed out amazingly. Except for Finlay Currie, who was as patriarchal and solid as an oak, Alfred was the oldest of us, as well as being the veteran of countless great films, German, American and British. I don't think he had ever been with such a young and independent unit as ours before *Colonel Blimp*. We teased him, and he loved it. He was a handsome man, massively built, and he grew visibly younger and more handsome as party followed party in the evenings. We made our headquarters at the Western Isles Hotel at Tobermory. Tobermory was a naval training base and the enlisted girls were having a very good time. I noticed one girl in particular, a bright, blonde Scottish girl from Glasgow. She was a secretary/typist, she said.

"Come and be my secretary after the war," I said. "You're just the sort of girl I'm looking for."

She thought it was a joke, but I was perfectly serious. She had three or four offers of marriage pending, and added my offer to the list.

We soon moved to Carsaig and settled in. Finlay Currie and John Seabourne volunteered to do the cooking. We Boy Scouts did the washing up, peeling potatoes and other chores. Wendy Hiller looked the joint over and decided that the twenty-mile drive back to Tobermory was worth it to spend the night in a comfortable bed. Pamela Brown decided to pitch in with us. We became intimate. It was a marriage not of bodies, but of two minds. Those weeks of storm and pale northern sunshine laid the foundation for a loving friendship that lasted thirty-four years. What I had seen first in that ridiculous play at the Torch Theatre was a spectacular young actress with resplendent chestnut hair to her shoulders, and great liquid eyes full of disdain, that could dart a glance backward like a nervous thoroughbred. She was tall, with a long back and lovely legs, but she moved on stage in a way that I couldn't understand, crossing the stage with swift strides and a queer loping gait as if she were a cripple and trying to hide it. It was only when we met and worked together in *One of Our Aircraft Is Missing* that I learned that she *was* a cripple, and that she *was* trying to hide it. She was a martyr to arthritis, and had been since the age of sixteen. It was hereditary, but in spite of this handicap she had won the Gold Medal for acting at the Royal Academy of Dramatic Art, and on the strength of that had gone to Stratford, which at that time was directed by Randall Ayrton, to play Juliet and Cressida. If she had found her crippled muscles difficult to hide on the tiny Torch Theatre stage, imagine what it must have been like to work on the huge stage at Stratford. She did the usual things, fell in love with her

Romeo, gave a bad performance as Juliet and a good one as Cressida. But the critics loved her from the start. There was no doubt that a blazing new talent would soon be coming to town, but the demon that was twisting her limbs and muscles gave her no rest, and I couldn't conceal the fact that she limped and that her face was wise with pain. At about this time she married Peter Copley, a descendant of the famous family of painters, a passionate and dedicated young actor. Unfortunately, his mother was French, lived in Hampstead, was a famous *femme de ménage*, and tried to make one out of Pamela, who was by heart and inclination a gipsy. Mrs Copley failed.

When Deborah and I were stepping out, we went one evening to see Pamela play the title role in a weird piece of American folklore called *Claudia*. It was wild miscasting, but she got away with it. She covered herself with suntan lotion and played acrobatics with the furniture, and did everything but stand on her head. We loved her. Two weeks later she had a major attack of the arthritis and had to leave the play and go into hospital for a year. It was rumoured that she would never walk again.

I think she was in the Clarendon at Oxford. Specialists persuaded her to take the famous, or infamous, gold treatment for arthritis which consists of injecting gold into the veins. The treatment gives you a fighting chance if you are prepared to suffer tortures. I knew about it, and although we never wrote to each other, I sent her books in hospital, and she sent me one or two in return.

She came with Peter to see *The Fifth Column*. That was the last I had seen of her for a year, until I caught sight of her chestnut head in the sunshine on the quayside at Oban. I had been there some days and the actors and actresses had all travelled up together. I heard her laugh at the actors' table at dinner that evening.

That was all, during the days that followed, until she decided to pitch in with the Boy Scouts at Carsaig. After five years of awareness of one another, we were at last intimate. Within three weeks we were passionately in love: not sexual love, it was more possessive than that.

She loved me because I treated her like a boy. I took her with me wherever I went on land or sea. I expected her to perform physical feats which she knew she couldn't do, but she did them. We went out in all weathers, we talked all night and we worked all day. I loved her because she never asked for an explanation. She either knew the answer, or kept quiet. I loved the way her great luminous eyes could see backwards like a horse's. I really believed that she could see the expression on the faces of people behind her. I loved her voice, deep and low, "an excellent thing in woman". I loved her silences – "a quiet woman is like still water under a great bridge".

We could sit for hours in silence, but yet remain closely in touch. It must have been rather unnerving for the others, especially for Wendy, who had every reason to expect that kind of rapport with the director for herself. She had done her homework on Joan Webster very well, especially in the physical changes that took place in the girl during these four Homeric days and nights. The humour was there, the invention, the imagination, but I felt that the spark was missing. Now, when I see her brilliant performance on the screen, I know I was wrong. I was just out of sympathy with anybody else playing the part but Deborah. What! You say? You just said you were in love with Pamela Brown. But my dear, innocent interlocutor, don't you know that there are many kinds of love?

The island of Scarba is almost joined to the island of Lunga. In between these two high and rocky islands, there is an arm of the sea, a sort of miniature Corryvreckan, about thirty feet wide. This passage of the sea is called the Pass of the Grey Dogs. In the middle of the passage is an islet which deer use for their astonishing leaps from one island to the other. The passage is easily navigable at slack water, but at the ebb it runs like a mill-race. On Sundays, when the rest of the unit were exploring the island, or taking their ease, Pamela and I and Ian MacKenzie would get John Seabourne to cut us some thick sandwiches and maybe a scone or two with jam, put out the big motorboat, cross the bay and arrive at Scarba at the slack. We would wait until the tide turned and then run the Pass of the Grey Dogs and round the end of Scarba just as Corryvreckan began to boil. We would be only a few hundred yards from the overfall beneath the sea, which was creating the whirlpools and eddies which were popping up all around us. Ian would creep into the main eddy below the sea cliffs of Scarba, and cruise about there as calmly as if he was on the Serpentine. I had my hand camera, my faithful Eyemo, and as the boat was pitching and tossing and sometimes whirling right round in the force of the current, I would tie myself to the mast, like Prince Breacan, to leave my hands free. This is how I got the shots of the eddies and whirlpools which we used with great effect in the back projection scenes in the studio. But my particular triumph was to snatch with the camera one of those mysterious boils which comes roaring up from unknown depths. As we cruised to and fro in the eddy from the whirlpool these boils would suddenly rear up like sea monsters and toss the boat about before subsiding again. By now, Corryvreckan would be roaring, and if the wind were against the tide, the minor races would be yelling and screaming and you could hear the din twenty miles out at sea. Deafened but exhilarated by all this clamour and keyed up by the tension of watching the surface of the sea for any surprises, we would spend a couple of hours until the tide slackened, when we would creep back up the Grey Dogs and so home, our cheeks roughened with wind and salt water, and our eyes full of the mysteries we had seen.

On one of these occasions I said to Pamela: "Do you realise that we nearly got drowned just then?"

"Yes," she said.

"Would you have minded?"

We had a disturbing encounter one day at Crinan, where the canal which crosses the narrow neck of the Mull of Kintyre opens into the ocean. We were standing on the quay by the hotel when we saw approaching three strange-looking objects. They were far away, but were coming directly towards us. I seemed to be looking at three men crucified, their crosses standing on barrels which rolled slightly, so that their feet were awash as they played follow-my-leader. The sun was low. It was slack water, and the sea heaved mutinously, but there were very few waves. The strange craft were about to approach us at a good speed, and very soon we could hear the thud-thudding of their engines, which sounded more like motorbike engines than anything else. Soon we saw that they were midget subs. Each skippper standing on the deck, holding onto the crosspiece, had earphones and a mouthpiece with which he communicated with his fellow sub-mariner down below in the body of the tiny vessel. I never saw such dedicated and absorbed young men. The hatchways were open, and as they passed beneath us to enter the canal lock, where there were steps up to the quayside, we caught a glimpse of the interior and saw the serious, intent faces of these young madmen. Lots of water had splashed over the deck and of course down below as well, and the particular sardine that happened to be in the can I was looking at was splashing about happily in about a foot of water. To my amazement, I recognised the leader of this pygmy flotilla. It was Henty Creer, once my operator on the exterior sequences on *The Thief of Bagdad*, and later second cameraman in our expedition to Canada on *49th Parallel*, when he had become such a bosom friend of Bill Paton's. He had volunteered for the Navy soon after our return and was now a lieutenant under training for this very hush-hush job. He was a little embarrassed on this occasion to find the whole camera crew hailing him by name, and asking him questions to which, of course, he could give no answer. He and the other dedicated young men were preparing for the underwater attacks which would eventually disable and destroy the German battleships which were wintering in the fjords of Norway. It was the kind of desperate solitary mission that reminds one of the knights of old, and Henty, like many others, gave his life for it. We had a short chat. He had heard from Bill from time to time. He was interested in what we were doing, but I felt that he was already living a life apart, had made his peace with himself, and had no illusions about the price he might have to pay for success. His fate was written on his forehead.

Early in November 1944, we finished all the exteriors, packed up and moved south back to Denham. Uncle Alfred had nearly half the sets ready for us, and after giving the crew a few days off we started work on the interiors. Erwin, Alfred and I went to the machine shops. We had brought back with us the actual open motorboat we used in the film. I was determined to construct a machine with two iron hands which could grip the keel of the boat, and mount it on a eccentric screw with variable speeds worked by a motor, which would toss the boat about in a realistic manner, or at least in a manner to which we were all accustomed. For we had spent many dozens of hours in an open boat and we knew what it was like. Later on, such machines were common for scenes involving aerobatics and for small boats, but at the time this was quite a new idea and our machine shop became really interested in it, and gave me what I wanted. The actors were able to work in a real boat, surrounded by wind and water machines, and working close up against a back projection screen, so close that they could almost feel the whirling waters of Corryvreckan. After about eight days, we all became utterly absorbed in this new plaything. One day, when wind and water were at full blast, the boat was pitching and tossing, Roger was roaring at Wendy, Wendy was screaming at Roger, and receiving buckets of water in the face from zealous prop-men, I looked up and saw a mildly surprised face, only a few feet away from mine, watching our eccentric activities with great interest. It was David Niven.

When the whole thing came to a gradual stop, and we dried off, he ventured a remark:

"Is this a private fight, or can anybody get in on it?"

It was at that very instant that I cast him for Peter, the hero of *A Matter of Life and Death*.

BOOK THREE

Colour

In January 1980, six and a half years ago, at Dartmouth College, New Hampshire, New England, I started to write A Life in Movies *because I knew that if I didn't, nobody else would – or could. I owed it to myself, and to the business to which I have dedicated myself to write down as truly as I could what it was like to choose to give my life to an entirely new profession that had just been thrown open to creative talent everywhere. For thousands of years the world's storytellers, whom Jan de Hartog gleefully describes as "the liars", had been telling each other lies, writing down lies and now were lying to each other on a silver screen. All authors since the beginning of time have wanted to have illustrated editions of their book; and all authors since the beginning of time have hated the illustrations when they saw them. Now they really had something to get excited about. Now all the other creative talents – acting, designing, composing – could give rein to their fantasies.*

It was at this time that I came into the business. I grew up with it, I grew out of it, I came back to it, I grew old with it. I have seen great technical inventions, like the coming of sound and the arrival of colour, convulse the business, ruin thousands of people, and enrich a few, and yet I have seen the film business arise Phoenix-like from the ashes, stronger, more inventive, more creative than ever. I have seen the curse of too much money and too much power in the hands of too few men ruin the industry again and again, and yet out of the devastation caused by this crass stupidity there have always been amazing creative talents to come springing up to revive the industry again. I have seen on one and the same day, a queue around the block to see a new movie – and the same night I have sat through hours of trash on television. I have seen – what haven't I seen? And I will try to write it down the way it was. There are a few other men who know from their own experience as much about the film business as I do, but, as far as I know, most of them can't or won't, put it down. It needs to be written. It needs to be recorded. It had never happened before and it will

never happen again – that such a medium as the movie will become
available to creative talent on such generous terms.

So I have planned generously. I didn't intend to write another "film-
book". There have been a lot of good ones published since the war,
particularly in Europe, but I hope to do better than that. It will, I hope,
prove to be the story of a young man of the twentieth century and his Muse,
his dazzling, dancing, fascinating mistress. A man who planned to write
the story of his love affair, only to find out that his mistress had walked out
on him. It didn't matter, he concluded – not if it made a good story, not if it
was a unique story, as he honestly believed it was.

I had planned it during the last ten years and had made several starts.
One of them was going to be a novel: none of them were any good, and I
began to think I had left it too late. The invitation from David Thomson to
come to Dartmouth College gave me just the necessary encouragement I
needed. But many things have combined since then to make my progress
slower than I would have wished. I never expected to see the book
published while I was alive, and I had no means of knowing whether it
would be published when I was dead, but I owe it to my cock-teasing
mistress to get it all down. I could arrange that it would always be available
for students and I knew that one day it would be of value, and would
somehow get itself published and even read.

A Matter of Life and Death is called *Stairway to Heaven* in the USA.
This change of title seemed to us to illustrate a fundamental difference
between the English and the American mind and outlook. We had been
pleased with our title. I believe the suggestion was mine. I loved the old
melodramatic phrase which crops up in every thriller written during the
last century, in every European language: and I liked the play upon words,
for in our film it really was a matter of life and death that was being
discussed, so Emeric and I looked a bit blank when the film was finished,
and two young, excited New York lawyers, Arthur Krim and Bob
Benjamin, who were determined to take over the film business and use
our film as their spearhead, came rushing down from the projection room,
into the studio and said to us: "Boys, we've got a wonderful title for your
film."

"We have a title already, Arthur." (This was Emeric.) "*A Matter of Life
and Death*, don't you remember?"

But this was 1946. Arthur and Bob brushed question and statement
aside. "You can't have 'Death' in the title," they screamed. "We're going to
market it as *Stairway to Heaven*! What do you think of that?"

What did we think of it? We had all of us survived a war with the
greatest and most fanatical power in the world, and won it. In the last
twelve years, sixteen million human lives had been sacrificed to overthrow

one man and his lunatic ideas. The words "life and death" were no longer the great contradictions that they had been. They were just facts. Out of this enormous holocaust, Emeric and I were trying to create a comedy of titanic size and energy. Two worlds were fighting for one man's life. It was indeed a matter of life and death. And now we were told that we couldn't have "death" in the title.

I don't recall that Emeric and I argued very much with Arthur and Bob. They loved our film and said so, and they were so proud of their inspiration and so sure we would be glad of this soapy title for our film. We had become rather anxious about Arthur Rank's and John Davis's promises and hope for world distribution, and it was exhilarating to know that these two young enthusiasts were going to start their career with our film. After all, there was a stairway in our film, a moving stairway, and it did lead to another world, even it if were not Heaven. Throughout the film, we were careful not to use that mighty word. And now these young Americans were juggling with it, as if it were a Hollywood musical.

Emeric made one last attempt to persuade them.

"Arthur, you say that no film with 'death' in the title has ever been a success, but what about the famous play which they made into a successful film also: *Death Takes a Holiday*?"

But Bob and Arthur were ready for him.

"That's the very reason it was a success. Don't you see, boys? Death takes a holiday – obviously there's not going to be any death in the picture!"

We gave in to American salesmanship, but we kept our original title for the rest of the world. I have often thought about this little conversation. Canada agreed with us. Europe liked our title, although most of them used the European version of the title, which translated is: "A *Question* of Life and Death". It was only the United States that had to be protected from the realities of life and death. But if I were a citizen of that great country, which has twice saved herself and Europe from tyranny and barbarism, I do not think I would like to be told the word "death" could frighten me any more than its great companion, "life", would dismay me. Americans have a marked capacity for judgment and for keeping their feet on the ground, and so are that much nearer Heaven.

A Matter of Life and Death was the title we had given to the story commissioned by Jack Beddington to improve Anglo-American relationships and which Emeric and I decided should be a love story. It is known to the Archers and their supporters as *AMOLAD*. Emeric had completed the first draft while I was trying to drown myself and my unit in the Western Isles. There were continuity problems on the script of *IKWIG* which needed our attention, but for the most part the shooting on the interiors and the trick work was straightforward, although the creation of the whirlpool gave me and Poppa Day something to think about. The two films overlapped rather more than was usual with us. Technicolor had become available again, our story and script were approved by the M of I, and by Rank and Davis (it was our most ambitious film yet), and it was agreed that Emeric and I would go to Hollywood as soon as the principal photography on *IKWIG* was finished. The object of our visit was to find the kind of American girl that we would like to see in our film: a professional, but one who was quite unknown otherwise. A great deal of interest had been aroused in Hollywood by our films, although they didn't understand them. And they suspected they might have been missing out on something. We knew enough about Hollywood to know that every studio and producer would be trotting out one of the favourites in their stable. We were equally anxious to discover an unknown actress whom we would be proud of in the part, and whom the Americans would be proud of later. She had to be young, pretty, the right age to be in the Forces, and real. That was all we asked.

Of the well-known actresses, there was only one that interested us and that was Betty Field. She was in a play in New York, one of John Van Druten's bits of nonsense, and we thought we would look her up. But otherwise the field was open as far as we were concerned.

The casting of David Niven as the British pilot speeded things up considerably. The end of the war was in sight, and he was due back in Hollywood when hostilities should be over, to serve out his contract with Sam Goldwyn. Before he had to report at the studio on Santa Monica Boulevard, he would have ample time to play in our film, providing that Sam Goldwyn agreed. David had trained and served with the Commandos, and had recently been seconded to the M of I to work with Carol Reed on *The Way Ahead*. It was a marvellous film and David was a revelation in it. We had all known and loved him as the charming playboy, but here was the real man, and a serving officer careful of his men. A lot of this was due to Carol Reed, the best realistic director that England has ever produced. I almost said documentary director, except that I would be misunderstood. Realistic is what I mean. Carol could put a film together like a watchmaker puts together a watch. In spite of his rich theatrical background, he was the best constructor of a film that I have ever known. Korda recognized his immense talent, but couldn't find the right stories for him except *The Third Man*, from a story and script by Graham Greene. In *The Way Ahead*, Carol Reed showed us a bunch of ordinary fellows – civilians – and how they became turned into fighting men who could work as a team or act independently. David Niven was the officer who trained them and led them, and his methods were not those of General Patton, but they got results all the same. We also saw, for the first time, the real David Niven: shrewd, kind, quick-witted and full of fantasy, the image of our hero Peter in *A Matter of Life and Death*.

During the war we had been forced to be insular in our casting and aimed only at whom we could get. Marius Goring had been shown the script of *AMOLAD*, with a view to his playing the important role of the Collector. He had been doing confidential work for the Foreign Office all through the war, but I hadn't forgotten his performance as Schuster in *The Spy in Black*, and how much he had impressed me with his intelligence and impudent charm. Nor had I forgotten his stunning performance in Clemence Dane's play *The Happy Hypocrite*. I knew that he was fluent in both French and German, and we were tempted to make his part a German in the story, but decided that would be too much of a good thing: the Archers were already suspected of having a German bias. We decided on a French aristocrat who had lost his head on the guillotine in 1793, but Marius didn't want to play this part. He wanted to play Peter, the hero of the story. He argued his case well. We were famous for our unconventional casting. We didn't have to cast stars in the leading parts all the time. He could play Peter on his head. Peter was supposed to be an artist and a dreamer, besides being a squadron leader in the RAF, but we were adamant. The Collector was a wonderful part. Take it or leave it. He'd better take it, because Peter Ustinov was waiting in the wings. He took it. We paid him back handsomely, but that was two years later.

Things were not going altogether well for Independent Producers Ltd. A few months before this, Rank had summoned a meeting of our group and asked us all if we would agree to Gabriel Pascal making George Bernard Shaw's *Caesar and Cleopatra* within our organization. None of us were keen about it. We all knew each other; we were all unanimously elected to the company. We had all created our own films in our own way and in our own time, and we were afraid of a buffoon like Gabby screwing up the works. His picture was going to cost half a million pounds, which was at least half as much again as our budgets. Knowing Gabby – and some of us had worked with him and for him – we felt he wouldn't stop at half a million, but would soon be asking for the other half. But we thought that GBS's *Caesar and Cleopatra*, starring Claude Rains and Vivien Leigh, could hardly go wrong, even in Gabby's hands. We were wrong. It certainly shook our little organization, Independent Producers, to its foundation.

One day, Gabby Pascal was casting young men for the parts known universally at Denham as "Caesar's Geezers". I was strolling along the long corridor and found myself among a bunch of young men waiting to be interviewed. Men were beginning to be released from the Services, and these were all tall, good-looking, fit young men, but I noticed one in particular whose good looks were so striking and whose air of truculence was so engaging that he stood out from all the others, quite apart from the fact that he was over six feet tall. I went straight up to him and asked him his name. It was James Stewart, and he was a Scot from the Borders. A month or two later, he was playing Apollodorus in *Caesar and Cleopatra* and was calling himself Stewart Granger; and a fine sight he looked in his armour and purple cloak, his muscular legs adorned with steel greaves. It was the scene where Cleopatra was smuggled onto the Pharos, rolled up in a carpet, and Larry Olivier was looking on from the wings.

"That's a good-looking boy, Larry, don't you think?" I said, teasing him.

"Too bloody good-looking," said Larry sourly; he has always been sensitive about his thin legs.

Stewart Granger was the best-looking leading man that I had seen since the regretted James Mason, and I made a note of him as a possible Peter. We had one or two talks about the part, and he was enthusiastic. But I couldn't quite make up my mind. And then David Niven strolled on the set and strolled off with the part. I knew that Sam Goldwyn would scream complaints about all the films he had lined up for David Niven, and that he would ask a large fee, or at least large for us, because he had kept David on a minimal retainer all through the war. Korda had done the same for Ralph and Larry. But in spite of all that, we had to have him. Everything happened as I expected. Sam Goldwyn drove a hard bargain, and we had to start making the picture rather sooner than we wanted to, but David played the part, and that was all that mattered.

I don't think that Jimmy Granger ever quite forgave me for casting the part away from him. Behind the public image that he was at pains to create – the truculent, damn-your-eyes seducer – there was another man, sensitive and imaginative. But he bore no malice and we each did the other a good turn later on, as I shall relate in its proper place for once. With Roger Livesey playing Dr Reeves and Raymond Massey playing Abraham Farlan, we had a starry cast. We only had to find our young American actress.

Both Emeric and I had so much enjoyed our stormy sessions with Dorothy and Ray Massey, that Ray was bound to be our first choice for the part of the Prosecuting Attorney in Another World. He and Dorothy cabled an enthusiastic affirmative: "For the Archers anytime, this world or the next."

Roger, being informed that Emeric was writing this new part especially for him, decided to grow a beard. He had completely altered his appearance twice for the greater glory of the Archers, first of all in *Colonel Blimp*, then in *IKWIG*. The beard proved to be red-gold in colour and completely altered his appearance and character. To complete his colourful new personality, I cast my two golden cocker spaniels in support. They had already appeared in *Colonel Blimp*, not only in the film, but on Colonel Blimp's coat of arms: two golden cockers *regardant*.

Meanwhile, it was not to be expected that the passionate friendship between Pamela and myself, which had been nourished by propinquity, would escape notice and a certain amount of comment in our respective homes. Our minds were in love with each other, but not yet our bodies. We had tried it once and laughed so much we had to give it up. It was at Carsaig. The whole unit had gone one evening to a dance at Tobermory in a hired coach, and we were left alone in front of the fire in the Laird's study. We ended up in the coal-scuttle roaring with laughter. That was all very well when we were seeing each other every day. But when we returned to the haunts of civilization, myself to the little house at 65A Chester Square, SW1; Pamela to 36 Soho Square, where she had an apartment over the offices of Rupert Hart-Davis the publisher, it wasn't so easy to suppress our need for each other. Pamela's part in *IKWIG* was a relatively short one, and it wasn't often that she was on call at the studio. We missed one another, and working five and a half days a week, never getting home until about half-past eight or nine, there wasn't much chance to share a joke or an idea. At first we tried meeting openly, but that didn't work. We were driven underground and that didn't work either. When we disappeared, Pamela's husband, Peter, and Frankie took to having long telephone conversations together. It would have been funny if it hadn't been so annoying – to both sides, I mean. All the time I had to shoot three to three and a half minutes a day of finished film.

It was during this time that the famous twenty-two takes took place. They became a legend. An actress of Pamela's imagination and capability doesn't usually need twenty-two takes to say one simple line in close-up. A director of my cocksureness usually makes up his mind after the first two takes how he wants a line to be read. It was the scene between Pamela and Wendy, which follows Joan Webster's last attempt to get to the island. To paraphrase the scene, Wendy says: "If you and Torquil are saddled with responsibilities that you can't get rid of, why don't you sell Erraig and why doesn't Torquil sell Kiloran? Then you could do what you like."

Pamela – I mean Caitriona – replies: "Yes, but money isn't everything."

We couldn't get this line right. We none of us saw it coming. It's a simple line, a cliché even. It seemed on paper to express what we wanted, but on film we couldn't get it right. Take 5 came up, Take 10 came up, Take 15 . . . Pamela exploded; "Well, for Christ's sake, what do you want? I've said it every way I can think of except standing on my head. How do you want me to say it?"

Then came the immortal response, which they all said I said, but which I don't remember: "There's only one way to say it, and that's the right way."

Finally – Take 22 on the board. By this time, the news had got around the whole studio, and all the Archers' backroom girls and boys had gathered around with great interest to watch this battle of great minds. For the twenty-second time Wendy gave the cue: "You can sell Erraig, and Torquil could sell Kiloran."

Pamela lifted her beautiful, luminous eyes to the ceiling, considered the suggestion, and then replied to it in exactly the same tone she had used in Take 1:

"Ye-ess, but money isn't everything."

"Cut. OK, print it," I said.

"Take 7 was good enough for me," said Erwin without humorous intent.

"Take 1 was good for me," said the camera operator with a grin.

Pamela's expression was enigmatic. Her voice was just as low and deep as ever, as she said: "Tell me, dear director, in your wisdom, what was the difference between Take 1 and Take 22?"

I answered briefly: "I liked Take 22, and I didn't like Take 1."

Pamela looked at Wendy, and Wendy looked at Pamela.

"Ah," said Pamela.

Of course, what was wrong was not the way the line was being read by Pamela: it was the line itself. When Wendy said: "You could sell Erraig and Torquil could sell Kiloran," Pamela should have answered: "Yes, but then we'd only have the money." See?

When, many years later, I told Pamela this, she hit me.

If we include editing and trick work, we were about four months in the studio in the winter of 1944–45, and during that time Poppa Day and his crew were working on the whirlpool sequence. The first and greatest problem of all was to build machines which would get a large inert mass of water, like the big studio tank, to move in a circular direction. When that was finally accomplished, there had to be wave machines for making waves and spray, and wind machines for beating up the surface of the sea, and cutting off the tops of the waves. There had to be boats made to scale with dummy passengers in them, and above all we had to create the centre of the whirlpool, and show the audience the terrifying moment when the tide turns and the whirlpool forms and the boat just manages to drag away from the abyss. Dozens of different shots were involved in the final sequence: shots of real whirlpools and boils, mostly shot by me tied to the mast like Prince Brecan, and blown-up to much bigger proportions, tank shots, close-ups of Roger and Wendy in the boat against back projection screens, shots of the model boat fighting against the tug of the whirlpool – and last of all the grand climactic shot, without which all the rest was pointless, the scene when the whirlpool forms and the boat skids around the lip and pulls away into safety.

For this last effect, which consisted of something like twelve separate negatives, twelve separate exposures, I relied upon Cecil B. De Mille's discovery in the first film of *The Ten Commandments*, of how to part the Red Sea and let the Israelites march through to the other side while Pharaoh's hosts were engulfed. De Mille was a great showman and he knew much would be expected of him. This was way back in 1923 or 1924, and the film was a silent one. He never surpassed it, even when he remade it as a talkie. The public was interested then in film miracles, and I remember reading all about it in popular magazines like the *Strand*. I think also that when I was with Rex Ingram, I discussed the parting of the Red Sea with Walter Pahlman, the trick-man on the unit, who had done all the tricks, as I think I have mentioned before, for the first *Thief of Bagdad*, starring and produced by Douglas Fairbanks. These men were pioneers who could and would tackle anything. They liked working for De Mille because he was a great showman and chose subjects that stretched the possibilities of cinema to its limits.

For his master shot of the Red Sea, De Mille chose a high angle, a God's-eye view looking down on the troubled sea, which then divides and draws back and allows the Israelites, hundreds of them, to march between the glittering walls of the spellbound sea. Working from this high angle, they built a big trough about thirty feet long, ten feet deep and six feet wide. It went into perspective at the far end from the camera, and vanished in the gloom. Out of the camera's range, on each side and high up, were water tanks with floodgates which could all be opened simultaneously. They coated the whole surface of the trough, the sides, the walls, the top, with some glittering substance which caught and reflected the lights and played and shimmered like water. This was before the days of plastics. Two high-speed cameras were mounted side by side to cover the shot. C. B. checked each one through the eyepiece. He reseated himself on his throne and called: "Cameras!"

Both cameras turned over simultaneously, revved up with long handles by the panting assistants; faster and faster the ratchets turned at high speed. The film was racing through the cameras at ninety-six frames a second.

C. B. picked up his megaphone. "*Water!*"

The floodgates opened, and about ten tons of water dashed down the chutes into the trough, the two opposing waves crashing into each other like fighting buffalo, leaping high in the air and then falling back into the trough, which filled and boiled in a matter of seconds.

"*Cut!*" roared De Mille, standing up from his director's chair, slapping his riding boots with his riding crop and walking off round the corner to work some more miracles.

Why two cameras? Was this because at high speed one of them might break down? It was because one high-speed camera was running normally, by which I mean it was running forwards, and the other high-speed camera was running backwards. The first camera showed what everybody could see: the tons of water crashing down over the shining cliffs of what appeared to be water and swallowing up the host of Pharaoh. The second camera, which was running backwards, or in reverse, showed what happened when Moses prayed to God to part the waters of the Red Sea: the surface of the sea boiled, sucked down what was like some enormous Corryvreckan, then rushed up the shiny walls of water on each side, and cosily re-established itself in the tanks from which it came. Of course, Cecil B. De Mille used double exposures, just as we did in *IKWIG*. He made a high-angle shot, always from the same angle, of the Children of Israel marching between the great shining walls of water, and then he made another high-angle shot of Pharaoh's hosts pursuing them with their chariots. These shots were superimposed between the walls of water. The editor only needed a few effective close-ups of apprehension on the faces of the actors and a few trickles of water beginning to pour over the edge of the miraculously held-back sea, ending with close shots of Pharaoh's chariots broken to pieces by the waves, and warriors drowning and horses struggling in the water, shot in a studio tank. Hail to De Mille! The greatest showman that the silver screen has ever had!

Years before, I had digested this miracle by the master for future use, so when Poppa Day said to me that he was having trouble with the centre of the whirlpool, I said: "Gelatine." For gelatine is what the miraculously held-back walls of the sea appeared to be. There were very few tricks in the cinema's miracle box that Poppa Day hadn't pulled off in his time, and he caught on at once. He ceased trying to make a whirlpool out of water and made it of plastic material like gelatine. It was mounted on an eccentric arm and could be whirled around at varying speeds in a tank of water. We used the trick of a high-speed camera running in reverse as De Mille had taught us, and at last our Corryvreckan rose out of the sea. It had only to be married with half a dozen other landscapes and waterscapes to see itself reproduced in a charming booklet published after the war, which had several photographs from frames of the film. It claimed to show us the only authentic picture of Corryvreckan in action. I never disabused the writer. The shots weren't authentic, but they were unique, and it cost us about £40,000 to get them on the screen.

But the director of the sequence was really Edgar Allan Poe. His *Tales* have inspired every imaginative writer over the past 150 years. It is not just the subject that thrills the reader; it is the style – like carved ivory – and the vision. His details are realistic, but he controls his realism as a strong rider controls a horse that's beginning to bolt with him. I don't know any other writer who seems so close to you when you read him. *A Descent into the Maelstrom* is a *tour de force* of imagination. Poe had never been anywhere near the Lofoten Islands, off the north coast of Norway. In one majestic sentence after another he describes the formation and appearance, almost at his feet, of the awful whirlpool into which his hero, the white-haired fisherman who now acts as his guide, had been sucked one day from staying too long in the eddy and, thanks to his own resource, had been vomited up alive. Even as a little boy *Descent into the Maelstrom* had always been one of my favourite stories, particularly at bath time, when one can contemplate a miniature Maelstrom as the bath runs out.

"Now, Master Michael, what are you doing sitting in the empty bath and catching your death of cold? Dreaming again, I suppose?"

My nanny was not to know an ambitious film director was planning the whirlpool sequence in *IKWIG* as the water drained away beneath his bottom. Incidentally, talking of miracles, some students of the cinema think that the greatest miracle achieved by C. B. in *The Ten Commandments*, was to persuade Theodore Roberts, his chief actor, whose trademark was a cigar like Ernie Kovacs's, to abandon it while he played Moses.

While I had been wrapping up the studio scenes of *IKWIG*, Emeric had been writing *AMOLAD*. Perhaps this is the moment to tell his story.

Squadron Leader Peter Carter, returning from a bombing mission over Germany, jumps from his crashing aircraft over the English Channel without a parachute, and miraculously survives the drop. His last words before jumping had been with June, an American girl working in a US Air Force station in England. Peter's body is washed ashore on the beach near where the American girls are billeted. At first, he thinks he is dead and in Another World. He soon realizes he is not when he meets June cycling back to her quarters along the beach. She has been crying all night. In the magic way of lovers, they recognize each other and fall in love.

In the Other World there is consternation. The alarm bells are ringing. Squadron Leader Peter Carter's life, which was due to end early that morning, has been prolonged for many hours through the carelessness of one of the many Collectors whose job it is to escort souls from one world to the next. The defaulting Collector explains that there has been a thick fog over England that morning, "a real peasouper" such as you get only over the English Channel. He himself is French. He is instructed to return to earth and report back at once with Peter Carter. But the powers that be are worried, for they know the strength of human love.

Peter's particular Collector is a young French aristocrat. It is not the first time he has lost his head. He was guillotined during the French Revolution. To his dismay, Peter refuses to go with him. Peter claims that it is not his fault that he's not dead, it is the Collector's. And now he is in love with June and she with him and that alters everything. The Collector threatens him and tries to persuade him, but he is no match for Peter, who is a poet as well as handy with his fists. Peter announces that he will appeal to the supreme court in the Other World, and the Collector returns there for instructions saying: "I shall return!"

The Collector's visits to Earth take place in space but not in time. So the whole argument between him and Peter has taken place in the fourth dimension, and June has heard nothing. When Peter tells her what he has experienced, she thinks he's mad or concussed. The local doctor, Dr Reeves, is a bit of a celebrity. Besides being a village doctor, he is also an expert on neurology and on injuries to the brain. He and June have a sentimental friendship and she decides to consult him about Peter.

After a talk with Peter's commanding officers, Dr Reeves takes on Peter's case. He has already suspected that in a previous crack-up Peter suffered injuries to the brain which can only be remedied by neurosurgery. Peter is living in two worlds at once: the world we know and an imaginery one which is created by his vivid imagination. The doctor treats both worlds as equally real, which they are for Peter, and even June is ready to believe it too. Dr Reeves says that the Collector will return because he said he would.

Sure enough, time stops again during a ping-pong match between Dr Reeves and June, and the Collector reappears. He is a cunning fellow and is still trying to get Peter to surrender himself, but finally he has to admit that Peter will be allowed to appeal. The trial will be in three days' time. The Collector disappears, borrowing one of Dr Reeves's books on chess to read. Peter starts to prepare his case and decide about his counsel. The counsel for the prosecution has already been appointed. His name is Abraham Farlan and he is the first American citizen to have been killed by a British bullet in the American Revolutionary War. He will obviously be a formidable opponent. Peter can choose anyone he wishes to defend him in the Other World, anyone who had lived upon Earth, but the hours and days pass and he still has not chosen his defending counsel.

While Dr Reeves is at the American army base to persuade a brilliant surgeon to perform on operation on Peter, Peter and the Collector are seated on a moving stairway between this world and the next. Peter has refused every suggestion of the Collector's for his defending counsel. What can Moses, Sophocles and Cardinal Richelieu know about our modern problems today? Suddenly, Peter realizes that he is being taken for a ride into the Other World and runs down the moving stairway. He only escapes from the Collector by the skin of his teeth. Dr Reeves insists that Peter has to be operated on tonight if he is to win his case. The doctor goes off on his powerful motorbike to speed up the ambulance, and is killed when he collides with it. June tells Peter that his friend the doctor has been killed, and Peter is happy. His counsel has been chosen for him.

At the entrance to the Other World, the Collector waits for Dr Reeves and gives him back the book on chess that he stole from his library, and tells him that he has been chosen by Peter to be his counsel. The doctor accepts and asks for leave to confer with his client, who is under anaesthesia at the moment. The Collector, who is now an open supporter of Peter's, stops all time and movement to whisk the doctor to Earth to consult with his client. After a brief discussion, Dr Reeves returns and takes his place in the court in the Other World.

The appeal, with its history of love between an American girl in the Forces and a British pilot, has attracted a huge audience. The judge and jury appear and take their places. Abraham Farlan takes his place. Thousands of young men and women, who have fought and died for what they believed in during the last few centuries, take their places. The trial begins.

While the American brain specialist fights for Peter's life on Earth, Dr Reeves fights for his life in the Other World. The battle between Abraham Farlan and Dr Reeves is well contested. The case is whether this young Englishman really loves this young American girl, or not. At the same time, almost every issue between the two nations, important or trivial, is brought up and examined. The battle between the two counsels rages to and fro. Finally, the judge agrees, at the suggestion of the jury, that the court shall adjourn and cross-examine Peter and June in the operating theatre where he is fighting for his life. The great moving stairway stretches across the sky and descends into the operating theatre. The judge and jury, the prosecuting and defending counsel, all descend to Earth.

The final struggle is intense, but when June shows that she is ready to forfeit her own life for Peter's, even the moving stairway refuses to move, and Peter wins his case. The judge instructs the jury that, "as Sir Walter Scott is always saying,"

> Love rules the hearth, the camp, the grove,
> This earth below and heaven above,
> For love is heaven and heaven is love.

In the hospital, Peter opens his eyes and sees June watching him. He smiles. "We won."

AMOLAD is my favourite Archers' film. *Colonel Blimp* is Emeric's favourite.

It can be seen that Emeric's interpretation of Jack Beddington's original brief ("Can't you two fellows think up a good idea to improve Anglo-American relations?") created plenty of scope for the director. Also for the designer and the cameraman and the special effects boys. Emeric's first draft of this story was full of fantasy, light-hearted miracles, mysterious appearances and disappearances. I decided that my job was to make each world as real as the other. I threw out all the double-exposures and ghosts waving curtains. Everything was to be as real as possible in both worlds. I went back to my brother-in-law, Joe Reidy, the surgeon, who had had priceless experience during the war. He put me on to medical textbooks which gave me the idea of staging hallucinations in space, not in time. I copied out chunks from medical reports. At the same time I was ferreting through the anthologies to choose deathless lines from English verse, which Peter could spout in the burning plane on the way to eternity. Emeric had followed up his idea of shooting This World in Technicolor, and the Other World in black and white, although we had both agreed that the opening of the film, in space, should be in full colour. Alfred Junge nodded his head. He had thought he had no more worlds to conquer. But now he had two more to create.

Now Jack Cardiff, the technician seconded to us by Technicolor, intervened.

"Why black and white?" he asked. "Why not monochrome? Technicolor can do that. Technicolor can do the whole job! We could shoot the Other World not in black and white, but in three-strip Technicolor, and print it without the dyes. That's the only way you can get the effect you want: colour fading from a rose and the colour flooding back into it without cutting away. Monochrome, not black and white!"

"What will three-strip without the three primary colours look like?" we all wanted to know.

"Sort of pearly," said Jack vaguely.

I looked at Alfred. "Did you hear, Alfred? Open wide them pearly gates!"

Jack had been Technicolor's brightest technician and their star demonstration cameraman for years. Like the other brilliant cameramen sponsored by Technicolor, he had been right through the plant, studying first the theory, and then the practice of the Technicolor dye-process colour system. Geoff Unsworth, Christopher Challis, Bob Krasker and George Menassian and Freddie Francis were all graduates from the unpretentious factory building, with the tall chimney, which faced the present London Airport. Kay Harrison was the managing director of the plant, and an adroit salesman of Technicolor, and George Dunn, an old-timer in the business, was his chief engineer. Kay was a salesman of genius, and he soon saw that Emeric and I were going to make the kind of films which would put British Technicolor ahead of Hollywood. Kay courted us, flattered us and gave us wonderful service. We had need of all the help we could get for the film we were going to make.

The fact that Jack Cardiff became the chief lighting cameraman on AMOLAD was the result of one of those painful decisions which I have had to make from time to time when extending the boundaries of our film-making.

Such a moment had come now. Although I had worked on two of the most ambitious colour productions ever planned, it could hardly be claimed, even by the warmest Korda partisan, that *The Thief of Bagdad* had been "planned" – it just growed; and while *Colonel Blimp* had been a pictorial success, I looked on it as an old-fashioned film, a relic of the prewar days of which the key was the exquisite photography of Georges Périnal. As for the design, the art direction and the costumes, I had insisted on Uncle Alfred equipping himself with a full team of painters, with the results that we had excellent colour combinations, probably the best harmony between costume and decor that had been achieved up to that point, although Rouben Mamoulian's *Becky Sharp* had been rightly much admired. But I was not satisfied with the modern episodes at all. This was not planning for colour; it was just letting colour happen. I digested the lesson, although I doubt whether Périnal or Junge did, and I swore that when my time came I would make them sit up. Technicolor between the wars had been the brainchild of Dr Kalmus and his wife, Natalie. At first, with a surplus of black and white films, they had a hard time selling the process to Hollywood. There were not many producers with the courage and showmanship of Douglas Fairbanks, Sr, who had employed William Cameron Menzies and Joseph Urban to design his sets, and had made one of the first big feature pictures in Technicolor, as I have mentioned already. But, at that time, Technicolor was only in the two primary colours, and it was Dr Kalmus's intention to include all three colours in his process, and he hoped he would live to see all films made in what was then called Natural Colour. His greatest salesman was James A. Fitzpatrick, who took Technicolor all over the world to make his travelogues, and who was infamous for the inevitable closing line: "And so we say farewell to beautiful Bali" (or wherever it might be).

But it made glorious Technicolor known to the whole world, and when a few first-rate theatre people saw the possibilities, as Mamoulian had, Hollywood began to think there might be something in it. I think that the first English Technicolor three-strip production was *Wings of the Morning*, a simple tale about racing and Ireland, based upon a story by the popular American Irishman Donn Byrne. It was followed by Korda's production of *The Divorce of Lady X*, a comedy starring Merle Oberon, Laurence Olivier and Ralph Richardson, and it was this film which introduced the great Georges Périnal to colour. But Korda didn't really understand colour or he would have used it in *Rembrandt*. The half-tones of *Lady X* were not what he was looking for. His Asiatic soul thirsted for the loaded palette of *The Thief*, while he set British hearts beating with the red uniforms of the soldiers in *The Four Feathers* and *The Drum*.

Now, in the spring of 1945, our time had come. We had a story and a script which called for wizardry and trick work on a grand scale. The way we imagined it, it had to be in colour. In Technicolor. We had four principal parts – two British, two American – which included a real star part for David Niven. We had the approval of the Ministry and the full financial backing of Rank and Davis. We had postponed the film for nearly nine months in order to have Technicolor.

Although we never put people under long-term contract, Erwin Hillier had every right to expect to be given the job. He had never lit a colour picture, but what did that matter? When I gave him *A Canterbury Tale*, he knew that he had my complete confidence. The same with *IKWIG*, a far more difficult job, and he made a triumph of both of them. I hesitated.

Over the years that we had been flirting with Technicolor, I had met Jack Cardifff several times. Kay Harrison had shown me his film *This is Colour*, which had been devised, photographed and directed by Jack Cardiff in association with his bosses. The film was made, of course, to sell Technicolor to the kind of producer who says: "Why should I want Technicolor? It's only one more headache." It was a brilliant little film with stunning colour effects obtained by the simplest means, such as pouring gallons of paint of one primary colour into a whirlpool of another. Naturally, Jack, as Technicolor's star technician, was in early on the discussions about *AMOLAD* and the trick effects which depended on going from full colour in one world to monochrome in another, and back again. Gradually, I realized that I had to have Jack, or someone as inventive and experienced as Jack, throughout the picture.

I compromised. I am no great believer in compromises: someone always gets hurt, deeper than in a clean cut. I knew that both men, Erwin Hillier and Jack Cardiff, were true artists and would rise to the challenge. But the size of the picture made me cautious – not usually an outstanding characteristic of mine. I asked Erwin whether he would work throughout the picture with Jack and share the credit, his name to come first. He asked for a couple of days to think it over. At the same time, I asked Jack whether he would work with Erwin on the same terms. He agreed. Of course, it was an easier decision for him to make than Erwin, who had two big pictures to his credit. And Jack, although he had shot sequences in big colour pictures, had no solo credit.

I told Bill Wall what was in my mind.

"Take Jack," he said. "He's a fucking genius. We'll need as many of the old gang as we can get together. Don't you worry, Guv'nor."

By the Old Gang, Bill Wall meant the tough and experienced bunch of electricians whom he had trained and worked with all through *The Thief of Bagdad* – Wimpy, Popeye, Jock and the others – and whom I had mostly met for the first time in Cornwall when I went down there with Sabu to kick off *The Thief of Bagdad*. Bill Wall had been gaffer, or chief electrician, on *Colonel Blimp* too, and it had been a treat to hear him yelling in his execrable French to Périnal across the set: "*Monsewer! Monsewer! Regardez. Ça va? Oui?*"

Erwin came back and said he couldn't do it. He was a proud man and had struggled a long time, as I well knew, to reach the top. He couldn't see this suggestion in any other way but a put-down. Perhaps he thought I would give way because we loved each other and had been through a great deal together, but I was moving into new worlds of light and colour after the drab realism and khaki of the war. I needed somebody to take off with me into the future. I gave the whole job to Jack.

There were still a few shots with actors to be done on *IKWIG* when I took off for America. Both Emeric and I had been on standby for some weeks, and we were suddenly told that there was only one berth available. It was decided that I should go and wait for him in New York. There was no question of not taking the berth that was offered at that stage of the war. During the war, there were only three ways to get from England to America: you went as one of the sitting ducks in a convoy; you flew in an unheated, unfurnished bomber over the Greenland icecap; or you went by the *Queens*. The last way was much the most popular, even though you slept eight, ten, or sometimes twelve to a cabin. The *Queens*, the *Queen Elizabeth* and the *Queen Mary*, were the fastest ships on the North Atlantic, and had already ferried over, in safety and without even a narrow shave, nearly a million service personnel. When fully loaded, and without undue squeezing, the *Queen Elizabeth* could carry between eight and sixteen thousand men with all their equipment. They usually sailed from "a northern port", which meant either Glasgow or Liverpool, and to another "northern port", which was Halifax, Nova Scotia. The policy for these enormous vessels was for the Navy to escort them with very fast armoured ships until they were well clear of the Irish coast, when they were left to protect themselves with their great speed. In the same manner, they were met off Newfoundland on the other side, and escorted in. As I have said, they were magnificently handled and had an unblemished record throughout the war. Not only their captains and crews, but the designers and engineers of the Cunard Line, had every reason to be proud of themselves. They had designed the ships to be the fastest and most comfortable vessels afloat, in order to win the Blue Riband of the North Atlantic. When the war came, they helped to win that too.

Emeric and I had two good reasons for going to America early in 1945: we had to find our ideal American girl, "June", for *A Matter of Life and Death*, and United Artists had bought the distribution rights of *Colonel Blimp* and wanted to discuss their handling of it with us. Our names were now known on the other side as provocative and puzzling but highly competent film-makers, and several distributors were interested in our new project, because, of course, it had names in it, like David Niven and Raymond Massey, who were known to their public.

The mighty Rank was now the fighting owner of a machine for production, distribution and exhibition of a kind with which the Americans were only too familiar and which they respected. United Artists had been bonny fighters in their day, and they realized the sort of quality that Rank was producing and offering and were the first to make approaches to him. It was part of our mission in going to New York so early in 1945 to follow up and examine a possible partnership with United Artists. They had always been the great independent with a top name for quality and for that reason were desirable as partners, but they were not theatre owners and had only a moderate amount of capital to invest in outside films, and for this reason Rank and Davis, to use John Lennon's inspired phrase "iced them warily".

The "northern port" in my instructions turned out to be, on this occasion, Glasgow. They usually staggered the ports of sailing and receiving, in order to fool the German U-boat squadrons, who were constantly patrolling the Irish Seas. The carrier in which I had a berth was the *Queen Elizabeth* with 12,000 troops aboard, most of them American wounded. They filled every companion-way and deck, most of them in pale pyjamas and a startling selection of dressing gowns – white-faced, sad-looking boys. Our two-berth cabin, sleeping eight at present, was comparatively luxurious. There was a table and a chair, at which I could write all day, and as I had the *AMOLAD* script to go over and in parts rewrite, I was glad of it. The other members of the cabin spent the day patrolling the ship, looking for pals, exercising in the gym, or taking Turkish baths. I wrote. It was like being in a busy monastery. The organization, discipline, meals, etc., were perfect. You would think that this glorious ocean liner had been built and intended to carry 12,000 men as a matter of course. We were all on board for twenty-four hours, then we sailed abruptly and without notice. We crossed the Irish Sea at full speed and arrived on the other side of the Atlantic in about four and half days. I believe that our average speed was about twenty-four knots. I wrote steadily all day and every day, with the usual breaks for meals and exercise. Emeric and I had had numerous conferences while he was writing the script, and I was working from his final draft. The next one – mine – had to be our definitive version, for it was going to be read by many people in America. Emeric had done the historical research and written the story and most of the jokes. I had my medical notes and brought to the script all that I knew and loved about England. I could also see that the spectacular elements of the script must be given due place and prominence. I was determined that our script should not be more than eighty quarto pages. Actually, it turned out to be eighty-four. My furious concentration on the script amused my cabin mates. I think they felt it gave our cabin a certain cachet. But it seemed to me that they were never in it day or night. Americans are great wanderers, gossipers, and loungers. And every deck was a village street with a thousand inhabitants strolling to and fro, smoking, talking and eating candy. When I got writer's cramp I joined the strollers and stopped by a map of the USA which hung on the flat by the main staircase: it was a big map with lots of names on it. A soldier came up, caught my eye and said "hello!" One of the nice things about American boys was the way they said hello – it wasn't to open a conversation, it wasn't because they hadn't anything else to say; it was just a recognition of a fellow human being with a stake in the universe. You could answer or not. We got talking about Minnesota, which was his state and of which he was proud. He was also proud of the other states he knew real well: eleven of them (he was only about twenty-one, tall, rangy, fair and good-looking). After the war he was going to get to know them all. He was on thirty days' leave and his home was Duluth on the shores of Lake Superior, where there was good hunting and fishing all around. I talked of the Lake of the Woods. He was going up there later when he'd got all 48 states under his belt. It was very significant, this passion the young Americans had for seeing every state in the Union. Several boys joined us and to each one he would say: "Well, buddy, where do *you* come from?" They were all Minnesota or Iowa. "I don't like that state", my boy said, "you drive north and south and east and west and northwest to southeast an' – anyway it's just flat." "Arkansaw is all bogs, and Kentucky's all mountains." They leaned all over the map, passionately talking, and owning it as casually as they owned their huge country.

By a coincidence, I am crossing today, Thursday, September 9, 1982, over the Atlantic to America, but I am being ferried in a TWA Boeing 747, and the journey from Frankfurt to JFK Airport will take about seven and a half hours. Because of the rheumatism that I have developed, I am travelling Club Class in great comfort, for if you can stretch your legs and walk about, it makes all the difference.

You will remember that when Emeric and I came to New York for our first peep, we arrived in the dark and left in the dark, like two thieves. Now suddenly we were steaming up the coast of America and silver dirigibles were escorting us on each side. One of them came silently forward, closing in on us, and there was a rush to the port side by every airman taking a walk on deck before breakfast. It was a fine sight with its beautifully proportioned and gleaming silver body, underneath the three-storeyed car with its cat-walks and big square port holes, and its two big propellers, one on each side, but it was treated irreverently by the airmen. I was surrounded by a group of English fighter pilots and aircrews, all with the D.F.C., their hair blowing wildly, their uniforms or battledress ragged but worn with panache; some were in the deep blue of Australia and New Zealand, some were in Air Force blue, but they were from all over the earth and their average age was twenty-three. The air was thick with professional jokes and when the skipper of the dirigible decided to show off they were highly delighted. It was beautifully manoeuvrable but to them, of course, it was like seeing a London bus in the sky. They were cruel to the friendly giant. "Do a stall-turn!" someone jeered. Then as he raised his bow to a 35° climb, a roar of applause. As he turned out of the wind and came right round us: "Now for the shootup. Look out, boys!" A few comedians flung themselves on deck. "Let me have him in my sights for two seconds," mused a pilot with a weird cavalry moustache, "just two seconds. Poor bugger!"

In New York Emeric had insisted that we be booked into the St Regis, presumably because Alex Korda nearly always stayed there. It had a large and comfortable bar for men only. And there were famous Maxfield Parrish murals of unspeakable coyness and ladylike eroticism, which had to be seen to be believed. They belonged to the never-never world of James Branch Cabell, the author of a pseudo-Rabelaisian volume entitled *Jurgen*, and were probably of the same date as the book. There was a dangerous school of American writing in the twenties. It inspired works like *Messer Marco Polo*, and I suppose that John Erskine's *The Private Life of Helen of Troy*, coming some years later, was part of the backwash. There was nothing else precious about the St Regis, which was a typical New York hotel with a busy lobby and filled with brass, copper, marble and solid materials of that kind, and soaring up to a height of thirty storeys on the corner of Fifty-fifth and Fifth Avenue. In the basement was an old-style New York men's hairdresser, or I should say barber, and a urinal with a bootblack to shine your shoes. To my delight, the hotel also had Salvador Dali sitting in the lobby. He sat in a large armchair where he could see and be seen. His thin moustache was waxed to two elegant steel points. Not a hair on his head was out of place. His boots had just been polished and he wore spats. His suit was bizarre but elegant, and he held an eighteenth-century cane between his long fingers. He was obviously waiting for a millionaire to drop into his lap. (I was to see him there again twenty years later, with hardly a whisker changed.) Though I had often seen him on the Riviera, I didn't know him, but I greeted him with effusion.

"Maître! Que faîtes-vous là? On m'a dit que vous étiez arrêtés, vous et Gala. Vous étiez tous les deux prisonniers à Cadaqués."

"Mais tu vois bien, mon cher, que nous sommes ici!"

Of course I knew Dali would not budge an inch without Gala.

"Que fais-tu à Baghdad sur le Hudson?"

I explained my mission and his manner changed perceptibly. He remembered me, if he remembered me at all, as a young freelance photographer on the Côte d'Azur. To learn that I was now a successful producer-director, with the money of the great Arthur Rank behind me, interested him. He became friendly, or at least as friendly as his contacts with other people allowed him to be. I liked Dali, and I admired him for his love and friendship for Lorca, but he never revealed his true self to the world. All the time we were talking, another Dali seemed to stand beside me, and whispered in my ear: "Clever, aren't I? Interesting, bizarre, unusual. A clown or a genius? Do you think I've overdone it a bit, that bow tie, for instance, too much?" Then with a surge of confidence: "But the manner, you must admit the manner is perfect."

There were several messages waiting for me in my room. At the St Regis, you got the messages from a porter, but they also shoved duplicates under your bedroom door. Emeric cabled his love and good luck. Kathleen Byron left a telephone number. Arthur Kelly's secretary from United Artists said that he would call for me at 12:45, and take me to lunch at the 21 club. Ray and Dorothy Massey were in California where Ray, tired of his triumphs in the legitimate theatre, was starting a new career in films.

Emeric and I had seen Betty Field co-starring with Fredric March in Joseph Conrad's *Victory*, and had admired her performance. She seemed to us to be a real actress, sincere, inventive, worth investigating. The John Van Druten play in which she was appearing currently was still on, but I decided not to go and see it on my first night in New York. I wanted to leave the whole day open for whatever might turn up. Arthur W. Kelly arrived punctually, and I went down and met him in the hotel lobby. He was plump, elegantly dressed, bright-eyed and bushy-tailed, and sported a light grey hat. He had a neat little hearing aid in his left ear. He wished to please and was quite charming. He explained that the famous 21 club was only two blocks away, and we could walk there in three minutes. It was a soft spring day, and we walked. That is to say, Arthur walked on the pavement and I walked on air.

The fabulous 21 club was located on the north side of West Fifty-second Street, only a couple of hundred yards from Fifth Avenue. The house was typical brownstone with lots of ironwork painted black, enlivened by the figures of dozens of miniature jockeys wearing the colours of various owners. These miniature figures always give me the creeps. They stood on the pavement on each side of the entrance door and thronged the balcony above it. They all had the eerie and disturbing face of a ventriloquist's dummy. If the intention was to convey a sense of the sporting days of New York, it was a failure. The figures were sinister. The big house had, of course, long ago been converted to the needs of a club and restaurant, regardless of expense. It was rumoured that there were rooms and corridors and tunnels communicating with the sewers. Today, it was a busy, impressive restaurant, with a clientele consisting partly of showbiz and partly of sport. Men were hard-faced; the women even harder-faced, but trying not to show it. The Schindler family, who ran the joint, were cordial, good-looking and poker-faced. I was introduced by Arthur as the English director of a great new colour film, *Colonel Blimp*. I was immediately dubbed "the Colonel", and "the Colonel" I remained for the rest of my stay in New York, for we lunched at the 21 club every day.

The 21 club had been a real speakeasy in Prohibition days, and to this it owed its glamour and its peculiar atmosphere. It had been primarily a men's bar to which women were invited at their own risk. Not that there's anything special about that. It's just that Prohibition made the whole play between the sexes harder, tougher, more realistic. When the Volstead Act was repealed, and liquor came back into the daylight, the main accent was on gambling and sport, which gave the club its peculiar cachet. But the new generation had seen the possibilities of the location and the clients, and had turned the visible part of the club into a first-class restaurant and it certainly was that.

In London before the war, the principal showbiz restaurant was the Ivy. It stood and stands on the corner of St Martin's Lane and Litchfield Street, which runs into Charing Cross Road. Once Jerry and I became film producers, we lunched there almost every day. There was a table by the front entrance – not a large table, a table for about six people – where Noël Coward and Ivor Novello used to lunch with their lady friends on matinée days. There were other tables that were almost always occupied by the same actors or actor-managers, or agents. There was one couple that I shall always remember. They were fat and elderly and very much in love and they always lunched at The Ivy. During those years I used to watch them growing visibly fatter and fatter. The chef at The Ivy was very good. Eventually they burst, I suppose, because they vanished. Some stranger appeared at their customary table. I hope they are together in some other world, fatter and happier than ever, and smiling to know that I remember them much more clearly than all the famous people who were customers of M. Abel and Mario, his *maître d'hôtel*, who started his own restaurant, the Caprice, after the war, and made it as famous in London show business circles as Sardi's in New York.

There are two sorts of clams which you eat in New York: Little Necks and cherrystones. Arthur Kelly was a gourmet and insisted that I try them both. They were served on an extravagant amount of ice. I ate six of one and half a dozen of the other and declared for the Little Necks. I am extravagantly fond of shellfish, although I have been poisoned many times by them. (One time was at the Edinburgh Festival, when I ate a bad oyster before a performance of *Romeo and Juliet*, in the round. Without warning, I fainted, just as Claire Bloom came on. This was reported to her by her friends in due course, but I still maintain it was the oyster.) People drifted up to our table, were introduced, and said "Glad to meet you", or "Say, what's it like over there? Is Britain starving?"

They looked rather astounded at this slim, very English young man, who Arthur said was one of England's great film directors and who looked more like an officer in the cavalry. The amiable Schindlers confused things even more by yelling out as they escorted some other party by: "How you doing, Colonel? OK, Colonel? Looee! Meet the Colonel! He's just arrived from England."

It was all noisy, bewildering, friendly, and completely gratifying after four years of blackout.

Arthur was a perfect host, and he was determined to feed me up, and the elaborate service, with white linen and heavy silver dishes, and telephones brought to your table, and the tremendous noise of New Yorkers talking, was almost more intoxicating than the food and drink. About three o'clock, accompanied by a barrage of "So long, Colonel! Come again, Colonel! See you tomorrow, Colonel!" Arthur and I left the Twenty-One Club and walked the few yards to Fifth Avenue and strolled down it. This was my idea of luxury, and it was also a very emotional moment for me. I had joined the film business through a great company like Metro-Goldwyn-Mayer, and I had always regarded myself as a maker of international films, of films for the world. MGM was my spiritual godfather. I had come to England in 1928 and battled my way through to 1945 as an English film director, neck and neck with my American friends, a citizen of the world. Now here I was in New York, the magic city, on my way to Hollywood, the magic encampment on the shores of the Pacific. Eight years before, when England had no use for me, I had planned to invade Hollywood by the back door, as a poor immigrant. And here I was, sponsored by the millionaire Arthur Rank, with one film finishing and another one starting, and with United Artists, of all people, the company who had fought for the independent producer, director and actor, as my host. We walked down Murray Hill. In those days, the New York telephone exchanges had kept lovely and evocative names which recalled the history of the astounding piece of rock that is Manhattan Island, which far from being flat as the world seems to imagine, twists, turns, rises and falls. Arthur's telephone number was a Murray Hill number, and it will always be a fairy tale name to me.

He introduced me to his secretary, Mrs Ramsay. I was impressed by the fact that she was already a lady of a certain age, very well dressed, highly competent. She was the sort of person you would expect to find running a big department today. *The New Yorker* notwithstanding, secretaries of serious companies were not the leggy buxomy bunch that Peter Arno would have us believe. I admire American women executives and secretaries. If I were an American businessman, I would run for cover. I knew at once that anything Mrs Ramsay organized would stay organized.

At this time, at the end of the war, in 1945, United Artists was still a very big name, but had lost some of its greatest talent – D. W. Griffith, Mary Pickford, Doug Fairbanks – so far as active production was concerned, and Charlie Chaplin was the only one who was continually producing. Arthur Kelly, Charlie Chaplin and his brother Syd, and their countless girlfriends, had all been friends since they were appearing in the music halls in London together. Now that Fred Karno and Mack Sennett had made Charlie a millionaire, the first thing he had thought of was to share all this with his friends. So Arthur W. Kelly was removed from the Chaplin Studio in Hollywood and made president of the United Artists Corporation and sent to New York with his wife, Bozo. Bozo was thin and lively and anxious. Arthur was enterprising and efficient and was soon over in London. There he saw the current projects and immediately saw that ours was the most likely to make some money for United Artists in America.

Arthur bought *Colonel Blimp* for United Artists on sight, and I think he had an option on our other films. Like most people in the film business in those days, he was delighted with it at first view. The film was charming, sophisticated, gripping and in the English language. Good! Splendid! Then the doubts set in. Where was the American public that was charming, witty, sophisticated and intelligent? We could have told him. It was the same public that had recognized Charlie Chaplin as a genius the moment he skipped onto the screen. It was the same public that had made David O. Selznick's production of *Gone With the Wind* the box-office champion of the world. It was the same American public that had instantly recognized the entertainment value of Alfred Hitchcock's films. It is the same public that still goes again and again to see *The Red Shoes* and *Stairway to Heaven*. The real point was not whether there was such a public (we were quite sure there was), but whether it would be allowed to see the films that it wanted to see by the distributors and exhibitors of America. A symptom of this was the desire to change the title of the film, that we had encountered already. Quite often the new title suggested by them was an improvement; but again, quite often, it was not. *The Invaders* is not such a good title for an epic film as *49th Parallel*; *Stairway to Heaven* is not such a good title for a comedy about life and death as *A Matter of Life and Death*. On the other hand, our second film together, *Contraband*, had been retitled as *Blackout* in America by David Selznick, and we had to admit that if we had wanted the film to be well received in America as the kind of film we intended it to be, we should have retitled it ourselves. Colonel Blimp, of course, was a national figure in England, but nowhere else.

I think the basic reason for the American salemen's uneasiness about British films was that they just didn't know how to sell them. At that time the majority of American films were mostly adapted from books, or headlines in the newspapers, or successful Broadway plays. The sales pitch was easy. It was just a question of spending a lot of money buying advertising space. But when films like *In Which We Serve*, Laurence Olivier's *Henry V*, David Lean's *Brief Encounter*, Anthony Asquith's *Way to the Stars*, the Archers' *Life and Death of Colonel Blimp* (these extraordinary films apparently produced under a hail of bombs by people nobody had ever heard of before and moreover in English), were screened by the American salesmen, they lost their nerve.

Before the war, when Alexander Korda had started to make his great films with big star names over the title, they had been equally frightened. He had gone to America with his films every year and had been refused the market. The major film companies were all producing fifty-two films a year, quality or no quality. But when Korda made *The Private Life of Henry VIII*, it was impossible to deny him. The news of the quality of a film like that crashes around the world in a few hours. Closed doors had to be opened to it. It made Charles Laughton a star in America, as well as everywhere else. But this was an exception. Getting desperate, Korda persuaded his backers to send him over to America to buy a controlling interest in the distribution company of United Artists. But even that didn't work. The idea had come too late, and UA no longer had the clout which four famous names had given it in the beginning. Ironically, it was Alex's last great production at Denham, *The Thief of Bagdad*, which made him a fortune in the United States, and a reputation with a whole generation of American filmgoers, because of its glamour, its colour, its optimism, its happiness, at a time when the whole world was trembling with fear. Curiously enough, when Thelma and I were recently in Moscow, we were told the same thing. The United States sent two big colour films to Moscow to entertain Russian children during the war, and one of them was *The Thief of Bagdad*. Time and again I have met people of fifty and over in Russia who remember *The Thief of Bagdad* scene by scene, and the same in the USA.

A further puzzle for the American salesmen was the content of the British films. By the end of the war, every Hollywood studio was pouring out combat films in which familiar faces glared or shouted at us from underneath uniformed caps or battle helmets, while around them the landscape blew up. The British, on the other hand, didn't seem to be interested in the fighting. They were more interested in themselves and their reaction to the war. Combat films were a rarity. They had more scenes

of civilian life than of combat. How to sell these films? Cautiously, the
American buyers tested the water with their toes.

Arthur Kelly had letters to sign and meetings to attend, so the rest of the
day was mine. I wandered about in a dream. Towards evening I found that
I was in the theatre district and I thought I would see a play. One theatre
announced the first night in New York of a play which had been a
sensational success in Chicago. It was called *The Glass Menagerie*. I went
in – and suddenly I became aware that I was watching a masterpiece. I had
never heard of the author, Tennessee Williams, but I knew the name of the
star, Laurette Taylor. She had toured the world for years in a famous
tearjerker, *Peg o' My Heart*. She had played at the Theatre Royal in
Canterbury and I remembered the poster vividly: a full-length picture of
the actress as the impossibly innocent eighteen-year-old heroine of the
play. That was thirty years before, and she was no chicken even then. Now
here she was starring on Broadway in the kind of part that old actresses
dream about when the offers get fewer and fewer. Five minutes after her
entrance, she had that tough audience, critics and all, in the palm of her
hand, and from then on she did what she liked with us, until the final
curtain. Then the storm burst, and that dear, wonderful lady got an
ovation that lasted several minutes. And she came to meet it like a queen,
as if it were her divine right.

As I recall, there were only four parts in the play: the frustrated
daughter, the brother, the man visitor, and the mother. I suppose I should
have taken more notice of the names of the people, the name of the theatre
– I just saw the billboard announcing the Chicago success and walked in
without even looking up at the marquee. When I realized that it was a first
night, I should have looked out for critics whose names I knew, and maybe
other people, but, to tell the truth, I was in a dream. It seemed only natural
to me that on my first day and night in this island city, I should have a
masterpiece served up for me alone, and should see a great star play a
part worthy of her and turn it into a legend. I was floating. To discover
an unknown playwright, as Tennessee Williams was then, was exciting
enough, but to share with that tough audience theatrical history in the
making, and to see the ageing star flare into incandescence when she heard
our love and appreciation and applause, was unforgettable. To share with
her the knowledge that audiences were hers again, to see the assurance and
graciousness with which she accepted the applause, after God knows how
many kicks from life, was a revelation. I seem to remember that, in the days
of her youth and beauty and success, she was not a very good actress. But
she had charm. Now she knew all that life had to offer in the way of kicks
and ha'pence, and she still had the charm. I stood and cheered with the rest
of the audience, I pushed my way through the lobby into the street and
walked a dozen blocks back to the St Regis in an exalted frame of mind. But

I was not surprised. I assumed that things would happen like that on Broadway on any night that I chose to be around.

My second night was not so successful.

As I have said, Miss Betty Field was one of our possibles, and she was playing currently on Broadway. I acted, perhaps, with incredible innocence. It must be remembered that, in London, stage and screen are closely connected, and most of the major studios, both film and television, are within less than an hour's drive from the centre of London. It's perfectly normal for an actor who is in demand to be in all three media at once; so we all knew one another, and during the war we had all worked together and helped each other, and we carried on this way once the pressure was off. Of course, I should have told Arthur Kelly what was in my mind, and he would have telephoned Betty Field's agent, the meeting would have been arranged, either at the agent's office or at some noisy restaurant, and Miss Field and I would have shouted banalities at each other, and that would have been that. Instead, I trotted down to the theatre where she was playing, bought a ticket, went in and saw the show, came out somewhat disgruntled, located the stage door at the end of a sordid passage, and gave my card to the doorman, with a message scribbled on it that I was a producer from London, England. Time passed. A not very prepossessing little man appeared about fifteen yards down the corridor and stared at me. The doorman volunteered that I was "some John looking for Miss Field." I reckoned that "some John" was Runyonese for "stage door Johnny" and I was evidently right, for Miss Field soon appeared, her arms full of flowers and accompanied by the little man, and brushed by me without a word. I murmured an introduction but I don't think it ever reached her ears; it was greeted with a snarl by the little man, who said something offensive about my English accent. They got into a waiting taxi and drove off.

I walked back to the stage door and inquired: "Why didn't you give Miss Field my message?"

"Listen, bud," he said not unamiably, "I'm fucking off home. Why don't you fuck off home too?"

I decided that there was merit in the idea and that Miss Field was not my type. As for the misunderstanding, it was entirely my fault. But there was a world of experience in her eyes and in her body which was a far cry from the kind of wisdom I hoped to find in our American June. The play too had disappointed me. Even for John Van Druten, it was pretty thin. Van Druten plays were fashionable. Their themes, their titles, their actors, were the latest thing. They were mildly interesting, and were well staged and presented by John C. Wilson. They were designed to run for a year, by which time a new one was coming off the assembly line. But with this comedy, the author must have miscalculated. It surely couldn't run a year. It surely shouldn't run at all. However, it was none of my business. I often wonder what might have happened if Miss Field had given me a smile, or handed me a flower, or said "Hello!" or "Hi!" in the way ordinary people do, instead of giving me that sour Broadway rat-race look. Anyhow that was the beginning and end of my career on Broadway as a stage door Johnny.

The next day Kathleen Byron came to see me. She had married a GI, had come over to America with him and was now anxious to get back and take up her career again in England, as an actress. She was another one of John Glidden's discoveries. I had first seen her in his office and then, as I have related, Vernon gave her the part of the Dutch schoolmistress who tells the children the story of Piet Hein who sank the Silver Fleet. It was a good, straightforward performance without any frills or mannerisms. She had remarkable eyes, and her nose was long and thin, as were the bones in her face. She had the look of a zealot, a martyr. I think that her great strength was in the power of her imagination.

We went for a walk in Central Park that day and for many days after that. It was early spring in New York, warm and almost cloudless. We were physically attracted to each other but it didn't seem important. She hoped to return to England if her husband could find a job there, and I told her that if she was there in the autumn, when the film went into production, she could play an angel.

Emeric would soon be here and Arthur Kelly was busy with plans for our journey to the West Coast. He was determined that we should do it in style. In those days, there was a recognized route for VIPs to Hollywood. You booked sleepers on the Twentieth Century Limited from New York to Chicago. In Chicago there was a break of about four hours until you joined the transcontinental express. We had a private drawing room, and for the next three and a half days, with its bell mournfully tolling, its immense cowcatcher scattering the herds of beef cattle to right and to left, the magnificent compound locomotive and its attendant coaches rolled across the United States by the southern route to avoid the Rockies, across the fabled Southwest, through towns named Wichita, Albuquerque and Santa Fe ("The Atchison, Topeka and the Santa Fe"). Finally we arrived in Los Angeles. If you were really VIPs perhaps you were put down at Pasadena, a green and white town before the Hollywood Hills began, which had gradually become the place for the important people to get off to avoid being mobbed by fans and press at the terminal. From Pasadena, the stars, after posing for photographs for the local fans, would be whisked away to mysterious hideouts in the hills, ranch-houses where a swimming pool took the place of a corral and the only beef was on the torsos of the temporary owners. In our case, Arthur explained, we would be whisked to the Beverly Hills Hotel where he had booked two private bungalows. He also warned us in a hushed voice that we were to be invited to dinner at

Pickfair, the twenty-acre estate created by Douglas Fairbanks and Mary Pickford when they were married.

It was sad to think that I could no longer meet my hero Doug. From the first glimpse of him on the screen, I had sensed a kindred spirit. His energy, his optimism, his agility, were mine too. But it was when he embarked upon his great productions *The Mark of Zorro, Robin Hood* and *The Thief of Bagdad* that I felt we had so much in common. A man of the theatre, he had great theatrical style and physical resources, which he brought to the creation of his costume parts. The thing which interested me most and endeared him to me was the way he went after great names in design for his productions. For the first time I heard the names of William Cameron Menzies, Joseph Urban, and Willie Pogany. They were given as much prominence by the publicity department as the star himself. From Fairbanks, I learnt to be satisfied with nothing but the best. Who else would have thought of casting Wallace Beery as Richard the Lion-Heart? And Doug always chose directors who *were* directors: men like Allan Dwan, Sam Taylor and Raoul Walsh. Even today it makes me furious to think that I only missed directing Doug Fairbanks by two years. He was making *The Private Life of Don Juan* in 1934, two years before I made *The Edge of the World* on Foula. Doug's picture was a failure—apparently it was about an ageing Don Juan, hardly a suitable thing for Doug, who had never been a bedroom athlete—but if I'd had the handling of it, I would not have allowed him to make a failure of it.

Three years later, in 1939, he was dead, as Hitler was putting an end to the old easygoing world of which Doug had been a hero.

Al Parker, who had directed *The Black Pirate* with Doug, adored him. He told me once that they were walking down Park Lane in London in the thirties, when Doug was already eclipsed by the all-singing, all-talking, all-dancing, all-murdering new Hollywood. It was late at night, and a muffled-up passer-by said "Goodnight, Doug" as he went by and turned into Brook Street. Doug called "Goodnight fella" and said to Al Parker: "You see? They still remember me."

When he told me the story afterwards Al almost spat the words: "And only five years before he had been the greatest star in the world."

In the great movie business which the talkies had created, and of which United Artists had been one of the founders, the writer and director were becoming as important as the star actor and actress. Hollywood was churning out war films and would continue to do so for the next five years. We had never made what I would describe as a combat film. We left that to John Wayne. And we had already been discussing the kind of big colour production that we would make after the war. We didn't talk about it, but we were confident about what we would do and what we ought to do. This gave us authority. Competence is rare in the film business. I dare say that if we had wanted to, Emeric and I, with the backing of Rank, could have taken over United Artists. They were still a big and successful company, producers and distributors of films, with many millions of capital at their backs, but of the founder creators D. W. Griffith was dead, Doug Fairbanks was dead, Mary Pickford, no dummy, was prudently silent. And Charles Chaplin, who had refused to be stampeded by the talkies, and had realized that a great clown needs sound-effects and music, but not dialogue, had continued to make enormously successful feature comedies, which were essentially silent films. He was the only one of the four still active, and being as far-sighted as he was, he was already acquiring all the negatives of his old films that he could lay his hands on, for it was already clear that fashions might come and go, but pantomime would be entertainment forever; and who knows, perhaps that perceptive and extraordinary genius could already imagine that a time might come, fifty years later, when some of the great silent films would be exhibited again, accompanied by orchestral music and sound-effects, and audiences would discover for themselves that a great entertainment medium had been kept like a prince in chains by greedy and vulgar men.

Do I digress? Well, I digress. This book is not a history of the movie business, but the story of one man's love-hate relationship with it. Art has its historian in every century. From Benvenuto Cellini to Kenneth Clark, we learn the most from their personal memories, experiences, opinions. Do I claim to sit with the Masters? Yes, I do. I served my apprenticeship and I became a master in my chosen profession in the twentieth century. I am writing this lengthy book because I conceive of it as my duty to do so, but I should be making a film about it.

Emeric arrived in New York and at once went shopping. Meanwhile I had had my final version of the script typed by a firm somewhere near Times Square, who rolled off about twenty copies. It was a very neat job with a small but legible typeface, and a dark green cover, and I still have one of them. Emeric looked a little dismayed when he saw how thin the script had become, but when he read it he was enthusiastic. He liked slashing straight into the love scene after the prologue and he liked the quotations I had chosen for David to spout, and the medical scenes and the new jokes. His ear is infallible. We decided this version was quite good enough to pass around, and so there was nothing further to keep us in New York.

On his arrival, Emeric had given me a letter from Frankie. She said that we were going to have a child, probably in September. It was a wonderfully typical letter, proud and laconic, careful to show no emotion. During Emeric's brief stay in New York we saw a lot of Arthur and Bozo. She is mentioned in Charlie Chaplin's book as the daughter of Jay Gould, the famous financier and racehorse owner. She was direct and funny, and we were to see much more of her later on in Europe. Arthur gave us a farewell dinner at the 21 club, at which Emeric was introduced as "the Senator". I regret to say that both the Senator and the Colonel got a little high that evening (not that Emeric ever shows it). Arthur saw us all off on the sixteen-hour journey to Chicago, smiling and urbane as usual. I believe that he had a fresh boutonnière in his lapel. No doubt he sighed with relief when the train pulled out. We had been lively guests.

In case anybody should wonder where the money came from for our shopping expeditions – Emeric is a great buyer of gadgets, particularly household gadgets, and I am a great buyer of ladies' gloves, coloured gloves, particularly luxurious items after five years of war, and I bought twenty-seven pairs for Frankie, short gloves, long gloves, elbow-length gloves – I should explain that on our arrival an envelope was pressed into our hands containing a thick wad of bills, which represented petty cash to United Artists and unheard-of affluence to us. We were told that this was "spending money." It seemed to us one of the finest inventions we had ever struck since we began in the film business. After all, what is money for but to be spent? Ever since we got into the big time, we had been paying handsome sums to artists and technicians on our films, without worrying about the fact that we were barely receiving a living wage ourselves. We were getting our own way and we were promised a percentage of the profits of the films, if any. In wartime that was fair enough, but we were beginning to suspect that we were selling our talents too cheaply. It was nice to have a lot of dollars to spend, and we spent them. At about this time, New York was full of tycoons on the make or break, and I remember Emeric was asked by one of them to take shares in an interesting project. He refused, explaining that he couldn't afford it. The promoter asked sympathetically: "Have you got a dollar problem?" To which Emeric answered truthfully: "No, we have a sterling problem."

Up to now, it had escaped our attention that our market value had increased, or that we had a market value at all. On present achievement, we had become part of the international world of films.

This was a little outside Arthur Kelly's scope. He was a film distributor, not a film-maker, but it was brought forcibly to our attention by Bill Burnside, who handled public relations for Arthur Rank in California and was a charmer and one of the best-informed men I have ever met. He was a little too much given to stating that everyone from the Aga Khan to Albert Schweitzer was his personal friend, but then it usually turned out that they were. He introduced me to the poems of Robinson Jeffers, and while I was reading them I told him that I wanted to meet Alfred Hitchcock again. Hitch had been in California all through the war. In five minutes he was on the line, and I heard once again that rich, plummy Cockney, voice:

"Hello, young man! Alma will call for you tomorrow morning at ten o'clock precisely, in front of your Beverly Hills Hotel. Be punctual, because they won't let her park there. Mr David O. Selznick is inviting you to lunch. See you tomorrow."

Miraculous to say, Alma was still Hitch's wife, and still wrote his screenplays under her own name, Alma Reville. I reported the Selznick invitation to Emeric. Bill looked pleased. "You two boys are *Hot*," he said.

Our transcontinental railway journey, so carefully prepared by Arthur, had been a fascinating experience in more ways than one. American railroad trains were massive, masculine and comfortable. It was a luxurious experience to feel the days and nights come slowly up and pass by under our wheels. The stops for passengers, water, and animals on the rail, were of a Biblical simplicity. It was heaven to sit in the Observation Car at the rear of the train and watch America go by, hour after hour and day after day. We crossed the plains and climbed into the high, clean air of New Mexico.

The most delightful surprise that we had on that transcontinental journey was the discovery that our fellow passenger in one of the other drawing rooms was none other than Fritz Lang, the German movie director who had been my idol ever since I saw his two-part saga, *The Nibelungen* somewhere about 1923 or 1924. *Metropolis, Destiny, The Girl in the Moon, The Spy* and *Doctor Mabuse*, and the sequels quickly followed, dazzling and bewitching me. Here was something new! It was a talent that could learn from legends, from history and from the theatre to enrich the cinema. Here was an artist of such detachment that he could make, plan and direct a subject like *M*, the film about a child-murderer (an actual human being who existed once in Düsseldorf), and who could yet show compassion for a deranged, sympathetic being. The part was played by Peter Lorre, a minor German actor who became a star on the strength of *M*. I have often thought that my own compassion for the killer in the film *Peeping Tom* echoes Fritz Lang's for the wretched little man in his film. I was half confirmed in this the other day when somebody who knows both films remarked upon the physcial likeness between Peter Lorre and Karl Böhm. There is no physical likeness between these two great actors, but in both cases the hand of the potter has slipped, and through no fault of their own both young men are driven to kill and kill and kill. And it is their calm acceptance of the curse upon them which disturbs people, and especially critics, who find themselves unable to praise or blame, so choose to blame. In my case I was hounded out of Wardour Street and Pinewood Studios and had to seek my fortune elsewhere. I seem to remember that there was an outcry against Fritz Lang when *M* was first exhibited in England; but he was a foreigner and a German, so it died down.

Anyway, there was this great director and charming man, our fellow

passenger, and we spent most of the journey in each other's drawing rooms, ordering extravagant and unlikely meals from the delighted chef, and drinking as much as was bad for us. We had many points of contact, for I knew all of Lang's films by heart, as a moviemaker should, and Emeric and he had many mutual acquaintances in spite of the age gap between them, and the fact that Emeric was an obscure screenwriter at the time Lang was one of the greatest directors in the world, and the pride of the UFA Studios. When Hitler's purges started, Lang had gone with many other Germans to Hollywood where he had made a new career, adjusting his peculiar vision of people and things to the American scene. He had hilarious stories to tell about his own experiences and those of other famous German actors and technicians known intimately by him and by Emeric. The adventures of Rheinhold Schunzel alone would have made a book.

We had a wonderful trip. But the fact that Fritz Lang had made many films in Hollywood, and many very good ones – but no great ones – struck a warning note. If the maker of *Metropolis* and of *Doctor Mabuse* was not allowed to have a free hand in Hollywood, who could?

The Beverly Hills Hotel is intimate, but extravagant, luxurious, casual and colourful. It stands on a terraced hillside where four magnificent avenues meet. I say stands, but it would be more accurate to say it wanders. It started as a hotel and has become a village. There are bungalows, tennis courts and swimming pools concealed among the palms. The hotel itself is on several levels and one can lose one's way very easily. It is very pleasant to lose one's way in the Beverly Hills Hotel.

The long avenues or drives which meet in front of the hotel are lined with stately palms sixty feet high. A coconut or date palm has to be constantly trimmed and tailored; the gardeners that oversee this, must curse the day that they were planted. Beautiful villas line all the drives, and the place is alive with guard dogs and private police, but there was one house I particularly wished to visit. It stands on an island where two drives meet almost opposite the Beverly Hills Hotel. It is the house that Harry Lachman bought when he first came to Hollywood with a great reputation from his work in England and France, and where he and his wife Quon Tai had given such fabulous and famous parties, only to have his new career blasted and ruined through some ridiculous argument with the head of the studio he was working for. Harry was a great painter and a true artist and he had a devil of a temper when roused. I had heard vaguely, through mutual friends, that he had gone back to painting and had also been highly successful in the antique business, bringing his excellent taste to the service of the new millionaires who were all battling each other for Second Empire furniture and third-rate paintings. I could just imagine Harry's sardonic eyes – he had beautiful, slanting, observant eyes – as he listened to the knowledgeable comments of his victims while pocketing their five-figure cheques. I looked forward to meeting Harry again, and I hoped he would be glad to see me.

Bill Burnside met us at Pasadena and drove us to Beverly Hills, and was thrilled by our coming, and was even more thrilled by the reaction which it had stirred among the big names of Hollywood.

"You see, they all feel guilty from having it so soft while the rest of the world was at war. They'll do anything for you. I have already spread the news that you are looking for an all-American girl to co-star with David Niven, and every studio is grooming some floozy or other for the part. Hal Wallis has already pigeonholed his latest discovery for the part."

"What's her name?"

"Lizabeth Scott. But wait until you meet David O. Selznick. He has a stable full, all raring to go."

I had rather expected this. It was one of the reasons why I had wanted to see Hitchcock as soon as possible. We needed a friend – a friend who was afraid of nobody; a friend to whom we could talk sensibly: Hitch.

Punctually at ten o'clock the next morning, a large, open, spotless convertible driven by a diminutive woman in slacks and shirt drew up at the Beverly Hills Hotel, where we were waiting. Alma had undergone the usual transformation of bright little self-effacing English wives who accompanied their husbands to California. She had always been popular as Hitch's constant companion and collaborator, but now she was a personality in her own right. Her brown hands and feet in her tan sandals were firmly in control of the huge machine. She reached over and opened the glittering door as we moved forward.

"Plenty of room for three in front."

There was room for four. I introduced Emeric as we climbed in and the door was closed behind us by the doorman ... *kerchunk!* ... like the sound of the closing of the breech block of a naval gun. The machine purred forward along the avenues of palm trees, just like in a Raymond Chandler story. Alma drove casually and chatted with animation. She said how delighted both she and Hitch had been that we had wanted to see them first on our arrival in Hollywood. She paid us compliments on our films, which she had seen, and she said how impressed and curious Hollywood had become over the splendid films that were coming out of wartime England, nearly all of them made by unknown names. Altogether she made us feel pretty good. After five years of saying to each other "Well, partner, we'll do better next time," we felt we could absorb any amount of praise.

At this particular point in his brilliant independent career, Hitchcock was unhappy. David O. Selznick had brought him over to America to direct *Rebecca*, and although it wasn't a Hitchcock film in the true sense of the word, it was such brilliant entertainment and wonderful melodrama, and produced with such richness and enthusiasm by Selznick, that it had been a smash hit and Hitchock had been with Selznick ever since. And although he yearned to be his own master (which was, of course, the only way Hitchcock could be Hitchcock), and although many subjects, like *The Paradine Case*, were assigned to him and were predictably disasters, there seemed to be nobody else in the Hollywood of those days capable of understanding him and working with his unique talent. It is greatly to the credit of Universal Pictures and Lew Wasserman, the president, that once they had persuaded Hitchcock to work with them, they gave him *carte blanche* in choice of subject and casting. It was obvious he had a real home for his enormous talent at the end of his life.

But that was twenty-five years later. In 1945 he was still with Selznick, working on *Spellbound*, while secretly making exclusive agreements with box-office stars like Ingrid Bergman and Cary Grant. In the Hollywood of those days, it was the big stars that called the tune, and Hitch felt he could play that game as well as Selznick. In spite of all the legends about Hitch – that he called actors cattle, and never told them how he was going to edit their performances – he was not only popular, but beloved by the big stars. They sensed an egotism as strong as their own. They joined forces with Hitch, not only to get their own way, but to make life more exciting. All this I learned later from Hitch over dinner, interlarded with sarcastic lampooning of the Hollywood great, dirty stories, and excellent food, for Hitch had always loved his stomach. He also loved telling filthy stories. The filthier the better; for like all artists who spend a great deal of time inside their own head, he was rather shy in company and so enjoyed embarrassing other people.

The Selznick International studios were situated in Culver City close to the mammoth studios of Metro-Goldwyn-Mayer – "*Ars Gratia Artis*" – founded by Louis B. Mayer, the father-in-law of David O. Selznick. Mayer's daughter, Irene, was a chip off the old block, and later on she would get a divorce from David; but at the time we were there, the alliance was politically sound, although domestically it may have been rocking a bit.

The Selznick studios had a frontage copied from an old Southern mansion, with white pillars. Wisteria and magnolia dripped all over the place and the social effect was pleasant and quite unlike Hollywood. Behind this façade there were offices and projection theatres and a busy little studio with several little stages, ideal for the kind of independent productions for which David already had a name. An assistant parked the car for Alma, and we went in to see Hitch. He awaited us in his office.

"Hello boys!" was his greeting. "I suppose you realize that you have commited an act of *lèse-majesté* in inviting yourself to visit this studio without waiting to be asked first. You have come to see me and not Mr

Selznick, who is pacing up and down now in his office, to find a way out of your diplomatic *faux pas*." "Don't mind him," said Alma. "Tell him what you've just been telling me."

The great, bland rosy face listened, while I explained the kind of girl we were looking for. Hitch mused:

"Simple, sensible and pretty, and looks good in uniform. Um. All the studios and all the agents know about you coming. Do you realize the sort of buxomy hopeful you will be asked to interview during the next few days?"

I mentioned Veronica Lake.

"Quite so. Mr Selznick, I fancy, also has a few young ladies awaiting your pleasure. There is one in particular he will want you to see. She is very talented as far as mammary development is concerned. At the request of Mr Selznick, I made a test of her yesterday. It was a . . ."

He paused. We listened, interested.

"There was a girl in that test," he said slowly, "who might very well be the girl you are looking for." He thought this over. "Sensible, pretty, could be the girl next door, can act, good voice, good legs."

He spoke on an intercom. "Bring me the file on those tests we did yesterday, please."

"Can we see the test?" I asked. "Can you run it for us?"

"It wouldn't tell you very much, Micky," said Hitchcock blandly. "She wasn't acting beside this other floozy up there on the screen. She was feeding Miss Ingrid Bergman's lines to her from behind the camera."

We stared at him, at each other, and at Alma, who nodded cheerfully.

"Is she a Californian?" I inquired.

"No. She's a lady."

The assistant returned with the file and Hitch glanced at it. "Yerss. Theatrical experience. Has been under contract to Mr Selznick for two years. Her contract is not being renewed."

He looked at us benevolently. "Would you like the name of her agent?" he inquired.

"What's her name?" I asked.

"Kim Hunter."

"Who's her agent?" I inquired warily.

"Nobody you have ever heard of." I doubt very much whether he had even heard of him himself. "But he will bring Miss Hunter to your hotel this evening between five and six. Don't say anything to anyone until you have met her."

There was an agreeable air of conspiracy about this which was very cheering. A telephone gave a discreet buzz. It was a direct line to the Presence. Hitchcock said: "Yes, David. Yes, they are here. Yes, they are anxious to meet you."

Hitch made no attempt to accompany us. With the end of the war in sight, he had no intention of playing second fiddle any more. As we got up, he said casually: "Boys, you are dining with us tonight. A production car will come and pick you up. I'm sure you would like to see the famous Mike Romanoff's."

"Will Michael Arlen be dining there?" I asked, remembering my gossip columns.

"I expect so. He usually is. I remembered that you admired his short stories, Micky, particularly the London ones."

"Yes," I answered, thinking that quite a lot of us in London had thought that this young Armenian writer, Dikran Kuyumjian, who called himself Michael Arlen, and who brought something quite special to the English novel, would develop into another Dostoevsky. But *The Green Hat*, his best-selling novel that had been made into a film with Greta Garbo, had called him to Hollywood and that had seemed to be that, for apart from *Man's Mortality*, a pessimistic novel of remarkable power and little commercial success, he had published little else.

David O. Selznick, with whom we were to work later, was a big man in every sense. He thought big, he talked big, he was big, but he wasn't quite as big as he thought. No one could be that. He sniffed benzadrine to keep awake and took sedatives to go to sleep. He had great ambitions and considerable artistic flair. You can sense his powers and his limitations in pictures like *David Copperfield, Little Women, Duel in the Sun,* and *Portrait of Jennie*, but he never had the guts to direct a picture himself. He shunned the responsibility. He preferred to spend hours and days of his life dictating memos telling other people how to direct films. This made him rather a pathetic figure. His *magnum opus, Gone With the Wind*, was a different case, and a remarkable achievement on his part. The mammoth book had become a mammoth success, and was obviously destined to be a mammoth film. Selznick was not afraid to produce a four-hour picture, although his father-in-law, Louis B. Mayer, thought he was mad.

Selznick also put most of his personal fortune into the completion guarantee for the film, and even sacrificed a percentage of his interest in the profits in order to get Clark Gable, the top box-office star of the day, to play Rhett Butler. I seem to remember that Selznick started to do the film with George Cukor, a subtle director and a fine diplomat, but that Clark Gable, coming into the picture, insisted on having Victor Fleming to direct. Fleming was a formidable character, a big, full-blooded romantic man, who liked working with the big male stars of Hollywood because they acted out his own fantasies for him. I have always admired his films enormously. But bringing Fleming into the making of *Gone With the Wind* must have made it difficult for Selznick to project himself as the real director of the film. Sensitive and unsure of himself, as he was all his life, Selznick was no match for those two extroverts Fleming and Gable.

I think I may say that we saw through his pretensions right away, and liked him for them. He was so eager to go one better than everybody over everything. He was so eager to understand things that were not to be understood, only appreciated. Art made no impression on him, only size. He saw himself as a common man, and if he didn't understand something over which perhaps the director had been slaving for weeks, or perhaps months, out it would go. That is what was happening on *Spellbound*, in which Bergman played the psychiatric doctor, and Gregory Peck the patient. Hitch, to my delight, had hired Salvador Dali to work with him on the dream sequences (or perhaps it was Selznick who had hired Dali, I'm not sure about this, I only know what happened later). Hitch showed us two or three versions of the nightmare dream sequences, and very exciting they were, but I hope that Hitchcock's script of these sequences, and the unused takes of the shots, exist in the Selznick archives. I am sure they would be valuable to students, for very little of them is left in the finished film. I was impressed by Gregory Peck, a new face in films, and asked Selznick what his plans were, knowing that Peck came from the New York stage, and wondering if later he might be visiting England in a play.

"Oh, he's all cut up," answered Selznick vaguely.

This blood-curdling phrase meant literally what it said. Young Peck had been signed to a twenty-picture contract by Selznick, and each segment of him, like slices of a pie, had been traded with other studios and producers, and with leading ladies ravenous for a new leading man. There was a ruthless, cold-bloodedness about the operation. To quote Flanders and Swann, "Eating people is wrong."

A great deal has been written and said about David O. Selznick. He was a monster, but in those roaring years before the war, when he was rising to power, Hollywood was terrorized by monsters, and, as usual, David was determined to go one better than anyone else. Socially, he was such a disaster that one could hardly believe it was true. But he was very likeable, I suppose because he aimed high. But how erratic was his aim! How naïve were the judgments upon which he based his decisions! Later on, when we worked with him, I tended to ignore his advice and opinions, which was a mistake. Hitch, that great diplomat, knew how to handle him and puzzled him so, that he retained David's respect long after he became his own producer. Carol Reed also handled Selznick very cleverly on *The Third Man*, which he was co-producing with Korda. Carol would phone him up in the middle of the night, and ask his advice on every step of the picture, and then go on entirely in his own way.

One last revealing glimpse of this mythical monster – Selznick took us into one of the sound stages where they were shooting sequences for *Duel in the Sun*. Gregory Peck was on the set and I think Joseph Cotten, but I don't remember meeting Jennifer Jones at that time. King Vidor, whose work I respected and admired, was directing. This was a Technicolor picture, I think his first. We talked about our mutual friend, Gordon Avil, John Seitz's assistant cameraman, who had been so kind to me in Nice at the Victorine Studios when I joined MGM in 1925. Gordon gave me my first glimpse of the simplicity and kindness of the top American craftsmen. King Vidor had given him his first chance to light a picture when he made the all-black, black and white film *Hallelujah*. I think I knew the cameraman already – it may have been Hal Rossen. We were introduced to the actors, and I noticed a prominent and familiar figure at the side of the set. I had the impression he was not seated in the production chair, but leaning on a table, or perhaps seated upon a shooting stick, watching us with a mournful, but sardonic eye. It was Josef von Sternberg.

We greeted the Master, the creator of the legend of Marlene Dietrich, with reverence, for we knew what a tremendous influence his films, both silent and sound, had had upon European film-makers. David muttered some introduction, saying: "Joe is helping out on the film."

I glanced at Vidor, who remained impassive. Only either a supreme optimist, or a complete idiot like David, would have tried to drive in double harness the romantic realism of King Vidor, the champion of the common man, and the romantic kitsch of von Sternberg, the exploiter of female eroticism. Sternberg's world never existed, and was fuel-fed by his sense of humour. Vidor's world – *Street Scene, The Crowd* – was as rich as Victor Hugo's. Both of these craftsmen were masters of the camera – their styles entirely different: Vidor a Goya, Sternberg a Renoir. I wondered if the two directors ever spoke to each other, and what they really thought of each other. This reflection had obviously not occurred to David, who seemed perfectly happy with the *mésalliance*.

I said to Gregory Peck: "I like those jodhpurs you are wearing. They are better than jeans. Do you have them made for you?"

He looked at me as if he thought I was mad, and said: "There's half a dozen stores west of Hollywood and Vine where you can buy them for $4.90." He then lounged elegantly away, obviously thinking he had been talking to a half-wit. Later on, I followed his advice and bought myself a pair of the admired pants. They were very well cut about the seat and on the legs, and they still are, but the waist, alas, is a tight fit today.

Before we left his studio, David showed us some sequences from *Duel in the Sun*. He was obviously very proud of the picture, and rightly, in the sequences which we saw, which were the rape scene and the duel scene at the end of the picture, in which Jennifer Jones is crawling up the mountain with a rifle to fight it out with her love. David showed us hundreds of feet showing the poor girl crawling on hands and knees up the most horrible

rocky path, dragging a rifle, her hands and knees torn and bleeding. David
didn't actually smack his lips over the power which he had over this
beautiful girl, tearing herself to pieces for the sake of her – shall we say art?
He was too interested in our reactions. I ventured the opinion that she had
guts. He nodded with pasha-like detachment towards the screen, and
murmured: "Yeah . . . she sure took a beating that day."

As we sat down and ordered a magnificent lunch at the Beverly Hills
Hotel, the telephone was brought to our table and plugged in. It was Kim
Hunter's agent and we arranged that he should bring her to one of the
bungalows at five-thirty. In the afternoon, while Emeric phoned dozens of
old friends, I strolled across to call on Harry Lachman and I nearly got
killed twice crossing the Drive, although the distance can't have been more
than two or three hundred yards. Nobody walks in Hollywood, and
particularly not in Beverly Hills. If the drivers do see you, they think it is a
mirage. Harry's house was large, ugly, and obviously very comfortable, it
also had a huge kitchen garden, as well as the front garden and short drive,
with the usual palm trees, oleanders, etc. He had bought it cheap when he
came to Hollywood in 1939, but it was worth a fortune today. Both he and
Quon Tai were away for a few days.

At half-past five, we were both sitting in Emeric's bungalow when the
agent arrived with his client. After a few words alone with us, he went to
the door and opened it, and the girl we had been looking for to play June
walked into the room. Hitch had been right. Kim Hunter had chestnut hair
and green eyes. She was brave, pretty and sensible, and very well put
together and weighed about one hundred pounds. Although only about
twenty-two, she was obviously an experienced actress. When she spoke,
her voice was delightful. When she acted, imagination and intelligence
showed in every line she spoke. Whatever accent she may have had for
American ears, it was charming to English ones. We asked her a few
perfunctory questions, mainly to put her at ease, as neither of us had the
slightest doubt about her – although, remembering Hitchcock's warning,
we told both her and her agent that we would let them know in a few days.
We asked Kim whether she had any objection to coming to England in
wartime, and she said: "Not in the least."

The war had brought her family to California, and if the war was now
going to take her to London, she couldn't be more interested. I found her
spirit delightful. That clever old Hitch!

It turned out later, when we were talking over dinner at Mike
Romanoff's, that she had been assigned to speak Ingrid Bergman's lines
during a series of tests for parts in *Spellbound*, which Hitch had been asked
to conduct.

I have just been speaking to Kim on the phone in New York in 1982,
and she said: "Hitch was rather like you. You are both rather like each

other in many ways. He would sit there in his chair with his hands together, twiddling his thumbs, and talking to these young actors about the part at great length, explaining who they were, what they were feeling, what they were supposed to be doing, making it as easy as possible for them, before actually shooting anything. After all that, he would turn to me and say: 'I'm sure that Miss Hunter would agree with what I have just said, wouldn't you, Miss Hunter?' and then I would turn purple and my feet would freeze and my palms were moist and I would stammer something, and then we would do the test."

But to an old hand like Hitch, I can see that two or three days of working on the main scenes of the picture with Kim understudying the lead would give him a very clear idea of her capacities. Anyway, we were all delighted with each other that evening at Romanoff's, and Hitch chose all the wines with great care, and we toasted him and Alma and Pat, his daughter. And Michael Arlen was dining at Romanoff's that night and I was introduced to him and told him I considered his novel *Man's Mortality* a much-neglected book. He agreed with me, but didn't seem too depressed about it. He was a rather smart-looking man and dining with a smart-looking woman, both of them carefully dressed. I didn't tell him I was proud to meet the young author of *London Venture, Piracy, These Charming People,* and *Young Men in Love.* But I was.

Although our mission was accomplished, we stayed a few more days in Hollywood, visiting the studios, meeting people and being made much of. Hollywood can be charmingly hospitable when it wants. Emeric had a number of people he wanted to see who were now living on the Coast, among them his first wife, Agi. I had two notable experiences I would not have missed for anything. The first was meeting Peggy Jackson, Jerry Jackson's widow, shopping in the Farmer's Market, known all over the world as the market where the stars do their shopping. It's a huge market, but we fell into each other's arms as naturally and inevitably as if it were Brewer Street, Soho. Of course, I knew that my old partner had died in Hollywood early in the war, I think in 1940, but I knew none of the details and was longing to hear about it and him. I loved Jerry always, and without him I would never have made the small name I had, which led to Joe Rock financing me to make *The Edge of the World,* the start of all my fortunes.

Peggy's story was short and bitter. When Irving Asher left Warner Brothers' Teddington Studios to produce four films for Korda and Columbia Pictures at Denham Studios, of which you will remember *The Spy in Black* was one, it looked like a good move. The empty seat he left behind him seemed a desirable one. He and Jerry were friends and had worked together and he recommended Jerry for the job. He got it. Although he had the job, he hadn't yet got a contract, and he was told he would have to come to New York in the New Year of 1939 and discuss it. Meanwhile he was confirmed as acting head of production, and got on with the job. It was during this time that he commissioned Emeric and me to write and direct the two films I have already written about.

For Jerry, who had always been an independent producer, it was a step up in money and in authority. He set to work at once to upgrade the quality of the production, hoping eventually to follow in Irving's footsteps into the big time. By this time he and Peggy were married and planning to have a baby.

I have told how Jerry came to the rescue when I started to shoot *The Spy in Black*, and convinced Irving that there are more ways than one of shooting a film. We kept in touch during shooting. Then he went to New York for Christmas, partly as a duty visit to his family. (I have already hinted that Jerry's New York Jewish family were less than enthusiastic about his marrying a *goy*.) It was also to confirm his appointment as head of Warner Brothers' British production, and sign a three-year contract. He went to New York at their suggestion. They paid for his fare and Peggy's, which was standard practice at the holiday season. So things looked good. But this was the Christmas of 1938, the Christmas which followed the Munich Agreement and the betrayal of Czechoslovakia, and, unknown to Jerry, talks were going on among the Warner brothers about pulling out of Europe before Dr Goebbels took them over. It was easy enough to make plans for the evacuation of a few distribution offices, but an active studio in production, with contracts with technicians and artists, was another matter. It must be remembered that to an American in those days, Hitler could not only gobble up Europe, but little England as well, and whenever he so pleased. I think that most of the American executives working in London were aware of this. Jerry had been living in England for ten years and had made his career as a producer in England, and like most Englishmen themselves he refused to admit the possibility of war and invasion. The attitude of England at this time can best be summed up as apathetic.

Jerry was single-minded. He wanted that job as head of Warners' production, that was all he thought about. He didn't understand why everyone was so pleasant to him in New York, but at the same time, whenever he wanted to see an executive, they had just left for Florida. His family, of course, didn't want him to go back at all, and were quite convinced that he would walk straight into a concentration camp. In the end, he had to return with Peggy to England, accompanied by lots of encouragement and good wishes from the top executives, but still with no contract signed.

Emeric and I saw quite a bit of Jerry while we were writing *Caesar's Wife* and *Fathers and Sons*, and we met briefly in Piccadilly just before I started work on *The Thief of Bagdad*. Americans in executive positions in Europe were already being warned to leave for the USA with their families, as they might find it difficult to get out later. Jerry couldn't make up his mind whether to stay or go. Like most people in the film business, he was concerned that the whole UK film business would vanish like a mirage if war was declared, and he felt that he should consolidate his position with the head office in New York before that happened. At the same time, as an American who loved England, and in many ways was more English than American, he hated the thought of going. Peggy's baby was expected in September, which made the decision even more difficult. We walked down Piccadilly. We had been through a lot together. I loved him, and admired him, and was sorry for him but it was a time when every man had to make his own decisions. That was the last time I saw him.

Jerry and Irving Asher had held several councils of war during 1939. Irving had finished and delivered his film for Alex and Columbia, and with considerable success, and had no doubt that he would be recalled to Hollywood, either to continue as producer with Warners, or with one of their rivals and associates, for at that time all the Hollywood companies were combining to keep the film business going and to find jobs for returning exiles. It was all very well for Irving, but it was small comfort for Jerry, who saw his job at Teddington diminishing day by day into a French Foreign Legion last stand, with him as Beau Geste. Warners would recall everybody, close the studio and he would have to shift for himself, having no contract. Having the comfortable knowledge that *The Spy in Black* was a smash hit in Leicester Square, and that the film was being rushed out in America (entitled *U-Boat 29*), Irving advised Jerry to go back to America and leave Peggy and her child in New York with Jerry's family so that he could come out to Hollywood, where Irving would introduce him around and possibly have a job waiting for him. He couldn't have been nicer, or more encouraging. Irving was fundamentally kind-hearted, but he was promising more than he could perform.

Sarah Jackson was born on September 8, one week after Chamberlain declared war. At that time I was already shooting the aerial sequences of *The Lion Has Wings*, planning to write and make *Contraband*, and promising to visit Mrs Seton Gordon on Skye before the end of the month. From that moment on I was going a blue streak, and by March or April Emeric and I were already on our way to Canada to write and plan *49th Parallel*. We might very well have been fellow passengers with Peggy and Sarah in one of the Drunken Duchesses, because she crossed with the baby and a nurse on one of them, and Jerry went on an American ship all alone. They were reunited in Montreal. Jerry can't have had an easy moment on the trip, because this was the time of some of the worst outrages by submarines on passenger ships.

Anyway, the first part of the programme in New York was a disaster. Jerry failed to get any compensation from Warner Brothers for the loss of his job in England, and they had nothing for him either in New York or on the Coast. Living with his mother and two sisters, in spite of the baby, was not a social success for the young marrieds, and when Jerry went to Hollywood he took Peggy and the baby with him. They had very little money. Over the years, Jerry had invested a great deal of money in Lee Planskoy's inventions for optical trick-work in films, and when the sudden move from Maidenhead to New York was decided upon, there were a lot of bills to pay. Irving's offers of a job proved illusory. He was having quite a struggle to establish himself. Jerry fell ill in November, and nobody diagnosed the cause of his intestinal trouble. He got better, then grew worse again. He had been seriously ill with this kind of trouble before. His family were alarmed, rightly, and insisted on him coming back to New York for treatment and perhaps an operation. It can be imagined what a big and expensive job it was in those days to take a dying man from one coast to another. Peggy had a difficult decision and decided to stay with the baby in Los Angeles. Jerry was in a coma most of the time, and soon after arrival in New York he died. Peggy was left alone and friendless in Los Angeles.

She survived, she and the baby. And when I met her again in the Farmer's Market, it was the old Peggy, pretty, brisk and matter of fact. As she told me her story I felt sorry for her for Jerry's sake, but I could see she had found herself. We had a lot of news to exchange. I went back to her flat and met Sarah and talked about Jerry and remembered him for half the night. We didn't meet again until she was married to John Monk, the screenwriter, and I was at Francis Coppola's Zoetrope Studios in 1980.

There can't be many people today who remember Jerry Jackson, but those who do will remember him with affection. He was introduced to me by Lee Planskoy. He took a chance on me and it came off. At a time when we were both finding just living difficult, he backed both Lee and me – me as a director, Lee as a technical wizard – and he took all the risks himself. Without Jerry's belief in me, I'd never have got back into the British film business in 1930. A whole lot of people, mostly critics, would have led much calmer lives. We made about twenty small films together, and when we parted in 1936 it was because I wanted to make *The Edge of the World*. Jerry had picked up the rudiments of the business very quickly, and he was rising rapidly as an executive until the war wrecked all his plans. We had worked and played together for five years. He had been more than an older brother to me. After a procession of girlfriends, he found Peggy, or Peggy found him. Marrying Peggy was the best thing he did in his life, and he knew it. He had energy, vision and guts. He should never have gone to Hollywood. He should have stayed in England, which he loved and where he was loved. Sarah, by the way, is now married and lives in Hampstead, London.

The other great event in our Hollywood trip was my visit at last to the MGM Studios, my Alma Mater in the film business. Eight years before, I had planned to take Hollywood by storm from a banana boat, and to sneak into MGM's studios by the back lot, to sleep in dressing rooms again, if necessary, as I did in Nice in the Victorine Studios in the summer of 1925, when Rex Ingram was directing *Mare Nostrum*. It was not such a crazy plan as it sounds. Moviemaking is a friendly and generous profession, and all over the world we who live in it and for it, have connections and memories shared, just like a deep-sea sailor with his tales of wrecks and voyages and a girl in every port. I was a veteran, a survivor of the legendary silent film industry. Three years working with an American company had not been wasted on me. Frank Scully had taught me to read and write for *Variety*, that fabulous showbiz newspaper. *Variety* and I shared our fiftieth anniversary together. And now here I was being met at the studio gates by Howard Strickling himself, a personal press representative of Louis B. Mayer, hailed as "Micky Powell!" and taken with Emeric directly to see Louis B., who welcomed us and gave us the freedom of his vast empire.

Howard, as slim, bony and dark-haired as ever, kept bubbling over with delight at his old friend of the days in Nice: "little Micky Powell", who had started as a grip with MGM and who was now one of Europe's great directors. Frank Scully, who was living in California, was still writing for *Variety*, and was publishing book after book, had to be mobilized for dinner. From these two I learnt everything that could be learnt about Hollywood, past, present and future. At this time, some of the big figures had slowed down or disappeared, but Louis B. Mayer and Metro-Goldwyn-Mayer were bigger and more active than ever. MGM was making, at that time, a movie a week. Fifty-two movies every year – count 'em! Emeric and I lunched with the producers in the producers' dining room. There were about twenty of them, and they each had from three to five pictures to look after. That meant they fought for, or were given, the subject. They engaged writers to make the adaptation, and then probably another writer to make a shooting script, which might, or might not, have been done in conjunction with a director. Emeric listened with his mouth open as Edwin Knopf explained how films were budgeted. Except for the shooting schedule, which was remarkably short, usually from five to eight weeks, the biggest item in any budget was usually for the story, adaptation and script. MGM dealt with what were called "known properties", and they brought in Broadway plays, big musicals, best-seller books, that were all in that class. Maybe the item in the budget covering all that was $350,000, maybe more, maybe less. If a figure was agreed, Knopf explained, they had to spend it. He might take a fancy to a Broadway play which was not a smash hit and buy it for $50,000. He could get an adaptation made for another $10,000, and the script for say $50,000. Now he was in a quandary. He went ahead and made the picture and it was a success – all very well – but if it turned out to be a weak sister or a complete flop, he'd be asked by Mr Mayer why the hell he had only spent $150,000 on the script when it was budgeted for $350,000. On the other hand, if he had hired every conceivable expensive name in Hollywood to work on the various adaptations of the script before going into production and then still had a failure, he could point to the budget and say well, the script was budgeted for $350,000, and I spent every dollar, so it's not my fault. And then Mr Mayer and the others would sympathise with him, and give him another big picture to make.

They were a remarkable bunch of men, the MGM producers – cultured, philosophical, realistic and experienced in show business; and over them all was this strange uncultured genius, who had created this dream factory, and who had usurped such dictatorial power over men and women, that he was dangerous to be with. Everyone trembled before him except Howard Strickling. To be alone with Louis B. Mayer in his office, which curiously enough was quite small, was like being in a pen with a raging bull. Emeric and I made a visit late one night with David O. Selznick to MGM Studios which were like a second home to him. A man like Mayer had his own henchmen, men like Eddie Mannix, or Benny Thau. These men never entirely left the studio. They could be found there day and night. Together with David, we roamed around the vast studio, watched and saluted by the studio police, across enormous stages crammed with expensive sets. Somebody was shooting on the lot that night: we could see the lights and hear voices. David decided he would like a game of gin rummy. He telephoned for three of these aides of Mr Mayer, and they, grumbling, got out of bed and came to the studio and played gin until four in the morning. The thought of such power in the hands of such men was blood-curdling.

As we trundled back across the prairies, I reviewed my twenty years in the movie business, and decided that I had been lucky. It had been a period of steady progress, and most of the time I had been my own master. My big chance came, and with it great responsibilities, which I had been equal to. The Hollywood oligarchy were looking backward, not forward. They had been so greedy and so powerful that they didn't know when they were out of date. Meanwhile, the great industry that they had created was organizing itself, led by the great technicians who had created the extraordinary entertainment industry. In England, it was different. Disciplined by war, England created a film industry on the European model, very personal and idealistic. Already we were being reinforced by film-makers coming back from all over the world as the war was nearly over. I felt that we were on the verge of great things. Yes, I had been lucky.

We spent a few days again in New York, waiting for our berths. I think our ship was the fabled *Queen Mary*, now a permanent resident of Los Angeles. The passengers were mostly young GIs going over as replace-ments. We had long talks with them in the public meeting places on the ship. They were already homesick for the United States, and again it was amazing how many of them had visited most, if not all, the states. We also played the game with them of writing down on sheets of paper as many states and their capitals as we could remember to make up the forty-eight. America had been a fabled country to us for many years, so Emeric and I often won this game. They howled with laughter at our pronunciation of Boise and Arkansas. Before I left New York, Kathleen Byron came to see me. She said she had thought over my angelic offer and would take a chance on it. Her husband agreed to her going and would follow her later when he had lined up a job. I liked her ambition and I liked her. I told her the part was hers if she could be in England around midsummer.

Arthur Kelly was as cheery and hospitable as ever, and preparing to release *Colonel Blimp*, but we didn't feel that United Artists understood the film, the motives of its characters and the long view of Anglo-German relations, which made the quiet anti-Nazi speeches at the end of the film so much more effective. *Esquire* magazine, labelled ostentatiously as "the magazine for men", had invented a cartoon figure of a lecherous little man who peeped through keyholes and up girls' skirts and dressed as a man-about-town, in their pre-war issues, and was now in uniform for the duration. This character shared some of Colonel Blimp's physical appearance: he had a heavy moustache and rolling eyes, but his sole reason for existing at all was to chase girls and make lecherous innuendoes, all of which were as popular as could be expected.

Arthur had hit on the idea of using this well-known image to popularize our own Colonel Blimp, quite missing the point of David Low's immortal character. He was extremely hurt when we criticised his brainchild.

When we landed back in England, we had been away nearly five weeks and we had a lot to do. We had *IKWIG* to finish and deliver; and within two and half months, at the end of August, we had to start shooting *AMOLAD*, the biggest and most exciting picture we had ever made.

Uncle Alfred had been assembling his staff. Gabby Pascal had finished shooting on *Caesar and Cleopatra*, and Caesar's Geezers were disbanded. There were a lot of good prop-makers and costume designers available, and he had had the pick of them. I noticed several familiar faces from *Colonel Blimp* delightedly rejoining the Archers for another colour production: little Josef Bato, a painter who had designed and mostly executed Deborah's costumes in *Blimp*; Roger Ramsdell, a superb art director; and Terry Morgan, a prop-making genius. And I noticed a new recruit among Alfred's staff, a tall, pale man with a head like a Roman emperor, big in every way. He must have weighed 180 pounds, and was probably German. He was going to be in charge of designing and executing all the costumes for the sequences in the Other World. Alfred was much too clever to introduce any of his staff to his director. If there was any credit to be had, you could bet it was going to be Alfred's, for having picked the right man to carry out his orders. I gathered that this new recruit of ours was a German painter and theatrical designer. He was looking at me with a worried, concentrated look. I waved to him and his face cleared to a broad grin, as he waved back. And the conference proceeded.

We had a lot of tricks in the film, but I don't like trick departments, and I decided magic and effects should be part of the art department, directly responsible to Uncle Alfred and to me, and to Jack Cardiff. I must now say a word or two about Poppa Day.

The movies were created for men like Poppa and his two sons. Poppa Day's hat was created not for Poppa Day's head, but to be danced upon. Poppa Day's spectacles were made to be broken, Poppa Day's hair had never seen a brush and comb, Poppa Day's clothes, when he was in the studio, would have disgraced a tramp; yet he commanded respect and admiration from all who worked with him, because he *knew*. I knew too, and Poppa Day knew that I knew. I can't remember that we ever exchanged a word on the subject. We just knew. When other people, even Jack Cardiff, made a suggestion, however good it was, and especially if we were likely to adopt it or at least part of it, Poppa would still look at me and I would look at him and *we knew*. He was ten or fifteen years older than me, but we both belonged to the miraculous period when everything had to be invented, when everything had to be discovered, when the motion picture wasn't just a machine that turned at twenty-four frames a second, but a miracle box which could record movements at any speed that the operator wished to crank, from two frames a second to thirty-two. If you lived and worked in the movies in those days, when the camera could lie and lie and lie, you could never take the sound camera seriously, tied down as it was to dialogue, sound effects and music. We never did. Our business was not realism, but surrealism. We were storytellers, fantasists. This is why we could never get on with the documentary film movement. Documentary films started with poetry and finished as prose. We storytellers started with naturalism and finished with fantasy.

Allan Gray was again the composer of the music. He was a very experienced writer of film music, which is a genre all its own. He had done a tremendous amount of work abroad, mostly in Germany. In spite of his romantic Scottish name, he was a German Jew. He was a delightful man to work with, and he contributed a great deal to the films of the period. He would read the script with great attention, find one or two plot themes and develop a musical theme to accompany them, keeping in close touch with the cutting room while the film was in production. This was the normal way of proceeding with a big film, only we kept in closer touch than was usual then. Many passages in *Blimp, A Canterbury Tale* and *I Know Where I'm Going*, were discussed in detail; and *Colonel Blimp* gained in sentiment, *A Canterbury Tale* in romance, and *I Know Where I'm Going* in Celtic magic, from Allan's sympathy and skilful orchestrations. Nobody who has seen *A Matter of Life and Death*, even if it is called *Stairway to Heaven*, will forget the musical theme of the moving stairway, with its remorseless beat as it mounted heavenwards. That single theme on the piano made the stairway sequences the most exciting scenes in the film.

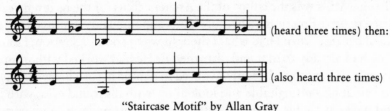

(heard three times) then:

(also heard three times)

"Staircase Motif" by Allan Gray

Besides Jack Cardiff, who was soon to prove himself the greatest colour cameraman in the world, we had another new recruit: Reggie Mills.

The editing and cutting of a film, the selection of the best performances by the actors from what the director and cameraman often think are the worst takes, the relationship with the director, the intercutting of close-ups and long shots, the use of dialogue and the use of sound – these are all in the hands of the editor as he sits in his cutting room looking at the images on the miniature screen before him, and trying to reconcile them with the words of the script, which lies open on his desk, and the scenes which the director has brought to the screen more in the breach than in the observance.

John Seabourne was all this and much more. From the start of the war he had been partly editor of my films and partly second-unit director. He had imagination, humour, humanity, and I knew I could depend on him. His contribution to our films was immense but varied. He edited *Contraband*. He was second-unit director on *49th Parallel*; but ill-health prevented him from editing the film and David Lean took over. David went on with us as editor to cut *One of Our Aircraft Is Missing*. He and Ronnie Neame left us to co-direct with Noël Coward *In Which We Serve*. John was restored to us, cured of his ulcers, to edit *Colonel Blimp*. He went on to edit the next two films, then collapsed from another attack, and we realized he would have to retire. It was the saddest decision I have ever had to make, especially as his son, young John, fresh from the RAF, was going to work for us on *AMOLAD*. On *The Edge of the World*, John and I were as close as brothers, and when I became too worried at the shortening of the days and the number of sequences with scenes unfinished, John would always have some story to tell, some idea to suggest, to interest me and to make me laugh and forget my worries.

While I concentrated on the whirlpool sequence in *IKWIG*, John was shooting most of the small-boat shots, sometimes in very broken weather and water, when he was seasick half the time, for he was not a very good sailor. Then he would come in from a filthy day off the reef to cook the dinner and tell the most outrageous lies to old Finlay Currie, who had stayed at home. Few people know or realize how much John contributed to the look of my films, to the feel of my films, and to the personal quality of my films. He loved all men and had something good to say of the worst. He had a keen eye and an inquiring mind. I learnt something from him every day, bless him.

Reggie Mills was the editor of the Archers' films for the next ten years. He used to drive Emeric mad because of his unpunctuality. He used to drive me mad because when I had what I thought was a good suggestion, I found that he had already tried it and discarded it. He had worked with masters and was a master himself. He always used to remind me of a brown owl. He would sit at his cutting table and look at me with his round eyes, with his round face, with his round spectacles, blinking amiably and cutting ruthlessly. He was extraordinarily precise in his timing, but I didn't know then how musical he was.

He loved opera and spent all his money on concerts and recordings. He lived in a world of his own and hardly ever made a public statement. When the rest of us were shooting our mouths off, he would sit musing and would seldom volunteer an opinion. If he did have one, he usually sought me out somewhere between sets or in the lunch break and, diffidently but precisely, explain how he thought such and such a difficulty could be solved. He was young, patient and far-seeing, and he soon saw that AMOLAD was going to be something out of the ordinary. He became a dedicated Archer and introduced a civilized note into our discussions. The crew, who were no respecters of persons, made fun of him, but knew how good he was. And when the big musical pictures came along, they were amazed at his technical skills. Later on, in the seventies he was to direct an enchanting film about Beatrix Potter and her animal characters, with Frederick Ashton doing the choreography and playing "Mrs Tiggywinkle". It is full of the charm and gentleness and musicality of Reggie and there's some very good dancing, particularly by a young dancer from the Royal Ballet, who plays Jeremy Fisher the Frog, Michael Coleman. The last time that I saw Reggie Mills was on Santa Monica Boulevard in Hollywood. I think I had been out to lunch at the Studio Restaurant, so we were near the Goldwyn Studios. I was about to commit suicide when a voice behind me said: "The lights are against you, Micky."

He was thirty years older, but looked much the same.

"How's the Zeffirelli picture going?" I asked.

He groaned. "I've got it down to two hours, and nobody else in the world could have done that."

It was the only immodest statement that I have ever heard Reggie make, which just shows the influence Hollywood has upon otherwise humble craftsmen like us.

Archers who had been called up and had served mostly in the RAF Film Unit, which was based at Pinewood Studios only a few miles across the woods and meadows of Buckinghamshire, had been demobbed and were returning to the fold. The chief of them, of course, was Syd Streeter. After *One of Our Aircraft*, I decided that Syd was too good to be just a chief of construction. He knew all the answers, so I made him production manager. With us a production manager title meant that you managed the whole production, and Syd took this all in his stride. George Busby had joined us earlier in the production office, and now these two worked together as a team of two men who really did know all the answers.

Now Syd was back again and already conferring with Uncle Alfred and Jack Cardiff and the master carpenter and the machine shop. It was a great start for the production.

Jack Cardiff had a strong team. All three of them were to be future Academy Award winners. Geoffrey Unsworth was operating cameraman, and that was no light job when, besides having to tell the story and follow the actors with his lens, he had to handle the huge Technicolor blimp for the three-strip camera, which had three negatives going through the camera at once. The huge camera and its lenses were inside this blimp. It was as big as a steamer trunk and about as easy to manipulate. Yet Geoff's operating (which means telling the story ahead of the actors) was as smooth as if the camera were an ordinary Mitchell. His wife, Maggie, had been our script-girl, on *Colonel Blimp*. After that she worked on all David Lean's films, right up to *A Passage to India*. Geoff lit scores of great pictures, including *Superman*, and he died while lighting Roman Polanski's *Tess*. He received a posthumous Academy Award for his lighting, which he shared with the French cameraman who finished the film.

Christopher Challis was the Technicolor technician on the picture. Later on he became chief cameraman for the Archers, lighting *The Tales of Hoffman, Gone to Earth*, and *The Battle of the River Plate*, among others. The team was completed by George Menassian, and "the Baron" (Johnnie von Klotze). George was handsome in a wild Byronic way. He was also full of fun. Like Byron too, he contributed dash and style to this sturdy English crew. Johnnie was a tall, blond boy, obviously an upper-class German, but educated in England. He really was a baron, and his fellow technicians never let him forget it. It was "Herr Baron! Just run the tape out to Mr Niven's nose, *nicht wahr?*" or "Bitte, mein Herr, give us a pound or two with this camera box, will you?" He took it in a good-humoured way, which was just as well, because he had to take it anyway.

Everyone on this marvellously talented camera crew had been through the Technicolor mill. It was not all in fun when I knelt down in front of the old Technicolor building in Hollywood on my way to the Zoetrope studios, for the documentary that Gavin Millar of the BBC *Arena* programme was making on Pressburger and Powell – it was a bit of an in-joke, because everybody in the business knows how much the development of colour in motion pictures is due to Technicolor.

It was a different pot of paint when I was the boss on *Colonel Blimp* and put Uncle Alfred and his staff of real painters in charge of costume, decor and even make-up. This last was greatly resented by the pundits of Technicolor, who liked to see the actors made up until they resembled nothing human. I started my experience with Deborah's Three Ages of Woman, aiming at complete naturalism, i.e. make-up so delicately put on that it looked like no make-up in 1902, a slightly more open-air look for the girl in 1919, to the full street make-up of the modern girl, Johnny, in 1942. The colour experts would have liked to have more to say about this, but I told them there was nothing more to say: that was how it was going to be.

But *Blimp* was, after all, a conventional film, a black and white film coloured. It had delighted the Kalmuses and their Hollywood technicians when they saw the final result lit by Périnal's superb photography, but so far as I was concerned we were just playing ourselves in. We had been waiting to get Technicolor back into our cameras, and now we had it, with superb experience in every department, and on a film fantasy. We were going to play with Technicolor on the screen in a way that nobody had ever played before. Abandoning the whole concept of "penny plain, tuppence coloured" we were going to make colour part of our story. I had fallen completely in love with Emeric's idea of the Two Worlds, one in colour, the other in monochrome, and I vowed that on the next film we would go even further, and further again on the film after that. The end of the war, coinciding with the activity of our powerful little group, gave a great opportunity to break down the conventional barriers and surge forward. The fact that *A Matter of Life and Death, Black Narcissus,* and *The Red Shoes* are still regarded, nearly forty years later, as three peaks of achievement in colour photography, speaks for itself.

But although we had got our four stars – David Niven, Kim Hunter, Roger Livesey and Raymond Massey – lined up for the picture and we were in active preparation, which included colour and monochrome tests for *AMOLAD*, we had still to finish *IKWIG*.

IKWIG was in trouble. We had viewed the dailies in the usual way, and I was shooting right up to the day I left for America. John Seabourne had picked up the few shots that had remained to be done while I was away, the trick shots were in and the first assembly of the film was ready for us to see when Emeric and I returned from Hollywood and New York. Perhaps our experiences, and the contact with so many professionals whom we had admired, made us more self-critical, for we didn't like what we saw, and realized we had a lot of work to do before we had a picture.

The shooting script that we had all liked so well had not worked out in practice. I had overproduced it, and there was far too much local colour. That was easy enough to fix, but some of the performances were weak and needed expert doctoring. Roger was fine, as usual, and Wendy's beautifully thought-out performance was a little too efficient and lacked surprise, but got better as the film went on. Pamela, on the other hand, seemed to both of us to be mannered and over-romantic. This was my fault. I had fallen in love with her face, with its tiger's eyes framed against the dark hills and the stormy seas, and with her poor pain-racked body which she handled so wonderfully that no audience could suspect that she was in pain. I had made it visually clear that Caitriona had been in love with Torquil ever since their childhood together. This subplot had to go. No doubt people who loved the film, and who have seen it many times, will howl with anguish when they learn what they have missed. But Emeric was firm and I have to admit that he was right. One glance from those great eyes of Pamela's early in the film told the whole story rather better than I could, with all my shots of her among the heather and the lochs. And yet, I wonder . . . ? One still photograph survives from this whole sequence, and it was taken by me. It shows Pamela in the Castle of Moy, as she watches Torquil read the Curse upon the stone. It has an eerie power.

We did an awful lot of work on the film before it began to assume the shape and the rhythm of the film you know now. The sound track was a production in itself. Almost everything we had shot on location with sound had to be revoiced, and nearly all those voices had to be brought down from the Western Isles. There were voices from Mallaig, from Tobermory, and from Colonsay itself, the island which we used for the unattainable island, Kiloran. John Seabourne had to return there, joyfully, to get more sound track. Allan Gray had done a lot of work on his music, but, of course, he couldn't have known what was in my mind for sequences like Wendy Hiller in the train on her way to be married and other more elaborate sequences like the Ceilidh, arranged and choreographed by dear John Laurie, and which had to be worked on and worked on until it had a rhythm of its own. John Seabourne and I recut the storm sequence and the whirlpool sequence several times before we were satisfied. It almost seemed in the noisy little cutting room that we were deluged with seaspray. At last, we were ready for the mix, which took about two weeks. A few days later we showed it to Rank and Davis in its cutting-copy shape. I can't say they were enthusiastic. They didn't understand it. They were English miles away from Emeric's subtle approach to a love story, which could have been etched by de Maupassant. We suffered from this again and again. We were showing them what we thought was an English-speaking film, and they were seeing what looked to them like a European film dubbed into English.

Today, *IKWIG* is perfectly clear to all audiences, and I was told the other day, that it has become a cult film at Harvard, God save us!

But in 1945, our distributors were cautious. We had all of us had the stuffing knocked out of us by the reception given to *A Canterbury Tale*. We had mistimed that picture and I had an uneasy feeling that they felt we had mistimed this one too. They weren't very sure that the public wanted a strange wayward story loaded with Celtic sounds and voices, and which seemed to them to have no relation to the facts of 1945. I think they thought we were an unpredictable couple. Today, of course, the picture stands on its own legs as a romantic and moving farewell to a European culture that was vanishing. It was also a wry salute to the materialism which was fast taking over Europe after the war.

IKWIG has had its admirers among the professionals. Only another writer can appreciate the skill with which Emeric plots his love story, by word and look, until both lovers are caught in the net. We played it straight, Wendy and Roger and I masking every emotion and refusing any tell-tale intonations. It worked. It's the sweetest film we ever made. Still Rank and Davis were puzzled and disappointed, and yet again, when we were in Hollywood again a year or two later, and Emeric paid a visit to an old pal at Paramount studios, he was told at lunch by the head of the story department, that they had a copy of *I Know Where I'm Going* which belonged to them, and which they showed to writers as an example of how a perfect screenplay should be constructed.

Allan turned in one of his best scores. Not even the most touchy Scotsman has ever protested at his orchestral simulation of the pipes. I persuaded Sir Hugh Roberton and the Glasgow Orchestra, men and women this time, to take part in the recording, and actually to appear on the screen in the Ceilidh sequence. We recorded some of their famous Mouth Music and we had three pipers of the Black Watch.

But Rank and Davis were not happy and I can understand why. The film was more popular in America than in England, maybe because service overseas had opened the eyes of many a GI to the strange diversity of the British Isles. An island in America is no more than an island, inhabited or uninhabited. Each island of the British Isles is a world.

Last night I went to a party in New York after a show and someone must have connected my name with an obscure British film director, because suddenly a big man, who I think was a press agent, was accusing me of being the author/director of *I Know Where I'm Going*.

"I was an usher at the Sutton Theatre. 1946! It is my favourite film of all time! Only a mild success? Nonsense! The theatre was crowded when I was there. People were coming again and again. Those women, those voices, those dogs and Nancy Price! I wanted to leave America right away and go and visit the Western Isles. The people! They were so crazy and so real.

Wendy Hiller, what a doll! And the music and the dancing and the kilts. Hey! Why is it that I can't find a record of a schottische. I just wanted to play that schottische music and go some place and dance it! It is as fresh to me now as it was forty years ago. I can't thank you enough!"

All this time he was thumping my hand and gazing earnestly into my face. I was overcome and fully repaid for all the work we had put into the speech and sound for the film.

The Nancy Price whom my new friend referred to was the celebrated avant-garde actress-manageress who managed the Little Theatre in the Adelphi, just off the Strand, in London. On that tiny stage she had presented innumerable productions. She was a magnificent looking woman, with the eyes of a great commander. Her daughter, Joan Maude, a red-headed beauty with green eyes and a spectacular body, was to appear in *AMOLAD* as the chief of the records department. The fact that the daughter followed so closely upon her mother's heels in our two pictures was pure coincidence. In *IKWIG*, Nancy Price played the chatelaine of a servantless castle who is giving a bridge party and carries the situation off with complete poise. The sequence is obviously based upon a real experience, and, of course, it was. Before we started to shoot the film, we scoured the island of Mull for locations and for help and advice. On one occasion we were asked to tea at just such a place as the Castle of Sornd. Even some of the dialogue in the scene is stolen verbatim from our hostess on that occasion. It was the authenticity of our eccentric characters which endeared them to our audiences.

Joan Maude I had met ten years before. It was in Oxford Street and as we strolled along I suddenly discovered that this serious young girl, luxuriant as a pre-Raphaelite "Stunner", was telling me with great earnestness how much she liked *Red Ensign*. She was at some pains to explain to me that the film was quite an ordinary piece of work but there was something serious in it, something she couldn't quite put her finger on which had impressed her. It was a first reaction by my puzzled public to a Powell film. And probably it was the first time that Michael Powell himself realized that there was something special about a Powell film, something going on on the screen, or behind the screen, which you couldn't quite put your finger on, something intriguing, aloof, but in the long run, memorable. Perhaps it is this that has always annoyed the English critics about my work: a tendency to take things seriously: a passion for getting my facts right; and a habit of verifying my quotations, except in this book.

Before we started shooting on *AMOLAD*, I had promised myself to pay fealty to Prince Charles Edward Stuart, the Young Pretender, who had become one of my heroes while I was following in his footsteps in the Isles. It was July 1945 and the two hundredth anniversary of the '45 Rebellion, when the Prince with a few friends landed on the west coast of Scotland and raised his standard at Glenfinnan, summoning the clans to join him. There was to be a ceremony on the spot attended by many notable Highland figures, including Seton Gordon, my friend, and Lord Sempil, my neighbour, and I was determined to be there although it was only a few days before the start of shooting.

Everybody thought that I was mad, except Bill Paton and Alastair MacTavish Dunnet. They knew. Alastair was a journalist, later the editor of *The Scotsman*, who had been sent by the Scottish Office to visit us on Mull and Carsaig while we were shooting *IKWIG*. We became friends and we still are. I shall have more to say of Alastair, much more, but in its proper place when I can spread myself. It may be thought and even demanded why I had become such a lover of Scotland when I had never crossed the border northwards until I was in my thirtieth year and planning *The Edge of the World*. Events had led me for that film to the Shetland Islands, and to the Orkney Islands for *The Spy in Black*. Now I had made *IKWIG* in the Hebrides, and the conquest was complete. The groundwork had been laid long ago by Walter Scott, John Buchan, Robert Louis Stevenson and Robert Burns – all great tale spinners and subtle propagandists for their mother country. Now with three films that had been distributed all over the world I had joined this select company.

Was it as a film subject that I was so interested in Bonnie Prince Charlie? Yes and no. There is probably no finer story of two people on the run, helped by a few devoted friends to escape, but it had been so romanticized on highly coloured postcards and biscuit tins, that, although I was tempted, I feared it. But I have a compass in my head that turns north, and something told me to go to Glenfinnan, and I went. It was an appalling 600-mile journey, six on a side in a crowded railway carriage, but it was worth it.

There were a lot of notables missing, for the war was still on. But there were enough to make it an occasion. The men wore the kilt, and the ladies the kilted skirt, and the colour blazed among the heather. I shall never forget Sir Donald Cameron standing on the steps of the monument, saying: "And it was on this very spot, that my ancestor, Cameron of Lochiel, swore devotion to the Stuart cause, and he wore in his bonnet this white cockade, which I am wearing now in mine."

And he touched it with his finger and we all looked in silence at this bunch of white ribbons. It looked to me as big as a cauliflower.

A film of the '45? Although instinct, backed by reason, said no, romance backed by that sturdy Jacobite, Dr Samuel Johnson, said yes. (Have you read Boswell's account of the meeting between the great Doctor and Miss Flora MacDonald? It is a moving piece.) When *AMOLAD* was in the can, and with the same crew, we planned and shot a sequence from a film that never was: *The White Cockade*. Emeric wrote it, Alfred Junge designed it, Jack Cardiff lit it, Hein Heckroth did the costumes, David

Niven played the Prince, Pamela Brown played Flora. I directed it. You would think there would be talent enough, but the piece was dead. The people in it never loved, nor laughed, nor trod the heather. Emeric had written a charming scene, but it never came to life. We never made *The White Cockade*.

On the day that Japan surrendered to General MacArthur, and it was broadcast to the world, we started shooting *A Matter of Life and Death* on location at Saunton Sands, North Devon. I had been here last with Bill Paton when we were looking for locations on *The Thief of Bagdad*. The sands were famous to holiday-makers but five years of warfare and mock-warfare had rolled over them and Braunton Burrows was thick with unexploded mines, bombs and barbed wire. A charming gunnery officer walked over to us, complete with walking stick, and apologized for the mess. It had been his gunnery range for the past two years.

"We'll soon get it cleaned up," he said optimistically. "Meanwhile, don't stray around too much and keep your eyes open."

It was just the right atmosphere for the picture to start in. We were standing on the low ridge at Saunton Sands, where the surfing waves roll in from the open Atlantic. It was a glorious day. I looked at the vast expanse of the Burrows, a wilderness of sandhills stretching for several miles. It had that pearly look of an English August morning, like nothing on earth, which was just as well because David Niven thought he was in Another World. As we stood upon the low cliffs above the sands and looked directly down onto where the waves were lazily breaking, we could see the blue sky and the cirrus clouds above us reflected in this enormous mirror made up of sand and water.

"Quick!" I said to Jack Cardiff. "We must shoot at once! Where's Niven?"

David was chatting with the gunnery officer, who was probably getting a free autograph for his children.

"David, we must shoot in the next ten minutes. Props, costumes, the full outfit as planned when you left the aircraft."

It wasn't ten, but twenty minutes, before David was arrayed in all the paraphernalia of a modern airman.

"Go on, for Christ's sake!" I screamed. "Get down on the beach!"

"What do I do?" asked David reasonably, for this was the first shot of the picture.

"Do? Nothing! Just float in on the surf and roll about. You are drowned anyway."

"OK."

"We'll bang off all the long shots from up here, and then we'll come down to the beach and shoot you there, so don't leave the water."

David came to attention and saluted. "You talk like my commando sergeant," he said. "This is going to be fun."

We shot the long shots in about ten minutes.

"Do you want to have a look at the set-up, Micky?" inquired Geoff Unsworth.

"No, what for? You're the operator, aren't you?"

The rest of the crew, who had worked with me before, grinned at Geoff, who hadn't.

"What lens are you using, 22mm?" I had asked for an extreme long shot with an angle right down onto the wet sand and the waves rolling in.

"Yes, Micky."

"That's all right then. *Stand by below! You are all in the picture. Get out of it!*"

David was surrounded by wardrobe people and prop-men and an assistant director. They all scattered as they heard me shout.

"*Roll 'em!*"

Johnny offered up the clapperboard. "*A Matter of Life and Death*, Scene 1, Take 1."

We were off!

In another forty minutes we had all scrambled down onto the beach bringing camera, reflectors, props, everything, and had completed the whole sequence with David when he opens his eyes, thinks he's in Heaven, gets up, starts to take off all his accessories, and has a little scene with his shadow on the beach.

"What's Micky in such a hurry about?" panted Geoff to Bill Wall. "Is he always like this?"

"What a fucking Londoner you are, Geoff," was the amiable reply. "Ain't your mother never took you paddling? Micky could see from the top of the cliff that the tide was going out, and when the tide goes out here it goes out a ruddy mile or two."

Already the place where we had been standing up to our knees in water was now quickly drying sand – and nine set-ups were in the can.

"OK," I said. "Alfred! Props! Come with me!" (For Uncle Alfred was with us; he was not going to miss the first shots on the picture.) "Geoff, come with me and bring the camera finder."

We scrambled up the soft sandy dune. We shot the scene where David sees the "Keep Out" sign.

"Where's the goatherd set-up, Alfred?"

Uncle Alfred, as the designer of the picture, had himself supervised the next little sequence and chosen the set-up.

"Just a little farther, Micky. Beyond those dunes."

The goatherd was one of my inspirations, like introducing a Coca-Cola machine into Heaven. The script called for a boy with some animals, who had to answer David Niven's question when he thinks he's in Heaven: "Where do I report?"

I made the boy a naked boy, playing on a reed pipe a little tune composed by Allan Gray, while his goats cropped the sparse marram grass on the sand dunes. It looked charming, like a scene from Theocritus. David kneels down and talks to the child, and gradually begins to realize that he is not dead, that he's alive, and has been washed ashore near to the very same place where June (Kim Hunter) has been posted. A Mosquito aircraft roars overhead, cued by my signal. He sees a little figure on a bicycle toiling along the sands and he knows – and we know – that it is June. We changed the set-up three or four times, shot the whole sequence between David and Kim, and she suddenly realized that her first scene in the picture, and one of the most important ones, was all over and in the can, without her actually knowing quite how it happened. If they know their lines, it doesn't do to give actors time to think – not on location anyway. But my charming Theocritean idyll was not appreciated by our American partners. The magic of the scene escaped them. They could only see sexual implications in the association of a grown man with a naked boy and rushed to protect their public. They cut the scene out in America, although there were important plot lines which played back to the earlier scene between June and Peter, and which helped Peter now to identify the distant cyclist as June. It has always riled me. And my friend and greatest fan, Martin Scorsese, agrees, and has been heard to splutter when a print of *AMOLAD* is shown on television: "It doesn't have the scene with the naked boy in it! It's that damn cut version again!"

In this great popular storytelling medium of the movies we tend to underestimate the public, who are usually ten scenes ahead of us in our storytelling. I have a great respect for the popular audience: they know what we are driving at before we know it ourselves. I direct on this assumption, which sometimes causes distributors to worry over scenes and themes which their public take in their stride. In America, with its vast size and twenty thousand cinemas, with its mixture of ethnic races and myriad accents, this disagreement between the director of a film and its distributor is intensified. I had no doubt that Joe Breen, the Hollywood censor, disapproved of my naked boy. He disapproved of almost everything.

I possess a copy of a little book, and certain avid collectors, loving friends of mine like Martin Scorsese and Thelma Schoonmaker, have one too. It is a rare book, but occasionally one turns up in the film bookshops. It has several unusual features and is worth having. It is totally devoted to the film *A Matter of Life and Death*. It has the format of a paperback, but is bound in cheap red boards. The body of the book is our script, told as a novel. This is done efficiently and clearly in about 30,000 words. But the remarkable thing about the little book, published in those days of economy in 1945, when paper was hard to find, is the lavish number of illustrations. I can sense a clear and appreciative mind in the compiler of the book. The reproductions of sketches by Uncle Alfred are faced by photographs of the same scene as it appears in the film. The moving stairway has its place as a remarkable feat of engineering, as well as imagination. The personalities – Niven, Byron, Livesey – are well-presented and contrasted. There is an editorial mind at work here. But the pages I'm most grateful for are the photographs of that happy first day of the picture at Saunton Sands and Braunton Burrows. Here is Jack Cardiff, wiry and agile, and Uncle Alfred, solid, smiling, with his head crowned with a French beret. Here is David chatting with everybody, the ideal, modern romantic hero. There are two or three pages devoted to the scene on the Burrows, and the charm of this classical scene comes over, vividly coupled with the dark shape of the Mosquito aircraft, skimming just over our heads to bring Niven's scattered wits into focus. And here is a slim, serious young man (but I was thirty-nine years old at the time) wearing the grey sweater with the roll-collar neck which I lent to Leslie Howard for his scenes in *49th Parallel*. Here is Kim with her bike ready for action. Oh! what a day that was! And it all comes back to me in this little book.

A few years ago in Sydney, Australia, Paul Hamlyn, who discovered how to industrialize marketing of expensive books, and became a millionaire in the process, said to me: "Do you know that the first book that I published was for you?"

"Was it, Paul?"

"I wrote most of it, too."

Paul and James Mason and I were waiting for a helicopter to touch down and take us to the grand opening of the distribution centre of Hamlyn Books in Sydney.

"You were making *A Matter of Life and Death*. Someone had done a paperback, a novelization of *I Know Where I'm Going*, illustrated with photographs from the film, and that gave me the idea. I don't suppose you remember our meeting."

"No, but I have the book."

"I worked very hard on it."

No wonder the little book has style and form. What luck I had to have a Hamlyn chronicle the start of my greatest picture. It was the kind of luck I took for granted, then.

Another gift of the gods was Hein Heckroth.

Alfred kept the members of his team anonymous and in the background. He was not only a great disciplinarian, but an autocrat. I would not like to state that he would sign his name to other men's sketches, because he didn't need to, he was a gifted sketch artist himself, but it was common practice in art departments. Those eyes of Uncle Alfred's that could twinkle so merrily could also be as hard as frost. That brain that could conjure miracles out of the art department, could also inspire discontent and jealousy. He was feared. I had been aware for some time in my almost daily inspections of costumes, settings, models, plans, etc., of a bulky, anxious figure in the background with pencil and notebook, always able to supply facts, figures and dates, and prompt to pass on to his underlings, with their notebooks, any alterations in the black and white period costumes: for the scenes in the Other World had large groups of men and women in costumes which covered two hundred years of American and English history. I never got to speak with Hein Heckroth, nor did I learn his name until I saw him on the credits on the film. He was kept well back, but Alfred was generous and gave him sole credit for the costumes. They were both German you see: Hein from Hesse, Alfred from Prussia.

Hein was a big man, well over six feet tall. As I have said he had a profile like a Roman emperor, but the most striking thing about him were his large pale eyes, reflective and reflecting, observing and imagining, inventing, joking, loving and – I almost said hating, but I don't think Hein Heckroth hated anybody. He might kill somebody who offended him or Ada, but he wouldn't hate him. He was too big.

Ada was Hein's wife. She came from a branch of the Rothschild family in Frankfurt am Main. She was a painter like Hein and they had fallen in love when she was the student and he the master. I knew vaguely – I was to hear much more later – that they had been living in England before the war, and had spent a year or two at Dartington Hall, where Hein had also been teaching. The phoney war ended and the real war began. Hein was interned and sent to Australia. After being screened he was allowed to return to England, and his theatrical contacts (for he had worked in the London theatre, but not in films) put him in touch with Denham and he got work on *Caesar and Cleopatra*. Of course, Uncle Alfred knew Hein by reputation and asked him to join our band of costume and prop-makers. This was how he came to be on *AMOLAD*.

Ada was small, black-haired and vivacious. She was devoted to Hein and Hein's interests. They had a daughter, Nandi, a red-headed young beauty, unmistakably the daughter of Hein. But all this I learnt later, as one does when working together in a big theatrical company.

From my one experience of directing a production for the legitimate theatre, I had learnt the value of *esprit de corps* and the necessity of getting all these diverse temperaments, on stage, backstage, and in front of the house, working to the same end. I had learnt a lot from that noble failure *The Fifth Column* – more, I fancy, than a theatre director does when he is invited to make a film. Making a film is like building an automobile. Amongst the hundred-odd people involved in the actual production there are at least three-quarters who come and go like artisans or craftsmen in a factory. They take a personal interest in the show, but it is not their show. Directing a play is quite different and much more fun, for everybody. In making a film it is the director who has the fun – at least that is my experience. In producing a play, with fewer people involved, and with the audience continuously in the minds of everybody, all of us – directors, actors and technicians – have fun. I am sure that this yearning to learn from the legitimate theatre – it had always been my great love – was of value to me, although my successes were very mild and would, by more professional practitioners of the art, have been considered failures. At any rate, this unity of purpose among all my collaborators towards an ideal film, became a religion for me. On the whole, the technicians responded to it with enthusiasm. The atmosphere that I created in the studio was delightful to some actors, hateful to others. For me, it became a way of life.

For the six years of the war, we had been coming to work by public transport, which often meant there was no transport at all. Denham Studios and Denham Laboratories are – or rather were – built on the rising ground on the right bank of the River Colne. It was a charming location in a thick wood, and the old red house looked across the levels for a couple of miles to where the land rose and Uxbridge town stood. There were several country seats of Edwardian merchant princes scattered about the flat land between the numerous rivers and streams and the Grand Union Canal. Denham Village, as pretty then as it is now, intersected by streams, including the Colne, lay about half a mile away, and was separated from the studios by a long high railway embankment on which Denham railway station was perched. It was a typical Victorian station, built of sulphurous brick, with a carriage road sloping up to the railway line and the level of the trains, and a long tunnel beneath the track for pedestrians and to preserve the right of way. A quarter of a mile separates the railway station and the studios, and the road was open to all weathers. The railway embankment was in full view of the commuters to the studio, and when you were late for a train you had the dubious satisfaction of seeing the train coming while you were running your heart out. There were only two possible trains after work in the evening, and if there was an air raid they stopped where they were on the railway line, so it was sometimes two or three hours before you got to St Pancras Station. It was not such a hardship as it might seem, because there were usually loads of extra girls returning to London too. And contrary to the impression conveyed by British movies, all the good little girls were not in the Forces. The London terminal stations, Victoria, Euston, St Pancras and King's Cross, were the main targets of the Luftwaffe, so it was usually a lively matter getting home for me, because I arrived at St Pancras and had to get across London to Victoria. Quite often in the early days I had to walk it, dashing in to the nearest doorway when the bombs started to fall too close. Later on that was impossible, for by that time we were putting up such an enormous barrage from the anti-aircraft guns around London, that we were much more likely to be hit on the head by a piece of shrapnel from our own guns, than from the enemy's.

I usually made it home by around eight o'clock at night. Going from Victoria to St Pancras in the morning was better. It was amazing how many taxis there were during the war, cruising the London streets, ignoring the bombs. For the best part of two years, I had a wonderful old taxi driver who was the spitting image of C. Aubrey Smith. He called for me every morning at 7:30, whether there was a raid on or not. I see him always in my mind's eye, with that great craggy face and nose, cap jammed over his eyebrows, muffler around his neck, the butt of his cigarette between his lips. We never chatted. It was just "Morning" and a nod.

All this time I had a car – in fact I had two cars. While I was away in Canada, going to and fro and making *49th Parallel*, the Auburn had been looked after by a mechanical genius, John Walker, who lived in Ebury Mews and had several garages. The petrol allowance was about five gallons a month, but it was possible to get extra coupons if you were excused from military service by some Ministry, in our case the Ministry of Information. I decided against it. Many people had been evacuated and the population was down to about two million. It had become really a charming city except for a few bombs. We fitted into the general picture better as pedestrians. I decided to turn the Auburn into a camera-car. It was a six-cylinder convertible coupé with a rumble seat at the back in which the cocker spaniels loved to ride, their long ears streaming in the wind as they leant further and further out.

The other car was a Bentley, three and a half litre, built in 1936. She was an open four-seater sports model with an aluminium body by Van den Plas. There was a hood which could be raised, preferably by two people, and locked into position, and side curtains which could be dropped into sockets. The overall colour was black, and the interior red, with lavish use of chromium everywhere, but the general effect was one of speed and endurance. Her top speed was ninety miles an hour and she weighed about one and a half tons. She had been left for sale by her American owner when he returned to the States, and had suffered some slight damage when the garage in which she was being kept in Ebury Mews was bombed. John Walker suggested to me that I buy her and keep her for the duration of the war. He would put her right and look after her and I could drive her when better times came again. I bought her for £500. She was licensed and I took her on the road in 1946, and we were inseparable for twenty-seven years. Except on one dramatic occasion. But that is another story.

On Monday, August 24, 1945, we started shooting at Denham Studios on *AMOLAD*. On the same day and date my elder son, Kevin Michael

Powell, was born. *AMOLAD* has ever since then been known as Kevin's Picture. The actors had been good enough to pick me up, and I drove out that morning in suitable splendour in a hired car, flanked by David Niven and Raymond Massey. Kim must have made her own arrangements, but I forget what they were. As the poor actresses have to come to the studios for make-up hours ahead of the actors, that probably accounts for her absence. I told them the momentous news in a typical Powell offhand, jerky way. However, they seemed to understand that I was bursting with excitement. I had been at the nursing home late the night before and early that morning, so the combination of Frankie's gift of a son and heir and the start of the biggest picture that I had so far tackled, made the occasion unforgettable.

It was a difficult birth and a long one. Frankie had treated the gestation and birth of her baby with her typical poker-faced calm. It fed her pride and her dislike of fuss that nobody should guess she was carrying a child, unless she chose to tell them so. A week before the birth, an old friend meeting her outside Fortnum and Mason's in Piccadilly chatted with her for half an hour, strolling along Piccadilly, without suspecting anything. A week later he heard that she had had a son. I don't think he ever got over it.

Kevin's Picture went smoothly from first to last. I think that the schedule was ten weeks of a five and half day week. We came in on Saturday morning and worked the morning as hard as any other day. But the afternoon tended to tail off if you wanted to get away early. That meant we were shooting about three to four minutes of cut film a day. "Cut film" refers to the actual amount of footage in the first cut of the film which you are shooting. I don't shoot many takes on scenes. I expect to get Take 1 and if I hit a snag I very soon change the set-up and break up the shot and get on with it. No point in having an ideal and then hammering away at it all day until everybody is exhausted and acting very badly. Sometimes you have to be very brutal, but it has to be done. The actors rise to the challenge of a new approach to the scene and everything seems to go quicker.

Usually, it takes me three or four days to get into the rhythm of the work. In the first days of a big picture, everything seems difficult and nobody seems to anticipate anything. I am not sure of what I'm doing, and the actors are still feeling their way into the parts. I work very carefully, very methodically, and without inspiration, or so it seems to me. Usually, to my surprise, the dailies on the first and second day are exceptionally good, because they were shot with such care and fear. But I still feel everything is an effort, and I have to stop and think things out. Then, all of a sudden, something clicks, I am sure of what I am doing and so are the actors and the whole vast jigsaw puzzle of a picture starts to gel, and to acquire its own momentum. People come to me with outrageous requests and even more outrageous suggestions, and I accept or reject them in a moment. The camera and its crew are no longer that bunch of people out there, but an extension of my own eyes and arms and head. We are rolling! We take off! Soon we are hurling scenes and sequences behind us that seemed almost insurmountable in planning. Every day there are a hundred decisions to make. We view the dailies either in the morning or at lunchtime or in the evening, but preferably at lunchtime. They may be glamorous or they may be tragic, or even miraculous. But we hardly ever stop to retake as we sweep along. To stop to consider, to discuss, would interrupt the rhythm, and besides the scene might never be in the picture. All of a sudden it's all over. In the case of *AMOLAD*, Reggie Mills had kept pace with us all the way through. This owl was an industrious owl. He would sit next to me in the darkened theatre when we ran the dailies, and he would sometimes follow me onto the set and ask questions, until I finally kicked him off. Five days after the last shot was canned, Reggie Mills had the first rough cut of the film, and when I saw it I stood up in the theatre and I looked at Emeric and everybody around me (actors, various people, electricians, lots of people used to come in – I liked everybody to see what was going on), and I said right out loud: "By God, we've brought it off!"

And satisfied with that, I left almost immediately for South America with Frankie.

It was wanderlust. It was restlessness. It was instinct after being cooped up in England for so many years. I yearned for exotic people against stupendous backgrounds. I had always been fascinated by the Spanish conquest of America, and particularly by the conquest of Peru. I had read everything I could lay my hands on about the Maya, the Aztecs, and the Incas, and it was the Incas and their mysterious empire and their total destruction by the Spanish Conquistador Pizarro, that fasincated me. I dreamed of making an intimate and savage picture about the clash between two rival superstitions, between the savage Spaniards and the civilized Indians. It was the Andes with bare, high murderous peaks, it was the world of the Indians, the Puño, the high grasslands ten thousand feet up in the air, dotted with incredible grazing animals like the llama and the alpaca and the guanaco, that attracted me. Above all there was a mystery of where these sophisticated rulers came from and the theory that there had once been constant communication by sea between South America and the islands of the South Seas. Ever since my abortive but enriching trip to Burma in 1938, I had been forced, by circumstances, to follow a general line of domestic drama. *49th Parallel* had been a last desperate attempt to escape this inevitable fate dictated by the war. That film, at least, had been a great adventure. I had plodded on with Emeric's advice and help, trying to make domestic films into international ones, and, with an eye on the future, always trying to tell the truth as we saw it. *Colonel Blimp* had an epic theme, but it was an intimate epic. Now, at last, with *AMOLAD*, we had returned to the Big Show, to the kind of film for which motion pictures were invented. With our talents proved, our powers at full stretch, and with the knowledge that with *AMOLAD* we had made a masterpiece, and with my head full of great stories and exotic backgrounds, it may be understood that I wanted to escape from postwar England where the inhabitants were already settling down with obvious enjoyment to a programme of austerity. There is nothing that the British enjoy so much as being deprived of something. We are great queue-joiners.

Long before the war, when Frankie was London's top model girl and was in every catalogue, and on every cover, she had counted among her admirers two Peruvians, Felipe Ayulo and Felipe Beltran. They had studied in London, spoke perfect English and, like all good Latin Americans, they came every year to New York and London: to New York to do business, to London to eat kippers and chase the girls. They were both attractive men. Felipe Beltran looked like a humorous and imaginative prosperous banker. Felipe Ayulo looked like a Spanish freebooter whose spiritual home was Paris. In both cases, the first impression was correct.

Frankie had never lost touch with her Latin American lovers, and never let me forget that she had both of them at her feet. I retorted that they came to London to stay at the Berkeley and eat kippers for breakfast and for nothing else, or at all events, for nothing more important. Although Peru was neutral in the war and Franco favoured the Axis, the upper-class Latin Americans of Lima were pro-British and pro-American. As soon as the mail service became more normal, Frankie heard from them again. I was already planning my escape over the walls of the prim Rank empire and encouraged her to write to both Felipes that we planned to fly to Peru to do research for a picture. An enthusiastic correspondence followed, culminating in our departure on the *Queen Mary* for New York, on the first leg of our long journey.

Vincent Korda was a fellow passenger, and we spent many happy hours in monosyllabic conversation with him. I remember little else, only undiluted happiness and Frankie's natural uneasiness at leaving Kevin at such a tender age. Before starting the film we had acquired a new home at 2 Ilchester Place, a corner house with three storeys, a basement and a garage. It had been occupied during the last years by the NAAFI (Navy, Army, Air Force Institutes), who had left us a legacy of black beetles. But we now got rid of them, and Bill and Myrtle, who were now married, undertook to look after Kevin, thus forging a bond between the three principals which continues to this day.

We only stayed a day in New York before starting on the long hop to

Peru. In those days progress across the States by air was slow and stately. We planned stop-overs at New Orleans, Houston, Texas, and Mexico City. After that, we were in the hands of Grace Airways, who were running an experimental schedule to Latin America, and might stop anywhere. Dick Grace, who had been a Hollywood aerial stuntman for Howard Hughes on *Hell's Angels*, was, like Hughes, one of the pioneers and great individuals of American air travel. Grace and his small company had opened up a mail and passenger service right down Latin America as far as Santiago de Chile. At this time their timetables were tentative because of the lack of aircraft, but they got you there just the same.

To say we were thrilled by planning and executing these giant hops across the Americas would be an understatement. We were like fugitives from a chain gang. Of course, in those days, the aircraft were small and didn't fly at astronomical heights, and we spent the whole journey dashing from side to side to see who had the most interesting view and to check with the map where we were. We had our little adventures. At New Orleans, after dinner at Antoine's, we returned to our hotel and to our first experience of air-conditioning below the Mason-Dixon Line. It was take it or leave it for the customers, for when we tried to open the windows, we found they were all nailed shut. Panting for air, which was supplied free in our draughty English house, we decided to leave the door open. It had a chain and socket on it, presumably for parlaying with insistent insurance salesmen. We left the door open on the chain and went to bed, but not to sleep. Within half an hour, a large hand came through the opening holding an even larger gun.

"What's going on?" a voice growled menacingly. It was the house detective. We explained, but he would have none of it. "Shut the door and shut up," he said. I obeyed. "Now lock it," thundered the voice through the panels. I locked. "I'll be around again," the voice growled. We sweated through the night.

Our next stop was Houston, Texas. It is an astonishing town plonked down on the shore of the Gulf of Mexico, as if by accident. Still in pursuit of new gastronomic experiences, we inquired about the local fish, red snapper. Everyone in Houston has their favourite restaurant, which is the only one where red snapper is properly cooked and presented. An enthusiast took us to his. It meant a drive of thirty miles to a shanty on the shore. Red snapper looks like red blotting paper. It also tastes like it.

We ran into an electrical storm over Texas. Like everything in that giant state, it was big. We were first made aware of it by the aircraft dropping vertically several hundred feet. In those days, there were no safety covers on the racks overhead, and everything in them was hurled into the air and fell on the passengers. For a terrible few minutes we were tossed about like a boat in Corryvreckan as the pilot struggled to get control of the aircraft and find a safe altitude. People all round us were screaming and being sick all along the floor. Frankie said nothing. Suddenly the pilot put the aircraft into a dive and penetrated through the boiling clouds, still tossing and rolling, until we burst out beneath the cloud ceiling at only about a thousand feet above the ground. We had been flying at about ten thousand feet. All around, just below us, was this immense purple landscape, while above our heads was the black ceiling of cloud which we knew only too well and which was full of turbulence. The pilot warned us that he would continue on course at this low level and we proceeded to mop up. Several people had become hysterical, and one woman had fainted. Passengers of today, cruising at heights which make even Texas look small, and looking down on these local disturbances, can hardly imagine the terror of such an experience.

At Mexico City we were in luck. There was a fiesta, a celebration of one of the innumerable revolutions which enliven Mexican politics. Everyone had come into town and there were parades and dances. I never saw such magnificent horses so beautifully caparisoned, nor such men and women. The big parade passed right in front of our hotel balcony, where we sat eating *huevos rancheros*.

Through the growing Rank Organisation, we had a contact in the city, an agent who was going to distribute our films. I had planned to spend two days to see the Diego Rivera murals and the museums and the Aztec pyramids, and was tempted to stay a week, but our time was limited and our goal was Peru. So leaving our hearts temporarily in Mexico, we flew on.

We passed over a vast land of sleeping volcanoes.

The volcanoes started to smoke. We were over Central America. Active volcanoes became more numerous and soon we were almost inside one. No wonder these passionate little republics are so touchy. Other people – the Irish, for instance – have hot heads and hot hearts. Central Americans have hot feet as well. We were travelling now in small aircraft and made frequent stops. We literally hopped from republic to republic. We could feel and see the immense changes that Dick Grace's pioneering airline was bringing to these fierce little countries. We were dazzled and confused by the size and variety of the Americas. We had too much to learn, too much to see. We passed over the spectacular riches of Venezuela and Ecuador as if in a dream. The cloud-capped, mile-high city of Quito was our last marvel. Then as we flew south along the Pacific coast, we descended to sea level and the city of Callao, the port of Lima, capital of Peru.

As we circled before landing, I was marvelling at my luck. This is not a personal record, but the story of one man's struggle with his art. As a craft it is new. As an art, the art of storytelling, it is as old as the hills. Now that I am old and a respectable back number, a Fellow of this, a Fellow of that, I have nothing to give in return for my education but this record of what I did and what I learnt in the pursuit of my chosen profession. If there is anything of value in these pages, it is that. When I was in my twenties, there were few of us film-makers. Literature was the thing. Magazine short stories were the training ground. Radio was the new medium. Talking pictures were a distant dream – facts incredible to the children of the media of today, to say nothing of the miracles of transport and communication which have changed the life of every creative artist.

I would like to describe how the two Felipes met us, and their friends and their wives and their welcome and their hospitality, but I must content myself with describing the result of my mission, which was to find a theme for a new film which would have spiritual or moral values entwined with an exciting story and new location. It was the Inca that had brought us to Peru, and we climbed as soon as possible to his city in the clouds.

In 1945, a cultivated citizen of Lima was also a citizen of the world. He or she knew New York, London and Paris, and had probably been educated in one of those cities. Spain, of course, was the parent country, the founder of their language and literature, the builder of their magnificent churches. They looked outwards from their own country, not inward. If they were important people, they lived in Lima the capital, a sombre town with a climate all its own. It is set back in the foothills, and the clouds come down on it in the winter months. It is only twenty miles from the coast and the bustling port of Callao, where the climate is entirely different. The coastal strip between the mountains and the sea is narrow, but rich, and stretches all the way down to the frontier with Chile. There are many large haciendas in the foothills above these plains, and south of Lima is the beautiful town of Arequipa, the second city of Peru. The two cities, Lima and Arequipa, seem to symbolize the two strains in the Spanish character: Lima proud, cruel and fanatical; Arequipa gay, imaginative and sun-loving. Arequipa is the junction of the railroad built and surveyed by the British engineers that climbs a staggering ten thousand feet in eight hours to that other Peru, the high grasslands and towns of the Puno. At the time of which I am writing, few citizens of Lima had taken this train to Cuzco, the old city of the Incas and the capital of the grasslands, for at that time the mineral resources in Peru were still being surveyed. Cuzco is two miles high in the mighty Andes and you have to get used to the thin air. It doesn't suit everybody. Coming suddenly from the coast, you can be seized by *soroche*, the mountain sickness. Very few of the coastal people have gone on from Cuzco to Ollantatambo, one of the great Inca fortresses which barred the way to the ultimate sacred city Machu Picchu.

When I was a child we used to play paper games, and one of the most popular questions was to write down the Seven Wonders of the World. The list of wonders was compiled by an unsophisticated world BG (Before

Guinness). But things were moving faster in the twentieth century, and even in my childhood there had to be a second series of wonders. One of these included Machu Picchu, whose existence was known only to about ten million South American Indians. But now Peruvian archaeologists and the Rockefeller Foundation had discovered it, and it was beginning to dawn on the authorities that Peru possessed a wonder that rivalled the jungle-covered pyramids of the Maya in the Yucatan as a tourist attraction. This was now our goal.

Although first discovered before the war, the menace of Hitler and the break in communication had kept Machu Picchu a secret known only to a few people. When we arrived in Lima we had never heard of Machu Picchu, but as we visited museums and archaeological collections, we soon did. When I planned this trip – or rather this trip planned me – it was Lake Titicaca, with its balsa-reed boats and its stone circles so like our own in the British Isles, that attracted me at first. But when I heard of this lost city in the clouds, the houses clinging like swallows' nests on perpendicular mountains, the whole city orientated and motivated by the rising and setting of the sun on a strange stone pillar in the centre, then I shifted my allegiance. Titicaca could wait.

Our hosts had put us up at the country club near Lima. After a delirious week of parties, invitations and festivities and museums, we announced that we were going to Machu Picchu. Our hosts thought we were mad, but seeing that we were seriously mad they planned our itinerary for us. We took the train down the coast to Arequipa, followed by the train which toils halfway up the Andes and across the plains to Cuzco. At Cuzco I nearly lost Frankie, because a baby deer walked into our rooms in the hotel, ate some cheese which we were carrying with us, paper and all, and was discovered curled up on the bed when we came in. I really thought that I would never get Frankie away from Cuzco. We inspected the great Cyclopean walls with their huge interlocking keystones that no earthquake has yet been able to dislodge. Finally, we drove on into the heart of the mountains and came to where the River Urubamba plunges down through mountainous ravines.

It was by this mountainous route that Pizarro's men found their way to the Amazon and on to the Atlantic. There was a resthouse by the roaring, dancing river, and there was a saddle of rock about a thousand feet high on the further bank. A trail suitable only for men or mules zigzagged up the side to the top of the saddle and it was there, on this dizzy-making razor's edge, that the city of Machu Picchu had been built.

We were lucky in the timing of our visit. The existence of this mysterious empty city had been known for a long time, but had only been visited by surveyors and archaeologists. The tourist rush was yet to come. The only way up to the city was by the zigzag track on the back of a mule.

When I looked down on Frankie directly below me from the back of my own mule, I saw that she was nonchalantly sitting on her mule, while below her again, one of the Indians wrapped in a serape was playing a guitar.

Once arrived at the city, we were allowed to wander about wherever we liked. There is a tremendous view on the other side of the valley, looking down on the Andes for a change, while behind you, looking the other way, you look up at them. Smooth bare pillars of rock soar into the air, sentinels of Machu Picchu. You turn and look to the south and west, where the valley and its tremendous battlements stretch away to the sea. There is no other village or town in sight. There is room for thousands of people on the terraces of Machu Picchu, but how were they built? How watered? Was Machu Picchu the holy city of the Indians, inhabited by only a few priests and priestesses? Or was it a vast refuge from the enemy and invader, like the Jewish Masada? At all events, to see it perched there, alone and empty among these stupendous mountains, is one of my wonders of the world.

Lake Titicaca, with its balsa-reed boats, its holy islands, its stone circles and the ruins of Tiahuanaco, is another. These great stones are similar to those in the Orkneys and the Outer Isles, and at Avebury in Wiltshire, at the other side of the world. Now if the same thinking produced these same results from people in different continents, isn't it likely that there was some form of communication between them? There has been a lot of nonsense talked in Britain about these great stones. They are dubbed primitive. Only primitive minds could label them such. When I stand in these wild and lonely places, in the middle of the gigantic monuments like Stonehenge, Carnac, Easter Island, the standing stones of Stennis, the stone circle of Tiahuanaco, I sense the same exultation and achievement and belief in all of them. The organization and the effort must have been immense, but at the same time, I can feel a cool intelligence behind it – an intelligence that knew astronomy and mathematics and could use them. Machu Picchu lies in the north-west corner of the great, high grasslands; Lake Titicaca some two hundred miles away to the south on the border of Bolivia. The lake is deep, about a hundred miles long, and one of the highest freshwater lakes in the world. Standing guard over it is range after range of mountains, many of them over twenty thousand feet. The outfall of the lake is on the Bolivian side and waters the city of La Paz. The frontier between the two countries runs through the lake itself. It is an extraordinary landscape and unlike any other I know. You feel dwarfed by the scale of things and are made drunk by the high altitude and the purity of the air.

I was to be forcibly reminded of this when we finally took the little train again to rattle down to the coast. The journey was an overnight one. We had sleepers, the air was very cold, and so was the compartment, and we were nearly three miles above sea level without an oxygen mask. Suddenly I was very ill. I had been gripped by the dreaded *soroche*, the mountain sickness. I spent most of the night on the floor of the lavatory, getting rid of everything in my intestines by every means at my disposal. The train roared and rattled, and I remember that the moon was full and looked down upon me. I was cold, and I felt as if I was dying. Probably I was. It seemed to me to be most unjust that Frankie should be immune, but she was. By the time we arrived at sea level, I was the nearest thing to a corpse. They had a chair waiting for me and wheeled me in and carried me to bed. They were convinced I was done for.

"Sleep," said Frankie and read a book. I slept, and in six hours I was normal. Such is the power and venom of the mountain sickness, striking down the little men that peep and pry into the secrets of the Inca gods.

Back in Lima, we were greeted by the Felipes as if we were things from outer space. Felipe Beltran and his wife had been to Cuzco, and Felipe Ayulo had interests in mines which were being developed high up in the Puno, and of course they knew about Machu Picchu, and Tiahuanaco, and were proud of them. But they were most incredulous when I babbled about the wonders I had seen and Frankie's eyes grew bigger and bigger as she nodded her head in agreement. But when I talked of the big film that was going to be made, possibly a modern film, possibly an historical film, but certainly a great film, they became really interested and even made up their minds to go there one day themselves, which was as likely as if a merchant prince of the City of London should decide to visit the Orkneys in the days before North Sea Oil.

Our time was running out. We planned to stop at Guatemala City on our return journey, and take a run around that glamorous small country. We wanted to stop in Mexico City again and we were awaited by Jimmy Cowan and his family in Canada, where we were to spend Christmas and New Year in up-country Quebec, before returning in the *Queen Mary* again to my anxious collaborators, waiting to hear what our next film would be.

Guatemala is one of those amazing countries like Japan, like Finland, like Austria, where everyone seems to possess a sense of form and colour and where everything made for a practical reason has a practical shape and therefore a satisfying shape. The people seemed to be artists and craftsmen by nature. The airport, built with local materials in the local style, was a joy to the eye. The runway was on top of the mountain, and was rather short for the aircraft we were using. It ended rather abruptly at the edge of a deep valley, which meant you were airborne, whether you liked it or not. I wonder what they have done about that runway now in 1982, when I am writing. Perhaps they are using jump-jets to get into or out of Guatemala. We hired a car with a talkative and well-informed driver, who took us up into the hills to stay at a lake with delightful chalets on the edge of the water. The mountains of Central America are cosy and volcanic, not austere and frightening as the Andes are. But we preferred the Andes. I forgave those tall gods for their curse of *soroche*, so long as they would permit me to return.

I have dealt at such length with our trip to Latin America because it was the turning point in my life and my professional career. When I flew with Frankie to Lima it was a conscious move westwards. I suppose that I had always had this feeling that the English-speaking movie was an American movie, and that it was a very rare British film indeed that could compete with theirs. It was not a question of inspiration – half the Hollywood films had English stories and English themes and English actors. It was a matter of market. The big market was there in America. Charles Dickens knew that, but he didn't like it. I knew it and did like it. Like most Europeans, I am fascinated by America and determined that it should be equally fascinated by me. I was familiar with all the dangers of being financed by Americans. I had seen the struggles of other British film producers who had taken that road and I wanted to meet the Americans on equal terms, financed by Rank or Korda: for Korda had returned to England and raised new finances and had bought Shepperton Studios. I had made one successful foray into American territory with *49th Parallel*, which was so much an American picture in style and panache, that Columbia Pictures had bought it and made a fortune. Hollywood had openly admired my invasion of Canada and had given Emeric an Oscar for his original story. With Arthur Rank ready to finance big films, it seemed to me that there could be no better time to poach on Hollywood preserves. When we went to the country of the Incas it was with vague dreams of a spectacular Latin American film. When we returned, I was definitely planning one. If the Archers had turned this plan into reality, I think that our future would have been different. We would have been more closely allied to Hollywood and more in tune with what was going on, still remaining based at Denham or Pinewood. It was all very well to be pro-British and insular during the war, but in peacetime we needed American allies and we left that too much to the businessmen. If we had written and made a Mexican or Peruvian epic, we would necessarily have used Hollywood as our advance base, and we would have got to know men and studios. We would have been more aware, competitive, less insular. This was in my mind when I spent those ten days with Jimmy Cowan in Canada.

Jimmy, who had been our press agent on *49th Parallel*, was one of the best-informed men in the Dominion; and having thoroughly enjoyed his time with us, he had followed up with other work for the Rank Organisation. He wanted to see a Canadian film industry emerge and hoped that we would be concerned with it. I felt that so long as our base was in England, and we avoided working in Hollywood studios, we would be able to compete on equal terms with our friends in Los Angeles as natural partners and locations in the great game of making international motion pictures. I had seen from the beginning that films were welcome everywhere and were the most wonderful ambassadors for their respective countries. If our films encouraged other countries to make their own films we must help them, not murder them. And we must send them our best films, not a lot of indiscriminate footage. All these thoughts were going round in my head as we sailed back to England. I wanted to discuss them with Emeric. But he was waiting for me eagerly with an entirely different proposal.

During the war, Mary Morris had come to me with a book which she thought would make a wonderful film. She also said that it had a wonderful part for Mary Morris. It was by an author new to me at that time, Rumer Godden. It was obviously based upon experience, both spiritual and physical, and told the story of a party of Anglican nuns who were sent by their order with a Sister Superior in charge, and at the invitation of the local ruler, to establish a community in his remote kingdom in the high Himalayas. For their residence they are given a beautiful but disturbing old palace where the former Rajah used to keep his womenfolk. The view is spectacular and the wind blows incessantly. Beauty is everywhere, but it is pagan beauty. The Sister Superior's chief contact with the ruler is through Mr Dean, a rude and dissolute Englishman who is the extremely efficient manager of the ruler's palaces and plantation. The Sister Superior and her nuns go through many traumatic experiences, again both spiritual and physical, before they admit that the place is too much for them and beat a retreat, leaving behind one of their number – the youngest nun.

This young nun, Sister Ruth, was the part Mary Morris coveted, very naturally. She had made her name in the theatre very early as the young Tudor Princess Elizabeth in a play called *Young Bess*. It had got her a contract with Korda, but had not led to any earth-shaking part. She had a most unusual personality and there was no doubting her extraordinary talent. She was small, compact, agile, black-haired, large-eyed, and she had the high cheekbones and Asiatic looks that would appeal to the Korda brothers. She was an exotic. I had met her first purely as a contract artist: she had to be employed on *The Spy in Black* in the thankless part of a lady chauffeur who was really a German spy in the 1914 War. It was a tiny part but I gave her a couple of close-ups and she filled the screen when she was on it. I met her again on *The Thief of Bagdad*, where she played Conrad Veidt's familiar. The part was not very convincing, chiefly because we made it up as we went along. But she introduced real magic into the film when she appeared, disguised as the ten-armed goddess who enfolds the Sultan, played by Miles Malleson, in her embrace, before plucking a dagger from its hiding place and stabbing him in the back. "She tickled," giggled Malleson. Mary was quite unforgettable in this exotic piece of mime.

Two years later, she came to me in the middle of the war, entreating me to make a film of *Black Narcissus* and beseeching me to let her play sister Ruth, the young nun whose lack of vocation and untimely death breaks up the community and drives them into retreat.

I read *Black Narcissus* and admired it without reservation. I could see that the story, so coolly told in excellent prose, would be wildly exotic and erotic on the screen. Each nun in the little community – there were five of them – was clearly characterized. The part of the Sister Superior – Sister Clodagh, an Irishwoman – was a star part if ever there was one. But although the setting was spectacular, the story itself was intimate and dramatic and depended upon marvellous casting and the interplay of passion and devotion. An easy thing to control in a book, but I very much feared if we went to a place like Nepal, for instance, it would swamp the story. Anyway, it was quite impossible to think about a story like this in the middle of the war, and I told Mary so. She agreed objectively, but she had known about my trip to Burma and our plans for *Burmese Silver*, and the war could not go on forever. The seed had been sown.

Now here was Emeric with the book in his hand imploring me to read it. Like myself, Emeric was searching for colour and excitment, and his wife, Wendy, had brought him *Black Narcissus* saying what a wonderful film it would make. Emeric had read it and entirely agreed, and after all, it is so rare that one entirely agrees with one's wife, particularly if one is Emeric. I told him that I had read the book and would read it again, but I wanted to talk about my discoveries in Mexico and Peru. I don't think he heard me. He had already started making inquiries about the rights to *Black Narcissus*, and was mapping out the sequences of the film. And every day we were running *AMOLAD* and making changes and approving trick shots and preparing the music and the mix. I couldn't get a word in edgeways.

The organization and future of Independent Producers took up a lot of our time. As founder members of the company, Emeric and myself were consulted on every important step. At that time, the members of the board were Emeric and myself for the Archers; David Lean, Ronald Neame, Anthony Havelock-Allan and John Bryan for Cineguild; and Frank Launder, and Sidney Gilliat and Ian Dalrymple. Gabby Pascal had been admitted on a one-picture basis to make *Caesar and Cleopatra*. The chairman and managing director of the Independent Producers was George Archibald. During the war, Rank had bought both Denham Studios and Pinewood Studios. Denham had continued in commercial production; Pinewood had been occupied by the Royal Air Force Film Unit. It was now coming back into civilian use and we were asked to choose which studio we wanted as our home: Denham or Pinewood. We could have either, but not both. After a lot of heart-searching, for Denham had been our parent studio for most of us for nearly ten years, we chose Pinewood. I have often wondered whether we were right or wrong. There is no doubt which of the two studios was the better designed. Pinewood Studios were grouped around a central covered courtyard and were connected by a covered way with the original house, a magnificent building which now houses the Pinewood Club, the restaurant and many executive offices. The garden and grounds were in good order and there was a large lake in the woods which surrounded the property. In the meadow on the other side of the studio was room for a studio lot of about fifteen acres. By contrast, Denham was a sprawl: a magnificent sprawl, but still a sprawl. But it had its own laboratories, which were in a separate block and which still exist as one of the best labs in the world – Denham Laboratories. It had two of the largest stages in Europe, it had a machine-shop and pattern shop second to none; it had magnificent grounds all along the River Colne with woods and meadows suitable for any type of location (scenes for *Elephant Boy* set in India, and for *Knight Without Armour* set in Russia, had been shot there); and above all, it had the glory of being the creation of the great and glamorous Sir Alexander Korda, and it had that indefinable confidence and expertise which a film studio has when a great number of films have been conceived and carried out there. The difference between the two studios was the difference between a frontier encampment with its circle of covered wagons, and the settled town with its streets and water and lighting which arises on the site later. It was the difference between Hollywood, with its energy, extravagant use of space and ugliness, and Pinewood, with its carefully thought-out plan, its magnificent mansion, and its formal gardens. For Pinewood had been planned and built after conferences between the management and the technicians who were going to use the studio, while Denham, designed by a Hollywood architect, had been unrolled at Alex's feet like a magic carpet in *The Thief of Bagdad*. At the time we were conscious of the difference between the studios, but it didn't worry us, although it was sad to see Denham, with its magnificent stages, gradually turned over to storage. We, the Archers, were to make three of our best films at Pinewood Studios, and with the last one we were already aware of what I might describe as a certain civil service mentality in the permanent staff, which jarred with the gaiety and confidence of our unit. In this strange business of ours, there is something after all to be said for lavishness, improvisation and a certain amount of waste.

But we all voted for Pinewood and moved into our new offices there in 1946. We all had pictures in preparation, some more advanced than others. Larry Olivier joined us for one picture, *Hamlet*. After his triumph with *Henry V* he could have gone anywhere, but he came to us, bringing with him an old pal from the before the war Korda days, Anthony Bushell, as his co-director, plus his team of artists and craftsmen. By this time I had given in and agreed to do *Black Narcissus*. My dream of invading the western hemisphere with vast global productions to challenge Hollywood's greatest was shelved. My maverick days were over. We had a beautiful new studio and our sponsors looked to us to fill it with work. Rank and Davis were excited about *A Matter of Life and Death*. The leaders of the film industry were already discussing plans with Buckingham Palace for a Royal Command Performance of a film every year, and an obvious choice for the first one was *A Matter of Life and Death*. Could I give up my part in all this excitement and bustle, in all these plans? Could I lead my unit out on great expeditions at a time when most of them were coming out of the Services and settling down and finding a house and raising a family? Could I give up the position which I seemed to have won, almost without noticing it, in the British film industry? Could I let somebody else make *Black Narcissus*? The answer was: I couldn't.

But I got my own back on them all when we had the first full conference of our team, after they had read the book and when we were still writing the script. They were all sitting around the big conference table, pencils poised, pads in front of them, eyes shining, tails thumping, waiting for me to define the objective which they would then seize and carry off to their various departments to work out. Emeric sat beside me, with George Busby, the production head, on the other side. Syd Streeter, just out of the Air Force, joint production head with George Busby and master of all trades, was polishing his glasses. The art department made a solid group headed by Uncle Alfred, flanked by Arthur Lawson, his associate art director, and the large, silent man, whose pale restless eyes never left my face, whom I still did not know by name as Hein Heckroth. Opposite them across the table, with some private joke of their own, was the camera department: Jack Cardiff, Chris Challis, who was to operate the big Technicolor camera in place of Geoff (who had other plans) and George Menassian, with his lined but eternally young Peter Pan face. Alfred was smiling tolerantly, like the headmaster with a schoolboy, as Chris propounded to him some impossible problem of lighting and design. Reggie Mills sat at the end of the table, still looking a bit incredulous at his luck in joining the Archers and having had a film like *AMOLAD* to cut. Allan Gray, composer of the music for our last four films, was not present for reasons which will become apparent. Betty Curtis and Joan Page at our end of the table presided over the minutes, and the script which was still in work. Bill Paton, solid as a rock, my personal assistant and faithful friend, was sitting by Chris Challis, with whom he had formed an imposing alliance. They were both heavyweights. He knew what I was going to say and looked around him with complacency and confidence.

George Busby opened the ball in his smoothest manner: "Michael, we are all waiting to hear what part of India you have chosen for the exterior location. Alfred and his department have a lot of photographs to show you. I have a map here." He spread it out. "I would like you to look at it. Of course, the choice is fairly wide, but we're not sure about wartime conditions. We have spoken to Miss Godden. She didn't seem to have any particular place in mind. She was rather vague and said it was a combination of several places. Have you any particular place in mind, Michael?"

I said: "Horsham."

George wrinkled his brown forehead and gave a half-smile. He suspected it was a joke, but wasn't quite sure what the joke was. "Horsham?" "Yes. Horsham."

By now the whole table was paying attention. As usual, Chris Challis was the first to speak.

"Do you mean Horsham in Surrey, Micky?"

"In Sussex. We are not going to India. We are going to make the whole picture here at Pinewood."

Alfred and his department were startled, but gratified. It was obviously going to be *their* picture.

"But why Horsham, Micky?"

"There's a famous house and gardens there called Leonardslee. It has one of the most famous sub-tropical gardens in England. You should see it when the azaleas are blooming. There are half a dozen others in Britain, but Leonardslee is the best for us."

I reminded them how British merchant princes and pro-consuls when they retired and come back to Britain to live, would bring whole trees and bushes wrapped in matting to remind them of India. Himalayan plants and trees do well in the British climate. Rhododendrons and azaleas grow like weeds. Leonardslee had a deep and steep little glen planted with cedars and deodars. You would swear you were in the Himalayas. There was water too. And it was all quite easy of access. "We can do the big exterior scenes there and Alfred will design the rest at Pinewood."

Alfred nodded proudly – in fact, majestically. Already his staff were shuffling and passing coloured prints from hand to hand. The camera crew were still unconvinced. Jack was afraid that the picture would look too small. Chris was disappointed at losing a hazardous and exciting location trip to Katmandu.

"What about the mountains, the Himalayas? You can't build them."

"Glass shots. Poppa Day and his two sons will paint them."

"Did you imagine painted backings? A big cyclorama?"

"Not much. I think the backing should be just impressionistic areas of colour. We'll use matte shots as well as glass shots, of course, but we'll keep them to a minimum. We can do that because we have the whole design of the film here in our hands, or at least Alfred has. The atmosphere in this film is everything, and we must create and control it from the start. Wind, the altitude, the beauty of the setting – it must all be under our control. If we went to India and shot a lot of exteriors, according to the usual plan, and then came back to Pinewood and then tried to match them here, you would have two kinds of colour and two kinds of style."

By now Jack was getting the idea. He nodded his head enthusiastically. "We create it here from scratch."

"Yes."

"We work the whole story up in a series of master shots? We don't use stock shots at all?"

"None at all. The only problem will be the big setting of the Palace. I have to have complete freedom of movement there. I can't split it up into separate sets. It has got to be a big life-size set built on the lot, and I don't see how we can handle the problem of the backing."

"No problem," said Alfred. "I have had this problem before. This is how it is done." He was sketching a set in profile. "We build this big set on the lot with all the ups and downs that Michael wants. It will be very big and much plasterwork, but no matter! We surround it completely with a wall of planks inclining at an angle of about thirty-five degrees. Although it slopes, it is so high that it hides all other buildings and trees. We cover it with canvas and plaster. Then the scenic artist paints on it the Himalayas."

"Why sloping and why thirty-five degrees?" inquired Chris.

Jack explained: "Because we'll be shooting at midsummer and from about eight in the morning until about eight in the evening, the sun will be constant as it crosses above the set. It will fall evenly on a sloping surface. There will be no shadows. It means we can shoot all day, just as if we were on exterior. Right, Alfred?"

"Right, Jack."

By now, the feeling of disappointment was over, and everybody was getting enthusiastic and producing ideas. Emeric looked at me reproachfully. "Michael! I have never been to India. You have forgotten that."

"Don't you think I'm right to have one style of colour and atmosphere for the story from first to last under our control?"

"Of course you are right. But now I shall never see India." But he did. He was to go to the Himalayas and see the whole of India with David Lean as companion. But that would be in the sixties.

"How do we know the gardens are in good shape?" demanded Syd. "After five years of war and occupation by the Army, there might not be much left of those beautiful gardens, Michael."

"Don't worry. I was there last Saturday. The owners must have had some friends in the right sort of places. The gardens are in good shape."

At the next full meeting of Independent Producers, with Arthur Rank in the chair, and George Archibald seated beside him, we disclosed our plans. Everybody was delighted. It meant that the studio would be fully occupied for the first year of its peacetime operation, and since most of our work would be on the lot, it left stage space free for the others. I was caught. My own personal integrity and my horse sense had betrayed me. I was trapped in a studio complex. Instead of battling my way up Machu Picchu, surrounded by thousands of Indians, my unit panting in the rear, I would be painting the Himalayas on glass! I was never again to have such an opportunity to extend my horizons. Not in a film, anyway. I had snatched every opportunity in the past to continue my visual education. I shall always regret the way things went on this particular occasion. The choice which was forced on me by circumstances, coincided with an increased awareness of art, a tricky sideline for a director of popular movies. Like other artists, I was beginning to take my audience for granted.

I must have driven Emeric nearly mad in those days. No sooner was I back from Machu Picchu than I was off to Dublin. The occasion was the belated christening of Kevin. Frankie had had a baby brother called Kevin who died prematurely, and we had decided that if we had a boy he should be called Kevin. We had never been to Ireland together, and since his godmother lived in Dublin, we planned that the baby should be christened there.

St Kevin was a prince of Ireland who dedicated his life to Christ and gave his name to the little church called Kevin's Kitchen, which stands on the shores of the beautiful lake of Glendalough. It is about twenty miles from Dublin. There are many legends attached to the saint's name, for he had been quite a boy in his early days, like St Francis. Now here we were in the early spring of 1946, and Kevin not yet christened. Frankie's family, four brothers and two sisters, and her beautiful mother were on the warpath. St Kevin himself was very cross. It was Dublin now or never.

Eileen, Kevin's godmother, bought a new hat for the occasion, and we drove down to Glendalough, having made an appointment with the priest. When he learnt that Kevin was the ripe old age of seven months, he was on the point of refusing to christen him. Did he realize that we had endangered the child's life with the threat of hell-fire? I was impressed, but Frankie, being Irish, told him to shut up and get on with the job. When Kevin was sprinkled with holy water, he sat up straight, rubbing the top of his head, looking exactly like Stan Laurel as he grinned his approval. We returned to Dublin in triumph.

I had promised to be back in a week, but meanwhile I had met John Betjeman, who was representing the British Council in Dublin's fair city, and using it, the Council, to further his own ends as a poet and *bon viveur*. He had put into my hands a book entitled *My Story, by Paddy the Cope, as told to Paeder O'Donnell*, and nothing would satisfy me but I must go to Donegal where Paddy was King of Dungloe. Now if you stand in Dublin and say to yourself, which is the farthest point away from me in the northwest of Ireland, the answer is Dungloe. I decided to ride there on horseback.

I passed the word to the late Lord Glenavy, then known as the Honourable Patrick Campbell, alias Paddy Campbell, a Dublin columnist of doubtful authority and weird sense of humour. Frankie, of course, knew him of old. He reported in his column that Frankie and her English husband had been seen racing our horses madly up and down the Curragh, as a preliminary to riding across Ireland to meet Paddy the Cope on his native heath.

The story of Paddy the Cope was another of those films which only I would want to make and which I certainly should have made. Paddy himself told his story to Paeder O'Donnell. The place is Donegal in northwest Ireland; the time, the early years of this century. Paddy was a little peasant, born and bred in the township of Dungloe. In those days the peasants of Ireland were either feudal tenants of the big houses, or else, if they were freeholders, or fishermen, were in the grip of the gombeen men, the local name for the middlemen, who were the suppliers of seed, fertilisers and tools necessary to smallholders. Their lives were miserable and short, or else they emigrated to America. Paddy was like any other little peasant, short and sturdy and quick-witted. But he was not what he seemed.

One day, Jesus Christ arrived in Dungloe in the form of a young man with a wispy beard, a knickerbocker suit and a bicycle. This was George Russell, known to all literary people as "A.E.", the friend of Yeats and Synge and George Moore. Russell was working with Plunkett, the apostle of land reform in Ireland. He was spending the spring and summer touring Ireland on his bicycle, and speaking to the peasants, telling them what their rights were and how they should organize. At Dungloe he spoke standing on the church wall, and a little mob of peasants listened to him. Among them was Paddy. Now there is nothing funnier in life than an intellectual telling a peasant how to live his life. But Paddy was different and Russell's words stuck. Russell stayed with the priest that night and departed next morning for the next township. The seed that he had sown had taken root in Paddy's head.

"The Cope" stands for the cooperative. The story of Paddy the Cope is the story of how he formed a cooperative with a few friends and started to buy directly from the big firms to bypass the greedy gombeen men. It is a thrilling, touching and hilarious story. The shopkeepers nearly break him and his friends by calling in their debts and insisting on being paid up to date. Paddy persists, and goes to a friendly bank manager who advances him money for his schemes. He gets the loan of a boat for a season of fishing, and becomes a Justice of the Peace. His enemies are not done with him yet, however, and he is tried on a trumped-up charge in his own court and sent to jail. But the governor of the jail refuses to have him and he returns in triumph, the whole countryside flaming with torches and humming with the sound of cheers and brass bands to welcome him home. Paddy himself was now about sixty.

Paddy Campbell's column was widely read. Ireland was agog working out the probable route of our equestrian saga, and giving Paddy, the ultimate goal, a lot of publicity, which he appreciated by all accounts. We were deluged with advice and warnings, of course, and took heed of some of them. We planned to ride, accompanied by a dogcart and a groom. There were two reasons for this. I had saddlebags on my horse, but there was room for a suitcase in the dogcart, as well as a sack of oats and a bale of hay. The groom, in thornproof tweeds, leggings and a hard hat, plus the sturdy-looking dogcart, appeared as if by magic. His name was Mattie Gaul. As for the horses we had to ride, they were both geldings and were two fine animals. You can imagine how in horse-mad Ireland this all had to be discussed again and again and alternatives proffered.

Meanwhile, Kevin, saved in the nick of time from hellfire, would proceed by train to Donegal, escorted by Frankie's brother William, Elspeth Dey, my new Scottish secretary, and a nurse. I had spotted Elspeth when she was being chased around Tobermory by young naval officers and had offered her a job after the war. She had never followed it up, but meeting her again in Glasgow (I stepped off a tram into her arms), I again offered her the job and she took it. This was her maiden flight, so to speak.

One morning, a formidable cavalcade clattered out of a stableyard in North Dublin and took the road. We were headed for Navan, West Meath. Unknown to us, there was panic ahead all along our chosen route, which went through Navan to Cavan, then to a town I forget the name of for the moment, and then finally to the coast at Bundoran. There we were to head northwards to the town of Donegal itself, and then by the coast road up to Dungloe. I suppose it was about 120 miles all told. We had chosen county towns because we were reasonably sure of finding a hotel big enough and old enough to have stable accommodation for the horses, as well as bed and breakfast for us and Mattie. Telephoning in Ireland in 1946 was a lengthy process, so we had wired the hotel asking for accommodation for man and beast. The landlord or proprietor was at his wits' end. The stables and loose boxes were there right enough, but full of old bicycles, chickens, broken-down governess-carts, rusty farm machinery, antique motorcars and tame rabbits. But to refuse us was not possible, for now everybody on the chosen route felt that the world's eyes were upon him, particularly the eyes of his fellow Irishmen. With a great squawking and flapping of wings, chickens were hurled into the yard, followed by broken-down washstands and jerry pots. Tons of nasty hay in the racks and mangers were burnt. The hoses were turned on, and a great scrubbing and brushing followed. There was plenty of straw and hay, but no oats, begorra! By the time we clattered into Navan in the failing light, all was ready and the whole town was out to see us pass down the main street. Greetings were shouted by the women and were acknowledged by us, and Mattie Gaul whipped up his elderly horse into a respectable trot and sat very straight with his rug tucked in over his knees in the prescribed manner. We arrived at the hotel and there were people waiting for us, waving torches and directing us into the stableyard. This was travelling in the grand manner.

I was justified. What had seemed a caprice to a lot of people in Dublin, became a compliment to all the towns through which we passed, or where we stopped. Everywhere they were watching for us, everywhere we were made welcome. Whole villages and towns turned out to see us pass through and to wave and wish us Godspeed. Lonely farms and tiny hamlets had all the people standing on the road waiting for us to pass by, alerted by the radio. In some obscure way, the whole thing was held to be a great compliment to Ireland, which indeed it was. It was how I had meant it. I was not seeking publicity, but looking for the soul of the people. I found it.

We had our little adventures. Frankie didn't ride all the way, but occasionally took over the dogcart while the groom rode her horse. At one place, which seemed to be the top of Ireland, we stopped at a coal mine. There were open shafts all around us, and while I was chatting with the manager I caught sight, out of the corner of my eye, of the dogcart with Frankie in it backing slowly and inexorably into one of these open shafts. Frankie sat holding the reins poker-faced with the open shaft yawning behind her, while the horse, as horses will, backed and backed and backed. We seized his head just in time. Frankie said something. I said: "What?" She said: "He was tired of waiting."

We arrived at the west coast in a gale of wind and rain. On the edge of the ocean was a huge building, half castle, half house, Victorian Gothic, and the gigantic Atlantic rollers were thundering at its feet. There was a formidable stone pier and a harbour made of great boulders. There was not a boat in it. The waves were breaking right over the entrance to the harbour. Great swells rushed and roared up to our very feet like hungry lions. The sun was sinking and the rain was driving almost horizontally. Everything, road, castle, harbour, was awash. We banged at the great door of the castle and demanded admittance and shelter from the storm. There was only a caretaker. I asked her the name of the place. She said: "The Mullagh More."

We talked as we dried out. I commented on the fine harbour and wondered why there was no traffic.

"Sure it was built by the great Lord Palmerston himself. It was part of a scheme to make the fisheries pay."

"And did he build the castle too?"

"He did. I think he did."

"Does anybody live there now?"

"Not since the war. It's been empty all the wartime. But now it's over, thanks be to God, we'll be seeing the family again. It's a great place for children in the summer. The girls used to run wild here, getting up to all kinds of mischief, the little devils."

"Who were they, then?"

"Edwina and her friends. But that was a long time ago, when I was a girl too. She married a great man and now she's a great lady. But she still runs wild without shoes or stockings when she comes to the Mullagh More. Did you hear of Lord Mountbatten? Him that's a cousin of the King of England?"

"Yes."

"That's her man, then."

I said to myself, so the young girl that ran in bare feet had been Edwina Mountbatten. Mountbatten. How perilous to be a "great one". Thirty-two years later, Earl Mountbatten of Burma, uncle of the Duke of Edinburgh, was brutally murdered on a picnic in a small boat, in this very harbour, while Pamela, his daughter, and John Brabourne, his son-in-law, and their family were either injured or killed. For fifty years, since Edwina's childhood days, the Mountbatten family had been associated with the Mullagh More – long enough to make them fearless of danger, and an easy target for the murderers of the IRA.

If I had not passed by there in 1946, I would never have connected the two events, but the place and the house were so dramatic, so unusual, that I never forgot them, and their association with the wild little girl who was later to become Lady Louis Mountbatten, who won the hearts of all India as Vicereine, and did not live to see her childhood playground turned into a family graveyard.

The next day we passed a green mountain, its face to the Atlantic, its back to the hills. It was Ben Bulben. Yeats is buried at the foot of Ben Bulben. He wrote his own epitaph:

Under bare Ben Bulben's head
In Drumcliff churchyard Yeats is laid.
An ancestor was rector there
Long years ago, a church stands near,
By the road an ancient cross.
No marble, no conventional phrase;
On limestone quarried near the spot
By his command these words are cut:
>   *Cast a cold eye*
>   *On life, on death.*
>   *Horseman, pass by!*

As we passed by, clattering along the road, Yeats was dead and his body was far away, waiting to be brought home to Ireland from the little hilltown of Roquebrune on the French Riviera above Monte Carlo and Menton. I have known it intimately ever since I was a schoolboy. Yeats was staying with friends there when he died, and the war came and it was no longer possible to bring him home. He lies now at the foot of Ben Bulben as he hoped, but there can't be many horsemen clattering along the road these days and stopping to read those lines as we did.

They are the words of a great poet, but they won't suit everybody. They don't suit me. I have a warm and interested eye for both life and death and prefer the Jacobean lines that I am fond of quoting:

> If I must die,
> I will encounter darkness as a bride,
> and fold it in my arms.

It was marketday in the town of Donegal (it is the name of the town as well as the county), and as we pushed our way through the crowds, I had the impression that I had never seen so many men in tweed caps in all my life. They were all fine, upstanding men in tweeds, breeches, gaiters and raincoats. You could tell by the set of their shoulders that a large proportion of them were soldiers on leave from the British Army. They all seemed to have come to town to see our little cavalcade arrive. The women in their black shawls were less conspicuous than the men. They were doing all the buying and selling anyway. We stopped for a cup of tea and a dozen boys fought for the honour of holding our horses' heads, and if Mattie had drunk all the Guinness which was offered him, he would have been afloat. The country hotel where we were to meet Kevin and the others was outside the town on the road to Dungloe. As we came out to remount, we were subjected to a hail of questions and improvised songs of praise: "Four days on the road and thirty miles a day, you'll never hear the like of it? . . . Dublin to Donegal! Well, that's a wonder! . . . and you're going to fill'um the cope man, Paddy the Cope, so? . . . well that'll be a famous fill'um . . ."

About half the population accompanied us out of the town and set us on the road. Within half an hour we were reunited with Kevin. After lunch, we rode over to find the Irish poet Monk Gibbon, who was living with his family in a cottage with its feet in the sea. I had read his book *The Seals*, which had an appreciative note by A.E. on the dust cover. It is an enchanting short book, a classic from its first page. It has the colour and clearness of a rockpool at low tide. It tells of a day spent on the edge of the sea – no ordinary sea but the sea of the west coast of Ireland. A hunter and his son have come at the request of the local fishermen to cull the seals and particularly the grey Atlantic seal, which is damaging their nets. Monk accompanies the hunters on their mission. The book becomes a meditation on life and suffering. It is a very personal book with glimpses of the author and his young family. The poet was slender, of medium height, with eager blue eyes, and he radiated his enthusiasm around him, an aura that was almost visible. To be dropped in on by a film director and his beautiful wife, both of them on horseback, reduced him almost to incoherence. I say almost, because he is a voluble man, never at a loss for words. He asked a hundred questions, answered them himself, and then asked a hundred more, and then it was time for us to go. We were only there an hour or so, but so bright and innocent was the personality of the man, and so infectious his interest, that he made a lasting impression on both of us.

The coast was low here, with green close-cropped grass at the water's edge. The sand was white, and the lazy sea sparkled green in the setting sun. As we explored a mile or more, cove after cove opened up, some of them with harbours, some with nothing but the sea-wrack strewn on the shore. There was the wreck of a large boat, whose ribs stood naked like those in "The Ancient Mariner". There were no villages, just farms and isolated cottages standing as close to the sea as they dared. We rode back to the hotel with our eyes and our lips and our tongues salt-encrusted.

The next day it was the little seaport of Dungloe and Paddy the Cope.

Paddy was dressed up to meet us, with a black jacket and tweed hat, as befitted such an important occasion. There were several girls who worked in the factory of the Cope, all in their best, and there were a few intimates, one or two of whom had figured in the book, and they were introduced accordingly. I can't remember whether we rode to Dungloe or went by car. I know the horses had to be boxed back pretty smartly to Dublin, and it would seem a shame, having ridden across Ireland, not to have ridden right to Paddy's feet. Maybe Mattie had to get the horses back pronto. Anyway, we didn't part with him that day because we parted with him the next, with congratulations on how he had taken it all in his stride. In reply he made a courteous speech saying that "it was the grand riders that we were – not a sore back on any of the horses after 125 miles!"

Anyway, if we arrived in Dungloe by car, I at least arrived in the kilt. I had seen in *IKWIG* what a handy nether garment a Scottish kilt is, and I was determined to have one for my expedition. It was warm, it was handsome and it was great on the hills. On arrival in Dublin, I went to the best sporting tailor and was measured for one. To what tartan was I entitled? I was asked by the tailor. I was married to a woman who was Irish born on both sides and who claimed to be a descendant of the rightful kings of Ireland. We settled for a saffron kilt. I wore it for the first time striding over the lower hills around Dungloe. My wearing the kilt discomposed Paddy considerably. He couldn't figure out how I could have ridden across Ireland on horseback in the kilt. I don't think he ever settled it comfortably in his mind.

Paddy was short and thick-set with a round, rosy baby face, bald, and with very shrewd eyes set deep in his head. He had charm and was quick on the uptake. Conversation with him was a joy. He had something to say about everything. He was proud of his story and understood why I would want to film him, and was quick to follow up a question with an anecdote as explanation. He took us to every one of the crofts and shops which figure in his story. It was a soft day with a weak sun and we saw a lot. Of course, much had happened since he told the book to Paeder O'Donnell. The Cope had prospered and they had a fishing boat now as well. The big building down by the jetty belonged to the Cope. They had correspondence now all over the world, partly business, partly friendship sparked off by the book. He went at least twice a year to Dublin and once a year to London.

It was important for us that he should agree to be adviser on the film. He would agree to be consulted on the casting, and particularly on the actors who played himself and his wife. Then we would need all sorts of facilities, most of which we could supply. He agreed readily to all this and could hardly believe it when I told him we would pay him for our consultations, as well as a separate contract for the rights to make a film of the book. I said I would pay him £500 for a ten-year option and he danced with delight. We got back to London and Chris Mann worked out a contract, and we sent it to him with a cheque. I hear that he went all round the township showing the cheque before he put it into his bank.

The next day we took the little train back across Ireland to Dublin. No crowds cheered and waved and shouted good luck as we steamed steadily along the single track. We were no longer romantic and glamorous cavaliers. We were just British tourists.

At Dublin we had an exciting invitation waiting for us. I had told Seton Gordon that we were going to Ireland and would be staying in Dublin. He had answered with a long letter forbidding us to leave Dublin until we had been to the island of Lambay and seen the seabirds there. "It's a sizeable island. It lies north and east from Howth and is about two miles out from the mainland of Ireland. It has a private ferry and the landing place is near Malahide. Rupert Baring, the new Lord Revelstoke, is a great friend of mine, and will be delighted to have you as his guests. I have written to Rupert and he will be writing to you at your hotel. You must on no account miss the birds at Lambay. Although it is so close to Dublin, it has one of the finest colonies of fulmars in the world."

We were intrigued and went to the map case. There it was, in plain view of Ireland's eye. Lambay is about a mile long north to south, and half a mile across east to west. The landing place and harbour is on the west, two or three hundred yards from the castle itself. From there the land slopes upward to end abruptly in cliffs about two or three hundred feet high. There is little doubt that, but for the war, we would have made *I Know Where I'm Going* in Ireland. Lambay's distance from the mainland, its physical characteristics, are almost exactly as called for in Emeric's story. Lambay had a radio telephone which Rupert Revelstoke used to talk to the lighthouse keepers and to the telephone exchange in Dublin, who would then forward the message. So on our first arrival in Dublin, before the great trek from sea to sea, we received a mysterious message saying "Fran will be getting in touch with you. She has a boutique (here follow directions)." Fran duly appeared, a shrewd and attractive lady, and brought an invitation from Lord Revelstoke to stay with him on our return from the west. It soon became clear that Fran's boutique was his advance listening post in Dublin.

On the appointed day a hired car came for us, sent by Lambay, which took us to the landing place opposite the island. It was not just at Malahide, but near enough to it to excite me, for it was at Malahide that the Boswell papers were discovered in a croquet box which has much the size and shape of a coffin, in a summerhouse where they had lain for years. It was an amazing literary discovery. If Boswell's diaries could be discovered in such a manner – who knew what other discoveries are mouldering in other such country houses? We had been told to be prompt, for we had "to catch the tide", and Neddy, the boat captain, notoriously waited for no man or woman. The boat was a big, rough coastal boat, very suitable for those rough waters. They were loading some animals into the hold – I think they were beef cattle going to be fattened on Lambay's good grass before the September sales. The tide was nearly at the full. We climbed on board and dropped into the cabin with our baggage and Neddy cast off almost immediately. The crossing took about twenty minutes. When we were about halfway across, I spotted through the glasses a solitary figure walking down from the Castle and along the high stone jetty. It was Lord Revelstoke. A red setter loafed along beside him.

The first thing I noticed about him was the way his black eyes danced, full of mischief. They were set in a weatherbeaten face. He seemed to be about our own age and size, but I believe he was younger. He looked us over with relief. He had a shy smile which was immensely attractive. He was dressed in a whipcord suit and wore a cap. He asked about Seton and about the ride to Donegal, about which, of course, he had heard full reports on the radio. We walked up to the house together, chatting, already friends.

Lambay Castle is a Lutyens castle, and when you have said that you have said everything. Edward Lutyens was a great architect. He was the architect of New Delhi, the capital of India, and many other public monuments and buildings. When asked to design a private house, he gave the client the house that he considered good for him, not necessarily the most practical and convenient. Lambay Castle was one of his mediaeval larks, like the castle on the Farne Islands, already mentioned, where Roman Polanski made his deliciously gloomy film *Cul de Sac*. Lutyens delighted in remote estates belonging to rich people where he could indulge his talent for organizing materials and men, and could gratify his taste for military architecture and monastic splendour. Lambay Castle, however, was not like that. I am sure that he described it to himself as "an intimate little job". It was built on the site of the old house, but resembled it in no particular. It was square with arquebus towers at each corner so that the defenders could cover the walls. Who Lutyens thought would be invading the island and storming Lambay Castle I have no idea, but I expect he thought that, in Ireland, you never know. The castle was attractive, built on bricks and stone and with lattice windows. The Great Hall where there was also a great fireplace, was one of the most charming and uncomfortable rooms I have ever sat in. Draughts came at you from every point of the compass. Draughts were one of Lutyen's greatest triumphs. At Lambay you had to leave the front door open or otherwise the fire in the Great Hall smoked. The bedrooms, however, were unexpectedly charming. The kitchen, like all Lutyen's kitchens, was vast and mediaeval, suitable for roasting oxen, baking bread and spitting partridges. It was also very cold, since the cook seldom used the vast fireplace, and cooked everything over an oil stove.

We stayed on Lambay for nearly a week. Emeric had sent me his completed draft script of *Black Narcissus*, and I had brought it with me. I worked on it every morning in the library while Rupert and Frankie explored the island. We had always written our own original stories, as well as the film script, unless you count *The Spy in Black*, which was in script form already when it was handed to us to transform, and I was nervous about tackling an adaptation from a book. The elements that make a book a success are not the same as those that make for a good film, and I had learnt to know the difference. Emeric had done a good job, and I was almost persuaded that we had written the original story ourselves.

I finally decided to give the part of Sister Ruth to Kathleen Byron. This was the part Mary Morris had wanted to play. Kathleen had done very well as the angel in *AMOLAD*. She was young, confident and unusual looking, with extraordinarily big eyes and a long pointed nose. I thought she could do it. Who was to play the Sister Superior, Sister Clodagh, I had no idea. I had dreamed for a short time of persuading Greta Garbo to return to the screen to play the part. It called for a woman in her thirties, Irish, of great authority, devoted to religion and to the religious order to which she belonged. Meanwhile, I wrote to Kathleen, telling her that she had got the part. Frankie saw the letter on the hall table waiting for the mailboat and brought it in to me in the library, where I was struggling with the part of Kanchi, the young Indian girl who brings the world, the flesh, and the devil into the nuns' retreat.

"What are you writing to Kathleen about?" asked Frankie with typical directness, flinging the envelope down on the table. I told her.

"Why couldn't you tell her when you got back? What's so special about Kathleen Byron that she has to have a special letter from you?" It was a good question. "Her nose is too long, she's got no bust, and her legs are bowed." Frankie needed nobody to write her dialogue for her. "I suppose you think you're a sort of god handing out parts in exchange for fucks. Can't you see it's not you she's after - it's the part?"

Having delivered this last shot, Frankie withdrew, or perhaps it would be fairer to say she stormed out, passing Rupert, who was lounging in to get a book, or to find Frankie for a further flirtation. He overheard the final remark.

"I say, I say," he said, shaking his head. "Family tiff, eh? 'Don't bring my wife into this', what?" It was one of Rupert's favourite quotations, and he uses it on every suitable or unsuitable occasion. "Don't bring my wife into this." He claimed that a member of his club had said this fiercely on one occasion, but he always made it sound light and slightly absurd.

At the north end of Lambay there was a gulf of cliffs with walls about two hundred feet high. This was where the fulmars nested. There were a lot of shag and cormorants swimming and diving or standing on the rocks, giving the alarm, and all the other usual sea birds, but the fulmars were a hundred to one. On a calm day we took the small motorboat and went round to the spot, and Rupert shouted and stood up in the boat as if he had a gun. In an instant, the air was white with fulmars travelling like bullets, deserting their nests on the ledges, skimming over the water, knocking the men's hats off, before circling again and returning to the cliffs above. It was an incredible sight.

Frankie wanted to know the difference between a cormorant and a shag, because they are very alike. The shag is a rather more untidy-looking bird, and not such a blue-black colour as the cormorant. In reply Rupert recited the following sloka, which he had composed, he claimed, himself:

> The common cormorant or shag
> Lays eggs inside a paper bag.
> Lest hoards of bears should come with buns
> And steal the bags to hold the crumbs.

There were very few trees on Lambay and consequently very little game. Occasionally, Rupert would take his gun and see if he could get "that woodcock". As far as I know, he never did. Of all game birds, the woodcock with its sharp zigzag flight is the hardest to hit. I don't think Rupert ever really tried. "That woodcock" was just one of the fantasies which made life on Lambay supportable for him. There were also two wallabies. The wallaby is a friendly animal, unlike the kangaroo, and an unconscious clown. The dogs could not bear them and made a great fuss of Rupert when the wallabies were around.

I finished my work on the script, and it was time to go. Time? There was no such thing as time on Lambay. An island has a timeless quality in which nothing matters but the tide. This is why so many rich and famous men have chosen islands as their second home. On Lambay, the Revelstokes; on Colonsay (the island that I chose to represent Kiloran in *I Know Where I'm Going*), Lord Strathcona and Mount Royal; on Mull, Lord Redesdale, the father of the Mitford girls. These were all great men or the sons or grandsons of great men, seeking for a little kingdom of their own. The Revelstoke title came from building the Canadian Pacific Railroad. Revelstoke was the highest point in the Rockies for the CPR, where the lines being driven from east to west and from west to east finally met. Rupert's family name was the famous one of Baring. The family were bankers, in origin German, and their present bank has a character all its own. They are a remarkable family in which the men and women are creative, eccentric and efficient. The late Lord Cromer, Viceroy of Egypt in all but name, was one of them, Evelyn Baring. Maurice Baring, the novelist and anthropologist (he published a delightful book of quotations entitled *Have You Anything to Declare?*), was Rupert's uncle. Rupert loved him and charmed me with tales about him. Maurice Baring had always charmed and irritated me by turns. He spoke several languages including Russian and I suppose he was influenced by Proust, but, of course, I had never heard of Proust at the time I was gobbling down his novels *C* and *Cat's Cradle*, and his autobiography, *The Puppet Show of Memory*. When we left Lambay with

thanks and regret, Rupert came with us, ostensibly to interview a family for
one of the cottages on the estate, but actually to escape for a while from
the little kingdom that he had inherited and of which he was chief. We
had an uproarious evening in Dublin. The next day Frankie and I left on the
steamer for Holyhead.

It was time I returned. I had a hundred questions to be answered, and not
least of them the casting of the actors in the film. Who was going to play Mr
Dean, the drunken but competent manager of the ruler's estate? Answer:
David Farrar. Who was going to play Kanchi, the sexy little piece who
attracts the eye of the young prince? Answer: Jean Simmons, a stunningly
pretty and talented sixteen-year-old, who made her film debut with
Anthony Asquith in *The Way to the Stars*. Both Larry and I wanted her for
our films: Larry to play Ophelia opposite his Hamlet; the Archers to play
Kanchi in *Black Narcissus*. Both wanted her at the same time and neither of
us would give way. Only the great Arthur Rank, who was fast assuming
Jove-like proportions, could solve the dilemma. Who would play the
young Prince? Answer: Sabu. Above all, who was going to play Sister
Clodagh? Answer: Deborah Kerr, said Emeric.

I laughed at the idea. I turned it down flat. She was too young, far too
young, ten years too young. Emeric was too old a bird to be caught with
chaff.

"If she were as old as Garbo, you'd want her to look ten years younger
than she is. Deborah is twenty-six and can easily look thirty-six. And she
won't mind doing it, either."

Deborah was under contract to Metro-Goldwyn-Mayer, who would
ask an enormous fee for her services. She had been under contract ever
since 1943 – didn't I know it! – and they had still not yet called her to
Hollywood. Now they would want to get back all the accumulated costs on
her contract. Emeric chose to ignore this and said that he had arranged a
dinner to discuss the part with Deborah herself at the Etoile, my old haunt
in Charlotte Street. The dinner took place. Deborah had been working at
Denham and at Pinewood during the past years, and I had hardly caught a
glimpse of her. Those soul-searing days when the irresistible force of
paganism met the immovable concrete of Christian Science were far behind
us and yet very near. With those passionate days vivid in our minds, there
was something ridiculous about peeping at each other over the top of a
menu while we discussed working together again.

My final conclusion was "You're too young."

Her final conclusion was "It's in your hands, Michael. If you say I can
do it, I can do it. How old is she?"

"Thirty-six."

"I know how to play her. They won't think about the age." A pause. "Who is playing Sister Ruth?"

"Byron, Kathleen Byron."

"Do I know her?"

"I don't think so."

"It's a good part."

"She's good."

"Whoever plays Sister Ruth will steal the picture."

"Are you crazy? Sister Clodagh is the best part you'll have in years!"

"Oh! I thought you said I was too young for it."

"So you are."

Emeric had been thoughtfully inhaling a *Tête de veau vinaigrette* as a preliminary to an *Entrecôte sauce béarnaise*: At this point he put in a word: "Do you think that MGM would loan you out, Deborah?"

"Oh, wouldn't they just! They're as mean as anything. You know I'm on a retainer and they take half of everything over that."

Emeric asked solemnly, with a mouth full of *sauce béarnaise*: "Are you expensive, Deborah?"

"What do you think?"

"I think you're expensive."

I went to see Ben Goetz, head of MGM-British. The studio at Elstree was the best-run studio in the country. He and his wife, Goldie, were very much liked and very popular. He was a big man, intimidating, until he took off his glasses to wipe them. Then he looked what he was, a kind, fatherly man. They asked £20,000 for Deborah for twelve weeks' work. I was dismayed. This was nothing like any of the salaries any of us had ever paid anyone, except Sam Goldwyn.

Ben saw my face. He looked sympathetic. "Is it budget trouble, Micky?" he asked tenderly, almost feeling for the spot with his immense hand. I nodded dumbly. We settled for £16,000. So my two mistresses, one ex and one current, were both working for me in the same picture. It was a situation not uncommon in show business, I was told, but it was new to me.

Sister Briony was played by Judith Furse; Sister Philippa by Flora Robson. Sister Honey – that was a pet name the nuns gave her – was played by Jenny Laird. Judith Furse was unforgettable with her huge body, commanding height and masculine voice. She was homosexual. I first saw her act on the London stage in Robert Morley's first play, *Goodness How Sad!* Judith's sister Jill Furse, dark, slim, talented and destined to die young, was also in the play. Their brother Roger Furse was a painter and theatrical designer. This talented and attractive family had been associated with the

Old Vic and the avant-garde theatre for some years. Roger Furse was a good painter and a friend of Larry's. Although he didn't design the film of *Henry V*, he contributed a lot of the best effects to it, and also to Larry's other Shakespearean adventures. Judith had played a small part in *A Canterbury Tale*. I had been looking for a chance to get her monstrous shape and towering authority into a real part on the screen. Sister Briony was the ideal opportunity.

Jenny Laird was a young Scottish actress whom I had seen often on the stage, notably in one of James Bridie's plays at the Westminster Theatre. I liked her directness and the way she got on with the job. Flora Robson, of course, was a famous actress, and Alex Korda had made her a star when he played her as Queen Elizabeth in *Fire Over England*. Now she had agreed to play Sister Philippa, the gardener amongst the little party of nuns, and I was almost afraid of my good luck.

We passed them in review. Sister Philippa quite obviously had green fingers – she reminded me of one of my aunts. Sister Honey adored children and especially babies. Sister Briony, a tower of strength in every sense of the word, had a medical degree. Sister Ruth was the brainy one; she was a Ph.D., taught school and had fantastic nightmares. Sister Clodagh, ah! Sister Clodagh! The veritable Admirable Crichton among missionary nuns. She is certain of her vocation and proud to be tested now in her first command. She was to be tested. Gradually the images of the actresses that I had chosen took over from the images in the book. They were a wonderful team, inventive, afraid of nothing. I identified with them so strongly that sometimes, when I run the film today, I expect to see myself coming round the corner or along the twisting corridors of the House of Women.

Ayah, the masterful old guardian of the place, who brings a touch of bawdy realism into the nuns' airy plans, is played by May Hallatt. I took a long chance in casting this diminutive English actress in the part, but it came off. There were sequences of her haunting the weird old place that were pure choreography, and she told me afterwards that she had no idea what I was driving at when I was miming them for her. Anyway, it worked.

Over Jean Simmons there was war between Larry and me, as I have already said. Messages flew to and fro between the opposing camps:

"Dear Larry, anybody can play Ophelia. I can play Ophelia. How about Bobby Helpmann? Love Micky."

"Dear Micky, how you could imagine that a typical English teenager, straight from the vicarage, can play a piece of Indian tail, beats me. I enclose a book of erotic Indian pictures to help your casting director. Love Larry."

"Dear Larry. Thanks for the book. I do my own casting, but it will come in handy for the make-up department. Micky."

"Dear Micky. Viv has read *Black Narcissus*. She wants to know if you are serious about Jean playing Kanchi?"

"Perfectly serious. Micky."

"Dear Micky. Arthur Rank suggests that our two production managers get together over Jean Simmons. Do you agree? Larry."

"Something is rotten in the state of Denmark. Love Micky."

In this way did the two plum parts of the year fall into Jean Simmons's luscious lap. She was lovely in both of them. I don't think that she was ever quite so good again.

The part of the ruler's estate manager and boon companion was the kind of part that makes a star of an unknown young man. David Farrar was not unknown, but he was not well known either. I had met him about a year previously when I paid a visit to Vernon Sewell at Elstree. Having made a success of *The Silver Fleet*, he was given a series of small films to do by the new company that had taken over the Joe Rock Studios. For the record, when I first went to Elstree in 1928, the little group of buildings was the studio of Ideal Films, and the sloping tiled roof still had Ideal Films painted on it in large letters. The day after that it became the Blattner Studios, then after Ludwig Blattner died and his son Gerry Blattner continued as studio manager, the place became the Rock Studios. After Joe Rock returned to Hollywood, I believe the place was financed during the war by Lady Yule. At the time I'm speaking of it was run by one Lou Jackson, who was in charge at the time of my visit in 1945. It was an Air Force film that Vernon was directing and I was introduced to the cast and was immediately struck by the dark and saturnine good looks of David Farrar. He had violet eyes. He was very relaxed and had the kind of physical appeal which is rare among British actors, but which is necessary for success on the screen. He spoke a rather artificial kind of BBC English, giving the impression that he would be much better in a much tougher and more realistic part. I didn't know his background, but I guessed that wherever he was born or brought up he might have acquired a strong local accent which he was doing his best to streamline. He reminded me in looks of Gary Cooper. He was an astonishing young man to find in a set-up like Lou Jackson's. Women of course recognized his quality at once. I sent for him, and we made a screen test in colour. He burnt up the screen. I realized that this intolerant behaviour was a product of real humility and genuine ambition. He and his actress wife had tried to run a little theatre together and they had aimed high. Emeric was as impressed by him as I was, and we did a thing that we never did before or since for any actor. We put him under contract for three films.

As if all this was not enough, we added Sabu to the cast. I had never forgotten my little friend of those months before the war, and I don't think he had forgotten me. At that time we had both been on the brink of great changes and new experiences. Although we had never corresponded, I knew what he was doing and he had heard of me. After Alex and Zoli had completed *The Thief of Bagdad* in Hollywood, they went to work immediately on *The Jungle Book* by Rudyard Kipling. It was made at what was later to be the Zoetrope Studios, which at that time was much bigger, and the available space was shared between Alex and Edward Small. As well as the present studio, they owned the neighbouring lot, which is now a car park, and Francis Coppola and his brother told me that they remembered seeing on their way to school the big *Jungle Book* sets and the monkeys creeping about and palm trees and other exotic props. On one memorable weekend the monkeys escaped into Hollywood, and it took the police and the fire brigade as well as the animal trainers to round them all up. By the time *The Jungle Book* was finished the tide had turned in Europe and the three Kordas turned with it. Denham was no longer available. Alex bought Shepperton Studios at Laleham, on the Thames. There was no part in the New London Films for Sabu, who had once been one of their great stars. He was now twenty-two. He had enlisted in the American Army after Pearl Harbor, and was an American citizen. He had married, and his wife Marilyn was, and is, a honey. In Hollywood he was in demand for jungle pictures, but now, after the war, none of the big companies were planning fantasies or fairy tales like *The Thief of Bagdad*, which had brought him the salary and the billing of a star. Sabu was quite cheerful about it. He showed his good sense by accepting everything that was offered. He knew very well that he had come from nowhere and he had no intention of ending up nowhere.

At this point, Bill Burnside in Hollywood searched him out and told him that his old friend Micky Powell wanted him to co-star with Deborah Kerr in *Black Narcissus*, in which he would play an Indian prince. The young General in Rumer Godden's book, and our script, was an attractive character. He was a boy with all a boy's charm and innocence, but with the power of life and death. He speaks English well but uses it in his own way. When Sister Clodagh is trying to establish her authority over the nuns and even over Mr Dean, the young Prince comes looking for her with the words: "I want to see the Superior Sister."

It is he who comes to the school where Sister Ruth is teaching and stinks the whole place out with a scent called "Black Narcissus" which he has ordered from the Army and Navy Stores in London. He is friendly and eager, but he also has charm and authority.

In fact, it was a part tailor-made for Sabu, who possessed all these qualities. When he replied enthusiastically, we enlarged the part. Sabu was shrewd and soon saw this was no ordinary film, and he was proud to be in it. As for me, I was delighted to help my little friend. I didn't look on Sabu as an exotic, as so many people did – an Indian boy from the Maharajah's elephant stable who had become a film actor. Sabu was much more than that. It is curious to me that so few people, audience or critics, realize how much Sabu gives to a film that everybody loves, like *The Thief of Bagdad*. It was because the leading part was played by a child, and by such a wonderful, graceful, frank, intelligent child, that the film delighted audiences all over the world. Magical tricks and colour and vivid spectacle help to make a fantasy work, but it is the human beings in the fantasy who make it immortal. In a fairy tale we need the kind of people we all know as well as hobgoblins or jinnies or magicians!

Esmond Knight, as the ruler of the mountain state, was the last actor to be cast.

In those days, when the war was just over, there was an immense floating population of Asians around London Docks, and we had no difficulty in building up a list of extras for the crowd scenes: Malays, Indians, Gurkhas, Nepalese, Hindus, Pakistanis, hundreds of them. We formed groups of different castes and races, and each group had a leader. We began to notice how clever the art department were being about the handling of these people. The costume department would encourage them to bring their own costumes or to pick out props and costumes for themselves from the common store. I noticed again how brilliantly the big man with the pale eyes, whom Alfred Junge kept so much in the background, was gradually creating an ensemble that was remarkably convincing. Of course, I had been in India and Burma and had something to build on too.

At this time, 1946, I was already groping my way towards a composed film, which I only finally achieved with *The Tales of Hoffmann* in 1951. Owing to my decision not to shoot in India and try and combine real location photography with studio scenes, I was left free to compose a sound-track which would be an organic whole of dialogue, sound effects, and music, very much in the way that an opera is composed. Film music and film sound effects are too often just a hodge-podge of flashy ideas, some old, some new, and effective only as far as the amount of money expended. This had been all very well for the kind of films that I had produced in the past, but it was not the way that I hoped to go on in the future. Films are too expensive a toy to be left to chance. We have seen only recently, in 1981, how a rather dull subject, simple to the point of simple-mindedness, can be transformed into a work of art and an exciting experience by using a musical theme creatively. I am referring to David Puttnam's film *Chariots of Fire*. For *Black Narcissus* in 1946 I had already decided to part with my excellent film composer, Allan Gray, in order to find a composer who thought operatically and whom I could entrust with all the sound effects for the film, as well as the music itself. If possible, I also wanted my composer to have experience of India and of Indian sounds. It was a tall order. But since I am talking of the film business with its limitless resources, I was able to find him with a recommendation from Carol Reed, who had met him in India when he was with a documentary film unit during the war. His name was Brian Easdale.

Allan Gray had composed the music for all our films, since and including *Colonel Blimp*. He had a keen ear for a tune and wrote all his own orchestrations. His main gift was a dramatic one. He had the capacity to enter into the idea of a scene or a situation, but it was still film music in the traditional way, applied on, as it were, mixed into the sound-track and the dialogue of the actors, like the rich glazing on a ham. I wanted someone with a more creative approach. I wanted someone who was my superior in musical thought, a collaborator who would lead me out of my depth and whom I could tempt even further out of his. I wanted collaborators who were the best in Europe and I wanted a continuous argument with them. Nothing else seemed to me to justify the kind of work that went into making a film.

I had been using music for years as a tool, which I pretended to be able to handle. I had never looked on music as a language, a philosophy, or a science. I had used it in my films as just another sound. When Muir Mathieson suggested that we invite Ralph Vaughan Williams to write the music for *49th Parallel*, I had a glimpse of what could be done in our medium by a great composer, but I didn't follow it up. Instead, it was Larry Olivier who commissioned William Walton to write the score for *Henry V*. These were genuine attempts at enlarging the scope of film.

In *Black Narcissus*, it was only a short sequence, perhaps ten or twelve minutes in a film lasting 112 minutes, but this sequence was really to be my first composed film. The technical phrase "composed film" is not my own. I have borrowed it from an ingenious Swiss film producer who produced a film called *The Robber Symphony*, and showed it in London at the Queen's Hall before the war. It was well received by the critics, both as a film and as music. He claimed to have written the music first and then shot the film to playback. I never saw his film, but the experiment interested me and stuck with me. I had unconsciously always been interested in the relations between music and film. In the silent days, when we quite often had a three-piece orchestra on set, I had noticed how the music affected the work of the technicians as well as the performance of the actors. When talkies came in and Hollywood started experiments with the film musical, we were all excited and interested but, as I have said, I had become accustomed to regarding music as something you brought to the film to increase its theatrical effect, after the actual shooting was finished. It can only have been a kind of restless ambition, a subconscious desire to experiment, which made me want to reverse the order of things.

In Brian Easdale, I had found the ideal musical collaborator. We understood each other over music the way Emeric and I understood each other over story. His suggestion of a new setting for "Lullay My Liking" for the Christmas carol scene in the House of Women was delightful and I accepted it at once. But I was still haunted by *The Robber Symphony*, and longed for a film subject where the music was the master. I felt that by working in harness with the composer, I would make a big step forward in the composition of my films. This may seem obvious now, but it wasn't then. We settled upon the sequence which followed the rejection of Sister Ruth by Mr Dean. It starts with Sister Clodagh haunted by her conscience and literally haunted by Sister Ruth, bent upon her murder.

In *Black Narcissus*, I started out almost as a documentary director and ended up as a producer of opera, even though the excerpt from the opera was only about twelve minutes long. Never mind! It was opera in the sense that music, emotion, image and voices all blended together into a new and splendid whole. By music, of course, I mean not only sounds produced by musical instruments, but the human voice itself. Although neither Deborah nor Joseph nor Sister Ruth used their voices for anything but screams, music dictated their movements and revealed their thoughts and intentions. The sequence started with little Joseph – I don't know why I have left Joseph out of my summary of the cast, because he was certainly one of the great successes of the film – bringing a cup of tea to Sister Clodagh as the colours of dawn spread over the snows of the Himalayas, and ends with Sister Ruth falling to her death. It was planned step by step, bar by bar, by Brian and myself. I wanted to get the maximum of suspense out of the cat-and-mouse play between the two women and we succeeded. The crew were amazed when Brian and I appeared with stopwatches and exact timings when we started to shoot the sequence.

I insisted on rehearsing and shooting to a piano track and consulting Brian with a musical score in my hand over each set-up. But it worked! It worked! I have never enjoyed myself so much in my life. For the first time I felt I had control of the film with the authority of the music. It was astonishing to everyone, but particularly, of course, to the camera crew that we were able to compress or speed up the movement of the action just by saying: "No, that wasn't fast enough. We've only got seven seconds for that bit of action."

I was so happy! I swore that this was the only way to make films; and so, of course it is, if they are silent films or musical films. But for me, film-making was never the same after this experience, and it was to lead me and my collaborators into tribulations as well as triumph.

Our editor, Reggie Mills, had been delighted, of course, by this development. He was far more musical than any of us, and he put the sequence together in about three days, editing with the score propped up in front of him and the piano track Brian had written and recorded himself on the side. But until Emeric and I were seated in the recording theatre, watching the screen while Brian, with earphones on his head to enable him to listen to the original piano track, conducted a thirty-eight-piece orchestra and a dozen voices, I did not realize what a breakthrough we had made. Here was the "composed film" that I had been dreaming about in which music, emotion and acting made a complete whole, of which the music was the master.

What else can I say about *Black Narcissus*, but that we made it and that, like Gloucester's Bastard in *King Lear*, "there was good sport" in its making. It is a handsome picture, and in design and execution it has not often been surpassed. Giving the nuns off-white robes, or rather the colour of oatmeal, was an inspiration. Their robes gave a key to the picture to which all other colours had to conform. The actresses had very little make-up, and what there was, unless they had weatherbeaten faces like Sister Philippa, was white and bloodless. This made the scenes where Sister Ruth confronts her Sister Superior with red lipstick, all the more shocking. It is the most erotic film that I have ever made. It is all done by suggestion, but eroticism is in every frame and image from the beginning to the end.

As predicted by Deborah, Kathleen Byron nearly stole the picture. Nearly . . . but not quite. Deborah is a modest lady, but she doesn't allow things like that to happen easily. She wrote to me some months later from Hollywood (she was working on a Clark Gable picture, *The Hucksters*), and said: "There is a new young actress in this picture, who is almost as big a menace to me as Sister Ruth. But not quite. Her name is Ava Gardner."

For after one good look at *Black Narcissus*, Louis B. Mayer had decided to send for his new star. But pronto!

The proprietor of the house at Horsham with the Himalayan garden, Sir Giles Loder, was the most relaxed and generous man I have ever met, and allowed us to run all over his beautiful garden with our unit of about a hundred people, without turning a hair. Leonardslee Gardens are one of the great sights of England. Although the actual area of the garden is not all that great, the scale of everything is so perfect that the audience never doubted for a moment that we were in the Himalayas. I have heard heated arguments, and in fact I have had them myself, with people who insisted that they knew the exact native state we had gone to, and the actual locations that we had used to make the film. It was a fine summer that year in England and we took full advantage of it. Alfred's great setting of the palace, with its gigantic sloping plaster backings, worked perfectly, as he said it would. The costumes – again in the hands of Hein Heckroth – were brilliantly imagined and executed. We exchanged a word or two in the heat of battle, but I still didn't know his name. Jack Cardiff and Uncle Alfred had many a scrap about colour, light and the direction of light, and the sum of their quarrels added up to a total that got them all Academy Award nominations in Hollywood. I believe the picture had half a dozen nominations and in the end it won three Academy Awards, as far as I remember: one for Jack Cardiff for colour photography, two for Alfred Junge as art director and set decorator. But although I knew naturally that we had got these nominations and awards, I still didn't know Hein's name.

When Larry Olivier saw Jean Simmons on the screen doing Kanchi's dance in the Blue Room setting of *Black Narcissus*, he couldn't believe it was the same girl who had played Ophelia. When I saw Larry's *Hamlet* with Jean Simmons as his Ophelia, I couldn't believe it either. When Stewart Granger, my old pal, who was sitting next to me at the first night of *Black Narcissus* at the Odeon Leicester Square, saw Jean eating a squashy fruit with a ring through her nose, he went straight out, proposed to her and married her. I always said it was the baggy umbrella she carried. It was the final erotic touch.

Arthur Rank took a print of *Black Narcissus* with him to Hollywood and screened it for the moguls there.

"Gee!" they said. "Everybody should see this movie." Everybody did. Everybody has.

Naturally, Hollywood being Hollywood, and censorship being censorship, they couldn't leave a picture with nuns in it alone. Some ridiculous organization that had been formed to screen European pictures so that they could cut out the good scenes that they considered bad for your morals, (and keep them to show privately to their friends) got in heat when they heard that we had nuns in the picture. The distributors became alarmed and rolled over with their paws in the air. In the end, we had to cut for America all the flashbacks to Sister Clodagh's love affair in Ireland before she took her vows. Don't ask me why. These cuts have since been restored on most copies, but I expect there are a few mutilated ones still going around. In spite of this rebuff, Hollywood realized that Arthur Rank was a man to be reckoned with, even if he was a Methodist lay preacher and a flour millionaire. They welcomed him as they had never welcomed Alexander Korda, for the time being.

The big event of that year was, for the Archers, not the making of *Black Narcissus*, not the signing of David Farrar, not the move from Denham to Pinewood, not the acquisition from Sir Alexander Korda of a script that Emeric had written for him before the war, entitled *The Red Shoes*, but the screening of our dear *AMOLAD* before the King and Queen and the Royal

Family at the very first Royal Command Film Performance at the huge Empire Cinema, Leicester Square.

The occasion was so exciting that the film passed practically unnoticed. There were many reasons for this. Royal patronage in England was very carefully controlled and really meant something. It was recognized all over the British Empire and Commonwealth and in the United States as the final accolade. In show business, the number of Theatre Royals and theatre knights attested to its power. The yearly Royal Command Performance was one of the big events of the living theatre, and even the Beatles many years later, were considered to be honoured by their inclusion in it. Except for the occasional charity show, films had not been so patronized – at any rate, not officially. But the war had changed all that. It was recognized now on all sides that films, under the guidance of the Ministry of Information, had done a wonderful job in the war. Films had been invaluable for training servicemen, films had been important for entertaining the troops. Films had been important as diplomatic weapons for the embassies abroad. Films had the direct patronage of Winston Churchill, who had most certainly been responsible for the knighthood granted to Alexander Korda. British films, thanks to an enlightened government policy and the talent which had been discovered and trained by Hollywood experts, and by exiles from every country in Europe, were second to none in originality and quality, although they still had to find a world market open to them, before they could compete with Hollywood on equal terms. British films were a Good Thing, so when the head men of Wardour Street got together and approached the Lord Chamberlain with the suggestion that a yearly Royal Command Film Performance would put the cap on all this achievement, the response from the Court was graciously swift. The new royal occasion was agreed to, the date was fixed, the place was chosen. The details were left to the film business to sort out for themselves, and since the first film was to be British, it was agreed that the American-owned Empire would be host on this occasion and that next year an American film would be chosen by the committee, and that Arthur Rank's Odeon in Leicester Square should be the host. So Rank had it both ways, as he deserved to, for *A Matter of Life and Death* was chosen as the first Royal Command Film.

I was delighted that Metro-Goldwyn-Mayer, who had guided my first faltering footsteps into films, should be hosting me now as the director of the most important film of the year. Nobody ever forgets their first employer, nor fails to identify himself with their future fortunes. I knew that I was, and had been, an unknown amoeba in that vast organization, but I was as proud of it as if I had been the president. We had been an expatriate unit under a great director making controversial films, which by no means pleased MGM's front office, and this split between the men in the office and the men on the studio floor had haunted me ever since. In those early days with MGM, I had absorbed a standard of quality which never deserted me. *"Ars Gratia Artis"* was the motto which accompanied MGM's famous lion on the screen and on their stationery. Art for the sake of art. Well – art is often a matter of opinion, but let us say that the motto meant "Nothing but the best will do". This was the lesson that I learnt from Rex Ingram. As soon as I had the opportunity and the backing, I put it into practice. Twenty years later, my heart had been warmed to learn that I was not forgotten by men whom I had admired close to idolatry: Harry Lachman, Howard Strickling, Frank Scully, and even Rex Ingram himself. Now my old employer was to be the host at my coming of age. My cup was full and running over.

The evening, like Gaul, was divided into three parts. In the first part, the royal party arrived through cheering crowds, while the makers of the film and the leaders of the film industry were lined up in the lobby to be presented, together with their wives and sometimes children (small child equals big bouquet). The second part was a live show on the stage of the cinema. This was to consist of actors and actresses, in some cases doing their stuff, in other cases just taking a bow. The third part was the chosen film. It was assumed by now that the Archers could do anything, so we were asked to devise the live show, as well as the one on the screen. The result was like amateur night in Dixie. We tried to do too much and in the end did too little. The vast Empire Cinema was quite unsuitable for any sort of personality appearance. In those days, before it was cut down, it seated about 3,000 people, and they were all there. I'm taking things out of order and I had better go back to the night itself. It was a night to remember.

Frankie and I had decided to give a party after the show. We asked a hundred people and a hundred and fifty came. We had just bought a large house, No. 2 Ilchester Place, Kensington, and had it done up. We had hardly any furniture, but that seemed a very small reason for not having a party. The house had three floors and people could sit on the stairs. We still had the little mews house at 65 A Chester Square, and now that the Bentley could be put on the road I had taken to driving across West London by a route that took me down Melbury Road and Addison Road to Shepherd's Bush, and from there out to join the main road to Oxford, which passed the gates of Denham and Pinewood Studios. I soon learned to jink down Abbotsbury Road, passing Holland Park on one side and Oakwood Court on the other. I noticed that this attractive corner house had a board up announcing that the lease was for sale. The house had a garage – which was a rarity in this corner of London, which was all owned by the Ilchester Estate, who were a little old-fashioned in their views. The family had lived at Holland House up until the war, and Holland Park was their private park, although open to the public through several rights of way. Melbury Road and the streets around it were famous for the number of Victorian painters who had lived and had their studios there: Holman Hunt, G.F. Watts, Luke Fildes, Lord Leighton and several others, good, bad, or indifferent, but all of them very rich. Their studios were magnificent and famous for their heavy Victorian bad taste, even when an architect like Norman Shaw designed the building. Ilchester Place itself was a development undertaken in the early twenties, between the wars, and consisted of a double row of Neo-Georgian red-brick houses facing each other across a short street which ended at the palings of Holland Park, and the ornamental gate to the house itself. It was typical of the thinking of the estate and of those days, that they all had basements and cellars and servants' quarters, but very few had garages. During the war, they had been deserted by their owners and occupied by the military. Frankie and I inspected No. 2. It was filthy from cellar to roof and infested with black beetles. There was a scum of grease on everything you touched. But it was a beautiful spacious house with a huge horse-chestnut tree in the garden and we loved it. We hoped that the owner, a Mr Joel, who had interests in racing, had seen the house in its present condition. He had, and was only too anxious to get rid of it. He had established himself in the West Indies and had no intention of returning to London at present. The house was leasehold, not freehold, but the lease ran for the next thirty-seven years, which seemed an eternity to us then, and must have seemed like an eternity to the estate since then, for I realize that as I write this the lease has just run out. We paid £5,000 for the lease.

Through the Chilean Embassy, Frankie had established relations with a cook, Carmen Veloz, a Chilean Indian who was a mistress of her craft. She had accompanied her employer from Chile back to England many years before, and had remained ever since, until he died. Through him she had many acquaintances and friends in London Latin-American society, and had innumerable foster-children. She was an adorable person and a magnificent cook. Like all real cooks, she loved parties, and was easily persuaded to be the suprema at this one. We decided not to beat about the bush on such an important occasion, but to give people roast turkey and buckets of gorgeous trifle.

"Everyone will be too excited to eat before the show," said Frankie wisely. "Besides, they will all be dressing up. It's the first party since the war, the first real party. It'll be midnight before they get here and they'll be hungry. What will you give them to drink?"

"Coffee – tea – and champagne."

"Can we get enough champagne?"

"On the black market. I have ordered a dozen dozen."

"We had better have whisky too."

"That's more difficult. But I'll see what I can do. Probably Emeric has got contacts."

Frankie summed up: "We'll give them a real hot supper, with a trifle full of sherry and brandy and the coffee has to be real, not ersatz. Carmen will get it through the Embassy. Real Brazilian coffee!"

The great night arrived, November 1, 1946. We had been working on the live show right up to five or six o'clock of the day itself, and then had to dash home to change into white tie, tails, etc. It was a fine evening. Emeric and I walked into Leicester Square Gardens to take a look at the front of the house. It was all up in lights already. ROYAL FILM PERFORMANCE TONIGHT . . . A PRODUCTION OF THE ARCHERS . . . A MATTER OF LIFE AND DEATH . . . DAVID NIVEN . . . RAYMOND MASSEY . . . ROGER LIVESEY . . . KIM HUNTER.

We looked at this splendid sight and looked at each other. We had done all that! We shook hands and raced for our respective homes to change into the soup and fish.

"Funny that there aren't more people about," said Emeric as we parted. "But I suppose it's too early yet for crowds."

Too right it was too early! To add to the unreality of the occasion, we had all been assigned huge black limousines to bring us to the show, and to take us home afterwards. We were timed to arrive from our various destinations at the Empire Cinema well ahead of the royal party in order to take our places in the long line of VIPs to be presented. By the time we got to Hyde Park Corner, the police and the special police had already taken over all direction of traffic, and told us which way to go after inspecting our car. As we approached Leicester Square our limousine slowed down to a crawl and we were literally passed from hand to hand by the police. There must have been 50,000 people out in the Square, and in the streets around it. When it dawned upon us, I began to shake with excitement for the first time. It was all for us. For the British Film Industry that had grown full stature in time of war. It was the public acknowledgment that we could compete with the best that other countries had to offer. As the big limousines discharged their passengers, there were roars of applause and shouts of well-known names from thousands of throats. Leicester Square was an astonishing sight. Somehow, the police managed to keep a narrow lane for the limousines, but everywhere was black with people. We were crawling along a foot at a time, when suddenly through the window as we approached the Empire, I saw a special constable holding back the crowd, or trying to hold it back. It was Claude Hulbert, the brother of Jack Hulbert, two great comedians who were also two great public servants. Before the war, when British film comedies had been the only competition we could offer to Hollywood, their films had been some of the best and funniest. Claude saw me, and panting as he held back the crowd, yelled: "G-G-G-Good luck, old man!"

He was a famous stutterer. I remembered that when I first came to

England, eighteen years before, and got the job of stills photographer at Elstree Studios, I had booked Claude Hulbert for a stills session, and he was very pleased with the result. His brother, Jack, was also out on special constable duty that night.

Then we were being helped out of the limousine and were conscious of thousands of faces asking "Who are they? Who's that?" and hearing comments upon Frankie's gown: "Cor, she must be someone famous!". And then we were in the lobby and were being lined up and drilled on the correct way to address royalty.

Meanwhile, royalty was having a rough time. In spite of all that the police could do, the crowd was so enormous by the time the King and Queen arrived, that their limousine had to be almost manhandled around the Square. At one point, the crowd pressed in so strongly in their desire to see the royal party, and to wish them luck, and to share with them their excitement over this popular occasion, that they rocked the limousine to and fro and the King was exceedingly annoyed. It was a wonderfully cheerful demonstration. Queen Elizabeth, who being Scottish born had a common touch, took it quite calmly. The two young Princesses, Elizabeth and Margaret Rose, were as excited as anybody, and could be seen chattering and waving as they caught the spirit of the crowd, who had now begun to sing "God Save the King" and "Rule Britannia" in various keys. Inside the theatre we only knew there was some delay and then suddenly we heard "They're coming, they're coming!" and we prepared for the great moment of introduction of ourselves and our wives. We were very conscious of our responsibility to the actors and technicians and accountants and secretaries and chair-polishers who worked together in this extraordinary business of ours, who would be opening their papers in the morning to see photographs and saying "Well, we did pretty well last night, didn't we?", and perhaps: "Micky and Emeric both have stunning looking wives."

The King was, as usual, shy and monosyllabic. But we all knew that he loved films and always had the new British films run for him, so it didn't matter. The Queen was very chatty. (She had an additional reason for being interested in films, for Alex Korda had, with typical flair, just bought the lease of the house at Hyde Park Corner where the Duke and Duchess of York, as they were then, used to live and where they brought up their family. I think that she half expected to find Alex Korda in the line to be presented.) She asked me about the film and I told her it was an original story by Emeric and that it was a love story and fantasy at one and the same time. Arthur Rank, with his great height and big generous body, made a perfect host. His wife, a tall sympathetic woman, was at once adopted by the Queen, who had a dozen questions to ask her. The affair was regal, yet informal, and we felt proud to be part of it.

The royal party went to a royal box which had been arranged for them in the centre of the dress circle, and the whole house rose when they appeared and a spontaneous cheer of welcome and affection burst out. Nearly everybody in that huge audience was in show business in some way or another, and they wanted to show their appreciation of this great new theatrical event. It was warm-hearted, direct, personal, sincere, and there was no mistaking it for anything else. It was the finest moment of the evening.

As I have said, the live show that followed was under-rehearsed and under-written. There were some wonderful cartoons by Vicky, the cartoonist, but on that vast stage they couldn't come over. One or two actors did their stuff, but most of them just came on, took a bow, bowed to the royal box and went off. I was in agony, but nobody seemed to mind.

The projection of the chosen film for the Royal Performance was almost an anti-climax. As the drama, all the colour, all the love, seemed to have gone into the events outside, rather than inside, the Empire. After all that genuine spectacle and emotion and drama, the film itself, even with the spectacular opening in space, which we had discussed with Arthur Clarke, seemed very small beer. Even the first scenes in monochrome in the Other World aroused in the audience only a puzzled interest, it seemed to me. They hadn't yet caught on to the idea that the whole picture was going to be a joke about life and death. Then suddenly a joke, a visual joke, snapped the house to attention, and from then on the film went like a bomb. (I don't want to be misunderstood here. American and English showbiz writers are not agreed about the use of the word "bomb" with regard to success or failure. To bomb in America means in England to lay an egg.) I had borrowed the idea from the Bing Crosby/Bob Hope comedies, where every joke was an in-joke. I made the joke quite deliberately, and I learnt a great deal from its success. We had seen the Other World in monochrome and we had heard the Conductor, played by Marius Goring, ordered to go down to earth and bring back Peter Carter, who had overstayed his time on earth. The Conductor arrives on earth in a grove of rhododendrons and the various colours of this great flower flood the screen as he moves through them. He sighs and says to nobody in particular: "One is starved for Technicolor up there."

Now in the original script, this joke had been suggested by Emeric, but in conventional terms, i.e. "One is starved for colour up there." When we came to shoot the scene, I didn't find the joke pointed or funny enough. I was also interested in finding out whether you can make an escapist joke like that within conventions of a naturalistic super-film in colour. So I deliberately changed the line from the script, changing "colour" into "Technicolor." To my delight, the whole audience, this huge audience of 3,000 people, gave a roar of laughter right on the joke, which is a professional one, and then without the slightest difficulty, or noticeable transition, they went right back into the film and went on following it in the normal way of involvement. I was thrilled. After that, I felt I could do anything and get away with it. Film was what I had always thought it was – wonderful fantasies superimposed upon life. For me from then on, there was no more realism in films, only surrealism.

The other lesson that I learnt may seem an ungrateful one, but it is one that has to be learnt by every film-maker: avoid charity premières (the Royal Film performance was in aid of the Cinematograph Trade Benevolent Fund). Lend the charity organisations your film by all means, but don't expect anything from the audience. They have come to see and be seen. They want to see who has bought the most expensive seats, and the film is a secondary matter. This is human nature. But a sensitive producer, director or actor, should expect nothing from charity premières. They will not get a fair impression of their work.

Still, it was a night to remember.

On the next day, *A Matter of Life and Death* opened at the Odeon Leicester Square, Rank's flagship, and Emeric and I both went to see the film again. We could hardly believe our eyes and ears. It was a totally different picture that we were seeing. This audience had rushed to see the film because it was "A Production of the Archers", who had given them seven box-office smashes in as many years. They bought tickets because the critics wrote of the film that it was: "Brilliant . . . fantastic . . . imaginative . . . pompous . . . confusing . . ." C.A. Lejeune sniffed: ". . . the film begins by quoting Marvell and Raleigh, and ends with a snappy excerpt from Sir Walter Scott. Between times it manages to work in a saw or two from Plato, George Washington and Benjamin Franklin, and to touch lightly and familiarly on Dryden, Pope, Coleridge, Shelley, Keats, Milton and Donne. . . ." Dilys Powell after judicious praise said: "(it) remains an audacious, sometimes beautiful, but basically sensational film about nothing." Paul Tabori wrote: ". . . soft Technicolor world and a monochrome Heaven, spiced with every possible trick of the camera, of directions and music. The actors are uniformly good: David Niven as the airman, Kim Hunter – a pretty and unaffected newcomer – as his girl, Marius Goring as the hapless Conductor 71 who lost his head in the French Revolution. Perhaps the greatest performances are those of Roger Livesey as a worldly-wise doctor and Raymond Massey as the anti-British Boston Yankee."

405 Greenwich Street, New York 1983.
On July 25 of this year David Niven died. I sent him a cable at Château d'Oex where he lived and lies buried: "Good luck on that stairway, chum," signed "Micky and Emeric."

Two days later Raymond Massey died in Beverly Hills.

July 1 is the anniversary of my wedding with Frankie. This year was the fortieth. On July 3 she had a stroke and was taken to St Stephen's Hospital in the Fulham Road. The Intensive Care Ward. She never regained consciousness. She died on Tuesday, July 5 at about four o'clock. She brought nothing with her into the hospital, and she left nothing behind her except two cheap rings. When we examined her things at the small hotel where she had been staying, we found no money, no chequebook, nothing of any value. She left the world as poor as any nun, and as lovely as a goddess.

Hour after hour, I sat by her bed and watched her breathing. The forest of wires and tubes that was keeping her alive vanished upwards into the shadows behind the lamps. Every so often she checked in her breathing and some pipe bubbled. That was all. She was clean and relaxed and young. I looked in wonder at that wonderful curve of her jaw and the large delicate eye sockets and the perfect nose, so full of breeding. Beautiful though Frankie's body was, her spirit was more beautiful. It controlled her body, it informed her glance.

A few years before, I had planned to return to Foula to make Return to the Edge of the World, and asked Belle Chrystall and Frankie to go with me and appear in the film as they were forty years later. Belle refused, but Frankie agreed at once. Forty years had not altered her carriage, or the sparkle in her beautiful eyes. She was twenty-seven when she came with us and appeared in the original film on that wild Shetland island, and I swear that she looks no older in the new scenes we made in 1978. She looked no older now.

I bent over her and whispered in her ear: "Frankie, I love you. Columba is here with me. He wants to speak to you."

That solemn, beautiful child, who had played the child in my film Peeping Tom, and who was now a tall, bony young man, bent over her and whispered in her ear, but she gave no sign of having heard.

When she died, Columba and I crossed Fulham and the Cromwell Road together, with the vague idea of finding her Catholic church in Kensington. We knew so little of our own village, where we had lived for thirty years, that we went first to St Mary Abbots Church at the foot of Kensington Church Street. It is a large, gaunt, but impressive church, approached and surrounded by numerous cloisters that appear to have no entrance or exit. We circled the church and found a small door which admitted us to the nave. A number of people who obviously knew each other well were preparing a performance of T. S. Eliot's Murder in the Cathedral. We soon discovered that we were on Anglican territory, but they very politely directed us up Church Street to the Church of the Carmelites, which was only a couple of hundred yards away. The church is *large, beautiful and modern: it was rebuilt after the war, having been the last church in London to be destroyed by enemy action. We found the Priory next to the church. The Fathers all seemed to be Irish. One of them received and directed us to an undertaker who had his business further along Church Street, and within an hour we had the funeral arranged for the Friday. It was a beautiful funeral. I had insisted on an organist and one had to be found and I asked if he would play some Irish airs. After the funeral Mass, the friar, who spoke the Mass most beautifully, said to me: "I thank you for the music. Jesus! I only hope they'll play 'Danny Boy' at my funeral!"*

Frankie was Irish through and through, but she was a Londoner through and through, too. She claimed to be a true Cockney, born within the sound of Bow bells, and I dare say she was, for her father, Dr Reidy, had his surgery in Commercial Road, became Mayor of Stepney and was one of the most devoted and beloved physicians who ever served in London Hospital.

London is an aristocratic city and indifferent to the lovers who die within her arms. She can put on a show second to none, as with the funeral of the Rt Hon. Sir Winston Churchill, MP, and she can arbitrarily, and with the consent of its Dean, find a corner in Westminster Abbey for her favoured sons and daughters. But for most Cockneys, the churchyards have no room, and there is nothing left for them but the acres of concrete, granite and marble which men call a cemetery.

As a citizen of the Royal Borough, Frankie was entitled to be buried in Kensington Cemetery, and this was arranged by Mr Hussey, the small, polite and almost invisible undertaker. He lived and had his business in a small house in Berkeley Gardens, just off Church Street. His front parlour was his office, his back parlour his mortuary. His furniture and properties were of a bygone age and would have delighted the heart of my art department set dressers. He apologised that the coffin had already been closed.

Three of Frankie's tall brothers came to the Mass and two of her tall sisters. Reidy is an Irish word meaning "long" and "tall". Frankie always claimed it also meant "royal". The kingdom of Dalriada, on Islay in the Western Isles of Scotland, was established by an Irish prince whose descendants claimed to be the rightful Kings of Scotland. I took Frankie to see the loch on the island of Islay, where an underwater causeway leads to the islet where the kings were crowned. Ever since then, she had claimed to be the rightful Queen of Ireland and Scotland.

Kensington Cemetery lies to the west of London and is bounded by the Chiswick flyover, the main highway to London's Heathrow Airport. How often we had arrived and departed by that high road. Now we were parting forever. Frankie lies within sight and sound of the thundering traffic.

David Niven lies in the churchyard of the Anglican church of St Peter in the Swiss village of Château d'Oex. His Swiss summer home is only a stone's throw away. The winters he passed at his villa at Cap Ferrat, within sight of our family hotel at St Jean. Prince Rainier of Monaco, his old friend, came to his funeral in Switzerland. Only a year or two before, David had supported his friend after the terrible death of his wife, Princess Grace. David's two sons, his two adopted daughters, and his beautiful wife, Hjordis, attended him to his grave. The boys had become American citizens and Californians, and I had hardly seen them since they were enchanting puppies at the time that we were making A Matter of Life and Death.

A matter of life and death; what an apt and beautiful title.

I loved Raymond Massey. Everyone loved his tall, gaunt frame with the eyes of a major prophet stuck in his head. But only his friends knew his cavernous laugh and the enthusiasm with which he tangled up his sentences when carried away on the wings of his imagination. When he started the inevitable whooping and crowing with excitement, so that his words and phrases became unintelligible, Dorothy would say: "Whoops! There he goes again". He remained my friend for many years, and I kept in touch with him through his two children, Dan and Anna. I had seen less of him when he moved to California and Beverly Hills, although I never failed to telephone him when passing through. He had a charming house on North Beverly Drive, a few hundred yards from the Beverly Hills Hotel. But in the last few years of their lives, he and Dorothy had been somewhat reclusive; and when I came to Hollywood again to join Francis Coppola, I felt rather stupidly conscious of the fact that I could not return his hospitality, and never went to see him and discuss old times during the whole eighteen months that I was in California. I convinced myself that he had no wish to see visitors, and I knew he was working on his autobiography. I wish . . . I wish . . . how many times I shall have to write those words in this long book.

Memories . . . memories . . . a matter of life and death.

Frankie loved parties and took care that every funeral that she had anything to do with was followed by the traditional Irish wake. Her mother married again after Dr Reidy died, and when this second husband was called to his father, we brought everybody back to 8 Melbury Road and had a tremendous party at which Kevin and Columba danced Irish jigs with their mother. Fanny, Frankie's mother, wiped her eyes and sobbed: "How John would have enjoyed this!"

So I knew Frankie would have wanted a wake to follow the funeral, and I hired the Belvedere Restaurant in Holland Park for the hours

between three and six, when we could have this lovely little appendage
of Holland House to ourselves. The two houses where we had once
lived, where the boys had been brought up, 2 Ilchester Place and 8
Melbury Road, were within sight of us. Most of the guests on this day
had been our guests in the days of our glory. The houses, the trees
and the gaunt silhouette of the vast mansions of Oakwood Court,
reminded everyone of those distant days. Old friends met again and lived
through the years, and as, fortunately, we were not within licensing hours,
nobody got drunk and started any fights, as too often happens at an Irish
wake.

   It was a lovely party and folk said again and again, how much, how
very much, Frankie would have enjoyed it. For she loved parties . . . she
loved the bustle and excitement and preparation as much as the party itself.
The one that she gave after the Royal Command Performance of A Matter
of Life and Death *was one of her best.*

There was no class distinction in Frankie's parties. We all talked with awe
next morning in the Studios and in Wardour Street of having seen Sir
Alexander Korda and J. Arthur Rank both seated on the uncarpeted stairs
with plates of roast turkey balanced on their knees, chatting and nodding
in temporary agreement. There was plenty of parking space in Abbotsbury
Road and in Ilchester Place itself, and the inhabitants soon woke up to the
fact that showbiz had arrived in their midst. Some of them walked over to
have a closer look. They were met by Bill and Myrtle, arms full of bottles of
champagne, who urged them to join the party – open house.

   Our nextdoor neighbour, whom we had not yet met, turned out to be
Lady Stamp, mother of the formidable-sounding Prunella Stamp, a
physical culture expert. I carved the turkeys while the beaming Carmen
circulated with huge plates of vegetables and mounds of chestnut stuffing. I
don't remember that anybody talked about the film or about the
wonderfully organized Royal Command Performance. All the men and
women who had helped to create the vast Rank Empire were there. There
was a general feeling that we had come through the war by a miracle, and
that great things were expected of us. All our own people were there: the
team which created *A Matter of Life and Death*, and was already creating
the miracle of *Black Narcissus*, beamed at each other, secure in the
knowledge that the financial backers trusted us and that we could do
anything. The champagne lasted – but only just. Somehow or other,
particularly with the help of the admirable Victor Finney, head of public
relations for the growing Rank Organisation, we had found a few dozen
bottles of Scotch, and this was a triumph; for as Robert Coote, David

Niven's friend, says in the film, Scotch whisky at the end of 1946 was hard
to come by.

It was a lovely party.

But behind the smiles and the roses there was trouble brewing. The
plain fact was that Sir Alexander Korda had returned from America to find
his supreme position in British filmdom usurped by King Arthur (Rank)
and Prince John (Davis). You would think that the two tycoons had every
reason to make an alliance in their fight with American distributors. Not
so. Alex could brook no rival. Since he was no longer the magician of
Denham, he announced publicly that he was glad to be disembarrassed of
that white elephant. He then immediately proceeded to acquire a white
elephant of his own, Shepperton Studios. He followed this up by acquiring
Worton Hall Studios at Walthamstow on the Thames – one of the older
British studios, with a record almost equal to Twickenham Studios for
turning out good pictures on low budgets. In addition to the original
studios, which were small but handy, there was a huge silent stage erected
before the war, which had somehow escaped the government scroungers in
their search for steel. It was not soundproofed or heated in any way, and
the owners of the studio seemed to have regarded it as a liability rather than
an asset. Not so Alex, who was well advised. He bought the studio lock,
stock and barrel. When I say "bought", I am, of course, employing a
euphemism with which every Korda or potential Korda is familiar. Kordas
are always "buying" things, but not with money. They acquire houses and
apartments and film studios and yachts in some mysterious way. Alex
could no more have bought Shepperton Studios than he could have bought
the Taj Mahal, or the penthouse flat that he occupied for so many years at
the top of Claridges Hotel. He could not have bought the magnificent
stone-built Victorian mansion in Piccadilly, near Hyde Park Corner. But he
only had to crook his finger, that magical finger, for someone to buy the
lease and present it to him on bended knee; whereupon he made it his
headquarters and the head offices of London Films, installed a luxurious
private projection theatre and then proceeded to invite the previous
owners, with their children, to private shows of films – his own and other
people's.

This "Hey presto! Now you see it, now you don't" style of living is
enchantingly described by Alex's nephew, Michael Korda, in his book
Charmed Lives. Of course, Michael's knowledge of the early days and of
the days of Denham Studios is based on family legend and hearsay, but he is
appallingly accurate in his assessment of atmospheres and personalities.
He was in his teens when the second Korda reign began. He conveys the

charming world of the Kordas and their strong family ties which bound them all together. I particularly like the frequent descriptions of the three Korda brothers foregathering at the end of the table, all arguing with each other in Hungarian and calling each other names, while their wives and families just sit at the other end of the table, or around the fire, listening with an indifference which they do not feel, as they desperately try to find out what the next move will be.

Arthur Rank had persuaded John Davis – or possibly, John Davis had persuaded Arthur Rank – that the growing Rank Organisation needed a logo, and since all the existing trademarks of Wardour Street were bombastic and in bad taste, they decided to go one better, or worse, according to taste, by employing a man with a gong, stripped as naked as Tarzan and swinging a club with which he struck the gong a resounding blow. This character was played by my old friend Bombardier Billy Wells, fighter and ex-champion of the world, who had a pub at the Piccadilly end of Park Lane, and whom we all knew as a stuntman and a sterling player of bit-parts in action films. "The Bomba" was a fine figure of a man and so was Arthur Rank – although his chest had slipped a little. I always thought that the general public had a hazy impression that the Man with the Gong was Arthur Rank himself. Still, there was no excuse for David Low drawing a wicked cartoon for the middle page of Beaverbrook's *Evening Standard*, the page which he had made his own, featuring a nervous Arthur Rank with nothing on but a towel draped around his loins, listening to a hail of directions relayed through a megaphone by an excitable Alexander Korda, directing him in shirt sleeves and wide-brimmed hat, smoking a cigar with the inevitable director's chair in the foreground.

That cartoon was uncomfortably near the truth. John and Arthur had the big battalions; Korda had the glamour. They were soberly building for the future, while Korda leaned heavily on the present. Neither man was capable of compromise, so war was inevitable. By combining and acquiring the vast Odeon chain of theatres with the Gaumont-British chain, Rank had about 700 of the best theatres in the United Kingdom, creating a powerful monopoly that delighted his supporters and outraged his opponents.

Unless Korda's films played these circuits they had no hope of making money in their home market. Korda muttered "Monopoly", and later on he shouted it. Rank said nothing, while John Davis bought another chain of cinemas. For the first time since movies became talkies, England had a vigorous film industry of her own and the directors, writers and producers were English. The aces in Rank's pack were the Independent Producers whom the Archers and Christopher Mann had brought together during the war years. Korda set about seducing us away from Rank, one by one.

Besides his two younger brothers, Vincent and Zoli, Alex already had one ace in his pack, Carol Reed. Carol had always been a bit of a loner and had consistently refused to join our group. He had handled the war years in his own way. He had joined the Army and had been posted to the Army Film Unit. He had been to all the most important battle areas. He made documentaries and training films. Finally, he made, with actors, a magnificent feature film, *The Way Ahead*. (Among the bunch of character actors chosen by Carol were not a few who reappeared twenty years later in *Dad's Army*. John Laurie was one.) When I say that the film was magnificent, I mean that is was magnificently British. If Colonel Blimp had been head of the Army Film Unit, it is the film he would have made. It proved – as needs proving again and again, year in, year out – that the script is the thing, and however brilliant a director may be, he is no better than his script.

Carol came from theatreland. He was the natural son of the famous actor-manager Sir Herbert Beerbohm Tree, the half-brother of Max Beerbohm. The Trees and the Terrys, the Esmonds and the Irvings, were London's great theatrical families. John Gielgud, of course, is one of them, (Ellen Terry was his great-aunt), and demonstrates today their versatility and toughness.

Stories about Herbert Tree abound, particularly about the years when he held the lease of His Majesty's Theatre in the Haymarket, and gave parties on the stage and in the famous Dome, which crowns that theatrical edifice. Tree was a gentleman, witty and malicious, given to striking attitudes, well knowing that they *were* attitudes, always ready with a crushing repartee for those familiars who were too familiar. His two daughters, Iris and Viola, adored him and were both delightful actresses. Carol Reed was born into and grew up in this environment. He knew everybody in show business. He became stage manager and chief production assistant to Edgar Wallace when that colourful genius burst into showbiz, took over the exclusive Wyndham's Theatre, wrote, produced and directed a gangster-thriller *On the Spot*, starring Charles Laughton as the gangster Tony Perelli, and scored a smash hit. Carol was with Edgar during the hectic years before he went to Hollywood, wrote *King Kong* and died. Basil Dean, a producer of spectacular realism and popular success, then called Carol to the Ealing Studios, whose star was Gracie Fields. There, Carol directed his first film, which was called *Midshipman Easy*, adapted from the nineteenth-century novel by Captain Marryat. One of his next films, made for Ted Black, brother of George Black the great variety showman at the Islington Studios, showed what a good director he was. It was called *Bank Holiday*. It was a love story full of tender observations and put together with loving care. With these two films, Carol Reed had arrived by the time that I had made *The Edge of the World*.

Carol was supposed to look very like his father. He was slim, very tall, fair, with protuberant light-coloured eyes. He had an "actory" kind of face which permitted him to show his emotions, although in society he always seemed to me to be far away. The last time I saw him he was standing in Panton Street, off the Haymarket, outside Stone's Chop House waiting for a cab. It was not long before his death. He had put on weight and was no longer slim, and at last I saw what other people, who had known his celebrated father, had seen. Carol had struck an attitude as he waited, and had become the Tree that I knew from Max Beerbohm caricatures. There was the suggestion of a cloak around his big shoulders and he looked distinctly Edwardian. I never saw him again.

A useful work-horse in Alex's new after-the-war team was Captain Anthony Kimmins R.N. Tony Kimmins had been a young Royal Navy officer, axed between the wars, who had turned himself into a highly successful commercial director of comedies for Basil Dean at Ealing. It was he who made some of the best George Formby comedies which are now collector's pieces. George Formby was a north country comedian who had worked the northern music halls. His act was a monologue. His assets were a fixed and toothy grin, and a ukulele upon which he played tuneless tunes. He was immensely popular. Although a passionate observer, he seemed to have no talent whatsoever; but the great public thought otherwise. His films with Kimmins were full of chases, races, harmless little numbers, and a simple little love story with a good, clean British girl. They raked it in. Tony Kimmins was recalled to the Navy when war broke out and retired after the war with the rank of Captain.

During the war he had often spoken on the BBC and done a number of important liaison jobs, and Alex spotted him as a man likely to be extremely useful and who knew most of the people in power. Tony Kimmins was one of those men whose great charm made people suspect his talent. But he knew exactly what he could do and he did it very well. When he first came into show business he had written a theatrical farce entitled *While Parents Sleep*, which ran for years and years, and later in 1953 he was to direct a film for Korda starring Alec Guinness, *The Captain's Paradise*, which was a little classic. But when in 1948, Alex loaded *Bonnie Prince Charlie* onto his broad shoulders, it was too much for him. He collapsed. And London Films collapsed with him.

But in 1946, the future was still bright. Alex's technicians and most of his general staff flocked back to him, and he was able to give Kimmins's film, *Mine Own Executioner*, by Nigel Balchin, a fine production. It was made at Worton Hall. The leading part was played by a young Irishman, Kieron Moore, who also scored as the lead of *A Man About the House*, in which my old friend Maggie Johnston gave a startling performance. Both films were great entertainment and made a good start for the new London Films.

Ralph Richardson, of course, went back to Alex. At Denham before the war, he and Larry had been Alex's particular protégés, and Alex had brought them on fast and very early. Alex's affair with Merle Oberon criss-crossed with the fiery romance of Laurence Olivier and Vivien Leigh. Ralph had scored as the blind Army officer in *The Four Feathers*, Larry had put the fire into *Fire Over England*. Ralph and Larry had both played light comedians for Alex in *The Divorce of Lady X*, and both of them had giggled their way through routine comedy-thrillers like Tim Whelan's *Q-Planes*. In that delightful film, Ralph's folded Whitehall umbrella played a part almost as important as its owner's. When war broke out, Alex kept them both on the payroll as long as he could. When both actors went into the Royal Navy, he somehow managed to give them an allowance for the whole time they were in the Service. Sam Goldwyn probably did the same for David Niven; but if he did, I can't believe that he did it with as good a grace as Alex, who held both men in great affection and, being a gentleman, felt that he owed them as much gratitude as they owed him. Alex may or may not have had a voice in the decision from high-up to bring both these splendid actors out of the Services and back to the theatre. If Alex and Winston Churchill had nothing to do with it this time, we can at least be sure that Laurence Olivier's *Henry V* put spurs to the decision. It was felt that such splendid public services as the Old Vic in London's Waterloo Road, or the Shakespeare Memorial Theatre at Stratford-on-Avon, both glories of the British theatre, should be revived. In 1944, the winning of the war and the defeat of Hitler had become a matter of time and logistics. The New Theatre was offered for the revival of the Old Vic, for the original theatre south of the river had been blitzed. The New Theatre is one of the finest theatres in London. Bronson Albery was the lessee and the theatre is now named after him – the Albery Theatre. Larry and Ralph and John Burrell, a theatreman and organiser of great talent, were to be the three co-directors, and they were given *carte blanche*. The result was one of the most exciting happenings in the theatre since the WPA, through the Federal Theatre Project, gave *carte blanche* to John Houseman and Orson Welles.

Talking of the film *Henry V*, its genesis was the visit that Tam Williams, Bernard Miles and I paid to Worthy Down, when we tried to persuade Larry, then serving in the Fleet Air Arm, that he should return to the theatre and put on a production with himself in the name part of Henry V in battledress. It may be remembered, my readers, that he failed to be stirred by this idea and jumped at the chance of getting his own back on the Services by playing Colonel Blimp.

Soon after that drunken evening, Two Cities Films got Larry seconded from the Royal Navy by the Ministry of Information to produce and star in a film production of *Henry V* promoted and financed by Del Giudice at Denham Studios. We were all thrilled to have another great big colour film in production and encouraged by the names we heard bandied about as designers, cameramen and actors. One day Larry came over to my set where I was making *Colonel Blimp*, and said:

"Micky, I want you to direct *Henry V*."

"Do you?" I said. "Tell me something about it."

We were on some exterior set: I'm not sure, but I think it was probably the scene of the concert in *Colonel Blimp* where hundreds of German officers are listening to German symphonic music. I had all these plaster casts of Germans sitting or sprawling or lying about, and the art department were busy touching them up and dressing them, and so we had plenty of time at our disposal. We pulled up a couple of chairs and Larry opened a big folder with sketches by Paul Sherrif and Roger Furse, and started to explain how he saw the film. I was enchanted at once by the opening in the Globe Theatre with Leslie Banks as Chorus, and I was more and more impressed as he explained how he proposed to mix theatrical with film conventions – an idea which I loved and which was done so frequently in the early days of films. But when he began to talk to me about going to Ireland for his battle scenes, where he could get hundreds of magnificent horses and, more important, hundreds of magnificent riders, I pulled him up short.

"Why don't you direct the film yourself?"

He had been hoping I would say it, but he hadn't dared to suggest it. "Do you really think I could?"

"Of course you could, you have got it all worked out already. You have a marvellous team all round you – what are you waiting for?"

In this way, one of the most important decisions in the making of a very important film was made. But I must record the fact – and it is a fact that has time and again put a curb on the more restive spirits of our marvellous industry – that this airy gesture of mine, to an artist whom I admired, a friend who had answered my call for help on *49th Parallel* when the whole world was shaking, would have been an empty one without the agreement of his financial backer. Larry had never directed a film in his life. From me he learnt to stand on his own feet and make his own decisions without reference to fees or billing. I had known Larry for years as a stormy, apparently impetuous young man. He knew exactly what he was doing when he provoked the storm. I had learnt the way his creative mind worked, both in the part of the trapper in *49th Parallel* and as a potential Colonel Blimp. I had heard already his views on the theatre, and I knew that he knew what to do when he became a theatrical manager himself. In the mysterious way that quality or novelty becomes instantly recognised in the vast complex of a studio like Denham, where four or five pictures can be on the floor at the same time, there was no mistaking the quality of the creative artists with whom Larry and Del Giudice were surrounding themselves. What I had heard convinced me that Larry was carrying the production on his back and would show the whole world "the mettle of his pasture", so I could guess that when he came to me, whom he admired, but who came from a different world, it was not for want of confidence in himself. Some distributor had said: "Entrust an actor on his first film with £350,000 and let him direct himself! You must be mad, Del." Del turned to Larry, Larry turned to me, I provided the answer. Del was encouraged to go into Wardour Street and fight with the distributor who had shaken his judgment in an artist whom he had admired. He fought and won. The result, as we all know now, was a wonderful blend of theatre and film, with a complete disregard for convention, and which for me opened the way to *The Red Shoes* and *The Tales of Hoffmann*.

There was a modicum of desperation in Del Giudice's decision. (By the way, what is a modicum? Don't tell me, I like to think of it as one of James Thurber's small animals.) He was an incomer to British films in wartime, an Italian lawyer who loved the arts and could sense what was happening to films in this extraordinary country, England. His company was called Two Cities Films. Two Cities gave Arthur Rank some tough competition. They had plenty of money to spend at a time when money was short and Rank was driving a hard bargain. Artists remembered wistfully the lavish days of Alexander Korda. Del Giudice took a magnificent country house in the Home Counties, not too far from Denham Studios and threw magnificent parties – so I am told. I was never invited. I think my informants were Roger Livesey and his enchanting wife, Ursula Jeans, who had always been a part of the Laurence Olivier/Vivien Leigh set. As Korda knew so well, flattery, adulation, and ostentatious wealth and luxury are the surest way to any artist's heart. If he's got one. Flattery, particularly, when laid on with a palette knife. I may be wrong, but I don't think that Arthur Rank and John Davis would have let Larry direct *Henry V* if they had been backing it. They had already saddled themselves, against the advice of the entire Board of Independent Producers, with Gabby Pascal's Caesar's Geezers. Gabby was a showman of some magnitude, but not a director. He knew as much about directing as a cow does about playing the piano. When first asked by the Rankers what his picture would cost, he snatched a figure out of the air. I think it was about £600,000, and in the end he spent over a million. By the time Gabby departed for Hollywood, where mendacious Central European promoters were not unknown, his arrogance and extravagance had nearly sunk Independent Producers at a vital time for Arthur Rank, who was preparing to go public with the Rank Organisation.

In Denham Studios, Ralph and Larry were two of Alex's contract artists: they were minnows from the hatchery of the River Colne. But in the theatre, it was another matter. In St Martin's Lane, Ralph Richardson and

Laurence Olivier were lordly salmon. St Martin's Court, the narrow paved passage for pedestrians only, which joins Charing Cross Road and St Martin's Lane, is walled on one side by two theatres, Wyndham's and the New Theatre. The stage doors face each other across a paved courtyard, and little passes in one theatre that is not swiftly known in the other, and within an hour or two by the whole profession. The news that Ralph and Larry had been relieved of further service with the Armed Forces, and had been given a mandate to create a new Old Vic, was at once seen and appreciated as the master stroke it was. ENSA had done its job. Actors and technicians were being demobbed every day. Very soon the only ham actor left in the combined forces would be General George Patton. The theatre needed leaders, and now it had got them. The Old Vic was at the New Theatre! It sounded good.

Why the Old Vic? Because Lilian Baylis, that woman of genius, had taken the Old Victoria Music Hall and turned it into a classical theatre. She stood for all that was good in the British theatre. Larry and Ralph had suffered from her tongue; so had Ninette de Valois and Bobby Helpmann. "Well, dear, we can't always be at our best can we?" was about the highest praise they ever got from her. She would have approved the news that classic plays and full-length ballets would soon be sharing the New Theatre in repertory. Others received it with incredulity. "It'll never work." It did work. The spirit of Miss Baylis could perform miracles; and what was a commonplace in the Continental theatre, became a commonplace in London.

My love of the theatre had been fanned into a blaze by my own experience, small though it was, and I kept pretty close to all this. Ralph and Larry were friends, of course, but Bobby Helpmann, that Australian wasp, was my chief informant about the constant crises. Three productions were being prepared: Ibsen's *Peer Gynt*, Shaw's *Arms and the Man*, and *Richard III*. The choice of the plays, the merits of the plays, and the parts in the plays, were discussed and criticised by all actors, and particularly by Bobby Helpmann, who having been leading male dancer with the Sadler's Wells ballet for ten years, had long ago signalled his intentions of becoming a legitimate actor, speaking the words. He had followed this up by speaking words on the stage in one of the ballets and by giving his remarkable mime performance as the Dago in Walton's *Façade*. This ambition of his to become a legitimate actor and to play Hamlet was known to all his friends, including Larry, who laughed him to scorn. Helpmann, and Michael Benthall, replied to this by staging a stunning *Hamlet* as a ballet, with a memorable decor by Leslie Hurry. It was the strongest statement that the homosexuals had made so far in the British theatre, and within a year or two, Bobby was to play Hamlet – rich in comedy and shrill in passion.

I have never been a regular first-nighter, but for ten years I went to most of the Old Vic first nights, starting with the memorable first night of the Olivier/Richardson/Burrell partnership. I took in most of the performances at Stratford – particularly when Tony Quayle was running the Shakespeare Memorial Theatre. My Shakespeare theatre-going ended more or less with Peter Hall and John Barton's productions of *The Wars of the Roses*. After a wonderful experience like that, I felt that I would like to ruminate Shakespeare a bit.

But the Olivier/Richardson first nights topped them all. The occasion was unique. The return of Ralph and Larry, two great stars, was comparable with the return of royalty to the cinema to see *A Matter of Life and Death* a year later. The Empire in Leicester Square and the New Theatre in St Martin's Lane were in the hub of London. Anything created within that magic circle bounded by Piccadilly and Regent Street to the west and Garrick Street to the east was bound to be of the first importance. The traffic jams attested to this. I went with Frankie to all three first nights. We had seats in the tenth row.

They opened with *Peer Gynt*. Sybil Thorndike, to everyone's surprise, died quietly as Aase. Margaret Leighton seemed to think that the Green Woman was a sort of Peter Pan. Larry made a late appearance with typical cunning as the Button Moulder. He had calculated his delayed entrance very accurately, and he got a terrific hand, but he had rather miscalculated the effect of the coup, for the Button Moulder's scene is short, and once he makes his exit he never returns. Actors who play the part usually like to double up some other part in the long cast. Larry was good, of course, but it seems to me that Ion Swinley was better in the production at Sadler's Wells, which we had seen when Alec Clunes played practically all the other parts. The desert oasis scene was a bore, as it usually is, but Ralph was magical as old Peer. We liked his lovely speaking voice, and his air of a lunatic at large was so moving that we forgave his loutish youth in the opening scenes, and gave him a standing ovation when the curtain rose again.

Ralph took his calls alone on the stage, in the actor-manager tradition, then with the whole company. Larry, with sure instinct, took his calls with the company. Then the three of them, Ralph, Larry and John Burrell took their call together, implying a shared responsibility for the production.

They used the Grieg music, alas!

It must have been a moving occasion for Ralph. The last time that he had appeared before the public on stage – you could hardly count his appearance with me in "The Ship-Shape Show" – had been in J. B. Priestley's morality play *Johnson over Jordan*. That had been in 1941. Larry's last public performance had been as Romeo in the short-lived production at the New York Fifty-First Street Theatre, in the same year. The last time they had played together, Ralph was Othello and Larry was

Iago at the Old Vic in the 1939 season. The audience on that first night knew this, and welcomed them back.

A week later came *Arms and the Man*. Ralph played the Swiss mercenary soldier, Captain Bluntschli. Larry gave us, to our delight, a heel-clicking, hand-kissing, saluting, wasp-waisted Sergius. It was his final comment on the military man. The play was a brilliant choice for two actors who had served in the Armed Forces and had never been so miscast before or since. Margaret Leighton wore some lovely dresses, which partly made up for her scanty costume as the Green Woman in *Peer Gynt*. The opening was terrific, the setting charming, everyone looked as if they had just stepped out of a bandbox, and we, the audience, loved it.

A week later came *Richard III*. Stories had been circulating about Larry's characterisation and make-up and the extra rehearsals that he had demanded. There were ear-witness tales that he hadn't found the Voice yet. There were eye-witness tales that Richard's crouchback was to be presented with two humps; or none. But nothing had prepared us for what we saw on the stage, when the curtain went up on that memorable night.

> Now is the winter of our discontent
> Made glorious summer by this sun of York.

The voice is cultured, the tone venomous. The figure is rich and noble, but twisted out of shape. The eyes are enormous, but as observant as a cat's and filled with sleeping cruelty. The nose – ah! that nose! – is long and pendulous. His pale face is shadowed by long dank hair which hangs to his shoulders. He stands alone upon the stage – not, if I remember right, in the centre, but on the prompt side and downstage where he can dominate the house and mark the slightest inattention, or movement. We return his look, terrified. Somehow he conveys the effect of a beautiful body and a brilliant mind, diseased and gone to the bad. He speaks. We shudder. His words drip like vitriol. We realise with relief that we're not going to have any theories thrown at us about Shakespeare's sources for a Freudian study of Richard Crouchback. We are to be presented with a full-length portrait of a villainous monster. We sit spellbound. However, a great actor is a conscious humorist. A show-off. He must have a taste for the bizarre, the unusual. He must savour the abnormal, else how can he portray the normal? He must be a conscious observer of the heights and abysses of human nature. He must have loved, in order to convey hatred and loneliness. He must suffer humiliation, before he can play a prince.

Above all he must be the right shape. The reader may have noticed that I have used and made this point before. I cannot emphasise it too much. An actor or actress may have all the qualities for a part, but if they are not the right shape, they will have to fight to keep the audience interested in them. Even Charles Laughton, an almost mystically talented actor, with an invincible personality, so powerful and grotesque, and with a reputation for originality and glamour that was second to none, could not triumph over his physical envelope in certain parts. After triumphing as Captain Bligh in *Mutiny on the Bounty* and Henry VIII in *The Private Life of Henry VIII*, he returned to the London stage to play Lear, but the audience refused to accept him.

Ralph was not the right shape for Peer Gynt. Alec Guinness was not the right shape for Macbeth. Larry was not the shape for Romeo, because his legs were too thin for tights, however much he might pad them. But as Richard III he was immense. He had lost a lot of weight directing and acting in *Henry V* ("My little bag of bones," said Vivien lecherously), and his pliant body responded to every thought and word as explosively as a firework. Not for him was the battle offstage ("A tucket sounds!" – put that tucket in the bag with the modicum), the desperate entry left with "A horse, a horse, my kingdom for a horse!" and the exit right, and death offstage. No! No! Larry is forced back *onstage* fighting desperately against his gallant adversary, Ralph, resplendent in armour and embroidered surcoats, banners waving with lions *regardant*, and falling, still fighting, is run through by Ralph and pinned to the ground. Recoiling like a serpent he twists around and bites the very steel that is impaling him. It was terrific! And when Ralph drew back with "the bloody dog is dead!" we were all so drained of emotion that all we could do was to nod our heads and mutter "Good show, good show." Ah! What a night that was! I thought we would never stop clapping.

What? You've seen the film? Well, then you've seen something. Imagine what that performance of Larry's was like when fourteen hundred people were sharing in its creation on the stage of the New Theatre, muttering to themselves: "Hit! Hit! That's how it must have been, that's how I want it to be. God! I hope that he will . . . he has! He has! Hooray!" And we were so exhausted, so drained, so battered, so dazzled by this superman, that at the end of the play, we could only give one great sigh of relief as the curtain slowly fell upon Bosworth Field. It released us from this wizard's spell.

I wish I could describe to you the stir, the excitement, that was spread around by this revival of the Old Vic; the surprise and love and wonder that was engendered when these three magnificent productions went into the repertory and played throughout the winters of 1944 and 1945. Broadway and Hollywood at once understood the gesture, and openly regretted that some of the best talent in show business, instead of doing what they did best, were flying or fighting or making documentary or training films.

The buzz-bombs were over, people were pouring back into London, and the house was full at the New every night. Of course, in the tradition of

Miss Baylis, everyone was working for a minimum wage, and I don't suppose that Ralph and Larry got much more than they earned in the Fleet Air Arm. But how richly they were rewarded in experience, in authority and in fame. In the spring, three new productions were presented: *Cyrano de Bergerac, Uncle Vanya*, and (in a double bill) *The Critic* and *Oedipus*. In *Cyrano*, Ralph gave a beautiful performance, lofty and romantic. In *Vanya* Ralph seemed to me to be a complete failure, but Larry was interesting as Astrov. In *The Critic*, Larry played Mr Puff with a turned-up nose, and every trick in the book. Nobody will ever forget him being hoisted twenty feet up into the air while he was sitting astride the scenery at the rehearsal scene. On the same night he played Oedipus, and invented a magnificent *howl*. It could have been used for an air raid warning.

Joyce Redman was the other female lead in the company. In *Cyrano* she played the girl in the tavern, I forget her name, but she has one good scene with Cyrano in which they shouted at each other across the stage, with lots of business; and as the play settled into a run, Joyce became aware that Ralph had forgotten all about her, or so she said. At last she could bear it no longer. At the next performance, she marched firmly across the stage right up to Ralph and played the scene shouting at him at a distance of about four feet. Joyce is about five feet nothing and Ralph was six feet two, so the effect must have been extremely funny. Ralph was completely confused and annoyed and floundered all over the place. Later they met backstage.

Ralph strode up to her and with a voice shaking with anger, said: "Why did you do that to me?"

With great spirit Joyce shouted back at him: "Because you never look at me!"

Ralph collapsed instantly, the professional and the gentleman, wounded to the quick as he realised what she said was true. "Oh my dear, I am sorry, so very sorry. You're quite right. I'm very sorry. I'll always look at you in future." And he did.

Dear Ralph! How gentle and inventive and crazy he was to work with. He did magnificent work in the theatre and in films and perhaps best of all in radio. Somehow he never seemed to get the parts that he was ideally made to play, for instance the Wizard in *The Wizard of Oz*, the scoundrelly solicitor Michael in *The Wrong Box*, and the White Knight in *Alice in Wonderland*. He was the best Falstaff that I have ever seen – full of fun, a ripe sunset of a man. Why didn't he follow up this vein more often? He did his best film work with Korda, but they were miniatures compared to the great sprawling canvases that he could have created. I happen to know this because he came over and sat down squarely opposite me in the Sandpit at the Savile Club, and without salutation or preliminary, both very necessary to Ralph, he launched into his subject:

"Micky, have you seen a film called *Fantasia*?" It is typical of Ralph that he had never heard of anything until he saw it with his own eyes or heard it with his own ears. His whole life was a constant surprise. The whole world could have been arguing and discussing about the Walt Disney-Stokowski masterpiece, as indeed it had been. To Ralph, it was born yesterday.

I said: "Yes, Ralph."

He continued in his light, dreamy voice. "There's a part in that film – oh! what a dream of a part! . . . a part that I would give my soul to play. Why don't they ask me to play parts like that? Why don't you ask me to play parts like that?" He mused.

I waited. Meanwhile, I hastily ran through the field of possible runners. Could it be – no! Who could it be?

"It's the Lizard," Ralph said solemnly. "He looks down and sees this lovely creature in negligée in her boudoir, and he falls *madly* in love with her. He *must* have her! He must! He comes twining and twisting down one of the pillars – oh! what a part it is! His eyes are shining, his lips are dripping with saliva. She repulses him. He insists! He seizes her by the waist! She kicks him in the stomach! Oh what a scene! Then . . . then . . . then . . ."

"Well, what then?"

"They dance!" said Ralph solemnly.

A light dawned: it was Ponchielli's "Dance of the Hours", a scene from *Fantasia*! Walt and his artists had decided to interpret the number with two monsters: a male crocodile and a female hippopotamus. With a sure instinct – oh that the rest of Hollywood were only like Walt! – he had realised that such swoopings and glidings, such delicate tripping, such passion, such fury, such bumps, boops and glides, could only be interpreted in all its finesse by two grotesque monsters. Go and see it, if you're in the business. You can learn more from seeing "The Dance of the Hours" by Walt Disney than from spending a year glumly staring at the television screen. How right Ralph was. What a part it was! My mind flashed back to the great discovery made by MGM: two great old actors on its roster, Wallace Beery and Marie Dressler. Some genius had the idea of pairing them together in a series of comedy dramas. They cleaned up. Such life, such truths had never been seen on the screen at that time, particularly at MGM. They too were ugly. They too were old. They too were beautiful, as life and death is. And audiences recognised this at once.

I nodded agreement.

Ralph had gone off into a dream of hope and ecstasy. "Micky, why don't you and the Dormouse write a part for me like that?"

Why, indeed? In these days of the ostrich, our heads in the sand, we are suckers for science fiction fantasy and fairy tales, made to order for Ralph. But the new generation knew him as a stage actor, an actor of realistic parts. They thought they were doing something wonderful when they cast him as a sorcerer magician, a familiar of dragons. He should have played the *dragon*!

I wrote this in 1983 when I had a dragon part for Ralph. It was the screenplay which Ursula Le Guin and I wrote together, adapted from her two books *A Wizard of Earthsea* and *The Tombs of Atuan*. Ged, the young wizard in the story, comes in his small boat to the island of Pendor to confront the Great Dragon and his sons, and the only weapons that he has are certain words of power and the knowledge of the Great Dragon's name. That may not sound much, but as Ursula Le Guin knows, to know someone's real name is to have power over them. Can't you see Ralph smouldering and smoking, one great leathery wing all asprawl, the spines of his back quivering with venom, bile on his great jaws terrible with contempt? Can't you hear the thunderous voice, can't you see the tower and castle totter into dust as he shoves it out of his way like a house of cards? Can't you hear the roaring of the fires behind those shuttered nostrils? All this, Ursula and I could give to this sequence with the collaboration and imagination of an actor like Ralph. Maybe Disney could have done it, but Walt would want to make the dragon a bit humorous – not we. As to this dragon, a primal force, merciless, cunning, superhuman, wise, observant of, but indifferent to the race of men – do you think that film financiers so quick to back the mediocre, will back two intellects like ours to make a film of *The Earthsea Trilogy*? Not bloody likely!

In 1946, however, we had the world at our feet. Arthur Rank and John Davis, impressed by half a dozen Academy Award nominations for *Black Narcissus*, and by the success of *A Matter of Life and Death* (although titled *Stairway to Heaven*) in the States, were anxiously waiting to know our next subject – and what it would cost. So far, very little money had been remitted back to England from America, and though a kiss on the hand is a very pleasant thing, a diamond bracelet lasts for ever. A flood of American films made during the war were competing with the British in overseas markets. Overseas competition was fierce. John and Arthur had created an empire with nothing in the treasury. Until they could go to the public and sell shares, they had to go to the banks, so it was with more than ordinary trepidation that they asked the formidable Archers what was to be the target. They must have paled and looked at each other with a wild surmise when we answered them – "a film about ballet".

I can't describe the plot better than Lermontov does in the film.

LERMONTOV: The Ballet of the Red Shoes is from a story by Hans Christian Andersen. It is about a young girl who is devoured by an ambition to attend a dance in a pair of red shoes. She gets the shoes and goes to the Ball. For a time all goes well, and she is happy. But at the end of the evening she is tired and wants to go home. But the red shoes are not tired. The red shoes are never tired. They dance her out into the street, they dance her over the mountains and valleys, through fields and forests, through night and day. Time rushes by, love rushes by, life rushes by, but the red shoes dance on.

CRASTER: What happens in the end?

LERMONTOV: Oh! In the end she dies.

On and around this beautiful tale, Emeric had spun a full-length screenplay for London Films in 1936 or 1937. Emeric, who had already made two careers, in German and French, was learning English at the time, so Keith Winter, a brilliant playwright, worked with him on the dialogue. For some time Alex had been looking for a script about a ballerina for Merle Oberon, and I think that it may have been G. B. Stern who suggested the Andersen story as a basis. Certainly, several writers had a crack at it. Alex, of course, had known Emeric and his work ever since the days of UFA in Berlin, and once he had brought this brilliant combination together, the script made progress. But it was never produced. This must have been about the time Merle Oberon was working on Sam Goldwyn's production of *Wuthering Heights*, and David Niven ran away with her. David told me that they drove across the country from Hollywood to New York, stopping at scruffy motels, and every time they stopped at a new motel, within twenty minutes a cable would arrive from Goldwyn saying: "Return at once. You're fired!"

It was certainly enough to make Alex hesitate about investing half a million in *The Red Shoes* for Merle and the film was never made. However, Merle and David's escapades no doubt had the desired effect, bringing the horse to water and soon after, Alex and Merle married. Before Alex gave up on the project I was asked to okay a certain ballerina as double for Merle in the ballet scenes. I went to see her. She had legs like swords. She was dark and had a marvellous body. I hoped that I would be allowed to direct the second unit.

Time passes by, life passes by, a war passes by and we are no longer an ambitious film director and an émigré Hungarian writer – we are the Archers.

Emeric said to me: "You know that script of mine that Alex has got?"

" 'The Miracle at St Anthony's Lane' ?"

"No, Michael. But I would be very happy if we made 'St Anthony's Lane' now that the war is over. I still own the rights. I optioned it many times, but it always came back to me."

"I remember. You wish you had a dozen stories like that which you could option and never sell. Then you could retire and need never write another story."

"Exactly. Well, would you like to make it?"

" 'St Anthony's Lane'?"

"Yes."

"No." A pause. My curiosity had been aroused. "So what is this script that Alex has got?"

"He commissioned it from me in 1937. Lajos Biro drew up the contract. It was a lousy contract. But I was very happy with the script. It was one of the best scripts I ever wrote."

"Can I read it? Would London Films have a copy?"

"Michael, leave that to me. I will get you a copy. We don't want Alex to get ideas."

We were seeing a good deal of Alex. He had already begun his campaign to break up Rank's Independent Producers. Naturally, he started with the Archers. We were alumni of London Films, and he behaved as if we still were his darling chicks. We were asked to dinner not once, but often, to the fabulous penthouse apartment at the top of Claridges where Alex lived and entertained. There were always interesting people at those parties, and no doubt we held our own. Emeric is the only man I know – including Alex's two brothers – who was not afraid of Alex. I have said elsewhere that Emeric is a lion for courage, but that is not the reason. He had no need to exert himself. He knew Alex for what he was, knew the real level of his intellect and had no compunction about using this knowledge in an argument. Those two Magyars understood each other very well. The only thing that Alex could never understand, was why from the beginning I had given Emeric so much power. A writer was a writer, and however much he got paid, was less than a director, and infinitely less than a producer. I think that he would have been incapable of understanding that money did not influence my decision when I made Emeric my equal partner. I know the best when I see it, and that was what it was worth to me.

As for myself, I loved Alex in the way I loved the film business. I loved him for his glamour, his good taste, his shrewdness, for the audacity and sheer fun that he got out of manipulating men and millions. Not that I didn't have fun. But it was a different kind of fun, the enjoyment of a craftsman who probes deeper and deeper into his art. Alex came to understand this and respected it. He often said that I was the finest technician he had ever known. It wasn't true, but I liked to know that he said it. My master in film, Buñuel, was a far greater storyteller than I. It was just that in my films miracles occur on the screen.

Anyway, these little dinners at Claridges were very pleasant, and gradually whittled away our single-minded loyalty to Arthur Rank. I never noticed it, but no doubt Emeric did. He knew Alex. I only knew that it was pleasant to be treated as an equal by a great gambler in the great world of international films to which I had never ceased to belong. I still read *Variety* every week and never glanced at an English trade paper. The whole world was my audience, and it irked me that films like *Colonel Blimp* were misunderstood by the distributors in the United States. I had led British films to equality with the Americans in the art that I loved. Now I wanted to see the two industries working together.

Alex, of course, wanted access to Rank's enormous chain of cinemas, but he didn't put it that way. He talked mainly of protection for British films, and government sponsorship to encourage banks to invest in British films, and the power to deal with the Americans from strength, which he certainly hadn't got, but Rank had. All this was very congenial to me. Arthur and John never talked film politics with us, and so long as they didn't insist on artistic control over our future films we were happy to leave it that way. Alex understood this perfectly well. He never made the slightest attempt to undermine our loyalty to Arthur. He made gentle fun of him, he flattered us and he bided his time.

We knew, or guessed – well, Emeric knew and I guessed – that the other members of Independent Producers were getting the same treatment. Carol Reed was already Alex's ace director, of course. Alex knew the ropes. In the next New Year's Honours List, Carol became Sir Carol Reed. He was popular and nobody minded.

I have said enough to show how desirable a prey Independent Producers must have seemed to Alex. He saw himself as head of this group of box-office conjurers – like Denham, only bigger and better. He quite forgot to ask himself the question – why did this group of young film-makers get on so well together, and produce such a high level of entertainment at such a reasonable price? We were all professionals, trained by men like Ted Black, Victor Saville, Mickey Balcon, Jack Harris, Walter Mycroft and Walter Forde, accustomed to work on tight budgets, and not to waste film. All this time, we had made the best of what we were given. A policy of hit or miss was more misses than hits. Now for several years we had chosen to make our own mistakes and the result had been hit after hit. This we owed to my successful bid to challenge Arthur Rank after making *49th Parallel*. But Rank should get all the credit he deserved. He found the money and put the onus back on us, where it belonged. And it worked. But could it work with Alex? Carol seemed happy enough, but then Carol had never really chosen his own films. Alex talked as if we had made a great discovery: that a film-maker should decide for himself what he wanted to make. Alex said that was how he proposed to run Shepperton Studios and the new London Films. We listened sceptically. But, after all, what did it matter to us? At that time we were happy.

Meanwhile, I had read Emeric's material, or at any rate the copy of his script which was in his possession. It had all Emeric's usual charm and ingenuity and rather stronger character drawing than usual. The viewpoint of the storyteller was from the outside, looking in. But the script was ten years old, and the prewar conventions of this kind of star vehicle showed up very plainly. There had obviously been instructions that this should be a romantic drama, and not a dance film. Occasionally the heroine, as seen from a box or from the stalls, danced "up the stage", later on she was made to dance "down the stage". There were excerpts from well-known ballets, but no ballet sequence that I would have liked to stage.

I said to Emeric: "I'll do it if a dancer plays the part and if we create an original ballet of 'The Red Shoes', instead of talking about it."

I am rather prone to these Olympian decisions. Take, for example, *Black Narcissus*: "It's a studio picture. We'll make the whole thing at Pinewood." Or *49th Parallel*: "No, thanks. I don't want to make a film about minesweepers. This isn't the 1914 war. I want to make a film in Canada." Or *The Tales of Hoffmann*: "It's an opera, isn't it? We'll let Beecham make a recording of the whole thing with singers and orchestra, and then shoot the film with dancers to a playback." Or *The Battle of the River Plate*: "We'll make all the movements of the ships at sea, otherwise it'll be just another naval thriller with model ships."

Emeric was so keen to have his script made that he would have agreed to anything, I think. It had delightful scenes that took me back to the Riviera and the Monte Carlo I knew in the twenties, when I used to drive my gambling father from Cap Ferrat to the Monte Carlo Sporting Club, or to bridge-playing villas where I was free to wander about, talk to the gardeners, read the books in the dustsheet-covered libraries, while my father played contract bridge with Lily Langtry, or billiards with Somerset Maugham. One scene in Emeric's script I admired in particular. It took place on the terrace of the Café de Paris opposite the Monte Carlo Casino where Diaghilev had his ballet season every winter in the lovely little theatre designed by the architect who also designed the Paris Opera.

Lermontov, who was based upon an impresario like Diaghilev, but more like Alex, is seated at one of the café tables while at a bigger table his creative team, choreographer, scenic designer, composer, are arguing about the staging of the ballet of "The Red Shoes". Lermontov pays little attention to what is being said, only putting in a word every now and then. All the same he gets what he wants, and his friends and collaborators are equally satisfied, and equally sure that they had thought of it all for themselves. As this scene was not in the final cut of the film, I would like to print it here. It illustrates the way Emeric and I worked together.

EXT. NIGHT. CAFÉ DE PARIS. TERRACE. (Allow Scene Nos. 279–287)
(SET & MATT SHOT)
The terrace of the Café de Paris. There are still quite a number of people

on the terrace, drinking and talking. From the interior of the Café we hear dance music. Lots of bright lights.

A table occupied by LERMONTOV, LJUBOV, RATOV and LIVY. RATOV is drawing sketches on the table while LJUBOV and LIVY look on with interest. LERMONTOV has his face slightly turned from the others and appears to be following some private train of thought.

RATOV: (To LERMONTOV) Boris! Please! (LERMONTOV turns.)

RATOV: Has it been decided whether we have four or five scenes?

LJUBOV: Five, of course! And for the simple reason that it just can't be done in four.

LIVY reluctantly withdraws his gaze from an attractive GIRL who is passing their table.

LIVY: If there are five scenes that will mean an extra interlude – and I don't think that's a very good idea.

LJUBOV: Why not?

As LIVY has no real answer for this, he contents himself with taking a drink of brandy from an enormous balloon glass in front of him.

LERMONTOV: Are you talking about "The Red Shoes"?

LJUBOV: (exasperated) We've been talking of nothing else for the last half hour.

LERMONTOV: Well, what's the trouble? (He bends over the table.)

RATOV: Now you see, Boris, here is Scene One, the girl's house.

We see the table with RATOV's sketch on it. Other sketches are on other tables, done boldly in black pencil.

RATOV: Here is Scene Two – the shop window where she buys the shoes; Scene Three – the hall where the dance is held; Scene Four – the Street, that of course, is where she cannot stop dancing – and a possible fifth scene would be the road to the church.

LERMONTOV: That all seems very nice.

RATOV: You like it? Then in two days' time I can let you have the first sketches.

LERMONTOV: But you know, Sergei. I think it could be simplified a little. For example, the street could be the same road as the road to the church.

LIVY: One less interlude.

LERMONTOV: And don't you think it would be more attractive if they held the dance in the open square?

LJUBOV: Yes! Much better! Much better!

RATOV considers.

RATOV: Then is there any reason why we shouldn't have the church on one side of the square?

LERMONTOV: No reason at all!

LIVY: You don't need a street scene.

RATOV: (doubtfully) No ... but I had planned to have a donkey going along the street. I thought it might give something to the scene!

RATOV looks hopefully at the others, whose faces register little enthusiasm.

LJUBOV: Anything a donkey might give would be most unwelcome!

RATOV grabs a new clean table. Starts sketching.

RATOV: I have it! It's really very simple We just have this beautiful square, in which the dance takes place – the donkey would look charming in the square.

LJUBOV makes an exclamation of disgust, but RATOV ignores this and continues.

RATOV: One one side of the square we have the church, on the other the shop where she buys the shoes ...

THE WHOLE GROUP.

LERMONTOV: But what about the third side?

LJUBOV: (triumphantly) That would be the girl's house, of course.

LERMONTOV: (with an ironic smile) Perfect!

LIVY: One set and no interlude music at all. Boris, you're wonderful!

LJUBOV: (a little offended) Well, I certainly think I contributed my share!

LERMONTOV: Of course you did! And so did Sergei and Livy! In fact you are all children of quite remarkable talent.

He smiles.

I looked forward to this scene all through the shooting of the film. We built a lovely life-size replica of the Café de Paris terrace at night, and it took me three days' hard work to shoot it. I remember how tough it was because I was suffering from catarrh. The set was a real old movie set and it looked it. No matter what Jack Cardiff and I did, it still looked like an old movie set. As for the scene itself, everything that had been said in it had already been either said or implied in every scene that I had directed since Julian Craster burst into Lermontov's apartment, interrupting his breakfast. The way that these artists, including Lermontov, thought and worked and invented in this closed world of music and dancing had been conveyed to the public in every scene. "The Ballet of the Red Shoes" itself was the fruit of all this collaboration and love. Nothing but their art existed for these dedicated artists. In the same way, while preparing and shooting the film, I was working with my own dedicated bunch of creative artists. Gradually the ballet ceased to be a naturalist conception and became completely surreal. At once, all the discussion in the scene in the Café de Paris became unreal and unnecessary. There was no longer anything to talk about or explain, because we were going to show the film audience what we had created. All that we needed now was their collaboration. And we certainly got that! When it came to the editing of the film, that whole magnificent scene at the Café de Paris was dropped without any discussion. It had served its purpose. It had alerted me and my friends that we were photographing images, not words, and that there was one contributor to our work whose collaboration was absolutely essential for the success of "The Ballet of the Red Shoes": and that was the audience.

There was a great deal of rewriting to be done. We figured on about four months' preparation before we started shooting on location in France in June 1947. We allowed four weeks for that, to include a few pick-up shots in London, followed by the studio scenes of the principals, some of which would also include the whole ballet company. Last of all came the "Ballet of the Red Shoes" itself. This scheme worked out all right, more or less. First of all, I have a good deal to tell about the months preceding it, which were not without incident.

First, we had to buy back Emeric's script from Alex, and we took infinite pains to avoid alerting that foxy gentleman, who would have upped the price if he knew how much we wanted it, or might even have refused to sell at all. We decided not to approach London Films ourselves, but to use our parent company, Independent Producers, as an intermediary to buy the film on behalf of the Archers. Our lawyers were instructed to say that they were acting more on behalf of Emeric Pressburger than for me, or for both of us. As it was one of Emeric's favourite scripts, he wished to buy it back for possible future production. Above all, this diplomat was instructed not to say that we contemplated making *The Red Shoes* our next production for Rank. We need not have worried. I have no idea at what figure of accumulated cost *The Red Shoes* stood – or should I say danced? – in the books of London Films. Certainly, Emeric had not been paid much for his original story script. But times had changed, and when a price of £18,000 was quoted, we were in no mood to argue. Alex bought another Monet and we got on with the rewrite.

Amongst the various versions of the story and script which were dumped upon our desk from the files of London Films, there was no doubt about Emeric's version being the master script. But it had never been revised by him. So far as I remember, it was in two distinct parts, which included a world tour by the Lermontov Ballet Company. We had to get this into shape and at the same time allow for "The Ballet of the Red Shoes", which was to be one of the dramatic peaks of the film. I made it plain that we were planning for a ballet about twenty minutes in length. Emeric thought, and hoped, rather less. Meanwhile, we commissioned a score for the ballet from Allan Gray, our long-time collaborator. At the same time we were working with Reggie Mills, the editor, and Brian Easdale, the composer, on *Black Narcissus*. We had a deadline because Arthur Rank was going to America, and it was planned to show *Black Narcissus* in Los Angeles in time to qualify for the Academy Awards in the spring of 1947. We had finished shooting by the end of July 1946, so there wasn't much time in hand.

I reminded myself that I had made two stipulations for taking on *The Red Shoes*: the part of Vicky Page had to be played by a dancer, and a dancer of exceptional quality; and a twenty-minute ballet, in which she would dance the leading role, would have to be invented. A score had now been commissioned and it was time to look for the girl.

My early interest in ballet, inspired by Diaghilev and my Russian friends in Nice, had been revived by my friendship with Bobby Helpmann and my contacts with the Sadler's Wells Ballet. I knew that Marie Rambert was re-forming her company at the little Mercury Theatre, but elsewhere the ballet world was in confusion after the war. Europe was rebuilding and re-forming, but America had kept some dance companies and dance teachers together, and it seemed to be the only likely place to find a young ballerina who was not exactly an actress, but who could at least open her mouth and speak the words in the script. At this point in my ruminations, Fate in the shape of Jimmy Granger took me by the arm in the noisy Pinewood Studios canteen. He had become a big star by now, and he aped the handsome brute, although his friends knew him for the innocent idealist he was.

"Micky! You're looking for a ballerina, aren't you?"

Jimmy always knew all the new girls as soon as they hit town, so I said: "Yes, Jimmy," and waited.

"Well, there's a new girl at the Wells. She's in Bobby Helpmann's new ballet. Go and see her. She's got it, whatever it is."

The ballet was "Miracle in the Gorbals". It was in the repertory already, and I would have to wait a week to see it. I spoke to Bobby.

"Oh – Moira . . . ye-e-es. You could do worse, I suppose. She's very spectacular-looking."

Bobby had read the *Red Shoes* script. I intended him to be my right-hand man all through the film.

"Do you think she could do it?" I asked.

"Mmm . . . she might . . . She's coming up very quickly. She ought to be out there dancing leads, but you know Madame."

I said that I knew Miss de Valois.

"Ye-e-es. She believes in bringing them on slowly. There's Margot too, you know . . . Ninette thinks the sun shines out of Margot's little arse. She wouldn't want anyone to stand in her light, would she?"

"What sort of voice has this girl got?"

"We-ell, she has a voice. She's Scottish, you know."

In due course, I saw "Miracle in the Gorbals". The girl was sensational. I asked that a meeting be arranged. A month went by – Miss Shearer was at class . . . Miss Shearer was at rehearsal . . . Miss Shearer was having costume fittings – then finally she managed to fit me in between a hairdresser's appointment and a performance. I, for my part, was attending one of the vast Rank get-togethers, three hundred salesmen in the Dorchester ballroom, to be introduced to the stars and the makers of stars, directors, writers, etc., and to hear about next year's programme. I had arranged to come out when I was told Miss Shearer was waiting in the ante-room. I had established a life-line of commissionaires, assistants, page-boys, to make sure that I was warned in time of my potential star's arrival. In due course, the signal came and I went out. The page-boy whispered to me as I passed him: "She's a corker, Mr Powell." She certainly was. And is.

She was tall, about Frankie's height, with the most glorious hair of Titian red that I had ever seen on a woman. And I've seen some. She had a cheeky face, well-bred and full of spirit. She had a magnificent body. She wasn't slim, she just didn't have one ounce of superfluous flesh. Her eyes were blue. Her hands – what's the use of describing her, you all know her. After a few minutes conversation, I offered her the part. I would have offered it to her the moment we met, but I didn't want to seem frivolous. As it was, she looked startled.

"Are you serious, Mr Powell?"

"Quite serious. The part is yours. We don't start shooting until June next year. But you understand, you have to prepare a long way ahead."

"You too, I suppose." Silence. Then: "What are you going to pay me, Mr Powell?"

I grinned. She was Scottish all right.

"Oh, a thousand pounds or so, and a retainer and expenses during the running-up period."

"I see. I would have to get Miss de Valois's permission, of course."

"Are you under contract to the Wells?"

"We have no contracts."

I remembered that this was true. It was one of Miss de Valois's proudest boasts: "Our dancers come to us. We don't go to them."

"Do you think she'll be sticky about it?"

"I beg your pardon, Mr Powell?"

"I mean, it cuts both ways, doesn't it? No contract, I mean. She can

hardly stop you doing what you want to do, so long as you give her plenty
of notice."

"The ballet is my career, not the cinema, Mr Powell. I must go now.
Goodbye."

"*Au revoir.*" We shook hands. "When will I hear from you?" Her hand
was slim and supple, like her body. She retook possession of it.

"You understand, Mr Powell, I shall have to make an opportunity to
speak to Miss de Valois. It may take a little time."

"Let me hear from you."

"Oh, and Mr Powell. Thank you for offering me the part."

She went off with her quick stride to her many appointments. That
page-boy was right. She was a corker.

Bobby Helpmann was pessimistic: "Ninette will kill it stone dead. She
will think you should have offered the part to Margot."

"I adore Margot, but she wouldn't be right for the part."

"Tell that to Ninette! Margot is the prima ballerina of her company.
You should have asked Margot first."

"She might have said yes."

"Yes. She might have. In any case, she would have come to me, and I
would have found some clever way of talking her out of it. Oh, dear! Why
didn't you let me handle it?"

A week later an agent rang up. He was not a very big agent, but I knew
him. He said that he represented Miss Moira Shearer. He understood that
Powell and Pressburger had offered the leading part in a dance film entitled
The Red Shoes to his client, at a proposed fee of £1,000, plus a retainer and
expenses. Miss Shearer would want a retainer of £1,000 to be paid
immediately, expenses to be agreed, and a fee of £5,000 for a twelve-week
film, half of it to be paid at the end of the first day's shooting and the
balance on the last day.

To myself, I nodded approval. She was Scottish all right. To the agent I
said, who did he think Miss Shearer was – Deborah Kerr? Anyway, we
understood that she had to get permission from the Sadler's Wells Ballet,
who had her under exclusive contract. Was this true? He said he would find
out and come back to me. Things seemed to be trundling along in the
required direction, so I condescended to listen to the piercing screams of
Reggie Mills and Brian Easdale, who were about to record the music of
Black Narcissus the following week.

The cutting rooms of Pinewood Studios would have done credit to
Alcatraz. They were cold in winter and hot in summer. A two-storey
cell-block, it flanked the car park, ensuring that each little cell received its
quota of carbon monoxide. The long narrow building had only two
storeys, and the most desirable cutting rooms were in the upper storey. I
once created history by vaulting over the railings of the catwalk onto the

flat roof of the building below, which proved to have a roof made of a substance about as brittle and strong as *crème brûlée*. I went straight through the roof onto the concrete floor below and stood there while bits of the roof fell all around me. Apparently unmoved by the incident, I walked with dignity to my Bentley, got in and drove off, churning the gravel before the studio police could catch up with me.

Emeric enjoyed the editing of the picture. He loved the cutting room and bristled over Reggie Mills's unpunctuality. Emeric is never late. He was once reported by Dilys Powell in an article as "the late Emeric Pressburger". He wrote her a charming letter in which he said: "Dear Dilys, I am sometimes early, but never late. Yours sincerely, Emeric." Reggie is always late. But since he is never late for a film, I don't think that matters. I think the time for starting work in the cutting rooms was nine or nine-thirty or ten, and on the dot Emeric would be there. Reggie would blink, and try to crank up his old car, and crank up his young wife and almost hurry to arrive at the cutting room, an hour late. Indignant top feathers having been smoothed down, these two incompatibles got on with the job about eleven. Towards the evening, perhaps, Emeric would like to work a little late. Reggie would gasp: "Emeric! I'm most frightfully sorry. But I've got tickets for the Garden tonight." (He had them nearly every night.) "It's Puccini, Emeric. It's *Gianni Schicchi* with Gobbi, Emeric."

What could Emeric do? He was a Mozart fan himself, Brahms, Schubert . . . we all loved music, but never discussed it. I loved Bartók, Stravinsky, Chopin, but I never said so. It had nothing to do with the film we were making. The composer was part of our team. He was telling the story as we all were: Emeric with his pencil, writing in his round hand his laboriously acquired English; Uncle Alfred with his formidable regiment of designers and draftsmen and his chiefs of construction; Jack, who in his years of apprenticeship to Technicolor, like a young painter in the studio of Verrocchio, had skimmed off every trick in the trade and was now a master himself, painting the scenes and actors with coloured light as they had never been lit and painted before; Chris, who had succeeded Geoff Unsworth as operator of the great three-strip Technicolor camera, the centre of noise and confusion, the cool heart and steady hand of the production; Syd, the meticulous craftsman, the master of all trades, Argus-eyed, for whom no phase of the production held any surprises; George Busby, arguing, persuading, coaxing and controlling; Bill Wall, chief electrician and gaffer on the floor of the studio, Jack Cardiff's third eye and arm, a genius of improvisation and disrespecter of persons; and last, and first, me and Bill Paton.

San Quentin, Marin County, California, October 20, 1983
   I am dictating this – for alas my eyes are no longer good enough to help

*me write and rewrite a half a million words – on the quarterdeck of a little
white-painted house that stands perhaps a hundred feet above sea level,
and which looks out over the Bay. By white-painted, I refer to the interior,
which is full of light and air, like the cabin of a ship. Outside, the house is
shingled from top to toe, and the sun has bleached the shingles in a pattern
of gold and silver. The elevation above the sea makes all the difference. The
waterfront is only one hundred yards away, and from our height we look
over the roofs of the shacks to the sparkling waters of the Bay and in the
hazy distance, to the dragon-shape of Corte Madera, and to the smugly
named Paradise Bay, where there is a vast marina. Thelma has gone to San
Rafael to hire some furniture, for there is a blessed lack of furniture in this
enchanting house. Still, I suppose the guests will have to sit on something.*

*I have called the place where I am working a quarterdeck, and so it is, if
your active imagination can supply it with brass fittings, an imposing ship's
telegraph, quartermaster at the wheel and the monosyllabic seaman with a
highly polished telescope. It is thirty feet long and six feet wide – the
quarterdeck, not the telescope! It runs from one side of the house to the
other. I walk up and down as I dictate, casting a professional eye at the sea
and sky from time to time, and judging to a nicety the moment when I shall
have to say: "Quartermaster, alter course thirty degrees to starboard," to
which he will reply: "Aye, aye, sir," and we shall save by our vigilance the
San Francisco ferry from being cut in half.*

*Our trip to Moscow, like Napoleon's, has proved an error. After our
first flying visit before Christmas, we had reckoned the job would take six
weeks. It took four months, and is still going on, though happily without
us. Time has no meaning in Russia. It never did. She's too big. We
scrambled out of the country, somehow, on April 30th of this year – 1983.
I speak professionally, not as a tourist, nor as an invader. In Russia I had
given up work on this half-written book, in despair. In Gloucestershire, my
good intentions were again frustrated, but this time because of happiness. I
think that these five months, culminating in my seventy-eighth birthday,
were the happiest days of my life, but I realised that I must get away for the
next three months to some retreat, if I were ever to finish A Life in Movies;
and for a long time I have realised that to write this book successfully was
what my mother would have wished, and what I was born for.*

*So here I am in Thelma's light and airy house, picking up trims from the
cutting room floor of memory.*

*It is 1946. Black Narcissus is in the editing stage. The Red Shoes are
quivering with impatience in the wings. I am forty-one years old and weigh
110 pounds. Thelma is six years old and living on the Caribbean island of
Aruba. By now, Independent Producers are a power in the land, and the
members of our group each have their own offices and their permanent
staff.*

I was impatient of the complacency of my associates about the mounting costs of our films. An American film, with half its costs guaranteed from America, could afford these prices. A British film could not. In spite of his vast empire, Arthur Rank was finding out the truth pretty rapidly. The increased budgets of our more ambitious films seemed reasonable only when set off against the promises made to him by American distributors. The answer seemed to us to be in quality, in a different kind of product; in *Henry V, Colonel Blimp, Brief Encounter* – MGs versus Cadillacs.

These thoughts had been occupying me ever since we regained contact with America and the American market. We were disappointed that they hadn't understood *Colonel Blimp*, but they hadn't. *A Canterbury Tale*, with its American soldier hero, was too close to home. *I Know Where I'm Going*, an escapist film, already had its fans. *Stairway to Heaven*, as they called it, was a hit from the start and is gathering new fans more than thirty years later. So much for the war. Now we were making someone else's story into a film, a novel by a woman writer, a typical Hollywood film subject. Nuns are always box-office, aren't they? Well, I was sleeping with one of the nuns and will always be in love with another. I reckoned that I could make one of the most subtly erotic films ever made. At the Everyman Cinema the other day, when Ian Christie introduced me and the film, I saw the sequence in which Kathleen Byron comes through the jungle at night to meet David Farrar, who rejects her, and I reckoned I had succeeded.

Black Narcissus was an almost perfect film. I say "almost", because there is always something lost in even the finest film, or perhaps I should write, especially in the finest film, when a scene or a whole sequence has to be dropped for reasons that at the time seem valid or even necessary. I wish that I had had the sense to make a private collection of these sequences. What a fascinating lecture I could give to film students with these martyred scenes as illustrations! What a banquet I would be able to set before them: the CPR train sequences in *49th Parallel*; the scene between Godfrey Tearle and Hugh Burden in *One of Our Aircraft is Missing*, which contains the germ of *Colonel Blimp*; the scenes of the love-lorn witch, Pamela, in *I Know Where I'm Going* when she follows Torquil, the man she loves, to the Castle of Erraig; the two dance scenes in *The Red Shoes* between Moira and Massine and Moira and Robert Helpmann – but I am anticipating. I was talking about *Black Narcissus*.

The scene that was later dropped was between Sister Clodagh, played by Deborah Kerr, and the Mother Superior of the order in Calcutta. The young nun is crying, as she confesses her failure to establish the new post and save Sister Ruth from her dreadful fate. The rain beats upon the window and the tears stream down her face as she confesses her failure and then raises her tear-stained face in disbelief as she hears the old Mother

Superior say: "Don't cry, my child. It is the first time I have been really satisfied with you."

Don't ask me if it came originally at the beginning of the film and the story was a flashback, or whether it was at the end, as it is in the book. I fancy that in the first assembly of the film it came at the end, when the rains came too. In that case there would have been the close-up of the rain falling on the huge leaf, and the camera sweeping round to show the curtain of rain blocking out the distant caravan, and then we must have seen the rain streaming down the window in the Mother Superior's office and the shadow of the raindrops mingling with the real tears on Sister Clodagh's face as she looks up and hears, humbly and incredulously, her Mother's words of praise.

If that was how we had it originally, I think we were bloody fools to cut it and substitute for it a highly romantic – or should I say High Romantic – shot of Mr Dean, with the prop rain making it impossible for David Farrar to keep his eyes open as he strained for one last look of his beloved Sister Clodagh. That is how it ends in the film. But I have a sneaking feeling that the scene with the Mother Superior might have come at the beginning of the film in one of the draft scripts, to make the sort of Chinese puzzle opening beloved of European film-makers. Anyway, I wish we had kept the scene, and I wish it was in my collection now. The present ending is the only conventional touch in the whole film.

Arthur Rank and John Davis were a bit startled by the outright eroticism of the film. There was no doubt about it being a big splashy production, and in high hopes they trotted off with it to Hollywood, where they ran into trouble with organisations like the Catholic League of Decency – though what Anglican nuns have to do with Decent Catholics I have no conception. The film collected three Oscars, as I've already recorded, for the art direction, the set decoration and colour cinematography. For his inventions, imagination and sheer audacity, there has never been another colour cameraman like Jack Cardiff. Georges Périnal was the best cameraman I have ever worked with, both in black and white and in colour, but Jack was something apart. The skin textures in the close-ups of *Colonel Blimp* would have delighted Fragonard, but Jack's lighting and composition in *Black Narcissus* and *The Red Shoes* would have infuriated Delacroix, because he couldn't have done any better himself, in imagination or in chiaroscuro. Anyway, Uncle Alfred was delighted for his department, and he even allowed Hein Heckroth and Arthur Lawson to take a few bows as well.

At this point in their career, the Archers were tall in the saddle and pretty arrogant about it. They had recovered from the shock of failure in *A Canterbury Tale* and were being courted by Sir Alex, who promised them the earth, moon and stars, and a charge account at Claridges if they would only leave Rank for one picture, just one picture, and make for him a remake of *The Scarlet Pimpernel*. They seemed to have the world at their feet, or at any rate a ballerina's feet, with *The Red Shoes* next on their list. But the gods smelt hubris, and two thunderbolts struck the Archers in quick succession. Moira's agent wrote to say that she had changed her mind about doing the film; and Allan Gray delivered the piano score of his "Ballet of The Red Shoes".

Moira first. Just as Bobby Helpmann said, it was a case of woman against woman: Scot against Irish, authority against artist. Miss de Valois was creating a national and international ballet company in the same way that Ralph and Larry had recreated the Old Vic. Her authority was based upon a mandate from the Arts Council and insufficient money. She had a small company devoted to their art and to her as artistic director, and she had three geniuses: Margot Fonteyn, Robert Helpmann and Frederick Ashton. In the circumstances, she was keenly aware of any breach of her authority, and my direct approach to Moira had been interpreted by her as just that. Nothing is secret in a theatrical company and more particularly in a ballet company, so Miss de Valois knew all about *The Red Shoes* and who they fitted. She had only to run into Bobby Helpmann backstage at the New Theatre, which the Sadler's Wells Ballet shared with the Old Vic. Miss de Valois bided her time. After a few months, Moira asked for an interview. What happened between them was something like this:

"My dear Moira, Michael Powell and Emeric Pressburger are two very clever men, and no doubt they will do what they say they will do, although" (a little arching of the eyebrow here) "it is difficult to see how they will get any first-class ballet company to be available to them as and when they will want their collaboration. The film world is a very wonderful world, I have no doubt, and they think money can solve anything, but you and I know, my dear Moira" (a flattering inclusion, this!) "you and I know that a dancer's career is based upon three things, talent, work and discipline, and such a break in your training could ruin – "

"But Miss de Valois, the film does not start until our holidays start. Surely it would be possible to – "

She's interrupted by a slow shake of the head for impetuous youth. "Let this red-headed beauty play the star part in a ballet film and get all the publicity and razzmatazz of a film of this kind with these two formidable young cinema men making it, and that traitor Bobby directing the ballet? And poor Margot left out in the cold when we already have an invitation to go and dance at the Met next year in New York? Not bloody likely!"

But Moira was not a redhead for nothing. "Then, Miss de Valois, you do not wish me to accept this offer?"

"My dear child! Of course you must accept it! It is a great chance for you, and no doubt these clever young men will surmount all the obstacles that I have mentioned, and perhaps they will start their film on the date they have mentioned to you. But suppose they don't start on the date that they have told you? Suppose that the film is still not finished when it is time for you to return to Sadler's Wells?"

Moira thinks this over. "But you don't object to my doing it?"

"My dear, you are as free as the air. Your holidays are your own, but naturally . . ."

A look between the two handsome women, blue eyes against steel grey ones.

" . . . if you leave our organisation to do this dance film, I can't promise that I will keep your place open for you, can I?"

A pause. Then: "Yes. I see."

Bobby Helpmann was unsympathetic. "I told you so. You should have let me handle it. Now the old girl has her dander up. She talks about gratitude and devotion, discipline . . . All balls! If you offered the part to Margot and played Moira in the second lead part, she'd sing a very different tune."

"I dare say."

"Well?"

"What do you mean, well?"

"Why don't you play some lovely little black-haired actress in the part and have Margot double the dancing. Moira can dance the Russian girl, whatever her name is."

"That's old hat. It's been done a thousand times. If a dancer doesn't play the part, I'm not interested."

"Well, you won't get Moira."

"Why?"

"Because she's scared."

"Of what?"

"Losing her place in the running. Don't be dumb. She is out to take Margot's place as prima ballerina assoluta. She wouldn't give that up for all the tea in China."

"But Ninette would never – "

"Why not, with that hair and those legs? Ninette has already promised Moira the lead in *The Sleeping Beauty*. She can't keep Moira in the back row. She's very spectacular, you know."

"Well, it looks as if I'll have to get somebody else."

"You won't play Margot?"

"No, she wouldn't be right."

The second thunderbolt was Allan Gray's score for "The Ballet of the Red Shoes". He played the whole thing to us on the piano, with remarks about the orchestration he proposed. Emeric and I looked at each other blankly. It was awful – for him, as well as us. He was an old friend, a valued one, but there was no point in beating about the bush. We paid him his fee and called in Brian Easdale. We were only three months away from shooting. By now, we had a rough scenario of the ballet worked out with Bobby Helpmann. He was to be the choreographer of the ballet, as well as dancing the leading male dancer's part of the Boy. Brian said mildly that he would have a look at it. Were we in a hurry for it? Yes, we said, we were. Could he have a week, perhaps? We looked at each other with renewed hope. Yes, we said, he could have a week. It was one of the longest weeks I remember. At the end of six days, he telephoned. Would we all mind awfully coming to his apartment, where he could play us some of the music? He didn't want to come to the studio because he was working rather hard and preferred to work at home. We all of us came next morning at ten o'clock. It was very like one of the scenes in *The Red Shoes*. He played us the adagio for the ball scene. Hein and Jack looked at each other and then they looked at me. I nodded. They nodded to each other. Brian introduced us to the four-square chorale for the church scene. Emeric nodded vigorously.

Brian said apologetically: "I thought perhaps for the Dance of the Red Shoes . . ." He started to play that magical hobgoblin tune that has set fingers tapping and feet dancing all over the world. Bobby Helpmann's austere and arrogant face broke into one big grin. Brian's room was one of those tall Belsize Park rooms with huge windows, unreliable heating and just room enough for Brian, his bed and his grand piano. He turned round on his piano stool and looked shyly at me.

I walked over, clapped him on the shoulder and said: "Thank you, Brian. When can we have the full score?"

"When do you want it?"

"Yesterday."

Everybody crowded round Brian and the piano.

"How long do you want the ballet, Micky?"

"Twenty minutes."

Emeric looked doubtful. Like me, he had been shaken by the Allan Gray episode. "Perhaps that will be too long, Michael. Even ten minutes is very long on screen."

I disagreed. "After all the build-up for about an hour of the movie to the girl's performance in the ballet, ten minutes won't be enough. I could do with twice as long as that."

"Split the difference. Make it fifteen."

But I was inexorable, although I don't know on what authority. It was just instinct. I said to Brian, "Make it twenty minutes," and to Emeric, "We can always cut it down."

In the end, and mainly through Emeric's pressure, the ballet ran seventeen minutes.

Those aficionados who read the credit titles on films may wonder why Alfred Junge, our chief designer and senior citizen, who always took a leading part in any important council of war, was not present at this historic occasion, while Hein Heckroth and Arthur Lawson were. The answer is that Uncle Alfred was no longer designing the film, and Hein and Arthur were.

The time has come to assess and examine Alfred Junge's contribution to the Archers. It was immense. He was a professional among amateurs, and he organised his department with maximum efficiency. He was a Prussian, and fought his pictures through as if they were campaigns. He left nothing to chance. He never overspent. His sets and costumes were always ready on time. His list of credits is astounding. He was probably the greatest art director that films have ever known. For all the qualities I have mentioned, I have never known anyone to touch him, to come near him. Ever since I had been in films I had longed to work one day with Alfred Junge. When at last I achieved this, we made together some of the most spectacular and fantastic films ever made. Alfred was always grateful to me for rescuing him from the Army Camouflage Department to design *Colonel Blimp* including scenes of the Berlin of his youth. It was all the more sad that when we parted it was by my doing.

Our triumph over *A Matter of Life and Death* was a joint one, shared equally with Emeric. He had asked miracles of us and we had performed. He had demanded scenes in a grey colourless Other World and we had created them. Emeric's story demanded an escalator, a moving stairway through the galaxies. Alfred had designed it, and with the help of Percy Day he had achieved it. For the stunning scenes that opened the film, Alfred had designed and painted his own galaxies, and other film-makers were borrowing from them for thirty years until Stanley Kubrick and George Lucas outdid us all. On *Black Narcissus*, my decision to make it a studio picture had delighted Alfred, and with the painters and craftsmen that surrounded him he had created a magic but believable country and people. In the years before the war, Alfred had been at Denham, chief designer for MGM on pictures like *Goodbye, Mr Chips* and *The Citadel*. But I had led him into a different kind of picture-making, and given him full range for his imagination. And now, over our most ambitious picture yet, we were at loggerheads.

It was a case of realism versus fantasy. Alfred was the realist. It might be assumed that the man who had designed *A Matter of Life and Death* would be the right man to design an original Freudian film-ballet, but it was not so. Everything in Alfred's Other World had been strictly literal and logical. His reaction to my introducing a Coca-Cola machine into his Heaven should have warned me. When I first saw Studio No. 4 at Denham filled to overflowing with Alfred's giant rocks and vast stadium full of costumed people, my heart failed me. I thought that I would never be able to get all this airborne. When I saw Alfred's painstaking reconstruction on the Himalayan mountains, and of the Palace of Mopu, I was equally disturbed that such meticulous realism, in what might be described as the geography of the area, would destroy the sensual and suggestive atmosphere that I was trying to create through Ayah and the House of Women. Fortunately, in both cases, my doubts proved groundless, but – don't tell anyone – it was a near thing. The goodwill of movie audiences pulled me through, but what was Alfred going to say when I told him that one of my key decisions in making *The Red Shoes* was that there would be no audience except the film audience. (How many people, I wonder, when they think of *The Red Shoes*, or when they see it, notice that there are no shots of the theatre audiences at all, except in the Mercury Theatre sequence.) And when I told him that once the curtain had gone up for the performance, we would no longer be in a theatre, but inside the heads of two young people who were falling in love, what would he say then? We both knew London and we both knew Monte Carlo like the palm of our hand, but once we had passed the stage door and were in the coulisses of the theatre, or on the stage – and to me, as to all artists, an empty stage is the most magical and suggestive area in the world, bar none – we were in a world where nothing was real and everything was fantasy and invention. What would he say then?

He said what I feared he would say: "Micky, you want to go too far."

And when one of my collaborators tells me that I want to go too far, that's the end of the collaboration.

By now, reader, it can be no secret between you and me that *The Red Shoes* was another step, or was planned by me as another step, in my search for a perfect film, in other words for a "composed" film. So I was in a thoroughly bad mood, having looked through a batch of Uncle Alfred's sedate and beautiful sketches for a lavish stage production, by which I mean an intimate theatre production, of the ballet, with wings and a backdrop, frontdrop and an orchestra pit and a genteel audience, and with Vicky Page and her dancing partner in the middle of a real stage in a real theatre, no less.

So, as I have said, I was in a bad mood when I met Roger Ramsdell for a drink in a pub near Baker Street. Roger was a friend of Roger Furse's and a lovely painter himself, as well as being a very polite man, so we drank our beer and he waited until I had finished grousing about the appalling limits that film people impose on themselves, before saying: "But you have just the man you want with you now."

I put down my pint. "Who?"

"Hein Heckroth."

"Do I know him?"

Roger grinned. "Of course you do, Michael, although I don't suppose you ever looked at him. Junge likes to keep his staff well in the background."

"What does he do?"

"Oh, come on, Michael, he's designed all your costumes on the last two films and he's working on this one."

"He is?"

I was mortified. What sort of producer was I not to know my own staff? What the hell was I up to prancing around in a golden bowl, living in an ivory tower, when I ought to be close to the ground, going around the departments finding out who did what? Roger told me that Hein was one of the very best painters ever to come out of the Bauhaus. He had wanted to make some money, and had designed a ballet for Kurt Jooss, *The Green Table*, a murderous lampoon on statesmen and politicians, which had made Jooss an international figure. Hein's wife, Ada, was a painter too. She was Jewish. To escape Hitler, they had both come to England with Jooss's ballet company. Later on they had taken refuge from Hitler and from Kurt Jooss at Dartington Hall. Hein was not known in England and was having trouble finding work. He did the settings for Kurt Weill and Bert Brecht's *A Kingdom for a Cow*, which went into the Savoy Theatre but didn't run. The war was too near. When France fell, Hein was arrested, like other enemy aliens, and in his case sent to Australia – an experience which he did not appreciate, for the Aussies took the war seriously and had no time for any bloody Germans. Eventually, Hein was screened and passed OK, and returned to England and Ada. Men of his experience and talent were rare during the war, and he got an introduction, probably by Roger Furse, to Gabby Pascal, who was making *Caesar and Cleopatra*, and gave him the job of supervising the costumes of Caesar's Geezers. Hein was a Hessian, six-foot-two and broad as a barn door. The Australians had taught him how to handle his geezers, and he soon got some discipline into them. Uncle Alfred, who had his spies everywhere, picked him up and he had been with the Archers ever since. I found him in our art department, working on the costume sketches for Junge's version of "The Red Shoes Ballet". He jumped up and stood to attention.

I pointed to the sketches and said: "Why in period?"

His large opaque eyes stared at me. "I do not understand."

I shuffled the sketches, glancing at the delicate Copenhagen porcelain costumes, at the colours in the Hans Christian Andersen period. "Very pretty, but why not today?" He still stared at me, trying to make me out. I said: "The Red Shoes girl is a girl like other girls. It's a good story, but there's nothing period about it. We are making this film for a twentieth-century audience with a twentieth-century girl."

He struck his great forehead with the flat of his hand as if he had just seen daylight for the first time. He bellowed: "You are right!"

I said: "I'm not satisfied with the designs for the ballets. Mr Junge and I do not agree. I want to see what she's feeling, I want to know what she is feeling while she is dancing."

He nodded, his eyes sparkling.

I said: "I don't want a theatre-ballet, I want a film-ballet. I want such a ballet as audiences have never seen."

He nodded furiously, but still looked at me. Why was I saying all these things to him?

I said: "Where do you live, Hein?" It was the first time I had said his name.

"In Chelsea. The Pheasantry."

It was a famous old building. Not a place where you would expect to find half the contributors to the *Yellow Book*. It was a nest of artists, writers, painters, sculptors.

"Perhaps we could talk there?"

He telephoned his wife. I met Ada and his red-headed daughter, Nandi. All three were painters. We talked European art and European theatre until two in the morning, and all the time I blessed Roger Ramsdell. Hein was the man I was looking for. We agreed that he should work at home for the present on just a few sketches and ideas. Then we would talk to Junge together. Until then, secrecy. But in a Prussian organisation, however rigid, there is always someone who has direct access to the commander-in-chief's office. Hein was at his drawing table etching the figures of boys and girls for the fair. The girls wore short skirts and the boys wore jeans and striped jerseys. Hein was just putting bowler hats and *apache*-like caps on their heads when the door opened and Alfred stormed in. Hein had no time to hide what he was doing.

Junge marched up to him and thundered: "I wish to ask you a question. As a German!"

This onslaught, and by a Prussian, brought out the old Hessian fighting spirit in Hein. He squared up to Junge and snapped: "As a German?"

"Yes, as a German."

By now, the whole department knew there was a big confrontation on. Hein shouted: "Ask it then."

The listeners trembled.

"Are you, or are you not making sketches for 'The Red Shoes Ballet' for Micky Powell?"

"Yes, I am."

"Thank you."

With one contemptuous look at Hein's sketches on the board, Uncle Alfred marched out, and as far as I know, the two men never spoke to each other again.

I regret to say that I laughed. It sounds heartless and was, but I happen to know that Uncle Alfred was being paged by MGM to come back to his old bosses and head the art department at the new MGM studios at Elstree. Alfred was just the man for the job: he had done it all before at Elstree, Shepherd's Bush and at Denham Studios, and in doing it he had trained God knows how many English art directors in the way they should go. He had grown to love the Archers, with their independent, piratical ways, and the way that he was treated as one of us. He had shed twenty years since he had joined us. But he had said that I wanted to go too far. There was no getting around that. He took the MGM job. We parted friends. Up till now, the disagreement had been in private.

After the big bust-up, George Busby came to me in great perturbation. "Micky, will you talk to Alfred? He wants to leave us."

"Let him go."

George looked me over. He never knew quite how to take me. "Seriously?"

"He wants to go. Let him go."

"That's just it. He doesn't want to go, and he wants me to tell you that he will work with Hein."

"But would Hein work with him? If he would, he's not the man I take him for."

"What's to be done, then?"

"Let Hein take over."

"But can he swing it?"

"Yes, I think he can."

George looked a bit more relieved. But he still persisted. "He's never designed a film on his own, you know."

I grunted: "Time he did."

"Shall I discuss a contract with him, then?"

"Yes."

"Six months?"

"A year."

"We're only ten weeks off shooting. The shooting schedule is twelve weeks. You agreed it. Six months with an option ought to be enough, don't you think?"

"We don't know how long all the trick shots and the matte shots of the ballet will take. A year is safer and it will make him feel more secure."

"Very well, Michael."

We called a meeting of the art department and all the leading technicians in the unit. I said: "Uncle Alfred is leaving us to go to MGM. Hein is taking over."

The camera department was very fond of Hein. Chris Challis moaned in mock horror: "Oh, God, another Prussian!"

Hein said placidly: "I am not a Prussian. I am a Hessian from Hesse."

"What's the difference?"

"There is a difference."

"England for the English is what I say. Niggers start at Calais!"

Hein understood that he was accepted.

I said: "Emeric, Brian and I have argued the ballet down to seventeen minutes. Hein reckons that with costume sketches that will be about two hundred drawings."

Hein nodded. "Or more."

Arthur Lawson nodded.

"For this reason, we leave the ballet to be shot last. But we record the music before we start shooting, so that we can discuss it visually. George and Syd have worked out the schedule. We start around midsummer on location at Monte Carlo for a month. We come back and go straight into the studio and clean up the story. Then we do the ballet. Any questions?"

As usual, Chris jumped in first. "Yes. The one we all want to know. Who's playing and dancing Vicky Page?"

"Ask Emeric."

Emeric smiled seraphically and announced: "Moira Shearer."

What happened was this. As soon as she had made her decision, Moira regretted it. She had enjoyed our brief courtship of her. She had enjoyed being chosen for a star part by the famous Archers. She had noticed the way the company looked at her, the way they talked to her already. She was not only a potential rival to Margot Fonteyn in the Sadler's Wells Ballet, one of the top ballet companies in the world, but she was also a potential actress in the mysterious and awful world of films. And then there was the retainer that she had returned in a burst of high-mindedness, and the fee of £5,000, which would come in very handy for a girl who danced for her living.

And then there was Bobby, with his worldly-wise views, and his open scorn of her idealism and kowtowing to Miss de Valois: "Well, you are a little idiot, Moira, to believe all that stuff that the old girl threw at you. You've a perfect right to take another job in the holidays. She had no right to try to frighten you off it. The bitch! She's afraid you'll put Margot in the shade with that film publicity and that hair of yours. Drop you? That's all nonsense."

Other people were equally outspoken. Jimmy Granger was one of them. Who did she think she was to turn down a part, a dancing part, offered to her by Michael Powell himself, after he, Jimmy, had put in a word for her? She must be nuts! Poor Moira began to think so too.

Then she heard that Léonide Massine was in town, and that I had sought him out to offer him the part of Ljubov, the choreographer of the Ballets Lermontov in the film. Massine, besides playing the part, would also dance the part of the Shoemaker in the ballet. Massine was one of the great names in the history of the ballet, and Moira admired him greatly. All this without her! Moira was shaken.

Then she heard that Alan Carter and Bobby Helpmann were gathering a company together for the film. They were not going to depend upon Sadler's Wells or any other European ballet company. We were going to have our own, with Bobby Helpmann at its head.

At this point, when Moira was still hesitating, Emeric came to me. He looked more than usually mischievous. "Michael, we must find another girl for the part of Vicky."

"You're telling me, but where?"

"In America. There are plenty of ballet companies there."

"I dare say, but what makes you think I'll find another Moira?"

"Michael, have you heard the phrase 'a sprat to catch a mackerel'? It is in the *Oxford Book of Quotations*."

"You mean a red-headed mackerel?"

"Yes. You go to America, you find another girl, you bring her to England with lots of publicity to make a test for the part, and Bob's your uncle."

"Is that in the *Oxford Book of Quotations* too?"

"No, I learnt it from Bill Wall. When I say 'Bob is your uncle', you say 'And Fanny is my aunt'."

In America I met a lot of Russians, all with ballerinas in tow. I met Sergei Denham. He found me a girl. I brought her back to England and we announced she was going to be tested for the leading role in *The Red Shoes* – and Fanny was my aunt: Moira changed her mind.

To hell with Miss de Valois! She wanted to play and dance that part. So, is it any wonder that Emeric had such a seraphic smile when he announced that Moira Shearer was Vicky Page? His sprat had caught his mackerel.

"Not a mackerel," I said, "but a whale!"

Emeric looked pained.

"What a way to talk about a lady."

What was the name of the girl I found in New York? I don't remember. What happened to her? She's fit and well and has a ballet school in Texas.

A week later, we made a test of Moira with Anton Walbrook, who had returned to the Archers to play Boris Lermontov, the enigmatic and formidable impresario of the Ballets Lermontov. This was against established Archers custom. I never make tests for leading parts, except make-up tests. We had *carte blanche* so far as Rank and Davis were concerned. But since the budget of *The Red Shoes* now stood at a little over half a million pounds sterling (and in those days, just after the war, a pound still bought a pound's worth), and since the leading lady was a dancer, not an actress, it did seem reasonable to show our sponsors that she could open her mouth and speak the words. It would also give them a chance to see that fabulous red hair and that lovely shape. It was the scene at the bar in Lady Neston's house in Belgravia, and I tipped off Hein and Arthur (we had decided to make Hein Heckroth and Arthur Lawson the joint designers of the film, and they had agreed with alacrity, because Hein had designed dozens of plays and ballets on the stage, and Arthur had been the executive assistant to Uncle Alfred since *Colonel Blimp*), saying that I wanted something more pretty than the usual two flats. They got together with Jack Cardiff, and within twenty-four hours I had George Busby crying on my shoulder.

"It's way over the budget, Michael. Jack wants a yellow backing, thirty feet upstage. I swear that half the expensive props that Terry Morgan has been sneaking over the last few days are not on Hein's list. Hein has n.g.'d Miss Shearer's own clothes, and the Wardrobe are doing something according to his sketches."

"What's it like?"

"Oh, all right. But there's not much of it. Jack wants a whole new range of colour filters. What shall we do?"

"Do? Give them to him. They're all crazy about her already. Let them shoot the works."

Anton conceals his humility and his warm heart behind perfect manners that shield him like a suit of armour. He responds to clothing like the chameleon that changes shape and colour out of sympathy with its surroundings. In tweeds and a Tyrolean hat with a feather, he was the perfect Viennese. In the overalls of Peter, the Hutterite, he was one of the disciples of Christ. In *Colonel Blimp*, stripped for the duel, he was the perfect soldier. Now, in white tie and tails, he was the supreme arbiter of elegance, whose approval or disapproval could mean life or death to an artist. The film would not start for several weeks yet, and then it would be on location in France, but Anton had agreed to partner Moira in the test. He was as curious as anyone else to see what he would have to deal with. Miss Shearer was surrounded by a swarm of acolytes when she came onto the exquisite little set and greeted me.

There were introductions all round, and then I said: "Ask Miss Shearer if she can spare a moment."

Syd himself went to get her. The buzzing group around her opened out and departed. She came over. Her wisp of a dress left her shoulders and arms bare, except for white gloves and a few jewels. Her cloud of red hair, as natural and beautiful as any animal's, flamed and glittered like an autumn bonfire. She wore hardly any make-up. She came with her quick stride to where I was standing with Anton, and held out her hand, saying: "How do you do, Mr Lermontov?"

Anton's catlike eyes met her blue ones. He bent over her hand and murmured: "So glad that we are going to work together."

By now, the whole camera crew had adopted Moira. The prospect of working with her for the next four or five months did not appear to daunt them at all. Jack said: "Can we see the scene, Micky?"

It was the same one that is in the film. We walked it through and made one or two slight alterations, then I said: "Let's take it."

Most actresses, or at least most young actresses, would insist on more preparation for such an important moment in their careers, and particularly when partnered by an actor as powerful, as subtle, as Anton. He goes underneath every line of dialogue, every emotion. Moira played it straight from her warm heart and stole the scene. I made two takes. Both of them were perfect. Alas! Where is that test now? What I would not give to have it in my collection!

I said: "I would like individuals."

We shot Anton's close-ups and Moira's last. By now, the whole camera department were her slaves. They already addressed her as Moira, and made jokes that made her eyes sparkle. She was adorably natural. Anton paused by me as he left the set and whispered: "She's sensational."

In a few days we ran the tests for the executives.

Arthur said: "Did you say she had never acted before, Micky?"

John said: "Is that red hair of hers real?"

I reassured them on both points. "She's a natural. I never knew what a natural was before. But I do now. It's Moira Shearer."

This important matter being settled, I could think about her clothes. There had been so much talk about Vicky dancing the "Ballet of the Red Shoes", Vicky dancing *Coppélia*, Vicky dancing *Swan Lake*, Vicky dancing *La Boutique Fantasque*, Vicky at class, Vicky in rehearsal, Vicky this and Vicky that, we had almost forgotten that Vicky had a life of her own. But she was, after all, an English society girl, the ward of Lady Neston, who was obviously pretty well-heeled, and on re-examination of the script it turned out that she had quite a wardrobe. Where would we go for this?

"Paris," said Frankie firmly.

It was only two years after the armistice, but Paris was the place. I have always loved France: not the tourist France, but the way that the French cope with life. From 1919 to 1939, I had spent my holidays there, and three years at a stretch while I was working at the Victorine Studios in Nice. My father yearned to get back. If Eisenhower had let him, my father would have gone ashore at Omaha Beach with the first wave. He tried to go with the invasion force as a guide and interpreter, but was turned down because of his age. And his comments on this piece of prejudice were outspoken to say the least. He was in Paris three months later, and in Cap Ferrat a week after that, and ever since then he had been urging Frankie and me to join him:

"You'd hardly notice any difference, Mick. Alice was here the whole war, she buried the silver in the garden, and because she could talk

German, they never bothered her. Marcelle and her mother ran the Manor House Bar at Chantilly and everything was all right there. Here, on the coast, all the hotels and pensions were commandeered for rest homes or hospitals, so there wasn't much looting. The Germans made inventories of furniture and linen and even listed the breakages. Poor old Bussell has gone – I'll tell you about that – but otherwise most of my friends are back."

Bussell, his wife and his two daughters, Lily and Violet, had been our nearest English neighbours when we first went to Cap Ferrat in 1921. I stayed with the family for the whole long summer my first year at the Victorine. He was a landscape gardener and general factotum for some of the big villas that needed an eye kept on them during the summer months, while their owners were in Paris or Vermont. He was a wonderful friend to me. He loved his garden and he loved life. On some trumped-up charge he was arrested, not long before the end of the war, and he died in a concentration camp. The thought of such a death for such a man was unbearable for me. What was worse was that it was a Vichy French camp, not a German one.

I had reacted with dismay to the fall of France, to Pétain and Laval and Darlan. Then we heard of shining lights like André Malraux and of the wonderful exploits in the Corrèze. But these glimpses of a France that still fought her enemy were soon blotted out by tales of collaboration with Germany by the French police and gendarmes. I couldn't believe it. None of us believed it. This was not the France we knew. Then, after the North African landings, the truth started to come out and those of us who loved France realised that there was a France we didn't know, just as there was an England that we did not know, where the same terrible treacheries and cruelties would erupt like some boil on the body politic. But in 1946–47 we hadn't yet got to the stage of self-examination. That would come later. Meanwhile, I had been in no hurry to return to France.

But now we were planning a picture that would take us to the Côte d'Azur for a whole month. George Busby, whom I had first met on the *plage* at Nice, was already there, lording it like a millionaire among his old friends, who had only known him as a bilingual bank clerk. We were to shoot at Monte Carlo, at Cap Martin and even at Cap Ferrat. We had to find villas like private palaces, untouched by war, and who should know them better than I?

Moira was to have her clothes designed by a Paris couturier!

"By whom?" I asked humbly, for this was Frankie's domain.

"By Jacques Fath."

Jacques and his wife were the favourite couturiers of all the people that we liked and admired most (except Monique, she went to Carven). Their cut was poised and elegant, young and modern. Jacques was invited to London, and came to a meeting with Moira in the paved garden of

2 Ilchester Place. Moira also lived in Melbury Road, so it was convenient. Jacques took one look at Moira and all his prejudice against English girls abandoned him. Such height! Such bones! Such hair! Moira looked suspiciously at this very blond young man, who was already sketching furiously on the back of envelopes. Was he going to be extravagant – make her a figure of fun? Already some of Hein's ideas had seemed a little bizarre. Perhaps it would be better in the film to keep her private life simple and go to Harrods or Harvey Nichols?

I could see these Home Thoughts from Knightsbridge passing across her vivid little face, and felt it was time to intervene.

"Jacques," I said. "You know the sequence where the girl is invited to Lermontov's villa and thinks she's going to be seduced, and puts on her grandest clothes, only to find that she has been summoned to an audition. Well, of course, this is a turning point in her career and in her life. She's going up, up, you see. No one knows how far, and I want to make something of it. There is a staircase in a garden above Beaulieu which I have known ever since I was a schoolboy. It is just a simple flight of steps up the mountain, but it has one hundred, two hundred, what do I know, maybe three hundred steps, going heavenwards, with no villa in sight. Now, Jacques . . ."

He was already sketching furiously on yet another envelope.

". . . I want you to listen carefully. This garden has been neglected since the war and all the way up the steps there are –"

"Weeds!" screamed Jacques Fath, sketching furiously. "Of course! Beautiful weeds, perhaps half a metre in height. Look! She must wear this crown, this little crown on her head." He sketched it. "And this cloak of eau de nil, made of very, very light material. As she climbs the stairs, this cloak will catch on the tops of these weeds and will spread out behind her as if it was borne by pages. What a conception!"

After that, there was no more talk of Harrods.

It was the summer of 1947. We were about to start on the most ambitious picture of our career, and the most expensive. Many people might have thought that it was our biggest gamble, but we would not have agreed with them. It was 1947. A great war was over and a great danger to the whole world had been eliminated. The message of the film was Art. Nothing mattered but Art. In a ballet, nothing mattered but the music.

At this point Brian came to us pale with emotion. He would conduct the rest of the music, but he thought the "Ballet of the Red Shoes" should be conducted by somebody else, by an older man, someone with a far greater experience of music and the theatre than he. Would we let him show the score to Sir Thomas Beecham? We stared at him in amazement. Only a true artist would have suggested handing over the baton to a greater man. He was right. In every department of the film we had either the greatest talent or the greatest name in the world. Sir Thomas Beecham, Bart., conducting the "Ballet of the Red Shoes" would be the final jewel in our crown. Sir Thomas read the score, asked a few questions, made a few caustic remarks and agreed to conduct it with the Royal Philharmonic Orchestra. I have known and admired Brian for many years, but I shall always think that this suggestion of his, so unselfish and imaginative, was the finest piece of collaboration that I have ever known from an artist.

Moira has up to now hogged the headlines, and it is time to talk of the rest of the marvellous cast.

Emeric is often too easily accused of basing the principal male character of *The Red Shoes* on Serge Diaghilev, to which he replies: "There is something of Diaghilev, something of Alex Korda, something of Michael, and quite a little bit of me."

There was also, in the film, quite a little bit of Anton Walbrook, whose enigmatic and elegant personality had enchanted audiences ever since his debut in *Maskerade* (1934) with Paula Wessely, the leading Viennese actress of that date. It was a joy to work with Anton. We had complete confidence in one another and seldom made mistakes. I should explain here that a great actor usually prefers to keep his effects up his sleeve until the actual moment of performance. The reason for this is obvious. The element of surprise, and by that I mean the surprise of the technical crew around him, as well as the actors who are in the scene with him, is an essential part of his performance in a film. But there is one person he should share his secret with – his director. A film director's job is to get an actor's performance on the screen, and for that he needs the confidence of the actor. It's a delicate balance and one of the most enchanting things about working in movies. It will be gathered that I am no lover of improvisation: I like to see both eyes of an actor, not his or her rear end. I can create an effect of spontaneity by the way I direct and cut the film. When the time came to shoot Anton's speech before the curtain at the end of *The Red Shoes*, we both knew that he was going to play the scene like a marionette, like the husk of the cool, confident, polished individual we had known. We had the problem that he was addressing the whole theatre, not a few people, and we had agreed that his voice should be bleached, mechanical, like that of a ventriloquist's dummy, yet audible to the whole theatre. I warned the sound department that they were going to get a shock, and that was all. Jack knew that Anton was to be ringed in the white floodlight of the great spotlight that we had specially built for the theatre scenes, and especially for the final scene. I said "Turn over!" and signalled to Bill Wall, who yelled "Spotlight!" The white circle of light came on and steadied on the opening of the curtain, and Anton stepped into it. He screamed: "Ladies and Gentlemen!" and everybody stiffened to that sound, like a trapped animal in agony. At the end of the scene he vanished abruptly. I kept the cameras turning a few more seconds before I said "Cut!"

Jack said: "Gosh, Micky! Aren't you afraid that it's over the top?"

I said: "No." But then, I had been prepared for it, and they hadn't.

Marius Goring was our final casting for Julian, the young composer of the "Ballet of the Red Shoes", whose love for Vicky, combined with Lermontov's possessiveness, drives her to suicide. Marius was an old friend. He had played the young U-boat officer in *The Spy in Black*, and then the Collector in *AMOLAD*. He was really too old to play Julian in *The Red Shoes*, although he had the background, artistic and musical, for the part. The more he tried to look young, the older he looked. He was certainly not the moody, formidable young man of Emeric's dreams, but Emeric loved him too. We decided that his tact and experience would be invaluable for Moira, whose performance as an actress would certainly not be improved by some selfish Adonis. We were proved right. Marius joined the club and fell in love with Moira, and she behaved towards him with trust and affection. It was odd casting, but it worked because we were all on the same wavelength.

Now for Lermontov's intimates. They were, in order of seniority, his designer Sergei Ratov, his choreographer Grischa Ljubov, his leading male dancer Ivan Boleslavski, his conductor and musical director Sir Edmund Livingstone, his prima ballerina assoluta Irina Boronskaya, and the ever-present, almost invisible Dmitri, Lermontov's valet, confidential man and spy.

We cast this group on the confident assumption that if Boris Lermontov was the greatest impresario in the world, but without any visible creative talent other than that of finding generous backers for his company, it followed that he would employ only the top talent, and that we should acquire the pick of the actors in the world to play them:

Sergei Ratov	Albert Basserman
Ljubov	Léonide Massine
Ivan	Robert Helpmann
Sir Edmund Livingstone	Esmond Knight
Boronskaya	Ludmilla Tcherina
and	
Dmitri	Eric Berry

The scheme worked and there was enough genius in each man or woman to enable them to appreciate the genius of the people they were playing. Fact and fiction combined to create a recognisable group of eccentric and talented individuals. One of the most successful marriages, to my way of thinking, was Basserman with the part of Ratov. We brought him from America. I had always admired him in films and I knew from my German friends of his work on the stage and that he had been the greatest Benedick of his generation. He was tall, with a great big bony frame, which he threw about recklessly, and a huge, handsome face with cavernous eyes. He had played all the great parts, and one could see how good he must have been by watching him play this small one. He was full of invention and never missed a line or a piece of business. I adored him. But he was married and apparently Frau Basserman was famous throughout two continents for the way she ran his life, and the way she ran him. I became aware of her one morning. It was the first day that her husband worked on a setting which represented the stage of Covent Garden. I seldom sit down on the set, and particularly when the whole of our ballet company and all of the principals were showing their paces. As I moved about, I began to realise that I was being followed by a small German woman who never stopped talking. I asked "Who is this?" to nobody in particular.

Syd, in a mild state of frustration, said: "This is Mrs Basserman, Michael. I can't get her to go away. She says that her husband will not come on the set until she's satisfied with the arrangements."

Hearing her cue, the woman nodded vigorously and attacked me in a mixture of English and German.

I said to Syd: "Send for George Busby," and went on with the work. She stuck to me like a burr. George Busby came on the set. I said: "Frau Basserman is not to come on the stage at any time while we are shooting."

George gulped, but said: "Yes, Michael."

"You will go with her to Herr Basserman's dressing room and tell him that if he is not on the stage ready to work within half an hour, he will have broken his contract."

The lady stammered, and said something that nobody paid any attention to, and George took her by the arm and led her away.

Within ten minutes, Basserman was on the set ready to work, and impeccably polite. God knows what that viperess had said to him, but the poor old man was pale and shaky. That was not the end of it. On his last day of shooting I announced, as I usually do when the actor merits it, that he had completed his part and would be leaving us. He got a round of applause. He flushed and bowed and waved his hand. Then he straightened up and looked at me. I was standing, as I usually do, by the camera. He walked over and stopped in front of me. There was silence, for they all thought he was going to make a speech and he did – but not what they all expected.

He said: "Mr Powell, I have promised my wife that I should tell you that your behaviour towards her was unforgivable. I demand an apology."

There were some audible intakes of breath from my unit. I said: "Of course. I am very sorry, Herr Basserman. Please tell her so from me."

He was trembling. He made a little bow and walked off the set. Phew! Can you imagine what a life that she-demon had led the poor old man, until she had forced him to extract a public apology from me? But her authority was never quite the same again. Within a few weeks, the foreign communities of London, New York and Hollywood had all heard the story and knew that Frau Basserman had been felled like a tree, and by a stripling.

Léonide Massine, who played Grischa Ljubov, Lermontov's choreographer, and danced the part of the Shoemaker in the "Ballet of the Red Shoes", was quite another glass of tea. None of his wives would ever claim to have run *him*. He was intensely musical, a superb mime and a good actor. He could pass from dignity to buffoonery in a flash, one moment a monk, the next a monkey. His name, his reputation, his achievement in ballet made him a formidable figure in public, and he knew how to exploit it; but in private he was a good friend who loved to pull your leg and didn't mind if you pulled his. I had worshipped him as an artist for twenty-five years of his brilliant career, and loved him as a friend for the next thirty years. We loved to work together. Together we created magic.

He had been in America during the war – he was an American citizen – and I had seen the two ballet films that he had made in collaboration with Jean Negulesco for Warner Brothers – the charming man who later made *Three Coins in the Fountain*. But when I heard that he had arrived in London just when I was casting for *The Red Shoes* I felt that Fate had brought us together just when I needed for the film all the genius of the world. He had taken an apartment in one of those tall stone and red-brick Kensington houses, just around the corner from Barker's department store, and we met there. He was preternaturally solemn and stared at me with a look that was centuries old. I explained what we were up to and that Grischa Ljubov was based, perhaps, partly upon himself. He bowed. Then I mentioned the ballet, spoke of Brian Easdale and Sir Thomas Beecham, and explained Bobby Helpmann's part in the proceedings. The temperature of the room went down perceptibly. Massine picked his words carefully. He had nothing against the Sadler's Wells Ballet and its leading male dancer, and of course it was my privilege to appoint whom I wished as choreographer. But if he were to dance the Shoemaker in the Hans Andersen story, he would obviously create the part himself, and would want credit for doing so. I was so mad about him by now – he brought half a dozen qualities to the film which had been sadly lacking – that I strode over this minor obstacle, merely saying that I was sure Robert Helpmann would agree to this. I knew that when Bobby and Fred Ashton were beginners, they had been pupils of Massine.

Inevitably, the question of the fee came up. Massine appeared indifferent. I took a deep breath and murmured: "£10,000?"

A perceptible warmth spread through the room. I had the impression that the difficulty about who was whose choreographer was a matter for compromise: give a little, take a little. I had been conscious for some time of family noises coming from the other rooms, and at this point the door flew open and Tania, Massine's wife, swept majestically into the room. She was a magnificent creature, evidently a dancer, but putting on weight. Two children tumbled in after her: young Léonide and young Tania. I am sure that the majestic Tania had been listening at the keyhole. I was not to know that I was transforming Massine's life. In the face of fierce competition in America, where he was too well known, he had decided to bring his family to Europe, where he had many friends and a few engagements, and proposed to eke out his slender income by restaging the famous ballets of which he held the copyright. My offer was a godsend to him, and when the film became a huge success it opened a new career for him.

I went straight to Bobby and told him the Massine tale. He purred: "But of course he would say that. At his age, I don't blame him." (Massine was about fifty, Bobby about thirty-five.) "Naturally, he wouldn't want to go down a step."

"Thank you, Bobby."

"Oh! Don't thank me. It's for the good of the show, as they say. He will be just wonderful as the Shoemaker. Nobody better. As for the acting – mmmm well, we'll see."

Bobby had a towering ambition to leave the ballet and become an actor, but so long as his dancing career could keep him in the limelight, he remained centre stage. I believed in him and wanted him with us, although the part of Ivan Boleslavski was that of a typical *danseur noble*, spoilt and monosyllabic. He had already played Hamlet in Michael Benthall's production, but he knew and loved the ballet world, and because of his ambivalent sexuality he wore the clothes and assumed the moods entertainingly. He knew how to run a company too. He claimed to have been with Pavlova during her last season in London at Golder's Green, and had learned from that great lady how to cut corners. He was a glutton for work. Besides playing Ivan, he was to choreograph the "Ballet of the Red Shoes", and dance the Boy in the story. In the other ballets, he had agreed to play Dr Coppelius and partner Moira in *Swan Lake*. Now Massine had joined us to play Ljubov, and in addition had agreed to dance the Shopman, the part he had created in *La Boutique Fantasque*, with Moira as the Shop Assistant. I gloated. The film already had a rich international flavour before we had even started.

Livy (Sir Edmond Livingston), the Ballets Lermontov's English conductor, was the eighth part that Esmond had played for the Archers. He was a Secret Service man, posing as a vaudeville agent, in *Contraband* (*Blackout* in the States). He was to play Lieutenant Hirth in *49th Parallel*, but decided on the Royal Navy instead. After he was invalided out of the Service, he appeared in *The Silver Fleet*, where he played one of the leading Nazis. In *A Canterbury Tale* he played three parts, and also spoke the Prologue. He played the villainous trader in *The End of the River*, a film of ours which is almost unknown, and about which I shall write in due course. In *Black Narcissus* he played the General of Mopu.

Livy was a cross between Sir Thomas Beecham and Constant Lambert. Esmond endowed him with the polished rudeness of an upper-class Englishman and the keen perception of a perfectionist. His conscious detachment from the emotions of Ljubov and Ratov made him the natural ally for Julian, the young composer played by Marius Goring.

Emeric's story was nothing if not true to life, and just as Miss de Valois had Margot and Moira to pit one against the other, so Boris Lermontov had Vicky Page and Irina Boronskaya. The part of Irina called for an impressive young dancer, a beauty, a good-humoured, lazy slut, destined to become the wife of a rich, easy-going racehorse owner, by whom she would have three children. No more and no less.

By now, I was so convinced of my good luck that I reckoned she would turn up, and she did – in a French film starring Louis Jouvet. There she was, sluttish and lovely, twenty years old, a face to dream about, skin like the petal of a rose, eyes like twin moons, sprawling all over M. Jouvet's bed, and apparently a dancer as well, or at any rate she danced or seemed to dance in the film, none of which I remember. What a dish! I ordered it to be brought to London. She arrived with a young man as beautiful and as remarkable as she was – her husband, Edmond Audran, the grandson of the poet. He was the most beautiful man I have ever seen. He looked and moved like a deer, and was tall and slim with broad shoulders. Kindness and friendliness radiated from him. The word that describes him best is "lovable". He was about twenty-four. These two beautiful human beings faced me expectantly in a hotel room. I was already more in love with Edmond than with Monique, which was how he referred to his wife, although her professional name was Ludmilla Tcherina. Her mother was French, her father a Russian general.

The part of Irina might have been written for the girl, but I asked her a few questions for politeness' sake. She and Edmond had met as ballet students, and had got married a year ago ("but we were dancing together long before that"), and now they were touring Europe as a team, going wherever engagements were offered to them. I asked them if they could get free from these engagements, and they answered with alacrity that they could. I described the part, and told her she could have it subject to agreement over money.

Edmond had been watching me closely and now spoke up. "Excuse me,

Mr Powell. What makes you so sure Monique can play this part, and in English? She speaks no English."

I said: "She can learn English. And I have offered her the part because I think she can do it, and because she appeals to me physically."

Monique giggled. Edmond made a very French face. "Ohhhhh!"

I said: "I can't work with women on any other terms."

"But if she is ugly?"

"Even an ugly woman has something attractive about her for some men."

He still looked quizzically at me. I knew that he liked me, so I said: "You'll come with her, won't you?" They looked at each other. I said: "Expenses paid, of course."

They looked at me, they looked at each other. It was touching to see them. Then we all burst out laughing, and were friends until the end of Edmond's short life.

A film director, like an impresario, has to have somebody in his unit who is solely devoted to his interests. Bill Paton had been that man for me ever since I beckoned him down from the Shetland Islands after *The Edge of the World*. In our case, it was a two-way devotion, just as it was with Diaghilev, who was devoted to two human beings ever since his childhood on his father's country estate near Perm. One of them was his old Nanny, and there is a very touching glimpse of her through the open door into another room of Diaghilev's apartment, painted by his friend Valentin Serov. The other was a huge *moujik*, who always dressed in the belted shirt and boots of the traditional Russian costume, with a big beard to match. I toyed with the idea of giving him to Lermontov, but there are occasions when fact and fiction don't mix, and I decided this was one. Our Lermontov was certainly a Russian of sorts, but not a provincial Russian nobleman, and he would never have allowed himself to be trailed around London, Paris and Monte Carlo by a bearded peasant, however devoted. Eric Berry played the part of Dmitri, Lermontov's valet, and thus supplied the link between *The Red Shoes* and *The Edge of the World* hitherto filled by Bill Paton.

At this time, May 1947, we were only a few weeks away from starting the film, when a rather disturbing thing happened. It must be understood that the Archers, like the other members of Independent Producers, were fully financed by Arthur Rank and had complete autonomy as to choice of subject, technicians, and actors. But this complete freedom to be generous to others did not, in our opinion, allow us to be as generous to ourselves. During the war, especially, it was a point of honour with all of us not to accept more than a living wage. The first film on which Emeric and I both had a percentage was *49th Parallel*. It was a very small one, but it still brings in a few hundred pounds a year.

On *One of Our Aircraft Is Missing*, we were dealing with British National Films, and had no percentage arrangement, but on *Colonel Blimp*, the first of a string of films for Arthur Rank, we stabilised our position and in return for not taking a large fee for our work, the Archers got 25 per cent of the profits, if any. In cash, Emeric and I took about £5,000 apiece. This ridiculous fee was for writing the original story and script, producing and directing and delivering the film. In America at that time, a creative partnership like ours would probably have been paid a half a million dollars for similar services. On the other hand, we would have had difficulty obtaining a percentage from it, since American distributors hate to account to their creative partners for their stewardship. This crazy arrangement went on right up until *The Red Shoes*. I seem to remember that we upped our fees, possibly to £10,000 apiece, for writing, producing and directing *A Matter of Life and Death*, and we certainly shared the same percentage, because we are still getting it. Of course, we registered the copyright of all our original ideas, and then assigned the copyright to Rank to make the film, while retaining the original copyright ourselves. What sounds crazy now, seemed quite sensible to us all then. Rank had created this enormous empire for production, distribution and exhibition, and it seemed reasonable to assume that after the war the money would pour in, and films of ours that were in the red and that had been waiting three or four years to cross the Atlantic, would be in profits in a matter of months. The Americans would be in no position to argue with the might of the Rank empire, particularly as Arthur was buying a controlling interest in one of the biggest distributing and producing companies, Universal Pictures. This was why Arthur and John had gone to America with *Black Narcissus* and several other big films under their arm, but they had found the Yanks were not the pushovers they should have been.

They had their own films to sell to Arthur, and that great little golden America was a mirage. We were the founders and leaders of Independent Producers, so on their return from Hollywood Rank and Davis asked us to come and see them. At that time, the Rank Organisation, as it was beginning to be called, was looking for a home. During the exciting years that I have described, they had a cramped headquarters in the building opposite the Dorchester, on the left as you come out of the main entrance. The public rooms of the hotel were handy for meetings, such as the one I have described when Moira came to see me, and since the Dorchester was one of the first London hotels to be built of steel and reinforced concrete, lots of VIPs lived there for the whole of the war. John had not yet found the palace at 38 South Street which has been the Rank headquarters for thirty years and more, and as the Park Lane premises were a wartime lease, the executive offices of the company were huddled into a peculiar building that was shaped like a slice of cheese on the edge of Bloomsbury, and smelled like one too. There were five of us present: Arthur, John, Emeric and I, and Christopher Mann. Chris was our agent, but he was also a trusted friend, who had assisted us at the birth of Independent Producers and attended most of our meetings.

We all slid about on ersatz buffalo-hide chairs, while Arthur walked up and down jingling coins in his pocket. Was it my imagination, or did there seem to be fewer coins than usual? He and John were embarrassed. They had left the production side to us, and we had given them the first Royal Command Performance, and had followed it up with three Academy Awards for *Black Narcissus*, and were now preparing to shoot another Technicolor production which was to be our most expensive and ambitious picture yet. They had never wavered in the confidence they had placed in us, and in our judgment, but in *The Red Shoes* there was not a single box-office name for the American market: and they must have been told so time and again by their salesmen.

Finally Arthur stopped his pacing and said, still standing and without any preliminaries: "I want you two boys to take less cash and more percentage."

We exchanged looks. We had expected to be told that our production would be cancelled. George Archibald, our chairman, had already warned us that the Rank purse was not bottomless.

Emeric, who had bought a Himalayan palace in Reddington Road, on the heights of Hampstead, spoke first. "I don't see how we can take less, do you, Chris?"

Chris coughed and murmured: "Korda is offering £50,000 for a picture and 50 per cent of the profits."

Arthur nodded. "I know. That's what he is paying Carol Reed. He'll go broke."

"Again!" interjected John pointedly.

Arthur was slipping into his native Yorkshire speech. "Alex has got t'brass for one year, maybe two, but if his films don't play the American market, he can't show a profit, and if he can't show a profit, how can he go to the public?"

We were listening. It was inside knowledge that John Davis was preparing a big flotation of Rank stock.

Arthur went on speaking bluntly and intimately, like he always did: "Quality tells in the end, but we're not going to get an easy ride in Yankeeland. They want my theatres for their pictures. They don't want to give us room in theirs for ours. It's going to be a fight and meanwhile we are short of brass. Next year we'll be all right, but now we've got to go to the banks and borrow the money for production and pay them interest. You boys are spending a lot of money on this new picture of yours, and we expect you to make sacrifices."

This was plain speaking and extremely unwelcome in those days of austerity, but I don't remember that we made any fuss about it. It must be remembered that we were carrying quite a few contracts with our own people, and with David Farrar, who was the first and only actor we ever put under contract. Anyway, we took the cut, and our share of the percentage of profit was raised from 25 per cent to 37½ per cent. It was a big sacrifice for us then, for after what Arthur had said we no longer expected our films to recover their costs in the foreseeable future; but twenty years later, when *The Red Shoes* was one of the top grossing box-office films of all time and was included in *Variety*'s "Golden Fifty", we were glad we had made the sacrifice, and even more glad that we ourselves had survived to benefit from it.

Earlier I mentioned *The End of the River*, and I should explain that it was an Archers Production and was in work at the same time as *The Red Shoes*. We were the producers, the screenplay was supervised by Emeric, and the film was directed by Derek Twist, who had made the final cut of the *The Edge of the World*. Both he and his wife, Nessie, had been in the Services during the war, but we kept in touch, and in 1946 he came to me with a book which I liked and passed to Emeric. There was nothing particularly novel about it, except its setting. It was the classic story of a man's life paralleling the life and flow of the river, in this case the Amazon. Derek proposed to go out to Brazil and research the project and we backed him to do this. When he came back from Brazil, full of enthusiasm, we were just finishing *Black Narcissus*, and so it was natural that Sabu should be suggested for the leading part in the film. Our distributors liked the subject and we decided to make it in black and white and lend Chris Challis to Derek as lighting photographer and associate director. Derek had found a remarkable entertainer personality, Bibi Ferreira, in Rio, who would play Sabu's wife. It looked a good proposition, but it wasn't.

Derek, as a director, was dull, and to be dull with the river Amazon as your backdrop, is to be very dull, indeed. He was a realist, but for him realism was ugly, not beautiful. We were to blame for not seeing he had a better script. The actors did their best, but it was all uphill when it should have been downstream. Even Esmond Knight as the heavy, even Sabu as the hero, couldn't save it. Sorry, Derek. We should have talked you out of it.

I am afraid we were failures as producers. As you know the Archers' famous credit title read: "Written, produced and directed by Michael Powell and Emeric Pressburger". Let's analyse it. "Written" came first, because if you haven't a good story and a good script, you have got nothing. "Produced by" came a comfortable second, because you can't turn a good script into a good film without money and know how. A producer has to find the money and have the last word. We two did better than that. We had the first and the last word. "Directed by" comes last, because it is a tradition in the film business to have the director's name last on the titles. I hope that you will all have realised by now, how right I was, when we founded the Archers, to go fifty-fifty with Emeric – credit, fees, the lot. Nobody understood it at the time, and nobody understands it now. "You could have written your own ticket," they say. "After you produced and directed *49th Parallel*, with all those box-office names, you were at the top of your profession." Quite true, but who got the Oscar for *49th Parallel*? Emeric, for the original story. Five years of war followed: five years of struggle and decision-making – seven films, all from original stories and scripts. What would I have felt like in 1946, with the war over, if the credit titles on *Black Narcissus* had read: "Produced and directed by Michael Powell", and on a separate card: "Screenplay by Emeric Pressburger"? Would that have been a true assessment of our contribution? Of course it wouldn't. I may have appeared the dominant partner, but where would I have been without Emeric's power of invention, wisdom and moderation? The press were intrigued and puzzled by the collaboration, yet in the theatre where would Hammerstein have been without Rodgers, Beaumont without Fletcher, and George S. Kaufman without practically everybody?

I can't understand, myself, the insistence of some directors on having absolute power. They miss half the fun of film-making. I know some directors who will line up the shots through the camera and then peer over the operator's shoulders during the take. I wonder what they hire an operating cameraman for? There are others who dash into the scene and show the actor how to do it. Directors are not usually good actors, except the strong, silent kind, and this exhibitionism of theirs can be very painful to watch. Personally, I ask the actors how they would like to do the scene, and when that is agreed, I say: "Let's do it." I then stand by the camera, because my job is to be the present audience for the actor. David Niven used to say that my excited little voice calling "Action!" was an absolute tonic at the beginning of a scene. A lot of directors try to look through the finders of a camera during a scene. This is a mistake. It is necessary to keep in contact with the whole of an actor's performance, whether you are shooting a close-up or a long shot. And in movies, no shot is complete without reference to the shot before it and the shot after it.

By June, the Red Shoes Company was 120 strong and buzzing like a beehive. We kicked off in Paris, and true to the Archers' tradition of sharing the good things of life with everybody in our crew, we invited our French actors to join us in a tremendous lunch at a brasserie near the Place de l'Opéra. After lunch, we decided the light was not quite right on the Opera, so we all had another round of liqueurs, with the result that we shot the only long-shot I have ever seen of the Paris Opera leaning drunkenly to the left. Next day we shot the sequence in the Gare de Lyon. Moira was still with Sadler's Wells, and so she flew over for it and then flew back to London again. She was as busy as ever with fittings, classes and rehearsals, and was not to join us officially until we were in Monte Carlo in three days' time. Jacques Fath's establishment was next door to the Hotel Queen Elizabeth, where I was staying, and I discovered that there was a charming little garden at the back where he sometimes held his shows. He was delighted that I wanted to use it, and appeared wearing an American buckskin jacket with many fringes, of which he was very proud. Monique proved easy to work with. She wore a white suit with a wasp-waist, and a huge black hat, and was accompanied by a very small dog on a lead. The boys, especially Bill Wall, who liked his women ample, adopted her immediately. The unit left that night for Nice.

I had other plans. It was the first time I had had the Bentley out on a long run and I planned to drive down and meet Emeric and the crew in Nice in two days' time. We had electrical trouble and arrived twenty-four hours late. I sent a telegram reporting: "Twice in trouble." Provoking a string of jokes from Emeric who met me on arrival and asked: "Who was trouble?"

I had recovered from my uneasy feeling about France and the French. I think that Edmond and Monique had something to do with it. They were so young and innocent and beautiful, so opinionated, and so – French. Everything that I had been missing over the bitter years came rushing back to me. I knew, as I have always known, that there is no culture like the French culture, taste like French taste, no *ménage* like a French *ménage*.

Moira flew down by the night plane. She was pretty near the end of her tether. With our fittings, and the ballet fittings, and make-up tests, she had not had a second to herself for about three weeks. She had to be up at six in the morning to start work in Monte Carlo.

"She's in the first shot. Ready at nine."

"Excuse me, Mr Powell" – it was the wardrobe mistress speaking – "the script says that Moira runs out onto the terrace and jumps into the railway cutting, wearing the Red Shoes. But how can she be wearing them? The ballet hasn't started yet. She hasn't even tried them on."

This was a poser, but it would never do to turn tail before a wardrobe mistress. "She's wearing the Red Shoes," I said firmly. "She is wearing the full costume for the ballet, plus the Red Shoes."

"But how *can* she be," wailed the wardrobe mistress.

"You just do your job and I'll do mine," I advised her kindly. "It's the Red Shoes that are dancing her away to her death, and so she's got to be wearing them."

By now, even Emeric was against me. "I'm not sure that you are right, Michael," he said mildly. "Vicky cannot be wearing the Red Shoes when she runs out to commit suicide."

"But it isn't Vicky who's running away from the theatre, it is the Red

Shoes that are running away with Vicky. We'll invent a reason for her wearing the Red Shoes when we get back into the studio. But tomorrow morning she wears the Red Shoes or I don't shoot the scene."

"Why not shoot it both ways?" suggested George Busby, the peacemaker.

But I already had an image in my mind of the shattered body of the ballerina lying on the railroad track, and her Red Shoes, red with blood, and I said: "No."

Next morning we were shooting the scene in the toy railway station of Monte Carlo, which still existed then, and which I had known since I was a child. Our cameramen struggled to maintain their position as the excited and sympathetic French crowd pressed in and around the two lovers. Marius knelt between the rails beside the dying girl, and with a passionate flinging out of his arms appealed to Heaven whether this was just. Moira, with her beautiful blue ribbons and her peach-coloured dress smeared with blood, whispered: "Julian! Take off the Red Shoes."

I was desperately trying to see what was going on, when I felt an arm around my shoulders and looked round into the face of the stationmaster, who had joined the crowd. Tears were pouring down his face as he watched the dying girl, and he stammered: "*Oh! Mon dieu! C'est terrible! C'est terrible!*"

Nearly all the British critics, having failed to understand the rest of the picture, picked upon this final scene as typical of the bad taste of the Archers, and particularly of Michael Powell. Why all this blood, they asked, why all this sordid realism in a romantic and beautiful fairytale? The poor bastards had obviously never read Hans Christian Andersen, the author of the original story, in which the girl got a woodcutter to cut off her feet with his axe, with the Red Shoes still on them, and danced to Heaven on the stumps. The whole point of the scene was the conflict between romance and realism, between theatre and life. But I suspect that what they really wanted was a happy ending. Our public knew better. When Alex Korda showed the film in his private projection room to the King and Queen and the two young princesses, he told me they were all devastated by the ending of the picture, as they were intended to be, and thanked him with tears streaming down their faces for showing them "such a lovely – boohoo! – picture."

I have often thought that the difference of opinion between Emeric and myself over whether Moira should wear the Red Shoes at the end of the picture or not was typical of our two functions and our two mentalities. Emeric was the writer and knew that she couldn't possibly be wearing the Red Shoes when she runs away. I was a director, a storyteller, and knew that she must. I didn't try to explain it. I just did it. I backed up this obvious fact with a few visual touches. When a ballerina is wearing a new pair of slippers, she likes to break them in herself. And I had Moira doing this in her dressing room before Julian shows up at the door. She had no chance of changing them before she's called down to the stage, but her dresser, played beautifully by Yvonne André, has the other pair of ballet shoes of the normal peach-coloured satin in her hands, ready to substitute for the Red Shoes for the opening scene. So much for realism. I now brought the Red Shoes into play as a magical image with a power over their wearer, exactly as in the fairy tale. I went close on the Red Shoes with the camera and worked out with Jack Cardiff a high intensity of colour and light, which seemed to give the shoes life. So I invented the action where Moira takes a step towards the camera and the shoes stop her dead and then turn her round exactly as if they were the masters. The flashing light and the flaring colour get more and more intense, and she starts to run in the opposite direction from the stage. The dresser screams: "Miss Page, Miss Page!" and then: "Monsieur Lermontov! Monsieur Lermontov!" The flying figure of Moira vanishes down the stairs. Here I introduced a cast-iron spiral staircase, often found in the older theatres, set it up in the studio and had Moira run down it. She did it in two and a half seconds.

"It's too short," said Reggie Mills, the editor.

"We must keep ahead of the feet," said Chris, the camera operator. "We'll put the camera on an elevator."

This was done. We shot it again and looked at it on the screen.

"We still don't see enough of her feet," said Jack. They made a brilliant suggestion: "What we ought to do is to have this spiral staircase on a turntable and have the turntable turning slowly as Moira runs down. This will keep her in full view of the camera all the time."

We mounted this twenty-five-foot-high cast-iron prop on an iron turntable, turned by a motor at variable speeds. We adjusted the speed to Moira's speed, which was fantastic. We shot it and ran the picture again.

"Now the shot is all right," I said, "but it's still too short."

"Simple," said Reggie Mills. "Shoot two takes and I'll cut them together."

If you watch closely, you will see where Reggie joins the two takes together, but you will have to be very quick to see it. The final length of the cut in the picture is six seconds. It gives her whole escape from the theatre, and Lermontov, a vertiginous whirling character before she bursts out of the stage door into the sunshine and to her death. There are dozens of images, cuts and moves in the "Ballet of the Red Shoes" that have this dual significance, and this was a deliberate attempt on my part to lift storytelling onto a different level and leave naturalism behind. I do it again and again in the film. An obvious sequence, which has nothing to do with reality, is the series of shots which take Vicky in her robe and coronet, as if on a magic carpet, from her hotel to Lermontov's villa, from obscurity to stardom. I used the landscape of mountains and sea that I knew so well as if it were an audience applauding a new arrival. But enough of that. I have brought you to the first days of shooting and to Moira's transformation into Vicky Page. I had nothing but admiration for her, but, of course, I did not say so. She did everything that I asked her to do, and even suggested something of her own.

"Mr Powell! I can jump over the balustrade onto a mattress, if you have one."

A mattress was found.

"Mr Powell! Shall I jump like a girl committing suicide, or like a ballerina?"

I thought. "Like a ballerina."

She is only in the air for about eight frames, but it is one of the most beautiful cuts in the film. By now the camera crew were her devotees. The whole sequence of her running out and dying on the track was completed by lunchtime. Moira spent the afternoon having fittings with Mme Jacques Fath and her dressmakers for the clothes in the film. Towards six o'clock she had hysterics, went to bed and slept for twelve hours. Her career as a film star had begun.

I am often asked why *The Red Shoes*, of all our films, became such a success in every country of the world. More than a success, it became a legend. Even today, I am constantly meeting men and women who claim that it changed their lives. This is natural enough, for women who were girls at the time, and who were growing up in countries that had been racked by war. But my friend Ron Kitaj, who was thinking of becoming an art student at the time, has told me the same thing. "It changed my direction," he said. "It gave art a new meaning to me." These are personal reactions, but I think that the real reason why *The Red Shoes* was such a success, was that we had all been told for ten years to go out and die for freedom and democracy, for this and for that, and now that the war was over, *The Red Shoes* told us to go and die for art.

When J. Arthur Rank and John Davis saw the film for the first time, they thought they had lost their shirts, collective and individual. I was not present at the screening, I was still working on trick effects for the ballet, but Emeric was and so was our agent, Christopher Mann. Dennis Van Thal, the head of London Management and my present agent, reminded me the other day that he was there too, so I have plenty of witnesses. The tragic and gory end to which their new star had come by the end of the film must have been the last straw. When the lights came on, they stood up and without a word to Emeric, who was sitting with them, they walked out, John muttering and Arthur for once not jingling the money in his pocket.

Next day we got a curt, official letter from John, asking us when we would be able to deliver the film to the distribution arm, and reminding us

that we were already nearly £50,000 over budget. This was mainly
attributable to a mistake on our part about the cost of maintaining a ballet
company throughout the film. We had budgeted the period of the ballet
itself, but we had overlooked how many scenes would necessarily have
members of the company in them. In the budget of a film, time is the most
important and expensive element. We were fully aware of this, but as the
weeks went by and we still had our company on the payroll, we had to
admit our mistake. Hein and his matte painters had about three more
months' work on the matte paintings and effects shots for the ballet. It had
by now become the most ambitious seventeen minutes that had ever been
screened. The main shooting with dancers had finished by the end of
September, and we estimated delivery early in 1948.

By this time, our same partners in America who were handling
Stairway to Heaven, as they called it, Bob Benjamin and Arthur Krim,
had seen our new film and were scared shitless. This was an art film with a
vengeance! And everybody knew art and money were two different things.
It only confirmed Arthur's and John's fears. The new stock flotation was
not going too well, and they were only just keeping their head above water.
The Red Shoes was not even given a première. Instead of playing the Odeon
Leicester Square, which had always been our showcase, it was booked into
the Odeon Haymarket. There was a midnight showing to an invited
audience, and I went to it with Kathleen Byron. At the end of the film I
asked her: "Is it good?" She said: "Yes."

The picture opened cold next day at the Odeon (it was the Gaumont
then), and it was yanked out of the West End after about ten days to go on
general release. The idea was to get the money back as quickly as possible,
but this was not the way to do it. There had been very little advance
publicity, and by the time the public in the sticks realised what sort of film
this was, it had gone. I think I am right in saying that our film made only an
average gross in the UK. Our distributors should have withdrawn it and
then reissued it in about eighteen months' time. Instead, they let it peter
out. Even the enthusiasm of European buyers failed to convince them that
this was anything else but an "art movie", that abomination of film
distributors that has to be sold, unlike the ordinary commercial film with a
few recognisable names, which sells itself.

Meanwhile, in another part of the forest, the jungle of Broadway, there
was a board meeting presided over by Krim and Benjamin. They had just
screened *The Red Shoes* and were violently divided. Their own company
was small, but they were doing well and would soon take over United
Artists. Most of them shared the opinion of Arthur Krim that it was an art
film, and would require tough selling. It was doubtful whether it could
recover the outlay that would be needed for a special campaign. One
member of the board disagreed. He was Bill Heineman. He had a wife and

eight children all mad about the ballet, and they thought that they knew what the public wanted. "If the public see this film, they'll go. Their kids will take them to see it."

This sounds good sense to you and me, but it isn't common, even today in the roaring eighties. Gossip has killed a lot of good pictures before any member of the public has seen them. Directors of the present generation, Martin Scorsese, Francis Ford Coppola, George Lucas, Michael Cimino, can endorse this in blood. Bill Heineman and his nine powerful allies kept on about *The Red Shoes* until he was given leave to try it his way. He searched around and found the Bijou Cinema on Forty-Fifth Street off Broadway and he guaranteed them a run of six months if they took the film. It was a 200-seat cinema and they took it, and he started an ad campaign. The film was classified as a British art movie and opened to brief notices to be read only by balletomanes, which meant about half the little girls in America. After it had run a year, Bill Heineman and his family were crowing "I told you so", and the theatre booked the film for another year. At the end of an unbroken run of two years and seven weeks *The Red Shoes* had arrived! Everybody wanted it. Everybody still wants it.

In America it can be seen in every medium, known or unknown. In Europe everyone knows *Les Chaussons Rouges, Zapatillas Rojas, Scarpeta Rota, Die Roten Schuhe*. Only in England is *The Red Shoes* just another movie to its distributors, an art movie that won't lie down, a bit of a nuisance because poor cinemas with enthusiastic patrons are always asking to rent it and they can't pay very much money. In fact, it's a toss-up whether the distributor's share of the box-office will pay for the handling of the film. Just fancy! We were told in the thirties, before the war, that the life of a film was about three years. After that, for all that anybody cared, it could be cut into mandolin picks. We believed it, but the fascination of the craft lured us on. Now, in the 1980s, the Red Shoes are dancing as magically as ever and Emeric and I are two old fellows, Fellows of the Royal British Film Institute. Prince Charles gave the royal charter to our president, Sir Richard Attenborough, and to us he gave two clay pigeons (the silver token of the Institute is contained in a round flat plastic box which does look remarkably like a clay pigeon for skeet shooting). Moira was there, looking as glorious as ever, but much more human and at last natural. Kathleen Byron was there as secret and as witty as ever. Wendy Hiller was there, a slim, Dresden china figure. I looked around and saw Emeric and Sheila Sim swapping memories of *A Canterbury Tale*, and at the other end of the table Valerie Hobson, a glorious grandmother, chatting with Googie Withers. But no Deborah! No Jean Simmons! And alas! Alas! No Pamela.

Columba came urgently to me. "Dad! You've got to introduce me to Susannah York."

That slender firebrand from *Sebastian* was there, but not Helen Mirren, who stripped so amply in *The Age of Consent*. What a bunch of actresses, of leading ladies, of lovely talented women! What a picker of thoroughbreds I was in those days, and still am.

I must explain my reference to Moira. We made three films together, and could have made two more, and yet we never trusted one another. What were the other two that we did make? *The Tales of Hoffman* and *Peeping Tom*. What were the two that we never made? *The Tempest* and *The Loving Eye*. Don't rush me, you'll hear about them, if I get that far.

Moira never made any secret of the fact that she played in *The Red Shoes* for money. She proclaimed it from the house tops. She was punctual, obedient, respectful, cooperative, efficient, inventive – for money. She was a dancer, not an actress. When she was not wanted on the set, she retired to her dressing room. Film-making did not interest Miss Shearer – except for money. She recognised that we were trying to combine two arts: the ballet and the movies. This was impossible. The ballet demands body and soul from its practitioners. The movies were purely representational. When Mr Helpmann invented such beautiful short passages, and after a few steps Mr Powell yelled "Cut!" she shuddered. Had he no sensibility? What did he mean by camera angle? When Mr Walbrook (a nod of approval here), a civilised man, in one of his scenes with her, spoke of simplicity, and said: "It can only be achieved by a great agony of body and spirit," she shivered. What did these numbskulls know of agony in their celluloid world? Why did Mr Powell never give her any direction in her performance? She thought she had done rather well with some of the dialogue scenes, but all he had remarked was "OK," or else "Try it this way, Miss Shearer." Sometimes she had caught him looking at her with an odd expression as if he were amused. She was not amused!

I never let love interfere with business, or I would have made love to her. It would have improved her performance. A dancer is rather like a nun. Not a nun like we had in *Black Narcissus*, but a devotee. Perhaps Moira was waiting to be insulted and had her answer ready. We were very much alike. I never pursued any woman but one; in my position they were more likely to pursue me. It was a curious relationship. I sometimes wondered whether she had a heart to break.

After Monte Carlo we went back to London, cleaned up the Covent Garden scenes and the Mercury Theatre scene and started work in the studio. We were shooting more or less in continuity and things went smoothly and fast. There is hardly anything that Marius can't do, or pretend to do, so Brian and I agreed that whenever there were scenes of Marius playing a piano, Marius would mime and Brian would play the piano offstage. This made the sound department very unhappy. I tried sweet reason first. Didn't they agree that there was something special about a scene rehearsed and recorded this way, in which the piano would be an extra voice? No, they didn't. They said it would ruin the smoothness of the picture. I lost my temper and said that I didn't want a smooth picture, I wanted something resembling life. They gave me up. We shot the piano scenes that way and that's the way they are in the picture. There were two other sequences that involved dialogue and music, and we gave them the same treatment. The scene between Moira and Marius where he plays the piano and she eats her lunch was easy and great fun; but the scene when Marius comes to the villa and plays the new Red Shoes music to Lermontov, Ljubov, Ratov and Livy was more complex because they all spoke and moved about and the piano cues were tricky. I worked all day to get it right under the cloud of disapproval from the sound department. But I was determined to shoot it in one big master shot without any self-indulgent close-ups or unreal pauses, and I got it. You can see the scene in the film today. There are lots of clever scenes in *The Red Shoes*, but this is the heart of the picture.

I have said that we were shooting in continuity, so that the big *Faust*-like scene in which Lermontov and Julian fight for Vicky's body and soul was her last scene in the shooting as well as in the film. Moira had been so fêted and adored by the crew and so gratified, although puzzled, by my tacit approval that she had concluded acting was a piece of cake. Then she found herself in a tiny dressing room fighting for her life between heavyweights like Anton and Marius, neither of whom was particularly inclined to let the other steal the scene, and she lost her nerve. We rehearsed it through a long day with tempers frayed and tears and both these good actors trying to coach a hysterical Moira. I was grimly determined to get a performance out of her, but as the day wore on I began to realise that it couldn't be done. She could act with her brains and her body, but not with her guts.

"It's five o'clock, Michael," said Syd in the tactful whisper of one who watches by a deathbed.

"Send everybody home," was my answer. "We'll shoot it in the morning, made up ready at nine."

"Made up and dressed?" asked the wardrobe girl.

"Yes. And full stage make-up for Miss Shearer."

I had realised that I would never get what I planned, and that I must settle for what I could get. The two actors met me in my office, which I never used except to hang my coat in. Marius still believed that he could get me what I wanted. "Give me an hour with her in the morning and you'll see!"

I said no, we should give up trying to make a film and barnstorm our way through. In the morning, we would run through the words and directions and set up the camera for a master shot and shoot it. They would have to carry Moira through. They looked a bit shocked at this plain speaking, but after the long day they were in no condition to argue.

At 9:30 in the morning we kicked off. The selfishness and cruelty of the two men who loved and killed Vicky Page suddenly flared into reality. They mishandled Moira as if she were a beautiful thoroughbred, pulling her head savagely this way and that. Because the two men were both refined and cultivated artists, the brutality of the scene was all the more disturbing. This was no longer acting. Moira, the centre of this savage combat, got frightened, missed her cues and started to cry. In the middle of the second take the make-up started to smear. The take ended.

The wardrobe and make-up sprang in. "She'll need a new make-up!"

"Nonsense!" I said. "Touch her up, we're going right away."

Take 3 came up on the number board. We were all jammed into this little dressing room set. It was abominably hot.

"Action!" I said with an intensity which surprised me. This was it. The men were terrific, and Moira turned blindly from one man to another like a broken doll between them. It was at last very moving. The mascara was running. She snatched at her lines wildly, and after Marius made his exit she seemed neither to see or to hear as Lermontov raised her to her feet and led her towards the door, saying: "Vicky, little Vicky! Now you will dance as you have never danced before."

As Moira staggered out, weeping, the whole stage burst into a roar of applause and sympathy. It wasn't art, but it was good entertainment.

But when art took over, that is to say when she started talking with her legs instead of her tongue, she could speak with authority. In spite of the respect that she had for Bobby Helpmann, she was prostituting her art. Even though Léonide Massine seemed happy with his part, even though Hein Heckroth's sketches were pretty and ingenious, even though he had dyed seventeen pairs of ballet slippers in seventeen shades of red in order to get the right red, she could not see how all this could result in an acceptable work of art. How could one take the cinema seriously, when Mr Powell and his camera crew set about tearing the set apart and inventing new camera angles, when it was discovered that Vicky's solo was short by sixteen bars of music? What was supposed to be the meaning of those faces of men painted on sheets of cellophane that fell like autumn leaves at Vicky's feet for her to trample on? On the last day of shooting she thankfully and humbly rejoined the Sadler's Wells Ballet, shaking the dust of Pinewood from her slippers and taking her place again in the ballet hierarchy.

But stars are made, not by producers, but by the public, and the press, who may not be denied. *The Red Shoes* was very long in the editing and printing before it was delivered to its American distributors, and the

Archers were shooting *The Elusive Pimpernel* when Miss de Valois's Sadler's Wells Ballet opened in New York in the autumn of 1949. *The Red Shoes* had been running several months and was already the new sensation. The press took it up:

"Say! That redhead who's in *The Red Shoes*, she's in this British ballet company at the Met."

"No kiddin'. In the flesh? And those legs! Wow!"

"There's a story there. Go get it."

At the studio where the company was practising, the press got the brush-off. Nobody was giving interviews. They would have to see Miss de Valois, the director of the company, at her hotel. They stormed the hotel. Yes, Miss de Valois would meet the press the next day at eleven o'clock in the morning. Miss Margot Fonteyn, the prima ballerina assoluta of the company, would also be there, as well as Mr Robert Helpmann, the choreographer and leading male dancer.

"But what about this Moira Shearer? Isn't she in your company? Isn't she the star of the movie *The Red Shoes*? We want to see her."

The spokesmen evaded the point. That could only be arranged through Miss de Valois, and it could be taken up with her next day. The press were disappointed and somewhat critical. The next day, the press met with Miss de Valois, but were no wiser. Bobby Helpmann is my chief informant about this bizarre episode. Ninette was adamant, he said, that Moira should not be allowed to push Margot into the background. It was just as embarrassing for Margot as it was for Moira, who behaved correctly throughout. In fact, so strong was her sense of vocation that she probably agreed with Miss de Valois's handling of the situation. Nobody else did. Margot, who was one of the greatest dancers ever to grace the stage, is correspondingly modest, but had to submit to being thrust into the foreground by Miss de Valois, at the expense of Moira, at every opportunity.

This obviously had a reverse effect. All sorts of rumours were circulating. The press couldn't understand why Moira should be playing supporting roles when she was so obviously a star. Bobby, of course, rejoiced in the situation and added fuel to the fire on both sides whenever he had a chance to do it.

I am laughing, or sneering, I can't tell which, but it was a tragic thing on the part of Dame Ninette de Valois (as she became in 1951). She should have known this would happen – or perhaps she did know, and looked forward to putting that glorious, tall, red-headed dancer, so spectacular on the stage, in her place. That she was jealous of Moira, I am quite sure, just as I am equally sure that Margot was not. Looking back, for Dame Ninette is still with us at the time of writing, she surely must realise that she did a great disservice to films and to the ballet. Moira could never have been a great actress, or even a good one, but she had a wonderful vein of fantasy, had beauty, humour and was a great dancer. She could have been a gift from Scotland to the English cinema at a time when our leading ladies looked like horses or Pekinese dogs. There were a dozen musicals like *Brigadoon*, a dozen dramas like *Mary, Queen of Scots*, a dozen fairy tales like *Undine* which she could have enriched with her spectacular talents. The life of a dancer is brief. Why this dog-in-the-manger attitude by a great woman towards a medium which is the greatest storytelling medium of them all? Now that London is no longer the capital of a world empire, the town is full of this kind of provincial snobbism. All art is one and in the three lively arts – playacting, dancing, and the movies – the audience is the thing. The world is hungry for art. *The Red Shoes* is an insolent, haunting picture, in the way it takes for granted that nothing matters but art, and that art is something worth dying for. I am sure that Miss de Valois thought that too, but only applied it to her little world.

The result was that by the end of the New York season, Moira was besieged by offers from all three media. She had thought it would be easy to plan a career and her life. She found that it was more difficult than that. She was in love. Ludovic Kennedy was a writer, a broadcaster and a crusader. He was also tall, dark and handsome and a Scot. Contracts worth fortunes were being dangled before the young couple's eyes, but once accepted, their whole life would be altered. This was the time when she needed strong support in her chosen career. Because of Miss de Valois's attitude, she didn't get it. She turned to the man she loved, and they were married. They spent some of their honeymoon in the South of France and I saw them there. She was still torn between the two careers, the one that she wanted and the one that she didn't. But at least when a decision was made, they would make it together.

The Archers also had to make a decision. Arthur Rank was no longer the intimate, slightly puzzled friend that he had always been. He had become the head of a vast empire. Our insistence on independence of choice no longer amused him. He was a studio owner, a producer, and a distributor. He was going the way of the Hollywood giants before the war. There was no more King Arthur and Prince John. They were the Rank Organisation, which needed films and called them products. The artists who had furnished the product were a bit of a nuisance because they were artists. They had to be disciplined, kennelled, threatened, murdered, and in extreme cases patted on the head. Meanwhile, executives for these multiple combines proliferated, and the amount of Rank overheads charged to our Independent Producers budgets increased accordingly. We call them invisible costs. Ask any mother of a family with a weekly budget to explain this term to you. We accepted all this in return for being fully financed. Continuity of production is the hope and aim of every producer worth his salt. We always had one film in production, one film being edited and one film in preparation. And no other way could we have kept our group together and our tails high.

But Arthur Rank had promised to open the world's market to our films, to force the American exhibitors to show our films, to use their contacts and exchanges throughout the English-speaking world. This he had not been able to do, and it looked as if he would never be allowed to do it. He had the big studios, but MGM were already building their own studio at Elstree. Korda had bought Shepperton Studios and Worton Hall, with its big silent stage. The American distributors put our films on their shelves, saying they were too British: a calculated insult, difficult to refute, because they *were* British. That was the point of a picture like *The Red Shoes*. It could never have been made in Hollywood in 1947. Hollywood had made films about art and life and love, but I can't remember a single one, and I have total recall. Gene Kelly told me that he ran *The Red Shoes* fifteen to twenty times for different executives at MGM before he got acceptance of his script for Vincente Minnelli's *American in Paris*, and then it was mainly because he had a foreign ballerina for the part – Leslie Caron. He was told that the success of *The Red Shoes* was due to the girl being foreign. An American girl in the same part would have bombed. He didn't argue, but took the money and Leslie Caron and ran. The film was a huge success. I never saw it, but Gene told me that it was full of quotes from *The Red Shoes*. Art! But it had Gene Kelly.

Now, we were all being asked to cut our costs. Not because we had been overspending, but because that golden American market, upon which we had all been depending, was not going to be open to us. The American market was not the whole world: but even there, American distributors and salesmen predominated, with huge backlogs of films held up by the war, waiting for release. Rank and Davis had counted on using these vast and experienced distribution outlets. But they were denied to them. To set up a British distribution company worldwide would, and did, take years. If only the Yanks had been capable of compromise; but the word "compromise" has never been a favourite of American movie salesmen, or indeed of American salesmen in general. My American dictionary, otherwise an excellent publication, can only give a few lines to the word. So we Rank producers were instructed to cut back just as we were expanding, an operation as painful as it sounds and reminiscent of hara-kiri.

The chilling reception accorded to *The Red Shoes* by Arthur and John decided our next step. At the monthly board meeting of Independent Producers – it was usually held in the Garden Room at Pinewood – we announced that our next film would be for Korda. We were free to do so, because our contract with Rank had always been picture by picture. The news caused consternation among our fellow producers, some of whom hinted that we were going over to the enemy, while others talked about the bad old days at Denham. We kept our own counsel, knowing that they themselves had all been approached and propositioned by Korda, but had hesitated to be the first to jump in at the deep end. Our chairman, George Archibald, asked if it meant that we were leaving Independent Producers for good. Not at all, we said, and at that time we meant it. We had signed a contract with Alex to make one film, and we regarded Independent Producers at Pinewood as our home. We had just completed our biggest picture for Rank and it would take four months to edit it and to complete all the trick-work.

It had been an expensive film. By the time it got to the public, Rank's investment would be around £700,000. They were scared stiff. Neither Rank, nor Davis, nor any of their advisers understood a frame of it. It was all about art, the dialogue was sophisticated, and there was not one single known name for the American market. We believed in the public and they did not. Only time would prove us right.

For some time, Alex, over the little dinners at Claridges, had been offering us big fees and percentages to tempt us away from Rank, as well as complete independence in choice of subject and in the people that we brought with us. But at the same time he was pressing me to agree to a remake of *The Scarlet Pimpernel* to star David Niven, a project which filled me with boredom. I had known and loved Baroness Orczy's book since I was a little boy. Everyone had read it and everyone had seen Fred Terry on the stage, with his wife, beautiful Julia Neilson, as Lady Blakeney. Once upon a time, I had Baroness Orczy's house pointed out to me when I was out riding my pony on the Isle of Thanet, and to have seen the Terrys in the piece was one of my favourite theatrical memories.

But all this nostalgia had nothing to do with making a major film of this old classic, after a war which had changed French and British relations forever. No! No! A thousand times no! I flattered Alex by telling him that nobody could direct a film of *The Scarlet Pimpernel* better than he did in 1936, with Leslie Howard and Merle Oberon. How could David Niven, with all his charm, improve on Leslie's reading of the little jingle "They seek him here, they seek him there, those Frenchies seek him everywhere"? I persisted, he insisted. With the Archers fronting for him in Technicolor, he could make a deal with Sam Goldwyn to finance half the cost, plus David's services. This would also ensure an American release for the film. I still said no, and added that I had greatly admired a film from London Films, directed by Anthony Kimmins, from a book by Nigel Balchin, called *Mine Own Executioner*. I thought that Nigel Balchin was one of the best writers, and certainly one of the best stylists, to come out of the war years. Did Alex know his book *The Small Back Room*? It had a great suspense sequence of a bomb disposal expert dismantling a bomb on a beach. The part of Sammy Rice would be ideal for David Farrar. Had Alex read the book? No, but if I wanted to make it, he would buy it for me.

Emeric's viewpoint was different. I was all for keeping our independence. He was all for tying Alex down to as many films as his financiers and lawyers would permit. He had suddenly realised, like me, that we had made a dozen pictures and had no capital. The way that Rank and Davis were fumbling the pass, it looked as if we wouldn't get any percentage out of our films for years. (We were right, it took about thirty years, with one or two exceptions.) Emeric knew and understood Alex of old and had no illusions about him as I had. He knew Alex had come back to England to make money and for no other reason. Alex had learned his lesson at Denham. Now he wanted to clean up. Emeric's Magyar taste for loot had also been awakened. One Hungarian genius sees another Hungarian genius, not as a genius, but as a Hungarian. Emeric respected and liked Arthur Rank, but he was bored by his small-town realism and the way he was handing over more and more power to John Davis, who was only too willing to accept it. Their walk-out together after the private showing of *The Red Shoes* boded ill for our future relations. Someone would have to be the master, and it was pretty clear that John thought it should be he. I had so little foresight that I really thought we would be able to return to the Rank fold after making one film for Alex. I loved *The Red Shoes* so much, and I was so sure of its success with the public, that I couldn't imagine that Arthur and John literally didn't understand a word of the film and consequently hated it. Uncle Alfred's words, "Micky, you want to go too far", had been prophetic. In the past, our more eccentric films, like *Colonel Blimp* and *A Canterbury Tale*, had been given a chance to prove themselves, but this was not to be the case with *The Red Shoes*. It was to be my first experience of the stupid viciousness of the people whom Bill Wall used to refer to as "chair polishers".

It seems incredible to us now that they hated the film because they didn't understand it, and they tried to kill it because they hated it. There's no other way to explain it. They were afraid that their newly acquired shareholders would notice that the Archers' new production, with a budget of half a million pounds or more, was a flop, so they rushed it out quickly as soon as it was finished, and took it off the market as soon as they could. They were not alone in their opinion. I remember now, as I write, that the film was shown in, I think, the projection room of Universal Pictures, with whom Rank was affiliated, and some big boss or other stood up when the film was over, and announced in the tone of one who deems it self-evident: "This film will not take in a penny in America." I don't give his name, because he has no other reason to be remembered. It can't have been comforting news for Arthur and John, and it helps to explain their astonishing behaviour to their partners.

I often think of those days, fateful for the new British film industry, which had been born from the unlikely alliance of the Ministry of Information and Arthur Rank. I don't see what else the Archers could have done. Emeric and I had made twelve films together, nearly all from original stories, and each one a little more ambitious than the last. Costs had mounted proportionately. *Colonel Blimp* cost £208,000; *A Matter of Life and Death* more like £320,000; *Black Narcissus* rather less I fancy, perhaps £280,000; but now we had really launched out with the *The Red Shoes*, and the budget was going to end up something like £560,000 or £570,000. It was certainly worth thinking about. Obviously, if we couldn't get the world market, then we were heading for disaster.

During the interval between the end of main shooting and the press show, we were told repeatedly by John Davis, through George Archibald, our chairman, that Independent Producers would no longer be allowed to remain so independent. It was a curious situation. During the war, and subject to the Ministry of Information, we had total artistic freedom. Now that peace was here, we were to be reined in, bridled and curbed. And all because our financiers could not find us the markets they had promised us. This was intolerable. But compromise was impossible with John. He had been so successful in tidying up the multiple interests of Rank in GFD, RFD, the Odeon circuit, the Gaumont circuit, that he felt that he could be equally successful in reorganising and controlling his creative partners. Other men have felt this before. If there had been no alternative, perhaps the Independent Producers would have battled with John and persuaded Arthur to relegate him to the areas now taken over by computers. But Korda was there waiting with tempting offers, and one by one, like ripe plums, we fell into his hands.

During these anxious months, I saw a great deal of Hein Heckroth. I admired his talent and his true aphorisms, usually delivered with a paint brush between his teeth:

"Film is the folklore of the twentieth century." And: "I am not a Communist, I am an Anarchist."

We had a good deal of time on our hands while the matte paintings for the ballet were being executed, and we talked for hours. I already knew all about his early life – he was a friend and contemporary of Kurt Schwitters and Kokoschka, so I used to encourage him to talk about his adventures in wildest England at Dartington Hall, and as an enemy alien during the early part of the war.

"Tell about when you were sent to Australia, when you were my prisoner of war."

"I have told you. Many times."

"Tell me again."

"When it was the fall of France they rounded us up, all the enemy aliens. Me. Alfred Junge. Emeric, too – they looked for him. All the boys who had run away from Hitler. They rounded us up all."

"It was a state of emergency."

"So they said. They listened with sympathy, much sympathy. They said: 'Did you really?'; they said: 'That must have been terrible!' And they slung us into concentration camp. Behind barbed wire."

"Emeric was with me. In Canada."

"I know. You were shooting your film. France had fallen. Hitler was at Calais. And you were in Pinniweg."

"Winnipeg."

"Pinniweg. Junge they sent to Liverpool. Me they send to Australia. All the headwaiters they send to Canada. Emeric they let go, if he reports to the police every week. This was the thanks we get for choosing England."

"I notice you're still here. What next?"

"On the boat out to Australia we are seventeen hundred men, with only thirty men to guard us. We are all clever men, otherwise we would be in Buchenwald. The voyage will take three months. I say: 'There will be trouble.' There were some good painters on the boat, writers also. We get together. About thirty. I am bigger than any of them and I am from Giessen. I am Hessian. I say: 'We must have discipline or there will be murder done.' I go to the Captain of the ship and tell him our plan. He makes a meeting with the British Commandant in charge of the prisoners, and I tell him: 'Do you want to be murdered?' He says: 'We are armed. You are our prisoners.' We – me and my friends – we all laugh at him. We really think he has made a good joke. He gets mad. He says: 'Return to your quarters!' I say: 'Major Harrison, we are here eight painters, four novelists, six critics, six composers, two poets, and eight mathematicians. What are you in private life, if I may ask?' I say it very politely, like an Englishman who wishes to insult an enemy. He is not insulted. He says simply: 'I am a stockbroker.' We say to him: 'Look, there are known Nazis on board. Leave them to us. We know what to do with them. For the rest we are going to make a university.' He is very alarmed. He says: 'What do you mean? You are forbidden to make assemblies. Please go to your quarters.' When we heard him say 'please' I knew we had won. We went back to our quarters. We named our faculty and we drew up our curriculum. We opened our classes. We told everybody to put their names down for the classes they wished to attend. Some did not wish to study. We told them that they must. We put their names down for them in the unpopular classes. Nobody was to be idle. Some of these turned out to be the best students in the ship."

"What happened to the Nazis?"

"They behaved good. After one or two fell overboard they behaved very good. They became model students. Some sharks they had indigestion. That was all. You know Bucholtz?"

"The chess champion?"

"We made him P.T. Instructor. He is a dedicated man. He made us very fit. No excuses were accepted without a doctor's certificate – did I say we had fifteen doctors, twelve surgeons, and forty-three psychoanalysts? – and he was so busy with 'Knees-bend! Breathe in! Breathe out!' – that he never had time to shout 'Heil Hitler!'"

"Do you mean to say . . ."

"Of course. He was an Obergruppenführer. He was a very good physical training instructor. He was also a very good student. Music of course. Composition and the hornet."

"The cornet."

"The hornet. In the last week of the voyage we held our examinations. All our Nazis graduated with honours. They all received diplomas. They were very fine diplomas, designed and executed by our art school. Bucholtz was going to tear his up. I said to him: 'Herr Bucholtz. It is better than a one-way ticket to Buchenwald.' He did not tear it up. His wife told Ada the last time they were in London, he has it still. Of course now he is an American and a famous man. An American cannot be a Nazi, especially when he is famous. He has it framed on the wall of his home."

"How did the Aussies treat you?"

"Tough. The Aussies were very tough. They were not polite like the British. They did not say: 'Did you really?' They called us a lot of stinking krauts. They gave us food which none of us could eat. They marched us six hundred miles into the outback and they put us in a camp with a double fence of ten-foot-high barbed wire all round it, with kangaroos and wabblies . . ."

"Wallabies."

"Wabblies – kangaroos and wabblies looking in at us. The guards shot them for meat. They were very good shots. They invited us to escape so that they could shoot us too. It was a waste of money keeping us, they said. A good German is a dead German. Some of them were Italians. New Australians. They were worse than the Old Australians. We were very unhappy."

"What did you do?"

"I kept my diary. I had started keeping it from the day we landed. I had hidden a lot of sketch books. It was an illustrated diary. Many illustrations."

"Where is it? Why hasn't it been published?"

"Roland Penrose has it. He took it from me when I came back, to get us some money. He was a good friend."

"But it's a valuable document. It's historical, quite apart from its artistic value. It's like Fromentin's North African diaries."

"I know. But he has lost it."

"Lost it!"

"Of course, it is not lost. Roland never loses anything. Even when they stole all his valuable paintings they were so well known he got them back. But he has so many things. My Australian diary is buried among them. One day it will turn up, sandwiched between a Magritte and a Miro and a pile of old catalogues of the I.C.A."

"I'd love to see it. So would the Aussies. Paul Hamlyn would publish it."

"Ada will get it, if there is money in it."

"How long were you a prisoner?"

"Seven months. Nobody could be bothered about us until after the Battle of Britain. When they saw that this house-painter was not going to lead poor bloody goose-stepping Hitler Jugend along Pall Mall, like he had led them into Prague, and into Vienna, then somebody thought about us, and a team was sent out to screen us. Of course, they had to come by sea. Junge was free by the Christmas of 1940. He and his assistants had organised his camp on military lines. He had started a camouflage school. They camouflaged their own camp so well that at first nobody could find them. Junge is very efficient."

"Were the Intelligence people good?"

"Very good. They asked many questions, but they knew all the answers already. They knew all about me and Hengest and the others who had been at Dartington. They had written and spoken about us. So had Penrose and Kenneth Clark. We soon were free. As enemy aliens of course. We had to report to the police. But we were no longer in a camp."

"And then?"

"We came home. As we could."

"You could have stayed in Australia."

"Some did. Not I. Ada was here, with friends. And I wanted to be in London to see the English kick the bloody Germans up the arse."

"You're a bloody German yourself."

"I am worse than German. I am Hessian. So I know. You have to kick us up the arse. That we understand."

"*Prosit!* You bloody Hessian!"

"*Slainthe!* You bloody Englishman!"

I used to go with Hein to the workshop assigned to us behind the Technicolor Laboratories at Heathrow, on what used to be called the Bath Road. It was there that our matte painters were working on the most spectacular shots of the ballet. There were several hundred set-ups in the "Ballet of the Red Shoes" and each one had been sketched out by Hein and then carefully drawn by draughtsmen so that we could shoot the live action

in the studio first. Naturally, we couldn't keep live actors under contract
while we painted the scenery around them. But by using the matte
paintings technique, we were able to do just that. In each set-up in the
studio there was a "live area" and a "dead area". A typical sequence was
the Shoemaker's Dance with the Girl, when the town explodes behind
them and around them in a sort of firework display, and then she dances
with a newspaper. The dancing by Robert Helpmann, Léonide Massine
and Moira Shearer had been filmed weeks before. Now, at the Technicolor
Labs, the matte painters were working on the "dead areas". Small
projectors, at a speed of one turn, one picture, were projecting the scene
with the live actor onto glass. Then, working from Hein's original sketches,
they painted, on a separate sheet of glass, the permanent decor which was
not going to change during this sequence of dancing. While they worked,
talked with Hein, or argued with each other, Léonide and Moira, those two
great artists, danced silently and continuously for them. Now, on another
glass slide, they started to paint the multiple dots of colour which
represented the firework explosions. When we entered, one of the painters,
a Pole, was cursing Massine for the astounding height of his jumps.

"I have more trouble with this bloody Russian than he is worth," he
stormed. "Confound him, he is always jumping into my painting!"

One of the other miniature painters, I think it was Ivor Beddoes, was
working on the Yellow Ballroom. In the studio, using a high angle, and
eight dancers, we had painted the floor yellow and lowered into the scene
some magnificent glittering chandeliers. Now Ivor was topping it up. He
was painting great swag curtains of purple and black and Hein nodded
approvingly at the freedom of his drawing. Technicolor would do anything
for us. They had been delighted and baffled by the magnificent colour of
our last three films: delighted because of Uncle Alfred's and Hein's use of
colour, and puzzled by my refusal to allow their experts to tell us what
we could or could not do. In the early days, they had been talking down
to technicians, art directors, and cameramen who worked in black and
white, and had told them what the limits of the process were. But now
they were dealing with painters, which was a very different thing. The
painters knew enough about the technical possibilities of the process,
particularly people like Jack Cardiff, who had worked in the laboratory for
several years, and they were able to tell Technicolor where they could get
off. Particularly when there was no setting or props to disagree or agree
about, but only seventeen minutes of painting, while in the theatrical
dancing scenes the music swept everybody along and there was no time to
criticise.

I had given myself twenty-four seconds for the Monster Sequence,
seventeen seconds for the scene in the street with the two girls under the
lamppost. Perhaps it was this austerity that had bewildered and frightened

Arthur and John. The images assumed that you had seen everything and it was now striking hammerblows on your conscience. The ordinary public, whose daily life is filled with images of danger and terror, can take this, but those who rely upon convention to maintain them in their superiority, to the extent that they are prepared to tell others what they should or should not like, cannot.

I was fascinated with the big Hessian. The more I learned about his stormy past, his stormy present and his possible stormy future, the more I loved him. We were much more in the position of pupil to master than of director to art director. He had come to me at exactly the right time.

Thanks to Arthur Rank's backing and to Emeric's wise collaboration, I was now at the very peak of achievement. Although I didn't know it, and Christopher Mann was careful not to tell me, for obvious reasons, I could go to America and command a salary of six figures, or I could stay at Pinewood, the leader of the Independent Producers, blarney it out with John and Arthur and persuade Emeric to write a comedy or two. I had always wanted him to write a comedy. He had that wonderful inverted Hungarian humour and a deep knowledge of men and women. I loved to pace and direct comedy, and it is one of my great regrets that we never did a real comedy together. I had ideas for making a realistic comedy in an unrealistic setting. And I longed to make a modern musical of Murger's *La Vie de Bohème* with designs and costumes by Delacroix, that is to say by Hein Heckroth.

All these plans were more attractive to me than remaking *The Scarlet Pimpernel* for Alex. And then, with Hein at my side, I began to say: "Why not?" Why not revive that idea of Dennis Arundell's to make a musical of *The Scarlet Pimpernel*? As a musical, the preposterous plot might do. I remembered that Alex had told me, at one of those little dinners at Claridges, that when he was directing the Leslie Howard–Merle Oberon version, they had got the Pimpernel into such an impossible trap that he could not possibly escape from it, and they spent the best part of three days with writers, trying to figure a way out. These conferences sent Alex in desperation back to the old, legitimate play and next morning he was all smiles as he announced: "Boys, I've got the solution. We just open the door and the Pimpernel walks in."

Dennis Arundell had actually written a musical play which he showed me, and which Bernard Delfont hoped to put on with Bruce Forsythe playing Sir Percy. It began to seem to me that I could become enthusiastic about a musical Pimpernel.

The next time that I met Emeric for a conference over *The Small Back Room*, I sounded him out. He was as confident about *The Red Shoes* as I was, and agreed, much more readily than I thought he would, to the idea of a musical Pimpernel. I have already explained Emeric's views about Alex, which were wiser than mine. He owed no particular loyalty to Rank, and much to Alex. On the other hand, he was not afraid of Alex, and quite prepared to go to the mat with him on any given subject. It was at that point that the news was broken to us quite brutally by George Archibald, that *The Red Shoes* was not to have a London première and would go out on general release. This would quite obviously signal to the whole film business that Rank and Davis didn't believe in *The Red Shoes*, and were rushing it out to get as much money into the box-office before unfavourable audience reaction or criticism killed the picture stone dead. This was war!

We tried to get Arthur and John to meetings, but without success. They said that there was nothing to have a meeting about. The picture had no hope of being a commercial success, and they were doing the best for it in the circumstances. We would have to toe the line.

There was only one answer to this. Before the news became general, we had a meeting with Alex and agreed to make five pictures for him. The first would be *The Small Back Room*, the second would be *The Scarlet Pimpernel* as a musical. They would both go into preparation immediately. We wrote a short letter to Arthur Rank, telling him what we proposed to do and he answered with equal brevity. Thus ended one of the most glorious partnerships in the history of British films. Perhaps all works of art that necessitate a collaboration between an artist and his patron, contain within them the seeds of enmity.

Writing my autobiography has meant abandoning my freedom of choice. I can only write it the way it was, or the way it seemed to me to be. I have reached the halfway line – I am eighty-one years old and in my book I am forty-three. If I am spared, I shall tell the rest, and then we shall see what I made of it. And then there will be nothing left for me but the open sea.

MICHAEL POWELL

A FILMOGRAPHY

By kind permission of Ian Christie and the British Film Institute.

Credit abbreviations are as follows:

d—director. *p.c*—production company. *p*—producer. *exec. p*—executive producer. *assoc. p*—associate producer. *p. sup*—production supervisor. *p. manager*—production manager. *sc*—screenplay. *adapt*—adaptation. *dial*—dialogue. *addit. dial*—additional dialogue. *ph*—photography. *addit. ph*—additional photography. *cam. op*—camera operator. *sp. ph effects*—special photographic effects. *sup. ed*—supervising editor. *ed*—editor. *asst. ed*—assistant editor. *p. designer*—production designer. *sup. a.d*—supervising art director. *a.d.*—art director. *asst. a.d.*—assistant art director. *set dec*—set decoration. *m*—music. *m.d*—music director. *sd*—sound. *sd rec*—sound recordist. *cost*—costumes. *choreo*—choreography. *asst. d*—assistant director. *t.s.*—trade show. *rel*—release. *GB/US dist*—British/American distributor (original).

1931

Two Crowded Hours

d—Michael Powell. *p.c*—Film Engineering. *p*—Jerome Jackson, Henry Cohen. *sc*—J Jefferson Farjeon. *ph*—Geoffrey Faithfull. *ed*—A Seabourne. *a.d*—C Saunders.

John Longden (*Harry Fielding*), Jane Walsh (*Joyce Danton*), Jerry Verno (*Jim*), Michael Hogan (*Scammell*), Edward Barber (*Tom Murray*).

43 mins. *t.s*—8 July. *rel*—28 December. *GB dist*—Fox.

My Friend the King

d—Michael Powell. *p.c*—Film Engineering. *p*—Jerome Jackson. *sc*—J Jefferson Farjeon, from his own story. *ph*—Geoffrey Faithfull. *ed*—A Seabourne. *a.d*—C Saunders.

Jerry Verno (*Jim*), Robert Holmes (*Captain Felz*), Tracey Holmes (*Count Huelin*),

Eric Pavitt (*King Ludwig*), Phyllis Loring (*Princess Helma*), Luli Hohenberg (*Countess Zena*), H Saxon Snell (*Karl*), Victor Fairlie (*Josef*).

47 mins. *t.s*—23 September. *rel*—4 April 1932. *GB dist*—Paramount.

Rynox

d—Michael Powell. *p.c*—Film Engineering, for Ideal Films. *p*—Jerome Jackson. *sc*—Jerome Jackson, Michael Powell and Philip MacDonald, from his novel. *ph*—Geoffrey Faithfull. *ed*—A Seabourne.

Stewart Rome (*Boswell Marsh/F X Benedik*), Dorothy Boyd (*Peter*), John Longden (*Tony Benedik*), Edward Willard (*Captain James*), Charles Paton, Fletcher Lightfoot, Sybil Grove, Leslie Mitchell.

48 mins. *t.s*—November. *rel*—7 May 1932. *GB dist*—Ideal.

The Rasp

d—Michael Powell. *p.c*—Film Engineering. *p*—Jerome Jackson. *sc*—Philip MacDonald, from his own story. *ph*—Geoffrey Faithfull. *a.d*—Frank Wells.

Claude Horton (*Anthony Gethryn*), Phyllis Loring (*Lucia Masterson*), C M Hallard (*Sir Arthur Coates*), James Raglan (*Alan Deacon*), Thomas Weguelin (*Inspector Boyd*), Carol Coombe (*Dora Masterson*), Leonard Brett (*Jimmy Masterson*).

44 mins. *t.s*—3 December. *rel*—11 April 1932. *GB dist*—Fox.

The Star Reporter

d—Michael Powell. *p.c*—Film Engineering. *p*—Jerome Jackson. *sc*—Ralph Smart, Philip MacDonald, from a story by MacDonald. *ph*—Geoffrey Faithfull. *add. ph*—Michael Powell. *a.d*—Frank Wells.

Harold French (*Major Starr*), Isla Bevan (*Lady Susan Loman*), Garry Marsh (*Mandel*), Spencer Trevor (*Lord Longbourne*), Anthony Holles (*Bonzo*), Noel Dainton (*Colonel*), Elsa Graves (*Oliver*), Philip Morant (*Jeff*).

44 mins. *t.s*—10 December. *rel*—9 May 1932. *GB dist*—Fox.

1932

Hotel Splendide

d—Michael Powell. *p.c*—Gaumont-British. *p*—Jerome Jackson. *sc*—Ralph Smart, from a story by Philip MacDonald. *ph*—Geoffrey Faithfull, Arthur Grant. *a.d*—C Saunders.

Jerry Verno (*Jerry Mason*), Anthony Holles (*Mrs Le Grange*), Edgar Norfolk ('*Gentleman Charlie*'), Philip Morant (*Mr Meek*), Sybil Groves (*Mrs Harkness*), Vera Sherbourne (*Joyce Dacre*), Paddy Browne (*Miss Meek*).

53 mins. *t.s*—23 March. *rel*—18 July. *GB dist*—Ideal.

C.O.D.

d—Michael Powell. *p.c*—Westminster Films. *p*—Jerome Jackson. *sc*—Ralph Smart, from a story by Philip MacDonald. *ph*—Geoffrey Faithfull. *a.d*—Frank Wells.

Garry Marsh (*Peter Craven*), Hope Davey (*Frances*), Arthur Stratton (*Briggs*), Sybil Grove (*Mrs Briggs*), Roland Culver (*Edward*), Peter Gawthorne (*Detective*), Cecil Ramage (*Vyner*), Bruce Belfrage (*Philip*).

66 mins. *t.s*—17 March. *rel*—22 August. *GB dist*—United Artists.

His Lordship

d—Michael Powell. *p.c*—Westminster Films. *p*—Jerome Jackson. *sc*—Ralph Smart. Based on the novel *The Right Honorable* by Oliver Madox Heuffer. *ph*—Geoffrey Faithfull. *a.d*—Frank Wells. *m/lyrics*—V C Clinton-Baddeley, Eric Maschwitz.

Jerry Verno (*Bert Gibbs*), Janet McGrew (*Ilya Myona*), Ben Weldon (*Washington Lincoln*), Polly Ward (*Leninia*), Peter Gawthorne (*Ferguson*), Muriel George (*Mrs Gibbs*), Michael Hogan (*Comrade Curzon*), V C Clinton-Baddeley (*Comrade Howard*), Patric Ludlow (*Hon Grimsthwaite*).

77 mins. *t.s*—2 June. *ref*—5 December. *GB dist*—United Artists.

Born Lucky

d—Michael Powell. *p.c*—Westminster Films. *p*—Jerome Jackson. *sc*—Ralph Smart. Based on the novel *Mops* by Oliver Sandys. *a.d*—Ian Campbell-Gray.

Talbot O'Farrell (*Turnips*), Renee Ray (*Mops*), John Longden (*Frank Dale*), Ben Welden (*Harriman*), Helen Ferrers (*Lady Chard*), Barbara Gott (*Cook*), Paddy Browne (*Patty*), Roland Gillett (*John Chard*).

78 mins. *t.s*—5 December. *rel*—6 April 1933. *GB dist*—MGM.

1933

The Fire Raisers

d—Michael Powell. *p.c*—Gaumont-British. *p*—Jerome Jackson. *sc*—Powell, Jerome Jackson, from an original story. *ph*—Leslie Rowson. *ed*—D N Twist. *a.d*—Alfred Junge. *cost*—Cordon Conway. *sd*—A F Birch.

Leslie Banks (*Jim Bronson*), Anne Grey (*Arden Brent*), Carol Goodner (*Helen Vaughan*), Frank Cellier (*Brent*), Francis L Sullivan (*Stedding*), Laurence Anderson (*Twist*), Harry Caine (*Bates*), Joyce Kirby (*Polly*), George Merritt (*Sonners*).

77 mins. *t.s*—18 September. *rel*—22 January 1934. *GB dist*—Woolf & Freedman.

1934

The Night of the Party

d—Michael Powell. *p.c*—Gaumont-British. *p*—Jerome Jackson. *sc*—Roland

Pertwee, John Hastings Turner, from their own play. *ph*—Glen MacWilliams. *sup. a.d*—Alfred Junge.

Leslie Banks (*Sir John Holland*), Ian Hunter (*Guy Kennington*), Jane Baxter (*Peggy Studholme*), Ernest Thesiger (*Chiddiatt*), Viola Keats (*John Holland*), Malcolm Keen (*Lord Studholme*), Jane Millican (*Anna Chiddiatt*), Muriel Akad (*Princess*), John Turnbull (*Ramage*), Laurence Anderson (*Defence Counsel*), W Graham Brown (*General Piddington*).

61 mins. *t.s*—Feb. *GB rel*—16 July. *GB dist*—Gaumont-British. *US rel*— floating 1935/6. US title—*The Murder Party.*

Red Ensign

d—Michael Powell. *p.c*—Gaumont-British. *p*—Jerome Jackson. *sc*—Powell, Jerome Jackson. *addit. dial*—L du Garde Peach. *ph*—Leslie Rowson. *sup. a.d*—Alfred Junge.

Leslie Banks(*David Barr*), Carol Goodner (*June MacKinnon*), Frank Vosper (*Lord Dean*), Alfred Drayton (*Manning*), Donald Calthorp (*MacLeod*), Allan Jeayes (*Emerson*), Campbell Gullan (*Hannay*), Percy Parsons (*Casey*), Fewlass Llewllyn (*Sir Gregory*), Henry Oscar (*Raglan*).

69 mins. *t.s*—2 February. *GB rel*—4 June. *GB dist*—Gaumont-British. *US rel*—floating 1935/6. US title—*Strike!*

Something Always Happens

d—Michael Powell. *p.c*—Warner Brothers-First National. *exec. p*—Irving Asher. *sc*—Brock Williams. *ph*—Basil Emmott. *a.d*—Peter Proud. *ed*—Bert Bates.

Ian Hunter (*Peter Middleton*), Nancy O'Neil (*Cynthia Hatch*), John Singer (*Billy*), Peter Gawthorne (*Mr Hatch*), Muriel George (*Mrs Badger*), Barry Livesey (*George Hamlin*), Millicent Wolf (*Glenda*), Louie Emery (*Mrs Tremlett*), Reg Marcus ('*Coster*').

69 mins. *t.s*—21 June. *rel*—10 December. *GB dist*—Warner Brothers-First National.

The Girl in the Crowd

d—Michael Powell. *p.c*—First National. *exec. p*—Irving Asher. *sc*—Brock Williams. *ph*—Basil Emmott. *ed*—Bert Bates.

Barry Clifton (*David Gordon*), Patricia Hilliard (*Marian*), Googie Withers (*Sally*), Harold French (*Bob*), Clarence Blakiston (*Mr Peabody*), Margaret Gunn (*Joyce*), Richard Littledale (*Bill Manners*), Phyllis Morris (*Mrs Lewis*), Patric Knowles (*Tom Burrows*), Marjorie Corbett (*Secretary*), Brenda Lawless (*Policewoman*), Barbara Waring (*Mannequin*), Eve Lister (*Ruby*), Betty Lyne (*Phyllis*), Melita Bell (*Assistant Manageress*), John Wood (*Harry*).

52 mins. *t.s*—4 December. *rel*—20 May 1935. *GB dist*—First National.

1935

Lazybones

d—Michael Powell. *p.c*—Real Art. *exec. p*—Julius Hagen. *sc*—Gerald Fairlie, from a play by Ernest Denny. *ph*—Arthur Crabtree. *sup. ed*—Frank Harris.

Claire Luce (*Kitty McCarthy*), Ian Hunter (*Sir Reginald Ford*), Sara Allgood (*Bridget*), Bernard Nedell (*Mike McCarthy*), Michael Shepley (*Hildebrand Pope*), Bobbie Comber (*Kemp*), Denys Blakelock (*Hugh Ford),* Marjorie Gaskell (*Marjory Ford*), Pamela Carne (*Lottie Pope*), Harold Warrender (*Lord Melton*), Miles Malleson (*Pessimist*), Fred Withers (*Richards*), Frank Morgan (*Tom*), Fewlass Llewllyn (*Lord Brockley*), Paul Blake (*Viscount Woodland*).

65 mins. *t.s*—17 Jan. *rel*—24 June. *GB dist*—RKO.

The Love Test

d—Michael Powell. *p.c*—Leslie Landau for Fox British. *p*—Leslie Landau. *sc*—Selwyn Jepson. Based on a story by Jack Celestin. *ph*—Arthur Crabtree.

Judy Gunn (*Mary*), Louis Hayward (*John*), Dave Hucheson (*Thompson*), Googie Withers (*Minnie*), Morris Harvey (*President*), Aubrey Dexter (*Vice-President*), Eve Turner (*Kathleen*), Bernard Miles (*Allan*), Jack Knight (*Managing Director*), Gilbert Davis (*Chief Chemist*), Shayle Gardner (*Night Watchman*), James Craig (*Boiler Man*).

63 mins. *t.s*—2 December 1934. *rel*—1 July. *GB dist*—Fox British.

The Phantom Light

d—Michael Powell. *p.c*—Gaumont-British. *p*—Jerome Jackson. *sc*—Ralph Smart. Based on a play by Evadne Price, Joan Roy Byford. *addit. dial*—J Jefferson Farjeon. Austin Melford. *ph*—Roy Kellino. *ed*—Derek Twist. *a.d*—Alex Vetchinsky. *m*—Louis Levy.

Binnie Hale (*Alice Bright*), Gordon Harker (*Sam Higgins*), Ian Hunter (*Jim Pierce*), Donald Calthrop (*David Owen*), Milton Rosmer (*Dr Carey*), Reginald Tate (*Tom Evans*), Mickey Brantford (*Bob Peters*), Herbert Lomas (*Claff Owen*), Fewlass Llewllyn (*Griffith Owen*), Alice O'Day (*Mrs Owen*), Barry O'Neill (*Captain Pierce*), Edgar K Bruce (*Sergeant Owen*), Louie Emery (*Station Mistress*).

76 mins. *t.s*—9 January. *rel*—5 August. *GB dist*—Gaumont-British. [Re-issued 1950]

The Price of a Song

d—Michael Powell. *p.c*—Fox British. *sc*—Anthony Gittens.

Campbell Gullan (*Arnold Grierson*), Marjorie Corbett (*Margaret Nevern*), Gerald Fielding (*Michael Hardwicke*), Dora Barton (*Letty Grierson*), Charles Mortimer (*Oliver Broom*), Oriel Ross (*Elsie*), Henry Caine (*Stringer*), Sybil Grove (*Mrs Bancroft*), Eric Maturin (*Nevern*), Felix Aylmer (Graham), Cynthia Stock (*Mrs Bush*), Mavis Clair (*Maudie Bancroft*).

67 mins. *t.s*—24 May. *rel*—7 October. *GB dist*—Fox British.

Someday

d—Michael Powell. *p.c*—Warner British. *p*—Irving Asher. *sc*—Brock Williams. Based on the novel *Young Nowheres* by I A R Wylie. *ph*—Basil Emmott, Monty Berman. *ed*—Bert Bates. *a.d*—Ian Campbell-Gray.

Esmond Knight (*Curley Blake*), Margaret Lockwood (*Emily*), Henry Mollison (*Canley*), Sunday Wilshin (*Betty*), Raymond Lovell (*Carr*), Ivor Bernard (*Hope*), George Pughe (*Milkman*), Jane Cornell (*Nurse*).

68 mins. *t.s*—17 July. *rel*—18 November. *GB dist*—Warner Brothers-First National.

1936

Her Last Affaire

d—Michael Powell. *p.c*—New Ideal. *p*—Simon Rowson, Geoffrey Rowson. *sc*—Ian Dalrymple. Based on the play *S.O.S.* by Walter Ellis. *ph*—Geoffrey Faithfull. *sd*—George Burgess.

Hugh Williams (*Alan Heriot*), Viola Keats (*Lady Avril Weyre*), Francis L Sullivan (*Sir Julian Weyre*), Sophie Stewart (*Judy Weyre*), Felix Aylmer (*Lord Carnforth*), Cecil Parker (*Sir Arthur Harding*), John Gardner (*Boxall*), Henry Caine (*Inspector Marsh*), Gerrard Tyrell (*Martin*).

78 mins. *t.s*—21 October 1925. *rel*—25 May. *GB dist*—Producers Distributing Corporation.

The Brown Wallet

d—Michael Powell. *p.c*—Warner Brothers-First National. *exec. p*—Irving Asher. *sc*—Ian Dalrymple, from a story by Stacy Aumonier. *ph*—Basil Emmott.

Patric Knowles (*John Gillespie*), Nancy O'Neill (*Eleanor*), Henry Caine (*Simmonds*), Henrietta Watson (*Aunt Mary*), Charlotte Leigh (*Miss Barton*), Shayle Gardner (*Wotherspoone*), Edward Dalby (*Minting*), Eliot Makeham (*Hobday*), Bruce Winston (*Julian Thorpe*), Jane Millican (*Miss Bloxham*), Louis Goodrich (*Coroner*), Dick Francis, George Mills (*Detectives*).

68 mins. *t.s*—25 February. *rel*—20 July. *GB dist*—Warner Brothers-First National.

Crown v. Stevens

d—Michael Powell. *p.c*—Warner Brothers-First National. *exec. p*—Irving Asher. *sc*—Brock Williams. Based on the novel *Third Time Unlucky* by Laurence Maynell. *ph*—Basil Emmott. *ed*—Bert Bates.

Beatrix Thomson (*Doris Stevens*), Patric Knowles (*Chris Jansen*), Reginald Purdell (*Alf*), Glennis Lorimer (*Molly*), Allan Jeayes (*Inspector Carter*), Frederick Piper (*Arthur Stevens*), Googie Withers (*Ella*), Mabel Poulton (*Mamie*), Morris Harvey (*Julius Bayleck*), Billy Watts (*Joe Andrews*), Davina Craig (*Maggie*).

66 mins. *t.s*—26 March. *rel*—3 August. *GB dist*—Warner Brothers-First National.

The Man Behind the Mask

d—Michael Powell. *p.c*—Joe Rock Studios. *p*—Joe Rock. *sc*—Ian Hay, Sidney Courtenay. Adapted by Jack Byrd from the novel *The Chase of the Golden Plate* by Jacques Futrelle. *ph*—Ernest Palmer.

Hugh Williams (*Nick Barclay*), Jane Baxter (*June Slade*), Maurice Schwartz (*The Master*), Donald Calthrop (*Dr Walpole*), Henry Oscar (*Officer*). Peter Gawthorne (*Lord Slade*), Kitty Kelly (*Miss Weeks*), Ronald Ward (*Jimmy Slade*), George Merritt (*Mallory*), Reginald Tate (*Hayden*), Ivor Bernard (*Hewitt*), Hal Gordon (*Sergeant*), Gerald Fielding (*Harah*), Barbara Everest (*Lady Slade*), Wilf Caithness (*Butler*), Moyra Fagan (*Nora*), Sid Crossley (*Postman*).

79 mins. *t.s*—24 March. *rel*—24 August. *GB dist*—MGM.

1937
The Edge of the World

d—Michael Powell. *p.c*—Rock Studios. *p*—Joe Rock. *sc*—Michael Powell. *ph*—Ernest Palmer, Skeets Kelly, Monty Berman. *ed*—Derek Twist. *m.d*—Cyril Ray. *orchestrations*—W L Williamson. *chorus*—Women of the Glasgow Orpheus Choir. *sd*—L K Tregallas. *sd rec*—W H O Sweeny. *p.manager*—Gerard Blattner. *p. assistants*—A Seabourne, Vernon Sewell, W H Farr, George Black, W Osborne, Sydney Streeter.

John Laurie (*Peter Manson*), Belle Chrystall (*Ruth Manson*), Eric Berry (*Robbie Manson*), Kitty Kirwan (*Jean Manson*), Finlay Currie (*James Gray*), Niall MacGinnis (*Andrew Gray*), Grant Sutherland (*The Catechist*), Campbell Robson (*The Laird*), George Summers (*Skipper*), Margaret Grieg (*Baby*), Michael Powell (*Yachtsman*).

81 mins. *t.s*—6 July. *rel*—10 January 1938 (pre-release in London—September 1937). *GB dist*—British Independent Exhibitors (Distribution). *US rel*—9 September 1938 [74 mins] *US dist*—Pax Films. *GB re-issue*—December 1940 [62 mins]

1939
The Spy in Black

d—Michael Powell. *p.c*—Harefield. *presented by*—Alexander Korda. *p*—Irving Asher. *sc*—Emeric Pressburger, from Roland Pertwee's adaptation of a novel by J Storer Clouston. *ph*—Bernard Browne. *sup ed*—William Hornbeck. *ed*—Hugh Stewart. *asst. ed*—John Guthrie. *p designer*—Vincent Korda. *a.d*—Frederick Pusey. *m*—Miklos Rozsa. *m.d*—Muir Mathieson. *sd*—A W Watkins.

Conrad Veidt (*Captain Hardt*), Valerie Hobson (*Schoolmistress*), Sebastian Shaw (*Lt Ashington*), Marius Goring (*Lt Schuster*), June Duprez (*Anne Burnett*), Athole Stewart (*Rev Hector Matthews*), Agnes Laughlin (*Mrs Matthews*), Helen Haye (*Mrs Sedley*), Cyril Raymond (*Rev John Harris*), Hay Petrie (*Engineer*), Grant Sutherland (*Bob Bratt*), Robert Rendel (*Admiral*), Mary Morris (*Chauffeuse*), George Summers (*Captain Ratter*), Margaret Moffatt (*Kate*), Kenneth

Warrington (*Cdr Denis*), Torin Thatcher (*Submarine Officer*), Bernard Miles, Esma Cannon, Skelton Knaggs.

82 mins. *t.s*—15 March. *GB rel*—12 August. *GB/US dist*—Columbia. *US rel*—7 October. US title—*U Boat 29*.

The Lion Has Wings

d—Michael Powell, Brian Desmond Hurst, Adrian Brunel. *p.c*—London Film Productions. *p*—Alexander Korda. *assoc p*—Ian Dalrymple. *p. manager*—David Cunynghame. *sc*—Adrian Brunel, E V H Emmett, from a story by Ian Dalrymple. *ph*—Harry Stradling. *addit. ph*—Osmond Borrodaile. *cam. op*—Bernard Browne. *a.d*—Vincent Korda. *sup. ed*—William Hornbeck. *ed*—Henry Cornelius, Charles Frend. *m*—Richard Addinsell. *m.d*—Muir Mathieson. *sd*—A W Watkins. *tech. adv*—Squadron Leader H M S Wright.

Merle Oberon (*Mrs Richardson*), Ralph Richardson (*W C Richardson*), June Duprez (*June*), Robert Douglas (*Briefing Officer*), Anthony Bushell (*Pilot*), Derrick de Marney (*Bill*), Brian Worth (*Bobby*), Austin Trevor (*Schulemburg*), Ivan Brandt (*Officer*), G H Mulcaster (*Controller*), Herbert Lomas (*Holveg*), Milton Rosmer (*Head of Observer Corps*), Robert Rendel (*Chief of Air Staff*), E V H Emmett (*Narrator—English version*), Lowell Thomas (*Narrator—US version*), Archibald Batty (*Air Officer*), Ronald Adam, John Longden, Ian Fleming, Miles Malleson, Bernard Miles, Charles Garson, John Penrose, Frank Tickle.

76 mins. *t.s*—17 October. *GB rel*—3 November. *GB/US dist*—United Artists. *US rel*—19 January 1940.

1940

Contraband

d—Michael Powell. *p.c*—British National. *p*—John Corfield. *assoc. p*—Roland Gillett. *p. manager*—Anthony Nelson Keys. *sc*—Emeric Pressburger, Michael Powell. Based on a screenplay by Brock Williams, from a story by Pressburger. *ph*—F A Young. *ed*—John Seabourne. *a.d*—Alfred Junge. *m*—Richard Addinsell. *m.d*—Muir Mathieson. *sd*—C C Stevens.

Conrad Veidt (*Captain Andersen*), Valerie Hobson (*Mrs Sorensen*), Hay Petrie (*Mate of SS Helving/Chef of 'Three Vikings'*), Esmond Knight (*Mr Pidgeon*), Raymond Lovell (*Van Dyne*), Charles Victor (*Hendrick*), Henry Wolston (*1st Danish Waiter*), Julian Vedey (*2nd Danish Waiter*), Sydney Moncton (*3rd Danish Waiter*), Hamilton Keen (*4th Danish Waiter*), Phoebe Kershaw (*Miss Lang*), Leo Genn (*1st Brother Grimm*), Stuart Lathan (*2nd Brother Grimm*), Peter Bull (*3rd Brother Grimm*), Dennis Arundell (*Lieman*), Harold Warrender (*Lt Cmdr Ellis RN*), Joss Ambler (*Lt Cmdr Ashton RNR*), Molly Hamley Clifford (*Baroness Hekla*), Eric Berry (*Mr Abo*), Olga Edwards (*Mrs Abo*), Tony Gable (*Mrs Karoly*), Desmond Jeans (*1st Karoly*), Eric Hales (*2nd Karoly*), Jean Roberts (*Hanson*), Manning Whiley (*Manager of 'Mousetrap'*), Eric Maturin, John Longden (*Passport Officers*).

92 mins. *t.s*—20 March. *GB rel*—May. *GB dist*—Anglo. *US rel*—29 November. *US dist*—United Artists. US title—*Blackout* [80 mins]

The Thief of Bagdad

d—Ludwig Berger, Michael Powell, Tim Whelan. *uncredited*—Zoltan Korda, William Cameron Menzies, Alexander Korda *p.c*—London Film Productions. *p*—Alexander Korda. *assoc. p*—Zoltan Korda. William Cameron Menzies. *p. manager*—David Cunynghame. *p. asst*—André de Toth. *asst. d*—Geoffrey Boothby, Charles David. *sc*—Lajos Biro. *adapt/dial*—Miles Malleson. *ph*—Georges Perinal. *col*—Technicolor. *ext. ph*—Osmond Borrodaile. *cam op*—Robert Krasker. *sp. ph. effects*—Lawrence Butler. *Technicolor d*—Natalie Kalmus. *sup. ed*—William Hornbeck. *ed*—Charles Crichton. *a.d*—Vincent Korda. *assoc. a.d*—W Percy Day, William Cameron Menzies, Frederick Pusey, Ferdinand Bellan. *m*—Miklos Rozsa. *m.d*—Muir Mathieson. *cost*—Oliver Messel, John Armstrong, Marcel Vertes. *sd*—A W Watkins.

Conrad Veidt (*Jaffar*), Sabu (*Abu*), June Duprez (*Princess*), John Justin (*Ahmad*), Rex Ingram (*Djinni*), Miles Malleson (*Sultan*), Morton Selten (*King*), Mary Morris (*Halima*), Bruce Winston (*Merchant*), Hay Petrie (*Astrologer*), Roy Emmerton (*Jailer*), Allan Jeayes (*Storyteller*), Adelaide Hall (*Singer*).

106 mins. *t.s*—24 December. *GB/US rel*—25 December. *GB/US dist*—United Artists. *prizes*—Academy Awards for Color Cinematography, Color Art Direction, Special Effects.

1941

An Airman's Letter to His Mother

p and ph—Michael Powell. *addit. ph*—Bernard Browne. Narrated by John Gielgud.

5 mins. *rel*—June. *dist*—MGM

49th Parallel

d—Michael Powell. *p.c*—Ortus Films/Ministry of Information. *p*—Michael Powell. *assoc. p*—Roland Gillett, George Brown. *p. sup*—Harold Boxall. *asst. d*—A Seabourne. *sc*—Emeric Pressburger. *dial*—Rodney Ackland. *ph*—Frederick Young. *cam. op*—Skeets Kelly, Henry Creer. *ed*—David Lean. *assoc. ed*—Hugh Stewart. *a.d*—David Rawnsley. *assoc. a.d*—Sydney Streeter. *m*—Ralph Vaughan Williams. *m.d*—Muir Mathieson. *sd*—C C Stevens. *Canadian adviser*—Nugent M Cloucher.

Eric Portman (*Lieutenant Hirth*), Richard George (*Kommandant Bernsdorff*), Raymond Lovell (*Lt Kuhnecker*), Niall MacGinnis (*Vogel*), Peter Moore (*Kranz*), John Chandos (*Lohrmann*), Basil Appleby (*Jahner*), Laurence Olivier (*Johnnie, the trapper*), Finlay Currie (*Factor*), Ley On (*Nick the Eskimo*), Anton Walbrook (*Peter*), Glynis Johns (*Anna*), Charles Victor (*Andreas*), Frederick Piper (*David*), Leslie Howard (*Philip Armstrong Scott*), Tawera Moana (*George the Indian*), Eric Clavering (*Art*), Charles Rolfe (*Bob*), Raymond Massey (*Andy Brock*), Theodore Salt, O W Fonger (*US Customs Officers*).

123 mins. *t.s*—8 October. *GB rel*—24 November. *GB dist*—GFD. *US rel*—15 April 1942 [104 mins] *US dist*—Columbia. *US title*—*The Invaders*. *Prizes*—Emeric Pressburger received an Oscar for the script of *49th Parallel*.

1942

One of Our Aircraft Is Missing

d—Michael Powell. p.c—British National. p—John Corfield, Michael Powell, Emeric Pressburger. sc—Emeric Pressburger, Michael Powell. ph—Ronald Neame. cam. op—Robert Krasker, Guy Green. ed—David Lean. a.d—David Rawnsley. unit manager—Sydney Streeter. sd—C C Stevens.

Godfrey Tearle (Sir George Corbett), Eric Portman (Tom Earnshaw), Hugh Williams (Frank Shelley), Bernard Miles (Geoff Hickman), Hugh Burden (John Glyn Haggard), Emrys Jones (Bob Ashley), Pamela Brown (Els Meertens), Joyce Redman (Jet Van Dieren), Googie Withers (Jo de Vries), Hay Petrie (Burgomaster), Selma van Dias (Burgomaster's wife), Arnold Marle (Pieter Sluys), Robert Helpmann (De Jong), Peter Ustinov (The Priest), Alec Clunes (Organist), Hector Abbas (Driver), James Carson (Louis), Willem Akkerman (Willem), Joan Akkerman (Maartje), Peter Schenke (Hendrik), Valerie Moon (Jannie), John Salew (Sentry), William D'Arcy (Officer), David Ward (1st Airman), Robert Duncan (2nd Airman), Roland Culver (Naval Officer), Robert Beatty (Hopkins), Michael Powell (Despatching Officer), Stewart Rome.

102 mins. t.s—18 March. GB rel—27 June. GB dist—Anglo. US rel—16 October [82 mins] US dist—United Artists.

1943

The Silver Fleet

d—Vernon C Sewell, Gordon Wellesley. p.c—The Archers. p—Michael Powell, Emeric Pressburger. assoc. p—Ralph Richardson. sc—Vernon C Sewell, Gordon Wellesley. ph—Erwin Hillier. cam. op—Cecil Cooney. ed—Michael C Chorlton. p. designer—Alfred Junge. m—Allan Gray. sd—John Dennis, Desmond Dew.

Ralph Richardson (Jaap van Leyden), Googie Withers (Helene van Leyden), Esmond Knight (von Schiffer), Beresford Egan (Krampf), Frederick Burtwell (Captain Muller), Kathleen Byron (Schoolmistress), Willem Akkerman (Willem van Leyden), Dorothy Gordon (Janni Peters), Charles Victor (Bastiaan Peters), John Longden (Jost Meertens), Joss Ambler (Cornelius Smit), Margaret Emden (Bertha), George Schelderup (Dirk), Neville Mapp (Joop), Ivor Barnard (Admiral), John Carol (Johann), Philip Leaver (Chief of Police), Laurence o'Madden (Captain Schneider), Anthony Eustrel (Lt Wernicke), Charles Minor (Bohme), Valentine Dyall (Markgraf), Lt Schouwenaar (U-Boat Captain), Lt van Dapperen (U-Boat Lieutenant), John Arnold (U-Boat Navigator), and personnel of the Royal Netherlands Navy.

88 mins. t.s—24 February. GB rel—15 March. GB dist—GFD. US rel—1 July 1945 [81 mins] US dist—Producers Releasing Corporation.

The Life and Death of Colonel Blimp

d/p/sc—Michael Powell, Emeric Pressburger. p.c—The Archers/Independent Producers. p. manager—Sydney Streeter. ph—Georges Périnal. col—Technicolor. cam. op—Jack Cardiff, Geoffrey Unsworth. ed—John Seabourne. p. designer—Alfred Junge. m—Allan Gray. sd—C C Stevens. military adviser—Lt General Sir Douglas Brownrigg.

Anton Walbrook (*Theo Kretschmar-Schuldorff*), Roger Livesey (*Clive Candy*), Deborah Kerr (*Edith/Barbara/Angela*), Roland Culver (*Colonel Betteridge*), James McKechnie (*Spud Wilson*), Albert Lieven (*von Ritter*), Arthur Wontner (*Counsellor*), David Hutcheson (*Hoppy*), Ursula Jeans (*Frau Kalteneck*), John Laurie (*Murdoch*), Harry Welchman (*Major Davis*), Reginald Tate (*Van Zijl*), A E Matthews (*President*), Carl Jaffe (*von Reumann*), Valentine Dyall (*von Schonbron*), Muriel Aked (*Aunt Margaret*), Felix Aylmer (*Bishop*), Frith Banbury (*Babyface Fitzroy*), Neville Mapp (*Graves*), Vincent Holman (*Club Porter, 1942*), Spencer Trevor (*Period Blimp*), Dennis Arundell (*Cafe Orchestra Leader*), James Knight (*Club Porter, 1902*), David Ward (*Kaunitz*), Jan van Loewen (*Indignant Citizen*), Eric Maturin (*Colonel Goodhead*), Robert Harris (*Embassy Secretary*), Count Zichy (*Colonel Berg*), Jane Millican (*Nurse Erna*), Phyllis Morris (*Pebble*), Diana Marshall (*Sybil*), Captain W Barrett (*The Texan*), Corporal Thomas Palmer (*Sergeant*), Yvonne Andre (*Nun*), Marjorie Greasley (*Matron*), Helen Debray (*Mrs Wynne*), Norman Pierce (*Mr Wynne*), Edward Cooper (*BBC Official*), Joan Swinstead (*Secretary*).

163 mins (later cut to ca 140 and 120 mins). *t.s*—8 June. *GB rel*—26 July (Charity Premiere 10 June). *GB dist*—GFD. *US rel*—4 May 1945 [148 mins](?). *US dist*—United Artists.

The Volunteer

d/p/sc—Michael Powell, Emeric Pressburger. *p.c*—The Archers. *p. manager*—Sydney Streeter. *ph*—Freddie Ford. *ed*—John Seabourne. *m*—Allan Gray.

Ralph Richardson (*Himself*), Pat McGrath (*Fred Davey*), Laurence Olivier, Michael Powell.

46 mins. *t.s*—5 November. *rel*—10 January 1944. *dist*—Anglo.

1944
A Canterbury Tale

d/p/sc—Michael Powell, Emeric Pressburger. *p.c*—The Archers. *ph*—Erwin Hillier. *ed*—John Seabourne. *p. designer*—Alfred Junge. *m*—Allan Gray. *cond*—Walter Goehr.

Eric Portman (*Thomas Colpepper, JP*), Sheila Sim (*Alison Smith*), Sgt John Sweet (*Bob Johnson*), Dennis Price (*Peter Gibbs*), Esmond Knight (*Narrator/Seven-Sisters Soldier/Village Idiot*), Charles Hawtrey (*Thomas Duckett*), Hay Petrie (*Woodcock*), George Merrit (*Neg Horton*), Edward Rigby (*Jim Horton*), Freda Jackson (*Prudence Honeywood*). Betty Jardine (*Fee Baker*), Eliot Makeham (*Organist*), Harvey Golden (*Sgt Roczinsky*), Leonard Smith (*Leslie*), James Tamsitt (*Terry*), David Todd (*David*).

124 mins. *t.s*—9 May. *GB rel*—21 August. *GB dist*—Eagle-Lion. *US rel*—21 January 1949 [95 mins]

1945
I Know Where I'm Going

d/p/sc—Michael Powell, Emeric Pressburger. *p.c*—The Archers. *assoc.*

p—George R Busby. *ph*—Erwin Hillier. *ed*—John Seabourne. *a.d*—Alfred Junge. *m*—Allan Gray. *sd*—C C Stevens.

Wendy Hiller (*Joan Webster*), Roger Livesey (*Torquil MacNeil*), George Carney (*Mr Webster*), Pamela Brown (*Catriona*), Walter Hudd (*Hunter*), Capt Duncan MacKechnie (*Captain 'Lochinvar'*), Ian Sadler (*Ian*), Finlay Currie (*Ruairidh Mor*), Murdo Morrison (*Kenny*), Margot Fitzsimmons (*Bridie*), Capt C W R Knight (*Colonel Barnstaple*), Donald Strachan (*Sheperd*), John Rae (*Old Shepherd*), Duncan MacIntyre (*His Son*), Jean Cadell (*Postmistress*), Norman Shelley (*Sir Robert Bellinger*), Ivy Milton (*Peigi*), Anthony Eustrel (*Hooper*), Petula Clark (*Cheril*), Alec Faversham (*Martin*), Catherine Lacey (*Mrs Robinson*), Valentine Dyall (*Mr Robinson*), Nancy Price (*Mrs Crozier*), Herbert Lomas (*Mr Campbell*), Kitty Kirwan (*Mrs Campbell*), John Laurie (*John Campbell*), Graham Moffat (*RAF Sergeant*), Boyd Stevens, Maxwell Kennedy, Jean Houston (*Singers in the Ceildhe*), Arthur Chesney (*Harmonica Player*).

92 mins. *t.s*—30 October. *GB rel*—17 December. *GB dist*—GFD. *US rel*—9 August 1947. *US dist*—Universal.

1946

A Matter of Life and Death

d/p/sc—Michael Powell, Emeric Pressburger. *p.c*—The Archers. *assoc. p*—George R Busby. *asst. d*—Parry Jones, Jr. *ph*—Jack Cardiff. *col*—Technicolor. *cam. op*—Geoffrey Unsworth. *p. designer*—Alfred Junge. *asst. a.d*—Arthur Lawson. *ed*—Reginald Mills. *m*—Allan Gray. *cond*—W L Williamson. *cost*—Hein Heckroth. *sd*—C C Stevens.

David Niven (*Peter Carter*), Kim Hunter (*June*), Marius Goring (*Conductor 71*), Roger Livesey (*Dr Reeves*), Robert Coote (*Bob*), Kathleen Byron (*Angel*), Richard Attenborough (*English Pilot*), Bonar Colleano (*American Pilot*), Joan Maude (*Chief Recorder*), Edwin Max (*Dr McEwen*), Abraham Sofaer (*The Judge*), Raymond Massey (*Abraham Farlan*), Robert Atkins (*Vicar*), Betty Potter (*Mrs Tucker*), Bob Roberts (*Dr Gaertler*).

104 mins. *t.s*—12 November. *GB rel*—30 December. *GB dist*—GFD. *US rel*—March 1947. *US dist*—Universal. *US title*—*Stairway to Heaven*.

1947

Black Narcissus

d/p/sc—Michael Powell, Emeric Pressburger. Based on a novel by Rumer Godden. *p.c*—The Archers. *assoc. p*—George R Busby. *asst. d*—Sydney Streeter. *ph*—Jack Cardiff. *col*—Technicolor. *cam. op*—Ted Scaife. *ed*—Reginald Mills. *p. designer*—Alfred Junge. *cost*—Hein Heckroth. *m*—Brian Easdale. *sd*—Stanley Lambourne.

Deborah Kerr (*Sister Clodagh*), Sabu (*The Young General*), David Farrar (*Mr Dean*), Flora Robson (*Sister Philippa*), Esmond Knight (*The Old General*), Kathleen Byron (*Sister Ruth*), Jenny Laird (*Sister Honey*), Judith Furse (*Sister Briony*), May Hallatt (*Angu Ayah*), Shaun Noble (*Con*), Eddie Whaley Jr (*Joseph Anthony*), Nancy Roberts (*Mother Dorothea*), Jean Simmons (*Kanchi*).

100 mins. *t.s*—22 April. *GB rel*—26 May. *GB dist*—GFD. *US rel*—December. *US dist*—Universal. *Prizes*—Oscar for colour cinematography.

The End of the River

d—Derek Twist. *p.c*—The Archers. *p*—Michael Powell, Emeric Pressburger. *asst. p*—George R Busby. *asst. d*—Geoffrey Lambert. *sc*—Wolfgang Wilhelm. *ph*—Christopher Challis. *ed*—Brereton Porter. *a.d*—Fred Pusey. *asst. a.d*— E E C Scott. *m*—Lambert Williamson. *m.d*—Muir Mathieson. *sd*—Charles Knott.

Sabu (*Manoel*), Bibi Férriera (*Teresa*), Esmond Knight (*Dantos*), Antoinette Cellier (*Conceicao*), Robert Douglas (*Jones*), Torin Thatcher (*Lisboa*), Orlando Martins (*Harrigan*), Raymond Lovell (*Porpino*), James Hayter (*Chico*), Nicolette Bernard (*Dona Serafina*), Minto Cato (*Dona Paula*), Maurice Denham (*Defending Counsel*), Eva Hudson (*Maria Gonsalves*), Alan Wheatley (*Irygoyen*), Charles Hawtrey (*Raphael*), Zena Marshall (*Sante*), Dennis Arundell (*Continho*), Milton Rosmer (*The Judge*), Peter Illing (*Ship's Agent*), Nino Rossini (*Feliciano*), Basil Appleby (*Ship's Officer*), Milo Sperber (*Ze*), Andreas Malandrinos (*Officer of the Indian Protection Society*), Arthur Goullet (*The Pedlar*), Russell Napier (*The Padre*).

83 mins. *t.s*—23 October. *GB rel*—1 December. *GB dist*—Rank. *US rel*—7 July 1948 [80 mins].

1948

The Red Shoes

d/p/sc—Michael Powell, Emeric Pressburger. *p.c*—The Archers. *asst. p*—George Busby. *first asst. d*—Sydney Streeter. *sc*—from an original screenplay by Emeric Pressburger. *ph*—Jack Cardiff. *col*—Technicolor. *cam. op*—Christopher Challis. *sp. ph. effects*—F George Dunn, D Hague (Technicolor composite photography). *ed*—Reginald Mills. *p. designer*—Hein Heckroth. *a.d*—Arthur Lawson. *m*—Brian Easdale. *m.d*—Brian Easdale, Sir Thomas Beecham. *singer*— Margherita Grandi. *dancer*—Alan Carter (also assistant *maître-de-ballet*). *sd*—Charles Poulton. *choreo*—Robert Helpmann.

Marius Goring (*Julian Craster*), Anton Walbrook (*Boris Lermontov*), Moira Shearer (*Victoria Page*), Leonid Massine (*Ljubov*), Austin Trevor (*Professor Palmer*), Esmond Knight (*Livy*), Eric Berry (*Dimitri*), Irene Browne (*Lady Neston*), Ludmilla Tcherina (*Boronskaja*), Jerry Verno (*Stage-door Keeper*), Robert Helpmann (*Ivan Boleslawsky*), Albert Basserman (*Ratov*), Derek Elphinstone (*Lord Oldham*), Madame Rambert (*Herself*), Joy Rawlins (*Gladys, Victoria's Friend*), Jean Short (*Terry*), Gordon Littman (*Ike*), Julia Lang (*Balletomane*), Bill Shine (*Her Companion*), Marcel Poncin (*M Boudin*), Michel Bazalgette (*M Rideaut*), Yvonne Andre (*Victoria's Dresser*), Hay Petrie (*Boisson*), George Woodbridge (*Doorman*).

133 mins. *t.s*—20 July. *GB rel*—6 September. *GB dist*—GFD. *US rel*—1 October 1951. *US dist*—Universal.

1949
The Small Back Room

d/p—Michael Powell, Emeric Pressburger. *p.c*—London Film Productions, The Archers. *asst. d*—Sydney Streeter. *sc*—Michael Powell, Emeric Pressburger, Nigel Balchin, from the novel by Nigel Balchin. *ph*—Christopher Challis. *cam. op*—Freddie Francis. *ed*—Reginald Mills, Clifford Turner. *p. designer*—Hein Heckroth. *a.d*—John Hoesli. *m*—Brian Easdale. *night-club m*—Ted Heath's Kenny Baker Swing Group. *sd*—Alan Allen.

David Farrar (*Sammy Rice*), Kathleen Byron (*Susan*), Jack Hawkins (*R B Waring*), Leslie Banks (*Colonel Holland*), Michael Gough (*Stuart*), Cyril Cusack (*Corporal Taylor*), Milton Rosmer (*Professor Mair*), Walter Fitzgerald (*Brine*), Emrys Jones (*Joe*), Michael Goodliffe (*Till*), Renee Asherson (*ATS Corporal*), Anthony Bushell (*Colonel Strang*), Henry Caine (*Sgt-Major Rose*), Elwyn Brook-Jones (*Gladwin*), James Dale (*Brigadier*), Sam Kydd (*Crowhurst*), June Elvin (*Gillian*), David Hutcheson (*Norval*), Sidney James (*Knucksie*), Roderick Lovell (*Pearson*), James Carney (*Sgt Groves*), Roddy Hughes (*Welsh Doctor*), Geoffrey Keen (*Pinker*), Bryan Forbes (*Dying Gunner*), 'A Guest' [Robert Morley] (*The Minister*).

108 mins. *t.s*—27 January. *GB rel*—21 February. *GB dist*—British Lion. *US rel*—23 February 1952. *US dist*—Snader Productions.

1950
Gone to Earth

d—Michael Powell, Emeric Pressburger. *p.c*—London Film Productions, Vanguard Productions. *pres*—Alexander Korda and David O Selznick. *p*—David O Selznick. *assoc p*—George R Busby. *asst. d*—Sydney Streeter. *sc*—Michael Powell, Emeric Pressburger, from the novel by Mary Webb. *ph*—Christopher Challis. *col*—Technicolor. *p designer*—Hein Heckroth. *a.d*—Arthur Lawson. *ed*—Reginald Mills. *m*—Brian Easdale. *sd*—Charles Poulton.

Jennifer Jones (*Hazel Woodus*), David Farrar (*Jack Reddin*), Cyril Cusack (*Edward Marston*), Sybil Thorndyke (*Mrs Marston*), Edward Chapman (*Mr James*), Esmond Knight (*Abel Woodus*), Hugh Griffith (*Andrew Vessons*), George Cole (*Albert*), Beatrice Varley (*Aunt Prowde*), Frances Clare (*Amelia Comber*), Raymond Rollett (*Landlord*), Gerald Lawson (*Roadmender*), Bartlett Mullins, Arthur Reynolds (*Chapel Elders*), Ann Tetheradge (*Miss James*), Peter Dunlop (*Cornet Player*), Louis Phillip (*Policeman*), Valentine Dunn (*Martha*), Richmond Nairne (*Mathias Brooker*) [US version only: Joseph Cotten (*Narrator*).]

110 mins. *t.s*—19 September. *GB rel*—6 November. *GB dist*—British Lion. *US rel*—July 1952 [82 mins. *addit. d*—Rouben Mamoulian.] US title—*The Wild Heart. US dist*—RKO Radio.

The Elusive Pimpernel

d—Michael Powell, Emeric Pressburger. *p.c*—The Archers for London Film Productions. *p*—Samuel Goldwyn, Alexander Korda. *assoc. p*—George R Busby. *asst. d*—Sydney Streeter. *sc*—Michael Powell, Emeric Pressburger, from the novel by Baroness Orczy. *ph*—Christopher Challis. *col*—Technicolor. *cam.*

op—Freddie Francis. *sp effects*—W Percy Day. *p designer*—Hein Heckroth. *a.d*—Arthur Lawson, Joseph Bato. *ed*—Reginald Mills. *m*—Brian Easdale. *sd*—Charles Poulton, Red Law.

David Niven (*Sir Percy Blakeney*), Margaret Leighton (*Marguerite Blakeney*), Jack Hawkins (*Prince of Wales*), Cyril Cusack (*Chauvelin*), Robert Coote (*Sir Andrew Ffoulkes*), Edmond Audran (*Armand St Juste*), Danielle Godet (*Suzanne de Tournai*), Charles Victor (*Colonel Winterbottom*), David Hutcheson (*Lord Anthony Dewhurst*), Arlette Marchal (*Countesse de Tournai*), Gerard Nery (*Phillipe de Tournai*), Eugene Deckers (*Captain Merieres*), John Longden (*Abbot*), Arthur Wontner (*Lord Grenville*), David Oxley (*Captain Duroc*), Raymond Rollett (*Bibot*), Philip Stainton (*Jellyband*), Robert Griffiths (*Trubshaw*), George de Warfaz (*Baron*), Jane Gill Davies (*Lady Grenville*), Richard George (*Sir John Coke*), Cherry Cottrell (*Lady Bristow*), John Fitzgerald (*Sir Michael Travers*), Patrick MacNee (*Hon John Bristow*), Terence Alexander (*Duke of Dorset*), Tommy Dugan (*Earl of Sligo*), John Fitchen (*Nigel Seymour*), John Hewitt (*Major Pretty*), Hugh Kelly (*Mr Fitzdrummond*), Richard Nairne (*Beau Pepys*).

109 mins. *t.s*—9 November. *GB rel*—1 January 1951. *GB dist*—British Lion. *US rel*—floating 1955. *US dist*—Caroll Pictures. US title—*The Fighting Pimpernel*.

1951

The Tales of Hoffmann

d/p/sc—Michael Powell, Emeric Pressburger. *p.c*—The Archers for London Film Productions. *assoc p*—George R Busby. *asst. d*—Sydney Streeter. *sc*—from Dennis Arundell's adaptation of the opera by Offenbach; libretto by Jules Barbier. *ph*—Christopher Challis. *col*—Technicolor. *p. designer/cost*—Hein Heckroth. *a.d*—Arthur Lawson. *ed*—Reginald Mills. *m*—Jacques Offenbach. *m.d*—Sir Thomas Beecham. *choreo*—Frederick Ashton.

Prologue and Epilogue: Moira Shearer (*Stella*), Robert Rounseville (*Hoffmann*), Robert Helpmann (*Lindorff*). Pamela Brown (*Nicklaus*), Frederick Ashton (*Kleinzack*), Meinhart Maur (*Luther*), Edmond Audran (*Cancer*).

The Tale of Olympia: Moira Shearer (*Olympia*), Robert Helpmann (*Coppelius*), Leonid Massine (*Spalanzani*).

The Tale of Giulietta: Ludmilla Tcherina (*Giulietta*), Robert Helpmann (*Dr Dapertutto*), Leonid Massine (*Schlemiel*).

The Tale of Antonia: Ann Ayars (*Antonia*), Robert Helpmann (*Dr Miracle*), Leonid Massine (*Franz*).

Singers: Robert Rounseville, Owen Brannigan, Monica Sinclair, René Soames, Bruce Darvaget, Dorothy Bond, Margherita Grandi, Grahame Clifford.

127 mins (reduced to 115 mins before release). *t.s*—17 May. *GB rel*— 26 November. *GB dist*—British Lion. *US rel*—13 June 1952. *US dist*— United Artists. *Prizes*—Special Jury Prize, Prize of the Commission Supérieure Technique, Cannes 1951.

1955

The Sorcerer's Apprentice

d—Michael Powell. *p.c*—20th Century-Fox/Norddeutscher Rundfunk. *p. designer* —Hein Heckroth. *solo dancer*—Sonia Arova (no further credits available).

13 mins. (cut from ca 30 mins). *GB rel*—14 July. *GB dist*—20th Century-Fox.

Oh Rosalinda!!

d/p/sc—Michael Powell, Emeric Pressburger. *p.c*—Michael Powell, Emeric Pressburger. *assoc. p*—Sydney Streeter. *asst. d*—John Pellatt. *sc*—based on Johann Strauss' operetta *Die Fledermaus*. *lyrics*—Dennis Arundell. *ph*— Christopher Challis. *col*—Technicolor. *cam. op*—Norman Warwick. *ed*— Reginald Mills. *p. designer*—Hein Heckroth. *assoc. a.d*—Arthur Lawson. *m*—Johann Strauss. *m.d*—Frederick Lewis. *choreo*—Alfred Rodriques.

Anthony Quayle (*General Orlovsky*), Anton Walbrook (*Dr Falke*), Dennis Price (*Major Frank*), Ludmilla Tcherina (*Rosalinda*), Michael Redgrave (*Colonel Eisenstein*), Mel Ferrer (*Captain Alfred*), Anneliese Rothenberger (*Adele*), Oska Sima (*Frosh*), Richard Marner (*Judge*), Nicholas Bruce (*Hotel Receptionist*).
The ladies: Barbara Archer, Betty Ash, Joyce Blair, Hildy Christian, Pamela Foster, Jill Ireland, Patricia Garnett, Annette Gibson, Eileen Gourley, Jean Grayston, Grizelda Hervey, Maya Joumani, Olga Lowe, Sara Luzita, Ingrid Marshall, Alicia Massy-Beresford, Eileen Sands, Herta Seydel, Anna Steele, Jennifer Walmsley, Dorothy Whitney, Prudence Hyman.
The gentlemen: Michael Anthony, Igor Barczinsky, Cecil Bates, Richard Bennett, Nicholas Bruce, Ray Buckingham, Denis Carey, Rolf Carston, Terence Cooper, Robert Crewsdon, Peter Darrell, Edward Forsyth, Roger Cage, David Gilbert, Robert Harrold, Jan Lawski, Raymond Lloyd, William Martin, Kenneth Melville, Orest Orioff, Robert Ross, John Schlesinger, Frederick Schrecker, Maurice Metliss, Kenneth Smith, Richard Marner.
Voices of: Sari Barabas(*Rosalinda*), Alexander Young (*Alfred*), Dennis Dowling (*Frank*), Walter Berry (*Falke*).

101 mins. *t.s*—15 November. *GB rel*—2 January 1956. *GB dist*—Associated British-Pathe.

1956

The Battle of the River Plate

d/p/sc—Michael Powell, Emeric Pressburger. *p.c*—The Archers/J Arthur Rank. *assoc. p*—Sydney Streeter. *asst. d*—Charles Orme. *ph*—Christopher Challis (VistaVision). *col*—Technicolor. *cam. op*—Austin Dempster. *ed*—Reginald Mills. *p.designer*—Arthur Lawson. *assoc. a.d*—Donald Picton. *artistic adviser*— Hein Heckroth. *m*—Brian Easdale. *m.d*—Frederick Lewis. *sd*—C C Stevens, Gordon K McCallum.

John Gregson (*Captain Bell*), Anthony Quayle (*Commodore Harwood*), Peter Finch (*Captain Langsdorff*), Ian Hunter (*Captain Woodhouse*), Jack Gwillim (*Captain Parry*), Bernard Lee (*Captain Dove*), Lionel Murton (*Mike Fowler*), Anthony Bushell (*Mr Millington-Drake*), Peter Illing (*Dr Guani*), Michael

Goodliffe (*Captain McCall*), Patrick McNee (*Lt Cmdr Medley*), John Chandos (*Dr Langmann*), Douglas Wilmer (*M Desmoulins*), William Squire (*Ray Martin*), Roger Delgado (*Captain Varela*), Andrew Cruickshank (*Captain Stubs*), Christopher Lee (*Manola*), Edward Atienza (*Pop*), April Olrich (*Dolores*).

119 mins. *t.s*—29 October. *GB rel*—24 December. *GB dist*—JARFID (Rank). *US rel*—November 1957 [106 mins]. US title—*Pursuit of the Graf Spee*. Royal Film Performance 1956.

Ill Met By Moonlight

d/p/sc—Michael Powell. *p.c*—The Archers/J Arthur Rank. *assoc. p*—Sydney Streeter. *asst. d*—Charles Orme. *sc*—based on the book of the same title by W Stanley Moss. *ph*—Christopher Challis (VistaVision). *cam. op*—Austin Dempster. *ed*—Arthur Stevens. *a.d*—Alex Vetchinsky. *m*—Mikis Theodorakis. *m.d*—Frederick Lewis. *sd*—Charles Knott, Gordon K McCallum.

Dirk Bogarde (*Major Paddy Leigh-Fermor*), Marius Goring (*General Karl Kreipe*), David Oxley (*Captain Billy Stanley Moss*), Cyril Cusack (*Sandy*), Laurence Payne (*Manoli*), Wolfe Morris (*George*), Michael Gough (*Andoni Zoidakis*), Roland Bartrop (*Micky Akoumianakis*), Brian Worth (*Stratis Saviolkis*), Paul Stassino (*Yani Katsias*), Adeed Assaly (*Zahari*), John Cairney (*Elias*), George Egeniou (*Charis Zographakis*), Demitri Andreas (*Nikko*), Theo Moreas (*Village Priest*), Takis Frangofinos (*Michali*).

104 mins. *t.s*—29 Jan 1957. *GB rel*—4 March 1957. *GB dist*—Rank. *US rel*—July 1958 [93 mins]. US title—*Night Ambush*.

1959

Luna de Miel (Honeymoon)

d—Michael Powell. *p.c*—Suevia Films-Cesario Gonsalez (Spain)/Everdene (GB). *p*—Cesario Gonsalez, Michael Powell. *assoc. p*—Sydney Streeter, Judith Coxhead, William J Paton. *p. sup*—Jaime Prades. *assoc. d*—Ricardo Blasco. *sc*—Michael Powell, Luis Escobar. *ph*—Georges Périnal (Technirama). *col*—Technicolor. *assoc. ph*—Gerry Turpin. *ed*—Peter Taylor, John V Smith. *a.d/ cost*—Ivor Beddoes. *asst. a.d*—Eduardo Torre de la Fuente, Roberto Carpio, Judy Jordan. *m*—Mikis Theodorakis. *sd*—John Cox, Fernando Bernaldes, Janet Davidson.

Ballets: El Amor Brujo. sc—Gregorio Martinez Sierra. *m*—Manuel de Falla. *sets*—Rafael Durancamps. *choreo*—Antonio. *soloist*—Maria Clara Alcala. *dancer*—Leonid Massine. *Los Amantes de Teruel. m*—Mikis Theodorakis. *cond*—Sir Thomas Beecham. *choreo*—Leonid Massine.

Anthony Steel (*Kit*), Ludmilla Tcherina (*Anna*), Antonio (*Himself*), Rosita Segovia (*Rosita*), Carmen Rojas, Maria Gamez, Diego Hurtado, Pepe Nieto.

109 mins. *France*—18 March 1961. *GB t.s*—31 Jan 1962 [90 mins]. *GB rel*—8 February 1962. *GB dist*—BLC. *Prize*—Special Prize of Commission Supérieure Technique, Cannes 1959.

1960

Peeping Tom

d—Michael Powell. *p.c*—Michael Powell (Theatre). *p*—Michael Powell. *assoc. p*—Albert Fennell. *sc*—Leo Marks. *ph*—Otto Heller. *col*—Eastman Colour. *ed*—Noreen Ackland. *a.d*—Arthur Lawson. *m*—Brian Easdale, Wally Scott. *sd*—C C Stevens, Gordon K McCallum.

Carl Boehm (*Mark Lewis*), Anna Massey (*Helen*), Maxine Audley (*Mrs Stephens*), Moira Shearer (*Vivian*), Esmond Knight (*Arthur Baden*), Michael Goodliffe (*Don Jarvis*), Shirley Anne Field (*Diane Ashley*), Bartlett Mullins (*Mr Peters*), Jack Watson *(Inspector Gregg)*, Nigel Davenport (*Sergeant Miller*), Pamela Green (*Milly*), Martin Miller (*Dr Rosen*), Brian Wallace (*Tony*), Brenda Bruce (*Dora*), Miles Malleson (*Elderly Gentleman*), Susan Travers (*Lorraine*), Maurice Durant (*Publicity Chief*), Brian Worth (*Assistant Director*), Veronica Hurst (*Miss Simpson*), Alan Rolfe (*Store Detective*), Michael Powell (*Mark's Father*), his son (*Mark as a child*).

109 mins. *t.s*—31 March. *GB rel*—16 May. *GB dist*—Anglo Amalgamated. *US rel*—15 May 1962 [86 mins]. *US dist*—Astor.

1961

The Queen's Guards

d/p—Michael Powell. *p.c*—Imperial. *assoc. p*—Simon Harcourt-Smith. *assoc. d*—Sydney Streeter. *sc*—Roger Milner, from an idea by Simon Harcourt-Smith. *ph*—Gerry Turpin. *col*—Technicolor. *ed*—Noreen Ackland. *a.d*—Wilfred Shingleton. *m*—Brian Easdale. *sd*—James Shields.

Daniel Massey *(John Fellowes)*, Robert Stephens (*Henry Wynne Walton*), Raymond Massey (*Captain Fellowes*), Ursula Jeans (*Mrs Fellowes*), Judith Stott (*Ruth*), Elizabeth Shepherd (*Susan*), Duncal Lamont (*Wilkes*), Peter Myers (*Gordon Davidson*), Ian Hunter (*Dobbie*), Jess Conrad (*Dankworth*), Patrick Connor (*Brewer*), William Young (*Williams*), Jack Allen (*Brigadier Cummings*), Jack Watling (*Captain Shergold*), Andrew Crawford (*Biggs*), Cornel Lucas (*Photographer*), Nigel Green (*Abu Sibdar*), René Cutforth (*Commentator*), Jack Watson (*Sergeant Johnson*), Laurence Payne (*Farinda*).

110 mins. *t.s*—9 October. *rel*—23 October. *dist*—20th Century-Fox.

1963

Never Turn Your Back on a Friend (*Espionage* series)

d—Michael Powell. *p.c*—Herbert Brodkin Ltd. *exec. p*—Herbert Hirschman. *p*—George Justin. *assoc. p*—John Pellatt. *asst. d*—Bruce Sherman. *sc*—Mel Davenport. *ph*—Ken Hodges. *cam. op*—Herbert Smith. *ed*—John Victor Smith. *p. designer*—Wilfred Shingleton. *a.d*—Tony Woollard. *m*—Malcolm Arnold. *sd. rec*—David Bowen. *sd. ed*—Dennis Rogers. *titles*—Maurice Binder.

George Voskovek (*Professor Kuhn*), Donald Madden (*Anaconda*), Mark Eden (*Wicket*), Julian Glover (*Tovarich*), Pamela Brown (*Miss Jensen*).

48 mins. 1963.

1964

A Free Agent (*Espionage* series)

d—Michael Powell. *p.c*—Herbert Brodkin/MGM. *exec. p*—Herbert Hirschman. *p*—George Justin. *assoc. p*—John Pellatt. *asst. d*—Jake Wright. *sc*—Leo Marks. *ph*—Geoffrey Faithfull. *cam. op*—Alan McCabe. *ed*—John Victor Smith. *p. designer*—Wilfred Shingleton. *a.d*—Anthony Woollard. *m*—Benjamin Frankel. *sd. rec*—Cyril Smith. *sd. ed*—Dennis Rogers.

Anthony Quayle (*Philip*), Sian Phillips (*Anna*), Norman Foster (*Max*), George Mikell (*Peter*), John Wood (*Douglas*), John Abineri (*Town Clerk*), Ernst Waldner (*Watch Factory Mechanic*), Gertan Klauber (*Innkeeper*), Vivienne Drummond (*Miss Weiss*).

48 mins.

Bluebeard's Castle

d—Michael Powell. *p.c*—Norman Foster Productions/Süddeutscher Rundfunk. *p*—Norman Foster. *sc/m*—Bela Bartok's opera *Bluebeard's Castle*. *libretto*—Bela Balazs (1911). *ph*—Hannes Staudinger. *col*—Technicolor. *p. designer*—Hein Heckroth.

Norman Foster (*Bluebeard*), Anna Raquel Sartre (*Judit*).

60 mins. Unreleased in GB.

1965

The Sworn Twelve (TV film for *The Defenders* series)

d—Michael Powell. *sc*—Edward DeBlasio *with*—E G Marshall, Murry Hamilton, King Donovan, Ruby Dee, Jerry Orbach. c 50 mins.

A 39846 (TV film for *The Nurses* series)

d—Michael Powell. *sc*—George Bellak *with*—Michael Tolan, Shirl Conway, Joseph Campanella, Jean-Pierre Aumont, Kermit Murdock. c 50 mins.

1966

They're a Weird Mob

d/p—Michael Powell. *p.c*—Williamson (Australia)/Powell (GB). *assoc. p*—John Pellatt. *asst. d*—Claude Watson. *sc*—Richard Imrie, from a novel by John O'Grady. *ph*—Arthur Grant. *col*—Eastman Colour. *ed*—G Turney-Smith. *a.d*—Dennis Gentle. *m*—Laurence Leonard, Alan Boustead. *m.d*—Laurence Leonard. *songs*—'Big Country', 'In this Man's Country' by Reen Devereaux; 'I kiss you, you kiss me' by Walter Chiari. *Cretan dance*—Mikis Theodorakis. *sd*—Don Saunders, Bill Creed.

Walter Chiari (*Nino Culotta*), Clare Dunne (*Kay Kelly*), Chips Rafferty (*Harry Kelly*), Alida Chelli (*Guiliana*), Ed Devereaux (*Joe*), Slim de Grey (*Pat*), John Meillon (*Dennis*), Charles Little (*Jimmy*), Anne Haddy (*Barmaid*), Jack Allen (*Fat Man in Bar*), Red Moore (*Texture Man*), Ray Hartley (*Newsboy*), Tony Bonner (*Lifesaver*), Alan Lander (*Charlie*), Judith Arthy (*Dixie*), Keith Petersen (*Drunk Man on Ferry*), Muriel Steinbeck (*Mrs Kelly*), Gloria Dawn (*Mrs Chapman*),

Jeanne Dryman (*Betty*), Gita Rivera (*Maria*), Doreen Warburton (*Edie*), Barry Creyton, Noel Brophy, Graham Kennedy.

112 mins. *t.s*—7 October. *GB rel*—13 October. *GB dist*—Rank.

1969
Age of Consent

d—Michael Powell. *p.c*—Nautilus Productions (Australia). *p*—James Mason, Michael Powell. *assoc. p*—Michael Pate. *asst. d*—David Crocker. *sc*—Peter Yeldham, based on a novel by Norman Lindsay. *ph*—Hannes Staudinger. *col*—Eastman Colour. *underwater ph*—Ron Taylor. *ed*—Anthony Buckley. *a.d*—Dennis Gentle. *m*—Stanley Myers. *sd*—Paul Ennis, Lloyd Colman.

James Mason (*Bradley Morahan*), Helen Mirren (*Cora*), Jack MacGowran (*Nat Kelly*), Neva Carr-Glyn (*Ma Ryan*), Antonia Katsaros (*Isabel Marley*), Michael Boddy (*Hendricks*), Harold Hopkins (*Ted Farrell*), Slim de Grey (*Cooley*), Max Moldrum (*TV Interviewer*), Frank Thring (*Godfrey*), Dora Hing (*Receptionist*), Clarissa Kaye (*Meg*), Judy McGrath (*Grace*), Lenore Katon (*Edna*), Diane Strachan (*Susie*), Roberta Grant (*Ivy*), Prince Nial (*Jasper*), Hudson Fausset (*New Yorker*), Peggy Cass (*New Yorker's Wife*), Eric Reuman (*Art Lover*), Tommy Hanlon Jr (*Levi-Strauss*), Geoff Cartwright (*Newsboy*).

98 mins. *GB rel*—15 November 1969. *US rel*—14 May 1969 [103 mins]. *dist*—Columbia.

1972
The Boy Who Turned Yellow

d—Michael Powell. *p.c*—Roger Cherrill. *p. manager*—Gus Angus. *asst. d*—Neil Vine-Miller. *sc*—Emeric Pressburger. *ph*—Christopher Challis. *col*—Eastman Colour. *ed*—Peter Boita. *a.d*—Bernard Sarron. *m*—Patrick Gowers, David Vorhaus. *sd*—Bob Jones, Ken Barber.

Mark Dightam (*John*), Robert Eddison (*Nick*), Helen Weir (*Mrs Saunders*). Brian Worth (*Mr Saunders*), Esmond Knight (*Doctor*), Laurence Carter (*Schoolteacher*), Patrick McAlinney (*Supreme Beefeater*), Lem Kitaj (*Munro*).

55 mins. *GB rel*—16 September. *dist*—Children's Film Foundation. *Prize*—Children's Film Foundation award, 'Chiffy', 1978.

1978
Return to the Edge of the World

Additional material on Powell's early career at Pinewood and a return visit to the island of Foula, with members of the original cast and crew of *Edge of the World*, commissioned by BBC Television and directed by Powell, co-producer Sydney Streeter.

1983
Pavlova – A Woman for All Time

Powell is credited as Western Version Supervisor on this GB/USSR co-production, written and directed by Emil Lotianou and co-ordinated by executive producer Frixos Constantine. Its origins lay in a project on the life of Pavlova that Powell had long tried to mount.

INDEX

A NOTE ON THE TYPE

The text of this book was set in Sabon, a type face designed by Jan Tschichold (1902–1974), the well-known German typographer. Because it was designed in Frankfurt, Sabon was named for the famous Frankfurt type founder Jacques Sabon, who died in 1580 while manager of the Egenolff foundry.

Based loosely on the original designs of Claude Garamond (c. 1480–1561), Sabon is unique in that it was explicitly designed for hot-metal composition on both the Monotype and Linotype machines as well as for film composition.

Composed in Great Britain. Printed and bound by
R. R. Donnelley & Sons, Harrisonburg, Virginia.